Your Book
of Financial Planning

Forrest Wallace Cato (left), communications director for the International Association for Financial Planning, interviews Loren Dunton and Venita VanCaspel, who has her own nationwide television series, "Venita VanCaspel's Moneymakers." VanCaspel's book, The Power of Money Dynamics, has been on the New York Times top ten best-seller list.

Your Book
of Financial Planning

The Consumer's Guide to
a Better Financial Future

Compiled and Edited by
Loren Dunton

President
National Center for Financial Education, Inc.

Reston Publishing Company, Inc.
A Prentice-Hall Company
Reston, Virginia

Library of Congress Cataloging in Publication Data
Main entry under title:

  Your book of financial planning.

    1. Finance, Personal—Addresses, essays, lectures.
I. Dunton, Loren.   II. Title: Financial planning.
HG179.Y67   1983   332.024   82-25062
ISBN 0-8359-9505-4

©1983 by Reston Publishing Company, Inc.
A Prentice-Hall Company
Reston, Virginia 22090

10 9 8 7 6 5 4 3 2

Printed in the United States of America

Personally
dedicated
to my sister Eileen Lourence,
to Jane, my wife of twenty-five years,
to my daughters Brooke Bacon and Page Lambert,
to my friends Val Lodholm and Bob Leary
and to the others who know how special they are to me.

Professionally
dedicated
to the authors and to those who helped the Society,
the IAFP, and the College for Financial Planning get started.
Also to those Corporate Sponsors and Board Members
who are putting some of their things aside
and helping people have a better financial future
because of the National Center for Financial Education, Inc.

Contents

In 1964 my wife Jane and I decided that our daughters Brooke and Page were the ideal age to benefit from a trip around the world. It was to be a poor-boy, getting-to-know-the-people experience—not a vacation, but an education. Even so, it meant an outlay of $25,000 or $30,000 just for the trip. As a high-income sales manager, I had been sold some cash value life insurance and had paid on it for many years. To take our year's trip around the world we had to cash in our life insurance, grateful for the cash it represented, knowing the money probably would have been frittered away otherwise. We also sold the stock recently earned in a small company as part of my sales consulting fees.

Of course the stock market had received some of my attention in earlier years. While a bachelor, I once bought Central Eureka Mining without knowing about assessable stock and learned a new word—three times. Then there was Berkey-Gay Furniture, which added still another new word to my vocabulary, "receivership." The only worse move I made other than following my stockbroker's advice was to choose my own stocks. I was soon completely fed up with the stock market.

Unfortunately, during those years when my sales and override commissions were high and expenses low, the only two mutual fund representatives who got in to see me didn't know how to sell. Instead of talking about a coordinated financial plan or other things like accumulating an estate, which would have appealed to me, they turned me off by talking about the stock market.

Like my father and his father, I had done no financial planning. We had all made good money and fallen for individual pitches for the wrong stocks, high-priced insurance, low-interest savings, and questionable real estate. A few of my college fraternity brothers, I learned later, had bought term insurance and mutual funds. They had started preparing for retirement while in their twenties and thirties. As for me, why I hadn't even thought about my

The Financial Planner: A New Professional

Loren Dunton

forties, and nobody ever told me about dollar-cost averaging. What I needed badly, had there been one, was a financial planner.

Looking back at my mistakes, I am appalled. For example, I should never have gone to an insurance agent for financial advice, as I did. Who can blame him for selling me the insurance on which he could make the most money? Or who can blame him for disparaging mutual funds when I asked him about those? He had been trained to do that. And can I really blame the stockbroker who sold me the stock? Buying it was fun and playing the market made me feel like a big shot.

How I wish now, though, that someone had been there to give me more objective advice—someone who would have found out how high my sales and override commissions were; who would have made me fill out a form or two, maybe even prepare a budget so I could have seen how much disposable income I really had; someone who could easily have intrigued a free-wheeling bachelor like me with the idea of putting money aside for the future; and who later would have wanted to meet my new bride to do a review of our finances. We needed someone then to help us devise a good financial plan. If we had been given such advice, fifteen years later we wouldn't have had to sell all of our stock or cash in our life insurance to make that world trip. But if an individual like that was around in the 1940s, no one told me.

Such individuals are around now, however. They are not only helping people plan their financial futures, but the outstanding ones are motivating people to spend less, save more, and invest wisely. These individuals are the practitioners of a new and valuable profession—they are financial planners.

Loren Dunton is founder and president of the National Center for Financial Education, Inc. He also founded the Society for Financial Counseling, Inc., the International Association of Financial Planners, Inc., and the College for Financial Planning, Inc., all non-profit organizations. In 1971 Dunton founded and published the *Financial Planner* magazine. In addition to his work in the financial world, Mr. Dunton is founder of the KWATRO Coporation, which markets his family of fast, "mental agility" games. He is a well-known lecturer and the author of many books and articles.

When Loren Dunton first asked me to participate on this book, I must admit to being somewhat skeptical. Could Loren convince some of the best personal financial planners in the country to take time from their busy schedules to write chapters in a book that was so unique it had never before been attempted? It was not an impossible task, but it was not easy.

I have talked with Loren several times during the many months this book has been in process and, like the other authors, I have become infected with Loren's enthusiasm. I feel quite fortunate to be one of the first people to see and review the entire book. It is easy to understand Loren's enthusiasm: this book responds to a very definite need. If read and heeded it will guide consumers to a better financial future.

The financial planning process is analogous to putting a jigsaw puzzle together. While the pieces of the puzzle have some meaning when viewed separately, they mean so much more once they have been put together. The pieces of the financial planning puzzle—the written plan itself, the possible implementation pieces such as insurance products, securities, etc.—have meaning when viewed individually. However, the meaning of the individual pieces is enhanced when viewed together as parts of a fully integrated financial plan.

Financial planning is not merely estate planning that provides for one's estate after death. It is not merely budgeting to determine how one's money is being or should be spent. Nor is it simply retirement planning, or the purchase or sale of equity products, or the informed acqusition of insurance in one of its many forms. Financial planning may include those things; but it is much more. Financial planning is a *process*. It is not something that is fixed at a point in time. It is not something that one establishes and then forgets or discards. As one planner stated so well, personal financial planning is not a destination; it is a journey.

The authors of the book are attempting

Foreword

Financial Planning: Yesterday, Today, and Tomorrow

William. L. Anthes, Ph.D.

to take you, the consuming public, on the journey to financial security. How do you start the journey? This book begins with chapters that discuss the setting of objectives and later chapters that prompt and motivate you to get started with your planning. The longest journey starts with a single step. In my estimation, the primary problem that most people have with financial planning is that they never take that step.

All aspects of financial planning are discussed in this volume: insurance, investments, tax planning and management, retirement planning, and estate planning. Read a chapter and you will learn. Read the entire book and you will learn how fully integrated financial planning can work for you

Whether you are now using the services of a financial planner or merely considering it, this book will add greatly to your knowledge. It will expand your thinking in such a way that any financial planning advice or recommendation you receive will be far more understandable. You will not become a financial planner; but you will have gained a financial planning perspective.

William L. Anthes, M.B.A., Ph.D., joined the College for Financial Planning as President late in 1979. During his first two years as President, the College averaged a 91% increase in enrollments each year and the staff nearly tripled. Before joining the College, Anthes was Director of the Evening Division and Management Center of Rockhurst College, Kansas City, Missouri. He has also held positions as Associate Professor of the College of Business Administration of the University of Nebraska at Omaha and as Faculty Consultant with the State University of Nebraska. His professional affiliations include the American Economic Association, the Colorado Financial Association, and the International Association for Financial Planning. A frequent speaker before business and professional groups, Anthes also has authored twenty-five published articles and research reports. He spends a great deal of time traveling to promote the College's Certified Financial Planner Program.

Financial Planning... An Overview

Forrest Wallace Cato, M.B.A.

The financial planning industry in the United States is composed of highly skilled professionals who practice as individuals or as members of small partnerships. Few national, or even regional, firms exist at the present time. Most financial planners work alone, attempting to solve the constant flow of problems brought on by differing client situations, evolving technology, new products, and changing economic conditions.

What impresses me most as I edit *Financial Planner* magazine and communicate with individual planners across the country is the tremendous creative spirit of our young profession. Its practitioners are willing to take on challenges that require not only a breadth and depth of knowledge far beyond any other in the financial services industry, but also the interpersonal skills of compassion, creative listening, on-the-spot psychological insight, and a sense of salesmanship. It is no wonder that financial planning attracts the cream of the various segments of the financial services industry. Only the truly confident, innovative, and intelligent can prosper as financial planners.

The concept of a financial planning profession originated with Loren Dunton, the founder of the International Association for Financial Planning (IAFP). He has been called "the man who created a profession without ever practicing it," and "the father of financial planning." A brief overview of this profession may be useful for the reader at the outset of the book.

How Does a Financial Planner Help People?

Most people find it difficult to objectively assess their own financial situation and develop their own financial strategy (one that will consistently enable them to reduce the ravages of inflation and their tax burden). The role of the financial planner is to review the client's current financial picture, identify problem areas, and recommend appropriate remedies. The planner helps

Forrest Wallace Cato, B.A., M.B.A., has earned national attention as a journalist and public relations practitioner. He is managing editor of the *Financial Planner* magazine and communications director for the International Association for Financial Planning, and has served on the board of the Sales Motivation Institute. His writings have appeared in *Reader's Digest, Better Homes & Gardens, New York Times, Wall Street Journal, Public Relations Quarterly*, and *Advertising Age*. He has also written about financial marketing and investor relations for the American Bankers Association, the Bank Marketing Association, the National Investor Relations Institute, and the Public Relations Society of America. Cato is former editor of *Trusts and Estates* magazine, former contributing editor to *Pension World*, and contributing editor to *Oil & Gas Tax Quarterly*. He is the author of a number of books and frequently speaks before financial groups and professional associations.

Editor's Notes:
Get Your
Thinking Straight

Whether you are an experienced investor or are still trying to accumulate enough money to become a new investor, the chapters in Part 1 can be invaluable to you. None of us is always able to think straight by ourselves, especially about money matters. Coming up are four chapters aimed at helping you get your thinking straight, or keeping it straight.

Part 1 opens with Venita VanCaspel's chapter, not because ladies usually come first, but because the subject she discusses is dear to everyone's heart—financial independence. Some of Phil Gainsborough's comments in Chapter 2 may shock you, especially those about Social Security, but you'll be glad he told you. You'll probably be challenged by what Bob LeClair says in Chapter 3 about setting your financial objectives; and if you haven't already set some objectives, this is the time to do so. In Chapter 4 Kemp Fain tells you about the all-important basic ingredient, self-motivation; he makes it as sensible, as easy, and as painless as it could possibly be. Maybe by the time you finish these four chapters you'll have your thinking straighter than it has ever been before.

Chapter 1

Venita VanCaspel is the president and founder of VanCaspel and Company, Incorporated. She is the author of several books including, *Money Dynamics*, *The New Money Dynamics*, *Money Dynamics for the 1980s*, and her latest, *The Power of Money Dynamics*. She has contributed to or been reported on in numerous magazines including *Financial Trends*, *Moneymaker Magazine*, *National Tax Digest*, *Fortune Magazine*, *U.S. News & World Report*, and *Money Magazine*. Ms. VanCaspel has appeared on many television and radio programs including "Good Morning America" and "The Mike Douglas Show." She is the moderator of her own National Public Television Show, "The Moneymakers," which is carried on 184 stations. She is also the first woman member of the Pacific Stock Exchange. She is a Certified Financial Planner. She is often introduced as the "First Lady of Financial Planning."

How to Keep More of the Money You Earn

Venita VanCaspel, CFP

Financial planning makes perfect: if you have the ability to earn, discipline to save, willingness to learn, and intelligence to invest, you can make your money grow and yourself independent.

The United States has one of the highest per capita incomes ever known, yet 95 of every 100 U.S. citizens who reach the age of sixty-five are flat broke. Why this tragedy—the tragedy of frustration, bitterness, and deprivation? Why do so many Americans retire in less than financial dignity?

It is because there is an educational void in our nation. Our educational system devotes millions to teaching our youth what they need to know to get a job and earn dollars, but we never stop to teach them what to do with the dollars that they earn. As a financial planner for twenty years, I have been a frequent witness to this senseless financial ignorance. During this time I have counseled a vast number of couples and individuals, and I have become convinced that anyone can become financially independent if they have a reasonable ability to earn, the discipline to save a small portion of their income, the intelligence to learn and apply some basic financial planning rules, and sufficient time.

Then why are so many failing to reach this attainable and vastly rewarding goal? There are five basic reasons: (1) procrastination; (2) failure to establish a goal; (3) ignorance of what money must do to accomplish that goal; (4) failure to understand and apply our tax laws; and (5) failure to buy the right kind of life insurance. My role as a certified financial planner is to help those who seek my advice avoid these mistakes by positioning their assets in the right places at the right times.

But the situation of many of those who come to me for financial counseling is ironic. They have accumulated sufficient assets already, or could easily do so within a few years, to enable them to reach financial independence—if these assets were properly put to work. Many of them have worked extremely hard for their money, but once they have it, instead of putting it to work for themselves they unknowingly give its earning power away to the various savings institutions. They have been taught that to become financially independent they must save and let their money grow.

So, they continue to save and let savings institutions grow, contributing to the beauty of their cities' skylines by building magnificent structures of glass, marble, and steel, while they reach retirement age without the necessary funds to retire in financial dignity. They lack the vital ingredient that a financial planner can supply—the knowledge of how to make their dollars work for them just as hard as they have had to work to earn those dollars.

Putting your money to work so that it can do more for you is the crux of a financial planner's job. But how do we planners accomplish this? The fine points will vary with every client, but the general approach I take is sketched out in the diagram of financial independence in Figure 1. I would work with a client to fill out this diagram, positioning his or her assets so as to minimize the potential for loss and maximize the potential for gain. First, we would need to determine what assets the client had to work with, the years left before retirement, the tax bracket, and the client's temperament. (Determining the latter is not an exact science, but it is essential to good financial planning.) Once this basic information is established, we can then begin allocating funds to the various compartments of the diagram that represent various forms of investing.

Buying Time

Time is the first problem we tackle. Since one of the great mysteries of life is its length, we can never know whether a client will live many years in retirement or die prematurely. This means we must plan for

DIAGRAM OF FINANCIAL INDEPENDENCE
BY VENITA VAN CASPEL
AUTHOR OF <u>MONEY DYNAMICS</u>

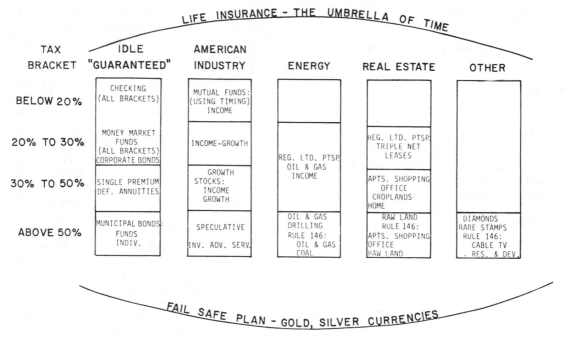

TAX BRACKET	IDLE "GUARANTEED"	AMERICAN INDUSTRY	ENERGY	REAL ESTATE	OTHER
BELOW 20%	CHECKING (ALL BRACKETS)	MUTUAL FUNDS: (USING TIMING) INCOME			
20% TO 30%	MONEY MARKET FUNDS (ALL BRACKETS) CORPORATE BONDS	INCOME-GROWTH	REG. LTD. PTSP. OIL & GAS INCOME	REG. LTD. PTSP. TRIPLE NET LEASES	
30% TO 50%	SINGLE PREMIUM DEF. ANNUITIES	GROWTH STOCKS: INCOME GROWTH		APTS. SHOPPING OFFICE CROPLANDS HOME	
ABOVE 50%	MUNICIPAL BONDS: FUNDS INDIV.	SPECULATIVE INV. ADV. SERV.	OIL & GAS DRILLING RULE 146: OIL & GAS COAL	RAW LAND RULE 146: APTS. SHOPPING OFFICE RAW LAND	DIAMONDS RARE STAMPS RULE 146: CABLE TV RES. & DEV.

Figure 1

either eventuality. We begin by buying the client time, for it does take time to accumulate a living estate. How do we buy time? Through life insurance, but with the lowest expenditure possible.

Life insurance is a necessary investment for anyone who needs time to build up an estate, and it can provide an all-important umbrella of protection for the family in the event of death. But because most people have an incomplete understanding of life insurance, they pour unnecessary dollars into it. I have found that if any one of the following is true of my clients' insurance programs, and if they are healthy enough to pass a physical, I can usually lower their cost without decreasing their protection:

1. If they have more than one policy. (A policy fee is charged each year for each separate policy. This charge does not go to pay for the actual insurance, but for administration.)

2. If their policies contain cash-surrender value.

3. If they have policies that are not on a current 1958 Commissioner's Standard Ordinary (CSO) mortality table. (Many are on the American Experience Table—which reflects death rates from the time of Abraham Lincoln. Even the 1941 CSO table is based on the death rate before penicillin.)

4. If they have "participating," "dividend-paying" policies. (Most clients actually think these are "dividends" and are

not aware that they are a partial return of an overcharge.)

Idle Money

After assessing my clients' insurance needs and helping them place a protective umbrella over their families, the second concern is to build a living estate and fill in the other parts of the financial independence diagram. The first block under the "Umbrella of Time" is labeled "Idle" or "Guaranteed Dollars." I encourage clients to keep as much money idle, or liquid, as they need for peace of mind—because peace of mind is, after all, a good investment. At the same time, I educate them about money so that they won't have too much of it idle and working for someone else.

The idle money allocation could be kept in a checking account or in a money market fund administered by one of the families of mutual funds. If the clients are in a high tax bracket and feel they must have the money guaranteed, some of it might also be placed in single-premium deferred annuities. I discourage four-to-eight-year certificates of deposit (CDs) because I think they force investors to make three bets they are likely to lose. Investors in CDs are betting that: (1) the long-term interest rates will not rise above the current rate; (2) we will not have inflation; and (3) they will not need to use their money for four to eight years. The same drawbacks apply to such hybrids as corporate bonds and municipal bonds.

Investing in Industry

The next block of the diagram for independence encompasses investments in U.S. industry. If the clients have the three "Ts" (Time, Training, and Temperament)

and "M" (sufficient Money to diversify), I suggest that they may want to select the stocks themselves. If they meet these qualifications, we then discuss whether they desire income or growth. I try to discourage speculation, especially in the lower tax brackets, but if clients insist, I offer recommendations.

I advise clients who do not have the three "Ts" and "M" and who do not intend to go it alone in the stock market to enlist the services of professional money managers. Also, if they have assets in excess of $250,000 that they wish to commit to the stock market, I recommend private professional management and help them select an investment advisory service. For clients with smaller amounts, I recommend one or more well-established families of funds that can cover a wide range of financial objectives, including one fund that is either a money market fund or contains only government instruments or cash equivalents and offers exchange privileges.

With this type of investment, clients can monitor their investments and use the mutual fund conversion service to move in and out of the market whenever necessary. There are times when the Federal Reserve Board tightens the money supply so greatly, and other government actions both domestic and foreign are so adverse, that it becomes extremely difficult to make profits in the market. When this happens, investors should be in a position to move out—for, after all, they are in the market to make money. When capital can command a high rate of return in the money market funds, there may be great merit in putting it there, and my clients should have their funds positioned so that they can move over and ride out these periods.

Then, when the pendulum swings back the other way, they will also be in a position to move back into the market without fanfare. They just have to complete and send in the same type of simple one-page exchange form that is used to move funds out of the market. By using a family of funds, investors have the flexibility to reposition this portion of their assets to protect them, without paying a commission.

Diversification is the first rule of successful investing, so let's turn to the next compartment in my diagram for financial independence—energy. A basic principle of economics is that you will enhance your potential for profit if you invest in areas where the demand is greater than the supply. In 1981, for example, where was demand greater than supply? Three areas seemed promising: (1) energy; (2) capital for business expansion; and (3) multiple-family housing.

Energy

The third compartment of the diagram concerns the first of these—investments in energy. The energy shortage has enabled my clients to make considerable profits over the past nine years by investing in oil-income and gas-income limited partnerships. In fact, I believe "black gold" should still be considered for a portion of every portfolio, except where constant liquidity for that portion of funds is a necessity. The energy area will probably continue to be promising since the price of energy seems likely to continue increasing as long as demand increases.

Let me again emphasize that I do not recommend that money be placed in limited partnerships if immediate liquidity of those funds is needed. Although the oil-and-gas-income funds do continually offer a repurchase price, it may not be the price an investor wants. Oil and gas investors must be willing to give up some liquidity in exchange for the potential of good cash flow, a tax shelter, and appreciation. I also emphasize to my clients the depleting characteristic of oil and gas investments. To date the price increases of the oil in reserves has far exceeded the depletion;

therefore, the remaining value has increased considerably rather than decreasing.

Business Capital

A second area where demand has been greater than supply is capital for business expansion. I have advised clients to take advantage of this supply-and-demand imbalance by putting some of their funds to work in triple net leases of office buildings of major corporations. (This investment falls within the fourth compartment of the diagram, headed Real Estate.)

Here's how it works. A registered limited partnership offering excellent potential buys the buildings of major companies such as General Motors, Sears, Safeway, J.C. Penney, New Jersey Bell Telephone, Alabama Power and Light, and other companies with assets of $30 million or more. Then the limited partnership leases the buildings back to these companies on long-term, twenty-five- to thirty-year, noncancellable leases. These companies agree to make lease payments each month and also to pay all the variable costs such as maintenance, insurance, taxes, upkeep, and so on. Many of these leases also have escalation clauses to hedge against inflation and increase cash flow.

The partnership owns the building and makes the monthly mortgage payments. This entitles it to deduct the interest it pays on the mortgage and to depreciate the buildings on a straight-line basis. The objective is quarterly cash distributions to the limited partners of 8–9 percent, of which 80–100 percent is tax-sheltered by the interest and depreciation passthrough.

This is a relatively low-risk investment, which has the added advantage of possible future equity buildup and appreciation. Ultimately, it's preferable to own a major company's building rather than its bonds. Rent payments take precedence over interest, and any court in the land will evict a tenant for nonpayment of rent. Not that this partnership would accept a triple net lease from a company such as Penn Central.

However, it's interesting to note that Penn Central was in bankruptcy for eight years but never missed a triple net lease payment. I use investments like this for people in the 20–30 percent tax bracket, through many higher bracket clients like the conservative nature of the triple net lease concepts and are pleased to have funds working there.

The Housing Market

Multiple-family housing has been another important area offering potential cash distributions, excess deductions, equity buildup (mortgage paydown), appreciation, and capital conservation. There is still a tremendous housing storage in the United States. The average home costs in excess of $74,000, but the average family income is around $17,000. This means that many families who want to live in a desirable area of their city and want access to such facilities as a swimming pool and tennis courts have no choice but to live in garden-type apartments. They may be frustrated potential homeowners, but home ownership is not one of the options open to them.

As an investor, though, you can benefit from the high demand for such rental housing by entering into a registered limited partnership, offered by general partners whose expertise is established, that buys and operates residential properties. Investors tend to be pleased with the "Now" benefits of quarterly cash distributions of 4–8 percent, which have been tax-sheltered, and with excess deductions of 6–9 percent.

Although there is no guarantee of returns, if the partnership does make cash distributions of 5 percent and does provide excess deductions of 9 percent, and if the investor is in the 30 percent tax bracket, this is equivalent to receiving an 11 percent return that is fully taxable. In a 40 percent tax bracket it is equivalent to 14.3 percent, in a 50 percent bracket it is equivalent to 19 percent, and in a 60 percent bracket it is equivalent to a 26 percent taxable return. These are the "Now" benefits, which we financial planners and our clients like. But even if there were no "Now" benefits, I would still recommend this investment because of the "Later" benefits of potential equity buildup and capital appreciation.

Past results with these limited real estate partnerships have been a delight. Yet, I think the potential for the future is even better because provisions of the new tax reform bill indicate building will now be based on need, rather than on the amount of excess funds savings institutions have on hand. Past performance was excellent despite a lower rate of inflation and, at times, overbuilding. Once inflation reached 15 to 17 percent there was underbuilding; and with our national vacancy rate under 5 percent and still dropping, the outlook is even better.

As vacancies continue to go down and replacement costs for buildings escalate, rents will be pushed higher. Rent is still one of this country's best buys, and it surely must escalate before there will be sufficient new building. This should allow the limited partnerships to make constant rental increases and still maintain high occupancy rates. Inspection of a large number of the properties owned and managed by the particular partnerships I recommend has shown that they do a superior job of buying at the right price, managing with expertise, and selling at the time the properties mature into a profitable position for capital appreciation.

Their expert managements have enabled them to continue to raise rents, to lower operating costs, and to increase cash flow. For clients who understand that investing in commercial, income-producing real estate entails giving up liquidity, who realize the past is no guarantee of the future, and who are in a 30 percent tax bracket or above, this investment makes sense.

Incidentally, I divide a client's dollars into two categories—"hard" and "soft." "Hard" dollars are their after-tax dollars. "Soft" dollars the ones that will have to be sent on a one-way trip to Washington, unless they are put to work in tax-sheltered investments. I recommend quite different investments for "hard" dollars than I do for the "soft" dollars that will belong to the IRS unless channeled to programs with tax incentives. I believe in using tax-sheltered investments if they offer the potential of tax deferral or of turning tax liabilities into capital gains, and if the investment area has social and economic value.

Tax Angles

This two-pronged goal brings us to an important lesson. Once you enter the higher tax brackets, you'll either be sending your hard-earned dollars to Washington, D.C., or you'll learn to "Defer and Convert."

Deferring, of course, refers to finding tax-sheltered investments that let you delay paying taxes on earnings until you move out of the investment at a later date. But if you'll have to pay the tax someday, why not now, you might ask? Inflation is one good reason. If, for example, inflation is 7 percent and you are in a 40 percent tax bracket, by deferring the tax payment for ten years, you not only have the use of that money for ten years but you will be paying it off with a 48¢ dollar. What's more, if you can convert it to the status of a long-term capital gain, you can pay it off with a 19¢ dollar. Long-term capital gains are taxed at a lower rate than other income.

The defer-and-convert tactic, while important in anyone's investment plan, must be tailored to each individual's temperament and biases. Beyond a certain point,

some clients will be happier paying the tax than playing the tax-shelter game. Others definitely prefer to turn their tax liabilities into potential assets to the maximum extent possible. I usually recommend that clients position their investments so as to bring their taxable income down to $30,000 if it fits their temperament. If not, surely down to $45,000. Even in a 50 percent bracket, they are giving Washington an opportunity to go into business with them, on a more or less 50–50 basis if the shelter has 100 percent deductibility.

Special Areas

After taking into account possible tax-deferred investments, we move to the final block of our diagram, which covers various areas that will appeal to some investors. Diamonds are portable, passable, liquid, and in demand. However, they can drop in price, as was evidenced in the early 1980s.

Rare stamps can also be an investment you may want to consider if chosen from reputable dealers. Stamps have escalated considerably in the past ten years.

Rare coins of high quality, uncirculated coins, and proof coins made prior to 1933 can also lend themselves to successful investing. During the past twenty years, they have risen in price approximately 20 percent per year, and during the past five years they have increased at an average annual compound growth rate of 28.7 percent.

Stability or Safety?

In addition to pointing out the value of diversifying assets, another key to helping clients position their assets properly is to impress upon them the difference between "stability" and "safety." "Stability" refers to the return of a known quantity of dollars.

"Safety" refers to the return of the same amount of food, clothing, and shelter. I attempt to have my clients' dollars in a "safe" position, but not a "stable" position. At the current inflation rate, there is no safety in being stable.

For example, let's say a client invested $10,000 in a stable and predictable AAA-rated corporate bond yielding 9 percent. Even if inflation could, by some miracle, be held to 5.2 percent, ten years hence the effective rate of return (measure of purchasing power) would be only 5.4 percent. Or stated another way, $900 earned ten years from now will only purchase what is today $540 worth of food, clothing, or shelter. To keep their purchasing power intact, bonds would have to have a floating rate that would increase to 14.9 percent in ten years. Remember that interest rates in this example assume only a 5.2 percent rate of inflation—less than half the rate today. And this interest would be subject to the normal tax bite ten years down the road.

I have never found a quality, fixed-dollar investment with a high enough yield to accomplish long-term "safety." The increase in the cost of living has always outpaced the return.

What If . . . ?

Even with careful planning and diversification, every investment plan involves some risk. Can a fail-safe plan be developed to protect investors in the event the preceding program aborts? To cover this contingency, the final element in the financial independence diagram is concerned with investments in gold and silver and in gold and silver stocks. Although I'm not a gold bug, money can be made with proper timing. Gold should be treated like fire insurance on a home. If your home doesn't burn down that year, you still shouldn't cancel your fire insurance policy, I think there is merit in having 5–10 percent of a person's

assets in gold and gold-related investments.

The accompanying diagram for financial independence (Figure 1) has served my clients well. With the proper placement and timing, their assets after taxes have grown in value, far outpacing inflation. Those clients who need income now can take the cash flow from each of their investments and use it for current expenses, and they can also set up a monthly withdrawal program with their mutual funds. For those who are still accumulating for the future, I recommend they sign a bank draft to add to their mutual funds on a monthly basis, and that they endorse their quarterly checks from the energy, real estate, and other partnerships over to the funds so as to recycle this money, bringing them the potential joys of compounding.

Remember, the Eighth Wonder of the World is compound interest. When we can add a bit of tax shelter to the picture, as we have been able to do, it could well move up to seventh place, and seven has long been considered a heavenly number.

Today's Biggest Misconception About Financial Planning

There is a great and ever growing need for professional financial planning services today. Unfortunately, a common misconception is that financial planners can help mainly upper-income people. Actually, financial planning can be very beneficial to middle-income people, particularly the great numbers—far, far too many—who have not altered their financial habits and are still operating under the Poor Richard theory: "Work, save your money; and don't borrow."

With inflation what it is today, to accept that theory is a serious mistake. The current interest paid by savings and loans is being obliterated by the current inflation level, which is giving them a negative purchasing power return; yet savers still are required to pay taxes on that interest earning. And to make a bad situation worse, the money is working for someone other than the saver.

Venita VanCaspel's Counsel

I tell most people that the Poor Richard theory will drag them to the bottom of the financial ocean, and if not changed in time, it will be too late for a planner to resuscitate them.

Early to bed and early to rise doesn't necessarily make a person healthy, wealthy, and wise. Money matters are very serious today, deadly serious. People at all levels are hunting! Historical clichés and long-standing platitudes must now be examined anew.

New Saying for a New Day

Inflation is the Robin Hood of the 1980s. It takes from the ignorant and gives to the well informed.

There is a new law of financial reality in the United States today. Either you will be a victim of inflation or you will be a beneficiary of inflation. Inflation does not destroy wealth, it repositions it to those who understand its workings. Nothing can make you as much money as inflation—and leveraged inflation can truly make you money. You must learn to embrace inflation, not fear it, because inflation will not go away!

Government is the biggest beneficiary of inflation. If you get a 10 percent raise in salary, the government gets a 16 percent raise in the taxes you pay. If inflation goes up 1 percent, the government gets $1 billion.

Why Fail in Your Finances?

As the economic situation worsens, so will some important statistics. Even now,

of every 100 persons who reach age sixty-five, only five are financially independent; 23 must continue working; and 75 must depend on friends, charity, or others. Of every 100 persons reaching the age of sixty-five, 95 are flat broke. This startling statistic will not improve unless more and more of our citizens learn to overcome the following basic problems:

Procrastination. Many people invest too much money in today's goods and services and leave the future without a plan.

Failure to establish goals. If you aim at nothing you hit nothing. Try setting a minimum goal of $300,000 and keep investing 10 percent of your income until you reach that $300,000. When you meet this goal, raise the ante.

Ignorance of what money must do to bring financial independence. We are raising a nation of financial illiterates.

Failure to understand and apply tax laws.

Buying the wrong kind of life insurance. The main purpose of life insurance should be to protect those dependent upon you until you have accumulated a living estate. Your goal is to become self-insured.

What Should an Investor Do?

When an investor opts for stability—which, as I said earlier, means the return of the same number of dollars—that investor is betting against four things (and I'll bet he is going to lose): (1) interest rates will not go up for the next four-six-eight years; (2) there will be no inflation; (3) the interest earned is not taxable (although it really is); and (4) the investor won't need any of that money before the maturity date. If the investor does and withdraws the funds, there is a substantial early withdrawal penalty. The investor should take that money out right now. Accept the penalty now. The same with corporate municipal bonds. Bail out now and recognize the importance of safety. Remember, inflation will not go away. The national debt is already in place. Deal with the world the way it really is and not the way you wish it was.

Most people are so illiterate when it comes to money they think they are winning when they are losing. Many older people are living in a financial world that no longer exists. And we aren't preparing our youth to deal with reality.

What Is a Well-Balanced Program?

Each person or family is different. Every recommendation must be based on a great amount of information, which can be obtained by having the investor complete a personal planning data sheet. This information will give the planner a definite picture of at least four factors that will affect financial decisions:

1. Assets and where they are positioned at present. This information often gives the planner insight into the person's temperament.

2. Tax bracket. Every investment must be made with the tax bracket in mind; otherwise the investor will probably make the wrong choices.

3. Time. How much time do we have to accomplish the investor's goals? Time is an important element.

4. Temperament. This is not an exact art and science, but it is absolutely vital to the investment. Consider temperament or the client won't have peace of mind, and peace of mind is a good investment.

There is always an investment for every season, but there is no investment for all seasons. The key words for the 1980s will be agility and diversification. Spread your risks. Look back, now, to the diagram of financial independence in Figure 1, which shows how this can be done.

First, note that your financial planner must tie your plan into your tax bracket. Second, note the section for idle guaranteed dollars. In my opinion, there are only two places for these—checking accounts and money market mutual funds. The next section to consider is U.S. industry. Here, we use a well-managed family of mutual funds and use a timing service to move between their aggressive mutual fund and their money market fund. In the energy category, which deals with the investment of hard, after-tax serious money, we use oil- and gas-income programs. In the real estate category, if investors are under a 30 percent tax bracket, we use triple net lease registered limited partnerships. Over this, we use multifamily housing partnerships. We also use miniwarehouse and budget motel partnerships.

We use tax shelters for those who are in the 50 percent bracket or above and who have sufficient net worth to qualify to bring their taxable income down to around $30,000. We try to use 200 percent deductible shelters whenever possible in order to get maximum use of tax dollars. The average client's greatest expenditure is his or her tax bill, so if we can lower that by attempting to turn tax liability into an asset, we have made a contribution to the improvement of his or her financial future.

Hard assets such as investment grade diamonds, mutual funds that invest in South African gold stocks, and the like can also play a role.

If the client has not already accumulated a living estate and has dependents, we also put the umbrella of time over his head through low-cost life insurance.

Do I Need a Financial Planner?

If you have only a small amount of money, you may need a financial planner to teach you how to save or to motivate you to seek a better-paying position so you will have funds to invest. The planner can only invest what the client saves.

If you have assets, a planner can help you reposition them for their maximum utilization.

It is great to know that everyone needs us—and most need us very badly. I want our clients to prosper, to benefit from inflation, to own a part of the economy. History proves that if the people don't benefit sufficiently from the economic system, then they will eventually fight to destroy it.

Choose a planner very carefully—just as carefully as any other professional adviser in your life. Reveal all about your finances. If you don't, the planner is greatly handicapped and cannot be of maximum help.

The client and the planner should be compatible and there should be a great level of trust. If not, the client should seek the services of another planner.

The planner most definitely should be a member of the International Association for Financial Planning and also a Certified Financial Planner. The IAFP adheres to a code of ethics and has standards of practice, plus a continuing education program.

Chapter 2

Social Security: It Won't Be Enough

Philip N. Gainsborough, CFP

Philip N. Gainsborough, B.A. (Economics and Radio and Television), has been working in the financial field for over twenty years. He is president of Gainsborough Financial Consultants, Incorporated, a firm developed to assist people in arranging their personal and corporate financial affairs, and he is on the Board of Advisers for Professional Designation in Personal Financial Planning at the University of California, Los Angeles. He has made frequent radio broadcasts, doing the daily market comment for E. F. Hutton and Company and the business and financial report for the Gary Owens Magazine Show. He has also acted as the co-host on the cable television program "Financial Strategies of the 1980s," and has hosted his own money talk show. His many activities have included guest appearances at various investment forums and the handling of financial planning seminars for large corporations. He has been national sales director for a public real estate syndicate and was involved in structuring and marketing several private placements. He was also on the staff of AMR International, conducting its sales and sales management seminars. Gainsborough is a Certified Financial Planner, a Registered Investment Adviser, a principal of a National Association of Securities Dealers firm, a member of the International Association for Financial Planning, and a member of the Institute of Certified Financial Planners.

Social Security, Franklin Delano Roosevelt's great postdepression experiment designed to insure the aged against poverty, illness, and destitution, is facing bankruptcy after less than fifty years. Not only has it failed to provide a comfortable old age for most pensioners, it now appears that those of us still paying into the system won't receive anything without a gigantic bailout from the U.S. Treasury. Even those now receiving benefits fear that their monthly checks, already too small to cover the most modest life-style, will shrink even further.

Unfortunately, you and I have been misled for over two generations into believing that Social Security payments will be adequate to provide for a comfortable retirement and that these payments constitute no more than a return of the payroll taxes that we have paid during our working years.

In reality, nothing could be further from the truth. From the very beginning, Social Security benefits for those retired have been *paid out* of taxes deducted from people working, who in turn have to rely at retirement on benefits from ever increasing taxes paid by their children. In fact, most people withdraw far more than they contribute.

To illustrate, Ida Fuller of Vermont, the first Social Security recipient, paid a total of $22 in Social Security taxes. She drew her last check for $112.60 in December 1974 shortly after her 100th birthday. By then she had collected $20,944.42, a return of 952 times her original contribution!

Originally, Franklin D. Roosevelt envisioned Social Security as only a supplement to other income when he said in 1935:

We can never ensure 100% of the population against 100% of the hazards and vicissitudes of life but we have tried to frame a law which will give some measure of protection to the average citizen and to his family . . . against poverty-ridden old age.

Roosevelt's political successors obviously did not heed his words about providing just a supplemental income stream. After decades of overambitious expansion to the point that we now deliver benefits to nearly 36 million people and promise financial independence to 120 million workers, Social Security quite simply is unable to pay its bills. The Old Age Survivor's Insurance (OASI) Trust Fund, with just $36 billion remaining, is projected to be exhausted by 1983. Why? Because today it is paying out $17,000 more than it collects in payroll taxes every minute of every hour of every day. Payments today amount to over 160 billion dollars, and by 1984 nearly 200 billion dollars will be mailed to recipients.

The question is not will Social Security be enough, but will there be any Social Security? The bottom line is, frankly, that the aged, the widowed, the disabled, and even the young have been promised more than the nation can deliver at any reasonable cost.

In all probability, however, some Social Security payments can be expected, but they will be far less than we will need. Therefore, we must have a plan, a financial itinerary, and an understanding of the problems, the benefits, and the potential solutions of the Social Security system if we are to retire with anything near our present standard of living. Additionally, nothing can take the place of timely, prudent individual saving and investment planning. These strategies remain crucial for those who hope to be able to choose the kind of life they will lead in retirement or to choose to fully retire. Social Security benefits alone never have and do not now provide for a gracious retirement. We must not assume that someone other than ourselves is going to take care of us.

For the balance of this chapter, it is my goal to outline the series of events that led up to this crisis, the potential solutions as proposed by various legislators, and the actual benefits that are allowed under the old age and survivor's package. In addition, I will describe and illustrate a planning strategy to aid in developing an achievable goal that will allow you not only to retire with a few basic needs paid for, but to retire with financial independence.

Evolution of the Crisis

What but a crisis could be the end result of a retirement plan to which one contributes at the very most $14,300 over a period of thirty years and is able to retire at age sixty-five on $753 a month, or $9,000 a year, for as long as one lives? (In 1980, the life expectancy for an individual reaching age sixty-five was more than sixteen years!) It sounds too good, but this is the promise our government has made through our present Social Security system: a return of over $144,575 (which does not include benefits keyed to the Consumer Price Index), or 1,011 percent on your original contribution.

Some have called the system a fraud and compared it to a pyramid club, a Ponzie scheme, or a chain letter. In these instances, members who join first are paid out of what is collected from the members who join later. In these schemes, not all the participants get all the benefits. This, it now appears, is the posture of the present Social Security system. Although many claim that those who promised the benefits knew this beforehand and knew there would never be enough money to pay them, let's examine more carefully what really caused the breakdown.

The Social Security Act of 1935 was modest. It covered workers in commerce and industry only (leaving out farmers, service workers, government employees, and the self-employed), plus their spouses and dependents. FDR implied that the act was not intended to guarantee a comfortable retirement, but was established only to ward off financial destitution.

Funding the System

The act was designed, therefore, to pay minimal benefits to elderly workers. Congress briefly considered the traditional annuity plan in which each worker's contributions would be set aside in a special fund, from which the interest income would pay future benefits. However, in order to cover those currently in need, Congress adopted a pay-as-you-go scheme in which payroll taxes collected from active workers were simply transferred to retirees. The system had to be funded entirely by a tax levied half on employers and half on workers so that it could be presented to the nation as a type of contributory insurance plan. To this day, paycheck stubs identify Social Security taxes as FICA, for Federal Insurance Contribution Act. It was a great idea, except that it made the system sensitive to adverse economic developments.

It is clear that FDR had in mind to help the penniless and the elderly who lost their savings in the Great Depression. However, he thought that in the long run Social Security retirement benefits would be just one leg of a three-legged stool that was to include private pensions and supplementary income from savings and investments. The initial philosophy was for the young and the employed to be taxed for the immediate support of the elderly with the expectation that when they, in turn, grew old, another generation would pay for them.

Expanding the Benefits

With a relatively small group of pensioners and a larger group of workers contributing, the system's cash balances grew rapidly in the early years, and Congress couldn't resist the temptation to spread these cash reserves in the form of new legislative benefits. This approach even became politically expedient. In fact, these new benefits were first initiated in 1939, before the first Social Security benefits were paid. The first to be added were death benefits that would continue to be paid to the widow and dependents. Since then, coverage has been steadily expanded to include farm and domestic workers, employees of state and local governments, employees of nonprofit organizations such as hospitals, self-employed people including doctors and lawyers, members of the armed forces, and even ministers and members of religious orders so long as they do not take vows of poverty. Retired millionaires collect as well as laborers; benefits go to almost anyone who has ever paid Social Security taxes and to some people who never have. In recognition of their important role in society, housewives who have not worked outside the home and thus have never paid into the system collect benefits equal to 50 percent of those earned by their husbands. In essence, Congress began trying to provide old age insurance for 100 percent of the population.

In time, whole new programs were added. In 1956 Congress started payments, financed by Social Security taxes, to disabled workers and in later years it greatly liberalized the definitions of who could qualify.

Another especially important expansion began, also in 1956, when Congress permitted women to retire at sixty-two rather than sixty-five, on 80 percent of the standard pension; men were allowed to do the same in 1961. Today two-thirds of all Social Security pensioners retire before the "normal" age of sixty-five. Although their pensions are lower, they not only collect benefits for more years, but they also pay taxes into the system for fewer years. When Social Security began, only 54 percent of all men and 62 percent of all women lived until sixty-five; those who did make it that far could expect to live another 12.8 years. By 1980, 68 percent of all men and 82 percent of all women could expect to live until sixty-five, and those who reached that age in 1982 will, on the average, live—and collect pensions—for more than sixteen years (see Figure 1).

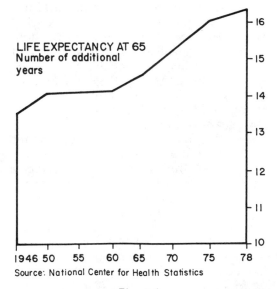

LIFE EXPECTANCY AT 65
Number of additional years

Source: National Center for Health Statistics

Figure 1

By 1963, as part of Lyndon Johnson's Great Society program, the Medicare program was enacted to help cover the hospital and medical bills of people sixty-five or older. Hospital bills are paid out of a portion of Social Security taxes assigned to a separate trust fund; insurance to pay doctors' bills is financed by voluntary contributions from the elderly who elect to sign up. The current cost of the compulsory Medicare program to Social Security is $34 billion annually.

Besides making even more people eligible for benefits, Congress, with the approval of the White House, kept raising the payments—eleven times between 1950 and 1972, six of those times during election years. It seemed a safe as well as a wonderfully popular thing for politicians to do. Into the early 1970s, tax collections almost without exception ran ahead of benefit payments, and the Social Security trust funds ran surpluses.

In 1972, Arkansas Democrat Wilbur Mills, chairman of the House Ways and Means Committee, was in the middle of what turned out to be a futile run for the Democratic presidential nomination. Mills pushed through Congress a bill raising Social Security benefits 20 percent. More important, the bill stated that beginning in 1975, Social Security benefits were to be keyed to the Consumer Price Index (CPI). If the CPI in the first quarter of any year averages more than 3 percent higher than it was twelve months earlier, benefits are raised the following July by an amount equal to the full increase.

From 1975 through 1981, the CPI jumped ahead at some of the fastest inflationary rates in U.S. history. Social Security benefits more than kept pace. The maximum annual benefit rose 200 percent during the 1970s and has risen 38.5 percent in the last four years. Although inflation is now cooling, benefits are still being boosted to make up for past price increases. The 7.4 percent increase due July 1 was created by inflation that occurred primarily in 1981. When the increase goes into effect, monthly checks will average $406 for a single pensioner and $695 for a retired couple.

Such increases have transformed the Social Security system into exactly what

Franklin Roosevelt never intended it to be: the primary source of income for most of the aged. In the early years, Social Security pensions averaged 30–34 percent of a retired person's last monthly paycheck; in 1981 the average was 55 percent. This increase is the result not only of indexing benefits to the CPI but also of the generous formulas used to calculate initial benefits, which have been written into the law.

In addition to the expanded benefits passed by Congress over the years and graciously accepted by all Americans, many other events have taken place that were not anticipated.

Projections Inaccurate

First, people are living longer. At sixty-five, the average life expectancy is nearly seventeen years. As medical technology develops, the present adult population over sixty-five increases. Now over 11 percent of our population is over sixty-five, but by the year 2020 it is expected to account for over 15 percent of the population (see Figure 2).

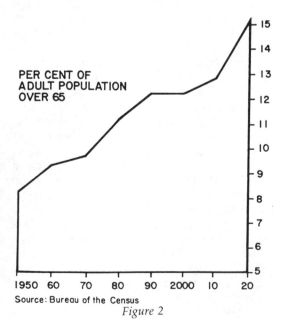

PER CENT OF
ADULT POPULATION
OVER 65

1950 60   70   80   90   2000   10   20

Source: Bureau of the Census

Figure 2

Also, the 50 million Americans in the age group over fifty-five represent 29 percent of voting age population. This group alone cast more than 33 percent of the ballots for president in 1980. Naturally, politicians are eager to appeal to this group.

The baby boom of the 1940s and 1950s, which brought a large number of workers into the system in the 1960s and 1970s, is almost over. Real wages have also declined. That is, inflation has been greater than the increase in taxpayers' salaries. With benefits tied automatically to the cost of living, expenditures have tended to exceed revenues.

Unemployment has also contributed to the deficit. When fewer people are working, fewer people pay Social Security taxes. Statistics show that in 1981, for every 1 million people laid off for just one month, Social Security lost $100 million in tax income. High employment, on the other hand, encourages early retirement, another unexpected expense. Over 235 state and city governmental bodies have withdrawn from the system, so that the total number of employees participating has been reduced.

Each situation by itself would disturb the system—together they are catastrophic. Senior citizens' groups and retirees across the country are strongly opposing most of the solutions being proposed. A typical response is:

I've worked for forty years. My wife and I have skimped and done without to raise and educate our children and I have had Social Security taxes taken out of my pay. Now, with my health going and retirement near, I'm being told that Social Security will be cut. It is not fair.

But was the system really designed to be fair? As A. Haeworth Robertson, former chief actuary of the U.S. Social Security Administration, points out in his book *The Coming Revolution in Social Security* (Reston, VA: Reston Publishing Co., Inc., 1982), the answer is no. He states:

Many participants can expect to receive much more in benefits, many participants can expect to receive much less. . . . Simply, the system was never designed on the principle of undivided equity or fairness for each participant.

The Social Security Tax

In the beginning, workers paid about 1 percent of the first $3,000 of salary, or a maximum of $30. It was not until 1950 that the contributions were increased to 1½ percent on the first $3,600. But beginning in 1956, the adjustments came almost yearly. By 1969 the maximum annual payment was $374.40, as individuals paid 4.8 percent on all earnings up to $7,800. All these increases received little publicity. From this point forward it became apparent that the system was in trouble, and the tax increases came swiftly, dipping into the pocketbook of all workers, until the tax reached today's height of 6.70 percent on the first $32,400 of wages, for a contribution $2,170.80. A tax increase of 580 percent in just 13 years! Projections for 1990 are 7.65 percent on the first $66,900 for a tax of $5,117.85. And, by the beginning of the year 2000, the tax will be $10,625.85, a percentage jump of 489 percent (see Figure 3).

Basically, the system is supposed to work like this. Out of the 6.7 percent of a worker's income paid this year, 4.75 percent will go into old age and survivor's insurance (OASI), 0.6 percent into the disability insurance (DI), and 1.3 percent into hospital insurance (HI). Those three funds are separate, and money from one program cannot be funded or funneled into another to pay benefits. Simply stated, one part of the system could be generating deficits while another enjoys a surplus. Although the system is a pay-as-you-go program, it does have safety reserves called trust funds. But these funds are only designed to absorb deficits; in other words, they are

Year	Annual Maximum	Social Security Rate	Tax
→ 1937	$ 3,000	1.0%	$ 30.00
→ 1950	3,000	1.5%	45.00
1951	3,600	1.5%	54.00
1954	3,600	2.0%	72.00
1955	4,200	2.0%	84.00
1957	4,200	2.25%	94.50
1959	4,800	2.5%	120.00
1960	4,800	3.0%	144.00
1962	4,800	3.125%	150.00
1963	4,800	3.625%	174.00
1966	6,600	4.2%	277.20
1967	6,600	4.4%	290.40
1968	7,800	4.4%	343.20
→ 1969	7,800	4.8%	374.40
1971	7,800	5.2%	405.60
1972	9,000	5.2%	468.00
1973	10,800	5.85%	631.80
1974	13,200	5.85%	772.20
1975	14,100	5.85%	824.85
1976	15,300	5.85%	895.05
1977	16,500	5.85%	965.25
1978	17,700	6.05%	1,070.85
1979	22,900	6.13%	1,403.77
1980	25,900	6.13%	1,587.67
1981	29,700	6.65%	1,975.05
→ 1982	32,400	6.70%	2,170.80
1990	66,900	7.65%	5,117.85
→ 2000	138,900	7.65%	10,625.85

Figure 3

simply a stop-gap measure in case the Social Security Administration is inaccurate at projecting the inflow and outgo of funds, taking into account factors such as trends in unemployment, marriages, birthrates, divorces, retirements, and disabilities.

An Abundance of Alarming Statistics

Today we find each pensioner is supported by three taxpayers. Compare this to FDR's Social Security program when one pensioner was supported by fifty workers. In Harry Truman's day the ratio was sixteen to one. By 2025, there will be just two workers for each Social Security beneficiary (Figure 4).

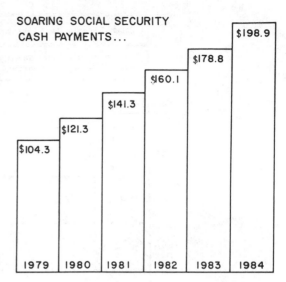

SOARING SOCIAL SECURITY CASH PAYMENTS...

Source: U.S. NEWS & WORLD REPORT, May 25, 1981

Figure 5

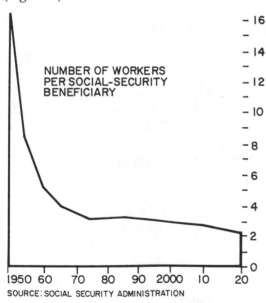

NUMBER OF WORKERS PER SOCIAL-SECURITY BENEFICIARY

SOURCE: SOCIAL SECURITY ADMINISTRATION

Figure 4

Board of Trustees report, unless changes are made. Today the Social Security trust has $36 billion (see Figure 6) remaining, and at the present deficit spending rate, the funds will be gone within two years.

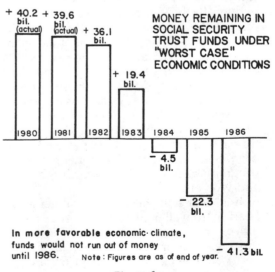

MONEY REMAINING IN SOCIAL SECURITY TRUST FUNDS UNDER "WORST CASE" ECONOMIC CONDITIONS

In more favorable economic climate, funds would not run out of money until 1986. Note: Figures are as of end of year.

Figure 6

Consequently, the cash payments are soaring. Estimated payments for 1982 are $160 billion (see Figure 5) and deficits are mounting, estimated at $6.6 billion in 1982. A crash course to bankruptcy is inevitable by 1985, according to a Social Security

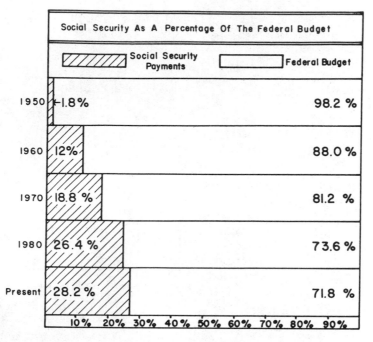

Figure 7

When compared to the total federal budget, the rapid escalation of Social Security costs is astonishing (see Figure 7). In 1950, Social Security and Medicare accounted for only 1.8 percent of the federal budget. By 1970, it had grown to 18.8 percent of the budget, and in 1982 the estimates were that over 28 percent of the entire federal budget would be used to pay benefits for Social Security and Medicare. These are now being referred to as "entitlement programs." In short, the system has expanded far beyond its current ability to pay, but then all the benefits seem valid, certainly from a humanistic standpoint. It is no wonder we all voted for the proponents of such programs as honorable and forthright men and women.

It is clear that the elderly will get a full hearing from all politicians who seek public office, and it is also clear that most retirement groups are being urged to oppose and vote against anyone who favors any cuts. But the fact remains that the current Social Security pension fund (OASI) is insolvent, and if steps are not taken soon, not only will Social Security not be enough, but it may disappear.

Possible Solutions to the Problem

Although it is estimated that about one-quarter of all American families pay more in Social Security taxes than they do in income taxes, it appears the short-term remedy is more taxes (see Figure 3). But is this the answer? Many economists believe that the employer's share of the tax is in effect paid by workers and consumers. As the employer's tax increases, he will either pass out smaller raises to his workers or increase the price of products. He may also hire fewer workers or eliminate them. Thus, the Social Security tax is believed to be a stimulant to both inflation and unemployment. If this trend continues,

Social Security could drain away 25 percent of American payrolls.

Raise the Retirement Age

Proposals for raising the beneficiaries' retirement age from sixty-five to sixty-eight and "early" retirement from sixty-two to sixty-five have also been discussed, as well as a further reduction in the percentage paid to early retirees. Although this first suggestion seems most plausible and the savings phenomenal in view of the fact that people are living so much longer, it has not met with political support. President Ronald Reagan proposed to reduce the incentive to retire early by reducing the benefits paid at sixty-two to 55 percent rather than the current 80 percent. Rewards of 8–10 percent for retiring after age sixty-five have also been suggested. Currently, this incentive remains at 3 percent, which is not much of a financial incentive.

Use General Revenues or Borrow from Other Trust Funds

Borrow from the Treasury, say some. Liberals and others opposed to any reduction in benefits argue for using income tax and other revenues to make any payments that cannot be financed by the payroll tax. Former Social Security Commissioner Robert M. Ball contends that the system could get through the 1980s with relatively small "borrowings," which could be repaid, with interest, out of the reserves that the pension fund will again begin to accumulate in the 1990s.

The argument against general-revenue financing has been stated succinctly by Social Security Commissioner John Svahn: "What general revenues? In an era of budget deficits that could all too easily approach $200 billion a year, the government simply has no funds to spare." Diverting money to Social Security would force the government to borrow even more from the financial markets than it is already doing to finance defense and general social spending. This tactic would continue to keep interest rates high, or push them even higher. Others advise borrowing from the other trust funds, but this too is just a short-run remedy and eventually these monies would have to be returned. How long could we continue to rob from Peter to pay Paul?

Eliminate Indexing

As most people will agree, the one element that has caused more problems than any other, but that many don't want to touch, is the keying of benefits to the Consumer Price Index. No one benefit has been so devastating as this aspect of the system. A one-year freeze on the cost of living has been proposed, but to have more than a brief impact on the trust fund deficit, any such plan would have to be combined with a cap on future cost-of-living adjustments. The idea favored by academic experts is to index benefits either to the rise in prices or to the increase in average wages throughout the economy, whichever is less. Such a system would keep benefits from racing far ahead of tax collections during periods of inflation. Other suggested minor reforms range from making Social Security benefits cover everybody, including the 3 million federal employees, to rewriting the benefits formula, or encouraging savings through tax-free or tax-deferred accounts.

Everyone seems to be well aware of the scope of possible solutions, but which political leader is willing to risk his career by supporting any of these proposals? The answer seems to be no one, since every suggested solution seems to offend some powerful group.

How the System Works

Simple in concept, but complicated in actual operation, Social Security basically replaces a portion of the earnings that are lost as a result of a person's old age, disability, or death, and pays a portion of the expense of illness of aged and disabled persons.

There are four primary categories of benefits for qualified workers:

1. *Retirement.* At age sixty-five, retirement benefits begin; if you retire at sixty-two, you may still receive benefits, but at a reduced level. Your spouse and children may also receive benefits on your retirement.

2. *Hospital Insurance.* Beginning at age sixty-five, you receive hospital insurance for the rest of your life. If you are not sixty-five yet, but have been receiving disability payments for twenty-four months or more, you also receive hospital insurance.

3. *Disability Insurance.* If you are unable to work because of physical or mental disability over an extended period, you, your spouse, and children may receive benefits.

4. *Survivor's Insurance.* If you die, your spouse, children, and elderly dependent parents may receive benefits.

Qualifying for Benefits

The method used in judging qualification of workers is relatively simple. You qualify for benefits if you have earned a specified number of "quarters" by retirement age. The required number of quarters depends on your year of birth. If you reach sixty-two in 1982, you will need thirty-one quarters of coverage. Each year the number increases, so that by 1991 everyone will need forty quarters to qualify.

Quarters are earned at the rate of no more than four per year and depend on the amount of salary you earned and paid Social Security tax on during each year.

The minimum earnings in 1981 for one quarter of credit was $310 (prior to 1978 it was $50 per calendar quarter). Therefore, if you earned $1,240 in 1981, but only worked two months, you still receive four quarters of credit. However, since you can earn a maximum of only four quarters per year, it will take ten years to earn forty quarters regardless of earnings in excess of $1,240 per year. In addition, this amount is subject to yearly increases as wages increase.

Calculating Your Benefits

Calculating your retirement benefits is a complicated process. In general, they are based on your average post earnings subject to Social Security tax. The closer your pay has been over the years to the maximum wage covered, the bigger benefit you get. Although most people rely on the Social Security Administration to calculate their benefits when they retire, below is a simplified step-by-step procedure to estimate your benefits.

Step I

Calculate your average earnings during your working years. The number of years you count depends on the year in which you were born.

YEAR BORN	YEARS YOU COUNT	YEAR BORN	YEARS YOU COUNT
1913	19	1921	27
1914	20	1922	28
1915	21	1923	29
1916	22	1924	30
1917	23	1925	31
1918	24	1926	32
1919	25	1927	33
1920	26	1928	34
		1930 on	35

Number of years you count: _____

Step II

List your earnings for each year from 1951 to present. Don't list any earnings above the Social Security tax ceiling for that year (listed below).

YEAR	ANNUAL MAXIMUM	YEAR	ANNUAL MAXIMUM	YEAR	ANNUAL MAXIMUM
1951–54	$3,600	1972	$ 9,000	1977	$16,500
1955–58	$4,200	1973	$10,800	1978	$17,700
1959–65	$4,800	1974	$13,200	1979	$22,900
1966–67	$6,600	1975	$14,100	1980	$25,900
1968–71	$7,800	1976	$15,300	1981	$29,700

1951–1958	1959–1966	1967–1973	1974–1981
$	$	$	$
		Total	$

Step III

Estimate your expected annual earnings from now through the year before you will be 65:

_____   _____

_____   _____

_____   _____

_____   _____

Step IV

Cross off the list those years in which your earnings were lowest until the number of years remaining is the same as the number of years you must count in figuring your average.

Step V

Add up your earnings for those years and divide by the number of years you must count. The result is your average yearly earnings.

Total $_____ ÷ _____ years you count
= $_____ Average Yearly Earnings

If this method is confusing, here are some figures to use as parameters: The maximum monthly payment an individual who retired in 1981 will receive at age sixty-five is $753 per month. This amount, however, will gradually rise as the taxable wage base increases.

The least a person who retired in 1981 will receive is $170 per month. This amount will be paid even if the benefit formula works out to a lower figure. The average benefit paid to a person who retired at age sixty-five in 1981 is about $375.

EXAMPLES OF ESTIMATED MONTHLY SOCIAL SECURITY PAYMENTS

Average Yearly Earnings*	$9,000	$10,800	$13,200	$14,100	$15,300	$16,500	$17,700
Retired Worker 65 or older or disabled worker under 65	640.80	695.20	764.00	788.30	818.40	846.80	873.60
Retired worker at 62	512.70	556.30	611.30	630.80	654.90	677.60	699.00
Wife 65 or older	320.50	347.60	382.00	394.20	409.30	423.50	436.80
Wife at 62 with no child	240.50	260.80	286.60	295.70	307.20	317.70	327.60
Wife under 65 and one child	480.70	521.50	573.00	591.30	614.00	635.20	655.30
Widow or widower at 65	640.80	695.20	764.00	788.30	818.40	846.80	873.60
Widow or widower at 60	458.30	497.10	546.30	563.70	585.30	605.60	624.80
Disabled widow or widower at 50	320.60	347.70	382.10	394.20	409.30	423.50	437.00
Widow or widower with one child	961.30	1,042.90	1,146.10	1,182.50	1,227.70	1,270.30	1,360.50
Maximum family payment	1,121.40	1,216.40	1,336.60	1,379.30	1,432.10	1,481.80	1,528.60

Figure 8

Family Retirement Benefits

In addition to your individual monthly payments, other benefits, calculated at a percentage of your rate, may be received by several members of your family. For example:

1. If you retire at sixty-two, your spouse of sixty-five will qualify for a separate monthly check equal to 50 percent of your age sixty-five benefit. If you and your spouse both retire at sixty-two, there will be a permanent 25 percent reduction in benefits.

2. A spouse may qualify for an amount equal to 50 percent of your benefit if caring for your child under eighteen, or a disabled child of any age if disabled before age twenty-two.

3. A child is also eligible to receive 50 percent of your benefit if unmarried and under age eighteen, or twenty-two, if a student.

4. In cases where both spouses have work histories, each will receive benefits according to individual earnings. However, if the wife, for example, would receive more as a "spouse" than on her own record,

she will receive the higher amount. A husband has the same option.

Family Death Benefits

Benefits to families of deceased workers are equally broad. If you have met the required forty quarters at the time of death, benefits are payable to certain family members, even if you died prior to retirement age. Possible beneficiaries include:

1. Your spouse, at age sixty, may receive reduced benefits; the full 100 percent of your benefit is payable at age sixty-five (unless you took a reduced benefit earlier).

2. A surviving widow of any age may receive an additional 75 percent if caring for children eighteen or under, twenty-two if students, or any age if disabled.

3. Your children are each entitled to 75 percent of your age sixty-five benefit.

4. Your dependent parents aged at least sixty-two.

5. Your spouse who lived with you or the person who pays for burial will receive $285.

If this sounds too good to be true, a warning is in order. All benefit payments are subject to a ceiling of about 175 percent per family, as well as maximums regarding how much dependents can earn.

Additionally, a surviving spouse who remarries before age sixty won't normally qualify for survivor's benefits, nor will a spouse who was receiving benefits to care for a minor child once the child is eighteen. However, benefits will resume once the widow reaches sixty-two.

To keep up to date with the development of your account, you should write the Social Security Administration every three years to make sure your payroll tax is being properly credited. Also, ask for the recent Social Security booklet *Estimating Your Social Security Retirement Check,* which gives current data concerning the system. You can get this by writing the Social Security Administration, Baltimore, Maryland 21235. Your letter must be signed and include your birthdate, your name and address, and your Social Security number.

Rewards of Working Past Sixty-five

One reason the coffers of the trust funds have been drastically reduced is that great numbers of workers choose early retirement. As a result, the government has introduced a few incentives for working longer, even past the age of sixty-five.

Foremost, for those who reached sixty-five in 1982, is the 3 percent benefit increase for each year a person continues to work through age seventy-one. This affords an even greater advantage to high wage earners since benefits are calculated on average earnings.

Conversely, retirement at sixty-two results in the permanent loss of 20 percent of your age sixty-five monthly benefit. Whether this loss is significant when balanced against the three additional years of payments received is questionable. On one side, considering that your yearly "income average" would remain the same, you would be better off until age seventy-seven,

even with the 20 percent reduction. However, if you are at the peak of your earning power, you will lose three years of high income, which could significantly affect your benefit level.

Moreover, Social Security benefits are now reduced $1 for every $2 over $4,440 of earned income for recipients under sixty-five, or $6,000 for recipients over sixty-five. Once you reach age seventy-two (age seventy in 1983), your earnings will *not affect* your check at all.

Medicare

Since many companies do not continue medical coverage after retirement, Medicare could become as important as your old-age pension. At age sixty-five, if you meet the minimum standard for length of coverage under Social Security, you will be eligible for Medicare. Your spouse at age sixty-five is also eligible. Retiring early does not give you Medicare coverage.

Medicare has two parts: Part A is hospital insurance that helps pay for medically necessary inpatient hospital care, subsequent care in a skilled nursing facility, and certain home health care. Part B is medical insurance that helps pay for medically necessary doctor's services and certain outpatient hospital services not covered by Part A.

There is a limit on the number of days Medicare can help pay for inpatient care. The limit, which is referred to as a "benefit period," lasts ninety days. You can have an unlimited number of benefit periods but a new benefit period does not start unless you have been out of the hospital for sixty days in a row. Each person also has a lifetime reserve of sixty days. Once you use a reserve day, you can never retrieve it.

For any part of a benefit period that occurred in 1982, your share of inpatient costs will be $260 for the first sixty days in the hospital, $65 *a day* for the next thirty days and $130 a day for the sixty reserve days.

Thus, your share of hospital costs for the first 150 days would be $10,000! (For day 21 through 100 in a skilled nursing facility, your share of the cost would be $32.50 a day.) What this amounts to is that if you had to be hospitalized for longer than 150 days, Medicare could no longer cover the cost.

Planning Retirement

Prior to the 1930s, retirement was a luxury few people contemplated. Most hoped they could remain in good health and work until the end of their lives, perhaps spend only a few years depending on children and other relatives. Since the life expectancy around 1900 was only forty-seven years, this was a viable solution.

No one could have imagined the leisurely, government-supported retirement of ten to fifteen years that we all expect today. However, with the current life expectancy at approximately seventy-three years and retirement age slipping from sixty-five to sixty-two, the government is financially responsible for a large portion of the 25 million people currently sixty-five and over. By 2000, about 32 million persons will be sixty-five and over.

Needless to say, the Social Security system will not be able to support 32 million people for even ten years with current benefit rates. The government's extravagant promise of financial independence for all who retire will have to be greatly amended if any benefits are to survive.

What does that mean for most Americans? Strategic financial planning, begun early in life, is the only possibility of ensuring a retirement commensurate with a comfortable life-style. Because of the possibility of being retired for one-fourth of one's adult life, it is imperative to begin planning early. Ironically, systematic counseling

rarely begins before age fifty, and by then many decisions are irreversible.

Retirement planning cannot begin too early as the decisions made in youth directly affect the chance of financial independence. It is no secret that the further away from retirement you are, the more difficult it is to estimate what it will cost. One concept held by both young and old, however, is that they should be able to maintain a standard of living after retirement not too much reduced from that of their economic best years.

This goal may be achievable with 50–60 percent of one's gross salary. Here's why:

1. You will have no Social Security deductions.

2. You will have no private pension or profit-sharing contributions to make.

3. There may be no need to pay dues, life and health insurance premiums.

4. Income taxes will be substantially reduced, as will be the need for clothes and transportation.

In spite of this, most people are still faced with a gap between income available for retirement and income needed or desired at retirement. A survey conducted by one psychologist found that three-quarters of those interviewed would like to retire earlier than the conventional age sixty-five, but less than one-quarter expected to be able to do so.

Following are some suggestions to help you set goals and plan retirement income. The investment vehicles and strategies to aid you in achieving such goals are discussed in later chapters.

To close the gap, you need an investment plan that contains two basic elements: a liquid reserve to deal with emergencies, and a fund working for future income. This fund should contain an element of growth to hedge inflation and some form of tax shelter.

To achieve your retirement goals, you

must give special attention to the planning process. It is prudent to estimate how much you will need at retirement and how many years before you retire. You will also want to consider what assets you currently have available for investment and how much you will be able to make available each month. This involves creating a budget now as well as estimating one for retirement. Understanding the pension benefits and vesting limits of all qualified plans will also aid you in projecting the amounts that must be saved and invested. Along with the rate of return that must be achieved to meet these projections will have to be other allowances for children's education, for helping elderly parents, and for possible inheritances.

In plotting retirement goals for my clients, I have found the following step-by-step formula helpful in estimating future retirement income needs and the current investment allocations required to achieve these goals.

Income Needs Analysis at Retirement

1.	Age at retirement		65
2.	Estimated Annualized Living Expenses		$ 20,000
3.	Number of years until retirement	20	
4.	Assumed rate of inflation	7%	
5.	Factor from Table 1		x 3.9
6.	Equivalent income at retirement		$ 78,000

Figure 9

Retirement Income Needs (Refer to Figure 9)

To calculate your future retirement income needs use the following steps:

Step 1. Decide at what age you want to retire.

Step 2. List all your potential annual living expenses at retirement. These should include housing, food, clothing, gifts, transportation, medical, taxes, and vacation.

Step 3. Note the number of years until retirement.

Step 4. Assume a certain inflation factor. We suggest 7 percent.

Step 5. Turn to Table 1 and use the factor that corresponds to the number of years until retirement and the assumed rate of inflation. Multiply this factor by your estimated annual living expenses.

Step 6. This result gives you an equivalent income at retirement as expressed in future inflated dollars.

Table 1
Compound Interest for Lump-Sum Investments

LENGTH OF INVEST-MENT (YEARS)	PERCENTAGE RATE OF RETURN OR OF INFLATION											
	2%	3%	4%	5%	6%	7%	8%	10%	12%	14%	16%	20%
1	1.02	1.03	1.04	1.0	1.1	1.1	1.1	1.1	1.1	1.1	1.2	1.2
2	1.04	1.06	1.08	1.1	1.1	1.1	1.2	1.2	1.2	1.3	1.3	1.4
3	1.06	1.09	1.12	1.2	1.2	1.2	1.3	1.3	1.4	1.5	1.6	1.7
4	1.08	1.12	1.17	1.2	1.3	1.3	1.4	1.5	1.6	1.7	1.8	2.1
5	1.10	1.16	1.22	1.3	1.3	1.4	1.5	1.6	1.8	1.9	2.1	2.5
6	1.13	1.19	1.26	1.3	1.4	1.5	1.6	1.8	2.0	2.2	2.4	3.0
7	1.15	1.23	1.32	1.4	1.5	1.6	1.7	2.0	2.2	2.5	2.8	3.6
8	1.17	1.27	1.37	1.5	1.6	1.7	1.8	2.1	2.5	2.8	3.3	4.3
9	1.20	1.30	1.42	1.6	1.7	1.8	2.0	2.4	2.8	3.2	3.8	5.2
10	1.22	1.34	1.48	1.6	1.8	2.0	2.2	2.6	3.1	3.7	4.4	6.2
11	1.24	1.38	1.54	1.7	1.9	2.1	2.3	2.8	3.5	4.2	5.1	7.4
12	1.27	1.42	1.60	1.8	2.0	2.2	2.5	3.1	3.9	4.8	5.9	8.9
13	1.29	1.47	1.66	1.9	2.1	2.4	2.7	3.4	4.4	5.5	6.9	10.7
14	1.32	1.51	1.73	2.0	2.3	2.6	2.9	3.8	4.9	6.3	8.0	12.8
15	1.34	1.56	1.80	2.1	2.4	2.8	3.2	4.2	5.5	7.1	9.3	15.4
16	1.37	1.60	1.87	2.2	2.5	3.0	3.4	4.6	6.1	8.1	10.7	18.5
17	1.40	1.65	1.95	2.3	2.7	3.2	3.7	5.0	6.8	9.3	12.5	22.2
18	1.43	1.70	2.02	2.4	2.8	3.4	4.0	5.6	7.7	10.5	14.7	26.6
19	1.46	1.75	2.11	2.5	3.0	3.6	4.3	6.1	8.6	12.0	16.7	31.9
20	1.48	1.81	2.19	2.6	3.2	3.9	4.7	6.7	9.6	13.7	19.6	38.3
21	1.52	1.86	2.28	2.8	3.4	4.1	5.0	7.4	10.7	15.6	22.7	46.0
22	1.55	1.91	2.37	2.9	3.6	4.4	5.4	8.1	11.9	17.8	26.4	55.2
23	1.58	1.97	2.46	3.1	3.8	4.7	5.9	8.9	13.4	20.3	30.6	66.2
24	1.61	2.03	2.56	3.2	4.0	5.1	6.3	9.8	15.0	23.1	35.5	79.4
25	1.64	2.09	2.66	3.4	4.3	5.4	6.8	10.8	17.0	26.4	41.2	95.3
26	1.67	2.16	2.77	3.6	4.5	5.8	7.4	11.9	19.2	30.1	47.8	114.0
27	1.71	2.22	2.88	3.7	4.8	6.2	8.0	13.1	21.6	34.3	55.4	137.0
28	1.74	2.29	3.00	3.9	5.1	6.6	8.6	14.4	24.2	39.1	64.2	165.0
29	1.78	2.36	3.12	4.1	5.4	7.1	9.3	15.9	27.1	44.6	74.5	198.0
30	1.81	2.43	3.24	4.3	5.7	7.6	10.1	17.4	30.1	50.8	86.5	237.0

Table 2
Compound Interest for Investments Made at the End of Each Year

NUMBER OF YEARS	PERCENTAGE RATE OF RETURN										
	3%	4%	5%	6%	7%	8%	10%	12%	14%	16%	20%
1	1.0	1.0	1.0	1.0	1.0	1.0	1.0	1.0	1.0	1.0	1.0
2	2.0	2.0	2.0	2.1	2.1	2.1	2.1	2.1	2.1	2.2	2.2
3	3.1	3.1	3.2	3.2	3.2	3.2	3.3	3.4	3.4	3.5	3.6
4	4.2	4.2	4.3	4.4	4.4	4.5	4.6	4.8	4.9	5.1	5.4
5	5.3	5.4	5.5	5.6	5.8	5.9	6.1	6.4	6.6	6.9	7.4
6	6.5	6.6	6.8	7.0	7.2	7.3	7.7	8.1	8.5	9.0	9.9
7	7.7	7.9	8.1	8.4	8.6	8.9	9.5	10.1	10.7	11.4	12.9
8	8.9	9.2	9.5	9.9	10.2	10.6	11.4	12.3	13.2	14.2	16.5
9	10.2	10.6	11.0	11.5	12.0	12.5	13.6	14.8	16.1	17.5	20.8
10	11.5	12.0	12.6	13.2	13.8	14.5	15.9	17.5	19.3	21.3	26.0
11	12.8	13.5	14.2	15.0	15.8	16.6	18.5	20.6	23.0	25.7	32.2
12	14.2	15.0	15.9	16.9	17.9	19.0	21.4	24.1	27.3	30.8	39.6
13	15.6	16.6	17.7	18.9	20.1	21.5	24.5	28.0	32.1	36.8	48.5
14	17.1	18.3	19.6	21.0	22.6	24.2	28.0	32.4	37.6	43.7	59.2
15	18.6	20.0	21.6	23.3	25.1	27.2	31.8	37.3	43.8	51.6	72.0
16	20.2	21.8	23.6	25.7	27.9	30.3	35.9	42.7	50.9	60.8	87.4
17	21.8	23.7	25.8	28.2	30.8	33.8	40.5	48.9	59.1	71.6	105.9
18	23.4	25.6	28.1	30.9	34.0	37.4	45.6	55.7	68.3	84.0	128.1
19	25.1	27.7	30.5	33.8	37.4	41.4	51.2	63.4	78.9	98.5	154.7
20	26.9	29.8	33.1	36.8	44.0	45.8	57.3	72.0	90.9	115.2	186.7
21	28.7	32.0	35.7	40.0	44.9	50.4	64.0	81.7			
22	30.5	34.2	38.5	43.4	49.0	55.5	71.4	92.5			
23	32.4	36.6	41.4	47.0	53.4	60.9	79.5	104.6			
24	34.4	39.1	44.5	50.8	58.2	66.8	88.5	118.2			
25	36.4	41.6	47.7	54.9	63.2	73.1	98.3	133.3			
26	38.5	44.3	51.1	59.2	68.7	79.9	109.0	150.3			
27	40.7	47.1	54.7	63.7	74.5	87.4	121.0	169.4			
28	42.9	50.0	58.4	68.5	80.7	95.3	134.0	190.7			
29	45.2	53.0	62.3	73.6	87.3	104.0	149.0	214.6			
30	47.6	56.1	66.4	79.0	94.5	113.0	164.0	241.3			

Investment Needs Analyis

1.	Annual Income from Social Security	
	Husband ($753 x 12) =	$ 9,036
	Wife ($376.50 x 12) =	4,518
		$ 13,554
2.	Inflation factor from Table 1	x 3.9
3.	Inflated annual Income from Social Security	$ 52,860
4.	Pension Income (estimate)	+ 16,000
5.	Total Annual Income Available	$ 68,860
6.	Income Needs at Retirement	- 78,000
7.	(Shortage) Surplus	$ (10,000)
8.	Investment Needs (shortage ÷ rate of return, ie 10%)	$ 100,000
9.	Annual contribution to accumulate needed dollars in 20 years ($100,000 ÷ factor from Table 2 57.3)	$ 1,745
10.	Lump Sum investment to accumulate needed dollars in 20 years ($100,000 ÷ factor from Table 1 6.7)	$ 14,925

Figure 10

Dollars Needed to Get Started Now (Refer to Figure 10)

To estimate the lump sum or annual contribution you will need today to produce desired income at retirement, use the information gathered in Figure 9 such as your desired age of retirement, the number of years before you retire, the inflation rate, and your income needs.

Step 1. List annual income from Social Security (if married include both husband and wife benefits).

Step 2. Multiply total Social Security benefits by the inflation factor chosen from Table 1.

Step 3. This result gives you the inflated income from Social Security.

Step 4. Add pension income. Note the estimates printed by most companies include years on the job, earned income, and date of retirement.

Step 5. Equals the total available income at retirement.

Step 6. From Figure 9, list total income needed at retirement.

Step 7. Subtract total income needed at retirement from total income available to give the surplus or shortage of income at retirement.

Step 8. If you have a shortage, you need to know how much capital you will have to accumulate to produce this shortage. To calculate the capital and investment needed, divide the shortage by the rate of return.

Step 9. For the *annual contribution* needed over twenty years to accumulate desired capital tomorrow, divide the capital needs by the factor in Table 2. This factor can be obtained by looking in the column that has your assumed rate of return and moving down the column until you are directly across from the number of years (years until retirement).

Step 10. For the *lump-sum investment* needed today to accumulate the capital tomorrow that will generate the income shortage, divide the capital need by the factor found in Table 1. Again, this factor can be found by moving down the column marked "percentage rate of return" until you are directly across from the number of years or length of time of the investment.

An old cliché is that most people do not plan to fail; they just fail to plan. Two reasons many fail to plan are simply that it takes too much time and is too complex. The tax laws are continuously changing, the investment alternatives are forever increasing, and the whole economy appears to be undergoing major surgery. Despite these problems and many others, we must be mindful of the fact that Social Security most assuredly will not be enough and will not exist as we know it today. If it is to survive, many changes will have to be made. The solutions mentioned earlier will have to be adopted. In addition, Congress will have to continue to pass new tax incentive retirement plans for individuals, such as the Individual Retirement Account (IRA) and the Keogh Plan for the self-employed. For the corporate executive and employees of corporations, qualified plans like the Money Purchase Pension Plan, the Profit-Sharing Plan, the Defined Benefit Plan, and the Salary Savings Plan will have to become more abundant. These will have to be less restrictive and more flexible, or they may have to allow unlimited contributions, with additional tax benefits and incentives unlike those we now know. These new retirement plans, to a greater degree, will have to assure us that all the dollars put aside today will be used for *our* retirement benefit tomorrow.

These changes will not come overnight, of course. There will be prolonged political debate, for as a former commissioner of the Social Security Administration has stated,

> A member of Congress who hopes for re-election will not vote to repudiate a promise to virtually his entire constituary. It is inconceivable that a majority of the members of each house of Congress ever will do so.

Thus, we have a political dilemma, and, in turn, are on a devastating collision course. No one can predict the end result, but what we do know is that the system has grave problems, that changes must be made, and that those changes will affect us all. Consequently, we must protect ourselves if we are to retire with a life-style comparable to that of our best earning years. To do this, we all need a comprehensive financial plan that includes the prudent and proper use of money and one that concludes that Social Security will simply be a supplement, and quite succinctly, not enough.

I hope that this chapter has given you a better understanding of the purpose of Social Security, the current benefits of the system, the problems and proposed solutions, as well as a method by which you can project and estimate your retirement income.

Chapter 3

Setting Your Financial Objectives

Robert T. LeClair, B.A., M.B.A., Ph.D., is a nationally recognized expert in the areas of finance and investment. He is dean of the Graduate School of Financial Sciences of the American College, Bryn Mawr, Pennsylvania, and a former chairman of the Department of Finance. Previously, he was a member of the finance faculty of the University of Illinois. LeClair has written numerous articles on retirement planning, mutual funds, securities options, financial management, and adult education. He is a co-author of *Money and Retirement: How To Plan for Lifetime Financial Security*. He has been active throughout his career as a lecturer and consultant for many firms and organizations, including Jewe! Companies, CNA Financial Corporation, Continental Illinois National Bank, the National Association of Mutual Savings Banks, the Pennsylvania Credit Union League, and the National Board of Medical Examiners.

Robert T. LeClair, Ph.D.

I used to think that money was the most important thing in life. Now that I am old, I know it is!

Oscar Wilde

The value of careful financial planning cannot be overestimated. Whether your purpose is to prepare for retirement, to educate your children, or simply to buy a new car, effective planning will bring you closer to your goal. The purpose of this chapter is to help you design an effective financial plan by setting useful and "workable" financial objectives.

You are the only one who can be held responsible for your own financial planning. You must take the responsibility for accomplishing your particular goals, or for failing to do so. It has been estimated that the average person will spend something like 85,000 hours during his lifetime earning a living and building an estate. And yet, that same person will typically spend only about 10 hours in actual planning for the most efficient use of his money. Think of it—only 10 hours out of an entire lifetime spent on planning! Is it any wonder that so few people are financially secure and have accomplished what they set out to do?

One reason why many people fail to reach their personal financial goals is that they aren't quite sure what those goals are. You may have some vague notions of what you and your family are trying to accomplish, but could you sit down at this moment and write them out on a piece of paper? Could you explain them in detail to other members of your family, or to a financial consultant who might be trying to help you reach your objectives? If not, you don't really have "workable" financial objectives. You aren't going to be as successful as you want to be unless you know where you are headed and how you are going to get there.

One of our great allies in undertaking any financial plan is time: time for plans to be made and evaluated; time for income to be earned and assets accumulated; and time for changes to be made when necessary. Unfortunately, the reverse is also true. No amount of determined planning can make up for the errors of omission that have already been made, or for procrastination, or for the loss of years of valuable time. *Now* is the time for you to begin planning and to start setting worthwhile financial objectives. If you need help in getting started, don't be afraid to ask for it from a financial planning professional. His or her assistance in planning a program suited to your needs and your individual circumstances will be well worth the investment in time and money.

Purpose of Objectives

Well-stated objectives can contribute to effective planning in a number of ways. Their foremost value lies in serving as a *guide* for your actions. Whenever you consider a particular action, evaluate an investment, or review your financial situation, you should do so in the light of your objectives. Will this particular investment help you to reach your goals? Will a change in strategy improve your chances of accomplishing a specific objective? Without formal objectives as a point of reference, many people head off in all directions at once. A written set of objectives can be as effective as a road map in keeping you on your course toward financial security.

Financial objectives also serve as a *benchmark* for performance measurement. You should be able to assess your progress in some formal way on a regular basis. It isn't enough to say, for example, "We had a pretty good year last year!" What does that mean? How can you make that kind of judgment without some idea of what "pretty good" stands for? Your objectives should be stated in a way that helps you to evaluate actual results. The next section of this chapter considers several ways in which you can build this measurement factor into your objectives.

Financial objectives should be the result of a planning *process* that involves everyone affected by those objectives. Two important ideas are involved here. First, good financial planning is an ongoing process. It is not a product that is sold or a service that is delivered at a particular point in time. The planning function should be a permanent part of your financial program. You can't do it sporadically and hope to do it well! Plans should be reviewed regularly, modified as necessary, and changed completely whenever your personal situation or economic conditions make it necessary. Second, everyone affected by the plan should be involved in the planning process. Are your spouse and children an integral part of the planning process? If not, they probably should be, and they should feel just as responsible as you do for accomplishing those goals. Working out a set of objectives provides a strong communications link among all members of the family. Everyone involved should have an opportunity to comment on stated objectives and to ask questions about them. Involving everyone in the planning process is the best way to achieve commitment toward those goals.

Finally, your objectives should be *reviewed* on a regular basis. This should be done at least annually, and more frequently if important personal or business factors change. Individual attitudes about the importance of certain goals can change. Economic conditions can also shift drastically, and such changes should be incorporated into new objectives. For example, would you be satisfied today with a 5 percent rate of return on your investments? Probably not, but 5 percent was an attractive return in the late 1950s. What about long-term utility bonds, once considered a "safe" investment? Today, volatile interest rates have made such investments highly risky in terms of capital value. Changes such as these make it important to keep your objectives current in both personal and economic terms.

Your NCFE Financial Data form (p. 494) lists factors to consider in setting your financial objectives. Whenever any of these factors change, you should review your objectives to see if they need to be modified to accommodate new conditions. This list can also be used as the basis of an annual review with your financial planner. Everyone involved in the planning process should review the list and evaluate the factors involved. Even the best-defined objectives can become outdated over time and made obsolete by changing economic conditions.

Establishing Effective Financial Objectives

We now turn to the crucial process of developing your actual objectives and three criteria you can use in evaluating their effectiveness.

1. Your objectives must be well defined and clearly understood. Unless you know and understand what you are trying to do, you will obviously have difficulty reaching your goals. You should be able to explain your objectives to others, including members of your family or a financial consultant.

One way of developing a clear statement of your objectives is to write them down. Do they make sense when you read them in black and white? Share your list with others and ask if they can understand what you have written. Does it make sense to them? Do these goals appear worthwhile to others?

Your financial objectives should not be mere expressions of wishful thinking. "I want to provide a good college education for my children" is an admirable statement, but a *poor* financial objective. Why? Because it fails to indicate what you need to do now in order to reach that goal.

Ask yourself, "How will I know if I am accomplishing my goal?" If you cannot answer that question, you should rewrite your objective! That question is always relatively easy to answer for objectives that are clearly defined.

Avoid vague terms such as a "good education," which are open to many interpretations. Does this phrase refer to a type of college, level of education, or some other particular aspect of education? Try to be as specific as you can be in setting your objectives, keeping in mind that they can and will change over time.

This stage provides an opportunity to get others involved in the process. Don't feel you have to do it all by yourself. Sharing the responsibility will make the job easier, help you to communicate your personal feelings and ideas to others, and increase everyone's commitment to the objective.

2. Objectives should be stated in *quantitative terms* whenever possible. They are much more effective when they are set down in numbers. Only by attaching specific numbers to your plans can you measure actual progress toward reaching those goals. Qualified financial planners can be extremely helpful during this phase of the process. Their experience and knowledge can help you to set realistic objectives that are consistent with your resources and the overall market conditions.

Goals stated in quantitative terms are generally better defined and easier to understand. Numbers may not be entirely accurate but they usually convey concrete information. It is much easier to tell whether or not you are earning a specific rate of return than it is to interpret "we had a pretty good year last year!"

Let's apply this idea to the educational funding objective we discussed earlier. This is one of the most significant financial decisions you may ever have to make. Today, funding a child's college education is second only to the purchase of a home in the commitment of dollars. You should estimate what those costs will be and set a specific objective in terms of dollars.

For example, your objective may be "to accumulate a fund of $40,000 for education purposes." Now you have a target to shoot for! Stating the objective in quantitative terms makes it less abstract, if a little frightening. The process by which you establish that number may be your most productive activity. It forces you to do some serious thinking about your objectives and to set reasonable and realistic goals.

Putting a price tag on a "good education" is not easy to do. You have to define your objective carefully, gather information on specific schools and their costs, and evaluate your own level of income. But, isn't that a better way to approach the situation than simply to guess at a cost, or hope that everything will turn out all right?

3. Stating your plans in quantitative terms also enables you to measure your progress in reaching your goals. This *time dimension* is the third essential element of good financial objectives. Each goal or plan should include a schedule of when it will be accomplished. You need to know how much time you have to work with, where you need to be along the way, and when you plan to reach your goal. Once you have set an objective with a time dimension, you can break the overall objective down into shorter time spans for review purposes.

Measuring your progress at regular intervals will keep you on track toward your target. These regular evaluations will also indicate whether you need to make changes in your strategies or in the objectives themselves. Have your plans worked out as you expected during the past year? Are you earning the rate of return you expected on a particular investment? Will you have to increase your educational funding contributions next year to make up for a lower-than-expected yield? This is the type of analysis that can be performed when you have a quantitative goal with a time schedule attached to it.

Let's add the timing process to the educational funding objective we've been developing. Up to this point we have said only that we wanted to accumulate $40,000. How much time do we have to work with before the funds will be needed? If we assume that it will be ten years, how can we incorporate this factor into our statement of objectives? As a beginning, we could simply say that our goal was "to accumulate $40,000 within ten years." This would be an improvement over our previous statement, but it wouldn't really help us much in planning. Why? The time period is too long and doesn't require us to measure performance along the way.

A better statement of our objective would be "to accumulate $2,280 annually for ten years." (This assumes an annual rate of return of 12 percent on the accumulated capital.) How is this an improvement over the previous objective? We have reduced the time period over which we are measuring performance from ten years to just one year. At the end of each year we can review whether or not we have actually accumulated an additional $2,280 and what rate of return we have earned on our investment. As well, we will be in a position to determine whether or not we need to change our annual contribution to reach our objective. If we have earned a higher-than-expected return, we can keep on with our regular program. If not, we may have to increase our savings to reach our goal.

Each annual review also gives you an opportunity to update the original statement to account for changes in your personal situation or in economic conditions. In this case, you can review college costs for particular schools and revise expenses projected for the end of the original ten-year period. You may have to increase your original estimate of $40,000, but at least you won't be totally surprised, as you might have been at the end of a longer period of time.

Even an annual time dimension may not be the most effective means of accomplishing your objectives. You may want to plan on a schedule of monthly contributions to an educational fund. You could revise the objective to be, "Set aside $175 each month for ten years to fund educational costs." Such a statement specifies a regular action to be taken on a short-term basis that will contribute to accomplishing a long-term goal. A monthly objective with an annual review is particularly effective because it keeps you from getting too far off the track without noticing it.

Evaluating Your Own Objectives

By now you should be evaluating your own financial objectives to see how they fit the three criteria we have developed. Are they written down in well-defined terms that are easy to understand? Are they stated in quantitative terms whenever possible so that they will be easy to measure and evaluate? Do they have a time dimension attached so that you can review your progress on a regular basis and make adjustments when necessary? If you can't answer yes to all of these questions, you should spend some time revising your objectives so that they meet these criteria. A little effort now will give you a better understanding of what you want to accomplish and how you expect to accomplish it.

Let's review our educational objective to see if it meets the test. Assuming that we have determined the appropriate school costs, our final statement could be: "Accumulate an education fund of $40,000 over the next ten years by investing $175 per month to earn a rate of return of 12 percent annually."

This statement presents a well-defined objective that can be easily understood by everyone involved. The quantitative terms make the objective a concrete one, by which we can measure our final results. If necessary, we could put down an annual schedule of the amount we should have at any point in time. By indicating a ten-year accumulation period, we know when we expect to reach our goal, and the monthly schedule should make it easy to keep up with our strategy. The only additional step needed is to review our actual returns on a regular basis to see how they compare with the objective of 12 percent.

If you decide to evaluate this objective on a yearly basis, you will have to review several important items. First, is the overall goal of $40,000 still realistic? Have college costs increased in line with your expectations or are they growing at an even faster rate? If they are, you may have to increase your objective or consider less expensive alternatives. Second, have you made the scheduled contributions of $175 each month? Did you make payments regularly or did you skip a month or two and then "catch up" later on? How much have you accumulated during the past twelve months, and is the total amount what you expected to have at this point in time? If it is less than you planned, you may have to increase your contributions or try to earn a higher rate of return during the remaining accumulation period. What rate of return did you realize during the past year? Was it more or less than you originally projected and what impact did the rate have on your annual target? If rates have fallen, you may need to consider alternative investments that offer higher returns but possibly involve more risk.

This type of review and planning may sound complicated and difficult, but with a little practice you will be able to do it easily. Well-written objectives can be readily evaluated and lend themselves to modification on the basis of regular reviews. The improvement you see in your actual results will motivate you to apply the system to all of your financial objectives.

Ranking Your Objectives

We have one more problem to deal with before we can complete our work on a statement of financial objectives. Like most of us, you probably have more than one objective on your list. Educational funding may be one of your concerns, but it may not be the only financial goal you would like to reach. Retirement may be another concern, or you may want to purchase additional insurance protection for your family. You may also need more in the way of savings for unexpected emergencies, or want to make additional investments of various kinds.

These may be desirable goals, but can you afford to pursue all of them at the same time? Again, if you are like most of us, the answer is probably no. We all seem to want more than we can afford at any one time and that problem makes it essential to set *priorities* on our objectives. Once you have developed individual objectives, you should arrange them in order of importance. This is another task that should involve your spouse and other members of your family. Everyone should have an opportunity to express their own ideas about the relative importance of these various goals.

Review your list of objectives and ask yourself, "If we could accomplish only one of these goals, which one should it be?" The objective you select should be assigned the highest priority and transferred to a new list. Ask the question again for the remaining objectives and repeat the process until you have ranked all of them. Your new list will be arranged in order of priority, and you can begin to focus on the most important objectives.

It may be essential to take immediate action on some of your objectives. Others may be less important and it may be possible to delay working on them for the time being. You may have to postpone certain objectives until after others have been accomplished. A common example of this situation is postponing retirement plans until after the children's education has been completed. Setting these priorities may be difficult because each of your objectives will seem worthwhile by itself. Determining which ones are more important and which deserve less attention will call for careful analysis and compromises by everyone involved in the decision-making process. A financial planner can play an important role at this time in providing objective advice and information.

Summary

We all wish that we had unlimited resources and could afford to achieve all our goals. Few of us are that fortunate, however, and we may have to eliminate some of our lower ranked objectives in order to accomplish those that are more important. Making such decisions is never easy, but if you have developed your objectives as suggested here, you will be in a better position to do so. Your plans will be more clearly stated and you will be able to measure the impact of one objective on the others. The time dimension of your statements will enable you to postpone some actions, if necessary, while emphasizing others.

A planned and systematic approach to accomplishing your financial objectives is almost certain to be more successful than any informal and irregular process. Plan for success by paying careful attention to your goals. You will be well rewarded for your efforts, both financially and in a true sense of personal accomplishment. *Good luck!*

P. Kemp Fain, Jr., B.Mech.Eng., M.S. (Management), and currently a Ph.D. candidate, is the founder and president of Asset Planning Corporation. He has been a stockbroker with a New York stock exchange firm and has served in several sales and management positions with a major financial planning firm. He has taught business and personal finance courses, and currently teaches a course in personal money management at the University of Tennessee. He is also the author of a monograph on financial planning, *Money Matters*. Fain is a Certified Financial Planner and Chartered Life Underwriter who is a registered financial principal with the National Association of Securities Dealers and a licensed securities salesman, real estate broker, and insurance agent. He is a member of the Institute of Certified Financial Planners and the International Association for Financial Planning.

Chapter 4

Motivating Yourself to Plan and Act

P. Kemp Fain, Jr. CLU, CFP

Money is probably more difficult to manage than it is to earn. If you manage your money well, not only can you have enough to spend now, but you can make steady progress toward your financial goals. Actually, the ultimate goal of sound money management should be to create financial independence for yourself. You undoubtedly know how important it is to manage your money well. But, do you know how to motivate yourself to make financial plans, and then act on them? First, you must recognize the biggest problem facing you—indecision! Further, you should know that your indecision is *based upon a lack of information*! This chapter shows you how to collect the information needed to manage your money efficiently. Once you have that information, your uncertainty will go away, and you will find it much easier to motivate yourself to plan and act.

By concentrating on this process, you should be able to acquire the lifetime skills and tools needed to successfully manage your own financial affairs. Most people want to know how to manage their money better, but they do not want a methodology that is complicated to use. When too much time or energy is required, one feels overwhelmed. The concepts in this chapter are simple, time-tested, and have wide application. In short, they work for me, they work for others, and they should work for you.

Perhaps you are saying that you're really not interested in money management, or that money does not matter that much to you. Whether you like it or not, you are forced to play the game of money management. The point is, "How well do you play it?" If you play the game well, you will reap many benefits: you will have more time to do the things that you enjoy doing; you will have the comfort of knowing that your financial situation is well organized and can respond properly to any emergency or contingency; moreover, good money managers seem to have the best life-styles, and they rarely become wards of the state. Too many people depend on others for their livelihood after they reach retirement age.

So, what can you do to motivate yourself to make proper financial plans and then to act upon them?

The methodology presented in this chapter will help you to take control of your financial life. It doesn't make sense to have insurance policies, company benefits, investments, government programs, and so on, and not know what they will provide for you! It doesn't make sense to overpay your taxes! It doesn't make sense to save and invest without a specific purpose! You should know what you have and what you want financially. You should understand the need for written objectives; without them, you're like a ship without a rudder and without power. A good financial plan is analogous to the rudder and your motivation is analogous to the ship's power. You might get somewhere without a rudder and without power, but you will be more likely to get where you want to go, when you want to get there, if you have both a rudder and some form of power.

In order to have the information that gives clarity of vision, which in turn makes it easier for you to act, you must know the answers to three questions:

1. Where am I now?
2. Where am I going?
3. How do I know when I get there?

I'm going to describe some simple tools to help you answer these questions in detail. More elaborate tools are available, if you should choose to use them, but those presented here are adequate and will get you started without extensive training.

Where Am I Now?

Before you can actively manage your financial situation, you must find out where you are. This information will allow you to set objectives, make plans, and then manage your finances so as to achieve the best possible results. To determine where you are, we use organizational tools and analytical tools.

Organizational Tools

These are the tools that help you assemble and organize the various aspects of your financial situation. Foremost of these is the *financial inventory*. It should include *all* things that are part of your financial situation. It will be difficult to prepare, however, unless all items pertaining to your finances are kept in one place, such as a desk, a file cabinet, or the like. The important point is: this information must be organized and accessible. Your NCFE Financial Data Form (pp. 495–501) shows a suggested format for a financial inventory.

If you do your financial inventory properly, nothing of financial importance about your life will be overlooked. You will note that one item called for is *living expenses*. Since this is a detailed, specialized item, a suggested form for your use is presented in Your NCFE Financial Data Form (pp. 495–501). You'll probably recognize that this is a type of budget. Its main purpose is to show how your money is spent. It can be used monthly or annually. It can also be used to analyze prior living expenses or to project these expenses for the future.

The next step is to examine your *balance sheet* (see Your NCFE Financial Data Form, pp. 495–501), for they will help you decide what you have and what you owe. This means itemizing in more detail your various assets, liabilities, and income. The financial inventory, living expenses, and the financial schedules are the basic tools for organizing your financial situation.

Analytical Tools

Two analytical tools in particular are important: the *balance sheet* and the *cash flow statement*. A suggested format for a Balance Sheet is illustrated in Your NCFE Financial Data Form.

Let's look at the various parts of the balance sheet to make sure you understand them. First, assets are everything that you own.

To help you identify your assets, we divide them into three categories: (1) fixed-dollar assets, which are fixed as to principal and/or earnings (for example, your checking and saving accounts, bonds, or life insurance cash values); (2) variable-dollar assets, which are variable as to principal or earnings (for example, stocks, mutual funds, business interests, real estate); and (3) nonincome-producing assets, or personal assets, which are the assets that you enjoy and use in your life-style (for example, your home, automobiles, clothing, recreational real estate, boats, and so on). By listing all your assets in the various categories, you can find your total assets, which should cover everything that you own. Liabilities, on the other hand, refer to everything that you owe. A convenient way to determine your liabilities is to divide them into short-term liabilities and long-term liabilities. Short-term liabilities are those that will be liquidated within one year (for example, charge accounts, or short-term bank notes such as ninety-day notes). Long-term liabilities are those that involve payments beyond a year (for example, a home mortgage, automobile loans, or furniture loans). By listing these two types of liabilities, then adding them together, you will find your total liabilities.

Next, subtract your liabilities from your assets to find your net worth. Net worth is a very important term in your financial life. It is the sum of all that you have accomplished financially up to the point of preparing the balance sheet. Since net worth includes personal assets (nonincome-producing assets), it should not be used for projecting into the future; for this projection you use capital at work, or the actual dollars you have working to produce other dollars. Your capital at work is found by subtracting the equity in your home and the value of your personal property from your net worth.

The balance sheet should be viewed as a snapshot of your financial condition at a given point in time. Typically, a new balance sheet is prepared at the end of each year. If you have made financial progress during that year, your net worth and capital at work will have increased. Eventually, your financial life will be recorded in a series of balance sheets showing your progress or lack of progress. In some respects, they resemble a series of electrocardiograms, for they indicate your "condition" at one point in time, but more important, they indicate the trend of this condition. A healthy condition is an increasing net worth, with increasing liquidity of assets.

The second analytical tool is the cash flow statement. A suggested format is shown in Your NCFE Financial Data Form. This is a record of what has happened over a period of time, usually a year. It can also be used to project what will happen over a future period of time. Gross income refers to the individual's or family's entire income. To find your net income, you have to deduct certain expenses. Taxes are calculated using the format outlined in the Internal Revenue Service Form 1040 or Form 1040A. As an alternative, taxes can be calculated by looking back at your last several tax returns and figuring out the percentage of income your taxes have represented. Usually, this figure is a fairly good predictor for future taxes. Living expenses can be taken directly from the form you have already prepared for these items (see Your NCFE Financial Data Form).

To find your net income you also have to deduct items that are basically nondiscretionary in nature. That is, there may be some latitude in the amounts, but all these items have to be paid. After finding your net income, you can deduct the discretionary items, which are expenditures you have a choice in making. The insurance category covers mainly personal insurance. Usually homeowner's and automobile insurance is placed with living expenses simply because it is not a discretionary expenditure. The same might be said about medical insur-

ance. Savings and investments include any regular contributions being made to savings accounts and investment programs during the year. The final figure is the margin, which indicates the margin of safety in the numbers. Since these calculations are estimates, the margin should be at least 5 percent, and preferably, 10 percent.

A cash flow statement reflects what comes in and what goes out between balance sheets. Obviously, if you are successful in saving and investing dollars during this period, then your net worth and capital at work should increase. Remember, there are only four ways that you can add dollars to your balance sheet. You can earn dollars, your dollars can earn more dollars, you can have dollars given to you, or you can steal dollars. Most of us don't expect to have dollars given to us, and we certainly don't intend to steal them! Thus, we are left with the mundane wealth-building methods of earning our dollars and then having our dollars work for us.

As you can see, work goes into money management. It takes time to gather the necessary information and to make the calculations required by the tools we have outlined. Fortunately, the work is really difficult only the first time. After that, revisions are much easier.

Now that you know your net worth, capital at work, and cash flow, you are in a position to answer the second critical question.

Where Am I Going?

This question refers to your financial goals. To answer it, you will have to apply the classic technique of management by objectives (MBO) instead of operating under management by crisis (MBC). Although many financial objectives might be reasonable for you, let's consider some basic ones you can achieve. Be sure to be specific and put your goals in writing. If you don't, they will merely be wishes, not goals. Most of us would be interested in the following objectives:

1. Adequate emergency reserve
2. Retirement/financial independence
3. Education
4. Adequate medical insurance
5. Adequate disability insurance
6. Adequate life insurance
7. Adequate property and liability insurance
8. Other accumulation needs

Adequate Emergency Reserve

First, everyone should strive to build an adequate emergency reserve. You may hear various rules of thumb concerning how much is adequate. Although such rules are not all that useful, they give you somewhere to start. Some people have secure jobs, other liquid assets, and the ability to borrow money if they need it, and thus need relatively small reserves. Others, such as commission salesmen, need higher reserves because their incomes are not secure. Though not a perfect "rule," about six months of income, according to most families, is a comfortable reserve. Your NCFE Financial Data Form shows a method for calculating your reserve requirements. If you have no other thoughts on the subject, use six months' living expenses for your goal. From this, you should subtract any cash and cash equivalents you have. We only count cash and cash equivalents because money needs to be readily available if it is to be an emergency reserve. Such things as checking accounts, savings accounts, life insurance cash values, money market funds, and the like, are cash equivalents. If your present cash and cash equivalents are not an adequate reserve, then you need to accumulate the deficit shown.

Retirement/Financial Independence

Second, you should decide when you want to slow down or retire. For most of us, that will occur between the ages of fifty-five and sixty-five. Because of inflation, it will obviously take more retirement dollars to equal the purchasing power of today's dollars. A useful format for developing your retirement/financial independence goal is shown in Your NCFE Financial Data Form. First, you will have to estimate the monthly income needed at your projected retirement age. Then, you will need to find out how much retirement plan and Social Security benefits you can expect. You can usually get this information from your company personnel office and from the Social Security Administration. Then, you should project earnings from your capital at work. If you still need some monthly income after these projections, you should plan an investment program to accumulate the needed income.

Education

If you want to provide an education for your children, you should definitely plan ahead for this need rather than wait to pay it out of your pocket. By preplanning, you can often save half the cost of an education (owing to the effect of compound return). One method of estimating education funds needed is shown in Figure 1. You should make this estimate for each child. Because of today's high costs of education, it would be wise to give this goal serious thought now, rather than later.

Adequate Medical Insurance

If the family breadwinner cannot work, either because of illness or an accident, a provision should be made for income to be replaced. Fortunately, a substantial income replacement benefit is provided by Social

Education

CHILD	AMOUNT NEEDED	MIDPOINT OF NEED	MONTHLY INVESTMENT EARNING % TO PROVIDE NEED
_____	$_____	_____	$_____
_____	_____	_____	_____
_____	_____	_____	_____
TOTALS:	$_____		$_____

Figure 1

DISABILITY INSURANCE

Monthly disability income needed (at least 60% of present income)	$_____
Less: Social Security benefits	−_____
Less: Employee benefits	−_____
Less: Personal disability income policies	−_____
Less: Earnings from capital at work	−_____
Monthly disability income still needed	$_____

Present amount $_____ vs. Needed amount $_____

Present outlay $_____ vs. Needed outlay $_____

Figure 2

Security. The format in Figure 2 can be used to estimate your needs in this area. If this analysis shows that you need disability income insurance, you should obtain information about various policies for comparison purposes before making a decision.

Adequate Life Insurance

If the death of a family member would economically deprive the family, then this person should be covered by life insurance. We are not concerned here with the type of life insurance to be purchased, but rather with how much life insurance is needed and how to compare costs. Two types of needs must be considered in calculating how much life insurance you require. These are the cash needs of the estate and the income needs for the beneficiaries. Cash needs are such things as an emergency fund, final expenses, administration costs, estate inheritance taxes, an education fund, a mortgage payment fund, and so on. Income needs are the monthly living expenses required by the beneficiaries. The format in Figure 3 may be used for estimating these needs. Such items

Adequate Life Insurance

CASH ASSETS NEEDED:

    Education $_____

    Mortgage   _____

    Final expenses   _____

    Emergency fund   _____

    Estate costs   _____

INCOME ASSETS NEEDED:

    Current income need of $_____ per
    month—estimated Social Security
    Income of $_____ per month =
    $_____ × _____
    (factor from below) $_____

TOTAL NEEDED: $_____

    Less:
        Capital at work $_____ + Face
        Amount of insurance $_____ −
        Cash value of insurance $_____ $_____

LIFE INSURANCE NEEDED (SURPLUS) $_____

Present amount $_____ vs. Needed amount $_____

Present outlay $_____ vs. Needed outlay $_____

FACTORS FOR VARIOUS CAPITAL EARNING RATES

FACTOR	CAPITAL EARNING RATE
200	6%
150	8%
120	10%
100	12%

Figure 3

as an education fund and a mortgage payment fund are dealt with in today's dollars. Final expenses are usually $5,000 to $10,000. An emergency fund should be considered for beneficiaries. If you do not have more detailed information, figure your estate costs at approximately 5 percent of your total estimated estate (net worth plus life insurance face amount). The income needed is an estimate based on the income prior to death. By adding all of these together, you will get the total amount of assets needed. By subtracting your capital at work and your net amount of insurance from the total assets needed, you will find the life insurance needed, or a surplus of life insurance.

Other Financial Needs

We have not dealt with at least three other basic financial needs—medical insurance, property and liability protection, and other accumulation needs. These are not as easily quantified as are the previous goals. Obviously, you should have good family medical coverage at the lowest possible price. This is primarily a cost-shopping job. The same applies to property and liability protection. As for "other accumulation" needs, the methodology is the same as it is for accumulating an emergency fund or an education fund.

Social Security

You will notice that I have included Social Security benefits in a number of places. To obtain estimates for your situation, you should call your local Social Security office or purchase a current table from which you can take the needed numbers. A thorough discussion of Social Security is presented in Chapter 2.

The foregoing discussion has been an attempt to show you how to think about some of the financial goals that people have. Once you have reviewed your goals, you should then set up a table similar to the one shown in Your NCFE Financial Data Form. This will help you take action!

How Do I Know When I Get There?

As we said at the outset, money *is* probably more difficult to manage than it is to earn. A successful money manager has to

YEAR	PERSONAL INCOME	TAXES PAID	NET WORTH	CAPITAL AT WORK
	$	$	$	$

Figure 4

be something of an economist, a mathematician, and an expert in consumer affairs. The financial environment surrounding most individuals or families today *is* very complex, and considerable skill is required to deal adequately with this environment. Of course, the goal of personal money management is to provide a better quality of life for the manager and his family while providing for the major contingencies of life. In today's jargon, the money manager hopes to "get it all together" for himself and his family, financially speaking. Thus, it is important to be able to measure the results of one's financial planning. This can best be done by using a table such as the one shown in Figure 4, which contains certain key indicators. Year by year, these key indicators of your financial situation should be entered into the table. Although each one is important in itself, it is even more important as part of a trend. For example, a real sign of progress would be an income that is increasing at a reasonable rate. A net worth that is increasing would also indicate that you are making financial progress. Feel free to add or subtract indicators that you think are important, but remember to enter the numbers regularly.

Summary

Do you remember that comment that I made earlier about the boat without a rudder and without power? Like that boat, you can get somewhere without a financial plan (rudder) and power (motivation), but it may not be the destination you want. Just as important as developing a financial plan is its implementation. A plan that is not implemented is really no plan at all! Most people make plans of one sort or another, but don't take action and implement these plans, usually because they are complicated and take time to carry out. I have tried to give you the simplest possible methodology that will help you collect the information you need to understand your financial situation. Now, you should be able to motivate yourself to take action. No one else can do that for you. If, after reading all this, you are able to develop a plan and start implementing it, then I will have met one of my major goals as a financial planner and investment adviser.

More important, you will have done something more vital for your future than deciding on a financial plan. You will have acted upon one.

Part 2

Editor's Notes:
If Accumulating Money Comes First

*F*ifteen years ago I became interested in discovering why some people have the money to enjoy their retirement, whereas others—who perhaps have earned more—don't. If there is a simple answer, it might be that those without funds for their retirement have simply put off accumulating money. If you have been doing that, the next four chapters should help you get started (or start again) in accumulating some capital.

As a first step, Lew Kearns suggests some new ways of thinking about money, savings, and interest. The information he gives us in Chapter 5 should be made available to everyone at a much younger age than most of us get it. In Chapter 6, Charles Atwell describes a plan that works, combining professional mutual fund management with dollar-cost averaging. This is not just theory or something for the big investor. It is a plan that can work for you, if it hasn't already—it's called dollar-cost averaging. Another strategy is discussed in Chapter 7 by Karen Knizley, who explores the advantages and disadvantages of renting or buying real estate. Part 2 concludes with Ken Rouse's advice in Chapter 8 on planning for tomorrow through "balanced living."

Chapter 5

What You Need to Know About Savings and Interest

Dr. Lewis G. Kearns, B.A., J.D., is an investment executive, financial consultant, educator, and writer. For twenty-five years he was senior executive of Wellington Management Company, one of the industry's oldest and largest management firms. He has also been a professor in three university graduate schools of business, and a consultant to some of the country's largest industrial corporations on the design and investment of employee benefit plans. He has advised investment companies and insurance companies on investment and annuity products. Kearns is a Certified Financial Planner.

Lewis G. Kearns, J.D., CFP

What Is a Saving(s)?

Saving is keeping. It is the preservation of a sum of dollars. It is normally not a method of seeking growth, or appreciation, or a tax benefit. It is an action with both negative and positive aspects.

The negative aspect is that a savings is a preservation *from* certain risks faced by the currency that is to be protected. The risks are well known.

Physical safety. Currency in a piggy bank, in a shoe box, or under the mattress can be stolen or burned, can disintegrate, or get lost.

Loss of the face amount. Because a savings account is a loan by the saver-depositor to the borrower-bank or association, the lender receives a written guarantee of the return of the dollars loaned. The saver gets the face amount back.

Loss of access or withdrawal rights. The saver wants to take out all or part of his deposit as and when wanted, without limitations or penalties on withdrawing the emergency money.

These negative aspects are defensive, aimed at protecting currency *against* certain hazards. But there are also positive aspects when savings are the means of preserving dollars *for* a specific purpose. The first and indispensable step is to decide on the purpose of saving by asking yourself, *What is the job that these dollars must do for me?*

Money, like any financial vehicle, is but a tool to be used to accomplish a goal or purpose. In the case of savings, the goals most suitably relate to dollar-defined goals. Dollars are to be preserved for a purpose linked to dollars. You might want to preserve:

$8,000 for purchasing a second car, or

$10,000 for a child's college tuition, or

$15,000 for a down payment on a residence, or

$5,000 to refurbish the bedrooms, or

$20,000 to supply a nest egg for starting that cabinet shop, or boutique, or Austrian pastry store

Whatever the case, you decide upon a goal and define it in dollars. Later we will discuss the hazards of inflation and erosion of purchasing power in relation to goals set in fixed dollars. For now, we assume that the dollar objective refers to the dollar requirements at a future date, but we do not necessarily assume that $10,000 put aside today will buy the same car at the future date of purchase.

Savings Are Rentals

If you want to borrow money, you are likely to go to a bank or association. The

Table 1

NAME OF PLAN	AMOUNT OF DOLLARS (MINIMUM)	HOW LONG (MINIMUM TERM)	AMOUNT OF RENT INTEREST (%)
Regular savings	25	None	5.25
Certificate of deposit	500	90 days	5.75
	500	1 year	6.00
	500	2½ years	6.50
	1,000	4 years	7.25[a]
T-rate certificate	1,000	2½ years	13.00[b]
T-bill certificate	10,000	6 months	13.70[c]

[a]Jumbo-size certificates of deposit live in a separate world. Today's newspaper advertises a bank one-year certificate of deposit with an interest rate over 15 percent—but requiring a minimum purchase of $100,000.
[b]Rate based on this month's 2½-year yield for Treasury securities.
[c]Rate based on this week's average yield for six-month Treasury bills.

bank may supply $10,000 for twenty-four months if you agree to pay interest at 13 percent per year. In other words, the bank will rent its property—money—to you for twenty-four months and will receive a rental fee from you of 13 percent per year.

Now reverse the roles. If a bank or association wants to borrow money, it may come to you. It may invite you to serve it as a borrower by means of inducements ranging from the amount of rent it will pay you for using your money, to free electric can openers, pocket computers, or quartz clocks. The renter bank will offer to rent your money under terms related to the size of the property (the amount of dollars), the duration of the lease (how long the bank can use the property), and the amount of rent (interest paid). These are presented in recognizably uniform schedules (see Table 1).

The longer the term and the larger the property, the greater the rent (interest), because the bank has more property to re-rent (lend) for longer terms, hopefully at higher rates.

"The Highest Rates Allowed by Law"

What law?

Do not hire a lawyer to look it up in the statute books, because it is not there. The "law" concerning interest rates is really a bureaucratic order, Regulation Q, which was adopted by the Federal Reserve Board over forty years ago, presumably to curb competition between banks, or between banks and associations, or between associations. It was feared that a bank which paid more rent (increased its interest rate) than its neighbors would be swamped with transfers from lower paying rivals. So Regulation Q became a welcomed ceiling—welcomed by the banks, that is—to avoid the nightmare of a "run on the bank" because of higher rates down the street. In theory, Regulation Q was to protect the depositor in assuring him the continuity and solvency of the depository of his funds. In fact, this function of protecting the depositor was more directly achieved by the installation of deposit insurance, in ever increasing coverages, through the Federal Deposit Insurance Corporation (FDIC) and the Federal Savings and Loan Insurance Corporation (FSLIC).

Maybe FDIC and FSLIC have made Regulation Q unnecessary as protection to depositors. On the other hand, maybe Regulation Q makes many bankers more comfortable by prohibiting competitive attacks in the form of higher rates offered by rivals. FDIC and FSLIC protect the depositor. Regulation Q protects the banks.

Regulation Q puts all commercial banks and all thrift institutions (savings banks and savings and loan associations) into a kind of dual lock step in which *all* payers must pay no more than "the highest rate allowed by (regulation)." Table 2 summarizes the maximums and the allowable margins between commercial banks and thrift institutions.

Table 2

TYPE OF ACCOUNT	COMMERCIAL BANKS (%)	THRIFT INSTITUTIONS (%)
Regular	5.0	5.25
90–day	5.5	5.75
1–2½ years	6.0	6.50
2½–4 years	6.5	6.75
4–6 years	7.25	7.50
6 Years or More	7.50	7.75

So do not bother shopping for higher maximum rates. Despite intriguing names like Super Saver, Prestige Deposits, Automatic Accumulator, or Tailored Savings, the maximum interest rates will be identical.

And they probably will remain substantially that way. Consider just the number of banks, associations, and branches, and their public use.

More than five times as many as all motion picture theatres.

More than four times as many as all barber shops.

Visited more often by the public than any place except a supermarket.

Nearly twice as many as all post offices.

Examined more often and by more regulators than anything except gambling casinos. But unlike the casino, the house cannot break the player, nor can the player break the bank. But like casinos, banks have house rules (such as the "highest rate allowed").

"With Interest Compounded Daily"

You may be a little discouraged to find that money costs the same at all the money stores, but you cleverly remember that there are different ways of compounding interest. Bank A trumpets that its "effective annual interest rate" is 5.12 percent, while Bank B advertises that it "compounds interest daily."

What are the ways in which interest can be compounded? Which works best for the depositor? Is there a difference between methods of crediting interest?

Compounding is not a simple process. Nor is crediting.

The ways of compounding and crediting interest do make a difference. Daily compounding, for example, means that the interest on an account is computed each day; the result is an increased base on which further interest is calculated. The fact that the interest has been compounded daily for twenty days does not mean, however, that the total compounded can be withdrawn on the twenty-first day, for example.

First, let us look at methods of compounding interest on a $1,000 deposit (Table 3).

In this case, the effect of daily compounding has been to increase annual interest by $1.20. It can be assumed that this additional $1.20 would be credited and withdrawable at the end of the year.

What about earlier or partial withdrawals? Here, crediting will follow one of several methods.

1. Day-of-deposit to day-of-withdrawal crediting. This is the best deal for the depositor, because it embraces both the most favorable compounding method (daily) and complete crediting at any withdrawal date.

There are three other less favorable methods.

2. Base the credit on the low balance. Interest will be paid on the lowest amount

Table 3

FREQUENCY OF COMPOUNDING	EFFECTIVE ANNUAL INTEREST RATE (%)	TOTAL INTEREST	TOTAL INTEREST AND PRINCIPAL END OF YEAR
Annually	5.00	$50.00	$1,050.00
Semiannually	5.06	50.60	1,050.60
Quarterly	5.095	50.95	1,050.95
Daily	5.12	51.20	1,051.20

of money in the account during the crediting period.

3. FIFO (first in, first out) adjustment of balance. Withdrawals are deducted from the starting balance, and interest is credited only on the lowered base.

4. LIFO (last in, first out) adjustment of balance. Withdrawals are deducted from the most recent deposits, and interest is credited on the reduced base.

It is worthwhile to know the frequency of compounding and the frequency of crediting. The method fairest to the depositor is one in which both frequencies are identical and are as short as possible.

Here are some questions to be asked about banks and associations:

1. What minimum initial deposit is required?

2. What minimum balance must be maintained?

3. What interest rate is paid?

4. How frequently is interest compounded?

5. When is interest credited?

6. What are the service charges or penalties for withdrawal?

7. Does your status as depositor carry preferred treatment for personal or business loans?

8. Are the locations of branches or automatic teller machines convenient?

9. What are the business hours of the bank or association?

Where Can You Get More than the "Maximum Rate Allowed by Law"?

Obviously, not from within the system regulated by the Federal Reserve.

Where else?

From a multitude of sources that want to rent (borrow) your money. There is no scarcity of borrowers prepared to pay much, much higher interest rates. The problem is not procuring a higher interest rate, but procuring along with it the features and benefits associated with a saving, as distinguished from an investment or speculating program, like the FDIC-FSLIC government insurance.

Nothing is riskless.

A passbook savings account is subject to the risk that its dollars will be eroded by inflation.

A United States Government Savings Bond will pay at least one percent more than a bank savings account if held to maturity; a Treasury bill, or T-bill, will pay still more interest if you can set aside a minimum of $10,000, which you will leave undisturbed for periods up to one year; a Treasury note has a maturity of from one to seven years, and Treasury bonds have a maturity of five years or more. All these Treasury obligations have the advantages of being backed by the United States government, and paying more interest than banks and associations. They have the disadvantages of requiring larger minimum purchases and, because they are securities actively traded on the government issue market, they will show market fluctuations before maturity.

There is no difficulty in establishing the current market value, however. Today's *Wall Street Journal* shows that the saver/investor who purchased some of the Treasury issues listed in Table 4 for $100,000 could sell them for the market values noted. The market fluctuation on Treasury issues represents a risk. Some of the issues could be sold at a gain, others at a loss.

Can you afford to purchase at the required minimum? Are you comfortable with the fluctuations in market value? If the answers are affirmative, join the growing ranks of Treasury issue students.

The list of possibilities just begins with Treasury issues. Time and space do not permit a complete presentation here, but

Table 4

TYPE OF ISSUE	TIME REMAINING TO MATURITY	YIELD TO MATURITY (%)	MARKET BID
T-bill	6 months	13.85	$ 99,920
T-bill	12 months	13.82	97,076
T-note	24 months	13.25	98,100
T-note	48 months	13.75	99,100
T-bond	5 years	14.75	102,140
T-bond	10 years	14.63	104,260

we can list some high-interest media that sophisticated inventors hold:

U.S. Government Agency Issues, such as FNMA (Fannie Maes), GNMA (Ginnie Maes), Federal Land Bank, Inter-American Development Bank, and World Bank bonds.

Large (over $100,000) certificates of deposit in banks. Regulation Q, which places a maximum on interest payable to *small* investors, does not require a similar limitation for *large* investors.

Commercial Paper, such as borrowings by corporations. A current partial list of such borrowers includes: American Express Co., Aetna Life & Casualty Co., Conoco, Inc., General Foods Corp., INA Corp., New York Telephone, Pepsi Cola Co., and United Technologies. These obligations are often privately arranged, and in very large amounts, such as several million dollars per issue.

Each of the above three normally carries a higher yield than the Treasury issues. Are they as safe as the Treasury issues? No. Do they fluctuate in value as interest rates change? Yes.

But why bother mentioning them if the average individual lacks the large minimum purchase money?

Because all of the three, plus other high-yield types, such as bankers acceptances and repurchase agreements, are indirectly available through the purchase of a money market fund.

Before we leave the subject of Treasury securities, here is a question list to help you analyze them.

1. What minimum investment is required?

2. Is the purchase made at a discount (new T-bills) or at face amount (new T-notes and T-bonds)?

3. What will your bank charge to make a wire-order purchase?

4. When is interest paid?

5. Can the issue be registered in your name?

6. When can the issue be called and paid off, before maturity? This is important because you may be confronted with the reinvestment of funds earlier than you planned or desired.

Money Market Funds: Pools of Private Paper for the Public

A money market fund is a mutual fund that seeks to obtain maximum current interest through investment in specified money market instruments. The fund invests a diversified group of high-yielding borrowings such as jumbo certificates of deposit, Treasury securities, government agency issues, the promissory notes of large corporations, and other obligations. All of these issues have short maturities, sometimes averaging as short as twenty-five days. Table 5 presents a capsule comparison of savings and money market funds that may be helpful.

Table 5. Bank or Association Savings vs. a Money Market Fund

	REGULAR SAVINGS ACCOUNT	12 MO. & 30 MO. CERTIFICATE OF DEPOSIT (SAVINGS CERTIFICATE)	MONEY MARKET FUND
Means of with-drawal	In person or by check	None until maturity, without penalty	By mail, bank wire, phone, or check
Penalties for early withdrawal	None	Interest penalty of 3 or 6 months	None
Current yield	5% to 5½%	Based on T-bills, fixed until maturity	Changes daily, depending upon the current money market
Safety	Insured by FDIC or FSLIC up to $100,000	Insured by FDIC or FSLIC up to $100,000	Based upon the credit standing of the issues
Price stability	No fluctuation	No fluctuation	Small daily varia-tions; some funds maintain constant fixed share values
Interest compounding	Daily or other bank practice	Prohibited by regulation	Daily dividends, compounded daily or other fund practice, or paid to shareholder monthly

How do you get complete information about money market funds? From your financial planner, investment adviser, or directly from one of the many funds that publish coupon ads in the financial press. Here are some questions you should ask about a money market fund:

1. Is there a sales charge? (In most cases there is none.)

2. What is the management fee? (These vary from as low as ⅒ of 1 percent to ½ of 1 percent.)

3. What is the management policy respecting the type of security held? (Federal securities only, commercial paper only, combinations, and so on.)

4. What is the minimum initial investment? The minimum periodic investment?

5. How are withdrawals made? (Mail, bank wire, phone, or check?)

6. Is there a minimum allowable withdrawal? How much?

7. What is the current yield, say, the last seven days, compared with other money market funds?

8. When are dividends reinvested? Credited to the account? Payable to you?

9. If the sponsor manages other portfolios, is there a right to exchange? At what cost?

10. What is the experience and size of the management?

11. Is the manager an independent entity or is management connected with another financial institution such as a bank holding company or a stockbroker?

When Is a Saving a Growth Investment?

When it accumulates fast enough to offset inflation.

How fast is enough to do that?

The answer depends upon the rate of inflation.

Interest rate theory holds that interest rates consist of two parts. One part is a figure representing the level of *expected inflation*. A lender needs a rate high enough to at least equal any decline in the value of the dollar. The second part is the *real* interest rate, which is to cover the lender's cost of doing business including a profit for the lender.

Let us do some remembering, and put these two together.

Remember when bank savings paid 1 percent or 2 percent or 3 percent? And there was no inflation? And banks were lending at 4½ or 5 percent? The interest rate was, on these facts, about 3 percent:

Real Interest   3%
Inflation   0
Total Interest   3%

Now to turn to the real current world. The lender's cost of doing business has increased. So has inflation. And the *expected inflation* is a real puzzler. But if we assumed an 8 percent expected annual inflation, the formula would look like this:

Real Interest   5%
Inflation   8%
Total Interest   13%

So you should seek an annual minimum interest rate of 13 percent. Any interest in excess of 13 percent will result in a *growth* of your dollars against your business costs and against inflation.

How fast should your account grow? Remember that *Doubling Takes Place at "72."* This figure does not refer to age or joys or troubles—just money. And 72 is the magic doubling number, into which is divided the annual interest rate compounded annually, as shown in Table 6.

What a difference the rate makes, especially in your personal goals and plans! For example, if you expect your money to double in six years, it must compound at an annual rate of 12 percent. If you must meet a $10,000 tuition bill in eight years, and you have $5,000 working for you, it must compound at an annual rate of 9 percent.

Yes, a saving can be a growth investment. With enough time. And an adequate total interest yield.

Table 6

CURRENT ANNUAL INTEREST RATE	THE MAGIC DOUBLING NUMBER	NUMBER OF YEARS IN WHICH MONEY IS DOUBLED
5	72	14.4
6	72	12.0
7	72	10.3
8	72	9.0
9	72	8.0
10	72	7.2
11	72	6.5
12	72	6.0
13	72	5.5
14	72	5.1

Now You Know

That the financial world is a smorgasbord of methods of saving. You will probably select more than one of these methods. Your appetite for very high yields should consider any digestive discomfort caused by market fluctuations or limitations on access and withdrawal.

You also know that you should start by personally answering these questions:

What is the dollar amount that I can set aside?

When will I need to have the dollars returned to me?

How many dollars will I need to have returned?

Your answers will form the foundation of your plan. And your plan will work if you do.

Chapter 6

Accumulating Money: Mutual Funds and Dollar-cost Averaging

Charles M. Atwell,
CLU, CFP, ChFC

Charles M. Atwell is a chartered financial consultant who has been in the seurities business for twenty-five years. He is the national director of Financial and Estate Planning for Waddell & Reed, Inc., for whom he has developed money management seminars that are conducted nationwide. He was formerly on the staff of the Securities and Exchange Commission and the National Association of Securities Dealers. He is an adjunct faculty member of the College for Financial Planning of Denver, Colorado, and is an instructor on wealth accumulation planning for the American College of Bryn Mawr, Pennsylvania. He has also taught financial planning courses at Rockhurst College, Penn Valley Community College, and the University of Missouri. He has appeared on both television and radio, and he conducts money management seminars for national associations. A Chartered Life Underwriter and a Certified Financial Planner, Atwell is a former president of the Kansas City Chapter of the International Association for Financial Planning. He also served on the national board of the IAFP for four years.

Accumulating money is difficult because of the various obstacles we all face. Fear of risk, lack of discipline, and procrastination are personal factors that prevent many people from achieving their financial goals. Furthermore, most people don't have the time, training, or temperament to explore the complex world of investing. Taxation, inflation, and the constant demand for a higher standard of living are financial obstacles we all face today and will face in the future.

In spite of all these difficulties, it *is* possible to design a financial plan that will overcome these obstacles. Investment strategies are available that greatly reduce the factors of risk and encourage disciplined investment. A carefully developed financial plan can include ways of making inflation and the tax laws work for you instead of against you. You don't need a degree in finance to be successful in accumulating money! What you do need, however, is a plan. Think of it as your game plan.

The money game is unique in that all human beings must participate whether they want to or not, although you can choose whether you want to be an active or a passive participant. To be an active player, you must begin with an evaluation of where you are now and where you are heading. Part of an effective financial plan is to write down all of your assets, liabilities, and potential future benefits and needs. Many people don't have a clear idea of their own net worth or a definition of their personal financial goals. A professional financial planner can be a tremendous help in analyzing how you can reach your objectives.

Establishing a financial plan is your first step in deciding to become an active player in the money game. Let's discuss some of the obstacles we've mentioned before you take the final step—the implementation of your plan.

Examing the Obstacles

Fear of Risks

Loaning Money. The money game is seldom static—even with "guarantees." Your money is safe in most thrift institutions up to the insured limit, but if inflation and taxes are greater than the rate of return, you can go broke safely! Part of your financial plan, therefore, should be to periodically reevaluate your plan in light of current monetary conditions.

"Never a borrower nor a lender be," your grandmother probably warned. But, in actuality, without borrowers and lenders the world would not go round and the money game would be over! Companies need money for expansion—and banks, savings and loans, insurance companies, and other institutions are actually intermediaries since they take your money (deposits, etc.) and lend or invest it to get a higher return than the interest they pay you for its use. If you wish to earn more money on your investment, and are willing to take some risks, you can choose to be an owner instead of a loaner.

Being an Owner. Many people play the money game by becoming owners of a portfolio of stocks and bonds. The possibilities are countless, because there are tens of thousands of different securities to buy, sell, or hold. There are management risks in deciding *what* to buy or sell, timing risks in deciding *when* to buy or sell, income tax risks in that the tax laws may change, and so on. Generally speaking, the greater the risk, the greater the potential reward. Underline the word potential!

The stock market gives us an opportunity to be part owners of American industry, and we should take advantage of it. There *is* a way to invest your dollars and minimize some of the risks involved. How would you like to have a full-time team of investment managers working for you, as millionaires have? That's what I have—I call them my professional worriers. They worry about what to buy and what to sell, if the market is going up or down, the future of the economy, and so on. "Ah," you say, "that's it! All I have to do to win the money game is to be a millionaire!" Not necessarily. You can have professionals manage your investments as well, starting with only $100 a month!

You cannot afford to let your dollars lie idle; they should be working for you. But where are you going to put them? Not in a cookie jar or under a mattress, I hope! In money management seminars we say, "People don't get rich making money . . . but by managing the money they make." Money that is earning 5 percent before tax when inflation is 10 percent is a guaranteed loss in the purchasing power of your savings. The most effective way to handle the "risk factor" in accumulating money is simply to acknowledge the existence of risk and choose an investment method that will minimize your risks while giving you maximum returns.

Inflation and Taxation

Inflation. Investments are available that capitalize on the inflation factor and are also taxed favorably. Real estate limited partnerships, for example, can show a high return since real estate has historically benefited from an inflationary economy. Investment plans that specialize in energy investments, such as oil and gas programs, can also benefit from inflation and help you to offset the bite that rising energy costs take from your money accumulation program. Ownership of shares of American industry is a proven hedge against inflation for millions of people through the use of full-time professional money management.

Taxation. Do you have an Individual Retirement Account? You probably should! An IRA should be a basic part of your plan to accumulate money. The amount you set aside in this account is tax deductible on your Form 1040 and can grow until your retirement years without any current income tax on the dividends and capital gains. April 15 can be a day of either punishment or reward; the tax system punishes the ill-informed and rewards the well-informed.

The Uniform Gifts to Minors Act provides another way to make the tax laws work for you. Under this law, which is effective in all states, you can give money to your child and name yourself or your spouse as custodian of the money for the child's benefit. This money, plus dividends and capital gains, can accumulate at the child's tax bracket, which is zero at the younger ages. One more tax strategy for winning the money game!

The tax code rewards investors with the dividend exclusions and the preferential treatment of long-term capital gains. Interest is taxed at regular rates, but dividends and capital gains are taxed favorably. It pays to be an owner instead of a loaner!

Charitable Giving. Some investment plans can make both inflationary factors and tax laws benefit the investor. Consider, for example, the case of an elderly woman who had stock valued at $60 a share with a cost basis of approximately 16¢ a share. Inflation had increased the total value of her stock to $1,300,000. If she had sold the stock, she would have had to pay an exhorbitant amount of taxes. She was also being taxed on the $20,000 a year that she was receiving in dividends.

She wished to leave her estate to charities, and when she heard about charitable remainder unitrusts, she gave stock worth $1,100,000 to a unitrust and also put $200,000 worth of stock into a living trust. The unitrust sold the stock without any capital gains tax and reinvested the money in income-producing securities programs managed by professional investment managers. As a result of these trusts, she is now receiving an income of approximately $100,000 per year, 90 percent of which is tax-free. Her unitrust provides for the eventual distribution of the trust to a number of the major charities. Her objectives, in addition to wishing to donate her estate to charities, were to substantially increase her income and minimize estate clearance costs. The use of these trusts made it possible for her to accomplish all three of these goals and avoid hundreds of thousands of dollars in unnecessary taxes and fees. She and her favorite charities will all end up winners in the money game!

Do-It-Yourself Investing versus Professional Management

The money game, like the game of love, is one in which emotions can run high. There are more losers than winners in the money game primarily because of these emotions—emotions that create the temperament risk. The rose-colored glasses through which we view our money and our love can blind us and keep us from making wise decisions.

If you buy a security because it is "going higher" and sell that security because it is down and "going lower" you will lose the money game. Suppose an investor hears about a "hot tip" to buy a stock at $10 per share "going to $100" when the Dow Jones averages are at 850 going to 2,400. The investor says, "How can I miss?" The major motivation here is an emotional factor—greed!

Let's suppose that this same investor buys the hot tip but finds his stock drops from $10 to $1 per share and the Dow Jones drops from 850 to 650. The investor now realizes that his "hot tip" was actually a "cold tip," like the tip of the iceberg that was big enough to sink the Titanic! He sells out and swears never to do that again! Once more, the major motivation is an emotional factor—fear!

Our emotions can get us into trouble if we don't know how to play the game. You can avoid the pitfall of letting your emotions turn you into a loser by letting a professional team manage your investments for you.

Do you know when to buy, how much to pay, and when to sell? Perhaps you'd like to try my buying and selling formula for buying sheep and selling deer to help you to accumulate money faster! Buy sheep when they are lying quietly and sell deer when they are up and running! The problem with this formula is how to distinguish between sheep that have finished resting and deer that are tired of running! As an investor, you are better off to let full-time professional money managers make these decisions for you.

Professional Management. Unless you have a minimum of $100,000, together with time, training, and temperament to study market trends, balance sheets, market indexes, economic indicators and the like, you should let the pros do your investing for you.

Many of the risks of investing can be reduced by choosing to have professional money managers work for you. Good management can also provide you with diversification of investment, flexibility, and liquidity that you could not achieve by investing on your own.

Your investment managers should be a team of professionals who know how to spread the investment risk over a broad range of securities that represent various industries. These managers should have access to the largest Wall Street firms for investment ideas and research.

The managers you choose should have full-time traders who can monitor all securities whenever the markets are open for trading. Extensive research should be conducted before any security is purchased and then monitored continuously as long as it is owned. Research analysis should include both fundamental and technical research to assist the investment managers.

Securities should be sold when they do not meet specific criteria, for example, earnings, growth, or dividends.

The securities should be managed according to specific written objectives, such as "long-term appreciation of investment, with income only a secondary objective," or "high current income." To achieve these goals, you may invest the money in different types of securities—common stocks, preferred stocks, and debt securities. The goals should not be changed without the approval of the investors.

To protect your assets, the cash and securities should be held by a bank and trust company and not by the investment people. If your investment managers qualify for special tax status, they will not have to pay any tax on your dividends and capital gains. The dividends and capital gains will be taxed only once—at your tax bracket—instead of being taxed twice.

Your investment professionals should send you frequent reports on how your plan is performing, as well as annual and semiannual financial statements, with listings of all securities owned, which should be audited by certified public accountants. You should also receive a statement of your acccount whenever you add to or reduce your account, every time a dividend is paid or credited to your account, or whenever a capital gain is paid or credited to your account whenever you add to or reduce activity of your plan. You should also be able to find out the daily status of your investment plan, and the investment managers should periodically bring you up to date on their expectations for the marketplace.

Diversification. How many securities could you purchase with $100? Probably one—with a substantial brokerage charge. Considerable risk is involved in owning only one or a few securities. You should have a portfolio of many securities to obtain diversification and reduce the effect of having the securities of one or more companies

drop in value. You want your investment team to avoid these securities or to sell "when the red flags go up." But securities will normally fluctuate. You need to look to the long term. Unless you have the time, training, temperament, and money to do this successfully you need professionals to handle these decisions for you.

Your investments could be spread over as many as one-hundred different companies, so that you have a limited amount in any one company. There is a time to own securities in some industries, and a time not to own some industries. Markets go in cycles—for example, from a growing economy cycle to a recessionary economy cycle. Your investments should be managed to take advantage of these cycles. At times they should be fully invested in stocks and bonds, and at other times in cash equivalent securities.

Flexibility. You should be able to choose from a wide variety of investment plans, ranging from conservative government bonds to young companies showing aggressive growth. This wide spectrum provides you with some flexibility in your choices by allowing you to match up to the one that meets your particular objectives and investment temperament.

You should be able to change from one plan to another without being charged. You might want to specialize in accumulating money in a particular industry, such as high technology. If so, your investment people can concentrate your investments in that industry. For example, a hedge against rising energy costs would be a plan that specializes in investing in the energy industry.

To be truly flexible, your plan should be set up so that you can add money at any time or terminate the plan at any time without a penalty, realizing that the amount of money received will depend on your cost and the current market value of investments.

The investment manager may charge a

management fee of less than one percent on an annual basis. You should be able to sell your investment back to the manager at the market value at any time. You should be able to reinvest income dividends and capital gains without a sales charge, but there can be a reasonable sales charge on the initial purchases to compensate the financial planner and the investment manager.

Liquidity. The availability of your money is an important factor to be considered. Life is unpredictable, and you never know when you will need to have your cash available for an emergency. A highly liquid investment plan is preferable, one that will send you any money requested within seven days or even send it to you regularly if you need additional income on a regular basis. Such a plan requires full-time supervision and management.

Implementing Your Plan

As you can see, it *is* possible to overcome the obstacles that prevent people from accumulating money. You can choose a plan that will help you to reduce your risks as well as help to make inflation and tax laws work in your favor. By choosing your moves carefully and using professional management, you can have a money accumulation plan that will help you to win the game! However, a well-developed plan is effective only when it is put into action. How are you going to implement your plan?

Mutual Funds: An Accumulation Plan That Works

A plan that has helped me to become financially independent has been to invest in a professionally managed portfolio of securities through mutual funds. You can have your own portfolio of securities— stocks, bonds, and the like—by owning shares of a mutual fund, which is a type of investment company that pools the investments of a group of individuals who share a common investment objective. The purpose of such a plan is to match your specific objectives with an investment company that has similar goals. With a family of funds to choose from, an investor has a number of different types of investment choices. A mutual fund reduces the inherent risk of investing in stocks and bonds. Mutual funds can be used for short-term or long-term objectives. They can help you accumulate wealth over the long term if you have a comprehensive financial plan!

The investment manager is responsible for investing the shareholders' money according to the objectives set for the fund. Included in a family of mutual funds would be the following: a money market fund designed for short-term savings or investments, which pays interest monthly as well as providing checkwriting privileges; a government cash fund designed for the most conservative short-term investors; a high income fund designed, as the name implies, to provide a high rate of current income; and aggressive growth funds designed for long-term accumulation plans.

Millions of investors have selected mutual funds for their savings and investments in seeking a higher return than would be available through other savings institutions. Some funds are managed for long-term growth. The investments and the cash of each of the funds are held by a bank or trust company for safekeeping. The investment manager stands ready to buy back or redeem the shares at any time. Families of mutual funds allow you to change from one fund to another without any charge. Most allow you to compound your dividends and capital gains by investing in additional shares without any charge.

When you purchase shares in a mutual fund, you receive a prospectus. The prospectus gives you information regarding the fund, its objective, its policies, and the interworkings of the manager and the fund itself. It also includes a list of the investments held by the mutual fund. Most families of mutual funds have been established for thirty or forty years and have proven records of performance.

When you invest in a professionally managed mutual fund, your investment is represented by the number of shares you own. The value of a share is the total value of the fund investments divided by the number of shares outstanding. This is called the net asset value, and is listed daily in the newspaper. The net asset value would be the amount received upon redemption of the shares. It could be more than you paid for the shares, or less.

The Internal Revenue Service has special provisions for mutual funds. The fund does not have to pay taxes if it pays out 90 percent of its net income. It pays out the net income plus capital gains to the investor, either in cash or through reinvestment in additional shares. However, the income is taxable to the individual investor even if he chooses to have it reinvested in more shares.

You can compound the number of shares you own by having your dividends and capital gains reinvested in additional shares. This method of compounding your shares should be used during the accumulation of your plan. Later on, when more income is needed—after retirement, for example—you can take payments of your dividends or capital gains.

Your financial planner can assist you in selecting the funds that will help you reach your investment goals. Many investors select several funds from a family of funds to cover all their bases—cash reserve, income, and growth of capital. Once you have found the fund or funds that will help you achieve your objectives, you need a method of investing that will substantially reduce the risks we discussed earlier. Stocks and bonds fluctuate in value daily. How can you reduce the timing risk of when to buy or sell?

A method that can make the most efficient use of your investment dollars is one that has worked for me for over sixteen years. It's called "dollar-cost averaging" and has proved successful for millions of people. It isn't a guarantee, but if you follow the rules for a long period of time, it can help you to win the money game.

Dollar-Cost Averaging

Dollar-cost averaging consists of investing a specific number of dollars at a regular time, such as every payday or every month, instead of buying a set number of shares. You choose the amount you wish to invest by paying yourself first on a regular basis. This method works equally well in a rising market, a declining market, or a fluctuating market. You buy more shares when prices are low and fewer shares when prices are higher.

Here's how dollar-cost averaging can work for you in any market, using $100 a month investment as an example:

IN A RISING MARKET	AMOUNT	SHARE PRICE	SHARES PURCHASED
Jan.	$100	$ 5	20
Feb.	$100	$10	10
Mar.	$100	$20	5
Totals	$300	–	35

Invested $300 ÷ 35 shares = $8.57 = average cost per share.

IN A DECLINING MARKET		AMOUNT	SHARE PRICE	SHARES PURCHASED
	Jan.	$100	$20	20
	Feb.	$100	$10	10
	Mar.	$100	$ 5	5
	Totals	$300	–	35

Invested $300 ÷ 35 shares = $8.57 = average cost per share.

IN A FLUCTUATING MARKET		AMOUNT	SHARE PRICE	SHARES PURCHASED
	Jan.	$100	$10	10
	Feb.	$100	$20	5
	Mar.	$100	$ 5	20
	Totals	$300	–	35

Invested $300 ÷ 35 shares = $8.57 = average cost per share.

This simple illustration does not show the average market price per share during the three periods, which would be $5, $10, and $20 added together and divided by three, or $11.66 per share. In all three periods, the average *cost* per share is $8.57, while the average *price* per share is $11.66. Stated another way, the average cost during the period given was 26 percent less than the average price per share. I used a period of three months; it could be three years or thirty years. This time to start is now, and the longer your dollars are working for you, the better it is for your future.

The key to using the dollar-cost averaging method successfully is discipline. This discipline will always produce an average cost per share that is less than the average price per share during the period—if you stick with the plan. When the price is up, you will buy fewer shares, and when the price is low, you will buy more shares. The danger is that you might be tempted to stop buying when the price is down. If the news is gloomy and the price is low, you need to "hang in there" or even accelerate the program. The market will fluctuate in value; this is to be expected. Dollar-cost averaging takes advantage of the fluctua-

tions in market prices to help you win the money game.

We have talked about being either a passive or an active participant in the money game. You also have the choice of being a conservative player or an aggressive one. Remember, the greater the risk you are willing to accept, the greater the potential reward. One way to be more aggressive in the money game is to play with someone else's money.

Leverage—OPM

Would you consider borrowing money to invest? Using OPM (other people's money) increases your risk, but it also multiplies your potential return. For example, you could use $5,000 of mutual funds as collateral and borrow $2,500 for investing and then have $7,500 worth of investments working for you. This is called using leverage aggressively, or multiplying your buying power. When the value of your investments goes up, you can borrow more money. If it goes down, you may have to put up more collateral or pay down the loan. Mutual funds have allowed me to become financially independent by providing collateral for bank loans; other people's money has helped me to win the money game. Remember, *loaner's* rewards are limited to a fixed rate of interest, while the potential for *owners* is unlimited because they are willing to accept risks. When you "loan" money to a bank, you receive 5 to 10 percent, and the bank earns 10 or 20 percent on that money. If you wish to earn more money on your investments, and are willing to take some risks, you can choose to be an owner instead of a loaner.

Using dollar-cost averaging and leverage money, as I have done, can be an effective way of accumulating money. However, you should always keep cash reserves for emergencies, and for a call from the bank or broker for either cash or more collateral. It's important to avoid being sold out because of such a call, which would probably mean that the price is at the bottom and will shoot back up. The risk is that you could lose your money as well as the OPM if sold out. For this reason, leverage is suitable only for very aggressive investors, because the risk is much greater.

There are tax advantages for investors who use leverage. The interest paid on the loans is deductible on your tax return, and the increase in value of leverage investments is not taxed until the investments are sold. These are long-term investments, so the increase in value, when taxed, is given favorable treatment as long-term capital gains. So, as you can see, the rewards for this type of investing can be high.

Another aggressive investment philosophy that I practice was perfected by Bernard Baruch, a self-made millionaire. It's called the "art of contrary thinking." When everybody on the radio and in the newspapers says, "It's the end of the world; the market is collapsing with no bottom in sight," it is usually time to get ready to buy. The art of contrary thinking helps you to buy when prices are low and sell when prices are high, and can make you a big winner. "Contrarians" buy on bad news and sell on good news—unemotionally!

As an aggressive investor, you can diversify your other investments by investing in real estate limited partnerships, oil and gas programs, and other tax-advantaged investments. These programs have a general partner as the manager and provide flow-through income to the limited partners as well as tax benefits. Tax-advantaged investments are covered in more detail in other chapters of this book.

If you choose to be an aggressive player in the money game, you should still continue to invest regularly in a professionally managed portfolio of securities, using dollar-cost averaging to give a solid base to your financial independence.

Is Now a Convenient Time to Start?

There is no convenient time to start your plan. Procrastination is your greatest risk in the money game. It is never too early to start playing actively, so I should like to ask you two questions. Are you satisfied with the number of dollars you have accumulated to date? Are you satisfied with your present financial position? If the answer to one or both of these questions is no, then you need a financial plan to help you accumulate money for your financial independence. And even if your answer is yes, you may need a plan to safeguard what you have accumulated.

Accumulating money is a financial objective shared by many and realized by only a few. By reading this book and increasing your awareness of the importance of intelligent financial planning, you are improving your changes of becoming successful at the money game. If you choose to be an active participant, remember—like it or not—it's the only game in town. Learn the rules, and play to win! The longer you wait, the harder it is to win. Your financial planner can be your coach!

I wish you success in planning for your financial future. It's your move!

Chapter 7

Renting vs. Buying Your Home

Karen J. Knizley is an experienced financial planner and tax accountant. She is the president of her own financial planning organization, Tax Coordinated Financial Plans. She and her staff provide comprehensive financial services to individuals, businesses, and institutions. She has appeared on television and radio and has given numerous lectures on the subject of financial planning and methods of saving on federal and state taxes. She is a Certified Financial Planner and is a member of the North Bay Chapter of the International Association for Financial Planning, serving as president in 1980–81. Most recently she served as chairperson of the board.

Karen J. Knizley, CFP

Individuals from all walks of life have long considered home ownership the "American dream." Obvious psychological benefits are attached to the pride of ownership. Having a home of one's own signifies roots in the community, as well as the attainment of a goal. In addition, there are economic rewards. Many a prospective homeowner has thought, "Why accumulate monthly rent receipts when, for the same dollars, I could be making mortgage payments and building equity in a home of my own?" Unfortunately, home buyers too often discover that the mortgage payment represents only part of the cost of ownership. Fire insurance, property taxes, maintenance, and repairs must also be budgeted, bringing the cost to the point where no money is left over to do anything besides own a home.

Today's inflated real estate prices and the high cost of financing make it imperative to weigh carefully any decision regarding whether to own or rent property. Purchasing a place to live may fit your current income, but unless you consider the potential problems and responsibilities of home owning, your "dream" may quickly turn to a nightmare.

I could relate many scenarios about the amazing decade of the 1970s and the profits made in residential California real estate. Those of you residing in Houston, Texas, or Orlando, Florida, may wonder what California real estate has to do with you. Everything! The "smart" real estate dollars today are being invested in the Sun Belt, just as they were invested in California in the 1970s. Many experts predict that the steady appreciation in values that took place during that decade is destined to repeat itself in the next housing shortage, and that southern cities will lead the way.

A Tale of Seventy-Nine Homes in Orange County, California

In 1975 I saw an ad in my Sunday newspaper announcing a lottery for the sale of seventy-nine new homes in Orange County, California. The prices ranged from $59,000 for a two-bedroom home to $140,000 for four bedrooms with a family room and a den. The reason for the lottery, I might add, was to prevent hundreds of people from camping out in order to be first in line to purchase one of the as yet unfinished new homes. As long as you were present by 9:30 A.M. on the day of the sale, your chances of success were as good as those of anyone else in the lottery.

I was amazed to see more than 2,000 people congregating at the proposed development site, fervently hoping they would have a winning hope. The process of logging attendees, issuing numbers, and calling out the fortunate names took the better part of that Sunday. It wasn't until quite late in the day that I realized just how fortunate at least half of the lottery winners were. Privately, these participants were selling their right to purchase one of the residences for anywhere from $5,000 to $10,000. What made the houses seem like a real bargain was that if past history were to repeat itself in that area of California, the houses would be worth a minimum of $15,000 to $20,000 more by the completion of construction in just a few months. What about financing? A prospective buyer is not concerned about whether or not a mortgage is available when the property most assuredly can be sold for a $15,000 profit *the day before escrow closed*. I know people who made a small fortune simply by "almost buying" homes.

In May of 1980, the decision to purchase one of these homes became a far more serious consideration. The seventy-nine homes had increased in price to $138,000 for the smaller model and $360,000 or so (depending on improvements) for the larger one. Even at those prices, people believed it was urgent to buy before inflation pushed costs higher. There were no line-ups to purchase any of the residences—at those prices, you don't exactly attract crowds—but in general the homes were not on the market more than a month or so.

Exactly two years later, eighteen of the original seventy-nine homes were for sale, some of which had been on the market in excess of six months. The prices had changed drastically over the two-year period. Now, they ranged from $108,000 to $229,900. From all indications, prices were still dropping, depending on how badly the owner wanted to sell. The property was the same as had been for sale two years earlier. The neighborhood had not deteriorated. No earthquake fault had been discovered. What was the cause of change in this environment? Interest rates? Todays buyer *must* consider the cost of obtaining financing. Today a new mortage on the seventy-nine homes will cost a much higher annual percentage on the amount borrowed.

Let's consider a 20 percent down payment (see below), and review the current cost of obtaining a mortgage and the resulting monthly payments. (I'll spare you interest rates of original mortgages. In comparison, they are depressingly low.)

Even if they could qualify for the loan, few potential homeowners would be so enamored of either of these houses to go the route of new financing, especially when rental rates in that particular neighborhood range from $550 to $1,600 per month.

Because houses did not sell and interest rates did not decline as everyone predicted, a new phrase crept into California real estate lingo: "creative financing." This incentive to purchase can take many forms, but by and large it meant the new buyer assumed the seller's original first mortgage after making a down payment, and then the seller carried a second mortgage for the balance at perhaps 12–13 percent interest for possibly three to five years. It seemed so easy; on a $100,000 home, for example, a buyer might assume an original 8 percent mortgage for $50,000, pay 20 percent ($20,000) down, and have the seller carry a second deed of trust for $30,000 at 13 percent. The new buyer usually paid interest only, or interest and a very small amount of the principal for the second mortgage. When the term of the loan was over (three to five years), the balance due was called a balloon payment. This particular approach to "creative financing" was short-lived because the U.S. Supreme Court recently ruled that all federally chartered savings and loans institutions can enforce a due-on-sale clause for existing loans. This means that the lending institution can insist that the old, low-yielding mortgage be paid off upon sale. New-buyer assumptions accounted for 42 percent of homes purchased in 1981 alone, and many of these transactions will be affected, since the ruling is retroactive. In addition, the Federal Home Loan Mortgage Corporation, known as Freddie Mac, made a similar ruling for its 700,000 to 900,000 mortgages nationwide.

The prospective homeowner must be careful. Although this ruling affects only federal savings and loan institutions, not

	TWO-BEDROOM		FOUR-BEDROOM	
Selling price	$108,000		$299,900	
Down payment 20%		$21,600		$59,980
Loan fee, 2 points		1,828		4,898
Closing costs		1,000		1,000
Total initial outlay		$24,428		$65,878
Monthly mortgage payment @ 16½% interest		$ 1,196		$ 3,323
Monthly taxes and insurance		133		317
Total		$ 1,329		$ 3,640

	TWO-BEDROOM		FOUR-BEDROOM	
Selling price	$108,000		$299,900	
Down payment		$21,600		$59,980
Loan fee		–		–
Closing costs		550		550
Total initial outlay		$22,150		$60,530

MONTHLY MORTGAGE PAYMENTS				
Assumed mortgage			$130,000	
$50,000 @ 8%	$	356	@ 8%	896
Owner-financed loan			109,920	
$36,400 @ 12%	$	364	@12%	1,099
Taxes and				
insurance	$	133		317
Total monthly				
payment	$	853		$2,312

those chartered by the state and specifically exempting Federal Housing Administration or Veterans Administration loans, other financial institutions are lobbying for similar rulings. In the absence of swift legislative response, state savings and loan institutions are expected to convert to federal charters.

This decision may not be as bleak as it seems on the surface, however. The affected savings and loan associations seem willing to negotiate an assumption by the new buyer at an interest rate somewhere between the old and current rates.

Next, let's assume the existing mortgage was assumed and that it carries an 8 percent interest rate. The down payment was again 20 percent. (See illustration above.)

The buyers, who had no idea the U.S. Supreme Court was even considering whether or not they could take over the original loan, now face substantially higher payments than they originally counted on. This is not their only cause for concern. Just about now, many second mortgages are coming due. When interest rates began to rise, buyers and sellers alike were convinced there was no way to lose. After all,

interest rates would surely come down long before the balloon payment on the owner financing was due and the loan could be refinanced. At the worst, if interest rates did not decline, eager buyers further assumed they could sell their dwellings for a handsome profit since these homes were worth three times their original cost after only five years.

These false assumptions have laid the groundwork for potential disaster in the California real estate market:

A. Interest rates have not declined substantially and the recent home buyer must either beg for an extension if the seller is amenable, or shop for the additional cash at a time when it costs more to borrow money than at any other time in our history.

B. If an extension or the loan funds are not available, the homeowner must sell, perhaps under "distress sale" conditions.

If you had purchased one of the homes in our illustration early in 1980, utilizing owner financing, it is time to make a decision about what to do. Several options are open to you.

	TWO-BEDROOM	FOUR-BEDROOM
Selling price	$138,000	$360,000
Assumed mortgage	51,000	132,000
Down payment	27,600	72,000
Seller financing due and payable	59,400	156,000

	TWO-BEDROOM	FOUR-BEDROOM
New mortgage @ 17%	$ 59,400	$156,000
Loan fee, 3 points ± 100	1,882	4,780
Closing costs	550	550
Debt service		
Monthly payments		
Assumed mortgage 8%	356	896
New mortgage	847	2,224
Taxes and insurance	133	317
Total	$ 1,336	$ 3,437

Option A: Shop for a New Second Trust Deed

What you must do now is find one entity or another to loan you $59,400 or $156,000, respectively. (See above.)

Keep in mind I've assumed that the financing was secured with a bank. If money is tight and you must solicit funds from a mortgage broker, interest rates can range anywhere from 20 percent to 25 percent, and the additional fee can be as much as 10 percent (called points) of the amount borrowed. These circumstances bring the costs up considerably.

Option B: Sell

This option presents a different set of problems. With eighteen homes for sale in the same neighborhood, it is definitely a

	Purchase			
	TWO-BEDROOM		FOUR BEDROOM	
Original cost	$138,000		$360,000	
Down payment	27,600		72,000	
Closing costs	550		550	
Loan fee	–		–	
Total out of pocket		$28,150		$72,550
	Sale			
Selling price	$108,000		$299,900	
Real estate commission		– 6,480		– 17,994
Closing costs		– 500		– 500
Balance due on mortgages	$110,400		$288,000	
Out-of-pocket loss[a]		37,530		– 79,144

[a]Not considering monthly payments, insurance, maintenance, improvements, or other costs.

buyer's market. Although I hope the market decline is only temporary, in our scenario the homes that sold for $138,000 to $360,000 when bought in January of 1980 are now selling for $108,000 to $299,900.

If you were to sell at this time, when buyers can practically name their own terms, conditions would be as shown on page 75 (bottom).

I don't see this as a viable option. As I mentioned earlier, when interest rates come down, the price of real estate should return at least to its pre-1980 peak. It would be a shame to give up at this point without attempting to exercise Option C.

Option C: Negotiate

Go back to the holder of the second mortgage and negotiate for time. Beg if you have to. It is helpful if you can offer the individual at least part of the balloon payment due. Remember, a mortgage holder may have more money in the property than you do, and would like to get some of it out for other things. Your chances of getting an extension are reasonable, as the person who sold you the home probably does not want to assume the existing mortgage and take the property back.

Friends and relatives are another possible source of the necessary money. Many have cash accumulated in savings accounts and money market funds and would be delighted to advance the amount necessary for a comparable interest rate.

Obviously this accounting is a worst-case scenario. It was not my intention to dissuade you from purchasing a home. The 1982 California experience is an example of what can happen when soaring expectations collide with a temporarily depressed market. Later I outline many potential merits of buying a residence. I do think it foolhardy to buy over your head on the assumption that interest rates will come down and stay down over the next few years, or that property will appreciate at the same rate it has in the past.

The Case for Renting

One of the most obvious advantages of renting is evident in the previous illustrations. As a homeowner of the larger model, your monthly payments will be a minimum of $3,431 with new financing, not to mention repairs and maintenance. As a renter living in that same $300,000 house, you might pay $1,600 per month in today's market and have someone else worry about the expense of faulty plumbing and broken water heaters. Some rental facilities offer swimming pools, tennis courts, and game rooms—amenities that most homeowners could not duplicate. Then, there's the freedom. A home requires upkeep. You must either hire someone to maintain your property, or spend leisure time doing it yourself. If your job might call for a transfer to another location, renting is vastly more advantageous. Many transferees having trouble selling their homes in this down market, have been faced with payments on the old homes plus rent or house payments in their new locations.

Disadvantages of Renting

One great disadvantage of renting is the limited availability of units to people with children and pets. In addition, the length of residency in a rental can be limited, especially if you prefer to rent single-family homes as opposed to living in an apartment complex. One renter I know experienced a horror story because she lived as a "gypsy." The first house she rented was put on the market and sold after she had lived there for only eight months. The new owners wanted to occupy the property, and she and her three children had to move. Her second residence was taken over by the owners' son, and again she had to move. By the time she moved into her third dwelling, she was afraid to unpack completely— a wise decision on her part, because after only six months the owners were divorced and one of them decided to relocate in the condominium she was occupying. Moving is expensive in terms of time, money, and nervous exhaustion. After this experience, personal ownership looked extremely attractive to this person and her children.

Another problem is that unless you are protected under rent control laws, you are at the mercy of the landowner when it comes to rent increases. You must either pay the additional rent or again go through the bother and expense of moving. I personally would be wary of moving to a community with stringent rent control regulations. In renting you know exactly how much your rent will be and how often to expect increases. On the negative side, however, I saw the city I grew up in and loved deteriorate rapidly because landowners were unable or unwilling to spend any money on necessary repairs and maintenance.

Many home buyers argue that owning a home is a way of building an asset base, whereas a renter has nothing. That statement isn't necessarily accurate when you consider the true out-of-pocket cost of owning versus renting. Many investments other than pouring your funds into an illiquid personal residence make it possible to accumulate assets.

Advantages of Owning a Home

As I've already mentioned, many advantages of owning your home have nothing to do with economics. Aside from the psychological benefits, there are practical reasons for owning a home. Space is one important consideration. People with children and pets may need a larger area than most apartments offer. In addition, all the disadvantages of renting a home are motivation for owning your residence.

Can History Repeat Itself?

Over the last ten years, many clients have proudly told me that purchasing a residence has been the best investment they ever made. No one can deny that the last decade was a banner time for real estate. I'm not sure that the past history of real estate can repeat itself today in the area of single-family homes. It's extremely important for you to analyze the location in which you want to live to ascertain its potential. In California, for instance, if we realize half the capital appreciation that we've had in the past, today's buyer will be able to sit back ten years from now and say "I made a good choice."

Tax Advantages

The single greatest advantage of owning, in my opinion, is the tax saving it offers. Why would an individual or family be willing to pay $1,000, $2,000, $3,000, or more per month for housing? In part, it is because such an expense generates considerable federal and state tax deductions. The bite is not so bad when you consider that tax deductions are in fact "subsidizing" the payment in the form of reduced taxes. The higher the tax bracket, the greater the benefit.

Let's consider the two houses in Orange County previously shown. We'll assume that your loan was the combination assumption and owner financing, that you are not depending on a drop in interest rates or rapid appreciation to bail you out of the balloon payment due in just three years, and that you have some idea now where you will obtain the capital needed to liquidate those notes. (Given the fantastic tax advantages, thousands of individuals purchase homes because of the tax benefits alone, only to lose their investment because the capital is unavailable when they need it.)

Tax Projection Two Homes
30 Percent and 50 Percent Federal Tax Bracket

Purchase price	$108,000	$299,000
Interest payments assumed mortgage @8%[a]	300	850
Interest payment on owner-financed loan, 12%[a]	364	1,099
Taxes	85	240
Monthly deductible expenses	$ 779	$ 2,189
$ 779 × 12 annual deduction	$ 9,348	
$2,1879 × 12 " "		26,268
Total annual payments including principal and insurance	10,236	27,268
Tax savings in 30% bracket	2,804	7,880
Net cost	7,432	19,864
Revised monthly payment (After taxes are considered)	619	1,655
Total annual payments including principal payments and insurance	$ 10,236	$ 27,744
Tax savings in the 50% bracket	− 4,674	− 13,134
Net cost	5,562	14,610
Revised monthly payment	464	1,218

[a]Of the mortgage amount, the part accounting for interest (not principal) is deductible. This part is usually the greatest part in the early years of a mortgage and declines as the mortgage is paid off.

At this point you may feel more confused than informed. Those high mortgage payments represent a substantial monthly payment for shelter alone. The after-tax figures are far more palatable, and make the difference in whether you should rent or buy. Because state and local tax laws vary from one area to another, the preceding illustration takes into account only federal taxes. Additional savings are possible through savings on your personal state taxes as well.

It seems that Congress is continually reviewing and changing the tax laws. At present the tax laws are favorable to the homeowner in that they allow deductions for taxes and interest. It is worth noting, however, that some tax laws being proposed would eliminate or limit interest expense deductions. These early drafts specifically exclude real estate mortgage interest for the time being.

Summary

The question of whether to rent or buy cannot be addressed easily in a single chapter of a book. What I've attempted to do is provide a rationale that is based on the pros and cons of either choice. More importantly, I want to stress that owning a personal residence is not the only way to accumulate assets that will increase your net worth. If you are contemplating purchasing a residence, take the opportunity to seek out the services of a professional financial counselor who can review your budget and goals. A person knowledgeable about the tax law and investments can outline all your alternatives and help you make an informed decision. No longer can we make decisions concerning our "dream house" without considering financial reality.

Chapter 8

Achieving
Financial
Independence

Kenneth R. Rouse, B.A., M.A., has been a respected financial adviser to business owners, entrepreneurs, professionals, and corporate executives for ten years. He is a senior partner in Financial Management Consultants (FMC). He has distinguished himself as an effective communicator, conducting in-depth seminars and workshops for corporations and associations, and authoring numerous articles for national publications. A Certified Financial Planner, Rouse is a member of the Institute of Certified Financial Planners and the International Association for Financial Planning. He is a member of the National Board of Directors of IAFP, and has served as president and chairman of the board of the Kansas City Chapter and as a member of the board of directors of the Rocky Mountain Chapter.

Kenneth R. Rouse, CFP

Who doesn't aspire at some point in life to become *financially* independent? Unless you are willing to be dependent upon others, the only alternative to working for the rest of your life in order to provide for your daily needs is to achieve financial independence. Even if you think today that you will always want to work, you may one day want to be in a position where working is by choice rather than necessity. You never know how you might feel tomorrow. The freedom to choose will come only if you have successfully employed your resources along the way. A sign in a Colorado gift shop expresses the predicament of far too many people:

"The difficult years have come and lit,
I'm too tired to work and too poor to quit."

Numerous surveys consistently show that less than 5 percent of the U.S. population achieves financial independence by age sixty-five. Almost 75 percent depend on someone else for financial support, and about 20 percent are still working. Certainly, a few individuals work past age sixty-five, even though they are financially capable of living on their accumulated wealth for the rest of their lives. Far more, however, are working out of necessity, to obtain their required food, clothing, shelter, and a few incidentals. There will probably be even more in the ranks of those working past age sixty-five if some remedy is not found for our ailing Social Security system. Few individuals under age fifty can count heavily on Social Security for much assistance.

The trend in current tax legislation is clearly to provide a greater opportunity for us to create our own future financial security. Our legislators are making it clear that we need to do some planning for ourselves, and they are trying to provide an increasing incentive for us to do so. The expanded limits of Keogh and IRA plans explained in chapters 29 and 30 are examples of this trend. Recent legislation has also encouraged investments in economically viable vehicles that are more likely to give us a "return of" and a "return on" our money. We are being discouraged from using the more gimmicky types of tax shelter programs, where the emphasis is simply on saving taxes. All of this says that you need to think seriously about saving and investing for your own future.

The key to financial independence, of course, lies in what I call "balanced living." It's a matter of learning to enjoy today and, at the same time, live with the confidence that you are doing what is necessary to be financially secure tomorrow. If you are overly concerned about tomorrow, and are obsessed with denying yourself today, the chances are you will be unable to enjoy tomorrow when it comes. No matter how financially secure you might be, you probably will not feel relaxed enough to enjoy the financial freedom you have created. On the other hand, if you try to ignore tomorrow and live only for today, tomorrow may bring some unpleasant surprises. Statistically, you are likely to be around when you are seventy or even eighty. It would be comforting if you felt confident that you could still afford to be around, and be able to enjoy those golden years.

One of my basic beliefs is this:

If we do not take inventory, plan, and take action today—
inevitably, we will panic and try to play catch up later.

The primary objective of this chapter is to provide you with some of the insights required to achieve financial independence. I hope this exercise will also stimulate you to create for yourself a "balanced approach to living."

Let's get specific! How do you go about developing a realistic objective of financial independence? How do you determine what it takes to be financially independent at any given point in the future?

Identifying the Resources

First you have to know where you are today. That means sitting down and putting together a complete and accurate balance sheet or financial statement. You need to list all your assets and all your liabilities. Don't forget about the loan from Uncle George, unless it really was a gift. If the day may come when the loan will have to be repaid, it is a liability and should be considered as such.

In the asset column, make a distinction between "personal" and "investment" assets. For purposes of financial security, it is important to identify items that will be able to provide future income. Personal property items, which are part of your "net worth," usually are not included in your "investment net worth." If you intend, for example, to sell or trade your gun collection or antiques and convert them to income-producing assets, it's all right to include them. Otherwise, if they are simply to be enjoyed, you shouldn't count them in your financial independence planning.

The question is, What do you have in terms of investment assets that can be put to work today to help create the pool of capital you need for your financial well-being in the future? How much of your accumulated wealth will be able to provide income for you when you are no longer providing income for yourself?

Quantifying the Dream

The next step is to select an age at which you would like to achieve financial independence, and determine the annual income you desire in order to be comfortable. A wild guess can be replaced with a somewhat more realistic figure if you will take the time to make a list of what you are spending today. Then subtract any items that would not be there at the age you have selected. For example, you may now be spending quite a few dollars for the support or education of children, which will not be required later.

On the other hand, don't forget to add items that may apply later but may not be on your list today. For example, you may wish to travel more. If time permitted and funds were available, you would certainly do so. Or you might have to add company benefits provided today, which you would need to consider if they were still important to you in later years. Automobiles, club memberships, and insurance programs are examples.

Once you have arrived at a realistic annual income figure in today's dollar values, you must inflate those dollars at a rate you think is reasonable. Subtract your age today from the age at which you desire to become financially independent. Using a compound interest table (Table 1), you can simply identify the number of years between today and your desired age of independence, select a percentage rate that you believe represents the average inflation rate for that period, and derive a factor. Let's say the period is twenty years and the assumed inflation rate is 8 percent. The factor would then be 4.66. This factor is used to multiply your annual income desired at independence (in today's dollar values) to determine a comparable annual income figure twenty years from now.

For example, if your annual figure was $30,000 in today's dollars and the twenty-year factor 4.66 as indicated above, the annual figure in twenty years would be $139,800.

If you are surprised at the numbers, consider that at the rate of 7.2 percent, inflation doubles the income requirement every ten years. Or, at the rate of 12 percent, inflation doubles the income required every six years. That's the mathematical "Rule of 72," according to which 72 is divided by the rate of growth to determine the number of years it will take income to double. Fortunately, this is true not only of inflation, but also of investment assets, as we will observe later.

An important, and often overlooked, next step deals with the impact of inflation

Table 1. Compound Interest Table
The Amount to Which One Dollar Will Accumulate at the End of the Specified Number of Years

YEARS	5%	6%	7%	8%	9%	10%	12%	14%	15%	16%	18%	20%	36%
1	1.0500	1.0600	1.0700	1.0800	1.0900	1.1000	1.1200	1.1400	1.1500	1.1600	1.1800	1.2000	1.3600
2	1.1025	1.1236	1.1449	1.1664	1.1881	1.2100	1.2544	1.2996	1.3225	1.3456	1.3924	1.4400	1.8496
3	1.1576	1.1910	1.2250	1.2597	1.2950	1.3310	1.4049	1,4815	1.5209	1.5609	1.6430	1.7280	2.5155
4	1.2155	1.2625	1.3108	1.3605	1.4116	1.4641	1.5735	1.6890	1.7490	1.8106	1.9388	2.0736	3.4210
5	1.2763	1.3382	1.4026	1.4693	1.5386	1.6105	1.7623	1.9254	2.0114	2.1003	2.2878	2.4883	4.6526
6	1.3401	1.4185	1.5007	1.5869	1.6771	1.7716	1.9738	2.1950	2.3131	2.4364	2.6996	2.9860	6.3275
7	1.4071	1.5036	1.6058	1.7138	1.8280	1.9487	2.2107	2.5023	2.6600	2.8262	3.1855	3.5832	8.6054
8	1.4775	1.5938	1.7182	1.8509	1.9926	2.1436	2.4760	2.8526	3.0590	3.2784	3.7589	4.2998	11.703
9	1.5513	1.6895	1.8385	1.9990	2.1719	2.3579	2.7731	3.2519	3.5179	3.8030	4.4355	5.1598	15.916
10	1.6289	1.7908	1.9672	2.1589	2.3674	2.5937	3.1058	3.7072	4.0456	4.4114	5.2338	6.1917	21.646
11	1,7103	1.8983	2.1049	2.3316	2.5804	2.8531	3.4785	4.2262	4.6524	5.1173	6.1759	7.4301	29.439
12	1.7959	2.0122	2.2522	2.5182	2.8127	3.1384	3.8960	4.8179	5.3502	5.9360	7.2876	8.9161	40.037
13	1.8856	2.1329	2.4098	2.7196	3.0658	3.4523	4.3635	5.4924	6.1528	6.8858	8.5994	10.699	54.451
14	1.9799	2.2609	2.5785	2.9372	3.3417	3.7975	4.8871	6.2613	7.0757	7.9875	10.147	12.839	74.053
15	2.0789	2.3966	2.7590	3.1722	3.6425	4.1772	5.4736	7.1379	8.1371	9.2655	11.973	15.407	100.71
16	2.1829	2.5404	2.9522	3.4259	3.9703	4.5950	6.1304	8.1372	9.3576	10.748	14.129	18.488	136.96
17	2.2920	2.6928	3.1588	3.7000	4.3276	5.0545	6.8660	9.2765	10.761	12.467	16.672	22.186	186.27
18	2.4066	2.8543	3.3799	3.9960	4.7171	5.5599	7.6900	10.575	12.375	14.462	19.673	26.623	253.33
19	2.5270	3.0256	3.6165	4.3157	5.1417	6.1159	8.6128	12.055	14.231	16.776	23.214	31.948	344.53
20	2.6533	3.2071	3.8697	4.6610	5.6044	6.7275	9.6463	13.743	16.366	10.460	27.393	38.337	468.57
21	2.7860	3.3996	4.1406	5.0338	6.1088	7.4002	10.803	15.667	18.821	22.574	32.323	46.005	637.26
22	2.9253	3.6035	4.4304	5.4365	6.6586	8.1403	12.100	17.861	21.644	26.186	38.142	55.206	866.67
23	3.0715	3.8197	4.7405	5.8715	7.2579	8.9543	13.552	20.361	24.891	30.376	45.007	66.247	1178.6
24	3.2251	4.0489	5.0724	6.3412	7.9111	9.8497	15.178	23.212	28.625	35.236	53.108	79.496	1602.9
25	3.3864	4.2919	5.4274	6.8485	8.6231	10.834	17.000	26.461	32.918	40.874	62.668	95.396	2180.0
26	3.5557	4.5494	5.8074	7.3964	9.3992	11.918	19.040	30.166	37.856	47.414	73.948	114.47	2964.9
27	3.7335	4.8223	6.2139	7.9881	10.245	13.110	21.324	34.389	43.535	55.000	87.259	137.37	4032.2
28	3.9201	5.1117	6.6488	8.6271	11.167	14.421	23.883	39.204	50.065	63.800	102.96	164.84	5483.8
29	4.1161	5.4184	7.1143	9.3173	12.172	15.863	26.749	44.693	57.575	74.008	121.50	197.81	7458.0
30	4.3219	5.7435	7.6123	10.062	13.267	17.449	29.959	50.950	66.211	85.849	143.37	237.37	10143.

during the years of independence. Let's call them the years of payout. This is the period between the age at which you desire to achieve independence, and your estimated ultimate age. Obviously, none of us know how long we will live. If we did, we could plan perfectly. However, it is important to do some projecting in this regard. A fairly accurate life expectancy table will help, and then we need to personalize this process by taking into consideration our own family history and personal health.

Let's say you are aspiring to achieve financial independence by age sixty, and your family history and personal health put you in the better-than-average group. Therefore, you estimate that your life expectancy is approximately age eighty-five. That means your accumulated assets and income-producing resources would need to provide the desired income you have projected for about twenty-five years (from age sixty to eighty-five).

At this point, let me emphasize that this is where much of the planning in the past has erred. Most plans that have been established to provide income for future years have failed to consider adequately the continuing impact of inflation. The simplistic assumption has been made that if you have $500,000 producing income at the rate of 6 percent net after taxes, you have the $30,000 a year desired, and you will be able to leave the $500,000 to your heirs.

We have already described the tremendous impact on the income requirement that we can expect in twenty years. Thus $30,000 a year today becomes almost $140,000 a year twenty years hence when affected by an 8 percent average inflation rate. What about the continuing impact of inflation from age sixty to age eight-five? Fixed incomes have played havoc with many personal plans, when the realization hit that inflation was continuing to take its toll every year.

Surprisingly, if you assume that you will be able to achieve an after-tax rate of return equal to the rate of inflation, you will be able to determine the total amount of assets required at the age of independence by multiplying the annual income desired (inflated amount in future dollars) times the number of years you expect the income to be required.

Example:
The income desired in today's dollars is $30,000 and inflation at 8 percent per year

Table 2. $3,500,000 Investment Equity

Average annual rate of inflation:	6%
Average annual (after-tax) rate of return on investments:	6%
First-year income from investments:	$140,000
First-year yield at 6%:	$210,000

YEAR	INCOME NEEDED	EQUITY BALANCE
1	140,000	3,561,600
2	148,400	3,617,992
3	157,304	3,668,329
4	166,742	3,711,683
5	176,747	3,747,032
6	187,352	3,773,260
7	198,593	3,789,147
8	210,508	3,793,357
9	223,139	3,784,431
10	236,527	3,760,779
11	250,719	3,720,663
12	265,762	3,662,195
13	281,708	3,583,316
14	298,610	3,481,789
15	316,527	3,355,177
16	335,518	3,200,839
17	355,649	3,015,901
18	376,988	2,797,248
19	399,607	2,541,499
20	423,584	2,244,990
21	448,999	1,903,750
22	475,939	1,513,480
23	504,495	1,069,524
24	534,765	566,845
25	566,851	0

will make that figure almost $140,000 twenty years from today. Assuming you will live for twenty-five years beyond your age of independence, you simply multiply $140,000 by twenty-five years, and the result is $3,500,000 of assets, which you need to accumulate by age sixty.

Table 2 illustrates the way the actual dollars interact when you achieve a rate of return equal to the rate of inflation. At first it is deceiving, since you earn more than required, and actually add to your assets. The tendency, then, is to begin feeling very secure. However, you can see what happens in those later years when inflation continues to sharply increase the income requirements. Once you use original principal, it doesn't take long for income to disappear.

At this point you may be wondering how you can ever acquire enough assets to get the job done. It would appear, on the surface, that achieving financial independence is close to impossible for many people. In order for them to become millionaires, the goal of a few select individuals would have to be a requirement for a huge section of middle America. Remember, however, that the same factor that appears to be your enemy can also become your ally. If inflation drives the requirements out of sight, cannot inflation also create unbelievable opportunities for us to multiply our existing assets and future potential?

Getting Results from Existing Assets

You are forty years old today, let's say, and you have been producing income for twenty years. You have saved and invested, in one form or another, and accumulated $100,000 of investment equity. At an 8 percent after-tax rate of return, that $100,000 should be worth $466,000 in

twenty years (Table 1 factor of 4.66 times $100,000). On the other hand, if you are able to achieve a 10 percent after-tax rate of return, your twenty-year result would be over $670,000 (Table 1 factor of 6.73 times $100,000). When you examine these possibilities, it becomes exciting to consider what strategic planning can do to improve those results. Consider, for example, what 12 percent after tax would do to that $100,000 of investment equity in the next twenty years. It would turn it into almost a million dollars (Table 1 factor of 9.65 times $100,000).

We have only increased our rate of return assumption from 8 percent to 12 percent, but the accumulation has more than doubled. That's the magic of the compounding effect. The longer you have money, property, or assets at work for you, the more you shorten the period when you have to continue working to support yourself.

An even more dramatic example of this point can be demonstrated if you assume $200,000 instead of $100,000 in current assets. If you have sucessfully accumulated $200,000 to date, it could be worth almost two million dollars twenty years from now, with inflation creating an economic environment in which a 12 percent net after-tax rate of return is possible.

Consider now what would happen if inflation was reduced considerably in the future, and consequently the need was less. The potential for "growing" assets would also be less. At a 6 percent after-tax rate, for example, $100,000 would become only $320,000 in twenty years (Table 1 factor of 3.20 times $100,000).

In summary, what you need to consider is how to at least keep pace with inflation, and if possible, get ahead and stay ahead. You can't do that by just working harder. That's what financial planning, and the execution of effective financial strategies is all about.

Calculating Future Value of Other Benefit Sources

Let's turn now to the next important step: once you have determined your targeted goal for asset accumulation and have calculated how much of that goal is likely to be achieved with favorable results from your current assets, it is important to consider the future value of dollars from other sources. Perhaps the most common would be retirement plans, deferred compensation, or profit-sharing arrangements. Whether you are in business for yourself or are employed by someone else, these benefits can be substantial.

Perhaps the most difficult aspect of planning for financial independence is to arrive at an accurate and understandable way of quantifying the value of these future dollars. It is not the purpose of this chapter to treat that subject in depth. However, in arriving at a figure, you should take into consideration factors such as:

The dependability of these assets, especially if you do not control the decisions

The tax effect on the benefits, when received

The impact of inflation on the value of fixed annual income benefits

For example, today a one million dollar distribution from a profit-sharing plan, received in a lump sum, may be worth considerably less than a million dollars. If all the contributions through the years were made on a tax-deductible basis, and you used the ten-year forward averaging method for calculating taxes due on the lump sum distribution, your taxes would be approximately $400,000, leaving you $600,000 net. This may still be the best option for receiving the benefits; it would depend on the other options available. Most plans allow a number of different settlement or payout alternatives. Again, it is important to convert those future dollars to a value that will help you complete the calculation of your need.

Determining Required Annual Savings

Earlier, you determined how much would be required at the age of independence for you to be comfortable so that you would not outlive your resources. Then, you calculated what your present investment equity would be worth at that time, and added any other sources of future dollars that might be available. Now comes the moment of discovery. Subtracting all anticipated sources of future capital from the capital required, does a shortage still remain? In our example, if we were able to reasonably expect $1,500,000 from all expected sources, we would still be $2,000,000 short. How do you go about accumulating another $2,000,000 over the next twenty years?

The resource we have not yet considered, and one that is usually our most important asset, is our personal service income between now and the time we aspire to become financially independent. If you are able to take a percentage of what you earn through personal service each year, and apply those "fruits of your labor" today to your future security, you are practicing "balanced living."

The question is "how much is enough?" How do you calculate the percentage you need to save and invest today in order to achieve your goal for tomorrow? This, like the other steps, has many variables. However, it is possible to find a range that is fairly close to the truth. A few basic assumptions will enable you to project the savings requirements and test whether they are reasonable in your situation.

First, let's establish several criteria. Even though, in many situations, incomes may occasionally go down as well as up, the trend is for personal service income to increase over the years. Since inflation has been a reality for some time and threatens to continue, we expect that we will have to bring more money home in order to pay the bills. If our incomes increase and keep up with the average inflation rate, we should be able to save more actual dollars in the future than today. The most realistic constant is not a dollar amount, but a percentage of our increasing compensation.

This calculation process can be very complicated, but for general planning purposes you may be well served by following these basic steps:

1. Determine the future value of 1 percent of your increasing compensation by multiplying 1 percent of your present compensation times the number of years you expect to continue working times the factor from Table 1 representing your expected rate of return on those new savings. (In this calculation, you are also assuming that your income will increase annually at approximately the same rate that you are using for a rate of return on your new investments.)

2. Divide the shortage of future dollars required for financial independence by the answer derived in step 1 above and you will discover the total percentage of your compensation that you need to save and invest each year in order to achieve your goal.

Example:
$50,000 present compensation
1% of $50,000 = $500
$500 × 20 years = $10,000
$10,000 × 6.73 = $67,300
(6.73 is factor for 10% rate of return over 20 years)
$2,000,000 shortage ÷ $67,300 = 29.72%

In this case, you would need to save approximately 30 percent of your compensation each year, assuming your compensation was increasing at an average of 10

percent per year and you were getting a 10 percent after-tax rate of return on your new invested equity.

Wow! Whatever the result of this exercise for you, you will likely feel a "wow" at the end. The bottom line for most people is an eye-opening discovery. Regardless of whether you come out feeling great or semidepressed, the value of this information can be significant. If you have been totally unrealistic in your aspirations, it is possible to go back and test the assumptions you made.

On the basis of where you are today, if you can't get "there" from here, what adjustments are you willing to make in order to develop a game plan that will enable you to win? Depending on your current age, the age at which you desire to achieve independence, and how much progress you have made to date, the challenge can vary considerably. For example, if you are age forty today, and hope to be independent financially by age sixty with the equivalent of $30,000 annual income in today's dollars, we have already calculated that with 8 percent inflation, you would need $3,500,000 in assets by age sixty to maintain a consistent life-style to age eighty-five. On the assumption that the after-tax rate of return on your investment assets was equal to the rate of inflation, your assets would be exhausted in twenty-five years (from age sixty to age eighty-five). Without changing any other assumptions, suppose you decided to postpone your date of independence to age sixty-five (five years later than desired). Following the same steps illustrated above, you would discover a need for over $4,000,000 by age sixty-five, and if this left you $2,500,000 short, you would be able to supply that need by saving less than 20 percent of your compensation each year.

Example:
$50,000 present compensation
1% of $50,000 = $500
$500 × 25 years = $12,500

$12,500 × 10.83 = $135,375
(10.83 is factor for 10% rate of return over
25 years)
$2,500,000 shortage ÷ $135,375 = 18.46%

In reality, your shortage at age sixty-five would probably not be $2,500,000 because there would be five extra years (from age sixty to age sixty-five) for existing investment assets and other sources of future dollars to grow. Thus, if the shortage was only $2,000,000, the calculation could be as follows:

$2,000,000 shortage ÷ $135,375 = 14.77%

What we have discovered is that you can, with reasonable expectations and assumptions, achieve your financial independence goal by age sixty-five if you are willing to save and invest approximately 15 percent of your increasing compensation over the next twenty-five years.

Each situation is different, and changes in basic assumptions will sometimes drastically change the results. However, it is precisely this kind of exercise that puts the rest of the planning process in perspective. The importance of *planning* for financial independence cannot be overemphasized. Otherwise you cross your fingers and hope. Most people who elect that alternative end up being disappointed.

Achieving Balanced Living

The primary objective of this chapter has been to provide you with personalized insight and practical tools to help you set and achieve goals that are appropriate in your situation. If you learn to listen to your feelings about the future, as well as your moods of the moment, you will be on the road to experiencing balanced living.

Finally, it isn't what *you know*, but what *you do* that really counts. Once you know what must be done to get from where you are to where you want to be, it's just a matter of taking those first steps. After that, the review of your progress and recommitment will come naturally.

Part 3

Editor's Notes:
Financial Planning
Is Not for Someone Else

*O*ddly enough, those who make the best incomes are often the ones who put off doing any real financial planning. Executives, professionals, and high-income salesmen in particular seem easily lulled into a false sense of future security by their healthy earnings. And, of course, the other people who aren't doing any financial planning are putting it off because they think they aren't earning enough. If you fall in either category, read the next four chapters carefully—they offer thousands of dollars' worth of knowledge and experience. But first you have to admit that financial planning is not just for other people.

In Chapter 9 Lee Pennington builds a strong case for financial planning by pointing out the mistake many people make in letting fear control their financial decisions,

or in letting their spending habits fall into "the conspicuous consumption syndrome." Those are just two of the interesting points he gets into. Jim Barry then introduces an exciting concept in Chapter 10, where he proposes that we organize our financial plans in the structure of a pyramid that will reflect the risks or rewards of various types of investments. Meanwhile, Larry Krause in Chapter 11 pinpoints the special problems of professional people and offers some tips on how they might improve their financial planning. In conclusion, Chris Hegarty and Craig Stone in Chapter 12 tackle the complex planning required of chief executives. They point out the myths surrounding executive rewards and reveal the great challenges in this area of financial planning.

Chapter 9

The Financial Plan as the Starting Point

Lee D. Pennington, CFP

Lee D. Pennington, considered to be one of the pioneers in the total financial planning process, has been in some phase of the financial planning industry for thirty years. He is president of Associated Financial Planners, Incorporated, and president of Pennington, Bass & Associates, Incorporated. In addition, he is involved in AFP Realty and is vice-president of AFP Insurance Agency, Incorporated. During his career, he has devoted much time and effort to the establishment and growth of other individuals interested in financial planning. He is a frequent speaker to civic and professional groups on subjects relating to money management and economy. Pennington is a Certified Financial Planner and is on the board of directors of the International Association for Financial Planning. He is also a life member of the Million Dollar Round Table and a member of the Institute of Certified Financial Planners.

You can become financially secure, free of worry, financially independent. Most of us *can* become better income earners, savers, investors. We don't have to end each month consistently broke or nearly broke. Operating that way month after month creates depression, guilt, and sometimes even fear. Why should you have to work all the days of your life? You have the opportunity to be in charge of your economic destiny. You should be able to determine your own economic future.

But how? That's the rub.

Most people do not have the experience to be able to make objective economic decisions. Many are uninformed about and do not know what process to use in making financial decisions. The process of decision making—knowing where to get the information, understanding how to assimilate it, and then making the hard choice—isn't easy, even for those with know-how and experience.

The amateur is really flying by the seat of his pants. Usually, if he does well, it is because he is lucky or has stumbled onto the method without realizing it. If education were the sole requisite to becoming economically successful, then all people with college degrees would be wealthy and those with advanced degrees would be wealthier. Progressive richness would be based on advancing degrees! Some people have the training and education to do a good job of financial planning for themselves, yet do not because they will not take the time. The inclination to undertake the total process is not there; they prefer to let someone else do it. Then, there are those who believe that quality, long-term financial planning can be accomplished either by themselves or through a professional. *They are the ones who make it happen*.

Why use financial planning as a starting point? Because it works and works well.

It should never be assumed, however, that financial planning is a panacea for all economic ills, no matter who does the planning. In a rapidly changing world, where tax laws are modified by politicians wanting to solve short-term problems and very little long-range planning is done, we can't assume anything will ever be the same as yesterday. Therefore, the purpose of financial planning is to create an economic situation within your family or corporation that is informed and flexible, and that has the best opportunity for survival under any conditions.

Decisions should be made by design and plan and not by wishful thinking. It is difficult enough to do well when you think and plan. It is doubly difficult to make it when you merely wish and guess. A few bad guesses and your economic future is seriously impaired. It sometimes takes years to recover from some of the economic mistakes caused by inadequate planning and forethought.

Many people think the way to financial success is to hit a one-time, "big deal" that will make them rich thereafter. This is rare. Other than hitting a Reno jackpot or a sweepstakes, there are only three legitimate ways to acquire wealth:

1. Work and earn
2. Money working for you
3. Inheritance

Work and Earn

Most of us believe that if we work hard enough and long enough, we will earn enough to make us comfortable. Certainly in this country, this is possible. Even so, it is extremely difficult for most of us to save and accumulate. We have, to a large degree, depended on government (Social Security) or company retirement plans to do our saving for us. In the 1980s, we have suddenly found Social Security under stress and benefits may have to be reduced. We have seen large companies with huge pension plans go bankrupt and all the money accumulated for the employees lost and gone forever.

Working and earning and depending on government or big company pension plans is a possible way to accumulate wealth, but not a guarantee by any means. Your greatest peace of mind will come from the money you have working for you.

Money Working for You

You may recognize that you can't work hard enough or long enough to acquire adequate wealth to do all the things in life you would like to do. Between the two great subtle thieves, inflation and taxation, you may spend your life working and saving and never accumulate much. Your purchasing power may remain static. Or it might even decrease. The answer to this problem is to get money (assets) to work for you. You want your assets to do three things:

1. Grow in value.

2. Produce income, preferably nontaxable.

3. Be readily convertible to cash if the need arises.

The perfect investment for all of us might be one that offers complete safety of principal, totally tax-free (or nearly so) earned income with the capital consistently growing in excess of the inflation rate, and a ready market where it could be converted to cash within a few days. All investments should be weighed against the criteria of what *you* believe to be the perfect investment.

Money should be at work, creating additional dollars while you sleep. You and I can work only ten to fifteen hours a day, but money can and should work twenty-four hours a day. Invested money operates in a geometric progression that continually doubles and triples—creating more money for additional investments. That is why you should understand interest rates and net return on invested money. In other words, be sure you are getting the most effective use of your assets.

Each dollar must be working effectively and efficiently. Efficiency is doing things right. Effectiveness is doing the right things. It is *efficient*, for example, to have money withheld from payroll and deposited to a 5¼ percent passbook savings account. This is easy and uncomplicated. Transferring this same money to a money market fund until a certain level is reached would be more *effective*.

Remember, money working for you is the key to your economic well-being. One of your objectives should be to create enough assets (which produce income) so that you work because you choose to work and not because you must do so. Money working for you will create this kind of freedom for you. I can't say it often enough: plan for what you want in the way of income without work. Freedom comes from money working for you, not vice versa.

Inheritance

You could be lucky enough to inherit money. Most of us will not. For the few who do, there are some principles I believe you need to follow. You must plan to keep your inheritance or it will surely get away. Remember the old saying, "A fool and his money are soon parted." A worthwhile plan would be to use this type of gift to enhance your own life and the lives of others. If you can make this kind of commitment to the use of your "newly acquired wealth," you will then go about planning its use and seeking quality guidance. The chance of having your inheritance grow is then enhanced.

Be a good steward of all you possess. Use only the earnings of your inheritance and keep the principal. Remember the centuries-old Chinese saying, "Do not eat the seed corn, or kill the goose that lays the eggs." You want to have a life of economic freedom. Money working for you is a good start.

Who Has Wealth, and How Do They Get It?

The people who are wealthy are the ones who *expect* to have it, and who believe they truly deserve it. By and large, they are the ones who acquire much more than the norm. These people may never be among the ranks of the very rich, but they form the top 10 percent of the population who earn well and accumulate reasonable wealth because they expect to and feel they deserve it. This is the first step: believe you are entitled to wealth.

What characteristics do these people have that make them different—set them apart? First, they believe in the planning process and put it into action. They learn by trial and error; they never stop planning, trying, and continually believing they will do well. They put their plans in writing. They set economic goals. They start on their plan, adjust when necessary, and continue toward the completion of the plan. They study, think, and plan. They never stop believing they are entitled to wealth and the joy it brings. This planning process alone makes a significant change in their economic life. Wealth can bring great joy if you think in terms of its use and not merely of its accumulation. I do not believe wealth will make you happy if you are an unhappy person, but neither will being poor. Don't use these excuses for not planning to become economically independent.

Many people may never achieve economic well-being unless it is forced on them by a semicompulsory savings plan such as a company thrift-profit-pension plan. Ironically, they do not believe they are actually entitled to have anything they don't work for. This is a self-fulfilling prophecy of what will and must happen.

They expect only so much, and they get what they expect.

Making an economic decision isn't easy, especially if it is based on inadequate facts. Although setting an economic objective, devising a plan or plans, and following through are difficult tasks, successful people still do them. Successful people form good economic habits. They save and accumulate. They study, think, and plan. They invest, they continually reinvest, and they continually plan their next steps.

Obstacles You Will Most Certainly Encounter

In developing your financial plan, it is essential to know the obstacles you will face so you can devise methods to overcome them. Four major obstacles you will need to consider are:

1. Inflation
2. Taxation
3. Inability to take risks
4. Indecision

Inflation and taxation are not within your control, but certainly you have the ability to plan around them. You are no doubt aware that the government creates inflation and the laws of taxation. To make these two thieves work for you, you will have to think differently about your money. You will have to know the effect of inflation and taxation on your total financial plan if you hope to have any chance for success.

First, you should assume that inflation will continue into the intermediate and long-term future. It will no doubt continue because of the growing problems in three critical economic areas: (1) transfer payments, which basically redistribute the wealth of the country; (2) defense spending, which we hope will protect the country; and (3) interest payments on the national debt. Politicians have some control over the first two, but none over the third. The only place the budget can be balanced is in the area of transfer payments and defense spending. The interest payments—money owed to the millions of Americans who have purchased Treasury notes, bonds, and bills—must not be tampered with. Otherwise, all confidence is lost in government, and the people will cease to lend money to Uncle Sam.

The government is funded primarily through taxation. The system is based on a progressive tax model, which simply means the more you make, the more you pay. Work hard, earn and save well, and then get penalized by Uncle Sam for achieving. This is the situation you face. Major obstacle? You bet it is.

Consider, for example, the person who has studied and worked hard in order to reach a point in his career where he can earn $50,000 to $100,000 a year. He has saved a few thousand dollars, which is in the local savings and loan, bank, or credit union. Perhaps the money is in a money market mutual fund. All of these vehicles for saving are fine, except that he has to pay tax on the interest or dividends. Taxation can take as much as 50 percent of the interest earned.

If he earns $50,000 to $100,000, his maximum tax rate will be 35–50 percent, according to various deductibles he might have. As a simple example, let's assume he is in the maximum 50 percent tax bracket and that he earns 13 percent on his savings. At the end of the year when he adds the interest or dividends earned, he will have to pay IRS half of the earnings from his savings. That means he has an effective return of 6.5 percent. At a return of 6.5 percent it will take him approximately eleven years to double his savings account. If we assume that he saves a reasonable amount by age thirty to forty (over and above the educational fund he has for his

children), then he can double his money at 6.5 percent. Put another way, if he has $10,000 saved, nets 6.5 percent compounded, he will have $20,000 in eleven years. Repeat the process three times and he will have $80,000 accumulated in thirty-three years. Not bad. Not good. But a start.

Remember that inflation will be reducing the purchasing power of this individual every day. He nets 6.5 percent after taxation on his original 13 percent return in his fixed-rate savings fund. Inflation has been in the 8–16 percent range since the early 1960s. You must take this factor into account if you are to understand what is really happening to your money. Inflation is in the 7–10 percent range at present, the precise figure depending on whose figures you use. The government's figures are always the lowest and are generally inaccurate. If inflation were exactly 6.5 percent, then at the end of the year this man's taxes would be one half of his return and inflation would have reduced his purchasing power by 6.5 percent and he would have broken even. He would not have made any money, but he would not have lost any.

If inflation is in excess of 6.5 percent, his purchasing power is declining even though he appears to be breaking even. He can actually go broke if the inflation rate continues to go up and no adjustment is made to offset the loss. Inflation is a serious obstacle in his planning toward economic independence.

There is nothing wrong with our saving methods. It is the system of excessive taxation and inflation that creates the obstacles. Our methods of saving must therefore change if we are to survive economically. The method of accumulation through savings that you have been taught is not at fault, as we have said, but you will most likely go broke if this is all you do. You must learn to invest if you are to succeed. You must earn enough on your money to offset taxation and inflation.

Consider now the two obstacles that can cause economic failure as much as taxation and inflation do: the inability to take risks and indecisiveness. Many people will not take risks and they will not make a decision. Therefore nothing happens. These people are the spectators in the economic world and eventually end up blaming almost everyone but themselves for their lack of wealth.

Most people in their desire for safety rely on methods that are familiar. Safety for safety's sake may not necessarily be a wise rule to follow in financial decision making. You can see in the preceding example that it is not. Risking means having a willingness to take a chance on a new method or process. Most people will not risk using their money or assets in a new and different way because they fear they will lose it. This is a legitimate fear and needs to be taken seriously. To lose your hard-earned savings is devastating and can create many problems for the future. No one would suggest you "shoot dice" or drill an oil well unless you can afford to lose the money. Most people can't afford it; therefore, most people should not take such risks. But if you will take the time, you can find low-risk investments that provide a return equal to or better than the "ultrasafe" investments, which might or might not have additional benefits, such as nontaxable income or capital gains.

What is the greatest problem I will encounter?

Indecisiveness and Procrastination

Do you put off saving or investing? Not take the time to study the documents, or evaluate thoroughly what you want and methods to go about getting it? Are you honest with yourself about what you are willing to do to achieve economic success? Or unwilling to study, think, and act?

All people procrastinate to some degree. The difference is one of degree and very little separates the successful from the not so successful. Remember, only one degree separates hot water from boiling water. That is to say, one degree of increased motivation to save and accumulate can change your life for the better. Don't put off starting a plan that includes saving, investing, and accumulating for your economic future. You are important and you should believe you are entitled to wealth.

"All right," you may say, "what if I plan—what next?" Many people plan but still fail to accumulate money. The reason is that planning and action must work together. No more procrastination.

What about spending? Is that a part of financial planning?

Quality financial planning means knowing what you are doing with your money; therefore, spending is planned. It can be a joy for everyone in the family to know they can spend because saving and investing is already accomplished. This frees you to spend. Most people in the United States are users, not savers or accumulators. They are victims of the Conspicuous Consumption Syndrome; they try to satisfy all of today's needs with their future money. For many of us, our education and life-style have held the promise of a steadily increasing income. It has been easy to "up-grade" our wants and expectations. But what happens when the economy no longer creates that automatic raise? We are then caught in a payback situation. This means months or years of tightening the belt, doing without, and occasionally becoming financially bankrupt. Certainly, spending should be a planned part of your program. We need to save and invest, but we need to spend also. The freedom to spend is one of the greatest rewards of financial planning.

What if I make a mistake?

Some who initiate their financial plan, budget, plan their expenditures, save, and invest, and then—*they make a mistake*. Savings are lost and net worth is decreased substantially owing to a bad decision. Confidence disappears. No one is to blame. Yet hesitation and fear set in and risk becomes more difficult to contemplate. The safest course of action for these people is to save only. No investing. This is their *biggest mistake.* They should not let fear control their lives because it will bring about a slow economic death. It is important to get right back into the mode of earning, saving, and investing. Mistakes are made by all investors. The key is to learn and start again.

Many obstacles can be overcome if your plan is flexible and you are tenacious. Do not allow yourself to have inflexible opinions or methods. Bend with the economic winds, since they change direction often. If you can't bend, you will break or you "get broke." Believe in principles, not methods.

"Now," you may ask, "how do I get started?"

Financial planning, the very act itself, will change your life if you will only start. There is something almost magical in the actual starting of the plan. Good things begin to happen: you become aware of opportunities; you become excited about savings; you become even more excited as you begin to invest. As the various avenues open up, you will find yourself saying, "I am an economic success."

The key is to let this happen. You will become tuned into opportunities you had not seen before. The very act of writing down your economic plans will put you on your way.

Planning Is the First Step

Determine what you seriously believe you are entitled to have in your economic life, write it down, break it into simple steps and start.

If you can't write down what you want to achieve economically on a short-term basis (next three months to year), in the intermediate range (one to three years), or in the long range (three years and beyond), then you haven't spent enough time thinking about it.

Short Term

An example of a short-term goal is to save the extra dollars over and above your emergency fund (which should cover three to six months' expenses). You may be saving for the down payment on a new automobile or something new around the home. The spending is planned and you save toward your short-term objective. Be cautious with your *saving*, but not ineffective.

Intermediate

Your intermediate objective may be to accumulate enough for a down payment on your first home, or to accumulate a fund for the education of your children. These savings extend further into the future than your short-term savings. Once again, this money needs to be invested as safely as possible.

Long Term

Your long-range objectives may be to retire in a place on the beach or in the mountains, or perhaps to take care of a parent you know will be dependent on you. According to the amount of time you have left to save and invest, you can be a little more adventuresome. You might put some money in an investment vehicle that has a little more risk, the idea being that if it should pay off, you will have achieved one of your objectives sooner than expected.

Net Worth—A Way to Determine Growth

Next, you will want to determine the specific *financial* goals in terms of your net worth. This is one way of keeping score on your economic growth. Net worth is assets minus liabilities. Therefore, in terms of net worth, you will want it to increase in excess of annual inflationary effects. Suppose that you now have a net worth of $10,000, and inflation is 10 percent for the year. You will want to increase that net worth more than 10 percent or you will have remained even. Net worth includes liquidity. This is the ease with which you can convert some of your assets to cash. It is important for you to have a certain amount of liquidity. Be certain these liquid funds are in the strongest interest-bearing account you can find. Increasing your net worth is an important objective. It will reflect your economic growth.

You should outline specific *goals* and *deadlines* so as to have a striving period and a success or plateau period. During the striving period you will be continually analyzing, resetting objectives, and determining your progress. As you reach your goals and seemingly a plateau, *enjoy* the results of your work! This period of satisfaction can last about six months to a year. At some point, however, you will want to formulate new goals and move onward and upward, or you will surely lose ground.

Don't panic if your economic life fails to evolve according to your particular pattern. There will be ebbs and flows, and extenuating circumstances may severely divert you from what you are attempting to achieve. You must, however, keep a clear view of the important goals, track them, and strive to achieve them at a specific time.

What specific steps must be taken to get started? The steps are:

1. Write down exactly where you are (prepare a financial statement).

2. Decide precisely what you intend to accomplish.

3. Make a commitment, orally and in written form, to yourself and to someone close to you.

4. Start your saving program.

5. Begin your investment program slowly and cautiously.

6. Gradually risk more as you learn more.

7. Seek professional guidance often and from reliable sources.

8. Remember, everyone pays for their education one way or another. (It is all right to fail occasionally. It isn't all right to stop trying.)

9. Believe you can succeed and that you truly deserve to have wealth.

10. Be willing to share with others.

The most important thing you can do for yourself is to begin. Begin at the beginning with a complete self-analysis of where you are financially. This includes preparation of:

1. A personal *financial statement*. Don't forget to include the value of your personal property (be conservative because these items are rarely convertible to cash), cash value in your life insurance, value of your retirement plan (yes—it does have a specific value at a specific point in time), money owed to you by relatives, and so on. Include the obvious: cash in banks, securities, real estate, equity in your own business. This does not have to be calculated to the penny. Just determine a conservative estimate of these values.

2. A *budget sheet*, which will ultimately help you determine your cash flow and funds available for saving and investing. Be realistic in determining how much you spend monthly. Don't forget to include the cash that "slips through your fingers." Look through your checkbook to provide accurate figures for the variable expenses such as groceries, entertainment, eating out, credit card expenses, and the like. Make savings a *fixed* expense, using 10–15 percent of net income as a guideline. (A sample is included in Appendix I.)

3. An *income analysis* that includes salaries, all dividend and interest income and loans from family. Include all continuing income, as well as bonuses, outside income from business—any income that is *certain*.

4. A *cash flow* showing monthly income less monthly expenses. Determine from this information the net amount you have for investing. This is also the time to budget out unnecessary expenditures that seemingly consume your income.

5. An *in-depth study* of all documents and insurance policies to determine exact contents. Each insurance policy (this includes life, disability, group health, and casualty) should be reviewed to determine its purpose, coverage, and any limitation.

6. A review of the *document checklist* to get an idea of the sources of your personal financial information (see the example in Appendix I). These are used extensively when a professional financial planner reviews your situation. For your purposes, gathering this information and reviewing it should provide an overview of what you have.

At this point in the process, contact the appropriate professional (attorney, CPA, insurance agent) regarding any questions or problems you have encountered in your research. This is vital to make sure your "house is in order," as you may lack expertise in the analysis of certain areas.

Making Decisions and Setting Goals

This is the time to make decisions about your financial future. As we noted earlier, you should *write down* short-term, intermediate-term, and long-term goals that are consistent with your present situation and conducive to your life-style and future. Commit yourself to these goals in the presence of someone close to you (especially if that individual will be instrumental in your success or failure).

Begin a Savings Program

This should already be a part of your budget, but if it is not, start a savings program immediately. It is one of the first steps toward your financial security. Understand that savings is not the key to financial success; it is only the beginning. Saving is better than not saving, but in an economy where inflation has averaged in excess of 8 percent per year for twenty years, you are truly fighting an uphill battle. Thus, saving alone is not good financial planning.

Now, Begin Your Investment Program

After you have saved at least three months' expenses for an emergency/opportunity fund, it is time to slowly begin investing. This means taking a disciplined approach to your investments. Begin with safe vehicles that provide stability and quality in your portfolio—perhaps a mutual fund with an excellent rating, sound stocks and bonds, and a money market fund for temporary purposes.

The next tier of investment vehicles could include real estate and oil and gas public programs, and more speculative stocks and bonds. At this level of investment, you must have professional guidance in seeking out quality programs.

For the more hardy, there are private programs, limited partnerships, and joint ventures that usually require a good deal of capital, involve more risk, but often generate greater returns. Also included in this level would be investments in gold, gems, and collectibles. The sophisticated nature of this type investing belongs to the financially secure.

Getting Help

Financial planning is a job for more than one or two minds, and certainly more than one educational discipline. Our economic situation today requires a team approach to estate building as well as estate distribution. The leader of the team should be a creative generalist in the area of economics, law, accounting, and product availability. Such people are rare, but are becoming less rare as more advisers become certified financial planners and chartered financial consultants. It is important to consult the generalist who has no particular product with which to "solve all problems." The Certified Financial Planner (CFP) and the Chartered Financial Consultant (ChFC) are two disciplines that are broad enough in scope to serve in the capacity of creative generalist. Certified Public Accountants, estate tax attorneys, stockbrokers, mutual fund salesmen, or life insurance salesmen may be qualified to assist you, but the odds are that most of these people will not have the general knowledge needed for investment decisions.

Those who carry out financial planning in a professional manner charge fees, commissions, or fees *and* commissions. I would like to put to rest the notion that one group may be more objective than another. They are all people who have opinions. And, if they are reasonably successful, they will have strong opinions. If they have strong opinions about methods to solve problems, they will be biased. If they are biased, they cannot be objective. The person seeking a top financial planner should actually be looking for a person of integrity. This is the one who doesn't claim to be objective, who will tell you where he is biased, and who will let you determine if you still want to work with him. Integrity is the key, not objectivity.

My Experience

When I first turned to financial planning on a consistent quarterly basis fourteen years ago, my net worth was exactly $37,000. I was thirty-seven years old and had accumulated exactly $1,000 a year for each year of my life. It appeared that I was an economic ignoramus. I wasn't. I had worked for thirteen years in an economic business where I was making twice the average family income at that time. I didn't know how to do financial planning or even how to get started, yet I knew I had to do something or at age sixty-five I would likely have $65,000, a thousand for each year of my life. Certainly if I continued on the same basis, that would be my future.

My first step was to start the planning process. What did I have? What did I owe? What could I do to improve? All my training had been to save in a fixed asset. A variable investment was beyond my wildest dreams. I didn't know how to spell variable, let alone how to use this type of investment to help my economic growth.

The second step was to set up a method to earn over and above my family's normal living expenses. This money was to be saved. It was imperative that a saving habit be started if I was ever to have money to invest. I saved by working harder and longer than ever before in order to have additional money to save. During this time, I began to study how others had accumulated wealth. There had to be a method that worked and one that I could learn. Most of the people who were successful didn't appear to be any smarter than I was. Therefore, I believed the wealthy had a method or a skill, not necessarily intelligence. How had they done it? Was there a special secret? Why did they always have the opportunities to do all these wonderful investment things and I never did? These were answers I had to have. What you are reading is the culmination of years of questioning, analyzing, thinking, and rethinking.

Keep in mind that money you have earned, saved, and invested is the most rewarding wealth accumulation method possible. What a joy to say, "I did it." This is an ego trip for you. You make it when you have reached those economic goals you have set that say, "I am wealthy." *Since wealth is relative, you must be the judge of what that is. To one person it is a $100,000 net worth. To another it is $50,000,000.* Wealth is what you determine it to be. Of course, your goals can change. Most of us limit ourselves because we do not set our sights high enough, but we can always raise them as we accomplish and achieve those predetermined objectives.

You Can Do Better

You can use financial planning as the starting point to achieve economic well-being for you and your family. This book contains hundreds of ideas that will give you a start toward achieving your economic objectives. *Starting* is the key. No more putting off, no more waiting until everything is just right to start saving on a consistent basis. Keep telling yourself you can do it. Take a step at a time. No one can jump across the Grand Canyon at its widest point, but there are many who have walked across. Some gave up along the way, some made it fast, and others made it slowly, yet they made it. Perhaps the greatest joy is in the effort and the trying. You can do better, by planning to do so.

I spoke earlier about the person who wants to be an economic success for the sheer joy of saying "I did it." It may well be that planning, thinking, creating, attempting, succeeding, and failing will bring you more joy than the actual accumulation. Part of your ego focuses on your economic well-being. If you use your money decently so it earns enough to avoid the devastating effects of inflation, taxation, risks, and indecision, then you have every right to be proud and feel proud.

Sharing

Using wealth in a positive way for the benefit of those less fortunate should be one of our objectives. If you and I have the ability to earn well, plan well, and accumulate well, then we should share not only our knowledge in these areas, but also some of the fruits of our labor. I would like to see all of us who do well economically begin to share with those who haven't done so well. I believe we should teach them how to do the same. Our economic system is a great one for those with a little luck and those who are willing to utilize the financial planning process. Our economic system is one of the few left in the world in which the person who starts with very little can still accumulate substantial wealth. Financial planning may not make you a person of wealth, but it will most certainly make you better off than you would be if you had not planned.

Chapter 10

Using a Financial Pyramid for Investment Planning

James A. Barry, Jr., CFP

James A. Barry, Jr., is a recognized authority on financial planning and a well-known national lecturer. He is the founder and chief executive officer of Asset Management Corporation. Prior to forming his own company, he was senior vice-president of Putnam Group, the second oldest professional money management company (formed in 1925) in the United States. Barry is the creator of a national seminar entitled "Managing America's Money," and he writes and publishes a monthly newsletter, "The Barry Report." He is the author of *Financial Freedom: A Positive Strategy for Putting Your Money To Work*. In addition to appearing on television and radio, he is the host of his own weekly radio show, "Business Sunday with Jim Barry." Barry is a Certified Financial Planner and a member of the Institute of Certified Financial Planners.

He is the founder of Florida's Gold Coast Chapter of the International Association for Financial Planning, and a member of the adjunct facility of the College for Financial Planning in Denver. He is also an officer of the Florida Association of Registered Investment Advisors and a member of the Florida Atlantic University Foundation.

Some persons assume their future is set once they've chosen their financial advisers. "What's there to worry about?" they'll ask. "My stockbroker picks securities for me, my accountant prepares my taxes, and my lawyer writes my will and trusts." Then they smile: "All I do is cash the checks."

As you probably know, all too often this doesn't happen. You become unhappy or frustrated with the experts you've hired to manage your money. You think you could do better yourself. But when you make all your investment decisions alone, you know you're missing opportunities by not having the time to explore fully the financial marketplace.

Although it's a common problem, many people become confused when they find they aren't getting satisfactory performance from their advisers. Unfortunately, it's human nature to trust "experts" too much. When you realize that an accountant can do your tax return quicker than you can, you tend to give the accountant your financial records and then forget the matter. "Taxes aren't my area," you would say. "But I've got an expert helping me."

When you end up paying more taxes than you know you should, you're disappointed. You don't realize that most accountants just record past taxable events instead of doing active tax planning. This isn't the accountant's fault: it's usually due to a lack of ongoing communication between the acountant and his client.

Use experts for their knowledge, but don't become dependent on them. Get involved with your financial planning. Mold outside advice to your specific needs. If you don't, your stockbroker will tell you to buy bonds while your insurance salesperson is saying you need more coverage.

Your financial situation can become buffeted from point to point as you wander among experts.

However, financial planning is a means of putting all the advice together in a way that helps you. No one investment program is right for everyone. I'd like to introduce you to a model that can help you decide which investments are best suited for your personal situation. Remember that the stakes are high when it comes to your financial planning.

If you had one dollar in 1940, you could have exchanged it for ten loaves of bread. In 1950—six loaves. Today, maybe one. That's what inflation is doing to your earnings.

Change is occurring rapidly in our society. Who would have thought five years ago that Sears would now be selling stocks and bonds? Who would have predicted the problems many savings and loan associations are having? Change frightens human beings. But in order to live as we'd like to today, you and I must change how we think about investing. Don't sweep your money problems under the rug, for we can't change what's happening in our economy. It's the job of money advisers like myself to painlessly get into your mind and somehow reprogram your brain. For the rules of the game have changed, my friends.

The Rule of 72 can show you if your investments are beating inflation. First, divide the number 72 by the annual rate of inflation. Your answer will tell you the number of years before inflation *doubles* the price of everything you buy (see Figure 1). For instance, at 10 percent inflation, everything doubles in price in 7.2 years. Is your income keeping up? If not, you must invest

Time Required for Investment to Double in Value at Various
Interest Rates—Compounded Annually

Interest (%) Rate	Years Required to Double Investment
1	70
4	18
5	14
6	12
8	9
10	7
12	6
14	5
16	4.6
18	4
20	3.8

Figure 1

so that the money you earn tops the inflation rate. But if you put your dollars in a bank earning 5¼ percent and pay taxes on that, then you're actually losing purchasing power. Next year, you won't be able to buy as many loaves of bread, for inflation will be around whether you're able to deal with it or not. Perhaps you have to learn about real estate limited partnerships, mutual funds, and other ways to make your dollars grow. If you don't, taxes and inflation will lower your purchasing power every day. You might not accumulate enough capital for retirement or the major purchases you'd like to make.

To reach your financial goals you must understand your money situation today, decide where you want to go, and then map out a path. Since your situation today and your goals for tomorrow are both unique, your plan must be personalized.

But you still must be able to look at your investments coldly. Too often we become emotionally attached to investments. Do you own a stock, bond, or piece of land just because your parents believed in it? Most people do. In fact, many persons have more money than they should in certificates of deposit just because their parents taught them to save at a bank. Perhaps

that was good advice when inflation was 2 percent annually, but it's not now.

Our financial pyramid is based on the idea that investments in which the principal is stable—as it is in bank accounts—are generally losing to inflation. Their yearly drop in purchasing power must be offset by investments entailing more risk and a higher possible reward. To increase your net worth your capital must grow enough to offset taxes and inflation every year.

Look at the diagram describing the pyramid concept (Figure 2). A base of conservative investments, designed to preserve capital, is along the bottom of the pyramid. Cash, bonds, bank accounts, and life insurance cash values are examples. As you go up the pyramid you find money market funds, stocks, and real estate. Such investments have more risk than your insurance cash value or savings accounts, but also offer a chance for capital to appreciate above the rate of inflation (see Figure 3). Most people should have the majority of their money in investments in this area. (Notice I'm not suggesting specific investments now. Later I'll show you how to pick investments to fit your specific needs.) At the top of the pyramid are high-risk ventures with potentially high rewards. Art,

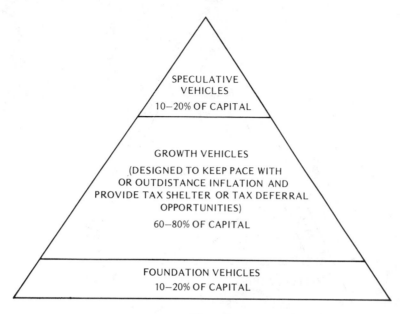

SPECULATIVE
VEHICLES
10–20% OF CAPITAL

GROWTH VEHICLES

(DESIGNED TO KEEP PACE WITH
OR OUTDISTANCE INFLATION AND
PROVIDE TAX SHELTER OR TAX DEFERRAL
OPPORTUNITIES)
60–80% OF CAPITAL

FOUNDATION VEHICLES
10–20% OF CAPITAL

Figure 2

gems, and commodities can bring good returns. But you could also lose a good portion of your original investment quite quickly. Looking at the pyramid should help you visualize risk management.

Many investors discover their needs are best met when they have around 15 percent of their portfolio in cash instruments for liquidity and safety of principal. Balancing that is about 15 percent in potential high reward areas such as hard assets, commodities, and oil and gas drilling programs. Of course, some of these riskier ventures also offer tax advantages. But never buy an investment solely for tax purposes.

Most persons then obtain acceptable growth by investing the rest of their portfolio in a home, growth stocks, well-managed mutual funds, a pension or profit-sharing program and closely held stock. Too little risk means you'll lose purchasing power. Too much means you'll spend your evenings worrying about your investments.

Although your portfolio is based on individual choices, the net result will depend on matching the strengths and weaknesses of all your investments. The pyramid can help you discover the right proportions of growth, safety, risk, and liquidity for you.

Your investments should be chosen with specific goals in mind. Begin this process by asking yourself the following questions:

1. When do I want to retire or be financially independent?

2. Factoring in inflation, how much yearly income will I need to live on at that time?

3. How many years do I have to earn money? How much do I expect to earn over that time?

The pyramid's construction reflects the risk-reward characteristics of various types of investments. The pyramid is flanked by "bad news, good news" arrows. The bad news about investments situated high on the pyramid is that they carry a risk of loss

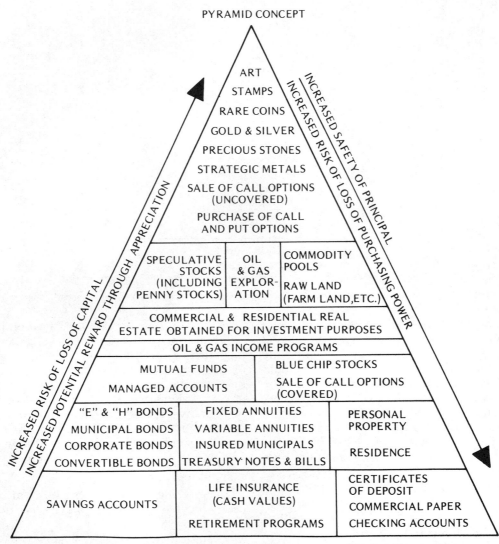

PYRAMID CONCEPT

ART
STAMPS
RARE COINS
GOLD & SILVER
PRECIOUS STONES
STRATEGIC METALS
SALE OF CALL OPTIONS (UNCOVERED)
PURCHASE OF CALL AND PUT OPTIONS

SPECULATIVE STOCKS (INCLUDING PENNY STOCKS) | OIL & GAS EXPLORATION | COMMODITY POOLS | RAW LAND (FARM LAND, ETC.)

COMMERCIAL & RESIDENTIAL REAL ESTATE OBTAINED FOR INVESTMENT PURPOSES

OIL & GAS INCOME PROGRAMS

MUTUAL FUNDS | MANAGED ACCOUNTS | BLUE CHIP STOCKS | SALE OF CALL OPTIONS (COVERED)

"E" & "H" BONDS | MUNICIPAL BONDS | CORPORATE BONDS | CONVERTIBLE BONDS | FIXED ANNUITIES | VARIABLE ANNUITIES | INSURED MUNICIPALS | TREASURY NOTES & BILLS | PERSONAL PROPERTY | RESIDENCE

SAVINGS ACCOUNTS | LIFE INSURANCE (CASH VALUES) | RETIREMENT PROGRAMS | CERTIFICATES OF DEPOSIT | COMMERCIAL PAPER | CHECKING ACCOUNTS

INCREASED RISK OF LOSS OF CAPITAL
INCREASED POTENTIAL REWARD THROUGH APPRECIATION

INCREASED SAFETY OF PRINCIPAL
INCREASED RISK OF LOSS OF PURCHASING POWER

Note: Bonds have traditionally been situated low on the pyramid, but the bond market debacle of 1980 showed that they are no longer entirely safe harbors for principal conservation. You should be fully aware of the recent history of bonds before you buy them.

Figure 3

of capital. The good news is that, if things go right, these investments will bring very large returns. The bad news about investments placed low on the pyramid is that the interest rates and dividends they pay usually fail to keep pace with inflation; the good news is that it is unlikely you will ever lose your capital in one lump sum.

Put in somewhat different terms, what the pyramid illustrates is that there is no such thing as a riskless investment. Those located low on the investment pyramid guarantee your principal, but time and inflation gradually erode the purchasing power of that principal. The higher you go, the less assurance you have that your principal will survive economic reverses, but the greater the potential for a large reward. The pyramid reflects highly individual value judgments. Where one or another type of investment should be placed is a highly subjective decision that is based upon such factors as a person's willingness to take risks and his or her knowledge of particular investment vehicles. The pyramid that I have created reflects my point of view; you might create one that is quite different, but still valid. Also the pyramid constructed here is by no means all-inclusive. It contains what I think are representative investment opportunities situated at various points on the risk-reward scale, but many additions could certainly be made.

When you build your own pyramid, you might want to add color to it to make it more graphic. Very speculative investments, for instance, might be colored red, middle-range investments might be toned down to orange, and your bottom rows might carry blue or green colors.

At or near the base of the pyramid we find vehicles that have traditionally been considered "safe" such as passbook savings accounts, bonds, and fixed annuities. These are generally thought to be secure investments, in which your principal will remain protected forever, barring a worldwide depression that might trigger the wholesale collapse of all the major economies. Right? Not quite. Although the options at the bottom of the pyramid do offer a high degree of safety, they do nothing to protect your principal against inflation, whose effect is greatest at the bottom of the investment pyramid.

Consider for a moment what can happen to $1,000 that sits in a 10 percent certificate of deposit during a year when inflation is running at 12 percent. Your end-of-year statement will report that your money has earned $100 in interest. There is certainly more to the story than that, but the rest of it is never reported. If it were, here is how one such report might read:

Dear Depositor:
First Federal is pleased to report to you that your $1,000 certificate of deposit has earned $100 during the past calendar year. Unfortunately, the inflation rate has been 7 percent, which means that the purchasing power of your principal has been reduced by $70. As you can see, this has resulted in a gain to you of 3 percent, or $30. We look forward to serving you in the year ahead.

At this point, you would probably start looking for somewhere else to put your money, and with good reason. But the story isn't finished yet. That $100 is fully taxable. If you and your spouse are filing jointly in a 40 percent tax bracket, the federal government will claim 40 percent of that $100, or $40. That means you are now left with only $60 in spendable income from your $1,000 "safe" investment, which has already shrunk by 7 percent and will continue to shrink for as long as inflation is rampant. You are actually losing $10 a year in purchasing power.

What do you think of the safety of such a vehicle now? Are you beginning to recognize that there are no totally safe investment areas left? Are you beginning to see that to keep a step ahead of inflation and the tax collector, you will have to venture out of these areas at the bottom of the pyramid and move toward investments that carry greater risk and greater reward? And are these thoughts making you somewhat uncomfortable? If your answers to all of the above questions are yes, you are to be congratulated. The uneasiness that you are experiencing means that you are coming of age as an investor, a process that never occurs without some discomfort.

Investments and Your "Comfort Zone"

The "comfort zone" is an investment area that for some reason—long-standing habit, perhaps, or automatic acceptance of your parents' investment philosophy—offers the investor a sense of security. But we have just established that there is no real safety in these "guaranteed principal" vehicles. It is time, then, to take the first step toward introducing constructive change into your personal investment pyramid, and to recognize that if you are to be a successful investor you must evaluate each investment you hold in terms of its TOTAL RETURN to you, not merely in terms of interest, dividends, or capital gains. Total return is the most important factor for you to consider as an investor.

This cannot be stated too often or too strongly: we are in uncharted economic waters today. We have never before experienced the kind of inflation or total taxation that we face today, although we're now waging a war on inflation that is currently successful. We have never before faced the energy crisis and worldwide political turmoil that we face today. These things mean more to you and me than an endless stream of disturbing headlines to be read over our morning coffee. They mean trouble, and big trouble, in our pocketbooks, both today and in the future. For the first time in our

history as a nation, we are facing problems that are not likely to go away through negotiations, military action, or plain old good luck. We're in a whole new ballgame internationally, and you, as a person wise enough to want to begin building for the future of your personal corporation right now, need to understand that the kind of financial planning that worked for our parents is not going to work for us. We're facing new problems, and we must come up with new solutions. New solutions are available, but in order to take advantage of them, you have to be willing to take some degree of risk with a portion of your investment dollar. In other words, it is time to venture out of your comfort zone—not altogether, of course, but to an extent appropriate to your personal circumstances.

Spreading Your Risk

How much of your investment dollar should you put into high-risk, high-reward areas in order to meet the challenge of keeping pace with and preferably outdistancing inflation? This judgment has to be made by you and the other adults in your family in consultation with your financial planner. My rule of thumb is to put no more than 10–20 percent of your money into the high-risk, high-rewards areas at or near the top of the pyramid.

If you are still actively pursuing your career and are years away from retirement, you can afford to venture into comparatively high-risk areas, because if the money you put into a speculative investment disappears forever, you can earn it back. The loss will be a shock and a disappointment, of course, but it won't spell irreversible financial disaster for you. Still, even if you have the best of recovery potential, you should probably hold your high-risk investments to 20 percent of your total portfolio.

If, on the other hand, you are close to

retirement years, you must be more conservative about risk taking because you have no way of replacing the dollars that might be lost to speculation. In this case, 5–10 percent of your investment dollars could be directed to the high-risk areas.

In either case, the bulk of your money should be placed into vehicles positioned around the center of the pyramid, where you will face moderate risks and reap moderate rewards. It is advisable to keep 10–20 percent of your investment dollars in vehicles at the bottom of the pyramid. As you know, inflation will take its toll in this area, but at least your principal will not be lost in one fell swoop. A financial planner who knows your emotional make-up and that of others in your family, your financial obligations, and your ability to replace lost wealth can help you to allocate appropriate portions of your investment dollar to each area of the pyramid as you progress toward and into retirement.

The pyramid is more than a graphic representation of the distribution of your investment money. It is also useful in generating cash flow statements for your family corporation. These statements are important, because they give you estimates of how much income your investments are likely to produce for you during the year, and thus enable you to do some tax planning in advance. It is *only* through advance planning—planning that starts on January 1—that you can hope to enter sensible and safe programs to lessen your federal income tax.

You should also diagram the percentages of your portfolio in the following areas: fixed, variable, liquid and nonliquid dollars. Fixed-dollar investments—such as bank accounts—will tend to keep your principal stable but offer little growth. Balance fixed dollars with variable-return investments that have growth opportunities. Figuring the percentages you own in each area might be interesting.

Liquidity

Because vehicles at the bottom of the pyramid tend to be liquid and those at the top tend to be nonliquid, by arranging your current portfolio in the framework of a pyramid you will also be able to see the extent of your liquidity at the present time. Although you certainly would not want every one of your investments to be liquid, for the sake of your heirs it would be prudent to make sure that at least some of them are. Think of the position of a surviving spouse who inherits an estate that is almost entirely nonliquid. It is not at all unusual for most of a business person's wealth to be tied up in the stock of his or her company, which is most often a privately held concern. This type of stock cannot be traded on the open market, and in fact, might lose a considerable amount of its ability to attract private purchasers when the original owner—very often a moving force in the business—dies. That stock may be worth $100,000 or $200,000 on paper, but what is its real value to a widow or widower who knows little or nothing about the business that has issued it and who needs to raise cash immediately to pay estate taxes?

To repeat: Think in terms of keeping enough of your holdings liquid to get your loved ones through the financial difficulty that your death could cause.

Rearranging Your Investment Pyramid

At this point, it would be useful to construct two investment pyramids, one showing your present investment distribution and one showing a more potentially profitable mix of vehicles. You can construct the first one yourself by simply penciling your current investments onto the pyramid in

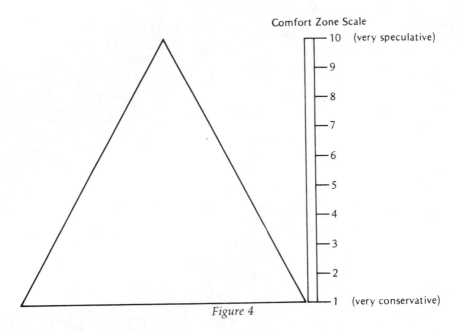

Figure 4

Figure 4. If you have any doubts about where a particular investment might fall on the pyramid, ask yourself if its main feature is safety of capital or growth potential. Place investments that preserve capital (or try to) near the bottom of your pyramid, and place those that involve greater risk and greater potential reward toward the top. You will notice that this pyramid has a scale running alongside it. This will help you classify your comfort zone. If your investments tend to bunch near the bottom of the pyramid, you are a conservative investor who avoids risk. Middle-range and higher index numbers indicate your increasing willingness to take calculated risks in exchange for greater potential returns.

If you find your pyramid is bottom-heavy, your object should be to redirect some of your money to higher positions on the pyramid. But that is more easily said than done, because it involves an emotional as well as financial adjustment in your life. Human beings by and large hate change.

Most of us avoid it, particularly if we have to take a fundamentally new approach to the way we do things. But sometimes we have to change in order to survive.

If you decide that your comfort zone needs to be pushed up the scale a few notches, you should proceed deliberately, but slowly. You should also consult a qualified financial planner, particularly in view of the dangers that face amateur investors dabbling in new, high-risk ventures. There are many sound vehicles in the marketplace that offer investors a chance to reap substantial rewards, but there are also incompetent and unscrupulous promoters. No one should buy into a high-risk program, particularly one that is advertised as a tax shelter, without first consulting an investment professional.

Let's say that you have a net worth of $500,000, which is producing $50,000 in income each year. If you want to retire in five years and then have $80,000 per year to live on, you must plan your investments accordingly. Either your net worth must increase by $300,000 over the next five years or else you must find ways to get higher returns from your investments. Personal goals will determine the amount of growth your portfolio needs. By looking at the investment pyramid, you can then find the sort of investments you need to have.

I urge you to become involved with your planning by asking yourself questions. With proper planning, you won't become upset with an unexpected change in interest rates or inflation. No one can predict or control such happenings. But once your roadmap is planned you'll feel secure and can then make changes in your portfolio to match the economic conditions and still accomplish your goals. Too many investors buy on impulse. Don't ask, "Is it a good investment?" Instead, find out if the purchase will most likely bring you closer to your economic goals.

If you've followed my guidelines here, by now you know where your investment portfolio is today. You also know what your economic goals are. Work to diversify your investments to reach economic goals. Develop an "ideal pyramid" for yourself which shows your portfolio as it should be.

But how do you choose specific investments? You do it by blending expert advice with your personal needs. Don't ask, "What's a good stock to buy now?" Instead, tell an adviser what your overall plan is and see what investments he or she recommends to help you reach your goals.

You Are a Money Machine!

Regardless of your age or financial situation at this moment, you are a money machine. Whether you are a student earning your first wages, an experienced professional approaching retirement, or someone holding down two jobs to make ends meet, whatever your situation, you should recognize that one of your key functions in life either is or has been the steady, reliable production of an income.

More important, consider for a moment how much your money machine has produced to date and how much of that total you have been able to conserve or increase through profitable investments.

If you're age thirty, and earning $20,000 a year, your money machine will produce $700,000 between now and retirement at age sixty-five. If you manage to receive a raise or two, your total lifetime income could very well top a million dollars. Think of it! Where could all of that money be going? Into a dark hole labeled "Expenses"?

Statistics tell a sad story about the financial situation of many older Americans: by one count, 90 percent are broke at age sixty-five, despite the abundance of retirement plans and investment programs available to them. At the root of this problem is procrastination, which few of us manage to overcome. We may want to put a sound investment program into effect, but the gap that yawns between intention and action is often as wide as the Grand Canyon.

You should realize that you earn two different *types* of money. The first type is what you receive every paycheck from your employer. And there's probably not a lot you can do to increase that amount very much. But the other kind of money is more important: it's the income you make from investment dollars at work. For money at work always lasts longer than people at work. Money at work doesn't get sick or take a vacation—and it should never retire or become disabled. But you are responsible both for bringing in the weekly paycheck *and* for managing your investment dollars.

There are three distinct types of money machines. Which one are you? First come the men or women who absolutely make things happen, no matter what the circumstances are. You and I have met them, and sometimes envy them. Second are the people who sit and watch things happening to them. Finally, there are the poor souls who can only scratch their heads and ask, "What's going on?" Americans historically have been in the first category of persons who make things happen for themselves, but it's up to you to decide what type of person you're going to be. If you decide to make things happen for yourself, and your investments, you'll be traveling a lonely road. Most persons live like sheep, going wherever they're led. When you strike out on your own, you can expect to see persons sitting on the side, envying you. They'll throw darts at you and say your successes are the result of luck. But keep at it. Don't let the "watchers" of the world deter you.

Step One: Finding Out Where You Are

When a doctor assesses your physical health, he begins with a health history. He asks you probing questions about what conditions run in your family, whether you smoke, whether you drink, if you get regular exercise, and so forth. This procedure enables him to assess your general health, right now. Similarly, as you begin your program to achieve better financial health, the first step is to evaluate your present financial condition.

Most financial planners will provide you with a comprehensive data sheet to help you make this assessment. Don't be frightened of its length. You may find, as you begin to fill in the blanks, that at this point in your life you do not have much information to enter on this sheet. Don't be discouraged if this is the case. Think of the data sheet as the blueprint of an idea that you will gradually be converting into a reality.

You will select the parts that you think should be in your financial game plan, and

you will begin working to obtain them. Right now, for example, you may not have a single entry to put on the page that shows stock holdings, but if you decide that stocks figure in your game plan, you will begin to acquire them, and soon.

A balance sheet, an expense sheet, and an income summary are three other essential forms. If you have not yet filled them out, you should do so immediately. These are diagnostic tools that will allow you to determine where your money is going. You will no doubt find that many of your dollars are siphoned off into unproductive areas each month. Once you track on paper the precise paths your dollars are taking, both into and out of your life, you will be able to make some important decisions about the kinds of changes you and your family can voluntarily put into effect in order to get your financial plans on target.

The rule of thumb to observe from the very outset is this: the first bill collector you pay is yourself. You are entitled to at least 10 percent of the net amount of every paycheck you bring home, and nothing should keep you from regularly collecting this debt to yourself. By keeping 10 percent or more of your earnings, you will build capital that can and should be used to launch your investment program. For instance, with a variable annuity, you might collect $1 million in thirty years if you could afford to invest just $50 a week and realize a 15 percent annual return. This is the kind of program that almost anyone can afford to begin right now, providing that regular payment of the debt you owe yourself becomes a priority item in your budget.

Your next task is to determine how much you are paying in taxes and to try to find legal means of cutting that bill down. You must learn to use your 1040 form as a tool that will tell you where your tax dollars are going. You must understand that form and spend time studying it. Your tax planning for the year should start on January 1 of the taxable year, and members of your family, especially your spouse, should take part in that planning. One of your objectives should be to develop familiarity with financial matters in your children so that they will mature into men and women who can automatically take charge of their own affairs. One reason so many adults fail to manage their money successfully, despite their earnest desire to do so, is that the financial arena is completely unfamiliar territory to them. You can give your children a priceless legacy by helping them to penetrate the mysteries of money at an early age. You'd be surprised at just how much a youngster can understand, especially if the information is presented in a way that engages his interest. Let your teenage son sit down with you and help fill out the family's 1040 form. Take your young daughter to a stock brokerage office and explain to her what the ticker tape made of lights on the wall is all about. Let the whole family "play the market" with Monopoly money and see who comes out ahead.

But let's get back to tax planning. Once you have studied the tax regulations (not only by reading the instruction booklet that comes with your 1040 form, but also by doing outside reading), you should be able to decide upon some strategic moves. Can you completely shelter some of your income from taxes? Can you at least put off the payment of some taxes under allowable provisions and let the dollars that would ordinarily go straight to Uncle Sam work for you instead, compounding interest? Are you in the right retirement program? Is the money that you have available for investment purposes right now spread across the pyramid in a way that will bring you optimal tax benefits? Can you reposition any of your investment dollars from a currently taxable to a tax-deferred status?

This assessment of the state of your financial health may hold some surprises for you. In taking your own psycho-economic pulse, so to speak, you will find out just how concerned you have really been to date about where your money is going and just how wise you have been about remedying current problems and planning for the future.

Step Two: Determining Your Objectives

Offhand you may say that you know what your financial objectives are—like everyone else, you want something called "financial independence." But what does the term mean to you personally? As you answer this question, you will begin to spell out your objectives. Remember that there are two types of objectives: short-term and long-term. A trip to Europe could be one of your short-term objectives, for example. Or perhaps a new car, or a boat. Long-term objectives might include a financially comfortable retirement, educational funds for your children, perhaps a second home for you in the Sunbelt or another vacation spot.

Becoming disciplined in the way you handle your money doesn't mean taking a monastic vow never to spend any of it on the things you enjoy. The difference lies in the way you approach this expense. The ineffective money manager acts on impulse, perhaps getting deeply into debt to gratify a whim of the moment; the effective money manager, after adequate thought and consultation with family members, decides to incur an expense and then develops ways to generate funds for that purpose.

You should write your objectives down and review them periodically with the whole family. They should be flexible enough to allow you to alter their specifications or perhaps to discard them completely.

Step Three: Evaluating Yourself on a T-Square

A T-square is a simple tool that you can use to identify two sets of facts that you must know about yourself: your weaknesses and your strengths. This is a way of evaluating YOB (Your Own Brain) to determine what kind of help you'll need to get from OPB (Other People's Brains). If you've ever spent time analyzing the lives of successful persons, you'll soon realize that most of them had help. They found the secret of what I call OPB and they surrounded themselves with it every day. OPB can magnify your daily efforts five to ten times.

By OPB I mean understanding the multiplying effect of using other people's brains to supply knowledge and experience you don't have. Let's face it—few of us are born geniuses. By getting help from others, you don't have to make excuses for important things you don't understand well. Your first step should be to take a piece of paper right now. On one side put a plus sign and on the other draw a minus. List under the plus all the things you're really good at—those areas in which you bury the average person. Maybe you're a good electrician, or a fine surgeon, or perhaps you play a tough game of tennis. When you're through, list your weaknesses under the minus sign. Maybe you have to admit that when you buy a stock, all too often it drops in price. Or perhaps you don't understand today's real estate market. And do you get upset whenever you look at your tax return, because of what you owe the government each year?

My advice is to build on your strengths, and don't let your weaknesses frustrate you. Surround yourself with other people's brains. Use other people's brains when approaching today's confusing economy. You'll find yourself getting stronger. When people work together, one plus one doesn't make two; they can make five, ten, or even more. That's the power of OPB which you need working within your financial gameplan. Instead of worrying about your weaknesses, do what you are good at and multiply all your efforts with other people's brains.

A sample T-square appears in Table 1. Be as honest as possible in filling out the weaknesses. Remember that the sole purpose of this tool is to give you insight into the areas in which you need help.

Table 1. T-Square

STRENGTHS	WEAKNESSES
Things you love to do	Things you hate to do
Things you do well	Things you don't think you'll ever do well, no matter how long you stay at them
Your talents	
Your abilities	
	Your shortcomings

If you are married, your spouse should fill out a T-square, too, and if you have children over ten or twelve, let them do some self-evaluating. (Incidentally, this T-square has many useful applications. You could, for instance, ask your son to fill one out to determine for himself if he is responsible enough to drive the family car.)

Evaluate your married children's marriages on a T-square when you are considering writing sons and daughters-in-law into a living trust or will. And, by all means, bring the T-square analysis into play as you examine various investment alternatives. You could develop a positive numbering system for the "strengths" side and a negative numbering system for the "weaknesses" side. Then, depending upon your comfort zone, you could set one number as the "buy" indicator on the positive side and another as the "don't buy" indicator on the negative side.

Filling out a T-square is another step in your self-administered psycho-economic analysis because it identifies the areas in which you need to seek outside help. The cardinal rule is this: *Don't try to build on your weaknesses. This only leads to frustration. Build on your strengths and let other people help you in the areas in which you are weak.*

Step Four: The Role of Advisers

If you are a football fan, you are undoubtedly familiar with the critical decision making every coach faces once a year. He has to pick the right players for his team if he wants a winning season. You may never have thought of yourself in this way before, but you are a coach too. The team you have to put together will consist of your financial advisers and it will last season after season if you pick your players wisely the first time. The important game your team will play involves your financial future.

Too many people unwisely trust luck to lead them to competent financial advisers, and, once they have found some likely candidates, they fail to ask any questions except, "How much do you charge?" This pattern can be attributed to at least two factors. First, because the various aspects of financial planning are somewhat complex, most people are eager to find someone who seems capable of handling this job, and so they may latch onto the insurance agent who calls out of the blue or the stockbroker who answers the phone in the local branch of a brokerage firm. Secondly, the value we place on higher education leads us to assume that anyone with a degree must be competent. Yet you should question the competence and dedication of anyone being considered for your financial planning team. A comedian once suggested that the Yellow Pages would be much more useful if the listings of various professionals such as doctors and lawyers included notations on their grades and rank in their graduating class. I think that this is an excellent idea, because it would help us to know which professionals are truly worthy of our blind trust and which are just barely qualified to be in business.

In the absence of an index of competence, you must devise some method of rating the professionals yourself. I know of only one method, and that is *asking questions.* You should go into your first meeting with your financial planner, stockbroker, insurance agent, and each of your other financial advisers prepared to ask everything you need to know in order to evaluate their ability to serve you well.

Since finding the right advisers is one of the most important steps you will take in the march toward financial independence, it is important to look at the types of financial advisers you are likely to need and the guidelines you should use in determining their probable ability to serve you well.

Attorneys

Many people view attorneys as all-knowing individuals whose advice and counsel should be sought on a wide variety of matters, from drawing up wills to evaluating "hot tips" on the stock market and tax incentive programs. Because lawyers attend college for six to eight years, they are often thought to be broadly educated men and women who are well equipped to give expert advice on questions that fall outside their area of specialization. It is not my intention to downgrade attorneys in any way, but something needs to be said about choosing attorneys for financial counsel.

First, you must determine what service you can expect of an attorney, keeping in mind that he must have the time and ability to gain extensive knowledge of your personal situation, in all its aspects, so that he is well equipped to counsel you on the matters that you bring to him.

He should understand your goals and objectives, your willingness to take risks with your money, your financial strengths and weaknesses. He must know the same about your spouse and any of your children who are old enough to take personal charge of assets they might inherit from you. In short, he must know all about your personal corporation and the things about your corporation that make it different from all others.

Owing to the complexities of the law in all areas of society, most attorneys today are specialists. It is advisable to avoid anyone who claims that he can handle any and all matters you might bring to him. In any case, your major concern will be the attorney's experience in financial matters. This is not to say that you should avoid a law firm that handles a number of different specialties and refers cases from one attorney to another in-house. This type of firm, in fact, is becoming more and more popular because of its built-in versatility. In any case, your major concern will be the attorney's experience in financial matters.

Which of your financial concerns are appropriate to bring to your attorney? Obviously, only an attorney is qualified to draw up legal documents, so any financial transaction that requires legally binding documentation should be handled by him. And I mean "handled" in the most complete sense of the word. Your attorney should be willing to take personal charge of every matter that you bring to him, regardless of its "routine" nature or modest dimensions. He should understand the part that each transaction plays in your overall plan, and he should give evidence of this understanding through his ability to ask intelligent questions.

Accountants

There is a common misconception that an accountant is someone you consult just at tax time. Since your accountant is the member of your team responsible for calculating your taxes, he, too, should have an accurate, running overview of your entire financial situation. To give him such a comprehensive overview, you should be in touch with him quarterly so that he can run a pro-forma on your income, an analysis aimed at predicting your tax obligation. If there is one time of year to be more concerned about seeking him out, that time would be January 1. Why? Because the beginning of the year is the best time to discuss whether you will need sound tax planning to reduce your income tax obligation during the year ahead.

Fees charged by accountants vary widely, depending upon the services you wish to have performed and the complexity of your case. Some fees paid to attorneys, accountants, financial planners, and other advisers are usually tax deductible. Accountants and all other financial professionals discussed in this chapter should offer one meeting free of charge, at which your needs can be explored and you and your potential adviser can become acquainted. Since financial planning calls for long-term associations, you should retain only those individuals with whom you feel confident and comfortable. If mutual good feelings do not develop at the outset, you should probably try someone else. All fee and billing information should be made clear to you during your first meeting with a potential financial adviser.

In the case of an accountant, you can expect a small fee to be quoted for a simple service, such as the preparation of an uncomplicated tax return. If your tax return is lengthy and complex, however, and if you have to consult your accountant once per quarter, for a record review and a pro-forma, your annual fee might exceed $1,000. When choosing your financial advisers, don't let the matter of their fees become the tail that wags the dog. Remember that your primary purpose is to obtain expert, individualized advice that will help you progress toward your goals. *Advisers who fill this bill will save you many times the amount of their annual fees in reduced taxes or will bring you many times those fees in profits realized from good investments.*

Stockbrokers

Your primary concern in selecting a stockbroker is to find one who does not simply take orders. Like all your financial advisers, your stockbroker should know you personally. He should know how much you know about the market and why you are inquiring about a particular stock. Above all, he should know your tolerance, both financial and temperamental, for taking risks.

Good stockbrokers earn their keep in many ways. As brokerage houses have diversified to deal in real estate, oil and gas ventures, insurance, annuities, commodities, gold and silver, and even rare coins, many brokers have added to their personal credentials by becoming certified financial planners.

Your stockbroker can help you make money by searching out investments suited to meet particular objectives, and he can help you save money by warning you to stay away from ventures that may, on their surface, look attractive. Because brokers are immersed in the investment world, they receive information that may never reach an outsider. Brokers use this inside information to advise their clients on the pros and cons of various investments.

It is important to find a broker who has had substantial experience. Ideally, he should also be a Certified Financial Planner. This credential will become increasingly useful in the 1980s, which promises to be an economically complex decade. When opening an account with a stockbrokerage house, try to identify the most experienced professional in the office through the office manager, other financial professionals in the community, or your friends who do business with the office.

You might also spend a day or two in the office, watching the ticker tape and observing who seems to be the busiest, most productive broker of the group.

Stockbrokers can also set up trust accounts for clients. A bank or other financial institution can be named to act as custodian or trustee after the client's death, while the client maintains full control throughout his or her lifetime. This service is normally offered at no charge or for a minimal fee.

Professional Money Managers

Not everyone needs the services of a professional money manager (for stocks, bonds, and money market instruments), but you should consider retaining one if you plan to enter a serious long-term investment program involving a percentage of your serious money—that is, money you do not want to subject to high risk. If you do hire a professional money manager, make sure he is registered as an investment adviser with the Securities and Exchange Commission. During the initial interview ask him whether he receives commissions on the sale or purchase of securities. Such commissions are not illegal, but since they might affect the advice he gives, you have a right to know about them.

Outside of integrity, it is most important to know about the performance of a professional money manager. You should therefore ask for a complete record of a potential money manager's performance on several different accounts during the past few years. You should know what the objectives of these accounts are—growth, for example, or income—and how well the money manager has guided each account toward its goal. The money manager should also give you information that will enable you to compare his performance with standard economic barometers such as the Dow-Jones Industrial Average and Standard & Poor's Stock Index. This will enable you to put his performance into an overall economic perspective.

Fees charged by professional money managers normally start at about one-half of one percent a year of the assets that are being managed, and run as high as 3 percent, depending on the size of the portfolio and the attention it requires.

If the amount of money you have to invest right now is too small to require the services of a professional money manager, you might consider investing it in a mutual fund. Unfortunately, mutual funds have received bad publicity in the past few years. In certain situations, they are ideal investment vehicles. One advantage is that many such funds have internal versatility. If you buy into a family of mutual funds, for example, you can switch your money—at will and without paying a commission—from that family's money market fund to its growth fund, or its bond fund and back again. There is normally no limit on the number of times you can make such a switch, so that as your needs change or as market conditions fluctuate, you retain the privilege of transferring your investment by the simple means of writing a letter to the mutual fund company. In some cases, you can make the switch merely by calling the company on a nationwide toll-free number. Remember that a mutual fund in a "family" is preferable to one that stands alone. A family of funds offers a place or refuge when one segment or another of the investment marketplace is depressed. The company manages the funds in much the same way that a professional money manager would manage your personal portfolio.

Life Insurance Underwriters

Probably no financial area is less understood by the general public than insurance, particularly life insurance. Your first step in obtaining insurance should be to understand the purpose or benefits of the insurance in question.

Here are some key questions to ask about a prospective life insurance underwriter. Is he an independent agent or does he represent a single life insurance company? Does he concentrate his efforts on selling permanent, cash value life insurance (policies with built-in "savings account" features), does he emphasize term life insurance protection (death benefits only), or is he willing to explore your needs and desires before he makes a recommendation? If he represents a single company, is he willing to shop among other companies for the particular life insurance product that you want if his company doesn't sell it? Above all, your life insurance underwriter should be willing and able to see your needs in a "big picture" framework. This type of underwriter will devote more than token effort to finding out what your current needs are and what your future needs are likely to be.

The premier designation among life insurance underwriters is Chartered Life Underwriter (CLU). To earn this title, an underwriter must pass ten very difficult examinations. A CLU, then, is usually a competent professional. Another way to investigate the professionalism and versatility of an underwriter is to ask whether he is licensed with the National Association of Securities Dealers (NASD). This license enables him to sell other products, such as variable annuities and mutual funds, and it will give you some insight into his view of the scope of his work. An underwriter with NASD credentials will be able to offer you access to many more investment opportunities than one who deals solely in life insurance.

Property and Casualty (P & C) Insurance Agents

All too often, this professional is overlooked whenever financial planning teams are assembled. Do not let this happen in your case. Few individuals will provide more valuable service to you than your property and casualty home and automobile agent. Those who have demonstrated comprehensive professional knowledge through study and testing beyond that required for state certification are entitled to write CPCU after their names—Chartered Property Casualty Underwriter. This designation is awarded by the American Institute for Property and Liability Underwriters to those who take a series of ten courses and examinations.

The P & C agent's primary role is to protect your hard-earned accumulated assets from sudden, devastating depletion because of a natural disaster, a lawsuit, or other misfortune. Think about this for a moment: you could work twenty, thirty years, or more to build security for yourself and your family and then see all or some of your assets go up in the smoke of a house fire or see them awarded to your neighbor in a dog-bite suit. Unlikely events? Maybe. Impossible? No. Just ask the man or woman who's been there; these things don't always happen to "the other guy."

It is up to you to anticipate problems and make sure you're not vulnerable to them. Your P & C agent can be of assistance here. For a premium that seldom exceeds $100 to $150 a year, this agent can sell you $1 million worth of personal liability insurance that will cover you against lawsuits. This coverage, called a *personal umbrella policy*, is in addition to the minimum $300,000 general liability coverage you should carry on your home and the $100,000 to $300,000 you should carry on your car. In the event of a serious misfortune, such as a traffic accident involving a substantial judgment against you, your umbrella policy will be available to pay off any sum that is over the amount of your auto coverage, but under $1 million.

Business umbrella liability policies are also available, but their cost is higher. The premium depends upon the type of business you are in and the various risks it entails.

As for your homeowner's policy—I have already said that you should have $100,000 to $300,000 worth of protection—in today's real estate market, you should have your P & C agent evaluate your coverage once a year. Your home becomes significantly more valuable during each twelve-month period. Furthermore, if you took out your homeowner's policy during your "salad days" and have now reached the main course in your life, it is definitely time to reevaluate your coverage. Even if you are still living in the same house, its contents have probably changed. Are furs hanging in closets that once housed cloth coats? Do you and your spouse now own valuable pieces of jewelry? Has the simple wicker furniture given way to French Provincial? If the answer to any or all of these questions is yes, you need to update your insurance coverage. And don't stop with your house. Apply the same kind of thinking to other types of insurance coverage that affect you. If you own a business, for example, you should examine the adequacy of the policies that cover your company. Remember that your coverage should change as your circumstances change.

You may need a homeowner's policy with special features, such as a "mysterious disappearance" clause to provide you with compensation for things that seem to vanish into thin air. This is especially useful for business people who often have to entertain guests they don't know very well. Many a piece of silverware or Wedgwood has mysteriously disappeared during such functions.

Some P & C agents urge everyone having valuable possessions to make a complete inventory of all expensive household items, and to include photographs and identification numbers. This inventory should be placed in your bank safe-deposit box to ensure that it is preserved in case your home is burglarized or destroyed. Many police stations will lend you an engraving pen that will enable you to mark your valuables for identification.

Bank Trust Officers

The bank trust officer, or some other representative of a bank trust department, is often useful to persons seeking confidential, trustworthy assistance in a financial management program. Unlike human beings, a bank will not die, become disabled, or go away on a month's vacation. The institution can be relied upon to provide competent, professional services for as long as you or your heirs wish the services to be performed.

When dealing with a trust department, you will receive accurate monthly computer printouts detailing all relevant financial data. You can give the bank varying degrees of responsibility for your funds, ranging from total control to the simple task of carrying out specific instructions.

In general, this type of association with a bank offers low return on investments, a consequence of the pronounced conservatism of most banking institutions. This problem can be solved by combining the accounting services of a bank trust department with the professional services of a money management firm. Under this arrangement, the bank simply acts in a custodial capacity, keeping track of transactions, issuing checks, and carrying out similar functions. The money management firm makes all the strategic investment decisions.

Similarly, you can appoint a financially astute friend or business associate to administer any trust built into your will that cannot, for tax or other reasons, be handled by your spouse. The individual can be made a co-trustee with the bank (with the authority to "fire" the bank if he sees fit), or he can be made sole trustee with the power to select a bank. It makes sense to

name a second trustee in your will, too, in case the individual who is your first choice dies or becomes disabled. Few people are aware of the many moderately priced services that are available at their local banks. A bank can be the executor of your will, for example. Or it can serve as your children's guardian in the event of the death of both parents. If you are in business, the bank can be asked to act as trustee in a buy-sell agreement between you and your associates.

A bank trust department can give you a wide range of investment, estate planning, and income tax planning ideas. Whatever your time of life or financial situation, you should find out about available services from a local bank trust officer—even if you think that you are not yet ready to take advantage of those services or that you will never want them. If only for the sake of obtaining information, ask this officer what his department can do for you, how it will carry out its duties, how much these services will cost, and how the bank could interrelate with other members of your financial planning team.

You should also become acquainted with other bank officials besides the trust officer. A loan officer, for instance, can provide sound business advice at no cost and may approve additional funds for you to put into your company if you are looking for financial assistance. If you have never visited your bank and talked with one of the vice-presidents about the institution's services, you should make such a trip a high-priority item on your calendar.

Tax-Shelter Experts

In recent years, many abuses have been perpetrated upon the unwary public by persons representing themselves as tax-shelter experts. The problem reached such proportions that the IRS addressed it in the Tax Reform Act of 1976 and in subsequent legislation. This does not mean that tax-shelter programs are, by definition, illegal schemes. It does mean that the IRS now carefully examines every program that comes before it. Remember, the factor that motivates you to buy into a tax shelter has to be its money-making potential and not its potential for saving tax dollars. Tax dollars may well be saved, but not unless the IRS can clearly discern the profit-making possibilities of the program.

You should deal only with the tax-shelter representatives who have untarnished personal reputations and who represent firms that are in verifiable good standing in the business community. The majority of tax-shelter programs are marketed by persons who claim to be or are financial planners, stockbrokers, or insurance salespeople. Obtain the prospectus (most often termed the "memorandum") of each tax-shelter program you are interested in and note the background of the general partner. Be suspicious of individuals in businesses they might logically be thought to know nothing about. If the tax-incentive program is an oil and gas drilling operation, for instance, and the general partner has had no prior experience in this area, ask whether this is a legitimate undertaking. If you have doubts, the IRS will too, and their concern might cost you a considerable amount of disallowed deductions, plus penalties.

You should investigate the "success pattern" of the general partner and others prominent in the program. If the general partner is reported to be a person with great versatility and experience in a number of unrelated areas, you should question whether his diverse activities might not indicate a lack of success in each area.

Always remember when investigating any investment program, tax-incentive or otherwise, that you and your advisers should learn as much as possible about the people behind the program. All enterprises stand or fall on the basis of the people who run them, so when you are weighing the value of a tax incentive program or any other potential investment vehicles, the cardinal rule is *to know the people to whom you're entrusting your money.* For all its computerized reports, the money business still is and always will be primarily a people business. Never overlook the human factor when making investment decisions.

In recent years, the IRS has looked with a jaundiced eye at many programs that have been described as tax shelters, including some dealing with lithographic plates, rare books, educational tapes, and the donation of artifacts to charitable institutions.

As the final point, remember that even if the tax shelter you are considering is legitimate and you do save tax dollars by buying into it, your chances of being audited by the IRS increase sharply once you have taken the deductions on your tax return.

These considerations should not deter you from looking into tax-incentive programs, but they should put you on your guard against possible misrepresentations. A reliable attorney and a reliable accountant are your best friends when you are examining shelter options. Let them advise you every step of the way.

Financial Planners

The financial planner is the quarterback on your asset management team. This person will, among other services, perform an in-depth analysis of your financial situation, coordinate the activities of everyone else on your team, create a balanced investment program, and, in some cases, implement that program by buying and selling investments for you. Before you select someone to fill this vital role, remember that the profession of financial planning is a relatively new one. It has been in existence as a recognized discipline distinct from others in the financial arena for only about ten years. Many people lay claim to the title of financial planner, but few are really able to perform all the functions that the job entails.

Anyone you are considering retaining as your financial planner should give you concrete evidence of his competence and his ability to relate to you as an individual. Again, you can learn a great deal about him by the questions he asks. Does he want to know about your hopes and plans? Does he ask about your financial background, where you are now, and where you want to go? Does he probe your comfort zones and your ability to face risk?

Is he as interested in your spouse's strengths and weaknesses as he is in yours? Does he understand that he must plan with the big picture of your family corporation in mind, and not just with an eye to the short-term profit? Do you enjoy talking to and dealing with him? Do you intuitively trust him?

One way to investigate the technical competence of a financial planner is to ask whether he has had training through either The American College or the College for Financial Planning. The American College offers the Chartered Financial Consultant designation to individuals who satisfy strict educational, experiential and ethical requirements. The education program consists of the following ten courses aimed at preparing candidates to effectively serve the comprehensive financial planning needs of the public:

Financial Services: Environment and Professions
Income Taxation
Economics
Financial Statement Analysis/Individual Insurance Benefits
Employee Benefits
Investments
Wealth Accumulation Planning
Estate and Gift Tax Planning
Planning for Business Owners and Professionals
Financial and Estate Planning Applications

The CFP has a five-course curriculum that leads to the designation Certified Financial Planner and qualifies one for membership in the Institute for Certified Financial Planners. This curriculum consists of:

Introduction to Financial Planning
Risk Management
Investments
Tax Planning and Management
Retirement and Estate Planning

Another indication of a financial planner's probable ability to serve you well is his involvement at the grass-roots level with others in his field. If he is active in the local chapter of the International Association for Financial Planning, he is most likely keeping abreast of current developments in the financial field by sharing ideas at meetings and reading professional publications.

You can obtain a list of qualified financial planners who work in or near your city by contacting either of these organizations at the following addresses:

> The American College
> 270 Bryn Mawr Avenue
> Bryn Mawr, Pennsylvania 19010

> College for Financial Planning
> 9725 East Hampden Avenue
> Suite 200
> Denver, Colorado 80231

The fees that financial planners charge to create investment blueprints for clients vary considerably. The fee that you will be charged for particular services from any planner should be agreed upon during your first, no-charge meeting. At this time, you should also be told exactly what you can expect to receive for this fee.

Before you decide to retain a financial planner, you should ask for two or three professional references, such as attorneys, trust officers, or CPAs in the community who can vouch for the planner's character and competence. In addition, the planner should give you a disclosure statement with details of his background and the backgrounds of key staff members. The statement should also tell you how long the firm has been in business and how its fees are set. The company's principals and top-ranking employees (or the corporation itself) should be registered as investment advisers with the Securities and Exchange Commission.

If additional fees might be charged in the future for services you do not now require, you should be informed of the probable amount and frequency of such fees. It is advisable to obtain a letter of intent from a financial planning firm before signing a contract. Even if you do sign a contract, you should be able to cancel it with no penalty within a specified time period, usually five days.

Select your financial planner carefully, because his expertise (or lack of it) in all phases of investments will have a far-reaching effect upon your life.

Step Five: Preparing a Written Financial Plan

Once your objectives have been defined, you must devise a means to attain them. You should have a written financial plan that will prescribe what steps to take at what times in the future if you are to realize your objectives.

The key concepts here are that your plan should be *written*, by either you or your chief financial adviser, and that it should outline action that is to be taken within a *specific time frame*.

Like your objectives, your financial plan should be flexible. A written plan does not have to be a rigid one. New ideas can be added as they occur to you and your advisers. Something that you should add to your daily routine is a half-hour or 45 minutes of reading about events and products in the financial arena. Publications that you will find informative and interesting include *Money, Time, Newsweek, U. S. News*

& World Report, and, of course, the *Wall Street Journal*. You can make your own list of favorites.

Sometimes you can give your daily study time over to a project rather than general reading. If you are thinking about joining a real estate limited partnership, for example, you might want to devote several days to a careful reading and rereading of material about it. Read with a pen in your hand and circle things you do not understand. Then take your questions to your financial adviser. Ask for solid, specific answers. That is what he's there for.

Step Six: Learning How to Monitor Your Program

At least once every three months, you should look over your financial program thoroughly. Set aside these periods on your calendar right now and then let nothing interfere with your commitment to use them for reviewing your program. During these reviews, evaluate your financial plan in terms of "the big picture." How are the various components performing? Are they living up to expectations? Are they moving you toward your objectives? Is it time to make some changes or should you leave the program alone?

The American Marketplace: An Ever Changing Challenge

Remember that no matter how competent and successful your financial planner is, *you* are always the chief operating officer of your personal corporation. As such, you should never stop informing yourself concerning conditions in the marketplace and the constant stream of new investment vehicles that makes the American financial arena a place of unparalleled excitement and opportunity.

This is not to say, of course, that we don't have serious economic problems in this country. One that I would put at the top of the list is our declining productivity. I believe that we can find solutions to the grave problems facing our nation, given our track record as a resilient people with the energy and will to bounce back from reverses.

We should also remember that an economic system rests upon the same foundation as religion: faith. Not gold, not silver, not the dollar, the pound, or any other currency. Faith in our economy and in the economies intertwined with ours is the force that opens the doors of the New York and American Stock exchanges, as well as the Pacific, Philadelphia, and Boston exchanges, every morning. We could do ourselves no bigger favor than to make a conscious effort during this difficult period in our economic history to strengthen our faith in our system. This is because recovery and continued growth are tied in no small measure to the unanimity of our belief in ourselves. And consider this: if the merchants of doom are right, and our system is irreparably damaged, then there is no place for any of us to hide financially. Not in Switzerland, the Cayman Islands, or the Middle East; not in gold, silver, or offshore drilling. The economy of the entire world is tied to ours, and the vital force that sustains our system is faith.

I, for one, am a believer, and I urge you to commit yourself to this faith, too. Remember that despite cyclical lows and the occasional doomsday cry of pessimists, the free enterprise system as practiced in the United States remains the greatest money-circulating machine that the world has ever seen. If properly used, the system can turn your personal money machine into an engine that will generate great wealth. One characteristic of capitalism remains constant: by its very nature it never stops pro-

ducing winners in the profit stakes. You can be one of these winners if you put the proper investment strategy to work for you.

A Few Final Thoughts

When you start your financial program, you're going to feel like a neophyte jogger who's just hit the street in his brand new jogging shoes. This new exercise (mental, in your case) is going to make you very uncomfortable for a while. Sometimes you're going to wonder why you ever broke out of your comfortable life-style and got started on this crazy new thing. You might take some kidding from other people (the "You can't do that!" crowd), and you will probably want to throw in the towel more than once.

All I can tell you is to hang in there. This is a worthwhile endeavor, possibly the most worthwhile and promising endeavor you have ever initiated. You are working toward a goal that is important not only to you, but to your family. When the highs start to come—and they will come if you stick with it—you'll be on top of the world. But you should also be prepared to face some deep lows when things don't go your way. At times like that, remember: you can't be right all of the time. No one ever is. Just try to be right most of the time and have enough staying power to hang on when you need to. The combination that will get you to your goal is:

Money + Time + Sheltering +
Good Rates of Return

Above all, believe in yourself. You are a unique individual, with special talents and abilities. The chances are good that you don't even know about some of these talents and abilities yet, or, if you do know about them, you don't realize the full extent to which you possess them.

You are your most valuable investment; you are your own greatest resource. Believe this philosophy and live it to the fullest. The things that we want and need begin to come within our reach when we discover our remarkable ability to redefine ourselves, to stretch beyond what we thought were our limits, and to show through our lives what becomes possible for those who say "I can."

Chapter 11

Financial Planning for the Professional

Lawrence A. Krause, CFP

Lawrence A. Krause, B.A., has been a financial planner for over twelve years and has a broad background in investment banking, securities, tax shelters, real estate, and business management. He is president of San Francisco-based Lawrence A. Krause & Associates, Inc., a professional financial advisory/financial planning firm. Earlier he founded and headed the Coordinated Financial Planning Department, Sutro & Co., Inc. He was also president and founder of Inventory and Business Controls, Inc. Krause frequently participates in radio and television interviews and writes a monthly column, "Hedging Your Dollars," for *California Business*. He is a Certified Financial Planner, a member of the Institute of Certified Financial Planners, and a member of the board of directors and secretary-treasurer of the National Center for Financial Education, Inc. He was voted "The Financial Planner of the Year" for 1982–83 by the International Association for Financial Planning, Inc., San Francisco.

Whether financial planning is for the professional, the owner of a closely held business, the corporate executive, the corporate employee, or simply you or me, the planning process is common for all: an objective and balanced approach that assists individuals and families to establish realistic financial goals and objectives and effectively pursue their attainment. The elements of financial planning are applicable to every person regardless of occupation, age, or financial status. To that extent, if we can all learn a few of the basic financial concepts developed throughout this book, our financial decisions can be made with more confidence and we can become more effective in this important area of our lives.

Why, then, write a chapter about planning specifically for professionals? Major diversity exists among members of the profession, for more than twenty (in some cases very different) occupations have been classified as "professionals" by law. Although the following list is incomplete by today's standards, the courts have held in specific cases that the following are "professionals."[1]

Operator of a Pool Hall
Insurance Agent
Private Detective
Minister of the Gospel
Operator of a School Bus
Teacher of Singing and Music
Pharmacist
Physician
Optometrist
Architect
Chemist
Newspaper Editor
Journalist
Landscape Gardener
Certified Shorthand Reporter
Engineers, including:
    Surveyor, Consulting Engineer, Civil Engineer, and Industrial Engineer

---

[1]C. Arthur Williams, Jr., and Richard M. Heins, *Risk Management and Insurance* (New York: McGraw-Hill, 1964), p. 147.

Lawyer
Dentist
Accountant
Veterinarian

And where is the world's oldest profession?

Obviously, relating financial planning to all professions would be difficult and would not be terribly meaningful for purposes of this chapter. Instead, if we concentrate on the more traditional category of professions that require extensive education, we can find common financial planning needs. Professions such as medicine, law, dentistry, the technical phases of business, as well as accounting, finance, engineering, are examples of professions that require a college degree. And because people in these professions tend to earn more money than both the noncollege person and other professionals, the problems of higher taxation on those earnings, higher taxation on their estate, and larger discretionary incomes become distinguishing focal points.

Other unique features of these professions include everything from (normally) an unusually high self-esteem to a high expectation by others; from a broad choice of business forms to a wide choice of retirement forms; from problems with spousal communication to difficulties with transferring their business or practice; from a relatively high personal aversion to taking risk to continually facing a high liability risk.

The most sensitive issue for the greatest number of professionals, however, is probably taxation. Say what you will about inflation, the fact remains that it has indeed given a great number of professionals a rather accelerated, if not queasy, view of life from the upper income tax brackets.

Common Financial Planning Mistakes

Professionals often respond in an unprofessional way to the vertigo induced by their tax bills. Investing in risky tax shelters is the most common financial mistake professionals make. Interestingly enough, experience has shown that in spite of a professional's stated aversion to taking risks, he or she is still overly susceptible to entering all manner of tax-shelter deals.

One doctor embarrassingly confessed that his CPA claimed the doctor held the office record for the largest number of K-1's (partnership returns)—he had more than *thirty*. Another doctor, who is also a tax-shelter junkie, not only has an excessive number of shelters, but also believes in excessive diversification. He has them all—from gold mines to master records, from movies to cattle, from oil to tax straddles.

Although in these instances the term "excessive" might be applied, they indicate the oversensitivity of many professionals to paying taxes. Concurrently, few people seem to understand—or even *desire* to understand— that tax shelters are highly risky investments.

It appears the above is partly a result of several contributing factors. The lack of understanding is an outgrowth of the "I'll do it myself attitude." And the lack of desire to understand is often due to "yikes, it's the end-of-the-year . . . I don't care how it's done, but I've got to get those darn income taxes down" syndrome. In other words, the problem is lack of planning.

Most professionals who do it themselves do so without the commensurate skill. Ironically, though they are "professionals" themselves, they often ignore the advice of or refuse to use other professionals. A private study has found, for example, that few professionals report that they trust (other professional) advisers.

Many specific solutions to income tax problems will undoubtedly be covered within the pages of this book. In addition, there are literally hundreds of books, magazines, newspaper articles and advisory columns and even television programs designed to instruct people how to handle their finances "a better way." But what they're really doing is telling people how to do it *their* way without taking each reader personally into account. Of course, they can't because each reader is unique. We can nonetheless draw some guidelines for the professionals, who face a number of common problems.

Professionals should first recognize that they are usually less qualified to evaluate investments than they think they are. We can illustrate this point by listing some of the questions and steps that are necessary to evaluate a tax-sheltered investment. This does not begin to take into account the person(s), their tax circumstances, necessary diversification, and so on.

Tax Features of Tax Shelters

1. What type of shelter is it?

2. What is the anticipated first-year write-off?

3. What is the potential for first-year excess write-off?

4. Is there sheltered income?

5. Is there capital gains potential?

6. What is the allowable depreciation method?

7. Is there an investment tax credit?

8. Is there recapture?

9. Is there phantom income?

10. Is phantom income a part of the shelter or a tax preference item?

11. Is there investment interest?

12. Is there a tax opinion and by whom?

13. Does it appear that the deductions are maximum? Will they be sustained?

14. If the IRS challenges the deductions, will the general partner pay the legal fees to defend the deductions?

15. Is there a request for an IRS partnership ruling?

16. Will the general partner make sure the K-1 (tax information for investors) is mailed on time?

17. Will an accountancy firm do the K-1's?

Economic Characteristics

1. How is the client obtaining the money necessary to make the investment?
2. What will the client do with any money the investment throws off?
3. What is the past track record of the general partner or promoter?
4. What is the past track record of the program?
5. Have any cash payments been made?
6. If so, how much and what percentage of the investment do they represent?
7. Is there opportunity for appreciation?
8. Does it make economic sense?
9. What is the risk and reward?
10. When will the investment make a return of capital to investor(s)?
11. Can the limited partner make any money?
12. Are the projections feasible?
13. Is there a break-even point that is feasible to achieve?
14. What is the requirement for attention and management?
15. What is the maturity or liquidation period?
16. Is the investment diversified?
17. Is it a blind pool or a specified offering?
18. Does the deduction include letter of credit, recourse or nonrecourse notes?
19. What is the integrity of the general partner or promoter?
20. Has his reputation been checked?
21. What are the reports of those who have visited the project?
22. Do the limited partners have the option of replacing the general partner(s)?
23. What is the commission, selling expenses, and so on?
24. Are there management expenses from cash flow and what are they?
25. How much money is actually going toward the investment?
26. Has the general partner invested more than the required 1 percent?
27. What is the sharing arrangement before payout and at termination, sale, or release?
28. Is the investment assessable? At what maximum percentage?
29. Is there a buyback provision? What amount?
30. What is the normal length of time for cash flow to commence?
31. What is the estimated internal rate of return?
32. What is the length of time for return of gross dollars?
33. When will the cash flow cease?
34. Is the investment an inflation, deflation, recession, or depression hedge?

Miscellaneous

1. What is the objective of the partnership?
2. What is total size of the partnership?
3. What is the amount of the investment?
4. What firms are selling this tax-sheltered investment?
5. Is there a limited or general partnership?
6. Is there a legal opinion and by whom?
7. Does the prospectus or offering memorandum provide all the pertinent information needed?
8. How did the offering reach you?
9. Is the offering a public or private placement?

10. Has the entire offering been read cover to cover?

To purport to understand the investment and tax merits of a tax-sheltered investment utilizing anything less than the above is equivalent to a doctor performing surgery with his or her eyes closed.

The "I'll do it myself" attitude usually exists because one's profession is largely based on education and ego. Thus, it becomes difficult to separate the professional from the notion that whatever he or she attempts will, with some study, find success.

It is understandable. We don't expect to be operated on by an insecure surgeon, nor do we want an insecure attorney handling our case. We also expect the architect to be highly competent; this is what we *expect* from all professionals. Thus, this mutual expectation by both the do-er and do-ee creates the belief by professionals that they have a high degree of skill in areas beyond their formal training. Furthermore, because of their necessary formal training, most professionals are highly sophisticated in their fields. This tends to create a problem, as many people seek a sophisticated solution to their personal financial planning problems when a simple, straightforward solution is all that's required. It does not follow that complicated deals are better simply because they are complex. Yet many professionals who do not understand the inner workings of a particular financial deal actually invest in and risk substantial dollars by doing so.

Another important force influences the professional's "why-do." That is peer pressure. This problem seems more prevalent among professionals than in any other group.

Many professionals are perceived by others, especially salespeople, to have an income usually in excess of reality, a burning desire to invest that income, and an immeasurable need to avoid paying taxes.

Therefore, a well-placed arm around the shoulder and a statement like "There are a few of us putting together this 'can't lose' deal that will save you thousands in taxes and we know you'd want to join us" creates enormous pressure. Too frequently, the result is a yes answer without the commensurate understanding.

If only professionals would at least *attempt* to find a competent adviser (not Uncle George, who does taxes on the side, or a friend who's an insurance agent by day and dabbles in financial advice at night). By finding an experienced financial adviser, the professional would likely be on a better path to financial success. Professionals then could also be effectively insulated from continual solicitations by saying that they first had to check with their financial adviser.

It works!

Peer pressure is external. But most professionals also face pressure from within. For example, they expect more from their offspring, and one of the forms in which these higher expectations are manifested is higher education goals—with their attendant costs. Thus, children of professionals can be expected to go to college and (often) graduate school. Meanwhile, the expense of all this education often plays havoc with the parents' cash flow because their lack of financial expertise leads them to pay these expenses with after-tax dollars. The pressure is self-inflicted and becomes aggravated unnecessarily. Although there are many procedural approaches to remedy this shortfall in cash flow, many professionals refuse to look beyond themselves for the solutions.

They also fail to discipline themselves to think in terms of net income rather than gross income. Self-employed professionals, in particular, experience this problem because they are not on a fixed salary. Since their income is derived as a direct result of their own efforts, and the professional can control the taxes paid on this income, the gross monthly income becomes a major *"why-do* I have a tax shortfall at the end of the year" problem. Because the professional tends to live as though the gross income was actually the net check, what should have been set aside for taxes is usually spent. For this reason, a self-employed professional *must* develop tax strategies *early* in the year to avoid this deception. (For that matter, planning is its own reward for *all* professionals.)

Still another contributor to a problem shared by many professionals is the "consuming" nature of their professions. The profession often consumes so much of their waking hours that their investments also tend to be myopic. Frequently, the professional's business and personal finances are so intertwined, that almost all of his or her net worth becomes (over)concentrated in business or business-related holdings. An example of this is the doctor who purchases a hospital or medical building, using all available capital for these investments. The lawyer, who in lieu of cash payments, becomes a partial owner in ten different companies owned by ten different clients is another common example. The assumption these professionals make is that given the high level of knowledge of their own (and their clients') business or practice—what better place to invest? Yet, if we examine most balance sheets, we still find many of these professionals are not reaching financial independence during their retirement years. Their assets are overconcentrated and still of insufficient size to produce the income needed for their later support. Indeed, most professionals are not only unaware of the assets and resources they do have, but also of the serious disorder of their financial matters.

What to do?

As stated earlier, most professionals need to understand the "why-do" and also need to devote considerable time to developing a personal financial plan. If time is not available because of the time and energy required of their profession, then a professional financial adviser should be engaged. Whether one attempts to develop his or her own plan or engages a professional, there are seven general areas that should be addressed and coordinated.

1. The Examination Stage.   In this initial phase, there must be a thorough "audit." Wills, trusts, insurance policies, deeds, mortgages, bank accounts, securities portfolios, investment documents, tax returns, and employee benefits must be reviewed. Loose ends should be eliminated, existing and potential problems identified, and some semblance of order established. Some examples of the audit would include ascertaining that real estate deeds reflect the proper titling; securities are in proper order; adequate homeowner's insurance is in effect; personal household goods, antiques, and jewelry have been appraised and insurance reflects those values; and all available fringe benefits from the practice of business have been correctly implemented.

2. Catastrophe Planning.   Professionals must protect themselves against the very large and unexpected risks that they face. This precaution not only lessens daily worries, but also lessens the possibility that a professional's assets will be wiped out by a disaster. In part, such risk coverage includes casualty insurance; errors and omission insurance; major medical coverage; business interruption insurance; possibly key man insurance or buy-sell insurance. Catastrophe planning can also include the hedging of investments against world economic turmoil. For example, the use of precious metals or a foreign bank account are but two methods which can be considered. Catastrophe planning must surely include adequate liquidity in the event of a prolonged recession, decline in practice income, termination of employment, family emergencies, or extended physical disability.

If a person is engaged in professional activities or performs services that require special care and skill, he or she will be subject to special liability problems. This is because it is no longer difficult to obtain a judgment against a professional person since a professional is held to a higher standard by American courts. He or she is expected to use "special knowledge and skill common to the profession." The slightest failure to exercise care may result in a costly lawsuit, and quite possibly, a sizable judgment.

Although professional malpractice insurance is carried by most doctors, many professionals do not protect themselves with proper liability coverage. For example, attorneys who should be more aware of the professional malpractice risk than almost any other professional, often do not carry professional malpractice insurance. A recent private study indicated that only 65 percent of the attorneys who were members of the bar in one large midwestern state carried professional liability insurance.

Any person who has any professional liability exposure should be sure to protect him- or herself with a separate policy. Insurance companies sell separate liability policies for druggists, dentists, surgeons, insurance agents, and many other professionals.

A typical individual's personal property and liability insurance needs are usually handled quite well by a homeowner's policy and an automobile insurance contract, but a common error made by many professionals is that liability limits are set too low. Normally, they should be raised to more closely cover the professional's assets. In addition to raising these limits, professionals should also seriously consider purchasing an "umbrella" or "excess" liability policy. Most individuals who practice a profession are deemed to have deep pockets. That is to say, they are perceived by the public as either making a good deal of money or having accumulated substantial

assets. An umbrella or excess liability policy covers an individual in the event he or she is sued for more than normal liability or for unusual causes, such as slander or libel. Such a policy must be coordinated with the normal liability protection provided by auto or household liability insurance.

The excess liability coverage does not relate to malpractice, but to conduct that causes people to sue as a result of suffering a perceived injury, either physical or mental. Often the professional's image is such that he or she is a highly visible target for such lawsuits, and therefore requires this extraordinary insurance.

Another area of catastrophe planning professionals tend to overlook is the need for disability insurance. If income stopped because of disability, bills and expenses could be paid from only four basic sources: savings, loans, charity, or insurance. If a professional were a sole practitioner and were prevented from working for a prolonged period of time, he or she could not afford to support himself or herself, or a family, for extended periods from savings. Borrowing the large sums of money often required to meet living expenses at a time when there is no income is practically out of the question. And no one really wants charity. Unless there are considerable savings, this leaves only one practical alternative to help assure financial security for the professional and his or her loved ones in the event of long-term disablement—long-term disability insurance.

My point is amply illustrated below. For a person under sixty, the odds on being disabled for a period of three months or more are far better than the chances of dying.

Here are the odds:

AT AGE	CHANCES OF DISABILITY VS. DEATH
30	2.7 to 1
40	2.3 to 1
50	1.8 to 1
59	1.6 to 1

Further, almost half of those who are disabled for six months will still be disabled at the end of five years. The ratio is fairly constant, irrespective of age.

Still another sensitive area for professionals is business interruption. Sole practitioners are especially vulnerable. The purpose of business interruption insurance is to keep the employees and office (rent) in operation until the professional can return to work.

Many of the above risks are covered by excellent policies offered through professional trade groups. These organizations understand the particular (and often unique) needs of their members, review their members' needs and benefits each year and because of a large membership (that is, they have clout) are continually able to gain more benefits at a more reasonable cost from insurance companies. Most definitely, professionals should (if they have not already done so) contact their professional associations and learn about the various insurance policies offered. This is especially true for disability and business interruption policies.

3. Investment Planning. All financial planners require that their clients prepare a cash flow statement and a balance sheet detailing their current financial position. Existing investments must be examined in detail—first to determine their appropriateness to the person's life objectives and comfort level, then for their investment value. Only then can new or alternative investments be considered.

For many professionals, however, the thirst for the quick kill is unabating. Sometimes it is to reinforce their egos; at other times it is just lack of prudent risk within the context of an overall financial strategy. Stripped of their boastful packaging, many get-rich schemes offer the identical risk to horse racing. But often it takes a professional adviser to do this stripping and to show his unwary client the weaknesses of the proposed investment.

Certain factors, therefore, should be taken into account by a professional when considering making an investment. The following list illustrates some of the common investment restraints that should be considered.

1. Current earnings and the nature or earning stability of the profession. A professional's income can be up and down, while others get a month-to-month set salary.

2. Income potential from profession.

3. Other sources of income.

4. Age, health, family responsibilities, ages of dependents, and other obligations.

5. Overall assets, liabilities, and net worth position (balance sheet).

6. Whether the professional has closely held business interests or other relatively nonmarketable assets.

7. Any likely inheritances.

8. Plans to use investment principal for particular purposes, such as education expenses, retirement, and estate settlement costs.

9. Estate plan. Who will inherit the estate and what kind of assets should be inherited.

10. The extent to which current investment income is required for current living expenses.

11. The degree and duration of price inflation (or deflation) anticipated and how other assets and sources of income will be affected by inflation (deflation).

12. The degree of liquidity and marketability needed to be maintained.

13. Ability to hold an asset when it is depressed in price.

14. Overall tax status.

15. The professional's and spouse's attitudes and emotional tolerance for risk.

Although the above list illustrates some of the common investment restraints, the only reference to risk is to emotional tolerance. But professionals have difficulty understanding risk-return trade-offs. The private study mentioned earlier documents this fact. When compared to business owners and executives, professionals fared very poorly at measuring risk. This seems logical. A business owner is required to render methodical, systematic business decisions on a daily basis. A professional, on the other hand, is an individual skilled in a profession. He or she usually does not have the time to perform the duties or functions of an office or position. Most professionals hire others (that is, hospital administrators, office managers) to fulfill that function. A professional's time is too valuable to step into that role. In spite of this fact, professionals consistently feel more qualified to render investment decisions (which includes understanding risk-return trade-offs) than they actually are.

4. Tax Planning. Proper tax planning should capitalize on incentives offered by the federal and state governments. If a "tax shelter" is considered, the object, while reducing taxable income (or, adjusted gross income) and moving the taxpayer into a lower tax bracket, is also to provide a reasonable possibility of making a profit. The idea then, is to convert what would normally go to taxes into assets. After everything else has been utilized to reduce taxes, that normally works best at the 50 percent tax bracket.

The following are some nontraditional tax shelters that should be considered before aggressive tax sheltering takes place:

Methods of Tax Deferral

1. Selling short against the box
2. Installment sales
3. Options—buy puts
4. Options—sell calls
5. Treasury bills
6. Tax loss "swapping"
7. IRA and Keogh plans
8. Corporate pension or profit-sharing plans

9. Deferred annuities
10. Deferred compensation plans
11. Ability to bill late
12. Utilizing a corporation with a different fiscal tax year

There are a number of methods of converting ordinary income to capital gains:

1. Tax-managed trusts
2. Reinvestment of capital utility dividends
3. Real estate, research & development, cattle breeding
4. Leveraged deep discount bonds

There are also several investment vehicles that allow professionals to avoid or reduce taxable income:

1. Municipal bonds
2. Treasury or U.S. government agency bonds
3. Offsetting capital gains with capital losses

Then, of course, there are the tax shelters. They allow an investor the use of what would otherwise be tax dollars as an interest-free loan for an indefinite period from the U.S. Treasury. But one should not be influenced by tax advantages alone. A bad tax shelter is a loan one cannot afford to maintain. It is important to remember that the first question to ask before you make a tax-sheltered investment should always be, "Is the investment economic without the tax benefits?"

5. Retirement Planning. The professional must begin retirement planning early enough to allow sufficient time to achieve objectives. To establish a plan because it is a "tax shelter," or because it is an easy way to accumulate a lot of money to "play" the stock market, usually only gets the professional into trouble. Too often it is forgotten that the primary objective of a retirement plan is to achieve a stable investment fund which will provide sufficient income at retirement.

In addition to retirement assets developed through the use of discretionary income, qualified (government encouraged) retirement plans are the primary source of these funds. Because of special tax incentives, the qualified plans best enable professionals (as well as all people) to achieve their retirement goals. But professionals have a broader choice of plans, for they may be able to select a Keogh plan (if they are self-employed) or one of the many corporate retirement plans available (if they are incorporated). As a result, decisions have to be made whether or not to incorporate; the answer to this question is not simple as there are additional elements to consider beyond just the retirement benefits. But it is the retirement benefits that draw all the attention when such a decision is made. This is because retirement plans offer more tax savings to a corporation than other tax strategies. Therefore, let's first examine these benefits in light of the Tax Equity and Fiscal Responsiblity Act of 1982.

In an effort to more closely conform retirement benefits for self-employed persons with those of corporate employees, the act proposes significant changes starting in 1984 to reduce the disparity. For example, in 1982 an incorporated doctor making $182,000 could have put away a maximum of $45,475. But in 1984, professional corporate contributions will be limited to $30,000. There have been increases in the maximum contribution every year, starting with $25,000 in 1975, but now we see the first decrease.

By comparison, $15,000 is the most this same doctor could set aside in 1982 and 1983 for a Keogh plan. However, Keogh contributions will also rise to $30,000 (capped) or 20 percent of income. This continues an unbroken string of increases since first created in 1962.

The largest annual pension that an employer will be able to pre-fund in 1984 is a defined benefit plan; the other major type of plan will be $90,000. The 1982-83 maximum of $136,425 will be reduced by 34 percent. Though a defined benefit Keogh exists, a professional cannot have a Keogh plan and a defined benefit Keogh. With the exception of the fact that an employer with a Keogh can also put away up to 10 percent of his or her own income in the plan each year (without increasing his or her contributions for employees), most of the other retirement benefits between the self-employed and owner/employee professional are pretty similar. That includes everything from the ability to be a self-trustee to Social Security integration; from a severe reduction of the amount an owner/employee can borrow from the pension or profit-sharing plan to a similar requirement when one must start withdrawing savings out of a plan.

6. Incorporation. Because many professionals believe the advantages of owning a personal service corporation are significant, the movement to incorporate their sole proprietorships and partnerships has reached stampede proportions. Today, however, before one considers whether to form a professional corporation, a sole proprietorship or a professional partnership, one should examine all forms of business alternatives carefully. All too often, a person may incorporate only because it is a "fad," only to discover later that a regulation has changed or a law has been passed that eliminates a major reason for incorporation.

For example, now that Keogh contributions are more in line with corporate retirement contributions, many professionals have to examine the other personal service corporation benefits versus their higher costs. Some of the benefits of incorporating include:

1. Medical reimbursement plans (the corporation pays the professional's medical expenses and he or she is not taxed on these payments).

2. Group term insurance (the corporation pays tax-deductible premiums and the

professional is not taxed on those premiums.

3. A split-dollar life insurance arrangement (which can drastically reduce the cost of his or her life insurance).

4. A lower tax rate that applies to corporations compared with those that apply to individuals.

5. A corporate taxable year which can differ from an individual's taxable year.

On the other hand, to have a corporation is to have increased Social Security expenses, corporate records, minutes and books, higher legal and accounting expense, and accumulated earnings tax on unappropriated retained earnings, an undistributed income tax and the age-old problem of double taxation (a corporation pays taxes on its income and the owner/ employee also pays taxes on the corporate profit distributed to him or her as dividends).

Should the professional form a personal service corporation or not? I would generally answer yes depending on the gross income. This is because the amount one can set aside in corporate retirement plans *still* greatly exceeds that whicn can be placed into a Keogh, and fringe benefits are also still attractive. However, for the professional making $50,000 to $100,000 annually, I would seriously question the value of having a corporation. For those who make in excess of $200,000 a year, I believe the overall benefits still far outweigh the negatives. Although the decision to incorporate is different for each professional, in order to take full advantage of the retirement plan benefits alone, the professional must have sufficient discretionary cash flow in order to fund the plans. Thus, the $200,000 income level is a logical one. However, the individual's income tax rate should be compared against the anticipated corporate tax rate and it should be determined if income is more important for current purposes. If so, assets should not be tied up for future years.

Since both the Keogh retirement plan and personal service corporation retirement plans offer attractive retirement benefits, it would certainly behoove a professional to establish his or her own checklist to closely examine current or long-term advantages and disadvantages of incorporation versus nonincorporation from both a tax and nontax point of view. But the subject of retirement doesn't only include qualified retirement plans or assets developed outside the plan. The professional also has a number of retirement options available to him or her that in some instances a nonprofessional does not have. These include the opportunity to work on a part-time basis and the ability to phase out of the profession or business.

Many professionals planning to retire can phase in to their retirement because they are in a position to dictate how many hours they wish to work and on what days. Besides continuing to guarantee the professional what may be necessary income, such flexibility also gives the professional control over how much income is earned. This in turn allows the professional to do tax planning, estate planning, and retirement planning.

Most nonprofessionals do not enjoy the option of phasing into part-time work before retirement. One day you are a full-time employee earning your maximum lifetime income and the next you are retired, living on a limited retirement income. The ability (and opportunity) to continue earning money from your work is better than any retirement plan, but this safety net is not often available to nonprofessionals.

Sound personal financial planning for personal service corporations and partnerships includes provisions for younger corporate shareholders/partners to buy out the interests of retiring associates at predetermined prices. The money received by a retiring professional for his or her share of the business often provides a sizable retirement fund. In the case of a sole proprietorship, an effective financial plan will include provisions for the proprietor to bring a younger person into the business. Once it is clear that this younger employee is interested and is sufficiently capable, agreements should be drafted pursuant to which the proprietor can sell the business to the younger associate and retire (or work part-time). It is important that the professional not wait until age 64½ before considering the sale of his or her interests in the business.

7. Estate Planning. The majority of professionals do not even have a will! Of those who do, many have wills that are out of date for they were executed when the professional was first married or at the time of the birth of the first child and have not been revised since. Estate planning can save thousands and sometimes hundreds of thousands of dollars. Yet, what should be "first" on the professional's security list is "last."

Despite the myriad of variations, sophisticated estate tax avoidance can be categorized according to three basic themes. First, the technique of estate freezing keeps free of tax the future growth in a professional's wealth by diverting that growth to the next generation. Second, the creation of tax-exempt wealth takes advantage of special provisions in the tax code that exempt certain assets from taxation. Finally, the reduction or elimination of tax on existing wealth is made possible by a package of techniques for gift-giving, manipulating valuations, and exploiting charitable deductions. All of these basic themes are well known to financial planners, although not everyone is, of course, familiar with the details of every variation.

The aforementioned professional does have certain problems and pitfalls that are relatively unique. One example concerns the basic principle behind estate planning: tax avoidance. For some reason, many professionals refuse to pass some rights and ownership in property to children in advance of the parents' death. This is a well-known estate planning technique yet people are loath to implement it.

A little-explored psychological and philosophical characteristic common to many professionals called "I am what I have" may be responsible for this behavior. So often the ego required to be a successful professional seems to make people feel that by giving up assets, they are abandoning a piece of themselves. Thus, it is difficult for them to implement certain estate-planning strategies, even though the strategies may mean a considerable tax savings. In other cases these psychological factors may simply give added cause for indecision where there is already a natural tendency to waver. This hesitation leads to delays in estate-planning implementation that may make the utilization of the most effective strategies impossible. By understanding at the outset that the fear of gifting assets may relate to the relatively unique psychological make-up of a professional, one may render the task an easier one.

Another psychological phenomenon that seems to influence estate-planning decisions of professionals is peer pressure and practice. Lawyers talk to each other and so do doctors, dentists, architects, and so on. Because of the common bond or "club" atmosphere that being a part of a profession encourages, the choice of estate-planning techniques (and investment techniques) varies among groups. There are also trends in estate planning that vary from time to time and place to place, just as there are trends in fashion.

As stated earlier, the majority of all professionals are sole practitioners. When a sole practitioner dies, the goodwill of his or her practice dies with that person unless another practitioner can take over immediately. Clients or patients disperse, his or her support personnel may take new employment, and the surviving family is likely to have difficulty in collecting outstanding bills. By the time the estate's representative can get around to looking for a buyer and negotiating a sale, there is apt to be little that can be salvaged.

A major protection for this type of occurrence is for the sole practitioner to be conscious of these possible events and to either have enough life insurance in force or enough outside (of the practice) assets to adequately provide for the surviving family. All too often the sole practitioner forgets about the vulnerability of the family when earning power is no longer in place. For many women whose husbands dictate family financial policy, the idea that they can intelligently invest in more than weekly groceries is still new. The inexperienced surviving spouse's best defense to mitigate the financial effects of the death is to learn basic money management strategies before it is too late. Whatever the level of eventual involvement, there need be no standard of income or expertise—only initiative—for women to begin.

Likewise, professional associates must plan for the disposition of the business in the event of one of their deaths.

If the practice is a partnership and there is an agreement, the professional partners can make adequate provision for the death of a partner. Generally, it is desirable that each partner assume the obligation to buy the deceased's interest in the partnership equipment and collect outstanding bills for the mutual benefit of him- or herself and the estate of the deceased partner. If warranted by the size of the practice and its income, provision may even be made for

payments to the surviving spouse of amounts exceeding the mere value of tangible assets (that is, "goodwill"). In a sense, professional partners can act as mutual insurers of one another without imposing too great a burden on the surviving partners. Alternatively, the partners may use various life insurance plans to fund death benefits that will enable the surviving partner(s) to pay the deceased partner's spouse an agreed-upon sum for the interest in the partnership.

A corporation, on the other hand, theoretically has continuity of life—it operates in perpetuity. That is, the corporation or business, regardless how small, continues to operate after death of an individual shareholder. If, however, a sole practitioner chooses to operate as a professional corporation, the estate problems remain the same as they were before incorporation. The laws of most states require that the shares of many types of professional corporations be disposed of on the death of the single licensed shareholder, unless stock is held by another professional licensed in the same field.

In conclusion, as the 1980s continue to unfold, a better understanding of one's self and one's financial goals and objectives, as well as the establishment of a personal financial plan, are becoming more important than ever, especially for professionals. Whether one does this alone, or engages a professional adviser, the professional's success—perhaps even financial survival— could depend upon a better understanding and management of the interrelationship of investment opportunities, tax planning, risk management, retirement, estate planning, and perhaps good advice from the right adviser.

Chapter 12

Financial Planning for the Chief Executive

Christopher J. Hegarty, Ph.D.
Craig M. Stone, CFP

Christopher J. Hegarty, Ph.D., is chairman of the board of Stone Financial Group, Inc., and president of C. J. Hegarty & Co. He was president of a national investment firm and founded and acted as sales manager of an international mutual fund complex. He also made the largest mutual fund sale in the history of the investment industry, which was $5.6 million. He has also been a consultant and adviser on a variety of assignments, including chairman of the Board of Governors of the National Center for Financial Education, Inc.; President's Council of the American Institute of Management; regent for the College for Financial Planning; member of the National Advisory Council of the International Association for Financial Planning; and a strategic consultant to the Stanford Research Institute (SRI International).

Craig Stone is well experienced in financial consulting to owners of closely held corporations. He is the founder and chief executive officer of The Stone Financial Group. He is a registered principal with a California broker dealer and is registered as an investment adviser with the Securities and Exchange Commission and in several states. He is also registered with the Commodity Futures Trading Commission as a commodity trading adviser. He is a Certified Financial Planner, a member of the Institute of Certified Financial Planners, the International Association for Financial Planning, and the National Association of Charitable Estate Counselors.

There is a myth that executive compensation is excessive. It is true that officers and owners of major corporations as well as smaller ones are compensated more than most of their employees. The common misconception, however, is that they are rewarded more and more each year, at the expense of employees. This is far from true.

A handful of top executives of Fortune 500 companies receive seven-figure compensation packages. These salaries are well publicized each year in national and local media. Because of this coverage, the public believes that most top executives are overpaid.

This perception is the reverse of what is actually happening. The after-tax, inflation-adjusted compensation of corporation executives has been going down for more than twenty-five years. The gap between the after-tax income of top executives and lower echelon workers is also getting smaller.

We predict that up to half of all middle managers will lose their jobs this decade. The survivors and big winners in the swiftly evolving growth industries of the coming decade will be those who keep management and administrative costs pared to the bone. Middle management ranks will be thinned.

The net result will be fewer layers of management. This will further lessen the pay differential between top management and employees. In corporate hierarchy, pay increases are the measure of success. An organization with twelve levels of management needs twelve pay plateaus. With fewer management layers, the pay differential between the highest and lowest echelons decreases. By the end of the decade we shall see even less of a difference between employee and management salaries.

These coming changes in corporate staffing and compensation have two ramifications that make financial planning for corporate owners and chief executive officers

(CEOs) important. On one hand, top managers of large corporations, with lowered overt compensation expectations for themselves and their staffs, will need comprehensive financial planning to maximize the value of what is received. They will also need to identify and implement wealth-building strategies secondary to direct cash compensations that are mutually beneficial for the firm and its employees.

On the other hand, we shall see a tremendous growth in small, individually owned corporations over the next few years. As middle management ranks are thinned, many former employees will be supplying services to their former employers, as well as to other firms, as contract consultants. This new breed of small corporation CEOs will also have to make use of strategic financial planning to survive and prosper in a changing economy.

Problems Facing the CEO

Because of the CEO's unique responsibilities to a wide diversity of people—not only employees but stockholders, bankers, suppliers, and customers as well—financial planning for the CEO must have a broad perspective. A daily rush of events demands exorbitant amounts of a CEO's time. It is rare that he himself has the necessary broad perspective to plan his own finances to best advantage. Objective third-party counseling is a must for effectively planning a CEO's finances.

The planning must encompass long-range development for the company, its stockbrokers, and employees as well as the personal assets of the CEO. In most cases, the major asset affecting the welfare of all these constituencies is the stock of the company itself. This asset, particularly in the case of management- and employee-owners, may have a low tax basis and thus a high latent capital gains tax exposure.

Current taxation has to be the overriding concern, however. The corporation earns $1.00; a 50¢ tax is levied; 50¢ is distributed as a dividend; and another 50 percent tax or 25¢ is charged, leaving 25¢. Upon the death of the CEO, another 50 percent estate tax is charged, leaving 12.5¢ for the heirs. The federal government has taken 87.5 percent of the original dollar of profit. State and local governments have taken an additional few percent.

However, we may take heart from a 1934 U.S. Court of Appeals decision that is a cornerstone of modern tax law. In Judge Learned Head's immortal words, "Anyone may so arrange his affairs that his taxes shall be as low as possible," and one "is not bound to choose the pattern which will best pay the Treasury." Choosing the pattern in which to arrange his affairs is the financial planner's primary responsibility to the CEO.

The CEO himself is in a high personal income tax bracket that requires planned sheltering. He would like to retain as much of his estate as possible for the benefit of his heirs. He has an interest in rewarding key employees. He has charitable inclinations, and will want to make gifts in an advantageous manner. He would like to slow down his work schedule but is not certain his family or employees are properly motivated to continue his business. Thus he is probably reluctant to give up control.

These problems are multifaceted and related. On several fronts at once, every dollar earned by this executive and his constituents is up against a complicated matrix of frequently changing tax laws. In today's world of specialization, most advisers to the CEO are not prepared to offer the comprehensive sophisticated planning required. The financial planner skilled in the art of planning for the CEO will have an overview of corporate and personal taxation, immediate and deferred employee compensation, estate planning, and charitable contributions. He will be the architect of the financial plan, and more important, the catalyst and motivator behind the teamwork necessary to create, implement, and monitor the plan.

Planned Solutions

Creative and competent planning for a chief executive officer's personal finances is as demanding and challenging as financial planning for the entire organization. There are potential conflicts of interest between the organization and the CEO. Outside professional advisers are a necessity. Many executives deceive themselves that their attorneys or accountants provide sufficient financial planning. Too often their focus is on controlling and monitoring the current financial structure. The nature of their services makes it rare for an attorney or accountant to provide full-service financial planning. Likewise, an integrated financial plan is most unlikely to come from an insurance or investment product salesman, however useful his services may be.

The ideal financial planning team acts as a financial architect to custom-design a financial blueprint. This master plan must then be carefully implemented—in cooperation with the client's existing legal, accounting, and investment advisers—and thereafter relentlessly monitored and updated.

In many organizations the control of finances is mistaken for financial competence, but the "audit" or "after-the-fact" approach often causes severe problems. Those to whom management gives financial controls are by nature averse to risk However, we are in an economic environment in which creativity is at a premium. There is danger in playing it safe; trying to avoid risk is sometimes the greatest risk of all.

True financial competence requires informed risk taking in tandem with precise controls. The U.S. auto industry refused to risk changing the cars it built, and lost a market share it may never recover. The same lesson applies to the financial plans of chief executives. Bold, intelligent, decisive actions—maximizing the benefits to the full constituency of concern—are necessary. The central challenge is often to create an integrated plan that maximizes the CEO's opportunities while advancing the long-term goals of his firm.

Enlightened shareholders in both public and privately held companies will soon require a major change in the way many CEOs are paid. The short-term incentives now used often damage the company's future as the CEO maximizes short-term returns. The creative alternative will be to escrow bonuses during the CEO's tenure, then pay up to double if predetermined long-term goals are met, or down to nothing if the company suffers a reversal. Such an incentive approach makes superb sense to the company, but will call for the CEO's personal finances to be planned with ever more agility, creativity, and foresight.

Many firms are now learning how to measure management performance as distinct from business performance. Business performance is commonly measured by current return on investment. But only for the short-sighted does "ROI" mean merely "return on investment." Management performance is evaluated by preparation for the future as well as the next dividend. "ROI" additionally means "return on individuals."

These new measures of performance will benefit the business, its stockholders, and its employees. At the same time, they will make it all the more difficult for the CEO to be sure of his long-term financial rewards. Without the security of large quantities of immediate compensation, careful planning and implementation of strategy will be all the more important in satisfying future needs.

The Founder vs. the Professional Manager

Chief executives are of many types. Some are founders who still run companies with an iron hand. Some are children and other heirs of founders who may have put their own individual stamp on the company, or who may have relied to a greater degree on professional managers. Some are management professionals who grasp an entrepreneurial opportunity and build independent control. And some are professional managers who are employees of the board of directors, with little equity interest in the company and little real control over long-term planning.

A founder, often the majority or only stockholder, is chief executive of an enterprise born strictly from his brains and brawn. His financial planning should differ substantially from that of a professional manager. The professional manager has normally come up through the ranks of business, often has an M.B.A., marketing, or accounting background, and is a manager of assets who endlessly and dispassionately weighs all sides of business equations, such as sales, production, finance, credit, and long-term planning. His financial and emotional needs are seldom like those of the founder. We can profit by a closer look at these two types of CEOs.

The founder is an entrepreneurial chief executive. This CEO should look carefully at long-term planning for the financial success of his firm only after defining the ultimate vision and purpose of both the company and the people he hopes will inherit or manage the company after his retirement or death, whether premature or normal. His financial planners must understand and plan with his probable reluctance or refusal to surrender control of his creation. Creative planning can allow him to pass the baton while retaining control.

An employee stock ownership plan (ESOP) provides an opportunity for a founder to sell a percentage of his equity to his employees at a profit to himself, with extraordinary tax and financial benefits for both himself and the corporation. At first glance, an ESOP may seem like some form of giveaway fringe benefit, but it functions very differently with careful structuring. On one hand, it shifts employee attitudes by giving them a stake in company success. Tremendous productivity gains under ESOPs are well documented. With IRS blessing it provides a number of legitimate tax benefits for the founder and the company. But often its greatest advantage is to provide a ready buyer—at full appraised value—for the founder's otherwise unmarketable stock, allowing him to cash out, either gradually or at once, under optimum conditions and even without his relinquishing control.

Suppose the CEO wants to slow down, reward his employees, see the business continue, realize cash, and retain control. This combination seems overwhelming, but a leveraged ESOP can provide partial solutions to every objective. The concept can be best illustrated by a diagram (see Figure 1).

In this case, the family owners of the original company (OC) sell all or a part of their company to the company employees (including family members). The OC makes an interest-free loan to a family trust. The trust purchases 49.9 percent interest of the new company (NC). The NC sells 50.1 percent of its stock to the ESOP retirement plan. NC now borrows from the bank the necessary amount of money to purchase OC stock. NC forms a wholly owned subsidiary (NCS). NC flows the bank loan proceeds through the NCS, which in turn buys assets from OC with cash and a note. NCS now becomes the operating company. As profits are earned, up to 25 percent of the payroll is contributed before tax to the ESOP. The ESOP now uses this tax-free

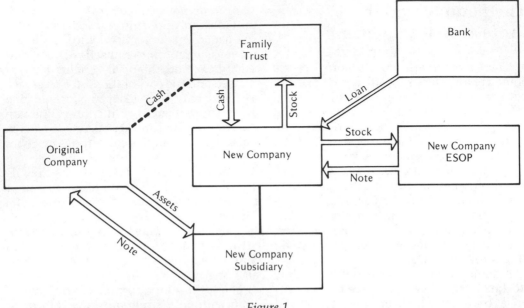

Figure 1

money to repay the loan to NC. These tax-free principal payments received by NC are used to repay the bank with before-tax income. The excess earnings from NCS go to the OC in the form of pretax note payments, since most of the payments represent interest payments on the OC note.

The net result of this transaction is that the CEO gets liquidity for diversification on a favorable tax basis (that is, long-term capital gains in installments). He can freeze the growth of his estate by having the family trust hold title to the NC stock. The cash for the buyout came from before-tax profits of the company. Through his stock ownership in NC and the ESOP he still controls the company. He can slow down, since his employees, who now own part of the company, will take a much more active interest in the company. If the company has a profitable year and wants to accelerate the note payments to OC, it can enter into a leveraged equipment-lease transaction and use the tax savings for note principal payments.

Such creatively structured ESOPs may prove to be the most exciting capital formation idea of the 1980s. A founder can sell his stock to a new company held in trust for his heirs, with the entire transaction financed using the leverage of an ESOP. The founder can remain in total control of the firm until death, even though he sells his interest for cash at capital gains rates.

A one-person executive corporation is an ideal financial planning tool for many CEOs of closely held companies. In one application, the founder resigns from his firm and forms an individual executive corporation, which then contracts with the company to fill the office of its presidency. In another variation, the CEO-founder remains as titular president, but at a sharply reduced salary, while his new executive corporation contracts with the company to provide many of the founder's services, in return for fees formerly paid him as salary. Simply by choosing a fiscal year end for the executive corporation of, say, January 31, and keeping late year fees paid by the business within the executive corporation past December 31 (when they are paid down to the individual as compensation), a year's tax deferral on substantial amounts of income is easily achieved.

As sole employee of the new corporation, the founder can be covered by a liberal defined benefit retirement plan, funded with substantially higher contributions than otherwise possible, immune from creditors, bankruptcy, IRS claims—in fact, every kind of judgment except divorce. The annual contributions to the plan are tax deductible by the individual corporation and are not taxable to the CEO. Legislation passed in August 1982 cut the maximum annual contributions for defined benefit plans, but they remain the best way to achieve both tax and retirement planning objectives. Voluntary employee benefit associations can be used for even greater tax benefits. The individual corporation, because of these tax-sheltering possibilities, will become an increasingly important component of CEO financial planning.

However, the individual corporation and its retirement plan must be executed precisely and based on sound actuarial statistics. It is wise to use a law firm specializing in the design and execution of these plans that has 100 percent success in meeting legal tests, actuarial standards, and IRS scrutiny.

An equipment-leasing trust can be a vehicle to fund children's educational costs with tax-deductible dollars. The founder can make a gift or interest-free loan to a trust established for his children, which in turn buys the cars, computers or other equipment the founder's business needs. In an arm's length transaction, verified by an independent appraisal, the equipment is leased to the company. The trust has important estate-planning advantages as well. The company's payments are deductible business expenses. This seemingly

simple approach requires careful planning and structuring, as the IRS will want to disregard the trust or the leases. The best financial planners can coordinate this strategy, in which the interplay of personal, estate, and business planning yields optimal results.

An estate freeze may be appropriate for a growing business. A founder can at any point stop the growth from occurring in his hands, where it will add to his or his spouse's taxable estate, and transfer the future growth to his heirs so as to bypass estate taxation completely. He can form a personal holding company, or simply recapitalize his business corporation, using at least two classes of stock. The founder retains voting control and a fixed preferred interest equal to present values. His children hold common stock, initially of little value, in which all future growth will occur. Estate tax, at 50 percent for estates above $2,500,000, is avoided. If the founder invests in real estate, the same estate-freezing concepts can be used in partnership form.

A founder has significant stock equity with a large latent capital gains tax liability. A *charitable remainder unitrust* can enable him to achieve liquidity with minimal tax consequence. Company stock is given to the trust. This action does not create an income tax liability. In fact, it creates a charitable deduction against current income.

The trust itself is tax exempt. Therefore the trustee (who must not be the founder or his beneficiaries) may sell the stock and reinvest the proceeds on a pretax basis. The founder and other beneficiaries will have been taxed only on income received. The character of such a trust creates ordinary losses when established. It defers taxes so more capital may be liquidated and reinvested in a diversified manner without tax erosion. The unitrust generates income for the lifetimes of the founder and his beneficiaries. Since the annual income distributed is based on a percentage of the trust's annual asset value, it serves as a hedge against inflation for the beneficiaries. For the CEO who is in a large public company, stock ownership can be transferred to a personal holding company, which can in turn create estate freezes or charitable remainder trusts. If the assets are other than stock, a multitiered family partnership may be appropriate.

The CEO who has already accumulated assets far in excess of his personal financial security needs can use a variant form of the charitable trust to pass wealth on to heirs with minimal estate taxation. With a *charitable lead trust,* the estate can actually be reduced. The lead trust can be created during life or by will at death. Assets are transferred to the trust. A portion of the income from the trust will go to charity for an actuarially determined period of time. At the end of the period the trust corpus will pass to heirs tax-free. The present value of the future payments to charity will produce a present gift value of zero. Therefore, one gives away the assets without gift tax and with an estate reduction equal to the gift. After a certain number of years, your heirs will receive the corpus of the trust, including any growth on the assets above the income that was distributed to charity— free of estate taxes.

Financial Planning for the Professional Manager

Normally, the CEO in the second category has a different set of financial goals and challenges and, just as important, his personal psychology and philosophy are different to a like degree. He receives a high current income, with bonuses based on performance and perhaps stock options. His ownership percentage, if any, is low.

Lacking capital participation, this CEO is much more likely to be interested in building his net worth than in limiting it in favor of his heirs, so the estate freeze is of little interest to him. Income tax planning will be a major concern, the degree of risk depending on individual preferences. The leveraged equipment-lease transaction described above often will suit him as an individual investor. It will produce large initial tax deferrals for up to eight years. Cash freed up from tax savings should be put into solid investments irrespective of tax benefits. We often recommend that a client invest his tax savings in high-quality commercial real estate. In the interests of diversification, tax-advantaged oil and gas investments may be appropriate.

Disability and life insurance will be primary concerns, as his family's security probably depends on his current earning power. A combination of individual and business key man insurance often works best. The company will likely prefer to confer value upon the professional CEO in the form of insurance than to give him equity ownership, especially when it can build a reserve for insurance in his retirement with deductible premiums that never create corresponding taxable income. Split dollar and other approaches can compensate the firm for the death of its CEO as well.

An individual executive corporation may be valuable to the professional manager, since it may allow the greatest possible retirement plan contributions, serving both his need for current income tax deductions and his dependence on deferred earnings, rather than corporate ownership, for retirement security. The directors of many firms have been reluctant to allow corporate officers to adopt personal executive corporations, but there are signs this attitude is changing, as indeed it must in the current environment of diminished employee loyalty, frequent job hopping, and heavy competition for managerial talent.

The professional manager will take interest in an ESOP because it can be one of his most powerful management tools. In appropriate situations, it is a superior method of corporate finance, while its benefits in employee morale and productivity are unparalleled. Only in certain circumstances will an ESOP figure heavily in the professional manager's personal finances. However, there are ways that ESOP financing can work superbly when a new management team takes over an existing business with limited capital available. The techniques are exacting, and the advisers and lending institutions must be well attuned, but the highest level of financial planners can recognize the need for the technique and coordinate its implementation.

Goals of Financial Planning for Chief Executives

The chief executive by definition is the key person in a network of productive interdependencies. His livelihood and that of his company depend on the productivity and well-being of his employees. The economic survival of other members of the network depends on the sound long-term planning of the chief executives.

Thus, the first goal of financial planning for CEOs is to create rapport among the associates of an enterprise. Enlightened financial plans will be structured in such a way that the entire community of interest is served.

A second important goal is to ensure the greatest chance for the firm's long-term success by focusing on legitimacy as well as legality. Interests of employees, stockholders, the founder, and his family must be taken into consideration.

Recognition and reward of true management performance on the part of the CEO should come through long-term incentive compensation which, for the benefit of all concerned, shifts the emphasis of economic rewards on quarterly profit margins. The CEO should find continuing rewards if the company prospers after his departure, and should be subject to the impact of business reversals occurring soon after he leaves.

Financial planning for chief executives must above all else encourage bold risk taking. CEOs, whether founders or professional managers, must realize that change is required and that destructuring is not always destructive.

As a final word, let us caution that this chapter is not the final word on financial planning for CEOs. We have presented but a few simplified concepts, none of which should be undertaken without the assistance of thoroughly competent advisers. Despite the complexity of planning at this level, it is urgent that more and more individuals, as well as professional financial planners, address the problems of pervasive tax erosion and inappropriate reward mechanisms that permeate most corporate financial arrangements.

Part 4

Editor's Notes:
Reducing and Sharing Your Risk

A *nyone preparing a financial plan, or even contemplating one, must give some thought to guarding against the type of catastrophe that could conceivably wipe out all that planning. There is always that risk and no way to eliminate it. You can, however, reduce the risk and get an insurance company to share it with you.*

Jay Smith begins this part of the book with an objective analysis of life insurance in Chapter 13 that should be of interest to all readers. Dave Goodwin next takes you into the realm of casualty insurance in

Chapter 14, where he explains methods of obtaining better coverages at lower premiums. In Chapter 15 Richard Austin points out that a successful financial plan should include a means of protection against the loss of income, and provides useful information on accident and health insurance. The subject of risk is then examined from a different perspective by Lewis Walker, who in Chapter 16 gives an overview of our changing economy, its forecasters, and what investors can do to reduce risk.

Chapter 13

What Everyone Should Know About Life Insurance

Jay A. Smith is an experienced life insurance analyst and stockbroker who has advised agents, financial planners, and stockbrokers throughout the United States. He is the founder of the Life Insurance R_x Corporation. A Chartered Life Underwriter, Smith is a member of the National Association of Security Dealers. He was one of the original founders of the College for Financial Planning and served on its board for three years. He was also founding president of the North Bay Financial Planners. His seminar forecasts are well known on the speaker circuit.

Jay A. Smith, CLU

The purchase of life insurance is not a simple matter, and can become even more complicated when it is part of an overall financial plan. There are more than 1,800 life insurance companies in the United States, each with its own rate books and specialized policies. Consumers are faced with increasingly confusing terminology as each company adds new features (or old features with new names) in an ongoing effort to stand out from the crowd.

Complex terminology alone is enough to cause uncertainty, even suspicion. Worse, over the last few years there has been publicity that some types of life insurance are not in the best interests of the policyholder. The Federal Trade Commission has indicated that millions of valuable consumer dollars have been wasted on unneeded or overpriced life insurance benefits.

The result has been confusion, even aversion, among consumers. This is unfortunate. In its pure form, life insurance is a marvelous tool for family protection and for financial planning. Its social benefit has been, and will continue to be, tremendous. However, in a free-market economy characterized by sophisticated sales techniques and computer aids, it is up to the consumer to be careful and informed. I hope that, after reading this chapter, you will be better able to buy a life insurance policy that meets your needs, or listen to an insurance agent or financial planner with more understanding. You should be familiar with some of the basics of life insurance if you are to take full advantage of its benefits, and not fall victim to its pitfalls.

The Beginnings of Life Insurance

It's been said that one of the earliest forms of life insurance was practiced by the Romans. Gladiators going into conflict knew that no matter what the outcome, their families would not suffer total financial deprivation.

Marine insurance also had early beginnings. Mediterranean traders divided their goods among several ships in order to guard against inordinate loss. Each ship carried the goods of numerous traders. If one ship went down, they shared the loss, so no one trader was wiped out. Later, groups of traders pooled a portion of their profits in an insurance fund, so that in the event of a loss at sea, the owners of the goods shipped could actually be compensated for their loss.

Trading guilds in England developed an early form of life insurance. Members chipped in and supported the widows and children of colleagues who died. In the New World, the first life insurance company was First Presbyterian Ministers Life, formed by a group of clergymen who paid dues to protect the welfare of survivors when one of their number died. First Presbyterian Ministers Life was the prototype of numerous fraternal life insurance companies that sprang up during the nineteenth century in the United States. The Lutheran Brotherhood, the Knights of Columbus, and Woodmen of the World are but three examples that are still with us today.

What is important to note about all the early forms of life insurance is that they offered only risk protection. Groups of people with a common interest banded together because they perceived a clear benefit in protecting any one of their members from loss and suffering. The earliest forms of life insurance had no cash value, dividends, or waiver-of-premium features, to name just a few of the terms commonly found in life insurance policies today. We would call these earliest forms of insurance pure term insurance. You paid your premiums for the period of time to be covered (the "term"), and if anything happened to you during that time, your beneficiary was protected. If you did not pay your premium for the next term, your beneficiary was not protected. It was that simple.

During the late nineteenth century, life insurance underwent some drastic changes and acquired numerous features and benefits that characterized most policies well into the second half of this century. The vast economic and social changes that took place were paralleled by corresponding changes in the nature of life insurance. As we developed more and more into a credit economy, the obligations of day-to-day living increased manyfold. Families incurred greater amounts of debt as they purchased farm lands and personal homes through debt mechanisms called mortgages. The potential losses and suffering of families left without the earnings of the principal breadwinner were greater than ever before.

The proselytizers of life insurance were quick to point out that through the purchase of life insurance it was possible to offset debt and the increased cost of living. The ruggedly independent American spirit was amenable to taking the risks of a mortgage or borrowing to start a new business. Thus, Americans were prime candidates to purchase life insurance to hedge against that risk of dying and leaving their obligations unpaid. The psychology of independent individual responsibility also played a role. The breadwinner could be proud that, through the medium of life insurance, he was taking care of his family both now and in the future. *His* family would never have to be dependent on neighbors, or the church, or the poorhouse.

The entrepreneurial spirit of the fast-growing force of life insurance agents was important, also. They were filled with enthusiasm as they offered to masses of Americans their socially commendable product. For just a few dollars a month, you could protect your property from foreclosure, and protect your family's reputation as solid citizens.

Policy Reserves

Perhaps the most significant change in insurance during the nineteenth century came from government regulators. As they observed some forms of life insurance being sold, they thought it unfair that a wage earner might pay his premiums year after year, then perhaps be unable to make payments one year and lose all his protection. Regulations were set up requiring life insurance companies to build up cash reserves beyond the amount required to offset the mortality risk of the policyholders. With the buildup of cash reserves in a policy, if a premium payment was missed, cash value in the policy was available to cover it, so that protection would go on uninterrupted. Further, should a policyholder decide to cancel his policy after years and years of premium paying, he could withdraw his cash reserves and have something to show for his faithful premium payments.

Level Premium Concept

Along with the cash reserve came the concept of paying a level premium throughout the life of the policy. This concept began the widespread practice of having to charge more for the policy than just the cost of mortality risk.

This charge was easy to justify, not only because life insurance companies were building cash reserves for individual policyholders, but also because they were taking on an awesome social responsibility. Life insurance companies had to live up to an image of financial indestructibility. There is no way in the world you would buy a life insurance policy if there was the least thought in your mind that it might not pay off. In the spirit of being safe rather than sorry, life insurance companies started building reserves with a vengeance. The statistical occurrence of death among thirty-two-year-olds might be only three per thousand in the first year, but what about abnormal occurrences such as war, famine, plague, or pestilence? Shouldn't those be protected against, also? Better to charge a little extra now, and create excess reserves, than run the risk (even if extremely remote) of profoundly disappointing bereaved families in the future. Besides, by building excess reserves the insurance companies were actually creating a "savings account" for the policyholder. Unlike a savings account with a bank (an insurance company charges you interest to borrow from your reserves), however, the buildup of cash value was a resource (forced savings) that many might otherwise not have.

Such was the thinking among insurance companies as more and more life insurance was sold. What was not clear to many insurance agents and insurance buyers was that for the insured, there is a point of diminishing returns in overprotecting against fainter and fainter possibilities of disaster. Life insurance companies began to build up larger and larger reserves, entirely out of proportion to the risk being covered. The actual statistical risk of mortality was covered with the first premium dollars. The overhead of running the company was met next. Everything charged in excess of overhead and mortality was, in fact, never intended to be used. The vast funds of excess reserves multiplied faster and faster, fed not only by new excess premium dollars, but by return on investment and the magic of compound interest. Insurance companies put money into everything that moved—railroads, automobiles, ships, and airplanes—as well as into everything that didn't move—real estate, stocks and bonds, machinery, and equipment.

How did insurance get to be the first trillion dollar industry? Few would argue that some of the leaders of the insurance industry were exceptionally astute businessmen. In retrospect, from today's perspective, we can say now that they must have been charging too much for their product. Like religion, the insurance industry dealt with emotion. What is too much

to pay for the protection of your loved ones? The premiums being charged each month seemed small enough, and the sums promised in the event of death seemed vast. Even if some might question the assumptions behind the rates of life insurance coverage, how could they contend with the vast statistical data base and complicated mathematical formulations of the actuaries—those highly trained specialists who calculated risks and rates for the insurance companies?

But today, the buying habits of insurance purchasers are changing. Financial planners and even some insurance agents are taking the emotion out of insurance decisions and replacing it with economic considerations. New insurance companies are being created, offering much more competitive rates. Existing companies are reducing their rates to meet this competition. The insurance buyer who knows what he wants and who takes the time to shop for it will save himself hundreds or even thousands of dollars.

Term and Whole Life: Two Basic Forms of Life Insurance

I mentioned that the earliest forms of insurance was term insurance, or insurance that protected against loss for a defined period of time, without any extra "bells and whistles." Because statistics show that your likelihood of dying during a given period increases with each year of age, the cost of mortality protection goes up with age. If you are an insurance company insuring a group of 1,000 thirty-year-old men against death during the next twelve-month period, and each insured person is carrying $1,000 worth of coverage, you certainly do not need to collect $1,000,000 in premiums (1,000 × $1,000)! Since statistical experience demonstrates that only 1.73 of the thousand men will die during the term covered, you need to collect only $1,730 in premiums to cover the mortality risk. If, however, you are similarly insuring 1,000 seventy-year-olds, you had better take in $39,510 in premiums, because statistics demonstrate that 39.51 of 1,000 seventy-year-olds will die during that given year. Thus, one year of term insurance will cost 22.8 times as much for a seventy-year-old as for a thirty-year-old. The mortality table of deaths per thousand men and women age 0 to age 100 is shown in Table 1.

The mortality table is the basis for all life insurance, term or whole life. It is different for males and females, smokers and nonsmokers, people with medical problems, and those without problems. That is why an insurance company takes all these things into consideration in computing the rates for whatever kind of life insurance you might buy. But one thing remains the same: the mortality table (and thus the cost of term insurance) always rises sharply as we get older. If you decide to buy term insurance only, year after year, the cost per $1,000 of coverage will naturally rise.

Annual Renewable Term

Today, term insurance is still commonly sold, and it is the least expensive form of life insurance protection you can buy. It is useful to understand the various forms of term insurance, so as to be able to compare any other kind of life insurance policy with the cost of pure term insurance in deciding whether or not the extra expense is worth the greater premiums. The most prevalent kind of term insurance sold today is *annual renewable term* (ART). With this kind of policy, your payment of premium dollars not only gives you life insurance protection for the upcoming year, but guarantees your right to renew the policy for the following year at a guaranteed agreed-upon rate. And no matter what age you start an annual renewable term policy, the annual premium will be substantially less than if you were to start a whole life policy at the same age. Since your mortality risk increases with every year, you can also expect the premium rate to go up year by year.

Table 1. Mortality Table
1980 Commissioners' Standard Ordinary Mortality Table

AGE	MALE MORTAL-ITY RATE PER 1,000	MALE EXPEC-TANCY YEARS	FEMALE MORTAL-ITY RATE PER 1,000	FEMALE EXPEC-TANCY YEARS	AGE	MALE MORTAL-ITY RATE PER 1,000	MALE EXPEC-TANCY YEARS	FEMALE MORTAL-ITY RATE PER 1,000	FEMALE EXPEC-TANCY YEARS
0	4.18	70.83	2.89	75.83	50	6.71	25.63	4.96	29.53
5	.90	66.40	.76	71.28	55	10.47	21.29	7.09	25.31
10	.73	61.66	.68	66.53	60	16.05	17.51	9.47	21.25
15	1.33	56.93	.85	61.76	65	25.42	14.04	14.59	17.32
20	1.90	52.37	1.05	57.04	70	39.51	10.96	22.11	13.67
25	1.77	47.84	1.16	52.34	75	64.19	8.31	38.24	10.32
30	1.73	43.24	1.35	47.65	80	98.84	6.18	65.99	7.48
35	2.11	38.61	1.65	42.98	85	152.95	4.46	116.10	5.18
40	3.02	34.05	2.42	38.36	90	221.77	3.18	190.75	3.45
45	4.55	29.62	3.56	33.88	95	329.96	1.87	317.32	1.91
					99	1000.00	.50	1000.00	.60

Based on experience of years 1970–1975.

Decreasing Term

You may also have heard of *decreasing term* insurance. Here, your annual premiums remain the same, but the face amount of coverage decreases year by year. If you are using term insurance to provide protection while you are building assets in other investments, such as mutual funds or real estate, a decreasing term policy may make sense. Your insurance costs are minimal and do not go up year by year. The face amount of coverage decreases, but this decrease happens at the same time that your other investment assets are supposedly increasing, so that the entire estate of investment assets plus term insurance should be growing *in toto*. By the time your decreasing term insurance decreases to nothing, you should have accumulated enough of a living estate to cover your needs and the needs of your family. Decreasing term is also commonly used as a form of mortgage insurance, decreasing at the same rate as the principal of the mortgage that is paid off. With the inflation rate rising, however, decreasing term sales have declined and are being replaced by ART, which gives the insured the flexibility of having his protection decrease only if he wants it to.

Level Term Insurance

Level term insurance is a modified form of annual renewable term. In this case you would buy a term policy for a predetermined period of time (one, five, ten, fifteen, twenty, twenty-five, or thirty years; or "level until age sixty-five") and the total amount of premiums to be paid would be divided by the number of years to be covered, so that the premiums are the same for every year. With this kind of policy, you are overpaying in the early years and underpaying in later years. However, it normally does not have the cash value accumulation feature of whole life policies.

Whole Life

Whole life policies (also known as *ordinary life* and *straight life*) are distinguished from term insurance by two characteristics. First, the premiums remain level for the period of the policy, just as with the level term policy. Second, the overcharge in the early years is enough not only to cover the cost of mortality, but to build up a cash value account in the policy. An insurance salesperson might point out to you the rising cost of term insurance versus this level benefit in whole life, saying, "When you're sixty-five and beginning to live off Social Security and your pension plan, you don't want to be saddled with exorbitantly high term insurance premiums, do you? Well, we have a way to solve the problem. It's a way you can pay a bit more now, in early years, and be guaranteed a level premium for life!" The salesperson then might draw up a chart like the one in Figure 1 to show you how a whole life policy works.

As you can see, the level of premium of $100 creates a cash surrender value that becomes a co-insurance or self-insurance feature. The excess over the actual yearly cost of mortality coverage in the early years will accumulate year after year. Not only are you building cash value with the extra premiums, but the insurance company credits interest on the cash value year after year. By the time the annual cost of term insurance rises so that it is more than the level premium you have been guaranteed, the interest earned on the accumulated cash value in the policy is enough to cover the difference. Thus, a whole life policy is simply a manner of paying extra premiums that are proportionately higher in later

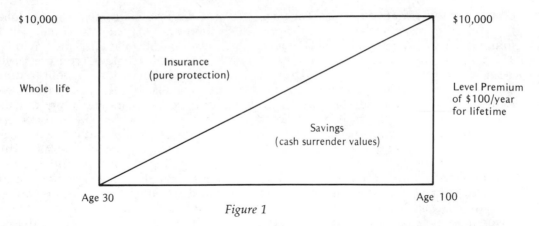

Figure 1

years. It is actually an ever changing combination of term insurance and cash value under the umbrella of a single life insurance policy. During your first year of coverage under a whole life policy, the accumulated cash value is next to nothing, so that if you should die during that year, your beneficiary would be paid out of the term insurance portion of the policy. After you have owned a whole life policy for a number of years, however, the cash value portion has increased considerably, so that the beneficiary will be paid in large part from the accumulated cash value, and in a smaller

part from term coverage. Thus, in a whole life policy where the face amount of benefits remains constant, the portion of term insurance coverage will gradually decrease as the cash value portion increases.

Once you understand rising mortality risk, term insurance, cash value, and how they combine in a whole life policy, you understand the basics of life insurance from the policyholder's point of view. The diagram of the actuarial triangle shown in Figure 2 will help you understand it from the insurance company's point of view.

The actuarial triangle has one positive

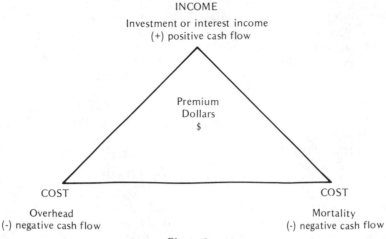

Figure 2

corner and two negative corners. The positive corner represents what *adds* to the premium dollars paid in by the policyholders. The two negative corners represent what is *subtracted* from premium dollars. The two things that can cost an insurance company money are the overhead cost, which includes commissions paid to agents, salaries paid to officers and staff, and costs of doing business such as rent, paper, printing, and postage. The mortality cost is what is paid out in death benefits. As premium dollars come in, a portion is set aside in very secure investments, such as Treasury bills, to cover the anticipated mortality for the period covered by the premium. Another portion goes to pay the overhead. Once mortality and overhead have been accounted for, the remainder is "excessive reserves." "Excess reserves" are the key to running a profitable insurance company, for it is anticipated that a good portion of those dollars *will never be paid out.*

How does this work? In most whole life policies issued before the late 1970s, the insurance company credits the policyholder interest of 3½ or 4 percent on the cash reserves being held. In the meantime, the insurance company is investing those cash reserves and receiving 8–12 percent or more. Thus, by deciding to buy a whole life policy, and paying more than is needed to cover the risk of mortality (which is what the rate of term insurance would be), you are giving the insurance company the use of your funds. The reason they can guarantee you 4 percent on your cash reserves is that they know they can obtain considerably more. This is the reason why whole life policies have been extremely popular for life insurance companies, and why they keep on promoting them with "new and improved" features.

Inflation

There is something else to take into consideration when deciding on what kind of life insurance to buy: inflation. To be sure,

term insurance will cost you more dollars per thousand in years to come, but by buying whole life insurance and paying the early years' overcharges, you are paying with today's dollars for a benefit (reduced premium rates in later years) which you will not see for years and years to come. You are paying with today's purchasing power dollars for a benefit you will receive in tomorrow's purchasing dollars. Thus, you are giving up the potential earning power for benefits you will receive at a later time in deflated values. Thus, you are giving up the potential earning power of today's dollars. The fact of the matter is, if you were disciplined enough (most people aren't, as Gus Hansch points out in Chapter 19) to take the difference in premium cost between a term policy and a whole life policy and put it in a 4 percent or 6 percent savings account, you would end up with more cash value than you would accumulate with an insurance company paying you 4 percent. And, instead of paying increasing amounts for a level benefit of term insurance, you could decrease the amount of term insurance each year by the amount you had accumulated in your own savings account, in effect avoiding the problem of ever increasing mortality costs (see Table 3).

There is a new form of life insurance, however, which in large part does this for you. It is called "universal life" and it is a kind of policy being offered by an increasing number of innovative insurance companies. But first, let's discuss some of the terms associated with the more traditional forms of life insurance.

New and Improved Life Insurance

Although life insurance in this country may have had its origins with a modest and retiring group of Presbyterian ministers, its great growth into a trillion dollar industry was the result of good old Yankee salesmanship. The many variations of policies available today grew not only out of consumer need, but also out of sales strategy. And, behind the ever more sophisticated salesmanship of life insurance agents was the ever present truth that the more dollars in excess of overhead and mortality costs you had as a company, the more profitable your company was. Thus, all the "bells and whistles" added to life insurance policies tend to have one thing in common. They all yield more premium dollars. Let's examine some of the more common features found in life insurance policies.

Endowment

The either/or policy is said to *endow* when the cash value builds up to the point where it equals the face value of the policy. A basic whole life policy endows at age 100. For example, if you purchase a whole life policy with a death benefit of $100,000, the actuaries set up the premiums so that at age 100, the cash value will equal $100,000 and the term portion will have disappeared. If you live to be 100, you receive (if you choose to) the $100,000, even though you are still alive; thus, either it is paid to a beneficiary when you die, *or* it is paid to you at the endowment year. This possibility (endowing at 100) does not excite most people because they figure that even if they are still alive, they are not going to have much fun with their $100,000 at age 100. Tell them they can buy a policy that endows at sixty-five, or fifty-five, and their ears will perk up. "You mean," the consumer might say, "if I buy this endowment policy and live to be fifty-five, I can get $100,000 in cash?" "That's right," says the agent, "or, you can keep it as a paid-up endowment policy, and never have to pay another premium."

Sounds like a great deal, doesn't it? But what does it mean to have a policy endow? It means that you have saved and paid, and paid and saved until *you* have built up a cash value equal to the face amount of

$100,000 (self-insured). All the insurance company has done is paid you 4 percent (plus possible dividends) on all the excess premiums you have deposited with them, while at the same time they have been putting your funds into Treasury bills, real estate, utility stocks, the money market funds, and the like, and earning 8–12 percent for themselves. They have been netting 6–8 percent on *your* money, while you've been earning only 4 percent in what amounts to a form of banking. Does it still sound like a great deal?

In the meantime, inflation has been going along at a rate of 8–10 percent, so you have actually been losing purchasing power on your money at the same time that the insurance company has been receiving extra income on your cash. When presented with the opportunity to purchase an endowment policy, remember that you are prepaying the total number of premium payments. You are agreeing to pay more of today's dollars for a benefit (insurance coverage in later years) that you will not receive for a long, long time. In an inflationary economy, it is *economic suicide* to pay for anything in advance. When you shorten the length of premium payments (which is all an endowment policy does for you), you increase the amount you must pay each year.

Because of the changing economics, endowment policies are rarely sold now. They were fairly popular until increasing inflation and interest rates made it clear that the only true beneficiary was the insurance company. But the basic principle that makes endowment policies unsound economically is a feature of many other types of policies that are still popular today.

Limited Payment Policies

An example would be a *limited payment* policy. A limited payment policy has the virtue of not prepaying so many early premium dollars into the insurance company coffers, but it is only a difference in degree. With a limited payment policy, you pick a date beyond which you no longer want to pay premiums. Two common examples of limited payment policies are "life paid at 65" (you pay no further premiums once you turn sixty-five) and "20 payment life" (you pay premiums only for the first twenty years of the policy). You have not prepaid so many dollars into the policy that the cash value has equaled the face value, but you have put in enough so that the interest on the cash value is enough to cover the mortality cost of a greatly reduced term portion of a whole life policy. You simply have prepaid your premiums for future years. Overpayment is what it's called. Overpayment is not desirable in an inflationary economy.

There is no magic formula in life insurance, just as there is no free lunch. For every benefit, there is a cost. In buying a limited payment policy, the benefit is that you know from a certain date that you will no longer have to write checks out to your insurance company, yet will still be covered by a whole life policy. It is easy to understand the appeal of this benefit. The salesman might say, "Listen, my friend, when you turn sixty-five and retire, all you are going to have for income is Social Security and your retirement plan. The last thing you are going to want to do is to have to write out checks to pay for life insurance.

I want you to have this limited pay policy, so you *know* that life insurance isn't going to cost you a penny after you retire!"

If you succumb to this sort of blandishment, all you agree to do is to prepay premiums, paying more each year than you would for ordinary life. Any policy that is paid up is self-funded in a shortened period of time so that the term portion is reduced and the interest income from the cash value is paying its cost.

Example:
    If a policy is to be paid up at age sixty-five, it requires approximately $7,000 for each $10,000 of face amount (see Figure 3).

The term (risk) portion of the policy, therefore, is only $3,000 (see Figure 4).

Question:
    Providing you are age sixty-five and insurable, what would a $3,000 whole life policy cost?

Answer:
    Approximateloy $65 for each $1,000, or $195.

Some simple arithmetic will show that if you were to withdraw the $7,000 (surrender your cash value) and invest in a safe guaranteed account earning a modest 6 percent, you would receive $420 per year in earnings. This $420 would enable you to buy $420 divided by $65 per $1,000 = $6,461 of insurance. Your total death benefit would then be your savings account of

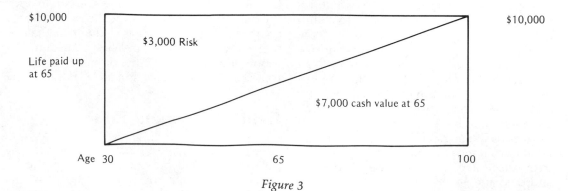

Figure 3

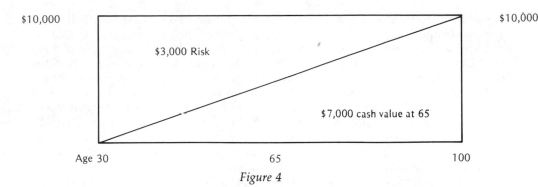

Figure 4

$7,000 plus your insurance of $6,461, or a total of $13,461 instead of the $10,000 you now have. Paid-up insurance is one of the costliest forms of buying protection.

Many insurance agents, financial counselors, and investment brokers are making themselves heroes to their clients by doing just this—showing how they can make better use of their assets through repositioning their insurance coverage. The process is called replacement, or sometimes twisting. Either is a dirty word to many of our largest old-line insurance companies carrying billions of dollars in limited payment policies bought five, ten, or fifteen years ago since they are ever conscious of their loss if policies are replaced.

Yet, if a limited pay policy is a bad deal at sixty-five, it is also a bad deal at any age. The fact remains the same: you are paying more of today's dollars than necessary for the coverage sought in order to swiftly build up cash values upon which you are earning only 4 percent. If you believe that inflation is going to be a factor over the period of time of a limited payment policy, why give up the time value (or, earning potential over time) of your money for the years the insurance company will be holding the cash? Why not just buy a normal whole life policy ("paid up age 100") and put the premium dollars saved in a bank, money market fund, or real estate? Better yet, why not buy term and put the premium savings elsewhere?

Knowing about whole life, endowment, limited payment life, and term will give you a clear perspective of the products that are available. Many other different types of insurance policies or methods of selling them are available for the most part in combinations of one form we've covered. You'll hear such names as:

Deposit term
Modified whole life
Graded premium whole life
Disappearing premium
Premium offset
Return of cash value
Minimum deposit
Revertible term
Joint whole life
Contingent life

and many more. All of these have particular benefits and you should investigate them thoroughly before buying one.

Participating (Par or Mutual) vs. Nonparticipating (Nonpar or Stock)

Once you've found the product you think is right for your needs and your budget, then the question will inevitably come up: Do you buy par (participating) insurance that pays dividends to the policyholder or do you buy nonpar, stock company insurance that does not pay dividends to policyholders but rather to stockholders? One can find sound reasons for buying either, yet the majority of life insurance sold in this century has been par insurance. The concept of par insurance is that you, the policyholder, share with other policyholders in the profits of the life insurance company. To whatever extent this profit is yours, the policyholder will receive a "dividend." In order to assure that a reasonable dividend can be maintained, the par company deliberately overcharges 25–40 percent per year (see Table 2). This overcharge is paid back to the policyholder over a period of years as a dividend, but since it is not a true dividend, it is not taxed.

A mutual company has no stockholders—they have only policyholders to whom to pay dividends. They have no obligation to pay dividends. However, they use the term *dividends* in their marketing of participating policies, not because there is any semblance between *the return of deliberate overcharges* which they *call* dividends and the real dividends that are paid to stockholders of a profitable company, but because it creates the illusion of the investment growth normally associated with owning stock. Although the distinction between dividends of a mutual insurance company and the real dividends of a stock company is not always made clear when the salesman is making his pitch, the insurance companies did make it clear to the IRS. When the IRS took note of the word dividend in these policies and decided that if dividends were being paid, they ought to be taxed, this is what was revealed by the life companies: according to the United States Treasury Department Decision No. 1743: reduced to understandable analysis, the contentions of the various companies are:

That dividends declared by participating companies are not dividends in a commercial sense of the word, but are simply refunds to the policyholder of a portion of the overcharge collected, which overcharge is merely held in trust by the company issuing the policy. Annually, or at stated periods, all, or a portion thereof, is returned to the person holding the policy. . . . It was vigorously contended by counsel representing certain of these companies that it was necessary in order to secure new business, to convince the prospective policyholder of the desirability of the same, and that this commercial necessity had resulted in the companies making misrepresentations of facts as to dividends to prospective purchasers of insurance, and that names and designations, having a single specific meaning in the commercial world and which were therefore attractive to prospective policyholders, had been adopted to represent transactions which they now hold are entirely different from what their name im-

Table 2. Comparative Annual Whole Life Premiums
(Par and Nonpar)

ISSUE AGE	WHOLE LIFE (PAR)	WHOLE LIFE (NONPAR)	AMOUNT OF OVERCHARGE	PERCENTAGE OVERCHARGE
20	$13.60	$ 9.04	$ 4.56	50
25	15.72	11.09	4.63	42
30	18.35	13.16	5.19	39
35	21.67	16.11	5.56	35
40	25.94	19.74	6.20	31
45	31.45	23.45	7.00	29
50	38.69	30.50	8.19	27
55	48.35	38.61	9.74	25
60	61.60	49.53	12.07	24

plies and represents, and from which the policyholder himself believed he was receiving and that business necessities had caused a continuance of these misnomers. *It was represented that, in fact, there were no dividends, but merely a refund of overcharge, which for reasons above stated, were usually referred to as dividends.*

If you bought a par and a nonpar policy for the same amount at the same time, you would pay about 25 percent higher premiums for the par policy. If all went according to plan (remember, dividends are not guaranteed), you would start receiving dividends after the second year, which could be used to reduce your premium payments. It could be up to the thirteenth year that the dividends would reduce payments to the level of the nonpar policy, and not until the twentieth to twenty-second year that "crossover" would occur. Crossover is the point at which the total cash outlay for both policies is equal. In other words, you have given up use of some of your premium dollars for *up to twenty-two years!*

However, the average time a policy is in force, according to industry averages, is seven years. Thus, most are cancelled or paid out years before the break-even point is reached. And, if that weren't enough, there is no certainty that planned dividends will actually be paid, as we see later in this chapter. A terminology familiar to investors is used to sell policies to people who perhaps may not be investors. The wise insurance buyer will think twice and ask a number of questions before signing an application for a participating policy.

Accidental Death Benefit

Double and triple indemnity has a nice ring to it. Not only are you covered, but you are doubly covered if death occurs by accident, and triply covered if accidental death is by common carrier (public transport such as plane, train, bus, or taxi). It costs just a few dollars more for double and triple

indemnity. The sales agent may say to you, "Well, I don't know, Bob, with your job, you're on the road a lot. Accidents do happen. I know your wife will sleep easier nights when you're away if you have this double and triple indemnity rider."

A few things should be considered before agreeing to such a benefit. The first is, why will the needs of your survivors be twice as great if your death is accidental, and three times as great if the accident is caused by common carrier? If the original death benefit of your policy is based on real needs, why pay extra for additional coverage? The next thing to consider is the policy's definition of accidental death. If you look, you will usually find a rigid definition using a phrase such as "violent external means." This definition excludes death by heart attack while shoveling snow (a common type of accidental death) as well as many instances of accidental poisoning (such as the gradual buildup of job-related toxins).

Double and triple indemnity riders are extremely profitable for life insurance companies—and they do not deny this. Accidental death, particularly as defined in the policies, is extemely rare. This is another example of an emotional sale. "Should (God forbid) an accident occur, and should your wife be left alone after identifying the remains, at least she'll have double indemnity. It's only an extra $13.00 per year."

What you are buying with such an add-on, or rider, is an accident policy. If your work is truly hazardous, you would be well advised to buy a regular accident policy from an insurance company that specializes in them. The cost might be slightly higher per $1,000 of coverage, but the definition of accidents would be much broader. Or, if you want extra coverage in case of accident, you might consider an additional term policy, covering death for any reason. Where a double indemnity rider on a whole life policy might cost $1.20 per $1,000, and cover only extremely unusual means of death, an extra term insurance policy might cost only about $1.50 per $1,000, and cover death from any cause. This is the type of advice you have a right to expect from your financial planner and what makes him or her well worth any fee or commission paid.

Waiver of Premium

Another common add-on to whole life policies is the *waiver-of-premium* rider. With this rider, your ongoing premiums will be paid in the event that you are disabled and unable to perform any gainful occupation. A waiver-of-premium rider is actually a form of disability insurance—enough to cover the relatively small (compared to the total annual living expenses) cost of policy premiums. This rider might often be sold to those who are not aware they can buy disability insurance in a separate policy from a company that specializes in disability insurance. If you buy a regular disability policy, you will be covered if you cannot work in your regular occupation. With a waiver-of-premium rider you are covered only if you cannot perform any gainful occupation. ("We know you were a concert pianist and lost both hands, Mr. Jones. You can still use your toes to dial and get into telephone sales. Sorry!") Telephone selling is a gainful occupation.

The cost of a waiver-of-premium rider is generally very small, and many agents insist upon adding it in good faith because nothing could be worse for them than to witness a disabled client have coverage lapse because of nonpayment of premiums. Again, an astute consumer who had other disability coverage might think twice before buying this add-on.

Nonforfeiture Values

Nonforfeiture values are guaranteed options for use of the accumulated cash value in a whole life policy. In essence, the non-

forfeiture clauses of a life insurance policy are lapsed or surrendered. This means that if you should decide to cancel the policy, the cash values accumulated will be surrendered to you. Another common nonforfeiture item is the reduced paid-up policy option. This is the right to stop paying premiums and convert the accumulated cash value to a paid-up policy for as much as the cash value will cover, according to established rates. (See previous examples of paid-up policy.)

Other nonforfeiture items include: the right to use cash value to pay ongoing premiums for as long as it lasts; the right to borrow cash value at a predetermined interest rate; and an automatic-premium-loan provision that automatically makes a loan from cash value to pay premiums should any regular payments be missed. These nonforfeiture options for use of cash value by law are spelled out in the policy. Read them carefully and ask questions about any nonforfeiture items you do not clearly understand.

Coupons

Certain kinds of life insurance policies can only be described as gimmick policies. The *cash coupon* policy falls into this category. Investors familiar with bonds know that with some, coupons must be periodically clipped and mailed to the trustee bank in order to get the interest payments. A cash coupon policy is a life insurance policy made to look like a bond. The coupon on this policy entitles you to receive, for instance, $150 on the coupon date. What this means is that a year earlier you paid in $244.75, of which $100 covered the life insurance policy; the other $144.75 is given back to you with 3½ percent interest. Thus a cash coupon policy is nothing but a gimmick that enables a life insurance company to borrow extra cash from you at a very favorable interest rate. Moreover, many policyholders neglect to clip coupons, giving even longer use of funds to the carrier.

Pure Endowment

A *pure endowment* policy is a cash coupon policy without the actual coupons. It is nothing more than putting up $96 at the beginning of the year and at the end of the year getting back $100. It's easy to find insurers willing to sell you pure endowment riders to your policy because as long as *they* can earn 10–20 percent on *your* money, it's pure profit for them. Pure endowment commonly comes in the form of "five-year pure endowment" or "ten-year pure endowment" and may be offered as an add-on to many life insurance policies.

Some life insurance companies are today selling a form of pure endowment life insurance to unsuspecting juniors and seniors in college. A team of agents will rent rooms in a college town, install phones, and begin calling students. Usually they recruit star athletes and student leaders as supplementary salespeople. Many fall victim to the pitch about "getting started early on insurance" and "building for the future." What these creative marketers actually induce naive students to do is go into *debt*. They arrange financing for the students for $200 to $300 for the first year's premiums, and the student pays interest only until year three. Then, the premium schedule is steep enough over years three through five so that the cash value buildup is adequate to pay off the loan by the sixth year (a form of pure endowment).

If a young person for some reason feels he needs life insurance, he should compare the cost of buying renewable term insurance for the same period of time. These dollars paid into the policy to create this pure endowment to pay back the loan, could be used more wisely, and he would have just as much coverage on his life.

Return of Premium

Another rider frequently offered is *return of premium*. What this add-on offers is that your beneficiary will receive not only the face value of the policy, but a refund of all the premiums paid in, too. This is nothing but an extra little life insurance policy sold on top of a normal one. You may be sure that such an add-on costs you more premium dollars. It does not make a whole life policy any better, but sometimes it makes it easier to sell.

Whole Life/Dividend Option Policies

Extra ordinary life or *"economatic"* are brand names for another kind of gimmick policy. This policy should more descriptively be called a whole life dividend option policy. It works like this: you buy a policy that initially consists of 30 percent term insurance and 70 percent whole life. For the first number of years, according to the formula that the company uses, your policy begins to yield dividends that pay the increasing cost of the term portion of the policy. Dividends in excess of what is needed to cover the increasing term costs go to buy additional amounts of paid-up whole life coverage, which gradually reduce the term portion. By the twentieth year, or so, you cross over, meaning that 30 percent of the policy is entirely paid up from this point on, and the excess dividends are used to buy more paid-up premiums, gradually increasing the face value of the policy.

Here's the catch with this kind of policy. For the first twenty years (if that's the formula selected), the declared death benefits are guaranteed, whether or not dividends are paid (remember, "dividends" are never guaranteed). But at the end of this twenty-year period, if dividends have not been paid, the face value of the policy reverts to the 70 percent figure that was the whole life portion at the beginning. In other words, once you approach the age when you are more likely to die, if the company has not been paying dividends, you may suddenly find yourself with less coverage than you thought. The salesman will assure you that dividends always have been paid in the past, but the plain truth is that many companies may soon be in a position where they may be unable to pay dividends as projected (see Summary).

Minimum Deposit

Minimum deposit (or *minidip*) policies are often marketed to high tax bracket individuals as a form of tax shelter. Artificially high initial premiums are paid, building up an unusually large initial cash value, which is then borrowed out of the policy to be reinvested, while the interest for these loans is made into a tax-deductible item.

These can be questionable from an economic standpoint, and although a salesman might approach you with a convincing array of computer printouts that "prove" how much money you are going to make, it is important to remember that the extraordinarily high initial premiums make an extraordinarily high commission for the agent. The IRS has ruled against deducting the interest in some forms of mini-dip, and it is easy to find more sensible things to do with your money. The key to not buying a minidip is an economic truism stating that any time you borrow money to pay for anything, you increase the cost of what you've bought.

Universal Life

A relatively new form of life insurance that has some of the advantages of term and whole life, without some of the disadvantages of each, is Universal Life.

It has often been said that if you could buy a life insurance policy based on low mortality rates and a cash accumulation side fund that paid competitive interest rates, it would be an ideal policy from the consumer's point of view.

James Anderson, FSA, a progressive professional actuary who has seen the effectiveness of traditional forms of life insurance decline over the last twenty years, first promoted the concept of Universal Life in 1975. Hutton Life was the first company to offer the product to the public in 1978, and now over one hundred companies are marketing this product. Until 1982, however, there were still some unresolved issues regarding the tax aspects of the product.

TEFRA (Tax Equity and Fiscal Responsibility Act of 1982) has cleared up the questions concerning Univeral Life. TEFRA places some limits on the cash value relative to death benefit that the contract can accumulate, but basically has removed the doubts of the skeptics regarding the legitimacy of the product.

Many of the "old line" companies that once opposed Universal Life are now in the process of creating their own versions of the product, in order to remain competitive in the marketplace.

Flexibility of Universal Life

Universal life is a policy that puts the consumer in the driver's seat. It is renewable and adjustable monthly, without penalty, so that you can change coverage at will, taking into consideration your overall financial circumstances, alternative investments available to you, and inflation. The policy is made up of a term portion and a cash accumulation portion. You pay low-cost per $1,000 term rates for the face amount of coverage you choose each month. Any amount you choose to contribute in addition to the cost of term coverage goes into the cash accumulation fund. The unique feature here is that not only are you guaranteed a return of 4 percent on the cash value, as with a whole life policy, but you are actually paid a rate of return greatly in excess of that, which varies up and down each month with the prime rate or economic conditions. The actual rates of return on universal life cash accumulation accounts have been running in the neighborhood of 11–14 percent. As with whole life policies, the interest paid on the cash value compounds tax-free. Taxes are payable only if you withdraw from the fund more than you have paid in premiums.

You have a number of options with universal life. You can have the death benefit of the term portion decrease periodically by the amount of increase in the cash value account, making the overall level of benefits rise with the increase in the cash account. Upon death, the beneficiary is paid both the current amount of term coverage plus the accumulated cash account, all exempt from income tax (although subject to estate taxes).

One option that motivates people to purchase universal life is, after the cash accumulation portion has built up to a sufficient degree, the policy will pay the premiums of the term coverage out of the income from the cash account. In this way, one is buying insurance protection with pretax dollars, a considerable savings over having to use taxed dollars (you may have to earn up to $2 to net $1 after tax in a 50 percent bracket, for example).

Perhaps the most attractive feature is that none of your decisions about what to do with a universal life policy is permanent. You can stop paying premiums whenever you choose, and the carrier will take them out of the cash account. You can start paying them again whenever you want. You can withdraw cash whenever you want, and pay no taxes on it as long as you withdraw less than you have paid in premiums. You can borrow against the cash value whenever you want, at an interest rate of 6–8 percent.

With every premium payment you make, that is, whenever you add new dollars from your other income to a universal life policy, deductions are made for a sales charge (commission) and management fees and mortality (term) costs. The remainder is credited to the cash account. You are sent a periodic statement, just as with a brokerage house or bank, which itemizes all costs, fees, mortality coverage, total credit to the cash account, and total interest payments.

Although Universal Life in its present form offers the buyer many advantages heretofore not available, innovators will continue to improve the product in its second, third, and fourth generations. With its flexibility and tax advantages, a Universal Life policy should be considered as part of a long-term financial plan.

How Safe Are Life Insurance Companies?

A number of things affect the profitability and the financial security of life insurance companies. As we saw in the diagram of the premium triangle (Figure 2), there are two drains on premium dollars: mortality payments and overhead. Over the years, one factor that has proven extremely profitable for life insurance companies is the use of outdated mortality tables. You should be aware that the life expectancy of Americans has increased in the past fifty years as we have made progress in health, nutrition, and medicine. Actuarial tables used to establish premiums for pure mortality coverage have traditionally been many years out of date. For example, the American Experience Table established in the late 1800s was used until 1941. Its statistical averages were based on years when medicine was extremely primitive by today's standards. The average deaths per thousand on twenty-year-olds were set at 7.80 per thousand. Yet, this mortality table

Table 3. Deaths per 1000 in Three Statutory Mortality Tables

AGE	AMERICAN EXPERIENCE TABLE	COMMIS- SIONERS' 1941 TABLE	COMMIS- SIONERS' 1958 TABLE	EXPECTATION OF LIFE 1958 TABLE IN YEARS
20	7.80	2.43	1.79	50.37
21	7.86	2.51	1.83	49.46
22	7.91	2.59	1.86	48.55
23	7.96	2.68	1.89	47.64
24	8.01	2.77	1.91	46.73
25	8.06	2.88	1.93	45.82
26	8.13	2.99	1.96	44.90
27	8.20	3.11	1.99	43.99
28	8.26	3.25	2.03	43.08
29	8.34	3.40	2.08	42.16
30	8.43	3.56	2.13	41.25
31	8.51	3.73	2.19	40.34
32	8.61	3.92	2.25	39.43
33	8.72	4.12	2.32	38.51
34	8.83	4.35	2.40	37.60
35	8.95	4.59	2.51	36.69
36	9.09	4.86	2.64	35.78
37	9.23	5.15	2.80	34.88
38	9.41	5.46	3.01	33.97
39	9.59	5.81	3.25	33.07
40	9.79	6.18	3.53	32.18
41	10.01	6.59	3.84	31.29
42	10.25	7.03	4.17	30.41
43	10.52	7.51	4.53	29.54
44	10.83	8.04	4.92	28.67
45	11.16	8.61	5.35	27.81
46	11.56	9.23	5.83	26.95
47	12.00	9.91	6.36	26.11
48	12.51	10.64	6.95	25.27
49	13.11	11.45	7.60	24.45
50	13.78	12.32	8.32	23.63
51	14.54	13.27	9.11	22.82
52	15.39	14.30	9.96	22.03
53	16.33	15.43	10.89	21.25
54	17.40	16.65	11.90	20.47
55	18.57	17.98	13.00	19.71
56	19.89	19.43	14.21	18.97
57	21.34	21.00	15.24	18.23
58	22.94	22.71	17.00	17.51
59	24.72	24.57	18.59	16.81
60	26.69	26.59	20.34	16.13

was used to fix premium rates up through 1940, when the death rate per thousand twenty-year-olds had descended to 2.43. Similarly, the Commissioners' 1941 Table, which reflected the death rate in this country before the introduction of penicillin, was used until the 1958 table was adopted. Table 3 shows the difference in mortality expectations for these different tables.

By charging premiums based on outdated mortality expectations in spite of dividend increases, life insurance companies have been far ahead on the mortality corner of the triangle. They've charged premiums based on a much higher rate of death than actually occurred during the years covered by their policies. Thus, they have never come close to using up their basic mortality reserves. Life companies will argue that dividends reduce this excess and by paying dividends, this difference was reduced. A comparison of old policies and new has proved this is not so in most cases.

Overhead, however, has not been as kind to life companies, who have experienced inflation along with the rest of us. But, because the life insurance business has tended to be extremely profitable, the companies have not been under pressure to streamline their operations. Life companies tend to be rather staff-heavy, and many have been slow to take advantage of the efficiencies offered by computer technology. This lack of imagination is cutting into their profits in today's time of high inflation and they have found it costly to catch up.

In the third corner of the premium triangle there is a delicate balance in the operations of life insurance companies. High interest rates have meant that life insurers have been able to get a good return on investment dollars like everyone else. However, high interest rates have also created two very important negatives. One is that as interest rates have shot up, the resale values of bonds held in their portfolios have dropped. If they have to sell the bonds in today's markets, they get only a percentage of face value. Thus, many insurance companies cannot liquidate reserves without having an adverse effect on the balance of their assets and liabilities. This would be all right if they did not need those funds, but there is another factor at play.

Potential Loans

Many life companies are carrying millions of dollars of cash value in policies with the insured's having the nonforfeiture right to borrow on cash value at rates of 5–8 percent. Knowing that money can be safely invested currently at 10–12 percent or more, thousands of savvy, whole life policyholders have taken advantage of their nonforfeiture clause, borrowed on cash values at 5–6 percent, then reinvested at a higher rate. Where are the insurance companies getting the cash to pay out these policy loans? They cannot sell their old bonds, for to do so would require that they take a loss. Many companies have only one alternative—to borrow, at current high interest rates of 12–14 percent only to lend it out to policyholders at the guaranteed low nonforfeiture rates of 5 percent or 6 percent.

The process of disintermediation of cash value reserves is already costing the insurance industry millions of dollars of interest each *month*. More than $50 billion has already been drawn out on policy loans. What concerns companies more than anything is that billions of dollars of cash value qualified for nonforfeiture policy loans have not yet been tapped. If the prime rate goes up to 20–25 percent, and if word spreads about how easy it is to borrow on a whole life policy and reinvest at a much higher rate of return, authorities think it could mean technical insolvency for many life companies.

Virtually any knowledgeable financial

planner or conscientious agent will point out that an excessive negative cash flow in the industry could have impact on dividend payments. This is the reason why consumers should be leery of expecting increased dividends from a policy. Any insurance policy in which described benefits are contingent on dividends (such as minimum deposit) being paid could be vulnerable. Not only the ability to pay dividends, but the very survival of many companies depends on the *vagaries* of the prime rate. In other words, when policyholders realize they can borrow at 6–8 percent and get a guaranteed return of 10–15 percent elsewhere on their policies, do you think they will do it?

Summary

Life insurance is not absolutely risk-free. Consumers should be cautious. There is no easy way for a consumer to know about the relative solvency of different insurers. The life industry has no GAP (generally accepted practice) of accounting. Real estate and other assets may be carried on the books at purchase value, depreciated value, or estimated current market value. Several nationally prominent companies participated in the ownership of many Braniff jets. These planes certainly caused concern to those companies whose assets were invested in this troubled airline equipment.

Because of these conditions, you should base your life insurance purchases on the assumption that there might be risk. When assessing cash value, be aware that most policies state in the fine print that even nonforfeiture policy loans can be delayed up to six months. Be aware that projected dividend payments may not be met. You should review your life insurance policies annually, just as you should review your stock portfolio or other assets. Your insur-

ance agent or financial planner should "shop" for you, comparing the rates of your current policies with those of other companies offering similar coverage (this has been difficult for many life agents who work for only one company). You should at least occasionally compare their recommendation with those of a financial planner or an independent life agent. If your agent cannot or will not shop for you, find a new agent or financial planner.

You, as a consumer in a free market economy, must take responsibility for comparison shopping if you are to get the most value for dollars spent. You surely do this when you buy groceries or a new car. Before you go to the store or dealer, you think carefully about what your needs are. You may write them down. As you walk the aisles of the grocery store, you compare prices and quantities before you put a desired item in your cart—or you should. At the auto dealer, you examine the list of options and the tested mileage per gallon, then take a test drive, and even then do not make a decision until you have compared other makes of cars.

You should exercise the same care and caution in purchasing insurance. First, with help from your financial planner or agent, you should determine how much life insurance coverage you need, and why. Then you should think about what kind of policies are best for you, whether renewable term, whole life, or one of the universal life policies. As you talk over your life insurance needs with a qualified professional, you should keep in mind that these are but one part of your long-term financial plan. When you know exactly what kind of coverage you desire, you should then begin comparison shopping among the policies offered by several companies. You should question any add-ons or riders offered that were not part of your original plan.

Properly understood and used as a part of comprehensive financial planning, life insurance can be of tremendous value to you. Be skeptical of anyone who offers the solution to your needs without first determining your individual situation or potential problems. It is, therefore, mandatory that as an individual with specific requirements, you seek help from a well recommended financial planner or agent. Be wary of either who offers the solution without first knowing the problem.

Chapter 14

Saving on Home, Auto, and Casualty Insurance

Dave Goodwin

Dave Goodwin is one of the nation's leading consumerists in all forms of insurance. After being in the insurance business for ten years, he sold his agency, and for the last twenty-two years has served as consultant to both buyers and sellers of insurance. He has taught at the University of Miami, served on the Consumer Advocate's Advisory Board, served on the Florida legislature's Ad Hoc Committee on Automobile Insurance, testified by invitation before state legislative bodies, and addressed the Consumer Participation Subcommittee on the National Association of Insurance Commissioners. He is author of *Stop Wasting Your Insurance Dollars*, and of the syndicated newspaper column, "Insurance for Consumers." He was insurance editor of *Boardroom Reports* and his work has appeared in numerous consumer publications. He has appeared on radio and television shows nationwide as an insurance expert and is a frequent podium speaker. Goodwin has been a member of the Board of Regents, College for Financial Planning, an auto section committeeman of the American Risk and Insurance Association, and chairman of the insurance committee of the Miami Beach Taxpayers' Association.

Assume nothing.
Shop.
Keep alert to changes.
ASK

The way to save many thousands of dollars and avoid much grief is to ASK. In property-casualty insurance (as in life-health insurance), if you follow the acronym's principles, you can obtain much better coverages at lower premiums. In some cases, you will be paid for occurrences that might otherwise be uninsured; you will avoid buying policies in companies on the brink of bankruptcy; you will have the benefit of leverage; and you will enjoy one of the greatest dividends any insurance program can provide—the peace of mind that comes with the knowledge that your insurance was built on an intelligently conceived and executed plan.

This chapter discusses home, auto, miscellaneous personal coverages (such as jewelry, hobby, boat, and so on) and some basic business insurance concepts. Cumulatively, your entire fortune—everything you own—plus everything you do and say, falls under the domain of property-casualty (p-c) insurance. Proper coverage is vital to your financial well-being. Many a financial whiz has been devastated by an insurance program that left him vulnerable to lawsuits or other catastrophes that were improperly, or insufficiently, or not at all insured. Many more—perhaps you—are just as poorly insured but won't realize it until they're either hit with a loss that exposes their insurance flaws, or have their insurance picture professionally reviewed, and regularly rereviewed.

Home

If you don't keep your home insurance attuned to inflation, you may find after a loss that the policy you faithfully maintained will leave you painfully short of replacing your loss. An annual review of insurance values is therefore important, and it can be an easy routine exercised about two months before your homeowner's policy is due for renewal. This review should focus on three basic elements of your homeowner's policy: the building, its contents, and liability. If you don't own the building, your renter's or condominium policy covers only the latter two components.

Building

You should first estimate the area of your dwelling (if you don't already know it) by checking your floor plans or calling your architect. Or, you can draw a rough diagram and pace off each dimension. If the dwelling is multilevel, show each floor separately. Label each section of the house by its construction, for example, frame, brick, masonry and so on. Then identify and diagram each section's roof covering, for example, tar paper and gravel, shingle, flat tile, or barrel tile. With the help of your insurance agent or a builder, you can compute today's replacement cost. Keep the diagram for future uses, and enter each year's replacement cost data.

Next, with your insurance adviser, list all the permanently attached items, fixtures, or appliances that are also insured as part of the building, and estimate their replacement cost. You should now have a figure representing today's cost of replacing your dwelling, excluding the land and foundation.

It is very important that you insure your dwelling to at least 80 percent of its replacement cost at the time of a loss. If it's insured for less than that, you will suffer penalties in your adjustment in two ways:

1. Depreciation will be calculated and marked off.

2. Co-insurance will be calculated and, like it or not, you will find yourself acting as a partial self-insurer.

Insuring to at least 80 percent of replacement cost *at the time of loss*—those last five words are the key—removes depreciation and co-insurance factors from your claim check. It's your obligation, not your insurer's, to keep abreast of inflation.

We recommend that you insure the building to 100 percent of its replacement cost. Not only will you be fully covered in case of total loss, but in the event of a partial loss you will have a comfortable margin to be sure that galloping inflation doesn't push you under the 80 percent co-insurance minimum.

Further, you can write your agent or insurer (and keep a copy with the policy, away from the house) asking for recommendations on how much you should carry. This could give you a strong moral argument if you're allegedly underinsured at claim time—assuming, of course, that you followed the advice you received.

Contents

Many agents offer free household inventory forms. Make a room-by-room inventory, estimating the cost of each item when new, its age, and its present replacement cost. A department-store catalog might help price your things. List everything—furniture, rugs, drapes, clothing—except for the scheduled items discussed below.

Calculate the value of your contents in two ways: (1) its replacement cost at today's prices; and (2) actual cash value (ACV), which is replacement cost minus depreciation. Now discuss your options with your insurance adviser. Some companies offer policies that will not deduct depreciation on a contents claim, in effect letting you profit from a loss by getting new contents to replace the old, much the same as new-for-old coverage on the building. As in insuring the building, you're supposed to carry enough contents coverage to reflect replacement costs in order to qualify for full replacement coverage.

Note, however, that inflated costs are a key figure whether you elect full replacement or ACV coverage, with depreciation. Don't feel that you can ignore coverage reviews, or inflation, just because your contents are (or aren't) aging gracefully. Replacement costs and inflation are always involved in any claim. Keeping current values insured is always important.

Scheduled Items

Jewelry, furs, silverware, fine arts, cameras, sport equipment, valuable hobby items such as stamp or coin collections are some—but by no means all—of the types of items that should be separately listed and insured for stated amounts. Current appraisals are essential here. With recent meteoric rises and dips in the price of diamonds, gold, silver, stamps, art, and other valuables, it is advisable to have appraisals made even more often than once a year on items that undergo sharp changes in value, up or down. If you're *underinsured* because of a rise in value, you're co-insuring; if you're *overinsured* because of a drop in value, you're wasting premium.

In appraising gold, silver, precious and semiprecious stones, try to have wholesale values shown and insured. Your premium will be lower than retail-based values, but in effect the coverage will be the same, since carriers have the option of replacing the lost item (which they usually prefer) in lieu of making a cash settlement.

Since the appraisal description is the basis for replacing an item, it is important that jewelry appraisals reveal a gem's good points, such as clarity, color, cut, lack of flaws, and the like. Weight and size alone on an appraisal will likely leave you shortchanged on a loss settlement.

Liability

Many people are careful to increase liability coverages on auto policies, yet their personal (nonauto) liability limits remain unchanged for decades.

Inflation demands that you carry high limits. If a neighbor's child is hurt and you're sued, part of the claim will be based on medical expenses, one of the fastest rising categories in the world of consumerism. Or if a neighbor's roof is burned because of your negligence, for example, the claim will reflect the soaring cost of construction.

Seven-figure liability awards are common now. You should consider carrying an umbrella (catastrophe) liability policy providing additional coverage of $1 million or more per claim. The policy supplements (but does not replace) your coverages on auto, homeowner's, boat, aircraft, and other nonbusiness liability exposures. Relatively few insurers offer the policy, and you may find premium variations from about $100 per year to as much as $500 for the same, or even an inferior, policy.

Space does not permit a discussion of the coverages offered by the various homeowner's package policies. Many insurers and agents offer brochures describing coverages and exclusions, and it is best to review them for generalities. Then ask your insurance adviser to discuss every possible alternative that may apply to you, including changes in deductibles, coverage for additional cash, flood, or earthquake. Then ask about premium credits for smoke or burglar alarms, fireproofed lumber in your house, or even for the age of your home if it's less than ten years old.

Auto

Automobile insurance relates to both the car and the driver. Many steps can take you to a better insurance policy at lower rates. Here are some:

You

Drive defensively; avoid tickets and accidents. Fight defensible tickets because each conviction costs heavily in premium and may keep you from getting insured in a top company.

Be careful in letting others drive your car. Your insurance record may be tainted with their driving sins.

Reduce your mileage if you can. Consider taking public transportation, walking for short trips, car pooling, and the like.

Don't leave packages in the car; put them in the trunk. Always lock the car and take the keys with you. Park in high-visibility, well-trafficked and well-lighted spots.

Your Car

Before buying a car, ask your insurer for the names of makes and models that are surcharged. Generally these would be the fiberglass, flashy, lavish, extra-expensive, hot-rod, superpowered or accident-prone models, or those comparatively expensive to repair.

Keep it clean and safe.

Consider antitheft devices and check for credits.

Premium and Rating Factors

Consider leasing a car with insurance provided, especially if you have a bad driving record. Warning: the coverages and quality of the carrier should be carefully checked. Obtain written assurance from the agent or carrier that you'll be notified in writing if any insurance changes occur.

If you own a business, consider having the business own and insure your personally used car. Also ask the insurer if you can get the lower personal rate.

If you own more than one car, insure them all with the same company. You'll get a discount on one or both and you'll avoid disputes between companies on certain claims.

Check on having your auto policy in the same company that insures your home. You'll avoid borderline claims and disputes between companies, and you may save premium. A few companies package home and auto coverages.

If you buy an additional car during a policy period, ask what free coverage your policy offers. You may have a free thirty-day period of protection.

Notify your insurer immediately when (1) you move, (2) you sell or replace a car, (3) the use of your car changes from business to nonbusiness, or from drive-to-work to pleasure-only, (4) your child or any other driver involving a higher premium moves from your home, marries, leaves for school, joins the service, or stops using your car.

If your policy carries a surcharge for any driver's age or marital status, have reductions made effective the day that status changes to a lower rated category. Don't wait for the next policy billing or anniversary date.

If you're surcharged for a driver's ticket or accident record, ask your agent to send a copy of the record to you so that you can check for its accuracy. You shouldn't pay for another driver's bumbles that may have been put on your record in error.

As soon as a ticket or accident "ages out,"— usually it takes three to five years—ask your insurer whether it pays to have the policy rewritten at a lower premium.

Pointedly and specifically ask about all discounts offered. Insurers vary greatly as to what they recognize for credits, and how much credit they grant for a given factor.

The Insurance

Find out about every kind of coverage available. You may not need or want all, but any kind of protection you don't carry should be an omission based on knowledge, not on ignorance.

Obtain an informed opinion about the financial strength of your carrier. Some companies will fail. Don't depend too much on state guaranty funds or other possibilities as a rationale to buy from a shaky company.

Call your state insurance commissioner's office about the number of lawsuits filed against the insurer you're considering. For a rough measurement of how tough or unreasonable a carrier is on claims, compare the number of lawsuit actions against other carriers for each $1 million of premiums written. An exceptionally high number might indicate trouble ahead; shop.

Ask for a twelve-month policy in favor of a six-month policy, if possible, so that you'll be hit somewhat later with rate increases.

Ask about premium financing. Some companies allow six to ten months to pay, with only token interest. But be careful: some interest rates are hefty.

Consider higher deductibles on collision and comprehensive coverages.

If your physical damage policy is written for more than twelve months when you are financing your car, be sure you're getting lower rates beyond the twelfth month; some raters forget to calculate the age factor.

If you want or need towing coverage, consider getting it from an auto club instead of your auto policy. Even a single, small, nondriving, not-at-fault claim may lead to cancellation.

If your car is not to be driven for at least thirty consecutive days, ask your agent in advance about suspension of liability coverages, but not of physical damage coverages. Be sure to notify the agent before anyone drives the car again.

Do not expect to use your policy for small

first-party (that is, nonliability) claims, particularly if the charges are around the amount of the deductible.

In case of accident or loss, report the claim to police and to the insurer. Do it promptly. Record the names and addresses of witnesses, and make your own notes while waiting for police.

Keep receipts for improvements or extraordinary expenses to your car(s). They'll help you obtain a better settlement for damage claims.

When planning an auto trip through other states, ask your agent if your coverage is adequate for each state. If you plan to drive in Mexico or abroad, get insurance information well in advance.

Have your agent make up a premium calendar showing the month and day on which each of your policies must be paid. This is a budgeting aid, but even more important, it is an easy way to guard against unintentional lapse. Auto policies have no grace period; don't assume you'll be insured without payment.

The purpose of auto insurance, like that of homeowner's, boat, life, medical, or any other coverage, is to prevent serious financial loss. It serves its purpose whether or not you have claims. It is not an investment. Don't feel that you should have claims in order to get your money's worth. You're better off carrying sensible protection and never having to use it.

Where to Get Your Insurance

A few decades ago, the insurance marketplace was relatively uncomplicated. You could buy policies from direct writers (companies like Allstate, State Farm, Liberty Mutual) whose agents were limited to selling the policies of their single carrier, or you could buy from independent agents (entrepreneurs representing several car-

riers such as Aetna, the Travelers, Kemper Group). You could buy over the counter, over your kitchen table, or through the mail, and generally property-casualty insurance was sold separately from life-health policies.

Now, for better or for worse, your market choices are much more complex. Some direct writers are selling through independent agencies, some companies traditionally selling through independent agencies are now selling direct, and both types of sellers are closely interweaving p-c with life-health products. In turn, all forms of insurance are meshed with investments, mortgages, health care delivery, travel and financial planning in the broadest sense. One stop financial planning is a reality.

In addition, changing technology is making vast differences in the marketplace. Through the computer you will soon be able to receive explanations about each type of policy, obtain premium quotations, compare them with the quotations of other companies, order the insurance, pay for it through electronic fund transfers, and have your home computer printer deliver your policy—all this from your living room easy chair.

But thanks to the time lag between technological development and widespread application, it will be some time before you can enjoy this scenario. In the meantime, you should watch for signs that your insurance company and your agent are (or are not) keeping abreast of current developments. In today's fast-moving business world, being current in both technology and in education is vital.

Examine the Alternatives

Examine the alternatives—ETA. That's the first step in building a sound insurance program, and in deciding how and where to buy the insurance.

We can't lay down a simple formula that

would be valid for every insurance buyer, in the sense that you could follow it straight to a specific company or agent. But we can illustrate some of the factors that will help you judge and weigh the options.

Human vs. Computer.   If possible, a competent individual should be working with you personally on your insurance. This can no longer be taken for granted, what with the advent of computerized, direct billing, WATS lines to distant company employees for policy information, group auto and group homeowner's policies (much like group or association medical or life coverages), and other impersonal mass marketing in all major forms of insurance.

The individual serving you should, of course, have the benefit of computer technology working for him and you.

Leverage.   Leverage means getting more than a dollar's worth of services for each dollar spent. In insurance, leverage is increasingly important because it can make the difference between having a professional who can afford to extend himself for you or having a distinterested beginner begrudging you minimal service.

Leverage is possible when you have all your p-c coverages handled by the same source, as opposed to fragmenting them among two or more competing firms. Your home, auto, boat, office, and related policies should be properly integrated if handled by the same agent or by his office. Your single source will make more commission on all those policies than it would on only one of them, and can afford to give you more service than a single policy's commission would otherwise warrant. Your agent would also have more leverage with your carrier when it's needed in underwriting, premium-setting, or claim situations.

Greater leverage can be obtained by having the same office—not necessarily the same person—handle your life-health coverages. The same principles apply: you have more clout on any insurance problem and your single source is more motivated to give you the best in service under risk of losing all your business if he slights you on even the least attractive (or least profitable) of all your insurance needs.

Still greater leverage can be had by adding to all your insurance the related products and services such as investments, savings, and financial planning. In practical terms, however, such broad-based leverage calls for more expertise than any single person has (barring a few exceptional individuals). Most firms are not yet offering all these professional services, although more are trying to do so. Even those individuals who are Certified Financial Planners—the broadest-based professional designation—often have no working knowledge of p-c insurance and fail to provide p-c expertise, directly or indirectly.

So we're back to searching out a competent p-c agent.

How to Judge a P-C Agent

Judging the expertise and market facilities of a professional is always difficult, but there are some telling signs you can look for:

Your agent should be knowledgeable in the types of property and operations you have, so that he won't be learning on your insurance problems.

He should come well recommended by people who have had both routine and difficult claims satisfactorily handled.

He should represent companies (preferably more than one) that are well rated financially and respected even by their competitors.

He (perhaps with one or more associates) should be competent in life-health insurance so that both you and he enjoy the benefits of leverage.

He should be abreast of current insurance

trends, through membership in at least one professional insurance organization and regular reading of several insurance publications. He should also be up to date on your needs and at least once a year should review all your insurance, updating policies and discussing possible changes.

Summary

Ask freely. Assume nothing. Examine the alternatives. Sample questions might be:

"What coverages are not included in your quotation?"

"What's the next step up in better coverage?"

"How much additional premium would the better coverage cost?"

"Conversely, how much can I save by eliminating some marginal coverage, or by reducing limits?"

"What are the differences between the policy you're quoting and that of your stiffest competitor?"

The principles discussed in this chapter might best be illustrated by a composite example based on actual cases.

Jack Ross, a lawyer, had his home insured through an agency related to the mortgagee and his autos through a direct writer. His life insurance was written by a cousin. Altogether, his premium totaled some $4,000.

The agency writing the homeowner's policy ("H") offered to double the building coverage for $340 in a new policy. (There had been no personal contact and no keeping up with inflation for eleven years.) With guidance, Ross asked if that was the best possible offer (the ETA principle). Agency "H" came back with an offer combining homeowner's with auto coverages for a total premium of $1,260, in effect

charging $920 for the autos. A review of the underwriting facts brought the auto premium down to $830 (ASK; assume nothing).

Now Ross asked his auto carrier for a quotation on the homeowner's policy. That agency ("A") quoted $330 for a slightly better homeowner's policy than that offered by "H" and, combined with its current auto premium of $800, seemed preferable. But, invoking the ASK principle, Ross asked and was told that the auto renewal premiums would rise to $910.

Ross now asked each agency to quote an umbrella liability policy, something neither had suggested. "H" quoted $65 for a $1 million policy, but would require higher liability coverages and increased premium on the underlying policies; "A" quoted $85 for the $1 million policy and $100 for a $2 million umbrella.

The final result was that by increasing the deductible slightly, Ross was able to get his homeowner's policy insured at full replacement values for both building and contents, a $2 million umbrella liability policy, the addition of a $4,000 jewelry scheduled item not previously insured and increased medical payments coverage on his autos. Total premium for auto, homeowner's, and umbrella liability policies was $1,340—about $80 less than the competitor's bid. (Of course, the premium was not the only factor considered in placing the insurance.)

The biggest improvement Ross achieved, however, was in his life insurance. Neither of his p-c agents mentioned life, although, ironically, it would have given them much greater commission than the total p-c commissions. Ross now carries four times as much death protection as previously, pays less premium, and has salvaged $12,000 of cash values from his obsolete and now replaced policies. The investment return of that money is more than enough to pay for all his p-c insurance!

Ross's story is typical. Many Americans

are up in arms when auto or medical insurance premiums increase, but they fail to recognize that they may be wasting fortunes in all the other policies they carry. A competent practitioner can usually create savings and a better program of protection if permitted to view all insurance as part of the total financial planning picture. Property-casualty coverages are basic necessities—think of your near terror if you were without auto and homeowner's coverages—and should be handled with high-priority professionalism.

Your role in getting such professionalism is helped greatly by following the principles of ASK, ETA, and leverage.

Chapter 15

Some Tips
on Health
and Accident
Insurance

Richard P. Austin has been a leading
insurance sales manager in both Florida
and California. He is second vice-president,
Life, Health & Financial Services Department, The Travelers Insurance Companies.
One of his responsibilities is health marketing and the development of health products.
Austin is a Chartered Life Underwriter, a
Chartered Financial Consultant, and a
member of the International Association
for Financial Planning. He was a charter
recipient of the National Management
Award of the GAMC and has earned that
distinction each year thereafter.

Richard P. Austin, CLU, ChFC

Strip away the ability to work and earn income and you strip away the ability of most individuals to provide the basic building blocks of any financial plan. An unexpected injury or illness could mean low or no income, and a drain of medical expenses on accumulated income that could be devastating. Think about your last medical bill. Maybe it was a dental bill for some bridge work, a hospital bill for the delivery of your last child, or perhaps the physician's fee for your annual checkup. Now think of paying 100 percent of that bill out of your own pocket. Was it a smaller expense easily paid for out of your current income? Or was it a larger expense that could not be easily covered?

It doesn't take long to recognize that a successful financial plan includes a means of protecting the plan from a loss of income. One such instrument is life and disability income insurance, which protects against the loss of human capital due to death or disability and helps prevent a drain on accumulated assets. Two basic rules should be followed when this type of insurance is under consideration:

1. *Always* insure against catastrophic loss no matter how remote the possibility of long-term disability or illness.

2. *Do not* insure against smaller losses if costs can easily be absorbed by current income. Coverage for smaller, more frequent losses is costly and, in most cases, unnecessary.

Health and accident insurance generally refers to those coverages providing the insured with benefits as the result of sickness or injury. More recently, preventive care costs and health maintenance provisions have been added. Health and accident insurance takes two major forms: (1) disability income insurance, and (2) medical expense insurance. This coverage includes hospital and surgical benefits, major medical insurance, and, in some cases, dental coverage.

Most of us separate medical expense from disability needs, placing priority on hospitalization, surgical, and major medical coverage. We assume our disabilities will be either minor and short-lived, or that government programs such as Social Security or group disability benefits will provide adequate resources for income. There's no guarantee on the first assumption and the second assumption is just not true!

According to 1978 government figures, financial losses resulting from disability were expected to affect about 16 million Americans in 1982.[1] Recent trends have also indicated that one out of every seven working individuals in their midthirties will be disabled for a period of ninety days or more before they retire at sixty-five. Almost 70 percent of their lost income will never be replaced.[2] When income stops, long-term disability amounts to economic death. Because disability income is more important than most of us realize, let's begin by examining insurance available in this area.

Disability Income Insurance

Disability income insurance can be defined as health insurance that provides income replacement payments when the insured is unable to work owing to sickness or injury. Some disability contracts cover both risks, some provide only for disability resulting from accidental injury.

If you have group health insurance, you may have some form of disability insurance. You still need to question its adequacy relative to your cost-of-living expenses. Whether you have group coverage or are self-employed and own an individual disability income policy, you can evaluate the adequacy of your coverage by estimating your monthly expenses and comparing the total figure to the total disability income

[1] 1978 Social Security Administration figures.
[2] Life Insurance Marketing and Research Association, Inc., *It Will Never Happen to Me* (Hartford, Conn., July 1980).

provided (see Your NCFE Financial Data Form in the Appendix).

If your cost-of-living expenses exceed your disability income provisions, you need to supplement your coverage. The total disability benefit available is based on: (1) the amount of the weekly or monthly payment; (2) the length of the initial elimination or waiting period; and (3) the maximum period for which benefits are payable.

The Basic Benefit Amount

The weekly or monthly disability income payment is the basic benefit provided by a disability income insurance policy. This scheduled payment is also referred to as weekly or monthly indemnity. The proper amount of indemnity is determined by the insured's income:

How much does the insured earn?

How much of that income will be replaced by employer-provided sick leave, state programs, Social Security benefits, or a private insurance policy?

How much additional income still needs to be covered by individually owned disability income insurance to meet projected cost-of-living needs?

Consider inflation. Consider increases in your responsibilities. You should arrive at a total benefit amount that will support your life-style realistically.

The Elimination or Waiting Period

This period works like a deductible. Your disability benefits begin when the elimination period ends. Although waiting periods range from zero days to two years, most disability income policies are based on elimination periods of 30, 60, 90, or 180 days.

The purpose of the waiting period is twofold. The longer waiting period discourages short-term disability claims, which, for the most part, are easily budgeted for by the insured, and so reduces the administrative costs of processing such claims incurred by the insurance company and the medical service suppliers. Lower administrative costs then trickle down to the consumer. The second, more direct result of an extended waiting period comes to the consumer in the form of lower insurance premiums.

Maximum Benefit Periods

The maximum benefit period is your indemnity limit—the longest period of time for which benefits are payable for any one disability. Generally, benefit periods range from one year to age sixty-five and would be the same duration for both accident and sickness under one contract.

The format of older disability contracts allowed the insured to stipulate different elimination and benefit periods for sickness

Older Contracts

DISABILITY	DURATION	ELIMINATION/ WAITING PERIOD	LENGTH OF TIME BENEFIT PAID	TOTAL BENEFIT
Pneumonia (sickness)	28 days	30 days	0	0
Broken leg (accident)	21 days	0	21 days	$360
Heart attack (sickness)	37 mos.	30 days	24 mos.	$14,400

Newer Contracts

DISABILITY	DURATION	ELIMINATION/ WAITING PERIOD	LENGTH OF TIME BENEFIT PAID	TOTAL BENEFIT
Pneumonia (sickness)	28 days	30 days	0	0
Broken leg (accident)	21 days	30 days	0	0
Heart attack (illness)	37 mos.	30 days	36 mos.	$21,600

and accident. A typical older contract might provide a thirty-day elimination period for sickness with a two-year maximum benefit period. For disability due to an accident, the same contract could provide lifetime benefits with no elimination period. On the basis of a $600 monthly disability income, benefits paid on typical disabilities would be as shown on the previous page.

The newer contracts are written with one elimination period, one benefit period, and one benefit amount for both illness and accident coverages. Taking the same typical disabilities, let's look at the benefit provisions under a newer contract that stipulates a $600 monthly income, a thirty-day elimination period, and a benefit payable to age sixty-five.

The newer contracts provide longer benefit periods and assume that income for the elimination period will be covered by the personal assets of the insured. Many people establish an emergency fund of three months' living expenses. If you can get by on an elimination period of longer than thirty days, your premium will be lower. Suppose, for example, that a forty-five-year-old male wants $1,000 monthly disability income with a benefit payable to age sixty-five:

30-day waiting period = $633 annual premium
60-day waiting period = $561 annual premium
90-day waiting period = $523 annual premium

Over a period of twenty years (coverage to sixty-five on a forty-five-year-old male), the insured can save over $2,000 in premium costs if he chooses a ninety-day elimination period over a thirty-day period!

Qualifying for Disability Benefits

Owning a disability income insurance policy does not mean you automatically receive benefits. You must qualify! Before you read any provision of a disability income policy, look at the definition of total disability. When you become disabled as the result of an accident or illness, you want to be able to receive benefits. To do so, you must satisfy the policy definition of total disability. The more liberal the definition, the better off you are.

Once upon a time an insured was not considered totally disabled until he or she was *unable* to perform *any* kind of work. Such a restrictive definition made it difficult for anyone to collect benefits. Today, policy definitions of total disability are more liberal. Eligibility for benefits is generally based on the inability to perform job functions in the insured's regular occupation. Even if the insured continues to work, the loss of speech, hearing, sight, or the loss of use of two limbs is recognized as total disability by many insuring companies. Total disability benefits are automatically paid in accordance with the maximum benefit limits specified in the contract. This is sometimes referred to as "presumptive disability."

Partial disability benefits are provided to the insured in some, not all, disability income policies. When an insured is unable to perform one or more of the important duties of his or her occupation, partial disability benefits are provided, following a total disability benefit period. Most contracts pay approximately 50 percent of the total disability benefit for six months or one year.

Some contracts have a residual disability benefit that pays benefits if recovery is not complete and partial disability remains. Emphasizing the loss of earned income rather than the inability to perform the

duties of a particular occupation, residual disability benefits are paid to the insured in the same proportion as the reduction in earned income.

These residual benefits may be subject to qualification periods, earned income figures prior to disability (the insured must earn an income 20–25 percent less than prior monthly earned income), and continued physician's care.

For a brief review of disability coverages, look at Table 1.

Additional Disability Income Policy Provisions

Waiver of Premium

While receiving total disability income benefits, you do not pay disability premiums if the disability income policy contains a waiver-of-premium provision. Some companies also waiver insurance premiums during periods of residual disability.

Recurrent Disability

All disability income policies include a recurrent disability clause. If a disability recurs within a period of six months, it is usually treated as a continuation of the same disability. If a period longer than six months has elapsed between disability periods, or if a disability results from a totally different cause than the previous disability, it is treated as a separate claim—with a new elimination period and a new benefit period.

Transplant Surgery Benefit

Many disability income contracts now include provisions for donor disabilities resulting from organ transplants. The policy must be in effect for a minimum period of time before this option may be exercised.

Table 1. Major Categories of Disability Benefits

Total disability	By definition, unable to perform duties of specified occupation, or any occupation for which the insured is "reasonably fitted by education, training, or experience."
Presumptive disability	Loss of speech, hearing, sight, or loss of two limbs—automatic total disability benefits.
Partial disability	Usually follows total disability benefit period. Insured unable to perform one or more of important duties of job. Benefit is 50% of total disability benefit.
Residual disability	Permanent disability, partial disability, or impairment. Benefits proportionate to percentage of earnings prior to disability that is lost. Must be 20–25% loss in earned income. Must be under physician's care.

Supplementary Coverages

Short-Term Additional Monthly Indemnity

This is an additional benefit over a short period of time during the first year of disability. It eases the coordination of benefits, eases transition to Social Security, and provides deferred disability income when other disability income plans have ceased.

Residual Disability

Supplementary income is provided for the partial and permanently disabled individual.

Future Increase Option

Sometimes called the guaranteed insurability option, this option allows the insured to increase the benefit amount without proof of medical insurability. The insured is generally required to provide proof of income qualification.

Partial Disability

Not always built into the basic disability insurance contract, this supplementary coverage provides a transitional income during the insured's job readjustment period.

Hospital Indemnity

This short-term, daily benefit is paid to the insured in addition to benefits offered under the basic hospitalization policy. The hospital indemnity benefit is usually a fixed amount elected by the insured, and not a percentage of the hospitalization policy's basic benefits.

Accidental Death and Dismemberment

If the death of an insured is caused directly by an accidental injury, a lump sum amount becomes payable to the beneficiary. If an insured should lose two limbs or the use of both eyes, total disability is assumed and a monthly benefit is paid in addition to the lump sum amount. Some insurers offer a common carrier benefit that pays double the regular benefit if the insured is injured while riding as a passenger in a common carrier provided for passenger service. Accidental death and dismemberment coverage is not automatically included in all disability income policies. Check your coverage. It may be available only as a supplementary coverage.

Rehabilitation Benefits

A recent trend has been to provide rehabilitation benefits to insureds to cover extra living costs incurred by rehabilitation programs and reeducation costs, that is, tuition, books, fees, special tutors. Reducing long-term disability benefit periods and motivating people to be productive members of a work community are the primary objectives of the rehabilitation benefit.

Cost-of-Living Rider

As a disability income policy rider, the cost-of-living provision allows for income adjustment over a long-term disability benefit period. The average increase is 5–10 percent on monthly benefits. A maximum increase is typically twice the amount of the basic policy benefit and is often tied to the actual Consumer Price Index.

Social Security Benefits Replacement Rider

In order to set up a specified amount of disability income without depending heavily on Social Security benefits, you may choose to supplement your income with this special rider. Let's say you want a total disability income per month of $2,000. Your basic contract provides $1,400 montly, and the rider $600, for the desired total of

$2,000. Then you become eligible for Social Security benefits.

During the first year in which you're paid Social Security benefits, you will receive the $1,400 per month from your personal disability contract, the supplementary $600, *and* your Social Security income—in excess of $2,000. After the first year, your supplementary rider benefit will be adjusted to your Social Security benefits so the combined amount will always equal $2,000 of monthly income (see Table 2).

Table 2. Benefits of Social Security Rider

	Basic Contract	Rider	Social Security	Total
Pre-Social Security	$1,400	$600	0	$2,000
1st year Social Security	$1,400	$600	$485	$2,485
Thereafter Social Security	$1,400	$115	$485	$2,000

Renewability and Rates

There are three basic types of renewal provisions:

1. Cancellable: Contract renewal is at the option of the insurer.

2. Guaranteed Renewable: The company guarantees contract renewal but reserves the right to change premiums.

3. Noncancellable: The insured has the right to renew the contract and the company cannot change the premiums or refuse renewal. (The best policy provides the insured with a noncancellable contract and an unchanging premium.)

Exclusions and Limitations

Some specific conditions are not covered by an individual disability income policy.

Disabilities eliminated from standard coverage are: (1) any self-inflicted injury or illness, (2) any disability caused by war, and (3) injuries incurred while the insured is a pilot or crew member of an aircraft. Most policies also exclude coverage during foreign residency because claims are difficult to process and administer. As a consumer you should know exactly which injuries and illnesses are excluded from coverage.

Preexisting Conditions

Preexisting conditions are those illnesses or injuries for which an insured has had treatment prior to the effective date of the disability income policy. In some cases, preexisting conditions can be defined as symptoms that would require an ordinarily prudent person to seek medical care. In many instances, preexisting conditions are excluded from policy coverage.

Occasionally, preexisting conditions may make it difficult for a consumer to purchase disability income coverage. Some companies write contracts specifically excluding preexisting conditions from coverage in order to provide some form of disability income protection to the insured.

Generally speaking, basic disability contracts state that after a policy has been in force for two years, statements contained in the policy application cannot be used to reduce or deny benefits. If you disclose all pertinent medical information on the application, and the insurance company does not disclaim it either at the time of application or within the two-year period, the company must honor subsequent claims.

Other Mentionables

State Insurance Pools. If a consumer applies for and is denied disability coverage by two insurance companies, and if the consumer is not eligible for Medicare, there is still a chance to secure disability income coverage. A few states offer coverage by way of an insurance pool. The cost of the coverage may be comparatively high but disability income is available. Check with the office of the insurance commissioner in your state for more information.

Workers' Compensation. Workers' Compensation usually provides for short-term disabilities, and then only for on-the-job related illness or injury. Make sure you know the limitations of your workers' compensation benefits. You may want to supplement the coverage.

Social Security Benefits. The Social Security program is quite stringent on eligibility. The disabled individual must be: (1) unable to do *any* kind of work, (2) disabled at least twelve months or have a terminal illness or injury, and (3) must wait a minimum of five months before receiving any benefits. You may want to provide yourself with a more liberal disability plan, including supplementary coverage. A Social Security benefits replacement rider should be considered.

Despite the protection that disability income insurance offers to our earned and accumulated income, the cost of the medical treatment of injury and sickness poses an additional threat to economic security. It is understandable, then, that the original form of medical expense insurance was an extension of disability income coverage. A fixed benefit was paid to the insured regardless of medical expenses. It was not until the depression that medical expense insurance was developed as a separate form of insurance coverage.

Medical Expense Insurance

Medical expense insurance is designed to cover: hospitalization costs and general nursing care; medical fees for physicians, surgeons, and private nursing care; and the cost of necessary medical and health care services, supplies, extended care facilities, medicines, dental care, plus prosthetic appliances. There are three major types of medical insurance: (1) the hospital-surgical policy; (2) the major medical policy; and (3) the comprehensive medical expense policy.

Hospital-Surgical Policy

The hospital-surgical policy may also be called a basic coverage policy. There are typically seven benefit provisions related to hospitalization and surgical care:

1. Hospital room and board
2. Miscellaneous hospital expenses
3. Maternity benefits
4. Surgery
5. Physician's nonsurgical services provided during a hospital stay
6. Extended care facility room and board
7. Outpatient diagnostic X-ray and laboratory expenses

Most hospital-surgical coverages have no deductible. Hospitalization coverage usually begins the first day of your hospital stay. Surgical coverage goes into effect with the first fee. However, some policies may have a small deductible.

If your hospital-surgical policy has a deductible, you may be able to choose a higher deductible, cover some portion of the hospital and medical expenses yourself, and save on the premium. Generally, the larger the deductible, the lower the premium.

The benefit amount paid for each service or fee under basic hospital-surgical coverage is limited by schedule, allocation, or specified maximum benefit amounts outlined in the medical expense policy.

Hospital Room and Board. Your medical expense policy will pay for the amount actually charged by the hospital, but not more than the policy's maximum daily hospital benefit. You should select a policy that will provide an adequate amount for hospital room and board in your geographic area. Most policies provide for semiprivate rooms, and some hospital-surgical policies provide special benefits for intensive care patients—surgical policies provide special benefits for intensive care patients, in other words, more extensive coverage for a limited period of time. Every policy must state the specific number of days coverage is provided. A covered period of confinement may range from 30 to 365 days.

PAY ATTENTION TO: your policy's definition of "period of hospital confinement." Confinement may be defined by cause, time separation, or both. Let's say you're hospitalized for a bleeding ulcer. Four months later you're back in for the same thing. Your hospitalization coverage might consider both hospital stays one period of confinement since the cause of hospitalization was the same each time. Another policy might consider it as two separate periods of confinement because of the four months between stays. A clear understanding of the provisions of your policy can make an enormous difference in benefits.

Miscellaneous Hospital Expenses. Many services and medical supplies are furnished to a patient during a hospital stay. Drugs, laboratory services, ambulance charges, X-ray or chemotherapy treatments, surgical dressings, plus the cost of an operating room—all fall under the heading of miscellaneous expenses. Pre-admission testing, physical therapy, hospital costs related to outpatient surgery, radiation therapy, and emergency care are usually covered under a basic, hospital-surgical policy. Hospital-employed professionals, such as radiologists, pathologists, and anesthetists are also paid for under miscellaneous coverage.

PAY ATTENTION TO: any maximum limits on miscellaneous expenses. Some policies offer a flat dollar limit, some follow a schedule of service fees. Anything over the allowable benefit is paid by the policyholder.

Miscellaneous expense limits are often a multiple of the basic room and board benefit. The more the room and board coverage, the greater the miscellaneous expense coverage maximum. Some policies have a built-in increase on miscellaneous benefits when the hospital stay exceeds a specified period of time. (If your stay is extended or intensive care coverage is required, benefits are extended to meet the need.)

Maternity Benefits. Never take it for granted that maternity benefits are provided in basic hospitalization and surgical coverage. Often maternity benefits are excluded (except for related complications). Usually there is a limited provision, a flat dollar amount that is based on the maximum daily hospital benefit. For example, ten times the daily hospital benefit is paid for a normal delivery:

Daily hospital benefit = $135
Maternity benefit = 10 × $135 or $1,350

The benefit is slightly higher for Cesarean deliveries and lower if the pregnancy ends in a miscarriage or abortion.

PAY ATTENTION TO: the specific amount of maternity benefits offered under your hospitalization and surgical coverage, if any. Depending on your geographic area and maternity care desired, you may want to increase your coverage.

Surgical Benefits. Surgical expense benefits are based on a schedule, or list of the most common surgical procedures and the benefit limit payable for each one. The benefit amount paid is the actual cost of the operation, but not more than the scheduled amount payable.

Surgical expenses are paid regardless of hospitalization. Fees or anesthesia administered during a surgical procedure may be handled in one of a few ways. Generally, the cost of anesthesia is covered as a miscellaneous hospital expense. In some cases, a separate scheduled surgical allowance is provided. The same is true of chemotherapy or radiation treatments.

PAY ATTENTION TO: the scheduled

amounts for common surgical procedures. One policy may provide only $300, while another policy offers $900 for the same surgical procedure. Choose a liberal schedule.

PAY ATTENTION TO: the maximum surgical benefit. This is the largest amount allowed for any listed operation. Benefits for multiple operations are usually based on the number of incisions. Two or more operations performed through separate incisions will bring a higher benefit than two surgical procedures performed through a single incision.

Physician's In-Hospital Expense. Many illnesses and injuries require constant medical attention, but no surgery. During your hospital stay your physician(s) may perform many nonsurgical services for which a fee is charged. The basic, in-hospital expense benefit for physicians' fees is based on a daily limit amount. The amount payable is the amount charged, but it cannot exceed the specified limit.

PAY ATTENTION TO: how the physician's in-hospital benefit is handled in your policy. In most policies in-hospital expenses and surgical expenses incurred by the same physician will not be payable under both provisions of the policy. The insured must choose the larger benefit and pay the lesser amount out of pocket.

Extended Care. This provision covers those room and board expenses incurred as the result of a stay in an extended care facility. In most instances the benefit is available only if the stay in the extended care facility follows a period of hospitalization. Benefits are similar in rate structure to hospitalization room and board.

PAY ATTENTION TO: the policy's definition of an "extended care facility." Most definitions require the facility to have six or more beds, to be supervised by a physician or registered nurse, and to care and treat primarily those individuals convalescing from sickness or injury.

Outpatient Diagnostic and Laboratory Expenses. To encourage people to use less expensive medical facilities and to practice preventive medicine, many policies now include coverage for X-ray and laboratory services provided by clinics and other private facilities. The benefit is usually a modest, flat dollar amount.

However, some policies hold that those X rays or laboratory expenses incurred within a limited period of time preceding hospital confinement may be covered under the policy's miscellaneous expense provision.

Major Medical Insurance

Major medical insurance was developed in response to catastrophic medical expenses and the inadequacies of basic hospital-surgical coverage. Coverage may be offered as an optional provision to a basic hospital-surgical contract or as a separate contract. With the emphasis on large medical bills, major medical expense provisions are based on a large deductible and co-insurance, or shared risk, between the insured and the insurance company. Five key factors determine the amount and distribution of major medical benefits:

1. Eligible medical expense
2. Deductible amount and accumulation period
3. Benefit period
4. Co-insurance percentage
5. Maximum benefit

Eligible Medical Coverage

Major medical plans cover all "reasonable and customary charges," including hospital, medical and nursing care, and any additional supplies or treatments as prescribed by a physician. Although hospital confinement is not necessary, the physician's prescribed care is.

Some major medical policies restrict benefits by "inside limits." Typically subject to the inside limits are hospital room and board expenses and surgical procedures, medical services of a physician, private nursing care, and the room and board expense of an extended care facility. Although allowances for hospital and surgical expenses are considerably higher than similar benefits under a standard hospital-surgical policy, maximum benefits are scheduled.

Deductible Amount and Accumulation Period

A deductible is the amount of expenses paid for by the insured before any benefit is paid. Deductibles range from $500 to more than $5,000, and must be satisfied either per illness or per calendar year.

Benefit Period

As soon as the deductible amount is satisfied and the first eligible medical expense is incurred, the benefit period begins. Benefit periods vary in length from one to five years, but if the insured remains hospitalized when a benefit period is due to expire, it is extended until the hospitalization period is over. A new benefit period may begin once the deductible is satisfied again.

Co-insurance Percentage

Major medical expenses are shared by the insured and the insurance company. This is called co-insurance. The typical cost split is 80:20 percent, the insurance company assuming the greater part of the cost.

Let's say you have a major medical plan with a deductible of $500. After the $500 deductible is satisfied, your major medical coverage will pick up 80 percent of eligible medical expenses with a maximum benefit of $5,000, $10,000, or $25,000. On older major medical contracts a $10,000 or $25,000 maximum benefit limit was common. The escalation in medical costs tends to make this kind of contract obsolete (see Figure 1).

Maximum Benefit

The maximum benefit is simply the maximum amount the insuring company will pay per illness or per the life of the policy. The more liberal, per cause arrangement is preferable over the per calendar year stipulation.

Comprehensive Medical Insurance

Comprehensive coverage provides benefits for medical expense prescribed by a physician, whenever and wherever incurred. Benefits pay for: hospital, surgical, and most other medical expenses incurred

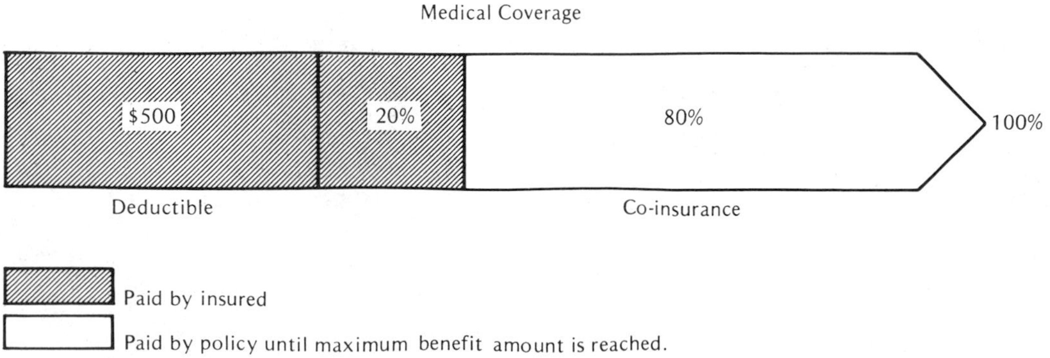

Medical Coverage

Deductible   Co-insurance

Paid by insured

Paid by policy until maximum benefit amount is reached.

Figure 1

Type A:

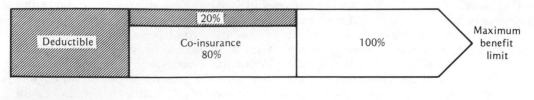

Paid by insured

Paid by policy

Figure 2

in or out of the hospital. In any calendar year there is an initial deductible of $100–500, depending on the policy. Co-insurance (80:20 or 75:25) between the insured and the company continues until the maximum, out-of-pocket expense for the insured is reached. This amount may be anywhere from $1,000 to $5,000, once again, depending on the policy.

Comprehensive coverage is generally structured in one of two ways:

Type A

Sometimes referred to as a modified major medical plan, this type of comprehensive policy shares medical costs with the insured on an 80:20 basis, *after* a relatively low deductible is met. When the

insured pays an amount of $500 or $1,000 the company will then pick up 100 percent of the medical costs per calendar year until the policy's maximum benefit amount is reached (see Figure 2).

It is not unusual for a policy to have a $1,000,000 limit. Such limits are a reflection of the high cost of medical care. Catastrophic illness or injury can easily absorb hundreds of thousands of benefit dollars. Some comprehensive policies have unlimited maximum benefits.

Type B

Sometimes called the modified comprehensive plan, this comprehensive policy pays for 100 percent of first dollar costs on hospital room and board, miscellaneous

Type B:

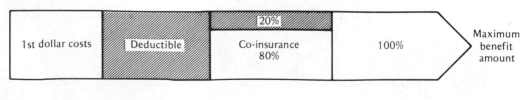

Paid by insured

Paid by policy

Figure 3

hospital expenses, scheduled surgical expenses, and in-hospital physician's fees. Additional expenses are subject to a small deductible. When the deductible is satisfied, medical expenses are shared 80:20. When the insured reaches a maximum limit for out-of-pocket expenses, the policy then pays 100 percent of all eligible costs until the maximum benefit amount is reached.

Hospital Indemnity Coverage (Hospital Income Insurance)

Hospital indemnity coverage provides a daily, fixed benefit during hospitalization, regardless of actual hospital expenses. Because the hospital indemnity plan is a simple, flat rate amount, it is commonly used as a supplement to other medical expense coverages. It is generally not a good idea to rely on a hospital indemnity policy for all your medical needs.

Interim Hospital Coverage

Many people find themselves between jobs or caught between life-styles or pursuits. For those of us undergoing transition because of student status, job change, or unemployment, interim hospital coverage

Table 3. Summary of Medical Coverages

	HOSPITAL-SURGICAL	MAJOR-MEDICAL	COMPRE-HENSIVE	HOSPITAL INDEMNITY	INTERIM-HOSPITAL
Hospital room and board	G	G	G	G	G
Intensive care	G	G	G	O	G
Hospital services and supplies	G	G	G	R	G
Anesthetics and administration	G	G	G	O	G
Physicians and surgeons services	G	G	G	O	G
Second surgical opinion	O	G	G	R	O
Psychologist's services	O	G	G	R	R
Physiotherapist's services	G	G	G	R	O
Private duty nursing	G	G	G	R	O
X-ray and lab exams	G	G	G	R	O
Radiation therapy	O	G	G	R	O
Ambulatory surgical centers	O	G	G	R	O
Convalescent facilities	G	G	G	O	O
Home health care	O	G	G	R	G
Prescription drugs					
out-of-hospital	R	G	G	R	R
in-hospital	G	G	G	R	G
Medical supplies and appliances	G	G	G	R	G
Medically necessary transport	G	G	G	R	G
Maternity/obstetrical	O	O	O	R	R

O = Occasionally
R = Rarely
G = Generally

is a necessary form of medical expense protection.

Generally, interim hospital coverage is a short-term policy written for 30 to 180 days of coverage, and the interim hospital plan acts as a basic hospital-surgical insurance policy.

The medical coverages we have been discussing are conveniently summarized in Table 3.

Basic Considerations in Selecting Medical Expense Coverage

Definition of "Hospital"

Many benefits provided by medical expense coverage are based on confinement in a hospital, extended care facility, or, in some cases, treatment or rehabilitation centers. Look for the most objective and liberal definition of "hospital."

Periods of Hospitalization

Hospital confinement on successive occasions is defined as one period of confinement if both stays are precipitated by the same sickness or injuries. Separation is usually determined by a specific period of time between hospitalization (that is, four months, six months), or is based on cause of confinement.

Medical benefits are based on a dollar limit and the length of confinement. Make sure you know how liberal your coverage is.

Preexisting Conditions

Many times people seeking health and disability coverage have medical histories that pinpoint a particular injury or illness as recurring. Because the medical condition exists prior to coverage, it is referred to as a preexisting condition and is often excluded from coverage. Exclusion generally depends on the seriousness of the condition and the potential for frequent claims. Conditions acknowledged on the application are automatically covered unless specifically excluded by a rider.

Deferred Medical Coverage

A probationary period of medical coverage is sometimes stipulated during the first thirty days or so from the effective date of your policy. This is done to discourage individuals who are aware of medical problems and want to cover anticipated losses. An insured seeking maternity benefits, for example, often has to be insured for thirty days under the policy before benefits are paid.

Elective surgical procedures may be subjected to even longer probationary periods. Six months is a typical waiting period for surgical procedures such as a hernia repair or a toncillectomy.

Policy Renewal and Rates

Although medical expense insurance can be written for short-term coverage, most contracts are for coverage to age sixty-five (usual eligibility for Medicare), or for life. Those medical insurance policies written for older individuals (sixty-five or older) generally provide supplementary coverages, such as hospital indemnity. There are also medical expense contracts designed to supplement, not duplicate, Medicare benefits.

Most of the better medical insurance policies today have some kind of renewal guarantees. That is, the insurance company cannot cancel the policy on an individual basis. But because of the rising costs of medical care and the new technologies used in medical treatment, most companies do reserve the right to adjust premium rates on a class basis.

Exclusion Characteristic of Medical Expense Coverage

Most medical expense policies automatically exclude the following coverages: self-inflicted injuries; losses caused by war; and normal pregnancy expenses.

These are the same exclusions found in most disability income contracts. However, medical policies have a few additional exclusions.

Government Medical Programs

Medical care or treatment given in a government-owned hospital is automatically excluded from coverage. Any expenses paid for by state or federal medical plans are also excluded.

Workers Compensation Plans

In order to avoid duplication of benefits, those medical expenses resulting from on-the-job injuries or illness covered by workers compensation benefits are excluded from individual policies.

Well-Baby Care

All states require medical coverage to be provided for newborns afflicted with injuries or illnesses from birth. Most medical policies exclude coverage of routine hospital care for a healthy baby until the child is discharged from the hospital, or a specified period of time (that is, fourteen days) has passed.

Limitations

Drug Addiction

Although some insurers consider drug addiction a self-inflicted illness, a few states have required that coverage be provided.

Benefit amounts and confinement stipulations vary from state to state. Benefit limits vary as well.

Alcoholism

The treatment of alcoholism is increasingly provided for in medical expense policies. Requirements of in-patient or out-patient care and the extension of coverage to treatment facilities vary from state to state. Benefit limits vary also.

Mental Disorders

Mental disorders and nervous disorders have traditionally been excluded from coverage. Recently, insurers are including such coverage in major medical expense provisions, usually on a co-insurance basis. Confinement requirements, benefit limits, and risk sharing vary from policy to policy.

Cosmetic Surgery

In many instances cosmetic surgery is still a negotiable item. For example, the removal of a mole at the suggestion of a physician may very well be covered by your policy. A face lift or nose job may not be. Perhaps a good guideline to follow is any cosmetic surgery performed as the result of a physician's request and as a preventive measure is eligible for coverage. Benefits, if provided, would be included in hospital-surgical coverage and major medical insurance.

Other Mentionables

Workers Compensation. Employers are required by state law to provide disability and medical benefits to any employee injured on the job. Coverage is also extended to occupational diseases. Hospital-surgical and medical expense benefits are paid but decisions on *unlimited* benefits are subject to the discretion of insurance and administrators. Most states prefer a lump sum settlement to lifetime benefits.

Read over your workers compensation benefits and pay special attention to long-term disability and major medical expense provisions. Additional individual insurance may be needed.

Group Health Contracts and Your Conversion Rights. As a general rule, most group health plans provide conversion privileges but limit the option to basic hospital-surgical coverage. There is usually a specified period of time (typically thirty days) within which the conversion option must be exercised. Conversion is guaranteed. Major medical supplements should be considered.

The new tax law provides coverage for those workers remaining on the job after they turn sixty-five. Employers of twenty workers or more are now required to offer workers over sixty-five the same benefits as other, younger workers, though to age sixty-nine. The over-sixty-five employee has the option of choosing Medicare or the employer's benefit package as his or her primary coverage.

Medicare. All persons age sixty-five or over are eligible for medicare coverage. Medicare coverage is made up of two parts: the basic hospital plan, and the supplementary voluntary plan (see Table 4).

Thirteen Common Exclusions

1. Services not reasonable and necessary for treatment

2. Services for which there is no legal obligation to pay

3. Services covered by government plans other than Medicare

4. Services not provided in the United States

5. Injury and sickness caused by war

Table 4. Medicare Coverage

COVERAGE	COST TO INSURED		LIMITS
PART A: BASIC HOSPITAL PLAN			
In-hospital expenses			No private accommodations
Room and board	1–60 days 61–90 days	$260. 65.	90 days per benefit period
Miscellaneous services	3 pts. of blood		
Physicians, surgeons & private nurses	No Coverage: Part B		
In-patient psychiatric care	Same as room-board		190 days/lifetime
Post-hospital care Extended care facility*	1–20 days 21–100 days	$ 0.00 $32.50	100 days per benefit period
Home health services	0		No limit

*Starting in 1984 Medicare benefits will cover hospice care for the terminally ill. The benefit period will consist of two periods of ninety days and one period of thirty days. A 5 percent co-payment (5 percent cost to the insured and 95 percent cost to Uncle Sam) on services and drugs will be required. The entire provision will expire on September 30, 1986, at which time the hospice care benefit will be evaluated and, perhaps, renewed.

Medicare Coverage

PART B: SUPPLEMENTARY AND VOLUNTARY PLAN		
Medical and other health services	$75 yearly deductible	No limit/per calendar year
Outpatient rehabilitation	20% of expenses	No limit
Physical therapy	Cost of 3 pints of blood	No limit
Home health services	0	No limit
Pre-admission testing	0	No limit
Ambulatory surgical services	0	No limit

6. Personal comfort items

7. Routine physical checkups and preventive care

8. Routine foot care

9. Custodial care

10. Cosmetic surgery except as required by a physician

11. Noninsured individuals

12. Dental benefits

13. Any benefit payable by workers compensation

Shopping Hints on Health and Accident Insurance

Compare Policies. Insurance policies vary in coverage. Compare definitions of total disability and hospital. Make sure you're getting what you want. Standard coverage in one policy may be costly supplements to another.

Don't Overinsure. You will wind up paying premiums for duplication in coverage. There's no such thing as duplicate benefit payments on the same claim. Know what policy covers which expenses.

Check for Preexisting Conditions or Exclusions. You don't want to eliminate coverage you need.

Know Your Maximum Benefits. Maxmium benefits are described in terms of dollar amount *and* time frame. Know how long you'll be paid benefits, and how much.

Check for Guaranteed Renewability and Noncancellable Coverage. Avoid the headache of cancelled coverage. You want to be in control of policy renewal.

Know Your Out-of-Pocket Expense. Is there a deductible? If so, how much? What is your expense limit on co-insurance? Know how much will be left for you to pay?

Check for Premium Adjustment Privileges. Can the insuring company raise your premium rates? How often? Under what circumstances?

Ten-Day Free Look. You have ten days to look over your disability or medical expense policy. If you decide not to purchase the coverage after all, return the policy and get a total refund of premiums paid.

Summary

Health and disability income insurance play vital roles in the success of your personal financial plan. This chapter has covered the basics of available medical and disability contracts. If you're considering purchasing, supplementing, or converting coverage, review the chapter and jot down any questions or concerns you may have and discuss these openly with your insurance representative. Remember, you are the client. You are entitled to satisfactory answers to all your questions concerning coverage.

When Considering Disability Income

DO insure catastrophic loss although the possibility may seem remote.

DO consider longer elimination periods on disability income to lower your premium.

DO consider staggering coverage to save on disability premiums. For example, opt for $500 after thirty days, add $500 after sixty days, and work up to a $1,500 disability income after ninety days.

DON'T accept just any definition of "Total Disability." Be sure the definition is liberal, otherwise you may not be eligible for benefits.

When Considering Medical Insurance

DO choose a higher deductible or shared risk, if possible. By paying some of the cost of medical care you will be able to reduce premiums.

DO look at premium differentials between scheduled benefits for hospital-surgical costs and 80:20 (75:25) shared risk contracts. Although scheduled benefits are paid 100 percent by the contract, benefits are limited. You may wind up paying expenses anyway. This is especially true for city dwellers where urban costs are higher than suburban costs. Social Security benefits under Medicare often fall short of current hospital-surgical rates, too. Pay attention to scheduled amounts. It may be worth sharing the risk.

DO be aware of conversion options under group medical contracts. You may need to supplement coverage when you leave the job or retire.

DON'T assume you're covered for anything! Many people think maternity benefits are automatically part of the contract—this is not so.

Being an informed consumer is in your favor. At this point you should feel confident about making the proper decisions in providing yourself and your family with adequate coverage. A "wise" guy (or gal) makes a "wise" buy!

Chapter 16

A Hard Look
at the Gloom and
Doom Approach

Lewis Walker, M.B.A., is a well-regarded seminar leader and speaker before business, social, professional, and academic organizations. He is president of Walker, Cogswell & Company, Incorporated, and is a registered securities principal affiliated with Investment Management & Research, Incorporated. He has conducted workshops and seminars throughout the nation on topics ranging from personal and business financial planning to preretirement planning, estate planning, and tax and investment strategies. He has been a contributor to numerous publications and has appeared frequently on radio and television. A Certified Financial Planner, Walker has maintained an active role in the International Association for Financial Planning and the Institute of Certified Financial Planners. He has served on the national board of directors for the ICFP and chaired the Ethics Committee.

Lewis J. Walker, CFP

Have you echoed the old complaint: "Just when I learned all the answers, they changed the questions!" As recently as the 1950s the answers to questions about personal financial planning seemed rather simple. That decade was one of recovery from the war years—both World War II and Korea—and a home in the suburbs and a transition to the two-car family were overriding personal goals. Money in the bank. and cash value life insurance were basic savings plans. Investors bought long-term bonds for safety and income; the more adventuresome dabbled in stocks and mutual funds. The buy-and-hold investment philosophy worked. Financial planning as a profession was unheard of. Neither the questions nor the answers were complex.

The 1960s contained the seeds of change. In 1964, President Lyndon B. Johnson decided to fight an expanding war in Southeast Asia and to wage war on poverty at home, without raising taxes. Johnson—who had been criticized for grabbing his dog by the ears—decided to grab the U.S. taxpayer in a fashion somewhat more subtle but equally as painful.

Lyndon Johnson was a student of history and remembered the actions of Franklin D. Roosevelt in the 1930s, when he was faced with a country deep in depression. Out of the Great Depression came the "new economics" championed by the followers of economist John Maynard Keynes, the modern theory of demand-stimulating policies spurred by the taxing and deficit-spending powers of the U.S. government. Taxation would be used to correct "market failures" and bring about a "more equitable distribution of income." The government would "create money" and increased government spending with easy money and ample credit would get the country moving, reasoned Roosevelt.

As the country recovered slowly from the Great Depression, World War II intervened, putting people back to work producing war materials. Consumer goods were rationed; citizens bought war bonds and grew victory gardens. Following the war, the national debt declined slightly and inflation moderated. As the nation entered the 1950s, consumer buying boomed, leading off with houses, autos, and appliances. A postwar baby boom was to create even more pressure behind classic Keynesian demand-side "easy money" economics.

In order to create the money needed to fuel his recovery, President Roosevelt had to abolish the gold standard. As long as money is tied to precious metals by some formula or ratio, politicians are hobbled. They cannot spend money they do not have because hard money limits the creation of money. Politicians have to ask citizens for more taxes, always an unpopular task. Roosevelt knew that he had to wrest control of the money supply from the free market and the citizenry, and put fiscal and monetary manipulative tools directly into the hands of the government. In 1934, Roosevelt called in gold. Gold coins disappeared, and Federal Reserve notes—unbacked receipts for government debt—became the money of the future.

In 1964, Lyndon Johnson abolished silver—not by calling it in, but by ceasing to coin money out of the metal. The effect was the same, however. Silver coins disappeared into cookie jars and bank vaults and paper silver certificates became a historical curiosity.

Richard Nixon completed the cycle of currency debasement in 1971 when the "gold window" slammed shut and foreign claims no longer could be settled in gold. Specie backing of our currency was totally eliminated.

Everyone acknowledges that the principal cause of inflation is a continual increase in the supply of money without a corresponding increase in the supply of goods and services on the other side of the equation. Beginning in 1965, in response to Johnson's war and welfare policies, the national debt, as it mirrored deficit spending, took on a disturbing upward slope (see Figure 1).

With no hard money constraints, money was easily created. Peopled wanted things,

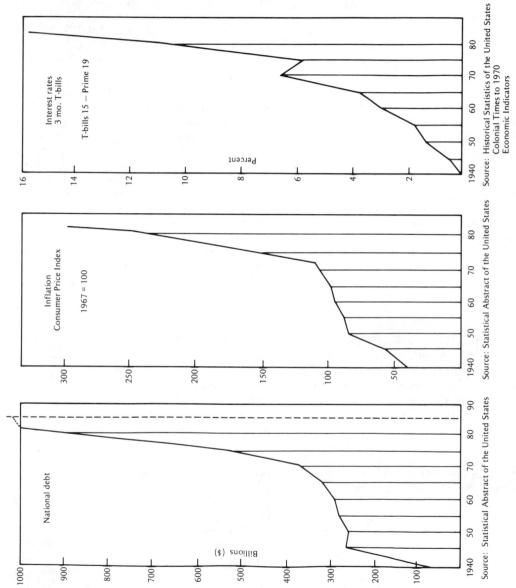

National debt

Source: Statistical Abstract of the United States

Inflation
Consumer Price Index

1967 = 100

Source: Statistical Abstract of the United States

Interest rates
3 mo. T-bills

T-bills 15 — Prime 19

Source: Historical Statistics of the United States
Colonial Times to 1970
Economic Indicators

Figure 1

201

and congressmen, fearing they might not be reelected, engaged in deficit spending to provide goods. The increasing supply of money caused higher prices, which spurred demands for higher wages.

And because of the progressive nature of the U.S. income tax system, rising wages pushed people into higher tax brackets, with little to no increase in real purchasing power on net take-home pay. Politicians found that they could increase taxes through inflation and yet appear to give "tax cuts" to the voters just before election. Most tax reductions were not true cuts at all, but merely decreases in the rate of increase.

The 1960s saw the beginning of what some have called the era of pendulum economics, which refers to cyclical swings of growing volatility: that is, a period of inflationary expansion fueled by ample credit and cheap money is followed by a government-induced "credit crunch" to cool things down, with a resulting recessionary slump and a deflationary phase.

Credit-crunch recessions hit the economy in 1967, 1971, 1974–75, and 1981–82. These cycles took on an ominous pattern. As the economy slid into recession, prices continued to rise, albeit more slowly. Inflation did not abate; the rate of increase in prices merely decreased for a time, and this effect was termed stagflation. Classical economists considered stagflation to be highly unusual in that the economy fell while prices continued to rise.

To cure the recession, at the bottom of the cycle the politicians returned to demand-stimulating policies, creating more easy money and greater federal deficits. Things looked better for a while, primarily around election time. But after each election inflation came roaring back worse than ever. Each interest rate peak was higher than the last peak, and the rates of change in interest rates became more violent. Inflation—the average increase in the Consumer Price Index (CPI)—doubled every five years.

Few people were disturbed when the average increase in the CPI doubled from 1.24 percent between 1958–1962 to 2.22 percent 1963–1967. They began to take notice when the rate went from 4.62 percent 1968–1972 to 7.92 percent 1973–1977. Remember Gerald Ford's WIN button campaign in 1975? Inflation was a beastly 5 percent.

In 1976, the country elected as president, James E. "Jimmy" Carter, an ex-Georgia governor who ran as a "Prairie Populist" who would go to Washington and change things. And indeed he did.

The expansion of the money supply and the national debt from the mid-1970s on was unparalleled in our history. Even John Maynard Keynes, in his defense, had warned that continued use of deficit financing during periods of business expansion would have ruinous consequences. Rampant inflation was such a consequence, and, as both an economic and political phenomenon, it became deeply entrenched as a way of life. For that reason, its control is neither easy nor painless.

Clever people learned new answers to old questions and they began to play the inflation game, leveraging themselves to the hilt and living on credit. Politicians learned that "bracket creep" would increase taxes while they could respond to public demands for solutions by intervening in the marketplace; in this way, they increased their power, influence, and importance. Bureaucrats happily complied with fuzzy congressional mandates, and government grew in size and scope to a level that would have horrified our Founding Fathers.

Out of chaos always comes opportunity, and a major new industry appeared in the late 1970s—gloom and doom. Sharp-eyed observers quickly capitalized on emerging trends. Conventional financial markets became destabilized. Savers were penalized with yields that were being eaten up by inflation and by ruinous tax policies that hit interest and dividends with marginal tax rates up to 70 percent. In many cases, yields to savers were actually negative after adjustment for inflation and taxes. Bonds, mortgages, and other fixed-yield paper securities lost value rapidly (between 1978 and 1982, some bonds lost 50–60 percent of their market value). Money flowed out of cash value insurance and banks and savings and loans, as investors sought to acquire "things"—nonpaper assets of all kinds, including real estate, commodities, diamonds, gold, silver, coins, stamps, art, antiques, even comic books.

Leverage was everyman's game. Things increased in value faster than the net cost to use the money required to control them. Interest was tax deductible; long-term capital gains were taxed at a far lower rate than earned and unearned ordinary income.

The gloom-and-doom books merely took emerging trends and projected them into the future. With inflation doubling every five years and averaging roughly 15 percent for the 1978–1982 period, it was easy to project 30 percent and 60 percent inflation rates in the not-too-distant future. Inflation would push more and more people into the 50 percent federal tax bracket, 50–70 percent on unearned income. Paper assets would be wiped out; the destruction of the dollar was assured. The Swiss franc seemed to be a far better bet than the Susan B. Anthony dollar. John Q. Public was now concerned about his very survival.

Economic survival became big business in 1979 and 1980. Inflation soared, investment markets fluctuated wildly, and the world's economy seemed to be at the mercy of robed oil barons with unpronounceable names. Entrepreneurs found that people would pay $150 to $300 per year (tax deductible!) for insider newletter advice on how to profit and survive in the inflationary world economy. Books followed, and economic survival vied with sex, diets, and physical fitness for top slots on national best seller lists. Syndicated television shows and investment seminars attracted flocks of investors eager to learn the new rules from the gurus of gold, silver, and internationalism.

But even the hard asset boom contained the seeds of its own undoing. What many of the prophets of doom ignored was the incredible ability of the U.S. government to interfere in capital markets, to postpone, delay, and confuse. And to the gurus of gold, 1981 was indeed a shock. They failed to reckon with the power of the Federal Reserve.

A Funny Thing Happened on the Way to Doomsday

Easy money fueled the 1976–1980 boom in real estate, commodities, hard assets, and stocks. The boom was aided and abetted by the Federal Reserve Bank and federal policy which, in effect, created a subsidy for borrowers. By placing ceilings on interest paid by banks and other savings institutions, the government limited the cost of funds to institutions and created a relatively cheap pool of capital. Savings and loans had a one-quarter point advantage over banks on passbook rates, which channeled a great deal of money into residential real estate. Rising values created equity that homeowners could tap for even greater degrees of borrowing power and leverage.

Another effect was more technical in nature, but equally important. Prior to 1979, the Federal Reserve attempted to control interest rates directly and to limit fluctuations in rates. Rates charged on federal funds (the excess funds that banks lend each other to meet reserve requirements) were relatively stable. Financial institutions were able to buy securities or make loans with assurance that money costs would not rise drastically in the short term.

But such polices increased bank reserves—reserves upon which loans are predicated. These reserves bloated the money supply, as did the growing government deficits being monitized through the banking system, with the result that the general price level rose through the 1970s. Inflation became a hidden tax on lenders and all citizens, and a generous subsidy for financial intermediaries and borrowers.

The Federal Reserve switched gears in October 1979, moving to control the money supply at the cost of letting interest rates fluctuate more widely. Banks were deregulated. Interest rate ceilings on deposits were removed; commercial banks and savings and loans were allowed to compete with each other. Faced with a rising cost of money and with the economy becoming more volatile, both borrowers and lenders increased risk premiums, causing interest rates to rise. The resulting fluctuations in capital markets had an incredible impact on investor behavior and on all investment sectors.

Interest rates soared to historical highs. Money market mutual funds grew by leaps and bounds to over $183 billion in assets by the end of 1981, as investors attempted to cash in on high rates. The housing and auto industry collapsed as cheap credit dried up. Leverage became expensive, and commodities—including gold and silver—tumbled, along with bonds and the stock market. The gurus of gold shocked their followers when some—as early as mid-1980—told their followers to sell gold and get into cash.

With the election of Ronald Reagan in 1980 and his taking of office in 1981, a new scenario was offered as an alternative to doomsday: supply-side economics.

An economist named Arthur Laffer drew a picture on a cocktail napkin purporting to show that increasing taxation at some point becomes self-defeating. The ideas of Arthur Laffer and others, such as tax-cutting crusader Jack Kemp, found a champion in Ronald Reagan. Their theories—dubbed supply-side economics—postulated a

move away from demand-side economics, which had centered upon increasing taxes and growing government deficits. Supply-side theory was embodied in the Economic Recovery Tax Act of 1981 (ERTA), which emphasized tax cuts and decreased government spending.

Although a liberal press that regards profits and free enterprise with suspicion pegs supply-side economics as "new and untried theories," such ideas are in fact not theory, and they are not new. English economist Adam Smith, generally regarded as the founder of modern economics, laid out the framework for supply-side economics in his epic work touting "hands-off" government, *An Inquiry into the Nature and Cause of the Wealth of Nations*, published in 1776.

As a disciple of Smith, French economist Jean Baptiste Say argued in 1803, in his *Treatise on Political Economy*, that savings and investment, rather than consumption, promoted growth and the formation of wealth. "It is the aim of good government to stimulate production, of bad government to encourage consumption," noted Say. On taxes, Say stated that "the best taxes, or rather those that are least bad . . . are such as are least injurious to reproduction."

Other classical economists and philosophers such as David Hume (1711–1776), James Mill (1773–1836), his son, John Stuart Mill (1806–1873), and David Ricardo (1772–1823) shared similar views of public finance. Ricardo, for example, who made a fortune in the stock market while still in his twenties, became the leading British economist of the early 1800s. He helped establish the theories of "classical economics" that were based on free trade and free competition. In his book *Principles of Political Economy and Taxation* (1817), Ricardo defined the conditions that would enable the economy of a nation to reach its greatest potential. He stressed that the accumulation of capital was the key to rapid economic growth; he argued that if businesses were allowed to seek high profits, capital would then form rapidly.

Compare these ideas with the modern approach—which has been characterized by taxation policies that inhibit capital formation and punish savers, massive transfers of income from producers to non-producers, and subsidies for the inefficient and most marginal of producers.

It was the virtual collapse of demand in the 1930s that led to the nation's abrupt departure from classical ideas. The resulting overapplication of Keynesian principles of demand stimulation through government intervention and deficit spending probably reached its ruinous nexus in the 1970s, an era of high and increasing tax rates, of dubious "tax shelters," disincentives to save and invest, massive government regulation and intervention in the economy, a growing underground sector, and low rates of productivity and real growth. In short, stagflation. Doomsday appeared to be knocking at the door.

But Look How Far He Can See

An Old World visionary, so the story goes, once told his followers that in a dream he saw the great cathedral in the town of Llow, eighty miles distant, burning to the ground. The next day a traveler from Llow passed through the village, and the citizens excitedly asked about the big fire.

"What fire?", the traveler asked. "There was no fire. The cathedral stands," he said.

Undaunted, the villagers were still proud of their visionary. "So what if he was wrong," they reasoned. "Look how far he could see!"

Clearly, President Ronald Reagan is seeking change. Less clear, however, are the long-term implications of the changes already made or those to be made in the future. Forecasts and opinions are far from unanimous.

The voices of gloom and doom are still heard. There are those who predict that we are headed for a massive depression, one that would make 1929 look like a picnic. They point to an "accident," a few major bankruptcies, a panic in the commercial paper market, a sudden jolt that would spin the economy into despair before the government could intervene.

Others—the "business as usual" school—point to a more realistic scenario. They maintain that the federal debt and the bureaucracy are virtually out of control. Politicians and the beneficiaries of welfare, subsidies, and government largess, they reason, will be unwilling to stand the pain. Politicians will bow to pressure and go back to easy money and short-term bailouts, using more inflated dollars. Ultimately they see a hyperinflationary blowoff with a final deflationary collapse.

The more probable scenario lies somewhere in the middle. The national debt is a problem of massive proportions. The debt now exceeds one trillion dollars ($1,000,000,000,000), a number beyond our imagination. That is equal to more than $138,000 in debt for *every* man, woman, and child in the United States. There is no way that the debt can be repaid in real terms. It will be repaid largely through inflationary repudiation and the scaling down of benefits. Inflation will continue to be a problem in the 1980s.

However, classical supply-side economics, if allowed to stand, will have positive results. Lowered taxation with inducements to save; lower deficits and decreased federal intrusion into capital markets; less federal regulation and manipulation of the free-market economy—such are the ingredients for long-term growth, and a braking of the runaway disaster scenario. On the other hand, if the return to fiscal and monetary sanity is halted through the return of big spending and big government, hyperinflationary fears will become a clear and present danger.

A visionary think tank in Washington,

D.C., the Institute for the Future, recently looked into its crystal ball and made the following forecast for the rest of the decade in terms of gross national product and investment, as adjusted for inflation as well as prices:

	REAL GNP (%)	REAL INVESTMENT (%)	CONSUMER PRICES (%)
1983	4.8	11.0	6.5
1984	5.9	16.0	7.0
1985	5.2	12.0	11.0
1986	1.5	2.0	13.0
1987	−0.5	−4.0	9.5
1988	0.5	1.0	6.5
1989	2.5	3.0	6.5
1990	4.0	7.5	7.5

SOURCE: U.S. News & World Report, February 22, 1982, p. 53.

As with any forecast, the numbers are subject to revision. In any case, the real significance of this forecast lies not in the specific numbers, but in their pattern: an economy recovering from the 1981–82 recession, a business expansion through 1985, a credit crunch leading into 1987, another slump, and another recovery. The cycles are still with us. Serious inflation will return. The battle is not over.

Lessons for Investors

The watchwords for investors in the 1980s will be flexibility and diversification. If there was one major risk in following the doomsayers, it was the risk of placing too much of one's faith and assets in a single commodity.

Hard asset prices generally reflect the degree of inflation of a nation's money. Any hard item—one that does not deteriorate in storage, or is in limited supply, or is a kind of art or antique—can be used as a hedge against an inflationary debasement of paper money. But the hedging process itself has its limits.

Who can forget early 1980? The Big Three—gold, silver, and diamonds—the favorite hedges of the hard-money crowd, appeared invincible. D-Flawless diamonds sold for over $60,000 a carat after appreciating more than 300 percent in three years. Silver topped $50 an ounce as the Hunt Brothers tried to corner the market. Gold passed $800 an ounce amidst confident predictions of $2,000 and even $3,000 per ounce.

But when a majority of investors switch to hedges in anticipation of even greater inflation and hedge-buying reaches an extreme, the pendulum usually swings away from hedges back into conservative values. Hindsight clearly tells us that the frenzy of 1980 was replete with warnings of the end of a classical bull market. The year 1982 saw gold hovering around $300 an ounce, silver well below $10 an ounce, and diamonds down as much as 50 percent.

Rising interest rates, decreasing international political tensions, and recession (not only in the United States, but in other industrialized nations) were major factors in declining investor interest in hedge investments. The bull markets of 1977–1980 had gone too far too fast and were due for a healthy correction.

Have such commodities been discarded as an inflation hedge? Not at all. In early 1982 the inflation-adjusted value of gold stood at $280 an ounce, and in that vein prices around $300 an ounce were far more realistic than the fanciful levels of the recent past.

"Trees don't grow to the sky" is a useful expression that reminds us that nothing goes on ad infinitum. On the other hand, "boats don't sink forever" is something to keep in mind when a sliding market appears to have no bottom. Even the Titanic found a bottom. Of course, it never came back up; lost causes should also be recognized and abandoned at some point.

Flexibility, diversification, creativity, and good counsel are the underpinnings of financial success. Investors must apply these concepts in a coordinated financial strategy tied to defined goals and objectives.

With the deregulation of savings institutions and the private sector competing with government at various levels, the cost of money will in general stay rather high. Money market funds will stay popular as repositories for liquid capital and as a defensive position in times of market decline. But money market funds and money market instruments such as Treasury bills (T-bills) are not a true investment; adjusted for inflation and taxation, they will do little to enhance the growth of purchasing power (see Table 1).

Table 1. Investment Returns vs. Inflation (CPI)

Investment	ANNUAL RETURNS YEARS				
	15	10	5	3	1980
Standard & Poor's 500	6.8	8.5	14.0	18.7	32.4
Bonds (Salomon Index)	3.2	4.2	2.4	−2.3	−2.6
T-bills	6.4	6.9	7.9	9.7	11.6
Consumer Price Index (CPI)	6.9	8.1	9.2	11.6	12.4

Even if taxation is deferred—as it is in annuities, single-premium life insurance, or retirement plans such as an Individual Retirement Account (IRA)—if the investment medium only approaches the rate of inflation but does not exceed it, in reality you have a guaranteed loss of purchasing power.

In effect, no guaranteed investment plan, whether from a savings institution or an insurance company, will preserve purchasing power over time on an after-tax, after-inflation adjusted basis. However, because of volatility in investment markets and periods of uncertainty, guaranteed investments will continue to play a role. When, as Mark Twain remarked, "return of your money is as important as the return on it," you might consider the newer types of high-yield tax-deferred annuities or single-premium cash value life insurance. Both vehicles have varying degrees of liquidity, safety, yield, and flexibility, as well as estate planning and tax-deferral advantages.

Since fixed-yield securities of all kinds, including mortgages and bonds, decrease in value as interest rates rise, fixed-income investments in the 1970s proved to be an excellent way to "slide into genteel poverty." Interest rates rose more years than they declined. A few periods of declining interest rates following credit-crunch peaks proved to be excellent times to buy bonds as severely discounted bonds rose in value. But bonds are no longer the safe-harbor, buy-and-hold favorite of widows, orphans, and pension fund managers that they once were. *Timing* is critical in the buying and selling of bonds. Shorter term maturities become more popular in uncertain times. Lenders are demanding protection against declines in face value and put provisions are being used to transfer the risk of loss to borrowers. Bonds indexed to inflation may emerge in the future.

Stocks—whether individual issues or mutual fund shares—also require a certain degree of timing. Awareness of cycles and the use of market-timing services can be employed to move money in and out of the market. One should not always be in the market. A certain degree of contrarian philosophy continues to be valid; if you're going to buy at bottom-of-the-market prices, you have to be willing to buy at the bottom of the market. And sell at the top.

"Things" will continue to play a critical role in investment diversification. Again, timing and responsiveness to change are vital. The real estate boom of the 1970s was fueled by cheap money (no longer available and not likely to return), leveraged tax deductions at marginal rates up to 70 percent (now reduced to a maximum of 50 percent), and galloping rates of inflation (while the inflation fight is not over, we cannot be sure that the overall inflation rate in the future will equal the 1975–1980 experience). Real estate investors in the 1980s cannot be assured of achieving historical profit margins merely by riding a wave of inflation. Values must be added to properties through better management, marketing, and rehabilitation. Financing costs may reduce leverage and tax advantages; all cash transactions could be more popular as pension funds and trusts increase their participation in real estate markets. Lenders will demand and receive participation in equity growth, gross rents, or sales.

As the oil glut of 1982 proves illusory, investors will see these times as a window of opportunity, when producing oil and gas properties were an enviable purchase. In 1982, the Hunt Brothers, as part of their recovery from the silver crunch, were forced to sell the family-owned Placid Oil Company holdings to one of the country's largest managers of investor-owned producing oil and gas wells. Financial adversity creates liquidation of assets that would not be for sale in better times; again investors who act and buy when others are not, are likely to gain on the other side of the cycle.

For tax and inflationary reasons on the part of investors, and financing reasons on the part of business, leasing programs will prove popular in the 1980s. Strengthened by tax law changes, leasing arrangements provide investors with an opportunity to own basic capital equipment—railroad rolling stock, fuel-efficient jet aircraft, barges, intermodel containers, new generation computers, and the like.

Hard assets will retain their importance, but lessons have been learned. Silver and gold are commodities. Prices are volatile and subject to leveraged speculation, unforeseen international pressures, changing industrial and consumer demand, and government interference. Russia, because of long-term climatic changes, is no longer able to produce sufficient grain to feed its people and cattle. With currency shortages in the West, the Russians have been heavy sellers of gold, and may be forced to continue such sales in the future. The oil producing and exporting countries may not have the cash surpluses they had in the past, and so may no longer be a potential source of demand. Timing and patience in the purchase of precious metals is always advisable.

Diamonds have been considered a storehouse of value and an international form of money for too long to be eliminated as a viable hedge. But some attention has been shifted to colored gemstones, which offer both pitfalls and promise. Rubies and blue sapphires saw price adjustments in 1981, while other stones advanced or held value. Brazilian stones (aquamarine; green, blue-green, pink, and ruby-red tourmaline; spinel; chrysoberyl; golden topaz); fancy sapphires from Southeast Asia (yellow, pink, golden); tsavorite, an emerald-green garnet from Kenya—such stones became popular with investors. The standards applied to these emerging stones are not as precise as they are in the judging of diamonds. But such stones are also rare, and prices per carat are far less than those of diamonds. Prices have room to grow, and the stones will have potential jewelry use. Diamonds and colored stones appreciate cyclically with varying rates of growth and, as we have seen, periods of potential flatness or decline. Buy and hold for the long term; ideally you should purchase gems in a slack market and sell at the top of the inflationary business cycle.

Rare coins and stamps also experienced declines in 1980–81 and provided valuable lessons. In the rapid advances of 1978–1980, "fringe material"—that is, lower grade coins or stamps, modern issues, and common date coins—were caught up in the frenzy but showed the greatest softness during the market adjustment. Truly fine and rare material stayed in strong hands, did not come back on the market, and proved the most durable.

For the future, here are eleven basic rules to keep in mind:

1. *Diversify.* Don't put all your eggs in one basket. And read more than one newsletter.

2. *Spread your risk* (a point of diversification). You will make mistakes; some investments will be better than others. Do not expose more than 10–15 percent of your investable assets to any one risk. Diversify within categories, also, so that stock, coin, stamp, or gem portfolios are balanced, as an example.

3. *Never buy a bargain.* If it sounds too good to be true, it is.

4. *Be willing to buy the best.* And pay top dollar for quality. Quality endures; junk does not.

5. *Watch cycles of growth.* Not all stocks, coins, stamps, or gems gain at the same rate or at the same time. And be realistic about value. A thing is worth only what someone will pay for it.

6. *Don't confuse collecting with investing.* Never invest in anything that you would not be willing to sell.

7. *Use a "stop loss."* Decide in advance what degree of loss you are willing to accept before you sell, and stick to it. Cut your losses, and protect your winners. Don't be greedy. And watch the tax treatment of short-term losses and gains (on assets held less than one year) versus long-term losses or gains (assets held over one year). Timing of gains and losses has important tax implications.

8. *Buy for the long term.* Short-run speculation is not suited to gems, coins, or stamps; and it is risky when applied to silver, gold, other commodities, or stocks. But be ready to sell in the short term, if need be. A 50 percent loss takes a 100 percent gain to get back even.

9. *Seek education.* The more you know, the more you are the master of you own destiny. Read, study, attend seminars, learn.

10. *If you are not an expert, hire one.* No one financial adviser can be an expert on everything. But he or she should have access to people who are. If you don't have the time, patience, or ability to plan, research, and monitor your investments, delegate the task to someone who can do it for you.

11. *Have faith.* The doomsayer notwithstanding, there is no final refuge. The Statue of Liberty is in New York harbor. The refugees and the flight capital of the world seek our shores. If we don't save our system, stabilize our dollar, and rebuild our economy, where can we go? And if you truly understand the laws in our books and the power of the U.S. government to seize, regulate, and control financial assets and currency, you cannot possibly believe that you would be able to walk into a supermarket on Main Street U.S.A. and buy hamburger with a South African krugerand!

An international metals expert recently quipped:

> My advice is to put 20% to 30% of assets into gold and hope that its price goes down. The world of $100 gold is marked by happy, friendly, and trusting people living in peace and plenty. The world of $1,000 gold is marked by war, famine, distrust, and human misery.

Something to think about. . . .

Part 5

Editor's Notes:
Basic Investment Strategies

If you are an investor, you probably have already formed, or are being guided by, some basic investment strategies. If you have yet to accumulate the money with which to invest, now is not too soon to be laying the groundwork. These four chapters contain some of the basics. Regardless of which group you fall into, you'll want to read them carefully. After doing so, you'll be better able to ask questions—or make decisions.

Chapter 17 opens the discussion of basics with Eric Medrow's explanation of the difference between an annuity and a life insurance policy. You'll also learn about the different types of annuities available to investors and their benefits. Next come Tom McAllister's guidelines in Chapter 18 for researching and evaluating financial products—he tells you how to spot those questionable "big deals." In Chapter 19 Gus Hansch turns to the continuing debate over term versus cash value insurance and raises the all-important question of self-discipline, the basic ingredient of any financial plan. Eileen Sharkey then winds up the discussion by pointing out in Chapter 20 that few people know what inflation is, what it can do, and why we should be concerned about it for our financial peace of mind in the future.

Eric H. Medrow is an experienced insurance consultant who has helped to research and develop new insurance products in the areas of deferred compensation and deposit term. He is president of H & M Associates, Incorporated, and he was previously vice-president, sales, for the Unistar Division of the Summit Organization. He has also held a number of positions with First Investment Annuity Company of America. He has provided consulting services to a number of firms in developing their variable annuity products. Medrow has written articles for and contributed to *Financial Planner, United Main Liner, Medical Economics, Financial Planning Practitioner*, and *Journal for the Institute of Financial Planners*. A Certified Financial Planner, he spent three years on the board of directors of the International Association for Financial Planning and is currently on the board of directors and is regional vice-president of the Institute of Certified Financial Planners. He is on the board of the American Association of Limited Partners.

Chapter 17

The Role of Annuities in Financial Planning

Eric H. Medrow, CFP

First, let's put the annuity in its proper perspective. Let's call a spade a spade by defining the difference between an annuity and life insurance. Basically, you purchase life insurance to protect your beneficiaries against the risk of your early death. The annuity, on the other hand, is the reverse concept. It protects against the risk of your living too long, or in other words, of out-living your ability to earn income.

Historical Development of Annuities

We can trace the first fixed-annuity contract back to the days of the Roman Empire, when the emperor rewarded his loyal and long-serving senators with a contract of income for the rest of the senator's life. Although it was a simple annuity contract underwritten by the empire itself, it certainly answered the income needs of the retiring senator.

By about the thirteenth century in northern Europe, the first variable annuity contract was designed. It pointed up the financial vagaries of the time and the need to live with the inflationary climate. A son and a father had arranged for an annuity contract between them to be denominated in Parisian livres and stipulated that this contract could be delineated in the sou of Tournai in the event that the purchasing power of the Parisian livre ever declined.

The annuity has become the keystone of modern financial planning and may well be the whetstone to sharpen people's interest in financial planning and lead the financial planner to better prepare his clients for the ravages of inflation.

The deferred annuity lay dormant for most of the early decades of the twentieth century, except for being occasionally used as a method to guarantee income, but it was not used often. The deferred annuity market really developed in the late 1950s and early 1960's. At that time, the University of Chicago did an interesting study on the effect of inflation on fixed incomes and how this related to the stock market. The first variable annuity was started by Teachers Insurance Annuity Association for the teacher market through its College of Retirement Equities Program Fund. Soon after that, a company was formed called the Variable Annuity Life Insurance Company or better known as VALIC. This company marketed the variable annuity contract through the teacher market on a more widespread basis until the early 1960s, when a landmark Supreme Court decision affecting both VALIC and the Prudential Life Insurance Company indicated that a separate account must be formed by the insurance company, which was to be registered with the Securities and Exchange Commission (SEC), and that only people licensed by the National Association of Securities Dealers (NASD) could market these plans.

It is interesting that annuity marketing began in the variable market in the 1960s, as opposed to the fixed-annuity market. This was mainly because of the tremendous growth in the equity markets at a time when inflation was still only 2–3 percent a year as a result of the prosperity that immediately followed World War II and the need to move into equity-type products to keep up with inflation.

By the late 1960s, some material changes in U.S. fiscal and monetary policies caused a sharp reversal of form by the major companies on the New York Stock Exchange. This was probably the main reason for the tremendous sale of fixed annuities that took place in the 1970s and into the 1980s. By the late 1960s, the Federal Reserve Board was manipulating interest rates to a far greater degree than it had even done in the entire history of that quasi-public body. At the same time, the effects of the Guns and Butter Policy and the Tax Reform Act of 1969 had the equities industry on its knees. The army of salesmen available in the New York Stock Exchange market required that this product void be filled, and by 1971, a small company located in Valley Forge, Pennsylvania, called First Investment

Annuity Company (FIAC), had been formed to fill this void with a product called the investment annuity. It took a decision by the New York Stock Exchange Board of Directors in April of 1972 to allow the New York Stock Exchange registered representatives to become licensed to sell insurance. By this time, the importance of investment annuities as a financial planning tool had come to be recognized by other securities salesmen, and in 1972 the firm of E. F. Hutton and Company, and A. G. Edwards and Sons, Incorporated, had their salesmen licensed to sell the investment annuity product.

After the initial marketing thrust by FIAC, other companies developed the single-premium deferred annuity (SPDA) contracts that would guarantee principal and rate of interest. By 1981 thousands of people signed up for over $5 billion on insurance company books in the form of SPDAs. This is a significant contribution to the formation of capital in this country; it also helps our consumers keep up with inflation and taxes created by many years of inadequate fiscal and monetary policy by our government.

Deferred Annuity (Accumulation Years)

The deferred annuity is a parking place for your retirement dollars—a place to stash away those dollars to protect them from inflation and taxation. The greater part of the dollars placed into annuity contracts today go into the deferred annuity. A deferred annuity means that your benefits do not begin until sometime in the future. Deferred annuities may be single-purchase annuities, in which one lump sum is placed into the annuity contract. This may be an insurance settlement, a bonus, or simple savings and investments that have been accumulating elsewhere and are subject to

taxation; they can be removed from exposure to taxation and placed into a deferred-annuity contract. In addition, flexible premium contracts are available as deferred annuities. These involved monthly or other periodic payment into a deferred-annuity contract, perhaps through a salary reduction plan, or a salary deduction plan, depending upon whether you purchased the annuity in a qualified plan market or simply used it as a savings device.

The Immediate Annuity (Distribution Years)

Just as the concept of a deferred annuity is relatively simple, the concept of the immediate annuity during the distribution years can be relatively difficult. Very little money goes directly into an immediate annuity contract, and there are really only two options available at the time an annuity becomes an immediate annuity; (1) the straight life annuity option and (2) the period certain only annuity option. Between these two options lie numerous variations on the theme. Let's review some of them.

First, an annuity option can be changed by the numbers of lives involved. The annuitant may elect a joint-and-survivor annuity, which will pay income to these two people as long as they are alive, and these options can be varied by the percentages of income to the survivor involved, for instance, 75 percent, 50 percent, 25 percent, or whatever amount of annuity payment is necessary. Since the annuity payment is based on mortality tables, these percentages of payback will be a function of those tables. The straight life annuity option does not have a refund feature, and will distribute both the principal and the income that have accumulated over the lifetime of these two or more specified people.

If you do not want to expose your assets

to the insurance company, you may elect a different option. What does that mean? By electing a straight life annuity option, the owner, on the basis of his life expectancy, exposes all of his dollars to the insurance company. In other words, if he were to die too soon, the remaining dollars would become the property of the life insurance company. The converse is that if the owner were to outlive his life expectancy, the insurance company would then have to pay those continued lifetime payments. This is the risk the individual takes. The insurance company's risk is spread over the lives of many people and by virtue of mortality tables, they will generally average their risk out and adjust it accordingly to obtain a profit.

The period certain only annuity would pay the proceeds of the principal and income accumulated in the annuity contract over a specific and certain period. Why it is called a period certain annuity as opposed to a certain period annuity, no one knows; however, this period certain annuity can only be for five, ten, fifteen, twenty, or whatever number of years the annuitant desires if it is available to him in the contract. A combination of the lifetime annuity and a period certain can be employed so that the lifetime guarantee would apply. If the annuitant died early, however, for instance in the eighth year of a ten-year period certain annuity, the following two years of the annuity (called the commuted valle) would be paid to whomever you have designed as your beneficiary.

Other options that are available give installment refunds, cash refunds, and the like. Remember, all these options are variations of only two pure annuity options—the straight life annuity option, and period certain only annuity option.

For financial planning purposes, it is recommended that you use immediate annuity without period certain options, or in other words, straight life annuity option, only in limited cases. It is better to find

other methods of distribution, which are discussed later in the chapter.

Fixed Annuities

Fixed annuities generally offer the least amount of risk while offering the traditional deferral of income on an annuity contract. In a fixed-annuity contract the insurance company guarantees are based on three factors: (1) it takes on the mortality risk, (2) it takes on the expense (administrative and all other) risk, and (3) it takes on the investment risk. Thus, whatever return on investment the contract guarantees must be paid to the owner.

When are fixed annuities used? In general, fixed annuities should be used to form the basis of the client's financial plan. In an environment of high interest rates, as has been the case in the late 1980s, the fixed-annuity contract is certainly an ideal investment. When a client can obtain a guarantee of 13 or 14 percent on his investment, and at the same time enjoy a tax deferral, this certainly underlines the appropriateness of the fixed annuity as an investment vehicle.

When investing in fixed-annuity contracts, you should carefully look at the investment philosophy of the insurance company guaranteeing the investment. Find out how some of the original contracts are being handled. Has the company upgraded the interest affixed to the older contracts as interest rates have moved up, or do they remain at their old rates? In a rising interest rate market, the contract holder risks the possibility of not keeping up with the rising interest rates.

Also, as interest begins to subside and the equity markets begin to move up, your fixed interest rate in your annuity contract may no longer be keeping pace with growth in the equity market. Because of the fiscal and monetary environment in the 1970s and early 1980s, this has not been the case, but who knows what the future may hold.

Variable Annuities

A variable annuity is generally set aside in a separate account by an insurance company so that the performance in the contract will not impinge on the general assets of the life insurance company, and thereby create an adverse effect on the capital and reserve structure of the insurance company. The insurance company guarantees the mortality risk and the expense risk in the contract. However, the investment risk is now passed from the insurance company back to you, so that the investment risk now depends on and varies with the investments in the separate account.

When is the variable annuity used? The variable annuity might be used after the purchase of a fixed annuity or other types of fixed investments by the client. Generally, the variable annuity is most suited to the needs of the younger individual who has the time to allow his money to grow tax-deferred ina variable account while taking on a measure of investment risk. Some of the investment media employed within the variable annuity by the insurance company might be money market instruments, option income, combinations of growth and income, high-yield bonds, preferred stocks, or short-term growth investments that will generate short-term capital gains.

Because of the nature of the variable contract, the owner of the annuity will translate his unit of value into an accumulation unit. The number of accumulation units will be determined on the day the contract is purchased, and this number will remain the same during the deferral stage of the contract. However, each accumulation unit will change up or down depending upon the net investment experience of the investment fund underlying these accumulation accounts within the variable annuity separate account. At the time that a variable annuity contract is available for distribution, these accumulation units will be valued again and either paid out in a lump sum or set up in one of the options discussed earlier. At this point, the accumulation units will be translated into annuity units and these annuity units will support the dollar amount of the monthly annuity payment on the basis of the growth of the unit.

Generally, a variable annuity is designed to keep pace with the cost of living and, therefore, should provide a constant in terms of purchasing power—that is, if the investment manager is doing his job right. The problem is that in periods of deflation or even sometimes during a recession, the variable annuity contract is not tied to the growth of the economy. One answer to this potential problem is to incorporate a timing concept into the annuity contract that would change the variable contract to investments that would be used in a fixed-annuity contract in these times of deflation or recession. In this way, a protective device can be built into the variable annuity contract.

Key Features for Use of Annuities in Financial Planning

Guaranteed Principal

In the fixed-annuity contract, principal is guaranteed. In other words, the client puts in 100 cents to the dollar, and his contract is always equal to at least 100 cents on the dollar, even if he takes it out the day after he's placed the money with the insurance company. This guaranteed principal may be subject to certain surrender options, depending upon the insurance company that the client uses.

Tax-deferred Income

All income has a current income rate feature that is deferred from taxation. That current rate might be guaranteed for three months, six months, a year, or three years. Some insurance companies guarantee the current rate for as long as five to six years.

Secondly, there may be a lower limit or bailout rate on the contract. This rate will be such that if the current rate ever falls below the bailout rate, then you may take your dollars out of the policy without being subject to any surrender charges.

A third element is the absolute guaranteed rate in the contract. This rate is usually based on a guaranteed rate established by the state in which the insurance company is doing business and is tied directly to a reserve and surplus fund that must be set aside by the insurance company to cover that guaranteed rate. Therefore, the higher the guaranteed rate, the more dollars must be set aside in the reserve account, and the less money is available for active investment. Therefore, the client should not dwell on the guaranteed rate in a contract.

Most contracts sold today do not require a sales charge and do not require any administrative fee placed against them. The contracts are generally available from any licensed insurance agent. It is important, however, to shop for contracts that have the best features available for the circumstances involved.

Liquidity

An annuity contract has a high degree of liquidity, either through partial surrender by the use of the contract as collateral for a loan, or through an IRC Section 1035 transfer.

If an contract holder elects to take a partial surrender from his contract, the surrender will not be treated as income to the contract holder until such time as the partial surrender equals or exceeds the original principal amount invested in the contract. It is suggested that the contract holder use this method only for urgent needs and that

the liquidations be in irregular amounts and at irregular times. The reason is that in the event of a tax audit, the IRS could deem the payments to be an immediate annuity and therefore taxable if there was a pattern of regular withdrawals from the contract.

The contract may be used as collateral for a loan. Remember, that while the contract earns tax-deferred interest, when a loan is placed with the contract as collateral, the interest would be tax deductible, and would therefore, create an interesting double leveraging effect.

If a client does not want to relinguish his substantial benefits in an annuity contract when he finds that one company cannot compete with another (either in the deferred stage or when he's ready to move into the immediate stage), he is able to elect an IRC Section 1035 transfer from one annuity contract to another annuity contract, and can do so tax-free.

Probate

An annuity contract with a stated beneficiary avoids probate. However, probate is not always something to be avoided since, in many cases, it is to the benefit of the client to have certain assets pass through the probate process. On the other hand, he may wish to place certain assets into the hands of his beneficiaries immediately and may wish to avoid having them probated, perhaps to avoid some of the probate expenses, both legal and administrative. In addition, he will be able to maintain privacy since no public announcements are made, as they are in the probate process.

Many people argue that the main reason for avoiding probate is that assets can be moved immediately from the owner to the stated beneficiary in the contract. It sometimes takes years to determine the appropriate distribution of assets in someone's estate.

Distribution

The way income is distributed to the retired owner of the annuity contract can be varied to suit the needs of the annuitant. The most efficient way to distribute the accumulated dollars in a deferred annuity is to combine a period certain only option with a continuation of the deferral process.

For example, let's assume the client has accumulated $200,000 in a deferred-annuity contract. He may need a specified annual income for the next five years. He may take 20 percent, or whatever provides the needed income, of his deferred annuity and set it aside in a five-year period certain only contract. The insurance company would then distribute those payments over a five-year period while the other 80 percent would remain in the deferred-annuity contract to accumulate tax-deferred. If the annuitant were to die at any time during that five-year period, the total value of the deferred-annuity contract, plus whatever years were left on the period certain contract, would go to the beneficiary.

If the annuitant were to go the total five years, he could then go back to the deferred-annuity contract, "break off another chunk," or take out another 20 percent and set it aside in a five-year period certain only contract while leaving the rest to accumulate tax-deferred. By this time, the deferred-annuity contract would probably have grown closer to the original $200,000 value, while at the same time, the client would have fewer years of need ahead of him.

Nontraditional Annuities

During the years of high inflation in 1978–80, a number of companies based annuities on gold or silver, or on some other strategic metal. They did so in the face of high rates of inflation that looked as though they were going to get even worse. The idea was, of course, that when you could no longer depend upon the dollar to keep up with the Consumer Price Index, gold would, as it had in the past, keep up with any increase in prices. There seemed to be less risk from inflation during these years with a gold-based annuity than with some of the other more traditional forms. Historically, gold has maintained its purchasing power in terms of other currencies, and so this seemed like a good idea at the time. During periods of high inflation, of course, gold and silver would seem to be a good bet for backing an annuity contract. In the 1981–1982 period, however, gold came tumbling down as the rate of inflation eased, and so a gold- or silver-based annuity would not have been a good bet.

Another hedge against high inflation would be an annuity based on foreign currency, which would be similar to the one mentioned at the beginning of this chapter; that is, it could be automatically converted from the currency of one country to the currency of another. For example, during stable economic times in Germany, a foreign currency annuity using the German deutsch mark as one of its options could be converted to that option for better stability. Another way of buying a foreign currency annuity would be simply to buy the annuity of the insurance company of another country, for example, an English insurance company, or a Swiss insurance company.

Another popular annuity form, and one that has been used by some American citizens, is an annuity based on the Swiss franc. About four or five Swiss insurance companies have made their annuities available to American citizens through certain sources. Since the Swiss franc has greater stability than most of the other foreign currencies, it seems that many people would be interested in purchasing Swiss annuity contracts. Although Swiss annuity companies traditionally pay a very low rate of interest, the increase in the value of the principal owing to the increase in the value of the franc would more than overcome the low income paid on the annuity. The Swiss economy has a longer history of fiscal responsibility than any other country in the world. This is probably due to the power of the initiative of and the referendum lying with the Swiss citizens, whereby a minimum of 50,000 registered Swiss voters can force a proposed or actual federal law to a popular vote, through which the law can be defeated. This, of course, cannot be done in our country or in most of the countries of the western world. This ability of the Swiss people to oversee their politicians has kept them vigilant and capable of reversing any irresponsible fiscal or monetary policies foisted upon them by the Swiss politicians.

Some people have suggested that annuities be combined—that is, the fixed account and the variable account. This is already possible where a potential contract holder can use a portion of his dollars to purchase a fixed-annuity contract and a portion of his dollars to purchase a variable annuity contract. This approach may become more popular in the future, depending upon what happens in our economy.

Probably the most underused form of annuity is the private annuity. The private annuity is so simple that even an insurance company is needed to create it. All that is necessary is a competent attorney who knows the IRS rules regarding private annuities and how they can be established for private citizens to avoid estate taxes and to spread out capital gains taxes over the natural lifetime of the person for whom the private annuity is created.

This is also a way to buy relatively illiquid assets, such as real property, funded with something liquid like mutual fund shares or deferred-annuity contracts, and thereby create a liquid situation where an illiquid situation had existed before. A number of financial planners are beginning to recognize that this type of annuity can be a useful planning tool.

Uses of an Annuity as a Financial Planning Tool

The Career Person

The person who is in the prime of his career and therefore in his highest income tax bracket would find a flexible annuity advantageous for setting aside dollars semiannually, quarterly, monthly, or even by direct deposit from his or her checking account to a flexible annuity account. This would have the benefit of accumulating tax-deferred dollars. The contract would be liquid since it could be used as collateral for a loan, or partial withdrawals could be made by taking the principal out first before paying any taxes. Thus the dollars in the contract would not be tied up but would be available for emergency needs or other major uses. This arrangement would generally supplement any qualified pension or profit-sharing plan that would be available through an employer; in the event that an employer did not offer these benefits, the annuity would make an excellent non-qualified retirement program for the career person. In the event of premature death, the assets would pass to the named beneficiary free of probate. This would not be the case with a savings account.

The Retired Person

The retired person looking for income could set up a systematic combination of deferred and period certain only annuities. Calculating from the amount of income that he would require to live, he would determine how much income he could receive out of a five-year period certain only annuity and pay taxes only on that portion that the IRS tables would indicate as income. He would not pay taxes on that portion that would come back to him as principal.

In the meantime, the remaining assets

would have a deferred status and therefore would continue to accumulate on a tax-deferred basis. For example, a retired person could take 20 percent of his assets, put that amount into the period certain only annuity, and allow the other 80 percent to continue to grow, tax-deferred. By the time the five-year period certain only annuity had run its course, the 80 percent left in the deferred annuity at a favorable interest rate would probably have grown to a point where it might be almost equal to what was available in the beginning. He would then "break off another hunk"—let's say another 20 percent—and set it up in a five-year period certain annuity and allow it to continue. If he or she were to die, the amount in the deferred annuity would go to the beneficiary, free of probate, and the remaining amount in the five-year period certain only annuity, would also go to the beneficiary also free of probate.

The Surviving Spouse

The same type of annuity plan suggested for the retiree would work well with the surviving spouse. If a surviving spouse has a family history of longevity—what I like to call a "family inclination to Methusalism"—he or she might wish to convert a part of these assets into a straight life annuity. Remember, when you use the life option in an annuity account, you are making a bet with the insurance company that you are going to outlive your life expectancy. If you are in good health, and you have this "family inclination to Methusalism," there is a good possibility that you will win your bet with the insurance company.

The Divorced

The use of an annuity in a divorce is an excellent financial planning tool. The person paying the settlement might prefer to use the annuity because he knows that his obligation will be over and done with, that the payments to the divorced spouse would now be in the hands of the insurance company. The person receiving the settlement then could either elect to take a deferred annuity, if that person is employed, or an immediate annuity if a supplementary income is needed.

The Lottery Winner

Whenever an individual wins a large lottery to be paid over a number of years, the state in which the lottery is held in most cases negotiates with an insurance company to pay that amount out of an annuity contract. The present value of the dollar will be much less to make a settlement today on an annuity that must be paid out over a period of life expectancy, or twenty years, or whatever the lottery has specified. This is generally an economical way to make the lottery payment, as well as take away the administrative burden of making these payments from the state agency.

The Free-agent Athlete

In recent years tremendous settlements have been negotiated by free-agent athletes. With recent negotiations in the National Football League, these same types of contracts can be envisioned in the world of the football athlete. A part of the contract settlement might involve the use of a deferred annuity to accumulate the dollars settled for by the owner of the athletic team. In this way, the athlete knows that his dollars are placed with an insurance company, and therefore, he feels that his dollars are safe. In addition, the owner of the athletic team knows that the dollars are being accumulated on a tax-deferred basis.

Instead of deferring the annuity in the name of the corporation, the owner of the annuity contract might be the athlete himself, so that each year the deferred annuity would be given over to the athlete. The athlete would then defer the income in the annuity contract during his high-income years and have the availability of immediate income when he retired, and, of course, he would probably do so much earlier than people in other careers.

Grandparents

Grandparents might find annuities useful in putting aside funds for the future educational needs of their grandchildren. The grandparents, or parents if they are in their high-income years, will accumulate these dollars tax-deferred. When the child or grandchild needs the dollars, he withdraws them by taking principal first and therefore not take any income, or he might take a five-year period certain only annuity option during his or her college years when the student's income tax bracket is very low.

The Financially Incompetent or the Handicapped

Many concerned parents are afraid that there will be no one to care for their children or their handicapped or incompetent adult son or daughter. The annuity is the ideal solution to this problem. First, funds can accumulate in deferred annuities over the years while the responsible person is still able to care for the handicapped or financially incompetent. In combination with a simple trust document drawn up by the family attorney, the annuity can trigger immediate income at the death of the responsible parent.

The Dependent Parent

In other cases, the younger member of a family may wish to take care of an older indigent parent and to have periodic payments made to this person. The annuity is ideal in this case, and it leaves the younger family member free to attend to his job and his more immediate family needs.

Litigation Settlements

Many times when court settlements are negotiated, an attorney will suggest that the settlement be made by means of an annuity. This makes the winner of the suit comfortable in the knowledge that he will be receiving his income from an insurance company as opposed to the individual, whom he may have to take back to court from time to time if the person paying the settlement falls behind in his payments. At the same time, an annuity may be a bargaining tool for a more favorable settlement for the person who has lost the suit.

Fund for Recapture Problem

An annuity could be used as a side-bar fund to a tax shelter, such as an equipment-leasing shelter or a real estate tax shelter with recapture facing the client down the road. The deferred annuity can be set up at the same time the tax shelter is purchased and can be used to pay the recapture when it occurs.

Municipal Bond Alternative

Municipal bonds and municipal bond funds offer tax-free income. However, the returns in a municipal bond fund are not as great as they would be in a fixed annuity. In addition, the compounding effect would not be available with municipal bonds. The compounding in the tax deferral available in a fixed annuity makes the deferred annuity an excellent alternative to the purchase of municipal bonds.

Charitable Gifts

The annuity is an excellent method of giving assets to a favorite charity. This can be done in either a deferred annuity or an immediate annuity, depending upon the needs of both the giver and the charity.

Using an Annuity as a Financial Planning Tool for Business

The deferred annuity can be used in a payroll deduction plan as an additional benefit, perhaps to obtain a highly skilled employee. It may also be used to fund a buy-sell agreement, to fund a key employee agreement, or a stock repurchase agreement. Also, it is available as a deferred compensation plan and can be used for excess retained earnings problems in corporations.

The movement to incorporate the annuity as a keystone for financial planning among financial planners continues to grow today.

What does the future hold? This very innovative and creative financial planning tool can only lead the fertile minds of this country's financial planners to grow in their capacity to serve the needs of the public.

Since this chapter was written, Congress has passed the Tax Equity and Fiscal Responsibility Act of 1982. Two of the changes limit the liquidity of single-premium deferred annuities:

1. Amounts paid out before the annuity starting date will be taxed first as withdrawals of income. Thus, there is an immediate tax on an early withdrawal from a deferred annuity contract. Effective: August 13, 1982.

2. In a nonqualified deferred annuity, a 5 percent penalty is imposed on amounts received from the annuity for a period of ten years or to age 59½, whichever is shorter. It became effective December 31, 1982.

Although the long-term value of investing in single premium deferred annuities remains the same for those requiring early liquidity, it may be beneficial to consider using a single-premium increasing life plan.

Chapter 18

How to Research
and Evaluate
Financial Products

Thomas Jay McAllister, CFP

Thomas J. McAllister is experienced in financial and tax planning for owner-managed corporations and professionals. He is president and owner of McAllister Financial Planning Corporation. He is also president and owner of Energy Development, Incorporated, and general partner of Empire Point Associates, Angels Limited, and Foxton Apartment Limited. Previously he was founder, branch manager, and vice-president and voting stockholder of Robert W. Baird and Company. He entered the investment business with Merrill Lynch, Pierce, Fenner and Smith, and is a graduate of that firm's training school. McAllister has written articles and done radio and television commentaries on the business scene in general, and he has written and spoken widely on the subject of Financial Planning for the helping professions and owner-managed corporations, and on the product research function in tax-incentive investments. He is a Certified Financial

Planner and currently serves on the National Association of Securities Dealers Qualifications Committee. He served three years as a member of the NASD National Direct Participation Committee, and he is past president of the Indianapolis Bond Club and the Indiana Financial Planners Association.

The greatest risk facing the professional financial adviser lies in the area of investment product recommendations. For this reason, many attorneys and accountants are reluctant to make such recommendations. Investment brokers and professional financial planners, on the other hand, make these recommendations as a normal part of their client relationships. But they do so at their peril, as pointed out by a prominent financial planner: "I can survive and prosper in my client relationships with a bad plan and good products, but I cannot keep my client base secure with the best plans in the world and poor financial products!"

A poor plan can be reviewed and amended—indeed, it should be, every year. Mistakes here are correctible. But an investment that goes sour can rarely be rescued, and even if it is rescued, the emotional turmoil involved is detrimental to the planner-client relationship. As a result, planners, too, tend to be conservative in their investment recommendations. Thus the client is left to make up his or her own mind about investments in areas that have traditionally been fraught with incompetence and dishonesty, particularly the field of tax-incentive investments, or "tax shelters."

By taking advantage of the desire to avoid paying Uncle Sam his exorbitant dues, unscrupulous promoters raise hundreds of millions of dollars every year. And the closer you get to the end of the year the more likely you are to see this type of offering. These deals are offered with misleading or inaccurate prospectuses, shady tax opinions, ridiculously optimistic projections (even from respected accounting firms), and little or no securities clearances with the various regulatory bodies.

Even if prospective investors manage to avoid the outright frauds and fly-by-night deals, they still have to sort through the numerous "start-up" ventures offered at this end of the investment business. These may be perfectly legitimate offers from honest, experienced, and highly qualified people. But some common threads running through them here and there stand out as sure signs of disaster to the investor:

1. Overoptimism and unrealistic assumptions

2. Inadequate capital

3. Inexperienced, though technically qualified, management

4. Lack of a best case/worst case/most likely case business plan

5. Character flaws in the principals

In addition to looking for these risks, which are hard to uncover in a new venture, be wary of invitations by respected friends and advisers who know of your previous investments and are absolutely sure this is a "better deal."

Protecting Yourself Against Risky Investments

Given that great jeopardy exists in selecting investment opportunities in the area of tax-incentive investments, what can you do to protect yourself? The answer is complex. One approach is to do nothing and pay your taxes, a course of action often advocated by attorneys and accountants who do not have to write the check to the

Treasury Department. If you wish to reduce the amount of these checks, then some risks must be taken. The first step is to find a competent investment broker who is well versed in this area and has access to quality products. As a general rule, the average stockbroker with a New York Stock Exchange member firm is not likely to have this type of expertise. They have their hands full just trying to stay ahead of the stock and bond markets. But most New York Stock Exchange firms do have in-house experts in the various areas of tax-incentive investments and these people are often available for client consultation. Product selection from member firms ranges from mediocre to excellent, usually in proportion to the dollar amount of the investment. Such firms have a great deal to lose in reputation and tend to do a very careful job when reviewing these type programs. Sometimes they are too careful. But you can quickly determine whether the firm and its representatives have done their "due dilligence," as it is called in the business, by asking appropriate questions.

These questions can also be addressed to the independent broker-dealer specializing in these investments or directly to the sponsor if the deal is being offered directly. One important point, however, is that there is no way to completely protect yourself in investing. Eventually you have to take someone at their word and all the cross-checks and bonds and contracts in the world may not prevent the individual from stepping across the line, grabbing the money, and running to Panama. All you can do is try to screen out the most obvious opportunities for this sort of behavior and use promoters and sponsors who have more to lose than gain if they misappropriate the money and run. This means using people with a good reputation, integrity, and substantial experience in their field of expertise and in their community.

The investigative process for tax-incentive investments can be divided into five areas:

1. Legal—securities law
2. Legal—tax law
3. Accounting
4. Industry expertise and reputation
5. Economic or investment opportunity

Securities Law

In the first area you should seek the advice of an experienced and qualified attorney familiar with securities law. Is the investment legal under the rules and regulations of the Securities and Exchange Commission (SEC). If so, is it legal in this state? Is the proposal completely revealed and are all the risks outlined? Does the attorney drafting the material on the offering have a solid reputation in his own field, and is the tax opinion offered by a qualified firm? If the offering is publicly registered (with the SEC) and offered by a New York Stock Exchange member firm, one can assume the answers to all these questions will be positive, but it is best to have your own attorney check on them, just in case. The danger here is a possible recision or cancellation of the deal, perhaps after the end of the tax year when a substitute investment is not available. When you are involved with nonregistered deals, so-called private placements—whether offered by a large firm, an independent broker, or directly—this check is vitally important and well worth the fee.

Tax Law

The second legal point concerns tax law. If the deductions do not hold up, the chances are that you will not come out whole. Is the tax opinion written by experienced, knowledgeable professionals? This is a complex and ever changing area, fascinating for some attorneys and accountants, and a jungle for others. You must have your own independent counsel check the basic tax assumptions and assure you that their opinion is correct.

You can often save this fee by reading the tax opinion yourself and determining which of three categories (certain, risky, and probable) the investment falls into from a tax standpoint. First, if the opinion says the proposed investment is deductible under a specific section of the IRS Tax Code, you can hire your own lawyer to see if he agrees. Second, if, on the other hand, the opinion says something like, "There exists a basis for taking this deduction or tax position," but neglects to recommend it, then you should probably pass. The third tax opinion falls somewhere in between and can be identified by phrasing such as "In the opinion of counsel the proposed tax position is deductible, but the law is not clear and the point has not yet been adjudicated." You must make up your own mind about the merits of this type of investment but, as a rule, it is more risky from a tax standpoint than the first type, and you should employ your own tax attorney for guidance.

Accounting

If the investment is in line with securities and tax law, you should engage a competent accountant to double check the numbers and assumptions presented by the offerer. Often mathematical errors will sharply alter the end results, even though they may be unintentional. Sometimes, however, the underlying assumptions are suspect and can sharply change the risk/reward ratio of the deal. Your accountant can usually provide another opinion on the tax merits of the deal.

Industry Expertise and Reputation

Industry expertise is a broad term with many meanings. To validate a securities offering, you need input from the industry itself, be it oil and gas, real estate, motion pictures, agriculture, or whatever. You may or may not have a personal knowledge of the industry, but it is always a good idea to find out whether or not the people making the offer are legitimate. What is their reputation in their own industry? Do they meet their commitments and keep their word? Does the proposal make sense within the industry as it exists now? Drilling for natural gas in a place several hundred miles from the nearest pipeline, for example, is hardly likely to prove profitable over the near term.

A great danger in this area is that many people downplay any deal that is not their own. For this reason, it may make sense to hire an independent industry expert to render an opinion for you. By and large, you can find answers to most of your questions just by seeking out knowledgeable, experienced experts in the field. Many answers can be had just for the price of a phone call or a lunch. Most people like to help other people, especially when the inquirer is uninformed and wants to learn about the expert's field.

Very few people will speak ill of someone who has given their name as a reference, and by the same token, very few people will give references that they believe will speak less than highly of them. For this reason, references are usually not the most reliable way to investigate a stranger. Rather, one should check with competitors, suppliers, bankers, and industry associations. In extreme cases, it may be worthwhile to check courthouse records to see what, if any, legal actions have been filed against an individual or his company. This information may also be available from local newspaper files. It is mandatory to establish the individual's honesty, reputation, and position in the industry and the community.

Economic or Investment Opportunity

Here, the decisions have to be made on your own. Does this investment meet your own particular investment criteria? Perhaps more important, are you psychologically comfortable with it? No investment is worth losing sleep over, and we all have our own "comfort levels" that should be considered before committing ourselves to a new venture.

Other Investigative Aids

Obviously you will incur substantial expense if you have to go through all the above steps and pay the various professional fees. This expense may not be justified for a relatively small purchase. Fortunately for the investor, it is usually not necessary to go to all this trouble and expense because the individual broker has already done so in nearly every case. In the ordinary course of events, therefore, you may ask your broker what his or her attorneys and accountants said and what they found out about the sponsor in their "due dilligence" study of the product. You will still want to check with your own advisers to make sure this proposal fits your particular circumstances. Indeed, most professional brokers will insist that you do so. But you can raise your own comfort level and at the same time indicate that you expect the broker to have done his homework.

Examine the Prospectus of an Offering

In order to properly evaluate the economic and investment opportunities in the tax-incentive investing field, as well as to decide whether or not it makes sense to spend professional fees investigating a given opportunity, you should read and understand the prospectus or offering memorandum. These massive documents are awesome indeed to the uninitiated, but they can be digested fairly quickly if you know the keys and how to take them apart.

The basic problem is that these prospectuses are drawn up by lawyers with other lawyers (the SEC) in mind. The legal language and thought processes may be difficult to follow. It is helpful to know that all the risks, no matter how remote, are spelled out in great detail, whereas few, if any, benefits find their way into these documents, at least on a surface reading. A well-known securities attorney once described a tax-shelter prospectus as "a long letter of response to the potential plaintiff's attorney." Because this is a fairly accurate statement, you must learn how to uncover the truly valuable information hidden behind all the boilerplate.

The Summary. To begin with, reading these documents is not like reading the newspaper. You must first look for a summary, either in the memo itself, or in a separate section. This summary will outline the deal—its structure, the benefits, projections, and so on. If such a summary is not provided, the first few pages of the prospectus itself will highlight the deal and give you enough information to determine whether or not it is of interest to you. If it is, you can continue your research.

Use of Proceeds. The next item to look at is the use of proceeds, normally somewhere in the front, but sometimes buried in the back of the prospectus. In the latter case, be cautious, because someone may be trying to hide something. Depending on the type of deal, the use of proceeds can help a potential investor or his advisers determine whether the terms of the offering are fair and reasonable. Obviously, abnormal fees or overhead charges going to the promoter or affiliates should be considered a red flag and should void any further consideration.

As a general rule of thumb, one can use the following percentages as fair and reasonable "front-end" charges on a tax-incentive investment. Up-front charges include sales commission, promoter or general partner fees, professional fees, and offering costs. Please note these are general ranges and that an investment should not be totally excluded just because it exceeds these ranges one way or another.

Oil and gas: 15 percent with 85 percent or more actually going to oil exploration

Income real estate: 20 percent (watch for hidden real estate commissions on these)

Troubled real estate—multiple write-off: 25–30 percent

Government housing: 50 percent (these are often 95 percent mortgaged so that fees look larger as a percent of equity)

Coal, income: 15–20 percent

Entertainment: 20–40 percent (movies, TV master tapes, plays)

Cattle: 15–20 percent

Agriculture: 15–20 percent

Research and development/venture capital: 15–18 percent

In addition to the front-end fees, some form of back-in compensation may be allowed after investors have had a return of their capital investment (usually plus 6 or 8 percent per annum). If the promoter puts up no capital, such back-in percentages should not exceed 25 percent or so, unless he has guaranteed a loan or contributed capital in some other way. It should be noted that the above percentages apply only to the investor's equity investment, not to the total amount of money employed in the venture. Thus, if a multiple write-off is involved with $2 or more of borrowed money for every $1 of equity investment, the compensation to brokers and promoters may be 30 percent of equity, but 10 percent or less of the total cost of the project or property.

Once satisfied that the fees and compensation involved are fair and reasonable for this particular deal, you then turn to the use of the remaining funds. Exorbitant legal and accounting fees sometimes indicate that the venture is taking an extreme tax opinion. If these fees appear out of line for the amounts involved, especially in relation to the total picture (that is, are other similar offerings being made concurrently by the same promoter, each having a separate legal fee that appears quite high), then one needs to look at the tax opinion itself.

The Tax Opinion. The tax risk of an offering is often discussed in a separate exhibit within the offering document. On exotic and aggressive shelters, it can run to dozens of pages. One rule of thumb to use is that *the tax risks of the investment are directly proportional to the number of pages in the tax opinion.* This is not universally true, but a very good indicator. As mentioned above, the tax benefits may be categorized according to their risk of IRS challenge, and a careful reading of the opinion will indicate which of the three is under consideration. The three categories—certain, probable, and risky—appeal to very different types of investors, but with the current IRS attack on "abusive" shelters and a 50 percent maximum tax rate, it would appear that higher-risk positions should be a thing of the past.

You may run across offerings that have no independent tax opinions at all, simply representations of the promoter or an affiliate. In every case, these should be left alone. Lack of outside independent opinions with their attendant liability is almost always a sign of either a scam or a start-up deal by someone naive enough to risk violating securities law. In any case, most state laws require an independent opinion of counsel on the structure of the deal as well as the tax positions.

If you invest in a deal in which the tax results are thought to be probable, but challengeable, it is best to secure a guarantee from the promoter that he will bear the burden of defense if the tax position is in fact, challenged.

For the most part, publicly registered tax-shelter offerings normally fall into the category of certain, since they are, by their very nature, intended to be reviewed by the staff at the SEC. The odds of the IRS mounting a challenge are normally much higher in nonregistered private placements.

Structure of the Offering. From the tax position, you must then move on to the structure of the deal itself, and the economics involved. Often tax-incentive investments are structured so that the investor gets the short end of the stick while taking all the financial risks. As long as these risks and the structure are disclosed in the offering memo, it is perfectly legal to offer such deals. *Caveat emptor*, or "let the buyer beware," is the guiding principle behind this part of the securities laws.

Among the things to look out for in this area are "functional allocation" structures in oil and gas, real estate commissions paid on both purchase and sale of property to the general partner or affiliates, and excessive management and maintenance fees in cattle and agriculture. Excessive royalties to affiliates or third parties are quite common in coal deals where the landowner ordinarily gets about $2.00 or 10 percent of the value of the coal mined. Oil and gas programs often feature a "daisy chain" in which the general partner does not originate drilling prospects but purchases them from other oil companies, which may or may not have originated them themselves. In such cases, the investors take all the risk and carry not just the general partner and the landowner, but several other oil people who have no money at risk. The key here is to determine the *net* working interest normally purchased by the fund. Anything below 75 percent is suspect; something in the area of 80 percent is normal.

The "Boilerplate." The rest of the prospectus is liable to be a lot of "boilerplate" which is included by the attorneys to protect themselves and their clients. After reading a few offering memoranda, you quickly learn to recognize these almost standard paragraphs

and can move right through them. Before investing, however, you should have your own attorney examine the prospectus to see if something significant is hidden in its pages.

Evaluating the Sponsor

Although it is often impractical for the investor to actually visit the sponsor or the property, there will often be meetings and seminars held to answer any questions potential investors might have. In addition, someone from your broker's organization will usually have made such a visit and can provide useful information on the deal. Beware of "free" trips and lavish entertainment. These are almost inevitably tip-offs to a bad deal.

All questions that you or your advisers put to the broker, to the sponsor, or both during your study of the deal should be answered satisfactorily. Next, you should assure yourself that the promoter is adequately staffed to handle this and any subsequent deals he has planned. Many investment sponsors and general partners tend to concentrate on the current or next deal to the detriment of past ones. You, the investor, have to make sure that your money will be managed in a prudent, attentive way by the sponsor, and that sufficient resources will be available to both manage the investment and communicate with the investors. On the latter point, it is a good idea to ask for copies of previous reports and to review them.

Communication itself can be a problem. Quarterly reports are the norm, but often are not sent on time, if at all. Annual audits and tax returns should be in the hands of investors by March 15, but these, too, tend to be late and cause anxiety and conflict between sponsor and investors and their accountants. A well-run program will get reports and tax information out on time and will have a reputation for doing so.

In most instances a close analysis of the

sponsor's financial statements is in order, even if these are not particularly germane to the investment at hand. If "funny" accounting seems to be in use, it will probably find its way into the partnership. Annual audits by recognized certified public accountants who have expertise in this particular field are a great comfort and protection for the investor, provided the auditors are independent of the sponsor.

In a given deal it may be necessary for you to meet the auditors and other outside experts who have been engaged by the sponsor or promoter. Geologists, petroleum engineers, appraisers, tax attorneys, and other such persons are often a critical part of the success of the program and should be interviewed, if only by phone. Your broker will often have taken this step and can give you a written report. Qualifications of these outside experts can be verified by checking out their individual reputations in their own industry.

Occasionally, despite the time, trouble, and expense that have been taken, a deal just does not "feel" right. The wise investor will take his money and go elsewhere. As a rule, you will find out later what was wrong with the deal. Even if you miss a good deal, another one will always come along later, if not with this sponsor, then with one who makes you feel more comfortable.

Your "comfort level" in this type of investing is all-important, since normally you are locked into the investment for a lengthy period, sometimes many years. If you make a wrong move, it is not possible to reverse yourself—as it is in the stock and bond markets—and get out with a modest loss. The steps outlined in this chapter may appear to be a lot of trouble. Remember, however, that short-cutting any one of them could leave you with a poor investment that is impossible to get out of and costly in terms of time, energy, and professional fees.

Chapter 19

Life Insurance: Taking the Risk Out of Financial Planning

Gus Hansch has been in the financial planning field for over thirty years and has been a featured speaker at numerous national meetings, conventions, and associations. He is chairman of the Hansch Financial Group, of National Association Services, and of Financial Profiles, Incorporated. He is also the creator of Business Profiles, a computerized financial planning service that provides a comparison of all forms of investment- and tax-saving ideas. He is the author of the financial planning book *Controlling Tomorrow*. Hansch is a Certified Financial Planner and serves as a member of the Board of Regents of the College for Financial Planning.

August C. Hansch, CFP

Let's put things into perspective. Many of us haven't been paying sufficient attention to what's been going on in a segment of the financial services industry that's been taking its lumps of late. Yet it's a fact—the giant life insurance industry is finally aware that what people now are looking for are places to put their planning dollars where they can do some good in today's, and probably tomorrow's, climate of incessant inflation, pervasive taxes, and high interest rates.

The result of this awareness is a diversity of life insurance plans of which you may not be aware.

Why Life Insurance?

It's easier to answer this question in the context of a broader question. "Why financial planning?" And the answer, of course, is that we design financial planning plans to make sure that our money is helping us be where we want to be today and in the future. To plan ahead we just look ahead, decide on goals, understand the risks, and act accordingly. To the degree that life insurance helps us meet certain goals and avoid certain risks, it belongs in our financial plans.

But what goals does life insurance help us meet? And what risks does it help us avoid?

Perhaps the most basic financial goal we all strive for is to provide ourselves and our families with a desired standard of living. That's why we work; the money we earn buys the necessities and the amenities of life.

As long as we're working, there's no problem. But what if we're not? What if we can't?

That's another goal of financial planning: to send money ahead to the time when our ability to earn it isn't as certain as it is today. To make sure that enough money will be there when that time comes, three critical elements must be taken into account.

Three Financial Planning Elements

The first element is *growth*. Because of today's inflation, our investments not only have to grow in order to help us in the future, they have to grow faster than inflation. Moral: a person in a 50 percent tax bracket, and inflation of 10 percent, has to earn a full 20 percent just to stay even!

The second element is *shelter*. Taxes being what they are today, growth by itself can't succeed if it's constantly eroded by taxes. So in addition to growth, we need to shelter those accumulations—as much as we can, anyway—from taxation.

The third element is *time*. It takes t-i-m-e for any investment to mature. And investments that offer the kind of growth and shelter we need often take longer to mature than other types of investments. So the more we seek growth and shelter, the more crucial the third element—time—becomes.

Among the options we've been talking about are some attractive investments offering both the potential growth and shelter an investor needs to get ahead. But they leave unanswered the all-important question of time. Fortunately, this lack of certainty can also be handled in a well-conceived financial plan—by means of life insurance. In a total financial plan life insurance guarantees that long-range objectives will be automatically met if the critical element of time is taken away by unplanned-for death.

And what's especially important to understand is that life insurance is the only product that can do that! It's the only financial instrument guaranteeing that lack of time won't keep us from meeting our basic financial goal: providing our families with the standard of living we want for them now and in the future. Unless you own life insurance, you just don't have that guarantee.

Life Insurance and Established Plans

You may be asking, What about plans that have already had time to accumulate? What about those estates already large enough to support us without working? Does life insurance belong in such a situation?

I believe so. Death doesn't just cost working people their livelihood. The expenses of death can also cost wealthy people a sizable portion of their estate. Time and time again, estates once adequate to live on are whittled down by death taxes, probate costs, administrative fees, and various other estate settlement costs. To pay these costs the surviving family is often forced to liquidate assets—often at sacrifice prices—that were earmarked for other purposes. Soon the estate no longer provides what the deceased intended—a suitable standard of living.

An adequate life insurance program can provide the funds to pay estate settlement costs at death. The estate is preserved, and so is the family's standard of living. Thus, life insurance not only *completes* an estate, it also *preserves* an estate. The event that creates the need—death—also creates the money with which to satisfy the need.

What Kind Should You Own?

Almost all financial planners recognize the need for life insurance. But they cannot agree on the *type* of insurance to be included in a well-rounded plan. Some say term insurance—or pure death protection—is the only form that's useful, regardless of the overall objectives of the plan. Others insist that permanent insurance—with its additional guarantees—is superior in every case. Still others say one of the new life insurance products meets everyone's particular needs best.

The fact is, different kinds of life insurance are designed to meet different types of needs and situations. Of the wide variety available, some will apply well or not so well to different individuals and different financial planning concerns and objectives. In other words, the kind of life insurance you should buy depends on you, on your

specific objectives, and on the rest of your overall financial plan. No one plan of life insurance is right for every situation. However, by defining your concerns, needs, and objectives, you can tailor a life insurance plan to fit your particular situation. By knowing your choices—and yourself—you can find the right life insurance plan for you.

Let's look at some of the various kinds of life insurance and what they can do.

Term Insurance

Term insurance offers protection only. You pay a premium that insures your life for a limited period of time. If you die during that period, your beneficiary receives the amount for which you were insured. If you outlive the period, the coverage expires and that's that. In this sense, it's like auto or fire insurance. You may or may not realize something for your premium payment, other than peace of mind.

Having term insurance coverage has been compared to renting your home, rather than buying it. The lease comes up for renewal at the end of a rental period, much the way the life insurance protection comes up for renewal at the end of the term. And no matter how long you stay in the rented home, no matter how many payments you make on it, you don't build up any equity or financial interest in it. The same is true of term coverage.

The advantage of term insurance is that the premiums are generally lower than for any other kind of life insurance you can buy, especially at the younger ages. All the life insurance company does is calculate the risk of someone your age dying within the coverage period, and charge you accordingly. The risk is less, of course, at the younger ages. And since the risk increases as you get older, the premium increases proportionately. With most term policies, you pay a higher premium every time you renew them.

So term presents a couple of disadvantages. One is the fact that you own nothing if you survive the term period. The other is that you'll have to pay a higher premium than the last time period because you're now older and therefore a greater risk.

What is more to the point, as far as the accomplishment of objectives is concerned, is that a surprisingly small number of term policies end up paying death benefits. One study, for example, revealed that in a group of term policies: (1) 45 percent were terminated or converted to other forms of protection the first year; (2) 72 percent were terminated or converted within the first three years, and (3) only 1 percent resulted in death claims. Thus, the great majority of term insurance buyers don't keep their temporary protection in force as long as it's needed.

Don't think there isn't a time and place for term insurance, however. If you're young, for example, you may need a lot of protection but may not have a great deal of discretionary income to put into a financial plan for the future. Or, your life insurance needs may exist for only a short duration, as security for a business loan, for example. These and other situations fit very well the temporary expedience of the lower premiums of term insurance.

But when it comes to lifetime protection, the increasing premium, lack of equity, and the potential lack of availability at later ages when the risk is greatest often makes term insurance a less-than-ideal solution. This is where permanent insurance steps into the picture.

Permanent Insurance

Permanent life insurance offers lifetime protection with premiums leveled over the entire period the protection is in force. In other words, the high premiums you'd expect to pay at later ages are reduced and the premiums you'd expect to pay at younger ages are raised. Those prepaid funds, earning interest over time, create a reserve from which the higher protection costs at the later ages can be paid.

The result is life insurance protection that is *both available and affordable* over an entire lifetime. And since life insurance needs normally last a lifetime, there's a strong argument that permanent life insurance is the most logical foundation for a financial plan.

In addition to providing a level lifetime premium, prepaid sums offer guaranteed, tax-deferred, steadily increasing cash values that are payable whether you live or die. Permanent life insurance thus provides not only protection and peace of mind, but it also offers "living benefits" from all the premium payments made over the years.

To return to our earlier analogy, owning permanent life insurance has been compared to owning rather than renting a home. When you buy a home, you're paying off a mortgage, not a lease. You can count on having your home for your whole life as long as you make your payments. There's no lease that someday won't be renewed, or that might be renewed only at a higher rent payment. And with each level mortgage payment, you come closer to full possession of a deed, not just a handful of receipts.

Certainly, traditional permanent life insurance has its limitations, as do all financial instruments. One drawback from a pure investment standpoint is that the interest rates earned by your cash values might look fairly low compared to what some investments are earning, especially today. One thing to remember is that your cash values grow free of current income tax, which means that their after-tax return is greater than it initially appears to be. Also, interest earnings on guaranteed investments will inevitably be lower than the rates paid on investments that carry more risk. One of the greatest strengths of life insurance is its safety, and there's always a trade-off between safety and return. If you need the guarantees of life insurance, you need not hesitate making the trade-off, particularly in a total financial plan that uses those guarantees to justify riskier, more growth-oriented investments in other parts of the plan.

Dozens of books have dealt with the real or assumed controversy between term and permanent insurance. Not all of them consider term and permanent in an adversary relationship, and neither do I. The issue is not which one is "better," but whether either one is *always* better for everyone in every situation. My answer to that is no. Term may be right for certain situations, permanent for others, a combination for still others. It's senseless to try to make individuals with unique and varied needs conform to a single product.

For a long time, term and permanent in various forms were about the only options available, but today the choice has broadened. Inflation and high interest rates have caused life insurance companies to look for ways to improve the growth and flexibility of their products. This means easing up on some of the guarantees of traditional cash values. Some of the new policies lean more toward high earnings than guarantees.

In effect, today's new permanent life insurance policies introduce a new approach to the word *guarantee*. The universal life policy for one, has drastically changed the definition of the guarantees of the cash values. For years, actuaries guaranteed death and retirement benefits by investing primarily in guaranteed, fixed-dollar investments, such as bonds and mortgages. They knowingly sacrificed the chance for higher returns from speculative investments in order to guarantee specific returns to widows and retired policyholders.

Now, universal life suggests that the risk of the loss of purchasing power in a guaranteed fixed investment, through inflation, entails a greater risk than the possibility of capital losses in a portfolio of the current high interest earning investments of today. And, so, we have an interesting debate within the insurance industry on what is safe and proper for cash value portfolios.

New companies (with no old bonds or 5 percent mortgages in their portfolios) advertise their high current interest rates, which make their policies look rather exciting. Obviously, if a policy projects 11¾ earnings on its cash values, it is going to look much better than another policy reflecting a 7 percent "portfolio rate," based on the average interest earnings of investments made over the past ten to twenty years. Today, even the most conservative old-line mutual companies are investing new premium dollars at today's high interest rates. Also, they are moving more and more into real estate ownership. The "portfolio rates" of the old-line companies will no doubt catch up with "current rates" before too many years go by and, from then on, you'll see most cash values invested in investments that create earnings comparable to the inflation rate of that time. Then, there'll be little to choose from between universal or ordinary life.

In the meantime, the old-line mutuals are selling stability, strength, and size, and the younger, smaller companies are advancing because they are young and have few old investments! It's an unusual situation that will vanish with time.

Now on to a further investigation of the specifics of the new policies.

Universal Life

If you've heard of only one of the new products, universal life is probably the one. The universal life policy offers death protection plus cash value accumulations, just like a traditional permanent product. But it adds a number of features not found in traditional permanent products.

For one thing, the cash values of universal life are credited with interest that reflects current rates on Treasury bills, other government securities, or money market funds. The money is continually rolled over into these instruments so that the cash value earnings usually reflect current economic conditions. And because the interest is part of a life insurance policy, these earnings accumulate without being currently taxed to the policyholder. The company usually pays only a modest tax on its total investment earnings. We will probably see an increasing number of new permanent life policies offering an opportunity to invest one's cash values in investments that pay current interest rates.

Universal life also offers flexibility of premium payments. As long as a minimum cash value is maintained to handle the cost of the protection portion, the timing and amount of premium payments is largely up to the policyowner.

Another feature of universal life comparable to some of the privileges of an ordinary life policy, is that adjustments can be made in the amount of the death benefit. One option allows you to maintain a level death benefit, which includes both cash values and pure insurance protection. Another keeps the insurance protection element constant in addition to the steadily growing cash values. The result is an increasing total benefit that has a better chance of keeping pace with inflation. You can switch back and forth between these two options, depending on your own long-range plans.

Finally, universal life cash values are more accessible than in traditional policies. Within certain limits, you can make withdrawals from your cash values without an interest charge. Or you have the option of borrowing them, just as you do in a traditional policy. So you can either make withdrawals or borrow from the policy, whichever method fits your tax bracket and personal plans. Of course, enough cash value must remain to pay your cost of protection.

Variable Life

Variable life is more like a traditional permanent life insurance policy, for it has fixed premiums and a minimum guaranteed death benefit. The difference is that the cash values are not fixed or guaranteed, either in respect to minimums or maximums. Instead, they're invested in a portfolio of common and preferred stocks, bonds, or money market funds, or a combination of those three that the policyowner chooses.

If performance on the stock portfolio funds is high, both the cash values and the death benefit of a variable life policy increase proportionately. If fund performance falls off, the death benefit may drop, too, but never below a guaranteed face amount. I believe that a new variable life with some of the privileges of universal life will inevitably be created by the actuaries.

Will these new products have a profound effect on the life insurance industry over the long term? Perhaps it's cowardly to say "it's too soon to tell," but it's accurate, too. Marketing thrusts have a way of coming and going with the times in which they're born. Consider one example.

Because the premiums for term insurance have always been less than the premiums for permanent, some think that you should "buy term and invest the difference." In theory, this is an attractive idea and for a disciplined individual would have worked well over the last twenty or thirty yeas. But the theory breaks down on the word "discipline," as I know from personal experience.

In the late 1950s, I arranged for some of my clients to buy large amounts of term insurance and then invest the difference in growth mutual funds. At the time, these funds seemed to be the best and safest way to invest in financial vehicles with potential for growth. Twenty-five years later, few of those mutual fund programs have been kept up. Even worse, most of those term life insurance policies have lapsed as well.

What happened? Somewhere along the way, my clients encountered unexpected cash demands. Whatever the reason for the demands, the easiest way to get the money was to dip into—or discontinue—the mutual fund deposits. Then came the stock market slide of the early 1970s and mutual funds slid along with it. Between those two factors, the investment side of the "buy term and invest the difference" equation ended up with zero results for many people.

On the other side of the equation, my clients now had term insurance premiums that were steadily increasing, and no "side" funds out of which to pay those premiums. Many of the term policies lapsed, of course. As a result, very few of those combination term and investment plans are still intact.

During that same period, I recommended that other clients use permanent insurance in their financial plans. In these cases, speculative investment growth was not a primary concern; none of them expected to get rich from life insurance. But the important point is, over half of those old permanent policies are still in force. In other words, the clients who chose permanent still have their protection, and in addition, those steadily increasing cash values have allowed them to take advantage of various opportunities and emergencies over the years.

As a result of this experience, I see a great advantage in a product that will do both jobs of accumulating guaranteed capital and maintaining a death benefit for one's family. Term insurance sales have been on the rise lately, but with the more aggressive investment stances in universal life, T-bill life, and new variable life plans, we will probably see some sharp increases in the sale of permanent insurance.

The good new policies will definitely find their place in the roster of expanding options. What's equally important, all of the new policies show that the insurance industry is not sitting on its hands through this volatile economic period. It's finding new ways of meeting the needs of policyowners no matter what the future brings.

It's impossible to know what interest rates will be next month, much less five or ten years down the road. Inflation is an equally slippery quantity. The insurance industry, once based on fixed assumptions and constants, is adapting to the times. It's saying that it might serve some policyowners better by taking new investment risks, since fixed benefits and guaranteed investments are not for every person or every situation. So the insurance industry has created choices to suit various needs and goals. Because these policies offer flexibility, you can readily change your plans to keep abreast of changes in the economy or in your personal situation.

Permanent Life Insurance: The Real Truth

Having briefly scanned the growing list of options available regarding life insurance protection, let's look at permanent life insurance more closely. Although it is not necessarily the best form of life insurance protection for every situation, it does have qualities that make it unique in meeting certain objectives, and that gives it a place in total financial planning.

Level Premiums and Guaranteed Growth

As already mentioned, permanent life insurance makes two guarantees that no other kind of life insurance combines in a single plan: (1) a fixed, level premium for life, and (2) guaranteed minimum growth of cash values.

A fixed, level premium means your cost of protection never increases. What are the disadvantages of plans that don't have level premiums? First, most term insurance plans have premiums that increase so rapidly at later ages that they usually become unaffordable. The annual cost of protection in universal life policies, as well as in ordinary life, also increases at the later ages (that is, its mortality deductions are based on term charges). Hopefully, enough premiums will be paid into the plan in the early years to cover these increasing costs. But because universal life doesn't *require* these deposits, one wonders how many policyowners will continue to make them. What if universal life policyowners who are not contractually required to pay premiums stopped making deposits into that cash value account? What if they suffered business setbacks, or wanted to visit the Orient? A buyer of universal life must have the discipline required to pay future premiums when necessary.

The fixed, level premium of permanent life insurance minimizes this risk, because the deposits to the cash value are built into the plan. In a sense, this means that people with permanent life insurance—if they want their protection to remain in force—are under a semicompulsory obligation to keep their cash values growing steadily at the same time.

Some people insist that they don't need this forced savings feature of permanent life insurance. And, they're probably right if they are disciplined savers, but how many can be self-disciplined over twenty or thirty years?

Putting up with a little forced savings buys a lot of benefits. For one thing, you continually add to a liquid fund that's available for emergencies or opportunities. Even if your other investments are successful, they aren't always liquid. In real estate, for example, many prosperous, high-earning individuals have been grateful for their permanent life insurance cash values when emergencies came up, because it was the only readily available source of funds they had.

Perhaps the greatest benefit of those forced savings is that insurance coverage tends to stay in force. Remember the figures we cited to show how many term insurance policies actually result in claims? Maybe claims are not made because term insurance doesn't have cash values and a fixed, level premium for life.

Variable life does have a fixed, level premium, but doesn't guarantee a minimum rate of cash value growth.

Let's now consider the benefits from your payments.

First, as we mentioned earlier, the return in a traditional permanent life insurance policy is more effective than the quoted amount, because it accumulates without being taxed. Someone in a 50 percent tax bracket would need to earn twice as much in before-tax income to equal a policy's protected return. And, in the future, as permanent policies improve, the situation will be even more favorable. In the meantime, you don't have to be shrewd with every dollar!

The "weaknesses" attributed to permanent life insurance might just end up being its strengths. The guarantees of permanent life insurance give you the opportunity to strive for more with the rest of your portfolio, to take greater risks, to invest a little more speculatively with the rest of your money as you attempt to keep up with inflation and high taxes.

The Goal: Total Financial Planning

Years ago, financial advisers lined up on both sides of the "why life insurance" question, according to their own orientation. In those days the lines were clearly drawn between the banking industry, the stock brokerage industry, the life insurance industry, and so on. Today those lines are becoming fuzzy. More and more professionals in one financial area are seeing their services in the context of other services available—and necessary—for financial planning.

Where does life insurance fit into this changing pattern? Basically, it takes much of the risk out of financial planning. Inflation is jumping up and down, but almost everyone agrees that it's not going to disappear.

Life insurance helps keep inflation from clobbering investors completely; it also gives them an opportunity to consider riskier investments. That is, it guarantees that no matter what happens, your family's standard of living will be protected; you can therefore get into the game and play it for all its worth. You'll probably win some and lose some. If you lose and can't recover from the loss, the life insurance portion of your plan can step in and create the capital necessary to take care of the people depending on you.

This idea can be illustrated by the story of the "very unidentical twins"—twin brothers—who came to see me for some advice. They were working in the same corporation, at the same kind of job. They had roughly the same family situations and were earning approximately the same level of income.

The first twin had only a small amount of term insurance, and steadfastly refused to add more protection. So in designing an overall plan, I didn't recommend any risks that had as much chance of losing money as gaining it. As a result, the plan focused on safe investments and guaranteed growth. The result was decent and unexciting.

But the second twin owned enough permanent life insurance to provide lifetime protection for his wife against the loss of his income. With that in place, he opted for a more aggressive plan, since most

risks, either to the investments or to the man, were covered. The second twin was able to earn enough money on his investments to pay all of the premiums on his life insurance, with a considerable amount left over.

Some general observations may now be in order. First, if a product is strong in tax-advantaged features—and has the potential to stay ahead of inflation—it often tends to be somewhat risky in the areas of safety, liquidity, or both. For example, real estate offers many tax shelters and the potential for really exciting growth, but it's also one of the most risky and nonliquid investments you can make.

On the other side of the coin, a product that is both safe and liquid may be short on the other advantages we've been discussing. For example, federally insured deposits in banks or savings and loans are thought by many to be the safest and most liquid financial vehicles around. But, they don't offer much in the way of tax advantages or growth potential.

What this means is that different concerns often conflict with each other. On one hand, we should rightfully be concerned with inflation and taxes, especially today. But on the other hand, it may not be a good idea to put that concern far ahead of everything else. As we've seen, safety and liquidity are also desirable.

In some situations, it may be necessary to satisfy one concern at the expense of some of the others. But as much as possible, we hope to design plans in which all of the components work together to meet the client's objectives, to produce what we might call the "sailboat effect." If you look at the four sailboats in Figure 1, you will see that the sail on each boat represents speculative investments, the hull represents guaranteed dollars in a savings account, and the life preserver represents a life insurance program.

The first boat was designed by a stockbroker. It's rigged with huge sails, a

Figure 1

narrow hull, and a tiny life preserver. This boat is built for speed. In calm seas with the right wind, it really moves—outrunning the tides of inflation. But what happens if the wind changes suddenly and the seas start to roll? The big, wind-catching sails may tear; the top-heavy boat may capsize; the fragile hull may not withstand the pounding of the waves. And that puny life preserver would hardly do anyone a bit of good.

The second boat, built by a banker, looks like the *Merrimac*—it has a thick, iron-clad hull, a small life preserver because the owner feels there's hardly any risk, and an insignificant sail. It plods along and makes no headway against inflation.

The third boat, an insurance salesman's boat, looks like a giant life preserver from a distance because that's all you can see. The sail is so small that the only possible danger is the chance of lying dead in the water, unable to get anywhere against the tides of inflation.

Then there's boat number four. It has a big sail, big hull, big life preserver—everything in perspective. It is a real dreamboat, the one everybody wants but thinks they can't afford to get.

What should your financial boat look like? It might be any of these, depending on what makes you feel most comfortable. Knowing how rough the economic seas have been lately, you'll probably want an adequate hull and life preserver. And knowing how the inflation tides are, you'll want all the sail you feel you can handle. Even so, no two boats should look alike.

We can make recommendations about certain alterations in the design, but ultimately it's the client who decides.

Ten Financial Controls

Ten financial variables, or "controls" can be used to set financial priorities in a comprehensive way. These controls form the basis of a sound financial plan. Let's look at each of these controls and where life insurance stands in relation to them.

The First Control: Inflation

We tend to think of inflation as a relatively recent phenomenon. The fact is, it's been around in one form or another since there has been money. It's had its peaks and valleys, of course, and it looks as though we're heading across one of those peaks now. A long, steep one.

How do we deal with it? First of all, we do not ignore it. Inflation probably poses its greatest danger to those who try to hide from it. The only potentially effective strategy to stay ahead of inflation is to make use of investments that offer either high growth potential, tax advantages, or both. But as you know from the "sailboat effect," investing solely in these instruments can mean giving up a measure of safety and liquidity. If you have a family, you probably don't want their future security riding wholly on something that may lose a great deal of its value if times are bad. And by the same token, a portfolio filled with only raw real estate isn't going to do your family much good if what they need is money right away for food, shelter, and clothing. It can take months or years to turn real estate into cash.

The part life insurance can play in your financial plan, then, is to guarantee enough safety and liquidity to permit investments in riskier, nonliquid investments that have the capacity to offset the effects of inflation.

Admittedly, life insurance *by itself* can't do much against today's inflation. But looking at the total picture, you can see that life insurance within a complete financial plan does help in the battle against inflation by giving you "a ticket to the ball game." It's the way decent men buy the right to invest in inflation-fighting opportunities without endangering their family's security.

The Second Control: Taxes

Of life's certainties, taxes are probably only slightly more popular than the other certainty, death. Nobody likes paying taxes. But are you doing anything to make sure you don't send money to the government that it doesn't want you to send? Let me explain that.

The tax code is full of incentives that encourage businesses and individuals to save or invest their money in ways that will benefit society. It can even be said that you have a responsibility to yourself and to society to take advantage of these tax laws whenever you can.

Suppose, for example, that you were to establish a qualified retirement plan in your business. For this you would get substantial tax advantages. But the general public benefits, too, because that plan makes it less likely that your employees will someday become burdens on society.

Or, take the depreciation allowances you get for investing in buildings and equipment. The government provides a tax incentive for those investments, because putting your money to work this way provides jobs and economic growth.

You should make use of every tax relief to which you are legally entitled. Life insurance fits here in two distinct ways. First, it is a unique security plan for your family, for it gives you the right to get into those higher—and potentially very profitable—risk investments that we discussed earlier. It's the base of your investment pyramid.

But in addition, life insurance has a

number of tax advantages of its own because over the years legislators have recognized that ownership of life insurance is good for society by substituting certainty for uncertainty. It gives families continued purchasing power if an income-earner dies, it keeps businesses functioning after the death of an owner or key employee, and it assures the completion of gifts to charities and other good causes. These are just a few of the reasons life insurance enjoys tax benefits. These benefits include the following:

1. Earnings on cash values accumulate without being currently taxed. This, of course, allows them to accumulate faster. It also keeps those earnings—which can be substantial—from bumping you into a higher tax bracket.

2. The entire death benefit payable to your widow is received income-tax free. That sets life insurance apart from other methods of receiving money.

3. A life insurance policy's annuity benefits—which can guarantee a lifetime income once they begin, even after the principal has been liquidated—also receive preferential tax treatment.

4. Life insurance allows still other tax-favored financial planning arrangements. Ownership of the policy can be arranged so that the death proceeds are received by the beneficiary estate-tax-free, as well as income-tax-free. Other types of property can also be kept outside the estate, of course, but only with life insurance is the arrangement so simple and free of undesirable side effects.

In terms of taxation, then, life insurance serves two purposes. First, it allows you to get into tax-advantaged investments with their accompanying risks and potential payoffs. Further, it is tax-advantaged property in its own right . . . but without the usual risks. Therefore, life insurance supplements other tax-advantaged investment strategies. It's not—nor should it be—the entire strategy. But it's a good base on which to build the rest of your tax planning pyramid.

The Third Control: Leverage

In basic physics, a lever is a tool that allows you to increase the force you can bring to bear on another object, so that you can do things you couldn't do with your bare hands. In finance, the principle is the same. But in this case, the lever is borrowed money that helps you to do bigger things than you could with just your own money alone.

But while this increases your potential for return, it correspondingly increases your risk of loss. If the venture goes sour, you could lose not only your own money, but the money you borrowed. Some people are nevertheless drawn to leveraging. They want to make it big, and make it fast. Leveraging is one way to go about it; many fortunes have been made using it.

Because the risks are greater in any investment that uses leverage, the potential liabilities—including those that an individual's survivors may inherit—are larger as well. That's why the use of leverage should be accompanied by increased amounts of life insurance to cover those potential losses. Many clients, then, also leverage further by borrowing on their cash values to increase their investment accounts.

The Fourth Control: Safety

Safety of principal refers to the extent to which you are protected against the loss of whatever you initially put into an investment. If an investment is safe, you're likely to recover at least your initial dollar amount even if economic conditions make the investment turn sour. Safety obviously sounds like a desirable part of any portfolio. And it is, in proper proportion.

But too much safety can be just as dangerous as not enough. Remember the "sailboat effect"? Safety normally is not compatible with high potential for growth. You can have your money very safe in a tin can in the back yard, but during an inflationary period, that money is losing purchasing power.

For that reason, it is wise to seek generous portions of equity investments and look to downside protection from life insurance cash values and controlled, moderate savings and accounts.

The Fifth Control: Liquidity

A liquid investment is one that allows you to convert your assets to cash quickly and easily. It's desirable, for example, when you have a sudden financial emergency or opportunity and need cash right now. Examples of short-range liquidity concerns are illness, accidents, educational expenses, and a business or investment opportunity or crisis. Long-range liquidity concerns are more likely to revolve around questions like "Could my family manage that real estate investment if something happened to me?" Or, "How can that warehouse full of inventory create enough cash to pay the costs of estate settlement if I should die?"

Liquidity, like safety, is a natural concern. But, also like safety, it isn't always compatible with growth objectives. Liquidity needs can hamper your chance to keep pace with inflation by investing in volatile or long-term growth areas.

That's because liquidity is generally an attribute of fixed-dollar investments, things like savings accounts, bonds, debentures, and life insurance cash values. And as we've been pointing out, concentrating on these kinds of instruments exclusively won't necessarily make you prosper. Fixed-dollar investments are for security, emergencies, and opportunities. They may or may not have tax advantages—life insurance being one of the exceptions—but they're not your typical builders of large

estates. Their real purpose is to provide a base for more aggressive investing, again, a ticket to the ball game.

A problem, of course—and it's not exclusive to the liquidity question—is finding the money to build as complete a financial plan as possible. Liquidity is necessary, but you don't want to ignore the nonliquid, more growth-oriented investments in your pursuit of it.

Fortunately, there's a way around the problem. The solution is to acquire a liquidity hedge that does away with the need to have actual liquidity.

I can't think of a better hedge than insurance in its various forms. Whether you're talking about life insurance, property insurance, medical insurance or whatever, the premiums guarantee that the exact amount of liquidity will be automatically created when a specific event creates the need for it. It's not necessary to maintain a large cash fund or savings account for a contingency that may or may not happen. The event that creates the need creates the money to satisfy that need.

And that's important, because the road to prosperity lies for the most part in nonliquid investments. By helping you to pursue actively such nonliquid investment positions without fear, an adequate life insurance program is an important step to achieving that prosperity.

The Sixth Control: Diversification

Most people just aren't comfortable putting all their eggs in one basket. And that, of course, is what diversification is all about. You trade one, overall, concentrated risk for a greater number of smaller, more widely separated risks, and greatly reduce the potential for catastrophic loss.

But you can't always eliminate risk completely. In fact, a greater number of risks can mean a greater chance of some loss among them. Also, while returns on some of those risks may really take off, they aren't *all* likely to rise. So the potential for high gains isn't the same either.

Life insurance cash values, with their high degree of safety, are excellent examples of diversification. First, life insurance companies invest in many different kinds of investments: mortgages, bonds, stocks, real estate, money market instruments, and so on. In addition, each of these is highly diversified in its own right. Mortgages, for example, are diversified by types: homes, factories, ranches, apartment complexes. They're diversified by location from, say, a building in Houston to a farm outside Muncie, Indiana. And they're diversified by time, with new mortgages being executed each day and added to old mortgages issued years ago. Interest returns vary, as a result, with the high rates of today balancing the low rates of yesterday.

But diversification goes beyond safety in its applications in a total financial plan. It gives your portfolio a chance to work in your favor no matter what happens to our economic conditions. During inflation, your equity portion will grow to offset rising prices. If recession sets in, your fixed-dollar assets will rise in purchasing power. That's the way it usually works.

So, beyond simply relating diversification to safety, you should relate it to portfolio strength. And because of their diversification as well as their many other excellent attributes, much can be said for the special strength of permanent life insurance cash values.

The Seventh Control: Professional Management

Whatever you do for a living, you're probably good at it. Generally, it's the successful people who pick up books on financial planning. But have you ever thought how limited your skills might be in someone else's area of expertise?

Consider the story of the $75,000 annual income executive who "moonlighted" for $20.00 an hour. This man had a keen desire to manage his own investments, and took a stab at it over a year's time. At the end of the year, he sat down and figured out how much time he had spent on his investments.

It wasn't difficult to total up the hours. Like many professionals and business executives, at the end of the day he'd leave the office, hop on a commuter train, open his Wall Street Journal and pore over the financial news during the approximately one-hour trip home. On his way to work in the morning he'd do the same thing. So, 2 hours a day, 5 days a week, 50 weeks a year meant he put a total of 500 train-riding hours into his investments.

Not bad, but divide the $10,000 net earnings by 500 hours and you end up with a $20.00 hourly rate. Not much to show for someone who is accustomed to earning far more than that in his own specialty.

Try the arithmetic on yourself. Isn't it likely that a professional investment manager—an expert in a highly complex field—could do better for you than you could do for yourself?

Where does life insurance fit into this overall picture? Consider the fact that it has come through under virtually every conceivable economic variable: recession, depression, war, ecological challenges, political changes, and technological advances. Yet, in over a hundred years—involving the lifetimes and premiums of hundreds of thousands of individuals—life insurance policies have consistently made good on all their promises. No other financial vehicle can make that claim. And all of it is done through the attention of trained professionals . . . people with the know-how to operate efficiently in today's complex financial arena.

The Eighth Control: Income Now

The likeliest candidates for seeking current income from their investments are those who have stopped working and earning incomes from a career or profession. They've already accumulated their estates; now they want the payoff. The prices on the kinds of investments that pay high income now normally reflect the money that these established estate owners can afford to pay for such investments.

Some high-income people who are still working for a living, however, also express a desire for income from their investments. Do they really need to add more taxable income on top of what they're already earning? Are they really in a position to bid for income-paying investments against those individuals who are much further along in the process of estate accumulation? It's more likely that these people take the risk of paying a lot of money for something they don't really need, not right now, anyway.

In most cases—and in normal times of reasonable current interest rates—investors in the estate accumulation stage shouldn't look for current investment income with the idea of supplementing their paychecks. In terms of long-range financial planning, they'd be better off investing in properties that grow internally and thus are not currently taxed. This allows such properties to grow in value faster than if they were taxed year by year.

As we've seen, the cash values in permanent life insurance are one kind of property that grows without being currently taxed. Others generally include the riskier types of tax-advantaged investments we looked at earlier.

The Ninth Control: Income Later

For a person in the accumulation stages of financial planning, deferring income, if possible, is normally a sound idea. Nobody expects to work hard, to invest for a lifetime, and then wind up dependent on others at retirement. Investing for adequate "income later" makes it much more likely

that you'll be able to retire in comfort and independence.

But accumulating growth-type assets is only part of the problem in providing income later. That's because the kind of assets that are more likely to grow to create a comfortable retirement income aren't usually income producing *in their own right*, for example, stock in companies investing heavily in growth and paying no dividends or commercial real estate projects that have high write-offs but little cash flow. As a result, they usually have to be converted into income-producing property before the objective of "receiving retirement income" can actually be achieved.

While that transaction is taking place, Uncle Sam usually steps in for his share. Whenever money moves, the government has a chance to tax it as income or a capital gain. And remember, at this point we're not talking about money earned and accumulated over a lifetime. Fortunately, there are some tax-advantaged financial instruments that can avoid such sudden tax shrinkage.

Life insurance, for one, offers such a tax advantage. A permanent policy's cash values—which have accumulated without being taxed over the policy's lifetime—can be converted into an annuity to create a guaranteed lifetime income at retirement. And that's significant because annuities themselves enjoy certain tax advantages during the payout period. So in essence, we're talking about a double tax advantage in life insurance when it comes to "income later."

Furthermore, that annuity will generally provide a higher guaranteed lifetime income for a given amount of capital than is available on a guaranteed basis from any other kind of investment.

The Tenth Control: Family Benefit

For a young, bullish investor with ambitious goals and a long time to work towards them, a particularly appealing investment is probably something that's growth oriented, potentially risky, tax-advantaged, nonliquid, not currently income producing, and not diversified. That's the kind of investment which under the right circumstances can lead to the accumulation of wealth. The trouble is, that investment, under the *wrong* circumstances, can also lead to disaster.

Let's look at it another way: A highly speculative, highly volatile investment program is something you may be able to sleep well with and handle yourself, but what about leaving it to your family if you should die? How would you feel about that?

That's where a concern for family benefit and ease of money management rightly figures into your financial plan. If you were no longer around to manage your investments, would your estate provide a comfortable standard of living for your family? Or would it turn into something unwieldy or even harmful for the people who are depending on you for their future standard of living?

Some people not wanting to leave their families in situations like that may balk at implementing those kinds of investments at all. Their intentions are good, but the results can be harmful. Reason? Safe, liquid investments by themselves don't offer enough growth potential. The solution is to own adequate life insurance so that you can make use of risky, nonliquid investments without transferring that risk to your family.

One of my most successful clients described this idea with a reference to the way he plays poker. "We play table stakes in our game, and we have some big hands. I know I'm no better and no worse a player than the average fellow there. And I also know I can't afford to lose any more than he can.

"So I play pretty conservatively through most of the game until, that is, I get ahead.

Then I change. I'll nudge my original table stakes over to one side, then concentrate on playing the money that's left in front of me. Knowing that *it's not my money*, I now have the right to have some fun!

"I'll abandon my conservative tactics. I'll draw to an inside straight. I'll indulge in a little bluffing. And you know what? I usually make more money when I'm playing unconventional poker than when I'm playing conservatively . . . when I'm concerned about potential losses.

"What's this got to do with life insurance? Simple. I consider my $1,000,000 life insurance policy my 'table stakes.' I have that pushed over a little bit to the left and I have that reserved for my widow. So it's easy for me to approach my investments as 'playing on the other fellow's money.' If I lose, so what? I've already made sure that my widow and children are taken care of. And even if I do lose, I'm alive and can always get back in the game.

"My life insurance estate has helped me be more aggressive in my overall financial planning strategies."

That's the approach I recommend. Invest to keep ahead of inflation, and for shelter against confiscatory taxes. But first, buy the right to invest speculatively. Buy adequate life insurance, so that if you're not given the time to let your investments mature, your financial plan will complete itself.

The Bottom Line

Growth plus shelter plus time—that's the formula for wealth. Your goal should be to make sure your financial plan provides for all three. But without life insurance, there is no way you can do it.

That's why life insurance belongs in your plan; that's where it fits. It's not like most of the other financial planning devices, but neither does it stand alone within the total design of your plan. On the contrary, it should be and can be an integral part of that design.

I hope I've made some headway in suggesting to you that modern permanent life insurance is the strongest, most automatic, and most risk-free method of guaranteeing a comfortable, lifelong standard of living for yourself and your family. For all the reasons I've discussed in this chapter, a carefully planned program of today's permanent life insurance allows you to enjoy the full advantages of total financial planning. I know I'm convinced of it, and I hope some of that conviction has rubbed off.

Chapter 20

Inflation and Your Financial Planning

Eileen M. Sharkey, B.A., is experienced in the areas of insurance, office management, and retirement planning. She operates her own financial planning and consulting practice, and is also a featured writer for *Senior Editions* magazine, a periodical for mature individuals. She is a frequent guest on radio programs in the Denver area. The founder and first president of the Rocky Mountain Chapter of the International Association for Financial Planning, she served concurrently as a member of the Board of Directors of the Institute of Certified Financial Planners. She is a Certified Financial Planner and currently teaches CFP courses as an adjunct faculty member of the College for Financial Planning. She is a national board member of the International Association for Financial Planning and is vice-president of the Institute of Certified Financial Planners.

Eileen M. Sharkey, CFP

It is impossible to do effective financial planning without paying attention to inflation. All our finances are affected by it, and it permeates every aspect of our economy. A thorough understanding of what inflation is and how it affects everything we do is essential for protecting our financial future.

The guidelines for families and individuals to follow in wise financial planning have changed drastically over the past ten to fifteen years. Many people are not aware of the changes and are falling behind as they find their thrift and planning are costing them money instead of earning it.

Perhaps it was once possible to purchase insurance from a neighbor, buy a stock on a hot tip, muddle along with too much month at the end of the money, and still be able to educate your children, enjoy a comfortable standard of living, and retire in dignity. If you have tried doing that without a well-defined financial plan in the last few years, you have probably realized that even though you are making more money than ever before, you feel "broke" all the time, panic at the thought of providing college education funds, and wonder if you will be able to retire at all!

Inflation is the major culprit responsible for our current economic woes. It is a kind of tax, an invisible tax, which robs us more ruthlessly than any of our highly visible Social Security and income taxes. Our politicians promise to reduce these visible taxes and fight inflation. (In reality, reducing taxes usually means promising fewer "goodies" to the voters—not a "winner" at election time.) Inflation works for Congress just as visible taxes do, except that you don't vote for the inflation! Your congressman won't ask you to approve the inflation tax increase because it's automatic and well hidden.

Why Is Inflation a "Hidden Tax"?

Take the example of a breadwinner with a family of four, earning $15,000 per year in the mid-1970s. By the start of the 1980s, $22,500 per year would be needed in order to buy the *same* goods and services purchased in the 1970s. In other words, our breadwinner would need 50 percent more dollars to *stay even* in purchasing power. How did this happen?

The Consumer Price Index shows that prices did not rise a full 50 percent during this period, so we would expect the worker to be better off in *real* terms (assuming his salary has increased 50 percent to $22,500 per year). *However:*

He now pays more dollars in Social Security and federal income taxes.

The *rate* of tax he pays is higher on *each* dollar he now earns in his new, higher tax bracket.

The cost of living has increased almost as fast as his income.

The result is that earning more dollars does not provide a higher standard of living if:

Each dollar you earn is worth less (buys less goods and services).

Additional dollars earned mean you pay more in taxes while you stay in the same financial place.

What Is This Thing Called Inflation and How Did It Sneak Up on Us?

John Maynard Keynes, the famous economist, speaking about the inflation following World War I, said

> There is no subtler, no surer means of overturning the existing basis of society than to debauch the currency. The process engages all the hidden forces of economic law on the side of destruction and does it in a manner which not one man in a million is able to diagnose.

A frightening comment. Two key points to ponder are, first, that inflation represents a devaluation (debauchery) of the currency—in our case, the dollar—and secondly, that very few people have grasped exactly what inflation is, what it can do, and why we should be concerned about it for our financial peace of mind in the future.

Price level inflation has been with us fairly consistently over the past forty years. It is the result of too much money chasing too few goods and services. What does this mean?

Consider the fact that from 1960 to 1978, the Gross National Product of the United States increased 90 percent, while the money supply increased 380 percent! The Gross National Product consists of all the real production of goods and services throughout the entire U.S. economy. The money supply is simply the number of dollars in circulation. In brief, the printing presses worked overtime creating pieces of paper called dollars, but there was no similar creation of goods and services to maintain the value of those dollars. Inflation then is not *caused* by unions, OPEC, big business, foreigners, or other convenient scapegoats, but mainly by our overworked printing presses. It is difficult to separate the causes from the side effects of inflation. (It was perhaps not any easier for Keynes back in the 1920s!) Our problem is also compounded by the speed at which money circulates through our economy and the reserve requirements of our banks and other lending institutions.

For example, I pay my secretary a bonus of $100 for typing this chapter and she deposits the check in her personal banking account. Her bank may then loan the $100 to a business, which uses it to purchase equipment. The equipment manufacturer now has $100 on deposit (from the sale of the equipment) in *his* bank, which in turn loans the $100 . . . and so on. How much "money" can we create this way? The $100 can be turned over a great number of times, limited only by current restrictions issued by the Federal Reserve Bank.

In many countries, banks are *required* to keep a certain percentage of deposits in reserve at all times. The Swiss, for example, have 40 percent in reserves to back every Swiss franc. U.S. banks are under the control of the Federal Reserve Bank, which has the power to authorize banks to keep *no* reserves to back money on loan.

The economics are complicated, but perhaps these examples will provide a preliminary understanding of the inflation problem, and the logistics behind devaluation of the dollar. When many dollars are issued without corresponding equity to back them, each of those dollars is worth less in purchasing power and this leads to a rapid rise of the "cost" or *prices charged* for goods and services.

The Consumer Price Index

In the twenty years from 1948 to 1968, the Consumer Price Index increased by 32 percent. From 1968 to 1978 (*half* the time), the Consumer Price Index nearly *tripled* its increases from the earlier twenty-year period, rising by 91 percent! The years since 1978 have seen similar increases. The index will continue to increase at these drastic rates until inflation is under control.

Planning for Inflation in Your Future

Between 1958 and 1966, inflation was held to under 1½ percent per year. In recent years, inflation has been between 8 percent and 18 percent. Obviously, the strategies that worked well in planning a sound financial future in the 1950s will not work well for us today.

Look what will happen to your dollar if inflation is only 8 percent:

Effect of 8% Inflation on the Dollar and Consumer Price Index

YEAR	VALUE OF DOLLAR	CONSUMER PRICE INDEX
1978	$1.00	$ 1.00
1989	.43	2.33
2009	.09	10.87

It is difficult to plan adequately for the future with this magnitude of inflation because the purchasing power of your dollar is decreasing while prices are increasing rapidly. Even a 5 percent interest rate will cut your purchasing power in half over fifteen years. You will need capital growth of more than 12 percent each year to keep pace with an inflation rate of 8 percent. Some projections indicate that inflation may even out at 6.2 percent for the next few years. If we do reduce the rate of inflation, will that make financial planning easier?

Suppose you want to retire in fifteen years on an income of $2,000 per month and we do *not* have any inflation in the economy. You could then sensibly plan to position your assets so as to provide $2,000 per month of income. If, however, we have an inflation rate of *only* 6 percent over the next fifteen years, instead of planning to retire on $2,000 per month, you would need to accumulate sufficient capital to provide an income of *$4,793* per month. You would not be any richer when you retired, although the *number* of dollars would have increased. You would merely be staying even with the 6 percent rate of inflation.

Developing a Strategy

Although inflation can affect everything we do with our money, not all the consequences need be negative. It may be helpful to think of money as belonging in different "baskets"—one basket of money for long-term retirement, another for current emergencies, another for anticipated expenses at various future dates, and so forth. We can then look at how inflation will affect money over definite periods of time and choose where and how we will position the "baskets" to avoid the worst results of an unstable economy.

For example, long-term planning for retirement is heavily affected by whatever rate of inflation is in existence during our working and retirement years. Money set aside for a vacation or purchase of a new car (within a few months) should not be so greatly affected, however. An important step in developing a strategy is to calculate the risks we need to take with different "baskets" to avoid inflation problems.

Risks and Rewards

In planning finances, you must always be prepared to take some risks. Risk is really defined as the exposure to loss. The first risk you face is that of losing your available money (capital) when investing in *any* operating business. For example, investing in the manufacture of buggy whips is not likely to prove safe or rewarding in the future! A second risk, and the one we are most concerned with, is that of losing your purchasing power because of inflation. There are many other risks. Spending all your dollars today means you risk having an uncomfortable retirement (or none at all)! Saving dollars brings its own risk in terms of where you choose to put your money for maximum safety *and* use. Because of the potential impact of taxes on any gain you make, it is dangerous to assume that increases in income and capital equal to the inflation rate will keep your money safe. If you invest only to fight inflation, you expose your money to unstable market prices, variable income streams, and significant business risks.

Remember, no single investment is a perfect hedge against inflation, or deflation, either, for that matter. No single asset can be counted on to fluctuate at all times so as to maintain absolutely stable purchasing power. Your objective, therefore, should be to get the best possible return, stretching your spendable dollars to preserve your lifestyle and recognizing those elements of risk essential to constructing a sound strategy for accumulating wealth.

Recognizing that there is no way to avoid *all* risks in an unstable economy, part of your strategy will involve the use of liquid assets so that you can move quickly as the economic and financial markets change. If you keep a significant portion of your assets liquid, then you can take advantage of the investment bargains that appear during times of economic dislocation.

It is usually a good idea to keep a "basket" for emergency funds. These funds will be safely "parked" rather than invested at risk, so do not anticipate a high yield for them. Try to get at least the market rate of interest by using money market funds in which the yield is pegged to the prime interest rate (rather than traditional passbook savings accounts with very low yields). Interest paid on money fund accounts is fully taxable, but the dollars are usually available to you in twenty-four hours without penalty. These funds are widely available and have been in existence for a number of years. You may want to investigate them more thoroughly if you are not already familiar with their uses and procedures.

The strategy outlined in the preceding paragraph will take care of your emergency cash and liquid reserves. The only way to stay ahead of inflation, however, is to devise a strategy that will help you achieve capital growth and income providing an *after-tax* yield greater than that of the inflation rate. Money funds and other fixed-dollar investments usually cannot keep up with inflation.

Inflation and Fixed-Dollar Investments

A fixed-dollar investment guarantees that the same number of dollars invested today will be returned to you in the future. In the meantime, you can earn interest on the invested funds. The interest may be subject to taxes. This type of investment is badly hurt by inflation because the dollars

may lose value before they are once again available to you.

For example, if you had purchased a government bond in December of 1968 for $37.50 and sold it in December of 1978 for $67.14 (some additional interest was paid to partly offset inflation), you might think you had made a good investment and obtained a good return. In *real* terms, however, the cost of living increased over those ten years to the point where you needed $70.00 in 1978 to purchase what $37.50 bought in 1968. This means your investment resulted in a *loss* in the purchasing power of your dollars. In addition, the interest that you "earn" on this type of investment may be partly or fully taxable, making it even less attractive during periods of inflation.

If you want to withdraw your money from a bond or similar investment before the agreed maturity date, you may suffer a larger loss in value. Some bonds paying a low interest rate that would pay you $1,000 at maturity date, will only pay $500 to $600 if you need to obtain the cash at an earlier date. In a bank account, you may be assessed penalties for early withdrawal and the interest rates earned will not keep up with taxes and inflation.

Before 1976, investors faced an uncertain future and so the rate of personal savings in the United States increased. The future is still uncertain, but investors now tend to pay more attention to the impact of inflation on their investment dollars, with the result that the amounts of money people are saving have declined significantly. Instead, investors are searching for inflation hedges in real estate, commodities, diamonds, and vehicles other than the traditional savings accounts.

Inflation Hedges and Fads

Over the years, many people have invested in various vehicles designed to maintain purchasing power at all costs and have not paid enough attention to their own priorities, or the underlying economics. For example, in the mid-1960s, a number of people invested heavily in convertible bonds as a hedge. Then in 1966 that entire market collapsed. It has not yet fully recovered. During the late 1960s, many stock exchange companies engaged in a wild flurry of leveraged acquisitions and mergers designed to increase their earnings per share, and many investors bought shares without regard to the increasing debt load of these companies. At the end of that decade, many people sustained heavy losses. The next fashionable investment "guaranteed" to offset inflation was REITs, Real Estate Investment Trusts. Again, the fad symptoms included heavy borrowing (high leverage); meanwhile, the credit crunch of 1974–75 destroyed many of the investments.

What is the current inflation fad? It may well be residential housing. The housing market has been characterized in the last few years by speculative fever, heavy borrowing, and the belief that house prices will always continue to rise. Like other fads and inflation hedges, many people have gone too far with leverage (borrowing) and may be exposed to the risk of financial disaster in another period of tight credit. It is interesting to note that in 1974, the home mortgage debt for the entire United States was $35 billion, but by 1978 it had grown to $100 billion. Since then, government guarantees of loans have increased investor and lender enthusiasm for leveraged real estate.

A number of alternative investments can be investigated without exposing you to excessive amounts of risk. Equities, such as stocks, real estate, and commodities, may all increase in value. An equity investment is designed to achieve a return of a *greater number* of dollars than you originally invested and is therefore suitable to combat the effects of inflation. Equity investments are generally calculated in terms of the *real* purchasing power of both your invest-

ments and of the income you receive from them. Stocks are a traditional form of equity investment, but you should be aware that stocks don't always move in tandem with prices. Historically, they have been an effective hedge against inflation, but the market prefers certainty and stability to the chaotic fluctuations associated with inflationary times. The stock market tends to give investors the best gains when the economy is quiet.

Real estate is another investment that has outperformed inflation significantly in the past few years. It may not do as well in protecting against inflation in the future.

Coins, art, metals, and gemstones (hard assets) are popular investments for times of inflation and hyperinflation since they are tangibles with unique and irreplaceable characteristics not available from current production. They should retain their value, since their worth is not dependent on a paper dollar that has a declining value.

Owning or participating in a small business venture can offer excellent growth potential. Many small businesses fail, however, and you should investigate them thoroughly *before* you proceed.

Other opportunities abound. Investigate cable television, oil and gas drilling, solar research, equipment leasing, and agriculture. These investments provide some tax advantages and inflation protection through managed ownership of high technology, real estate, and energy development. Like all tax-sheltered investments, they should be treated with caution—Congress can always remove the tax advantages before you are through with the investment.

Coping with Deflation— or, Nothing Lasts Forever, Even Inflation!

Some investments that will help you weather a recession or deflation include bonds, savings accounts, cash values of life insurance, annuities, and other fixed-dollar assets that decrease in value during inflation, but maintain their position in a recession. Municipal bonds and second mortgage notes may provide high income.

Working with a Game Plan

The key to keeping ahead of the economy is the proper positioning of *all* available assets. Before you start to challenge the inflationary spiral, you need to take into account the stability of your family earnings, the adequacy of your insurance coverages, and your family's short- and long-term capital needs.

Here are some guidelines that may help you in our volatile economy:

1. Invest a percentage of your assets in tangible, physical economic goods, such as real estate.

2. Use some borrowed paper dollars (margin accounts, loans, leveraged items) or other currencies to increase the total holdings of your assets.

3. Stay *liquid*—don't overborrow. Because today's markets are very volatile, some investments are best left to professional traders who can accept the risks involved. Even in an inflationary economy, periods of recession will occur where the damage of inflation to the real value of income and savings is not as important as the load of debt that you carry.

4. Be prepared to take your losses! When you buy the investment, make a firm commitment that if your investment drops in value beyond a certain percentage, you will immediately sell. Whenever your original reasons for buying an investment are no longer valid, or if the market turns against you, recognize the change in circumstances and be prepared to move. Recognize the importance of timing and going with established trends.

5. Work from a plan! Determine your investment strategy in advance and stick with it (until your strategy changes in accordance with your needs and desires). Try to avoid investing for emotional reasons, such as a hot tip from a neighbor. Keep your funds liquid in a money market fund until you are ready to make an investment. Try to determine ahead of time how a particular investment can help you achieve your goals. Look for things that the market considers risky, but that *you* think are reasonably safe. Avoid trading small increases in income with *real* risks of loss.

6. Limit your risk exposure. Consider limiting yourself to 10 percent of capital in any one investment area. This should give you some protection against adverse market conditions. You could also consider hedging your investments, by putting perhaps 20 percent of your capital into investment areas that would do well if the markets were to go *against* your major holdings. In an unstable economy, try to maintain about 40 percent *equity* in any hedged investments.

7. Keep a cash reserve of at least 10 percent of your investable capital to take care of emergencies and to take advantage of sudden, unexpected bargains.

8. Be prepared to set up your own retirement plans. Because the Social Security system has been in financial trouble for a long while, you should not assume that Social Security will be available in its present form when you are ready to be a beneficiary. Use the time you have to plan your retirement wisely, making full use of the IRA, Keogh, and qualified pension and profit-sharing plans that are available to you. Unless the fundamental causes of inflation are cured, you must recognize that you may not be able to retire at age sixty-five. You may want to arrange your career to enable you to keep on earning, perhaps on a reduced, part-time basis for as long as possible. This will reduce your risk of outliving your resources.

9. Invest in yourself, in your own skills

and knowledge, and your own business, if you can.

Depending on the amount of money you have or can make available, you will have to make some compromises and trade-offs. Whether you are an old hand or a newcomer at managing money, it makes great sense to pay attention to basics. You cannot make your money work effectively unless you develop a sensible plan and accept the fact that you will have successes and failures. When you have made a mistake, the only thing to do is admit it, and change as quickly as possible. Enjoy the successes!

Inflation is characterized by instability and uncertainty. In such a climate, there are no long-term investments, and all your options involve increased risk. Alternative investments are always available to you. Be prepared to evaluate them closely, and hire experts to help you analyze them, if necessary. Proper positioning of all your assets for maximum safety and growth will protect your purchasing power and secure your economic and emotional future in a recessionary or an inflationary spiral. As Ben Franklin said: "The use of money is all the advantage there is to having it." Use it wisely and you won't lose to inflation.

Part 6

Editor's Notes:
Making Your 1040 a "10"

My early research in the 1960s as to how people were coordinating their financial affairs while doing business with an insurance agent, a stockbroker, a mutual fund representative, or a banker made it obvious that there was little coordination, and almost none of what existed really saved taxes. Even those who brought in an accountant were doing it too late to effect any real tax savings. (Not so with wealthy people, of course.) However, as more and more professionals assumed the mantle of financial planner, more and more clients started benefiting from the type of coordinated financial plan that took into account tax liability from the beginning of the year. The following chapters get into the subject not only of tax shelters but also of the two most basic investments: real estate and stocks and bonds.

In Chapter 21 Jim Miller provides basic and helpful information on what many people still think of as the meat-and-potatoes of an investment plan—stocks and bonds. Lucile Lansing moves on in Chapter 22 to a discussion of investments that enable people of average means to invest in real estate. Next, because of the increasing interest in and importance being attached to domestic oil and gas exploration, Chapter 23 is devoted entirely to oil and gas investments. Beverly Tanner tells you what to look out for and what might be right for you. This part concludes with the interesting and informative picture of tax shelters given by Lesley Bissett in Chapter 24. Of particular value to all investors are her words of caution!

Chapter 21

Stocks and Bonds

James Miller, Ph.D., is editor of *The Digest of Financial Planning Ideas*. He was founding executive director of the National Center for Financial Education, and was formerly a stockbroker for a major Wall Street firm.

James Miller, Ph.D.

The stock market on the whole lost value between 1965 and 1980. Let us say that in 1965 you bought ten shares each of the 400 stocks making up Standard & Poor's industrial average, and held them until 1980. Your investment would have only about one-half the purchasing power it had fifteen years earlier, even if all dividends had been retained and reinvested. Take into consideration taxes and commissions, and your investment would be worth even less.

Bonds have fared worse. For instance, if you bought thirty-year Triple A (highest quality) bonds in 1968, and held them until the present, banking all the interest payments, you would have lost 65–70 percent of your purchasing power over the life of the investment.

Any small investor considering stocks or bonds as a potential investment should be aware of such facts. Since 1965, the majority of investors in the stock and bond markets—including the full-time professional investment managers—have lost purchasing power.

Until the 1982 fall rally the Dow-Jones Industrial Average, the most widely followed indicator of stock market performance, was approximately at the level it reached in 1965. Adjusted for inflation, the current market values of these 30 "blue-chip" stocks were approximately *70% below* their 1965 values.

This situation is the reverse of the period from 1945 through 1965, when we had a rapidly expanding economy and, relative to recent years, low inflation and interest rates. The fact is, the nature of our economy has changed drastically, and with it, the nature of stock and bond investing. The U.S. economy of 1945 to 1965 was characterized by relatively low cost of capital, developing markets at home and abroad, a consumer base with ever increasing amounts of disposable income, and both technological and marketing dominance over other nations. Since then we have seen high inflation and a much higher cost of capital, mature or declining markets for our basic industries, a consumer base with diminishing purchasing power, and foreign nations surpassing us in both technology and marketing proficiency. In broad terms, the performance of the stock and bond markets has reflected that of the economy as a whole.

The question remains, how will stocks and bonds perform over the *next* decade? We have no way of knowing for certain. We cannot accurately foretell the success of government fiscal policies in bringing down inflation and interest rates, nor future technological developments, nor potential extraordinary expenses of war, nor the consumption capacity of developing nations, nor the nature of competition from other developed nations. For this reason, you should recognize that any investment in stocks and bonds is a venture into the unknown. No matter how carefully selected your investments are and no matter how plausible the scenario for their success, the fact remains that you stand a fair chance of losing money with either stock or bond investments.

This does not mean that you should not consider stocks or bonds. But it does mean that you should understand clearly what risks you are running. It also means you should take every precaution to put the odds in your favor. Finally, it means that the portion of your money you invest in stocks and bonds should be clearly demarcated as risk capital. You should not put all your investment capital into stocks or bonds, but should move into these markets only after placing some funds in more secure vehicles, such as bank certificates of deposit, or real estate partnerships. As with any investment, stocks and bonds should make sense in accordance with the needs and goals of your long-term financial plan.

What Are Stocks and Bonds?

You can do two things with money you have set aside for investment. You can lend it to someone else for use in some form of enterprise, or you can buy ownership of some enterprise or commodity. More succinctly, you can buy debt or you can buy equity.

When you place money in a savings account, you are buying debt. The bank becomes your creditor, and owes you the principal placed in the account as well as an agreed-upon rate of interest. Because of the contractually predetermined amount of interest to be paid, debt is often referred to as a *fixed-dollar* investment. Whether you own a savings account, or a bank certificate of deposit, or treasury bills, you know beforehand to the penny exactly how much income you will receive from your investment. Bonds are a fixed-dollar debt investment. If you buy bonds, you are lending money to a corporation, or to the federal government, or to a local government agency in exchange for a fixed rate of return on your money.

Stocks are a form of equity. When you buy stocks, you are buying direct ownership of a corporation. Stocks are a *variable-dollar* investment. You do not know beforehand how much income you will receive. You may look at the past record of dividend payments, and may read analysts' projections of future earnings and dividend payments, but the corporation is under no contractual agreement to pay any income at all to its owners, the holders of the corporation's common stock. Rather, as an owner, you take full risk for the success or failure of your corporation. Decisions about company management and about dividend payments are made by the board of directors, who represent the shareholders. Your shares of stock give you voting rights, in proportion to the number of shares you own, which can be used to replace directors whose decisions you do not like. Thus the ultimate authority in a corporation lies with its stockholders.

Risks of Bond Investing

Although bonds are similar to savings accounts in that the income is fixed, there is a significant difference. Your principal is *not* guaranteed with a bond. Put your money into a savings account, and at any time you choose, you may withdraw the full amount deposited. Your deposit is guaranteed by an agency of the federal government, so it is protected even if the bank should fail.

Unlike savings accounts, bonds are traded on the open market. The bond issuer is under no obligation to return your original investment to you until the due date of the bond. In the meantime, should you wish to withdraw your funds, you have to sell the bond in the marketplace to a buyer who wants to take over the income stream from the bond. There is no guarantee you will get all of your original investment back. What you get for your bond is determined entirely by what the third-party buyer is willing to pay.

The main influence on what buyers will pay for bonds on the open market is interest rates. If your bonds have a *coupon rate* (their interest rate based on the face value, or *par value*, of the bond) of 7 percent, at a time when new bonds are being issued at 12 percent, there is no reason why a buyer should pay you the full par value. If he pays you about $585 for bonds with a par value of $1,000, the yield on his money will approximate the 12 percent he could get from new bonds.

Thus one principal risk of buying bonds is that if interest rates rise after you purchase them, the market value of your investment will be reduced. By the same token, should interest rates fall subsequent to your purchase of bonds, their market value will increase, and you will be able to sell them for more than you paid. For taking interest rate risk, you have a corresponding potential reward.

A second risk in bond investing is *loss of purchasing power*. Suppose that you buy some bonds with a yield of 12 percent at a time when inflation is running around 8 percent, and that inflation averages 8 percent over the next five years, up to the time you decide to sell. At that time, yields on your grade of bond are still at 12 percent, so when you sell the bonds you get back the full amount you paid. But, after five years of 8 percent inflation, the dollars you receive back have lost considerable purchasing power.

A third risk with bonds is the financial stability of the issuing party. It would be impossible for an individual to scrutinize the financial records of all the issuers from which he might buy bonds. Fortunately, that is unnecessary, because there are two rating agencies, Moody's and Standard & Poor's, that do this for us. Issuers and their bonds are rated on a scale from triple-A on down. The safety-conscious bond buyer will stick to bonds with a single-, double- or triple-A rating. The safest bonds of all are those issued by the U.S. Treasury, which are backed by the full faith and credit of the U.S. government. Those willing to take more risk in exchange for a higher rate of return may look at bonds with a B in their rating. C-rated bonds carry considerable risk of default by the issuer.

The Vocabulary of Bonds

Par value is the face value of a bond upon which its nominal rate of interest, or *coupon rate,* is based. The coupon rate is so called because many bonds have a full set of coupons attached for each semiannual interest payment through maturity. These coupons must be turned in by the owner to receive the payments.

Market value is the price already issued bonds are selling for on the open market, and will most often vary considerably from par value. When the market value is higher than par value, bonds are selling at a *premium.* They are at a *discount* when market value is below par.

Call protection refers to the period of time during which the issuer guarantees it will not call in the bonds. Bonds are called in and redeemed by the issuer at times when

interest rates have lowered considerably since the date of issue. By calling in the higher interest bearing old bonds, and at the same time issuing new bonds at lower rates, the issuer can save considerable interest expense.

Yield refers to the income from bonds. *Current yield* is the ratio of the coupon rate to current market value. A $1,000 par value bond with a nominal coupon rate of 5 percent that has a current market value of $500 has a current yield of 10 percent.

Yield to maturity is the overall return on investment, adding the total interest payments over the remaining life of the bond to the difference between the purchase price and the par value, then dividing by the number of years remaining to maturity. Bonds bought at a discount will have a yield to maturity greater than the current yield. Yield to maturity will be less than current yield for bonds bought at a premium.

Yield to call date is similar to yield to maturity, but figuring is based on the years left until call protection expires, rather than on the ultimate maturity date of the bond.

Municipal bonds, or *munis,* are bonds issued by state or local governments or governmental agencies. Income from munis is constitutionally exempt from federal taxation. A muni bond issued in your own state will generally be exempt from your state taxes, as well. Because of this tax-exempt feature, the coupon rates of muni bonds are substantially lower than similarly graded corporate bonds. To take full advantage of muni bonds, you should be in the 50 percent tax bracket; otherwise their *equivalent yield* to you will not be equal to what you could get from corporate bonds of the same grade.

Investment Strategies for Bonds

When you compare the yield of corporate bonds to that of a savings account, the bonds may appear quite attractive. If you want to purchase corporate bonds for their current yield, you should consider purchasing them in the form of a *unit trust*, offered by most major brokerage houses. A unit trust is a portfolio of high-grade long-term bonds, assembled by the brokerage firm. In this way, you can purchase a unit of a diversified portfolio of bonds with as little as $1,000. Your commission costs will be less than buying bonds individually, and because of the diversified portfolio, you will have greater safety against the nonperformance of a bond issuer. Tax-exempt unit trusts are also available for investors in high tax brackets. These are portfolios of municipal bonds.

The major risk with unit trusts is interest rate fluctuation. If interest rates climb after you purchase units of a unit trust, you may want to kick yourself, because you will not be able to redeem your units for as much as you paid. Further, you would have been able to lock into a higher yield simply by waiting. On the other hand, if interest rates fall after you purchase a unit trust, you will pat yourself on the back. You will have locked into a higher yield than subsequently available, and if you wish to sell your units, you will get more than you paid. The point is that you are taking a gamble on which way interest rates will go.

Another possibility is to buy deep discount high-grade bonds two to five years before their maturity date. For example, take a bond with a 5 percent coupon rate maturing in three years that you buy at 80¾ (bond prices are quoted as a percentage of par value; the purchase price of a bond quoted at 80¾ would be $807.50 for a $1,000 par value bond). Your yield to maturity will be 14.16 percent. The return from your investment will consist of six semiannual payments of $25 (the coupon payments) plus a payment of $1,000 when the bond matures. The $150 in coupon payments will be subject to full taxation. But the difference between your purchase price and the full redemption value ($1,000

− $807.50, or $192.50) will be long-term capital gains. Thus 60 percent of that amount, or $115.50, will be excluded from taxation.

Because a significant portion of your total return from the bond is excluded from taxation, your after-tax rate of return will be favorable compared to, for instance, a unit trust also yielding 14.16 percent and likewise held for three years. Should interest rates rise after you purchase the bond, you can avoid selling it at a loss simply by holding on to it until maturity. If interest rates swing against a unit trust, however, you will sell at a loss should you decide to liquidate your holdings.

Risks of Stock Investing

When you buy common stocks, you are facing only one risk—the market value of your stock may go down. The factors that can cause a drop in a stock's price are innumerable, among them the management of the company, the market into which it is selling its product, and the quality of its competition, not to mention new technology, foreign competition, and government regulations. Interest rates and foreign exchange rates, too, can have their effect on profitability. Then there are broad business cycles, changing consumer habits, and demographic patterns. These are but a few of the numerous factors that can affect the profitability of a corporation. No matter how profitable the company is, however, there is also the mass psychology of the stock market, which, depending on current perceptions, may overvalue or undervalue stocks.

Mutual Funds

Because of the complexity of factors affecting the valuation of stocks, most investors are wise to refrain from purchasing individual stocks. However, as we are coming out of a recession, and many segments of the economy are in all likelihood entering a period of increased profitability and market growth, there is good reason to make stocks a part of your overall investment portfolio. Rather than purchase individual stocks, the preferred route for the vast majority of investors is mutual funds. By purchasing shares of a mutual fund, you can save in commissions, you have full-time professional management overseeing your investment, and you are far more widely diversified than possible as an individual investor.

Many mutual funds allow the regular purchase of shares for relatively small amounts of money, so mutual funds can be part of your monthly savings and investment program. You can arrange to have the distributions from your mutual fund automatically reinvested. In later years, should you want your income supplemented from your mutual fund holdings, you can arrange for regular periodic redemptions of your shares. The investor interested in the most reasonable, safest, and most conservative method of acquiring equity in American corporations, should read carefully the chapter in this book on mutual funds, and, in consultation with his financial planner, embark on a program of buying mutual fund shares.

How to Pick Stocks

Most small investors who choose to purchase individual stocks do not do so because they are conservative investors looking for safety. They buy stocks because it is exciting. They can check the value of their holdings at the close of each day of trading, feeling elation if their stocks have gone up, and despair if they have gone down. They develop a relationship with a broker, or several brokers, and are fed a constant stream of information about new

offerings, growth companies, and advancing technologies. The psychological involvement this kind of investor has with the market is akin to that of a gambler at the casino. The conflicting pull of greed and fear color their investment decisions.

All this is to the good, for in the process the investor can learn a great deal. Following the progress of a variety of individual companies is extremely educational. It is fascinating to learn about new products, and new technologies. You can read articles in *Forbes*, *Barron's*, or the *Wall Street Journal* and get glimpses of the drama of market share battles, takeover battles, and internecine battles for corporate control. To take a chance on a company, or management team, or new product that you believe in is to involve yourself directly in the dynamic world of business. With a bit of common sense, it is possible to help reduce the odds against you and increase your chances of profiting monetarily as well as educationally and emotionally.

First, you should note the two factors that can have a great effect on the return on your investment—commissions and taxes. Every time you buy or sell shares, in a transaction involving less than $10,000, you lose 2–8 percent of your investment capital to the broker. If you buy or sell odd lots (fewer than 100 shares), the commission erosion can be even greater. Taxes are also a consideration. Any profit you earn on a stock held less than a year is subject to full taxation. Hold the stock longer than a year, and 60 percent of your capital gains can be excluded from taxable income. Thus, you are making the odds against you greater if you indulge in frequent short-term trading. You will erode your capital with commissions, and any profits you make will be eaten by taxes. You put the odds in your favor if you only purchase stocks that you are willing to hold on to for a year or more.

Next, you should recognize that big institutions are influencing the market. Large institutional investors follow 300 to 400 of the largest corporations, most of which are traded on the New York Stock Exchange. These tend to be mature companies past their prime growth. The stocks listed on the NYSE as a group have not shown as much growth as those listed on the American Stock Exchange (AMEX), which lists mid tier stocks, or those sold "over the counter" (OTC), where small public companies get their start. Thus you can increase the odds of investing in a company with strong growth potential by seeking out OTC or AMEX stocks.

A third consideration is the price-earning ratio (P/E). This is simply the price per share divided by the after-tax earnings per share. A high P/E (20 or above) indicates that the stock is very popular with investors. The mass opinion is that the company will grow rapidly over coming years; thus people are willing to pay a high multiple of earnings for the privilege of owning the stock. The problem with high P/E stocks is that when they fall into disfavor, the drop in stock price can be drastic. Schlumberger and Halliburton were perceived as well-managed companies with tremendous growth potential because of absolute need for the oil drilling service they provided for the big oil companies. Their high P/Es and correspondingly high prices held through 1981. Then came the 1982 oil glut and a great decrease of drilling activity. In the fall of 1982, both companies were selling at approximately *one-third* of their 1981 highs. The moral—stocks with relatively low P/Es have less downside potential.

This leads to a corollary—be a contrarian. Look for industries and stocks that are not the most popular investment of the moment. When a particular segment of the market has experienced exceptional growth over a year or two, everybody starts paying attention to it. More and more investors jump in, and push stock prices even higher. The P/Es in that industry will increase. What happens is that the stocks become overvalued. No company or industry can sustain spectacular growth forever. People buy in at high P/Es because of *past* growth. For those who buy in at the top, just before the growth curve slows, the losses can be traumatic. Once earnings falter, people realize they have been overvalued, and the great sell-off begins.

Those who purchase stocks at the tail end of a growth curve are disobeying the most basic tenet of stock market investing—buy low, sell high. How do you know when stocks are low? Generally, stocks are undervalued when the overall economic picture is gloomy. During a recession, when there are increasing bankruptcies and unemployment, when major companies are suffering earnings declines, assets are taken out of the stock market, and the market becomes unpopular. If interest rates are high at the same time, investors think, "Why take a chance during such awful economic times when I can get such a good return with CDs or T-bills, and not take any risk?" That is precisely the time when you should be bargain hunting, looking for well-managed companies with future growth potential (even though they, too, may have suffered earnings declines during bad economic times). Recently, for instance, the large semiconductor manufacturers were complaining; their margins dropped because of overproduction, and, dampened by recession, the demand for computers fell off. Their earnings were down, and the prices of their stocks fell. Yet, as you look ahead over the next decade, can you believe that semiconductor manufacturers, who make the basic building blocks of computer technology, are going to suffer over the long term? On the contrary, they should do very well over the decade. The fall of 1982 may be looked back upon as the last great opportunity to get into semiconductors on the ground floor.

How do you know when stocks are high? When the economic scene is rosy, earnings have increased over a number of quarters, inflation and interest rates have declined and the press is full of reports about an expanding economy, you should be thinking of selling. This is the kind of period when stocks become overvalued. More and more assets shift into the stock market, prices increase, more and more people profit, and the overvaluation snow-balls. This is the time you should be liquidating some of the stocks purchased in gloomier times, and salting away your profits in real estate, T-bills or CDs. You should be very cautious about purchasing more stocks when the economy has such a rosy glow.

Finally, keep informed. If you venture into purchasing individual stocks, you pre-sumably find it an interesting hobby. You will do best if you avidly pursue informa-tion about company management, chang-ing industries, and developing technol-ogies. Familiarize yourself with the *Wall Street Journal* and *Barron's*. Read *Forbes* and *Business Week* regularly. If you are really serious, you will want to subscribe to *Value Line*, which gives you quarterly updated financial and management evaluations of major companies in a wide variety of indus-try groups. Have your broker send you his company reports on industries you follow,

and Standard & Poor's sheets on specific companies you are interested in.

There are risks in investing in both stocks and bonds. For many people they would not be appropriate. If you have only $10,000 of investment capital, you might do better to keep it in risk-free yet relatively high-yielding investments such as bank CDs or T-bills. If you are in a position to start diversifying from such basic safety investments, publicly offered real estate partnerships or oil-income partnerships have less downside risk, plus tax benefits, to boot.

For the conservative investor who wants to achieve the high current yields available from bonds, or the growth potential of stocks, unit trusts and mutual funds are the way to go.

Buying individual stocks and bonds is only for the very wealthy—or for the hardy venturer who is comfortable with risk, and willing to put in the necessary time to look after his investments. The monetary re-wards may be great, particularly if precau-tions are taken to keep the odds against you down. But in addition to potential profits, the rewards of excitement, involve-ment, and knowledge can make the ven-ture worthwhile.

Chapter 22

Real Estate for the Small Investor

Lucile Lansing, M.B.A., is president of Lansing Financial Group. She has been a broker for over fourteen years, and is now a registered principal with Private Ledger Financial Services, San Diego, California. Before starting her own full-service brokerage firm, she was registered with Dean Witter Reynolds. She holds a Master's Degree in Business Administration from Pepperdine University, where she attended the Presidential-Key Executive Program.

One of her main interests is in educating the public on money matters. She is a frequent lecturer on the subjects of tax planning, financial planning, and investing in the eighties. She has personally marketed several millions of dollars of real estate limited partnerships, both public and private.

Lucile Lansing, M.B.A.

Real estate is a popular form of investment for many reasons, for both the small and the large investor. Most people are more familiar with the "language" of real estate than they are with that of other investment categories. They have observed that the home they purchased a few years ago was their most successful investment. However, like other generic types of investments, real estate is cyclical. Just because it *has* been the best investment since World War II does not necessarily mean this trend will continue. Some basic changes in economic philosophy have taken place since 1979; with these changes will come some great opportunities, but also some disappointments. We will discuss both the opportunities for the small investor and some areas of caution.

Changing Times

The best opportunity for accumulation of wealth occurs with the early recognition of change. We are currently experiencing the greatest shift in economic philosophy in fifty years. Those of us who usher in the next century will look back and see two basic changes in economics in this century: one in the mid 1930s, with the advent of what is commonly called "Keynesian Economics," and the other in the early 1980s, with what is commonly called "supply side economics." The debate over the supremacy of one philosophy over another is beyond the scope of this chapter; however these changes do affect our investment decisions.

Modern economists agree that the level of national income and employment in the United States is "manageable." Whether or not they will be managed is in part a political question. We have learned since World War II that great depressions such as that of the 1930s are now obsolete. However, minor business cycles are inevitable, and we shall continue to have recessions from time to time. Many investors, even today, are frightened by headlines and the indiscriminate use of such terms as "depression." It is important to understand that the Great Depression was brought about by a number of factors that were unique to that transition period in the United States. It was the unenlightened response of our government to the economic conditions of that time which caused the prolonged Great Depression. Profiting from that painful experience, our present enlightened monetary and fiscal policies, following a prolonged recession, make a recurrence of the Great Depression very unlikely. The *real* enemy today is inflation. Those with an indelible memory of the Great Depression are often inclined to sit on the investment sidelines, ignoring the even more insidious threat of inflation, which can erode the purchasing power of fixed-income investors as surely as the unemployment of that Depression.

Fundamentals

The basic economic facts that concern real estate investors are: supply and demand for the type of real estate being purchased and inflation expectancy. There are, of course, other guidelines for choosing specific investments; those will be covered later in the chapter. But for now, let's address these two basic economic issues. They are fundamental when considering real estate as an investment, and a great help in deciding which segment of the real estate market to choose.

Inflation

Someone said inflation was their baby's first word! We all know it's here, but exactly what causes it is not well understood. We need to recognize the causes in order to predict, with any degree of accuracy, whether it will cool before the next ice age.

While history may not exactly repeat

itself, the lessons of history may be instructive. Since Lyndon Johnson's attempt to fight a war abroad and provide increased entitlements at home without raising taxes, we have had significant and continuous inflation. This tendency to incur a federal deficit that is an increasing percentage of the Gross National Product (GNP) seems to have been reversed somewhat by Jimmy Carter's appointment of Paul Volker as Chairman of the Federal Reserve Board (monetary policy), the election of Ronald Reagan as President, and a Congress (the fiscal policy) that appears to be committed to lowering the percentage of increase in the federal deficit (over the GNP). Only history will tell whether this is, in fact, a permanent new trend, or only a temporary interruption of former policies.

But monetary and fiscal policies are only part of the issue of inflation, since inflation is not entirely an invention of politicians. America seems to have shifted from the work ethic of our forefathers to the entitlement ethic. We have come to believe in continuous plenty accompanied by not as much hard work. These entitlements must be paid for. The proliferation of special interest groups who continually pressure legislators to accommodate their requests for funding may succeed in creating an ever larger deficit.

When these deficits are funded by the central banking system, including the Federal Reserve, it results in the permanent expansion of the money supply, which in turn results in a higher rate of inflation. This is called "monetization of debt." When the U.S. Treasury continuously refinances without actually retiring net outstanding debt in order to fund the programs created by Congress, the impact on inflation is the same as if the U.S. Mint printed greenbacks. Money creation in excess of the creation of real goods and services leads to inflation.

Whether the expectation of continuing inflation is realism or pessimism depends on the intelligence and will of the American people and its leaders. The practice of transferring wealth from lenders to borrowers, and from the private to the public sector, determines in part whether real assets (like real estate) or financial assets (money equivalent) will be the more valuable at any point in time. At this moment in history there is no evidence that any major industrial nation has solved the issue of inflation, though some, including the United States, seem to have reversed the trend of increasing percentages.

Supply and Demand

Value is a function of supply and demand, as well as the most fundamental base for considering any investment.

During World War II few houses were built. The end of the war saw the return of Armed Forces personnel, the availability of raw materials, and the availability of labor for construction. Building boomed, and the owning of one's own home became an integral part of the American dream. Prior to 1945 it was unheard of to purchase a piece of real property for 10 to 20 percent down, with lenders offering mortgages payable over thirty to forty years at low interest rates. In some cases veterans were able to purchase homes with almost nothing down. After the war, great housing tracts were constructed in the suburbs, and some multi-unit residential projects were also built.

Partly because of changing lifestyles, partly because cheap energy was no longer available, we have witnessed some fundamental changes in location of and demand for housing. First, the migration to the "sunbelt" is not to be understated. Second, there is now an increased demand for amenities, such as swimming pools, tennis courts, and clubhouses. This demand has created a demand for multi-unit residential garden type apartments strategically located near workplaces. Some years ago a fifty-unit apartment project was large; but by the mid 1960s, 300- or 400-unit buildings were common. Economies of scale dictated the minimum project size to support these amenities. Simultaneously, the neighborhood store became passé and regional shopping centers become commonplace. With the rising cost of land, office buildings likewise became towering high-rises. Some wise sellers of buildings reserved the "air space" for further negotiation.

The issue of existing supply and demand is a function of many things. Available technology, the shape of that demand, and the ability of the developer or owner to satisfy or anticipate that demand are critical factors.

Another important factor to consider is changing demographics—more single adults and smaller family units may move the demand pattern for residential housing toward condominium and apartment living with amenities such as swimming pool, clubhouse, and tennis courts.

Another important demographic consideration is that the baby boom of the 1950s and 1960s is now resulting in a family foundation boom. The family formation demand for new housing will have a much stronger impact on real estate values than the baby boom did twenty or thirty years ago. It is becoming increasingly important to think about a proposed investment in terms of the time and place and people it is intended to serve.

Ways to Invest in Real Estate

Every investor makes two fundamental decisions with respect to real estate investment. The first is a portfolio decision; that is, what proportion, if any, of one's discretionary income and savings should be in real property. The second decision is whether to acquire property for one's own account, or whether to invest in group ownership with professional management.

Individual Ownership

The direct ownership of property must be considered as a part, or even full-time job. One must have the economic resources to meet unexpected costs arising from repairs, vacancies, adverse economic conditions; the ability and willingness to take on entrepreneurial risks; and the specific knowledge needed to acquire (including the art of negotiating and evaluating current and future economic conditions, inflation expectancy), manage, and time the sale of such property.

A very important consideration is the psychological needs involved in choosing the form of investing. If you are a "do-it-yourselfer," like to tinker on Sunday, and can deal with tenants, you may enjoy owning a "fix-up" or a duplex, or a single family home as a rental. But this does not mean you will necessarily make more—or as much—money as a passive investor in a well managed, well chosen real estate partnership. If it is important for you to drive by, kick the bricks, and totally control your investment, you may be very uncomfortable in a pooled investment. However, if you place a high price on leisure and do not enjoy the responsibility that goes along with individual ownership, you will want to explore alternative ways of approaching the real estate market.

During the 1970s particularly, inflation made money for most small direct estate speculators and investors. Whether the 1980s will offer the same opportunity is a fundamental question. The inflation rate was cut in half between 1980 and 1982, and this trend might continue well into the 1980s. Most lenders are no longer willing to loan money at low rates for long periods of time. Careful thought must be given to *real value* more than at any time in the past ten years. An ample amount of sophistication seems essential for the individual owner/investor today to equal the profits of the 1970s.

Pooled Investment

Before 1970 it was very difficult for the small investor to participate in the ownership of properties larger than the single family home or duplex because of the large amount of capital required to acquire and sustain one's investment in higher-priced properties. However, now it is possible to buy several buildings spread over a broad geographical area, and sometimes diversified by types of properties. Many of the risks and difficulties in real estate investing can be reduced or eliminated through *careful* choice of a real estate syndication firm that raises money from the public and then invests on a pooled basis. And these investments are often available for as little as $1000. Investment may be made either through a real estate investment trust (REIT) or through a limited partnership.

Advantages of Pooled Ownership

Diversification: Diversification of type of property and locations of the portfolio properties provides for less risk than in single ownership.

Economies of Scale: Ownership of several thousand units or management of large portfolios of properties provides for more cost effectiveness. This, in turn, allows for bulk purchases of supplies such as paint, carpets, and drapes. It also allows for the hiring of specialized personnel, operation of computer systems, and so on.

Income: Some, though not all, pooled ownership forms of real estate investments pay monthly distributions, some partially sheltered from taxation.

Limited Liability: The investor's liability is limited to the invested amount. The managing syndicator is responsible for all uninsured or uninsurable risks and takes on all excess liability.

Management: This is the most crucial factor. Good management will be reflected in the track record. Since real estate ownership is a complex, time-consuming business, it is very difficult for a small investor to compete with professional management. Whether or not freedom from management responsibilities is important is an individual consideration.

Real Estate Investment Trusts (REITs)

One way for individuals to participate in large properties is through a real estate investment trust. In simple terms, a REIT is a mutual fund of real estate. This type of real estate ownership is bought as a stock through any securities firm or financial planning firm. There are two basic types: an equity REIT and a mortgage REIT.

The *equity REIT* typically owns large buildings, such as apartment houses, office buildings, and shopping centers. Most of them make cash distributions to investors on a regular basis. Income distributions to the investors in equity REITs (as opposed to mortgage REITs) may be partially or fully offset by depreciation on the properties held in the trust. Therefore, the after-tax return to the shareholders may be higher than an equal return from some other investment that offers no tax benefits. The taxation of REIT income is substantially the same as that from a limited partnership, except that excess tax losses may be passed on to a limited partner owner but not to a REIT shareholder. The amount of tax benefit is limited to the amount of the distribution.

The *mortgage REIT* is simply a portfolio of mortgages that are acquired and managed by the trust for the benefit of the shareholders. Most people buy mortgage REITs for the income they produce. This income typically does not carry with it any tax benefits.

Standard & Poor's and other financial reporting companies, such as *Value Line*, provide reports that fully describe the specific investment philosophy of the particular trust you may be interested in. These reports are available at all securities firms.

Though many of the older REITs have had a checkered career, explained more fully later in the text, some REITs formed after 1974 have had an outstanding track record. Careful screening of the REITs may uncover some potentially attractive investments with a great deal of intrinsic value.

Modern mortgage REITs have offered income-oriented investors a most interesting new opportunity to invest for income and still receive some inflation protection. Some lend short term (one to three years) with high interest rates and good current yield to the investors, and offer a profit-participation in rent increases and/or participation in the appreciation upon sale or refinance of the property. This type of income security can be very attractive to the investor who wants both income and inflation protection.

The market price of these securities fluctuates depending on current interest rates, much like that of other income securities such as Treasury notes and bonds or corporate bonds.

Limited Partnerships

Limited partnerships, sometimes called syndications or pools, are groups of small investors who invest their funds on a joint basis with a professional real estate syndication firm or individuals who act as the general partner. The investors ordinarily provide most of the capital. The general partner is responsible for investing the funds, managing the property, administering the partnership, and ultimately for selling the property and distributing the proceeds. The general partner accepts all liability for debts of the partnership in excess of contributed capital.

Choosing a Partnership

Private versus Public. Private partnerships are generally small groups where the investor buys a limited interest in one or more specific properties. Since private partnerships are not regulated by either the Securities and Exchange Commission or by the State Securities Commissioner, the small investor or his adviser should be sophisticated enough to evaluate the merits of the entire transaction. Since federal laws (SEC Reg. 146) require large income or net worth in order to qualify as an investor in these private partnerships, and each must be evaluated separately, these offerings are beyond the scope of this text.

Registered Partnerships. Public, or registered, partnerships are sponsored by syndication companies. The six largest, in alphabetical order, are: American Property Investors, Balcor Co., Consolidated Capital, Fox and Carskadon, JMB Realty Corporation, and Robert McNeil Corporation. Public offerings are registered with both the SEC and the State Securities Commissioners. Offerings are approved only if they meet prescribed guidelines which include limitations on compensation to the general partners and limitations on limited partners' rights and privileges. In addition, the brokerage firms and the financial planning firms who market these partnerships go through a review process, called "due diligence," to assure themselves the offering represents a fair investment opportunity. The minimum investment in most programs is $3000 to $5000.

Several real estate syndicators have returned to their investors very attractive yields—15 to 35 percent annually—plus tax benefits. There are few alternative ways of investing that offer all the benefits of a well-run, well-structured real estate limited partnership.

Historical Foundation for Caution

In order to understand the current real estate environment and to be able to make more intelligent judgments about the risks and future opportunities, it is important to look at the past with an eye for inherent risks to be avoided regardless of the manner in which one chooses to invest in real estate.

During the twenty-five years following the end of World War II, real estate inflation in the U.S. was both dramatic and uniform, so that examples of investment losses by both large and small investors were rare indeed. However, beginning in the sixties, real estate became less predictable. Examples of overbuilding began to appear in certain regions, as demonstrated by "90-day free rent" ads appearing as an inducement to fill large vacancies in apartment projects.

In the late sixties and early seventies real estate investment trusts were made popular by Wall Street traders. For a while, these REITs showed high earnings by borrowing funds in the short term at low rates and lending them at higher rates in the long-term market, often on construction projects. The REIT debacle in the early 1970s was caused by a combination of short-term rates rising above the long-term yield, the bankruptcy of many of the REIT borrowers faced with unparalled inflation and cost overruns, and vast overbuilding in the 1972–73 period, which created record vacancies. The accounting rules prior to 1973 allowed corporations to generate fictitious profits through zero-down-payment sales of property at inflated prices, and pre-1974 tax rules allowed for the deduction of pre-paid interest expense. All of these factors combined to bring about the first big losses to real estate investors, particularly banks and insurance companies, since World War II. Since the accounting standards and tax rules have now changed, it is not likely that this particular set of circumstances will be repeated, but there will always be the risk that a given market or a given type of property will be overbuilt.

Concerns and Risks

Improved property, such as apartment projects, shopping centers, and commercial property, experiences cycles of overbuilding and underbuilding. For example, 1972, with approximately one million surplus housing units under construction or indicated by building permits, was one of the worst years to invest in real estate. But by 1975 there was an 800,000-unit deficit in residential unit construction, vacancies were being absorbed rapidly, and the market was ready for a rapid rise in rents. The same can be said of apartment projects in 1981–82, because of the shortfall in housing starts. Keep in mind that these figures are national, and are used to demonstrate a principle, whereas the individual investor will be more concerned about a particular region, which may have a different set of statistics.

In the very long run, the value of improved income property tends to fluctuate around an equilibrium level suggested by depreciated replacement cost. For example, if at a moment in time market demand and supply causes selling prices to be above depreciated replacement costs, then builders ordinarily rush in (provided adequate financing is available) and build new units until such time as values approximate depreciated replacement cost. Conversely, when values are below depreciated replacement cost, as was the case in 1981–82, relatively little building takes place, which causes rents and values to increase until it is profitable for builders to start building once again.

Therefore, the fundamental question that every investor must ask is whether the purchase price of his investment is at, above, or below depreciated replacement cost. Some judgment is required to make this analysis, because physical depreciation and the land portion of the total cost cannot be determined precisely.

The advantages and disadvantages of any existing real estate financing must be clearly understood. Most homeowners are used to financing that has, in the past, been set at a fixed rate, payable in monthly installments continuously until paid. However, beginning in the late 1970s, many lenders were on the brink of financial failure as their cost of funds exceeded yields on older loans. Their defensive measures included adopting variable interest rates (which could be adjusted upward or downward according to some index measuring cost of funds) and/or relatively short-term due dates, often three to seven years, which allowed them to adjust the interest rate when the loan came due. In addition, some lenders, perceiving that their interest rate was high at the time it was made, negotiated a "lock-in" provision that prevents the borrower from prepaying the loan and refinancing at a lower rate for the term of the lock-in period, usually ten to fifteen years from the time the loan was made. Any of these provisions may expose the real estate owner to substantial risks if the finance market moves in the wrong direction or, as is the case with a lock-in provision, prevents the real estate owner from taking advantage of changing conditions.

When investing in a limited partnership a small investor should be particularly skeptical of the management capabilities of a syndicator. Such skepticism should be dispelled only if the syndicator demonstrates a considerable experience record (called a track record in offering circulars)

for managing an investment and for paying reasonable returns.

An investor should ask, "How did the syndicator do over that period of time with that type of property, compared to others who managed the same property, in the same market, during the same time?" In this regard, there are certain "track record traps" to be aware of. One is that a syndication company may have experienced considerable turnover in personnel, in which case an old successful track record does not necessarily mean that the current organization can continue to perform in the same manner. Another trap is that of the "red hot" market, such as Southern California in the late 1970s. A good track record in such a market does not necessarily indicate that the syndicator can duplicate that result at another time under different market conditions.

Development projects carry a considerable extra risk, compared to existing projects. This does not mean that development projects are unworthy of investment, but rather that the investor must be in a position to afford the risk, and that the project should offer extra returns to compensate for the risk. The early 1970s proved that well written development contracts, substantial contractors with bonds, and well reasoned projections do not eliminate development risks. A number of things can go wrong to make a development project unprofitable: the contractor or developer may seek the protection of the bankruptcy courts to stave off foreclosure proceedings; contractors or subcontractors may default; a drastic change in market conditions could occur during construction or at the time the project is completed.

A small investor usually invests in a real estate syndication on the advice of a broker. An investor has a right to expect his broker to have performed a "due diligence" examination of any real estate offering in order to resolve the fundamental concerns set forth above. Generally speaking, the more technically competent advisers or brokers have performed extensive due diligence of their own and are happy to share their findings with you.

Clichés are not a substitute for understanding risks or opportunities. For example, the well worn cliché "Real estate investment protects you against inflation" did not protect the 1981 home buyer from suffering a substantial loss in 1982 in most U.S. cities while general inflation continued at a high rate. The irony was that the same general inflation fear resulted in such record high mortgage interest rates that sellers found it almost impossible to find a purchaser who could qualify for a loan. This resulted in a decrease in sales prices, even while general inflation continued. However, the cliché foretold good fortune for those owning income-producing properties during this period because of increased rents, made possible by higher mortgage rates. What was bad news for the home buyer became good news for those owning income-producing property because potential competition and overbuilding was no threat in the marketplace. The exception to this segment of the marketplace was office space, which obviously was not competing for those who want an affordable place to live.

Another cliché is that the most important consideration in real estate is location. Those who bought well located, highly leveraged apartment projects in the overbuilt sunbelt in 1972–73 commonly faced foreclosure proceedings in 1974–76. While location is an important factor, others, such as purchase price as related to replacement cost, are equally important.

Summary

The decision of whether or not to invest in any particular generic type of investment is made daily, whether by design or by default. For example, if one has funds on deposit which are yielding what appear to be acceptable rates—such as money market funds offered between 1979 and 1982—let's look at what we have left to keep, or the bottom line:

$10,000 deposit
+ 1,000 interest at 10% for one year
$11,000 at year end
− 300 taxes, at a marginal tax rate of 30%
$10,780 (looks good so far . . .)
− 700 subtracted for inflation (at an annual rate of 7%
$10,000 (So where is the benefit?)

Obviously money market funds have a place in every investor's savings plan (though these are not to be confused with money market *certificates*, which are time deposits and therefore are not liquid). The example above is given to point out that inflation forces us to consider our savings as a holding pattern before we know where to land on some investment opportunity, or to view our savings simply as overnight emergency money. Obviously savings are not investments. These figures only illustrate that failing to decide can have the effect of making a decision—the decision to allow our hard-earned money to be lazy. Our money can work as hard as we worked to get it if we are willing to make some decisions.

Just how much of one's portfolio should be invested in real estate, if any, depends on numerous factors, including age, income, tax bracket, personal concern about the need for protection against inflation, how much of one's assets needs to be kept in a liquid position, and many other variables.

This chapter has made an attempt to cover some of the potential benefits and to point out how overbuilding, economic cycles, and inflation rates can affect your real estate holdings.

The *advantages* of real estate are:

1. *Appreciation:* Real estate has increased

in value fairly consistently over the past four decades.

2. *Cash flow:* Many types of real estate provide current income.

3. *Equity buildup:* Mortgage payments are partially payments of principal, so the invested equity in the property may increase significantly over a number of years. In some cases this equity is contributed by the tenants, as in the case of income-producing properties with positive cash flow.

4. *Tax advantages:* For most taxpayers, the interest expenses on leveraged real estate are deductible against income. Gains on sale are almost always long-term capital gains, with a favored tax treatment. Tax laws allow us to depreciate the building. Depreciation is based on IRS rules, which overstate the reduction in the value of a property caused by age. Depreciation is used to offset income without specific cash cost to the investor. Congress passes laws from time to time delineating the useable life of certain types of real estate. Depreciation when used to offset other income is a way of turning ordinary income into a long-term capital gain. Since the new tax law (ERTA) is not as simple as it used to be in the treatment of long-term capital gain, each individual should consult an accountant or visit a library before determining the exact amount of tax to be paid on long-term gain. It suffices here to say that it is a most favored tax treatment.

Taking the depreciation advantage one step farther, a person may now depreciate real estate and yet, on the demise of that person, the heirs inherit the property on a stepped-up basis. In a community property state, the surviving spouse takes on not only the portion inherited from the deceased spouse, but also finds that the portion held by him or her gets stepped up to current market value. Therefore the inherited property has a new "cost basis," and if sold at some subsequent date less tax will be paid on the gain. Readers are encouraged

to consult with their attorney for the laws governing real property in their state.

5. *Leverage:* In physical science, leverage expresses the magnification of power using a rod and fulcrum. In a real estate transaction, by analogy, leverage refers to the magnification of economic return which results from borrowing a part of the cost of the real estate. The power of leverage can substantially amplify both profits and losses. The proper use of leverage can be a major tool in accumulating wealth.

6. *Estate tax planning:* As explained in the section on tax advantages, definite estate tax advantages exist for those who pass property from generation to generation without the incidence of successive rounds of federal estate tax, state inheritance tax, and probate costs. Every reader is urged to explore the form of ownership, titling, and means of passing property to heirs free of estate tax. Since each state has its own laws governing this area, it must be explored on an individual basis.

7. *Deferral of tax by installment sale:* Federal tax law allows a seller of real property who receives payments in the year of sale of less than the total sales consideration to spread the tax payment proportionately over the same period that they are paid. The economic benefit to the seller is that he is entitled to receive interest income on a profit (included within the note receivable) without the obligation of paying an immediate tax.

8. *Conversion of ordinary income to long-term capital gain:* This may be accomplished either through the deduction of repair and maintenance costs or through depreciation (explained previously).

A limited partnership form of ownership allows for tax benefits to flow through to the limited partners, as they would under individual ownership.

Disadvantages of real estate include:

1. *Illiquidity:* Real estate is generally

purchased and held for a number of years. Unless held in a publicly traded security, such as an equity REIT, it is difficult to convert this asset into cash until the property is sold or refinanced, assuming there is trapped equity.

2. *Liabilities,* including liabilities for debts incurred to manage the property and liabilities on the mortgage itself. Not to be overlooked are uninsured liabilities, such as liabilities for punitive damages, since not all liabilities for real estate ownership can be insured against. (Remember that a limited partner does not assume these excess liabilities. They are borne by the general partner.)

3. *Management intensive:* The proper purchase, development, financing, management, and sale of real estate is complex, competitive, and difficult to do well.

4. *Other risks* include leverage (since most real estate is purchased with some cash and some mortgage debt, where the mortgage holder has first call on the property); vacancies; management incompetence; overbuilding (where supply exceeds demand); government regulations, either through zoning or rent control; low or negative cash returns requiring additional capital investment; and economic trends.

Both pitfalls and opportunities exist for the small investor participating in group ownership versus individual ownership of income real property. The opportunities and excellent potential results offered by group ownership require some due diligence on the reader's part, but the results can be very rewarding. Some help in becoming familiar with the many avenues open to the small investor today may be obtained through brokerage firms and financial planning firms.

With adequate knowledge, proper caution, and foresight, the small investor can look to real estate as a valuable tool in increasing his net worth.

Chapter 23

Investing in Oil and Gas

Beverly Tanner, CFP

Beverly F. Tanner is a distinguished financial planner who was one of the first women to receive the Certified Financial Planner designation. She is the founder of Intravest Centaur Corporation, director and vice-president of Cal/US Venture Capital Association, Incorporated, and vice-president and partner of Planned Investments, Incorporated. She recently completed a financial planning guide to tax shelters, *Shelter What You Make, Minimize the Take*, written after the Economic Recovery Act of 1981. Tanner is a regular guest speaker at both consumer and industry events and lectures at colleges and universities nationwide. She was the first woman to be elected to the board of directors for the International Association for Financial Planning, where she is currently serving her fourth term. In 1981 she was named Certified Financial Planner of the Year.

Fossil fuels and their by-products are essential to modern life: world agriculture is increasingly dependent on petroleum-derived fertilizers; petroleum is important to plastics, packaging, industrial chemicals, drugs, and cosmetics; petroleum products are used in highway construction, building materials, genetic research, and micro-technology. But most important, oil and gas are our primary source of energy. Petroleum is a significantly cheaper source of energy than nuclear fission. In developed countries, where per capita energy consumption is high, our search for alternative thermal, solar, and nuclear sources of energy has repeatedly confirmed the low cost and high efficiency of fossil fuels. In underdeveloped countries, where per capita energy consumption is still quite low, the growth of technological, industrial, and transportation infrastructures will require increasing quantities of energy—far more than will be saved through efficiencies in the developed countries.

The United States needs to import approximately one-third of its oil to meet domestic energy consumption. For strategic and foreign exchange reasons, government policy and public sentiment at this time both lean toward cutting back the percentage of imported oil. This means that tax incentives favoring domestic petroleum development will in all likelihood remain intact.

What all this adds up to is that, despite periodic "gluts" caused by warm winters, market manipulations, or shifts in consumption patterns, the worldwide demand for gas and oil will continue to be high. In the near future, as the United States and other economies recover from a recession, the consumption and price of energy will probably increase faster than the rate of inflation.

If oil and gas prices do, indeed, increase in price at a relatively fast rate, there will be an effect on consumers. Your heating, energy, and transportation costs will rise, then prices in general will rise as increased energy costs are passed through.

For this reason, the consumer or family in a position to diversify their savings and investment program should consider one of the many forms of oil and gas investment. Specifically, if you have more than $10,000 in savings and liquid investments, and are considering going beyond banks and money market funds in your investment program, there is likely to be some form of oil or gas investment appropriate for your particular plans and needs. Investments in domestic exploration development and extraction are particularly attractive. There is less political risk, there are government tax incentives, and, in the case of natural gas, the expiration of current price controls in 1985 will cause a one-time revenue enhancement in the near future.

If you can invest in oil and gas in a manner that provides good return at today's energy prices, the same investment will provide an even better return when energy prices go up in the future. Investing in oil and gas, if properly done, is a way of letting price inflation work for you instead of against you.

Wildcat wells, high risks, and shady dealers frequently come to mind when oil and gas investing is mentioned. Wealthy celebrities with sophisticated tax attorneys have lost money in a few of the more notorious oil "deals." Many other investors have lost money, legitimately as well as illegitimately, in other oil investments. Because of these kinds of associations, it is important to understand that high-risk drilling partnerships are only one of many legitimate forms of oil and gas investing. Some oil investments are as safe as your local utility stock, and some quite a bit safer.

Oil Stocks

The most common form of oil and gas investment is direct ownership of the common stock of public companies. Over the last decade, oil stock prices have risen much higher—and dropped more precipitously—than the stock market as a whole. The unpredictable ups and downs of the stock market are the main drawback to using common stocks as an oil and gas vehicle. It is possible to make tremendous profits from oil stocks if your timing is right. However, when you see premier oil service companies selling at one-third of their highs, you realize that you can also lose a great deal in oil stocks if your timing is wrong. For this reason, common stocks are not the most attractive way for the smaller investor to invest in oils.

If you are willing to bear the risks of stock ownership, there are several kinds of companies to consider. The oil service companies provide construction and drilling services to the industry. Their stocks have been even more volatile than other energy-related stocks. Two of the premier service companies, Schlumberger and Halliburton, recently sold at about one-third of their 1980 high. The astute investor whose timing is impeccable will buy these stocks during an oil glut when energy demand is dampened by a recession, and sell them during a period of apparent energy shortage and oil price increases. He may choose oil services stocks precisely because they are more volatile, and will provide a better run for the money.

A slightly more conservative oil investment would be stock in one of the medium-sized companies involved in domestic extraction and distribution. The stocks of these companies will not be as volatile as the oil services companies. The added attraction of these stocks is that they may be acquired by another company at a hefty premium over what you pay. Witness the fate of Conoco (purchased by Du Pont) and Marathon (now owned by U.S. Steel). The attractiveness of these medium oil companies lies primarily in their known reserves. It costs $12 to $15 per barrel to explore for and develop oil in this country. If already known reserves can be purchased for half that price by taking over an oil company, you have made a good deal. Analysts and investors interested in these companies look at the per-barrel cost of reserves as reflected in the stock price. When the stock price values the company's reserves at less than $5 per barrel, the company is ripe for takeover. Pennzoil, Murphy Oil, Kerr-McGee, and Getty oil are among the more prominent medium-sized oil companies.

The big oil companies have no takeover potential. If you buy Exxon or Texaco, you are buying current dividends and long-term stability. Their dividend yields have reached 10–11 percent. This might be right for institutions or tax-sheltered retirement accounts, but most individual investors can put their stable growth dollars in a better tax environment than the common stock of the big oil companies.

Lotteries

If you truly have a gambler's heart, another little-known form of oil and gas investing is to enter the bimonthly lotteries for federal leases. Under the Federal Simultaneous Oil and Gas Drawing program, the Bureau of Land Management allots American citizens the right to share in the income that might be derived from the extraction of oil and gas from federal land. A number of prespecified parcels of land, ranging from 10 to more than 10,000 acres, are placed into each drawing. An individual citizen can submit only one entry per parcel, but can enter the drawings for as many parcels as wanted. This assures that each person who files an application has an equal chance to win the lease being allocated. Successful applicants, whose entry number is drawn in the random selection process, have the exclusive right to explore, drill for, and extract all oil and gas deposits on the parcel. This right extends for ten years, and as long thereafter as oil and gas are produced in paying quantities.

As with any lottery, this is a pure gamble. But it does have a significant advantage over other forms of gambling—you can deduct your losses. Another advantage is that it costs only $75 to file for a parcel lottery. Since leases won under this system have been sold to oil companies for as much as $800,000, your return on investment could be substantial if you win a lease. There are filing agents who, for a fee, will direct you to the upcoming parcels with the highest likelihood of hydrocarbons (and thus will command the highest prices from the oil companies) and file your entry for you.

As with any transaction where tax deductions are involved, however, the advantage is with the high bracket taxpayer. If your taxable income is $15,000, the deductibility of the lottery entry will save you only a few dollars in taxes. You will be bearing 80–90 percent of the risk yourself. If your taxable income is more than $41,500, every dollar you deduct will save you 50 percent in taxes. Thus, you will be bearing only half the risk. Through tax deductions, the government pays half your entry fee for you if you do not win the lease. These lease lotteries are not recommended as an investment for most people. They really come under speculation and not investment.

Oil Income Partnerships

A relatively conservative form of oil investing that has advantages over the stock market is the oil income partnership. During the first half of 1982, when the price of oil stocks plummeted, and investments in oil drilling partnerships dwindled, investments in oil income partnerships surged ahead and set new records. The two biggest risks usually associated with oil investing—stock market risk and drilling risk—are eliminated from oil income partnerships. When you invest in such a program you and your partners are buying ownership of successfully drilled oil on tap ready to

flow into buyers' distribution networks. The value of your asset does not change with daily stock fluctuations. It is determined by the price commanded at the wellhead by your product. The primary risk in an oil income partnership is that the price of oil will drop in the future. However, if the price of oil increases in the future, you will reap the rewards directly. A good time to buy into oil income partnerships is during a glut, when spot market prices have dropped off a few dollars per barrel. Those are the conditions under which many people invested in oil income programs during the first half of 1982.

The advantages of the oil income partnership are that you have no drilling risk or stock market risk. You are buying proven reserves of completed wells, and part of the partnership income—about 15 percent—is sheltered from taxation through depletion allowances. The reserves are bought at approximately a 50 percent discount from the spot price, so there is a built-in profit as the oil or gas is extracted from the ground. Income is regularly distributed several times per year, and it can be reinvested without commissions. Most oil income partnerships maintain a buyout offer, which is updated and renewed with each income distribution. You always know what your share is worth, and you can sell it back to the general partner at any time.

One disadvantage is that it takes a year or two before the partnership purchases its quota of reserves. If you were to take out your money during the first twelve to eighteen months, you might not get your full purchase price back because too few reserves were purchased to make up for the start-up costs and commissions. You thus have to think of an oil income partnership as illiquid for the first two years. The other disadvantage is that the partnership is subject to the risk of a decline in oil prices. Should oil and gas prices decline from their level at the time you purchased your partnership, your income from the partnership could drop. However the chances that energy costs will increase at least as fast or faster than inflation in the long run are far greater than the chances they will decrease. It is prudent for most investors in a position to diversify to take this risk with a portion of their holdings, if the nature of the investment is consistent with their personal financial plan. Given a choice of three alternative ways of investing in oil—common stocks, income partnerships, or drilling partnerships—income partnerships seem to have the least risk of loss and the best prospect for stable growth in value.

Only two sizable firms offer oil income partnerships. Petro-Lewis is the senior of the two, and has a track record of solid payments to investors going back a dozen years. Damson's record only goes back to 1976, but it is now recognized along with Petro-Lewis as one of the two quality purveyors of oil and gas income partnerships.

Drilling Partnerships

Drilling partnerships are an entirely different kind of investment from oil income partnerships. When you become a partner in a venture to drill for oil, even in a conservative developmental program, you are taking a very expensive shot at the unknown. *Developmental* drilling partnerships concentrate their efforts in areas near successfully completed wells. Nationwide, the average success rate of developmental drilling is about 80 percent. The success rate varies considerably in different geological areas. In the tight sands formations of eastern Ohio, about 95 percent of developmental wells are successful. In many other areas the success ratio for developmental wells is in the 65–70 percent range.

The risk is not merely finding recoverable hydrocarbons. Drilling costs can vary, depending on the final depth of the well, the exact geology encountered, and the efficiency of the drilling contractor. Sometimes partially completed or even completed holes have to be abandoned because of drilling bit problems, or cave-ins, or uncontrolled explosions in the fracturing process. All these variables affect the cost per barrel of the oil developed by the drilling partnership. None of those variables are encountered in an oil income partnership. Thus with any drilling partnership— even conservative ones that are developing known fields—you are taking a significant step up the ladder of risk.

Why would anybody want to take on this added risk of drilling for hydrocarbons when they can safely invest in known reserves? One important reason is the "unlimited" upside potential. Some publicly offered oil drilling partnerships have returned original limited partners more than twenty times their investment over a ten-year period. This level of performance is the exception rather than the rule, however. Two and a half to three times the original investment over ten years would be more typical of a successful developmental partnership. Many do not achieve that level of success. A review of the return graphs in a rating guide such as *Invesearch* will reveal that many developmental partnerships return less than two times the original investment over ten years, and that a great number of investors lose money.

In pure economic terms, an oil drilling limited partnership is not a good investment. But our economic and political policy is to develop domestic oil and gas reserves, so Congress has created tax incentives to encourage American investors to take on the risk.

Unless your income is well into the 50 percent bracket, drilling partnerships, whether developmental or exploratory, are not for you. But if you do have a taxable income of over $70,000, you probably should consider drilling partnerships as one alternative to paying half of every dollar to Uncle Sam.

The way the tax incentives work is relatively simple. Say you have substantial annual income subject to 50 percent federal tax and $10,000 pretax sitting in the bank. If you leave the money there to the end of the year, you will pay a 50 percent tax, and will have $5,000 after taxes to invest. Put the remainder in a bank at 10 percent, paying a 50 percent tax on interest earned, and at the end of ten years there will be less than $8,200. Put the same 10,000 pretax dollars into a drilling program that allows 80–100 percent write-off in the first year or two, and you will have ongoing deductions for depreciation, depletion allowances, and interest expense. A partnership does not have to perform very well to leave you better off than if you pay the taxes and bank the rest. Since most partnerships return at least the original amount invested over their lifetime, your chances of coming out ahead by using this alternative to income tax passivity are excellent.

If you do start investigating oil and gas drilling partnerships, you will find many pages of the offering prospectuses devoted to detailed explanations of the tax allowances. This can be somewhat intimidating. The subtleties of oil tax law are complex. For this reason, you should invest in a drilling partnership only in consultation with a financial planner or other qualified professional who can clearly explain to you the effect it will have on your individual tax situation.

If you have the temperament to take higher risks in return for greater rewards, you may also want to consider *exploratory* drilling partnerships. Exploratory wells, drilled outside of developed fields in areas where geologists predict a high likelihood of hydrocarbons, have a much lower success ratio than developmental wells. In a developmental partnership you are virtually certain to find recoverable hydrocarbons in some of the wells drilled. In an exploratory partnership, there is a chance of complete loss of the money invested.

However, successful exploratory partnerships can return many times the amount invested.

A chief reason for the high potential profitability of exploratory drilling is that if it is successful, the value of the acreage will increase substantially. Before a field has been explored, owners of the oil and gas rights simply cannot command a high price, no matter what quantity of hydrocarbons geologists hypothesize may be underground. Once actual oil and gas reserves have been proven by successful completion of a well, the values of leases in the area shoot up.

Thus exploratory drillers generally put down holes in areas where they have bought surrounding lease rights as well. If the area does have recoverable hydrocarbons, the original exploratory well, and the offset developmental wells they may drill later, will have an extra margin of profit because of the relatively low cost of leases they bought before the area was proven. Latecomers who buy into the field only after exploratory drilling has been accomplished will pay premium prices for their leases, and thus will have a higher cost per barrel.

There are also *balanced* drilling partnerships, in which the money of investors goes half into exploratory wells and half into developmental wells. Other combinations are possible as well.

Developmental programs have much to commend them. If investors want some of the excitement and extra upside potential of exploration, they can still find these qualities in a mixed partnership, but the exploratory element will be kept to 20–25 percent.

If you have a particularly substantial net worth and a sizable income, *leveraged* drilling programs may fit your needs. Generally, leveraged programs will be privately placed offerings rather than public partnerships registered with the Securities and Exchange Commission (SEC). The technique is similar to leverage in real estate. You borrow money, putting up only a minor portion yourself. This increases the tax deductions in relation to the cash you put up. Using your substantial net worth, you obtain a letter of credit from your bank that enables the partnership to borrow most of the funds for your portion of the investment.

Consider an exploratory leveraged drilling partnership in which $100,000 invested will yield a $70,000 tax deduction its first year, and another $30,000 in deductions over the following two years. Instead of putting up the full $100,000 to buy your share, you put down $10,000 immediately, and with your letter of credit as collateral, sign a note to pay $10,000 in a year, a second note to pay $10,000 in two years, and a third note to pay $70,000 at the end of four years. The partnership expects discovered reserves in the ground will be sufficient to take out production loans and get you off the hook for the last $70,000. Under that scenario, you have paid out $30,000 in cash and received $100,000 in tax deductions, which saved you $50,000 in federal taxes alone.

However, there is a big "it" in that scenario, and this is where a leveraged drilling investment is unlike a leveraged real estate investment. The loans you take out to leverage a real estate purchase are collateralized by the asset itself. The loans taken out to leverage your drilling partnership are not collateralized by the asset you are seeking, the oil, because the banks cannot be certain it is really there. These loans are collateralized by your other assets, which the bank knows it can get its hands on. The investor is thus fully at risk for the entire $100,000 of the investment, because if oil is not discovered in sufficient quantities to cover the final $70,000, the last note will have to be paid out of the pocket. Leveraged drilling partnerships are not for most investors.

Assessments

Most investors find the partnership form of oil and gas investing has significant advantages over the stock market or lotteries. Depending on your tax situation, you might choose income programs, drilling programs, or some combination of both. The income partnerships offered by the two major suppliers, Petro-Lewis and Damson, are fairly straightforward and much less risky than drilling programs. Since the terms of drilling partnerships can be quite complex, and the dollars you put into them are at risk, partnership offerings should be examined carefully by you and your financial planner before you make any decision to invest.

You should, however, be aware of potential "assessments," which you may be called upon to pay to the partnership in the future. These assessments, which range from 10–25 percent of your original investment, are called only if the partnership finds oil or gas. This is because the original partnership funding is used to drill as many different wells as possible. Only the wells actually hitting recoverable hydrocarbons will be completed. The completion costs (permanent well casings, pumping equipment, and connections to pipelines) have to be met through assessments. In the case of exploratory drilling, assessments are often used to drill offset wells in the neighborhood of successful wells.

Although the idea of requesting the investor to pay out more cash if a drilling program is successful may seem contradictory, it is actually quite sensible. Original dollars invested are spread over as many wells as possible to maximize diversification of the program, and thus the total reserves tapped. Additional dollars are called upon for completion or for offset drilling only after success is assured.

In general, assessments are voluntary.

If you cannot or will not put up additional money, the partnership will fund your share elsewhere—from other partners or from a bank. In the case of additional offset wells in an exploratory program, one common practice is for the funding source providing your share of the assessment to receive 300 percent of their investment back before you can again participate in your share of the income stream from the new well. Another alternative in both developmental and exploratory programs is simply to dilute your ownership share in the partnership as a whole if you do not pay assessment.

Although an assessment means putting out more cash, it is generally a good idea to go ahead and make the additional investment. Your assessment dollars are going into the partnership after the major risks of drilling have been taken. Occasionally, an offset well next to a successful exploratory hole will not pan out, but your assessment dollars are at much less risk than your original investment dollars. Assessment dollars for completion of successful wells have little investment risk.

Risks of Oil and Gas Partnerships

As you look through an offering brochure for an oil and gas partnership, you will notice several pages devoted to the subject of potential risks for the limited partners. It is a good idea to look these pages over so you will have some idea of the ways things can turn sour. It is important to remember, however, that because of SEC disclosure regulations, the attorneys overseeing the writing of partnership offerings make certain that just about every conceivable mishap is described in great detail. This protects the company making the offering from any accusations that investors were not properly forewarned. It

also makes for a somewhat gloomy view of the risk factors.

Drilling partnerships that are "blind pools"—that is, partnerships that raise funds before specific leases to be purchased have been identified—may have trouble finding good leases. There are many oil companies with skilled geologists and landmen in the field at all times. The competition for quality leases can be tough. If the partnership's management is not adequately staffed in this area, or if the partnership's lease-purchasing period falls during a time when competition is particularly acute owing to rising oil prices, they may not get leases at reasonable prices.

If the partnership acquires attractive prospects at fair prices, it still faces drilling risks. Even in areas of proven reserves, no one knows beforehand if a well will be successful. It may turn out to be a dry hole. Even if oil or gas is found, problems with the well itself might prevent extraction. Nationwide, two out of ten developmental wells are not successful, and 17 out of 20 exploratory wells fail to produce.

Management risks exist in oil and gas drilling, as in any business. One of the most common is conflict of interest. The general partners should be completely experienced in oil and gas drilling. But this will mean that they have interests in numerous producing properties and drilling prospects that are not in your partnership. How quickly the prospects of your partnership are drilled could be determined by other business priorities. Another area of management risk is how efficiently the partnership is operated. If a partnership puts only 60¢ on the dollar into the ground, the management fees, overhead, commissions, and offering costs will eat up too much of your investment. At least 80 percent of your investment should be going into the ground. Finally, there have been cases of outright fraud in oil and gas drilling. What all this means is that the background, experience, other business interests, and actual drilling track record of the management team should be scrutinized.

If a drilling program is not adequately funded, it may not be able to achieve enough diversification. Spreading risk is an absolute in oil and gas drilling. Even companies like Exxon rarely drill a well entirely with their own money. Rather, almost all wells are drilled as joint ventures. A typical drilling partnership will take a 10–25 percent position in as many wells as possible. If inadequatedly funded, they will either have to invest in fewer wells, or reduce their percentage of participation. To go into fewer wells increases the risk of the limited partners. To take too small a percentage of participation reduces the partnership's control over drilling activities. Thus, a drilling partnership should be funded with at least $600,000 if it is to achieve adequate diversification.

Another risk consideration is illiquidity. Even in an income program, you will probably not get your full investment back if you withdraw from the partnership during the first two years. Drilling partnerships are even more illiquid. That is, you can sell your share if you choose to do so, but the price you will get for it from the general partner or another investor will be at such a discount from value that you will do much better to leave your money in the partnership if at all possible. In several stock exchange offers, limited partners have been able to liquidate their partnership shares in exchange for new shares of common stock in a corporation formed specifically to buy up partnership interests. The common stock is valued, before issue, so that the limited partner receives stock holdings equal to his portion of partnership oil reserves. However, the unfortunate experience has been that once this common stock hits the market, sellers are more eager to sell than buyers to buy, and the price drops rapidly. A limited partner who receives a "$10" share of stock for every $10 of known reserves often finds, when he goes to sell his stock, that he can get only $2 or $3 for it. For this reason, any dollars you put into a drilling program should be long-term dollars. Your investment will lose much value if you decide to liquidate it. You will do much better to keep those dollars in the drilling partnership and seek liquidity elsewhere.

This does not apply to income partnerships after the first two years have elapsed, however. The general partners are willing to repurchase partnership units on the basis of the current price of oil and the known reserves. There will be some discount from total value, but generally speaking you will get more back than you originally put in, and when you add to the repurchase price the income you have received from the partnership in the interim, the total return will be satisfactory.

A risk common to drilling partnerships not spelled out in offering brochures is buyer's remorse. Investors who enter into a partnership without understanding its long-term nature sometimes change their minds two or three years into the investment. Once they have received their tax write-offs, if the program is not spectacularly successful, they feel disappointed at the income, or lack thereof. They want to get out and go on to another investment. Nonetheless, even in a subpar program you will still do far better by staying in and taking full benefits of the partnership over its lifetime. Buyers of drilling partnerships should be thoroughly versed in all its aspects and give careful consideration to possible long-term results *before* investing.

There are also some tax risks. If the partnership is not properly structured according to current tax law, the IRS might question or disallow the deductions you have taken. In addition, tax laws frequently change, and you have no absolute assurance that deductions allowable at the time you enter the partnership will remain allowable.

The most significant tax risks, however, are related to the intermeshing of the partnership's tax benefits with your personal tax situation. Two of the potential consequences on your taxes are the triggering of "tax preference items" and the "recapture" of previously allowed deductions. You should have your financial planner detail explicitly the potential effects on your current and future taxes. The following description of oil and gas taxation can only provide a cursory summary. The consequences of an oil or gas partnership on your present and future taxes should be discussed thoroughly with an accountant or financial planner.

Taxes

The tax benefits peculiar to oil and gas investing fall into two main areas: (1) intangible drilling costs, and (2) depletion allowance. Intangible drilling costs, or IDCs, provide immediate tax write-offs in the first two years of the investment. Depletion allowance, which is a variation on the depreciation allowance encountered in real estate, provides tax benefits over the life of the investment.

Intangible drilling costs include all costs of drilling that produce nothing tangible or salvageable. Labor, drilling "mud," drill bits, fuel, and all the other expendables that go into the ground are all IDCs. Of every dollar a limited partner invests, 50¢ to 75¢ will be IDCs. To understand the special significance of being able to deduct IDCs, it is instructive to compare oil drilling to real estate construction.

The money a builder puts into labor, fuel, paint, and so on during construction is incurred as immediate costs, but the builder cannot claim most of these costs as deductions in the year they are incurred. Rather, he must capitalize them, adding them to the tangible "bricks and mortar" costs of construction. The costs are then depreciated over the lifetime of the structure.

In oil drilling, IDCs are written off the year they are incurred, even if the well is successful (all the costs of unsuccessful wells may be written off in the year incurred). This special tax incentive is the principal reason investors who need immediate write-offs invest in oil and drilling partnerships. If the investors or the partnership borrow money, and the investors are fully at risk to repay the loan, the IDC tax deductions can be far greater than 75 percent of the cash invested: multiple write-offs can be achieved.

Depletion is an ongoing tax deduction over the lifetime of the well. There are two forms of depletion. *Cost depletion* is much like depreciation. It is based on the actual costs of accessing the oil. If you own an estimated 100 barrels of oil underground, and it costs $200 to obtain those reserves, your basis for cost depletion is $2 per barrel. During a given year, if you produce and sell ten barrels, you may take a depletion allowance of $2 per barrel, or $20.

Percentage depletion is much more advantageous to investors, especially when energy prices are rising. It is based on gross revenues from the sale of oil, rather than the cost of obtaining oil. For instance, if you had qualified for percentage depletion in 1981, you could have deducted 20 percent of your yearly gross revenue if that deduction did not exceed half of your enterprise's taxable income. Thus if you had sold your ten barrels at $30 per barrel, your gross revenues would have been $300. Your percentage depletion allowance would have been $300 × 20%, or $60, if the taxable income from the enterprise was at least $120.

The difference between the $20 cost depletion allowance and the $60 percentage depletion allowance is significant. Another difference is that cost depletion entails a limited deduction. Once all the original costs of obtaining the oil have been deducted, the allowance ends, even if the well continues to produce oil. Thus with cost depletion, oil revenues will at times be entirely exposed to taxation. With percentage depletion, however, you can continue to take your percentage deductions year after year as long as the well continues to produce revenues.

Under former oil-depletion allowance laws, it was possible to write off two or three times the actual cost of the reserves. The large oil companies did precisely this, until Congress closed the loophole. Under current law, the depletion allowance is going through a phased decrease from its traditional level of 22 percent, down to 16 percent in 1983, and 15 percent in 1984 and thereafter. This decrease applies only to small producers. Percentage depletion has been eliminated altogether for the large oil companies. Since most developmental and exploratory oil drilling limited partnerships qualify for percentage depletion, the tables have been turned. Now the middle-class taxpayers can benefit from depletion, while the large oil companies have to seek other means to shelter their profits.

Another way in which an investor can improve his long-term tax situation with an oil and gas drilling program is sometimes termed the "family maneuver." An investor buys partnership units and holds on to them for a couple of years, taking full benefits of the initial deductions. A successful program may then begin paying out income that is subject to taxation at the investor's high rate. At this point, the partnership is gifted to a minor child, and the income stream is subject to taxation at the child's rate. If the child has no other income, there will be little, if any, taxation.

Plan Ahead

Before considering any investment, you should be aware of your personal and future tax liabilities, you and your family's investment goals, and the risks involved in the investment. This is particularly true with oil and gas partnerships. Since one of the primary benefits of drilling partnerships is their tax advantage, it follows that you *must* be thoroughly versed in your own tax situation and the possible tax consequences of the investment. Investing in an oil and gas drilling program should only be done in consultation with a professional who can examine your tax situation and clearly explain how the specific partnership under consideration will affect you.

Oil and gas partnerships are long-term investments. Before investing, you should have a long-term financial plan with specific goals. Only then will you be able to determine if such an investment meets your long-term needs.

The General Partners

If you and your financial planner have determined that some form of oil and gas partnership is appropriate for your needs, you should next scrutinize the track record of the general partners. Newcomers to the oil and gas business, even if they are honorable and have the best of intentions, can make expensive mistakes. You should generally look for at least three or four years of good records preceding the partnership being offered. A great performance one year, or even two, may just be luck. Trust only the most experienced operators. There are too many other risks in the business, all of which are amplified by inexperience. You may miss one or two good programs, but the losses in all likelihood would have been greater. There are too many instances of an operator hitting it big one year, attracting much larger investments for the next, then being unable to put the money to efficient use because he was incapable of analyzing a greater number of leases and drilling a greater number of wells.

Make sure your financial planner or investment counselor subscribes to *Invesearch* or a comparable rating guide. *Invesearch* is a useful tool for comparing different programs according to several criteria. It summarizes every publicly registered offering as to its prior performance, staffing, where it intends to drill, its inventory or reserves, and its specific strengths and weaknesses. *Invesearch* also compares all drilling programs against model performance curves representing returns of 2 to 1, 3 to 1, and 4 to 1 over a ten-year period. In this way, you can see at a glance how a particular partnership offering stands up to the competition.

What to Look Out for

Once you have determined that the principals operating the partnership have a better-than-average record and are fully experienced in oil and gas, you follow up with some specific questions. What is the minimum investment? What is the size of possible assessments, and when are they likely to fall due? What is the estimated tax write-off for the present tax year and for future ones? What is the projected income flow, and does it seem reasonable in the light of prior performance? How many years until payout (that is, the point at which the partnership has paid out to the investor an amount equaling the original investment)? How much of the limited partners' investment is actually going into the ground?

An important issue to probe is the sharing arrangement between the limited partners and the general partner. How much is the general partner putting up in cash compared to the amount put up by the limited partners? How are the revenues to be allocated? A common practice is for the general partner to receive a 15 percent "promotional allocation." In other words, if the general partner puts up 25 percent of the total drilling and completion costs, he will ultimately receive 40 percent of the revenues. Often, however, the allocation is more in favor of the limited partners until payout, and then shifts in the direction of the general partner after the investors have received back their original investment.

Is It Right for You?

If the answers to these questions are satisfactory from the perspective of your financial plan and your tax situation, it is then time to start asking some personal questions. If you are considering a drilling program, can you live with its illiquidity? Do you have enough other liquid investments set aside? Financially, could you afford the risk of loss? More important, can you stand the emotional strain of living with the risk day to day? In other words, can you sleep at night with the risk?

Oil income partnerships do not carry either stock market risk or drilling risk. The principal risk is the price of oil. If it goes down, your income stream could decrease. But the likelihood of oil prices increasing over the coming years is much greater than the likelihood of a decline. Although this is an acceptable risk, it does not mean that you should put the only investment dollars you have into an oil income program. Even income partnerships should be part of a diversified investment portfolio.

Ownership of common stock of oil companies is a less desirable form of participating in oil and gas ownership for the small investor. Oil stocks are for those who are willing to take on the added risk of unpredictable stock market ups and downs, and those who are knowledgeable enough to follow closely the management of the companies they have invested in. There is always the possibility of significant gains in the stock market. It's all a matter of timing.

Drilling partnerships are only for investors

who have taxable income in the 50 percent bracket or above, who have other investments to fall back on in the case of loss, and who have the right mental attitude toward risk taking. Drilling partnerships should be entered into only with careful scrutiny, and the consultation of an objective investment professional. For investors with the right mental and financial profile, however, drilling partnerships can become an important part of long-term financial planning.

Chapter 24

Lesley D. Bissett is a well-known supporter of the cause of financial planning for women. She is regional vice-president of Integrated Resources Equity Corporation and is responsible for the product education and training of the firm's representatives in the western states. She has written many articles on investments and financial counseling for the woman and has been a speaker at the national conventions of the International Association for Financial Planning. Bissett is a registered principal of the National Association of Securities Dealers and a life and health agent for California. She serves as vice-president of the Los Angeles County Association for Financial Planning and was recently elected to the national board of directors of the International Association for Financial Planning. She has also been listed in *Who's Who of American Women*.

Tax Shelters— Not Only for the Rich

Lesley Bissett, CFP

Suppose we could create the dream investment, an investment that

Offers stability and safety through diversification.

Is professionally managed.

Can meet all your needs for income and growth and can generate tax-free or tax-deferred income.

Is strongly recommended by Congress as a place to put your money instead of giving it to Uncle Sam.

Well, there *is* such an investment! It is called a *tax shelter*, and it is a very important method of holding on to your hard-earned money.

What Are Tax Shelters?

Years ago, Congress decided to attract money to support various key industries by offering tax incentives for investments by the public rather than by providing government funding. These incentives are known as tax shelters.

Tax shelters are neither gimmicks nor loopholes. They came about as a result of a conscious decision by Congress. Congress said, in effect, "If you help us support our key industries—housing, beef, oil and gas, construction, and many more—we'll give you a break on your income tax." Tax shelters are thus a way of reducing your taxes while furthering some social or economic objective that benefits the public at large.

Only for the Rich!

Ah, but you say, tax shelters are only for the rich, and I'm not rich! Not so! Let's take a case in point. If you earn, as a single taxpayer, $34,000 per year, 50 cents out of every dollar you earn above that level goes to taxes. If you are married and you and your spouse have a combined income of $47,000, you, too, are donating 50 cents of every dollar above that level to Uncle Sam.

Charity begins at home, but many people miss out on tax-shelter investments because they do not realize they are in a position to benefit from them. Contrary to popular belief, tax shelters are not just for the rich. In fact, countless tax-shelter investments are suitable for a broad range of taxpayers in an equally broad range of financial situtations. *The key is recognizing what you need and what kind of investment can provide the solution.*

Increasing Spendable Income

Taxpayers earning $25,000 per year will not get the same benefit from a tax shelter as a taxpayer earning $60,000 per year, but they can still benefit. To see how, let's examine an imaginary situation in which three brothers named Chico, Harpo, and Groucho (remember, this is an *imaginary* case, only, and bears no relationship to actual persons) each filed a joint federal income tax return with their spouses in 1980. After subtracting all deductions, exemptions, credits, and so on, they showed the following taxable income:

Chico—$25,000

Harpo—$40,000

Groucho—$60,000

According to the income tax rate for 1980, they each owed the federal government the following:

Chico—$4,633

Harpo—$10,226

Groucho—$19,678

However, on January 1, 1981, Chico, Harpo, and Groucho invested in Happy Haven Apartments, a tax-oriented real estate limited partnership. It was formed to build and manage garden apartments in Atlanta, Georgia. Each of the brothers invested $5,000, and each is entitled to a one-third share of the venture.

On January 1, 1981, Happy Haven Apartments borrowed $1,000,000 and, along with the $15,000 loaned by Chico, Harpo, and Groucho, they carried out their project, which was completed before December 31, 1981.

The costs for the Happy Haven Apartments project were as follows:

Land—$70,000

Construction—$900,000

Miscelleanous items—$30,000

The miscelleanous items consisted of interest, real estate taxes, business expenses, and the like—*items that are deductible for federal income tax purposes. This is the item the limited partners* (Chico, Harpo, and Groucho) *can deduct from their reportable income.*

Since Chico, Harpo, and Groucho were the only three investors (in reality, limited partnerships have hundreds of investors, and miscellaneous expenses are much greater than the above illustration), each can deduct one-third, or $10,000. (They may also get an annual distribution, which could be, assuming full rental of Happy Haven Apartments, tax-free income for several years.)

Now let's look again at their *taxable income*:

Chico—$25,000 − $10,000 deduction
= $15,000

Harpo—$40,000 − $10,000 deduction
= $30,000

Groucho—$60,000 − $10,000 deduction
= $50,000

Thus, each was able to deduct $10,000 from his reportable income as his share of the limited partnership's deductible expenses, and *each then had a lower reportable income for federal income tax purposes.* According to their *new* taxable income figure, their taxes were as follows:

Chico—$2055

Harpo—$6238

Groucho—$14,778

Chico saved a total of $2,578 on his income

taxes through his investment; Harpo saved $3,988; and Groucho saved $4,900.

What was the true cost of their investment? Because Chico, Harpo, and Groucho saved on their taxes, the *true cost* of their investment was not really $5,000. Chico invested $5,000 in Happy Haven Apartments, but he saved $2,578 on his taxes; therefore, the true cost of his investment was $5,000 minus the tax savings ($2,578), or $2,422. Harpo invested $5,000 but saved $3,988 on his taxes, so his true investment was $1,012. And Groucho, who invested $5,000 but saved $4,900 on his taxes, found the true cost of his investment to be only $100!

The tax shelter accomplished three important objectives:

1. It reduced the tax bills of Chico, Harpo, and Groucho.

2. At the same time, they acquired potentially profitable investments.

3. These investments were paid for, in part, by the government.

As an extra added attraction, some tax-shelter investments offer *investment tax credit* (often referred to as ITC or pass-through). The ITC makes a tax-shelter investment even more attractive because it is a *direct credit* against taxes owed to the government. Let's see how the ITC works.

If, instead of investing in Happy Haven Apartments, the brothers had invested in Uncle's Leasing Investors, an equipment-leasing (airplanes, office equipment, and so on) tax shelter, they might have received investment tax credit. Let's say that their investment tax credit for the tax shelter amounted to 5 percent. After their taxes due were computed, the 5 percent investment tax credit would be figured into taxes owed.

Chico owed $2,055 minus $250 (5,000 times .05 = $250), which equals $1,805, for a 12 percent saving on taxes owed.

Harpo owed $6,238 minus $250, which equals $5,988, for a 4 percent reduction on taxes owed.

Groucho owed $14,778 minus $250, which equals $14,528, for a 2 percent decrease of taxes owed.

This illustration brings to light a very important point: *investment tax credit benefits the lower bracket investor more than the higher bracket investor.*

Evaluating Tax Shelters

As a prospective buyer of a tax shelter, you will have your choice of a broad variety of products, each with a different risk level and objective. A consultation with a Certified Financial Planner can help you determine the investment best suited to you.

Investments are offered in real estate, oil and gas (covered in detail in separate chapters of this book), equipment leasing, fast-food franchising, cattle, low-income housing, solar energy, cable television, and many, many more. Many of the better-known tax shelter investments are covered later in this chapter, but first we must examine the steps to take in determining which tax-shelter investment is best suited to your needs.

Buyer Beware!

Never buy a tax shelter from a person who is not licensed with the National Association of Securities Dealers (NASD), and who does not present you with a prospectus at the time of the meeting. It is against the law for anyone to sell you a tax shelter without giving you a prospectus. While a prospectus can be difficult reading, you should make the effort to learn about the investment (the summary page is helpful) and to raise any questions you might have *before* you make a purchase. Follow these guidelines when examining your proposed tax-shelter investment.

1. Is the sales representative licensed by the NASD?

2. Does the broker/dealer (company) with whom the representative is affiliated have a good reputation? Ask for a copy of the broker/dealer's annual report and *read it carefully and closely.*

3. What is the underlying capital or net worth of the general partner? Is it sufficient if there should be losses in the limited partnership?

4. How many previous programs has the general partner offered?

5. What is the track record of the general partner on previous programs? Ask to see the annual reports of the previous programs.

6. Will the general partner give you a list of satisfied investors who are in the previous programs so that you can contact these persons yourself?

7. Is it an SEC or an intrastate offering? (More about this later.)

8. Is it a public or a private offering? (More about this later.)

9. Do you qualify? (Covered later.)

Suitability Requirements

Each tax-shelter investment requires the prospective client to have a stated net worth (not including home, auto, and furnishings) and annual income. If you are a person earning $30,000 per year, for example, you should not be investing in a tax shelter requiring $50,000 of taxable earnings. The suitability requirements are actually a consumer protection device put on each investment by the Securities and Exchange Commission (SEC) and the state commissioner of corporations. Not only do suitability requirements differ for certain tax-shelter investments, but the same investment might have different suitability requirements in states other than your own. Pay close attention to these restrictions—they are put there to protect *you!* The financial planner who begins your meeting by asking about your financial situation is determining just what investments your suitability might fit.

SEC-Registered Programs or Intrastate Programs?

There are basically two kinds of tax-shelter investments. First, some tax shelters are registered with and come under the scrutiny of the Securities and Exchange Commission, and can, if the general partner desires, be offered in many states other than the home state of the general partner. Usually, SEC offerings are "blue-skyed" (that is, approved for sale) in thirty or more states. The sales representative must be licensed in each state where he offers the program.

The second type, intrastate offerings, are not registered with the SEC and are only approved for sale in the home state and can only invest in that home state. Therefore, the limited partnership that is an intrastate offering does not have the opportunity to take advantage of deals on a nationwide basis. An intrastate offering in real estate must be closely examined because it is common knowledge that certain states in the country no longer offer promising real estate investments—the good buys are long gone. There are still many fine intrastate tax shelters in existence today, but you need to determine the potential value of the product within the tax shelter.

Public Offering or Private Offering?

Unless you are in the 50 percent tax bracket, you should not be in a private offering. A private offering is a tax-shelter program usually called a "146" program because it falls under the Securities and Exchange Regulation Rule 146 for private placements. These programs are exempt from registration requirements and can only be offered to a *limited* number of *qualified* investors according to set standards, rules, and procedures. A private placement offering is limited to thirty-five investors and generally the investor must prove that he has knowledge and experience (or his attorney or accountant has knowledge and experience) and can bear the economic risk. There can be no public advertising about the program, and no seminars or written public communication is allowed. The investor must satisfy rather large suitability requirements and have a consistently high income now and in the future. In general, the high investment in a private placement is spread out over several years, and the representative offering the program must be assured that the client can come up with the next portion of his investment in the years to come. In return, the client will receive "deep shelter," which can be a permanent sheltering of income from the investment. Typical of the client who would like to invest in a private placement but cannot by law is the young physician who has just begun his practice and is receiving $100,000 to $150,000 per year. He is not suitable for a private placement because he has no net worth. Both the net worth and income suitability requirements must be satisfied, and they are significantly higher for the private placements than for the public programs.

In 1982, the Securities and Exchange Commission set forth new rules and regulations that replace the current exemption under Rule 146. A private placement under the new Rule 506 may have no more than thirty-five purchasers who are *not accredited* and an *unlimited* number of accredited investors. Accredited investors are those:

1. With a net worth (either individual or joint *including* home, automobile, and furnishings) of $1,000,000 or more.

2. An investor (not including spouse) with a gross income (less business expenses for a sole proprietor) of $200,000 for the *last*

two years (and who expects $200,000 this year).

3. An investor who purchases $150,000, provided the $150,000 is payable within five years from date of purchase and the net worth is at least five times the purchase.

4. Any entity 100 percent owned by accredited investors.

This is a partial summary of the investor qualifications. A consultation with a qualified investment counselor will provide the final determination of qualification.

Companies specializing in the syndication (putting together) of tax-shelter programs often introduce a tax shelter in the form of the private placement, and then put together a public offering for which the suitability requirements and minimum investment are substantially lower.

Public offerings are not limited as to the number of investors, and you will see a great deal of written communication and seminar material on the specific tax shelters. The public programs offer a wide variety of investments, each with a specific objective. There are many tax shelters for the "warm and breathing category" whereby the investor need only have a net worth of $20,000 (exclusive of home, auto, and furnishings) and an annual income of $20,000. Generally, the higher the element of risk, the higher the suitability requirements. Be cautious about any program having low suitability requirements but a high degree of risk. For example, suppose you were offered a tax shelter in raw land (the riskiest form of real estate) and the suitability requirements were less than $15,000 of net worth and $15,000 of annual income. Compare this offering to a garden apartment (which is SEC registered, whereas the raw land deal is an intrastate program) tax shelter where the suitability requirements are $20,000 of net worth and $20,000 of annual income, and you have possible cause for concern about the raw land program.

Key Factors

Before we look into the specific types of tax shelters, let us summarize the key factors in evaluating tax shelters:

Avoid Questionable Promoters. Don't be dazzled and enticed by high write-offs (100 percent, as high as 500 percent). If your program is in the hands of a sponsor whose reputation is less than perfect, you are adding to the likelihood that you will lose all of your money.

Do Your Tax-Shelter Planning Early. Tax shelters should be purchased at the *beginning* of the year, not at the end. Yet, a majority of investors wait until November and December to make their purchases. This type of action leads to investments in programs that are significantly less promising in economic potential than the earlier programs. You will also be subjected to the riskier, less reputable programs that do heavy promoting at year end, when it is easier to sell a not-so-reputable program because many clients are desperate for shelter and will take anything available.

Recently the IRS developed a task force strictly for examining the tax shelters of questionable worth. You might consider the tax shelters of this type as an "audit looking for a place to happen" and then ask yourself if it is worth investing in a program of this type. The tax shelters that will come under the IRS scrutiny will generally be the nonregistered type being sold by nonlicensed personnel.

Be Reasonable in What You Expect the Program to Do. The programs with high write-offs usually fall in the category mentioned in the paragraph above, and should be regarded with suspicion because "funny economics" may be behind the supposed tax deductions. Generally, a modest write-off and good projected return on your money is a reasonable expectation to have about a tax shelter.

Find a Good Adviser and Follow His Advice. For every client who does well, there are twenty clients who do not because they failed to follow their adviser's recommendations. And the same twenty clients usually lose a good portion of their money and inadvertently attach a "red flag" to their tax returns. If you think that your financial adviser's approach is not compatible with your own philosophy, then get another adviser. But you must be prepared to act on his recommendations.

Types of Tax-Shelter Programs

Equipment Leasing

The use of modern equipment is indeed bolstering the progress of business. However, obtaining the necessary equipment to stay competitive can mean a substantial outlay of capital. As a result, for many companies the practice of leasing has become an attractive alternative to purchasing equipment. Leasing usually requires a minimal cash outlay and it may be possible to build flexibility into the terms of the lease in order to coincide with the cash availability of the user company. Lease costs may also be lower than those of a loan taken out to purchase equipment; furthermore, the Economic Recovery Tax Act of 1981 has made it possible to depreciate equipment on a more rapid basis, the benefits of which are passed on to the investors.

Equipment-leasing transactions can be designed to provide a combination of tax and economic benefits that will be attractive for individuals with middle- as well as upper-income brackets. Tax savings may be realized through depreciation and interest deductions, and, in some cases, the investment tax credit. Economic returns may accrue through cash distributions from rental payments and from the ending or

"residual" value of the equipment at the time of sale.

A variety of equipment can be included in the partnership portfolios:

Transportation: aircraft, railroad rolling stock, heavy-duty trucks, tractors, trailers, and so on.

Office Equipment: computer peripheral equipment (not actual computers—they are possibly subject to obsolescence), photocopiers, word and graphic processors.

Miscellaneous Equipment: manufacturing equipment, oil drilling rigs, construction cranes, large display units for department stores, medical equipment, farm machinery.

Generally, the public equipment-leasing programs stress safety with income (tax sheltered), which is in the area of 10 percent. The objective is a return of your entire original investment within five or six years, with a continuing return for several more years. The investment tax credit will also be available in some transactions. The partnership would try to structure the leases so as to realize favorable residual value of the equipment at the end of the lease terms, thereby providing a possible inflation hedge for investors. In addition, proceeds from the sale of the equipment in excess of the depreciated cost basis will be taxed at the lower ordinary income rates provided for in the Economy Recovery Tax Act of 1981. Another benefit of the tax act is the reduction in the amount of investment tax credit to be recaptured on an early sale of the equipment.

Here are some points to consider before investing in an equipment-leasing program:

1. Are the leases operating leases or full-payout leases? Full-payout leases return at least the purchase price of the equipment to the lessor during the initial lease term. Operating leases return less, and thus represent a greater risk; however, the risk can possibly be offset by management obtaining better renewal rents. Generally, the partnership will use a combination of the two types of leases.

2. What is the financial stability of the lessee? What criteria has the management established to determine whether the lessee is capable of continuing to make the lease payments on a consistent basis? The stronger the lessee, the less the risk of a default on lease payments. The lease agreement may be constructed to pay off the equipment within a three- to four-year period, and the continued payments of the lessee long after that period will provide cash flow to the investors. The strength of the lessees will be a guideline to the risk involved in the partnership investment.

3. Is the industry using the equipment profitable? Will the equipment in the partnership avoid the pitfalls of obsolescence? If there is a chance of obsolescence, the re-lease or sale of the equipment would be extremely difficult.

4. What ending or residual value will the equipment have?

5. Are the tax benefits compatible with my overall financial situation?

6. What about the general partner?

How long has the general partner been engaged in this type of activity, and how qualified is he to conduct this type of business? (Ask for a copy of the annual report.)

How have the previous programs of this type fared? Any IRS audits?

Has the general partner done all he promised in the prior programs?

Does the general partner deliver the appropriate tax information and investor reports on a timely basis? Are the investors of the prior programs kept informed on all transactions?

Will the general partner provide you with a list of satisfied investors of prior programs? Contact some of these people.

Is there enough capital behind the general partner to handle partnership emergencies without a panic assessment (asking the investors to come up with more money)?

How long did it take for the investors in past programs to get their money back?

What are the fees and commissions in the program—how much is up front?

Is this program a diversified program? A program set up for one piece of equipment does not offer the safety or diversification of a partnership containing several different kinds of equipment. Examine the program for diversification of equipment and industries.

Equipment-leasing programs were once thought to be for the rich. However, several programs are available for the middle-income taxpayer. Because equipment is necessary for the success of our economy, equipment-leasing programs should be given close attention by the investor. The economy runs on business, and business runs on equipment.

Equipment-Leasing Income Fund. A relatively new type of equipment-leasing program to be offered to investors is the leasing income fund. High predictable cash flow with inflation protection are two key benefits. An equipment-leasing income fund invests primarily in office-related types of equipment such as terminals for management information systems, photocopying equipment, graphic processing equipment, electronic printing systems, and the like. Most of the equipment is vendor-leased; that is, the manufacturer arranges the leases with user companies and provides all maintenance and remarketing services. The partnership management retains the responsibility for credit approval of the lessees.

The investors receive the cash flow from the lease payments, the partnership's objective being to provide at least a 14–15 percent return on investment to the limited partners. Excess cash flow is usually invested, on behalf of the limited partners, in additional equipment. Most of the cash distributions will be taxable, but the investors will receive the benefit of depreciation deductions on the equipment and, in some cases, the investment tax credit. The investors will receive additional cash distributions when the partnership equipment is sold (in approximately eight to eleven years).

This type of program may offer the opportunity to reinvest cash distributions, in part or in whole. It is the type of program suited for the investor who wishes a good to high rate of return, some tax savings, and the ownership of tangible assets that can provide a potential hedge against inflation.

Cable Television

Cable television, as an investment, is so new you will find little information about it in any book published prior to 1978. Yet no other type of investment will have as great an impact on our future as cable television. Previously, cable TV programs were offered as private placements; however, with the rapid growth and success of the industry, public programs are now being offered to the investor.

It is important to determine if the partnership's objective is to build new systems or purchase existing systems. Should the partnership elect to build the cable TV systems, the risk is greater, owing to the ever increasing government rules, regulations, and restrictions of government agencies such as the Federal Communications Commission.

The objective of a lower risk cable TV partnership would be to purchase existing systems, upgrade the equipment, increase the numbers of subscribers (and the services available to the viewers), and then sell the system at a substantial profit.

Naturally, all systems within the partnership should have the co-axial (two-way) cable, which allows signals to be received and *sent*. Over the next few years, the three main sources of revenue (in addition to increasing the number of subscribers) in a cable TV partnership will be:

1. Advertising. Where we once subscribed to cable TV to get rid of advertising, most major companies will spend the greatest portion of their advertising budgets on cable TV, mainly because athletic events will become an important part of cable programs.

2. Pay per view packages. Within three to five years, most major sporting events will be carried only on cable television, and subscribers will have to *pay* an extra fee to view the event. The Super Bowl, World Series, Olympics, Masters Golf Tournament, Davis Cup Tennis Championships, will all be programs that will only be seen on cable TV. This prediction has been made by several notable sports figures.

3. Buck Rogers technology, the two-way communications capability. Currently bank-at-home services and shop-at-home services are available, as are home security and medical alert systems. Subscribers will be able to give their opinions on political issues as well as entertainment vehicles (Academy Awards, Emmy Awards, most popular shows or entertainer, and so on) simply by pushing the appropriate button while sitting in the comfort of their living rooms.

A cable TV limited partnership may very well be an investment in the "future" of cable television. Generally the programs will offer a good write-off (in the area of 100 percent over three or four years), with minimal or no cash flow. This is a promising growth vehicle for the young investor.

Because the cable TV limited partnership is a new entity, the experience of the general partner will be a key factor. If the general partner has no prior experience, is he affiliating with a cable systems company that can provide the expertise?

The aspects of cable TV that make it so attractive to consumers also make it attractive to investors—both corporations and individuals. Stories of major companies buying into cable TV have become common place. Westinghouse recently purchased Teleprompter; Capital Cities Communications bought Cablecom-General; the *New York Times* acquired fifty-five cable franchises in New Jersey; and Newhouse bought Daniels Properties Inc. Dollars spent have exceeded $1 billion.

If you do not fit into the above category as a corporation, or do not meet the high suitability requirements for a private placement, the public cable television programs may be the investment suitable for you.

Fast Food Franchising

A limited partnership whose prime objective is income is the fast food franchise. This type of investment generally provides little or no write-off, but instead returns partially sheltered cash flow to the investors. Naturally, the amount of the cash flow received by the investors will depend on the success of the program. The investor, therefore, should consider the following points before investing in a fast food franchise limited partnership.

1. First consider the franchise itself. Does it have widely accepted identification with the general public? Some franchises are household words in the vocabularies of all food-consuming beings, whereas unknown franchises presented in one or two states of the country may have difficulty competing with the specialties served by the superstars. It is also important to examine the criteria the franchise parent company uses to establish a facility, as they may be used as guidelines to project the success of the facility.

2. The investor should learn as much as possible about the facility (that is, the store) itself to determine whether the program meets the three most important criteria of a successful franchise limited partnership: *location, location, location*. Investigate how many people live and work in the area, the volume of automobile traffic (does the store have a "drive-thru" window?), the number of other similar food franchises in the same area, and *their* sales results in the previous years.

3. What amount of support (advertising and promotional programs such as coupons offering 2 for 1, contests, and so on) will be provided by the parent franchising company and what will the management of the limited partnership facility offer as an inducement to increase sales?

4. Examine the general partner. Does he have the capital to assist in an emergency, or will the partnership result in disaster for the investors because the capital was not there to give the program a boost "over the top"? What has been the experience of the managing general partner? Does he own similar stores in previous public or private programs? What is his track record? Does the general partner own the franchise rights to the entire county, or can someone else build the same facility in the same county?

5. The investor should examine the payment of proceeds to the management. Is the fee subordinated (paid *only* after a projected annual return is received by the investors)? A worthwhile program may contain an incentive bonus fee that would be paid to the management only if sales reach a certain dollar amount. The incentive bonus certainly creates a desire on the part of management to achieve their objectives.

6. Does the franchise include the real estate? Some franchises consist of only the store itself. A franchise that includes the underlying real estate may increase the potential for appreciation in the investment.

With sound management, strong capital, and a superior location, fast food franchise limited partnerships offer steady income with partial tax advantages. Generally, these partnerships are long-term in nature and are suitable for investors seeking steady income, little (if any) write-offs, and possible appreciation.

Research and Development (R&D)

In a typical R & D partnership, an inventor or promoter wishing to develop a potentially patentable invention or idea transfers all rights to a partnership in return for an interest as a general partner. The limited partners contribute the capital to finance the necessary research and development. Usually the partnership contracts all research activities using an outside organization to perform the active R & D to achieve a marketable product. The research contract may require a cash prepayment that accelerates the partner's deduction and provides working capital for the research organization.

The partnership arranges to sell its product or patent rights to another entity rather than manufacture and market the product itself. The sale would in this case be under a royalty agreement. It is important to note that the sale may be pre-arranged; however, the sale should not be closed until the research has been successfully completed. This is important in establishing that the partnership is bearing the risk of development and therefore has economic substance.

The party that performs that R & D can be the same party that contracts to buy the developed product and may even be related to the general partner.

In recent years, investors have found it increasingly difficult to raise capital for the development and marketing of an invention. Since few companies have been able to raise money by new issues of stock, the solution to R & D financing has been through the use of limited partnerships. There are distinct advantages to both for the inventor and the investor:

1. Acting as general manager, the inventor is responsible for the day-to-day management decisions. Limited partners do not interfere but have veto power over sale of partnership assets.

2. General partner/nee/inventor does the negotiating—he can sell the research results. He exchanges a percentage of royalty sales for research financing without suffering significant diminution of his control over his invention.

3. If the partnership is properly structured, the investor can get up-front immediate deductibility of that portion of his capital contribution which is expended for research and experimentations, and possibly obtain long-term capital gains treatment on his investment return when the results of the research are commercially exploited.

Generally the IRS code provides that most R & D expenses can be deducted when incurred. This allows the investor to deduct the cost of his investment while developing a potentially profitable product. A further provision of the code allows any gain on the sale of the patent rights to be taxed at long-term capital gains rates, should the product become successful.

Research and development transactions are a highly specialized field and it is important that the investor deal only with companies devoting all or a major portion of their efforts to this field. It is important for the investor to listen closely to the advice of the experts. A practical guideline in measuring whether the partnership meets the requirement is to ask who bears the economic loss if the research contract is ultimately unsuccessful. If the full brunt of the loss falls on the partners, they should be deemed to bear the burden of the research. If a projected budget is in the prospectus or offering circular, great care should be used; and any expenses for marketing or promotion by the research corporation should be reconciled with the corporation capital and estimated profit on the contract. If a thinly capitalized contractor is paying for nonqualifying expenses with partnership payment, the partnership Section 174 deduction could conceivably be reduced by the excess of these expenditures over the contractor's normal profit margin on the R & D contract. This is of even greater concern when the contracting parties are related. Accordingly, there should be an accurate accounting by the contractor for actual expenditures made under contract.

Some R & D programs require minimal initial cash contributions with additional contributions either in the form of personal guarantee of partnership loans or an irrevocable letter of credit, or some similar device.

How does a potential R & D investor identify a promising investment program? These suggestions may be helpful:

1. The general partner should have had successful experience on past similar projects. The general partner gets another "plus" if he has put up his own money in the program.

2. Do the limited partners receive any interest in any side products or technology growing out of the original project?

3. Is the risk of the program lessened by spreading out the capital over several projects?

4. Which part of the program is most heavily weighted? Avoid partnerships concentrated mainly on the *research* aspect. It's the *development* that is going to make the investment successful.

With significant front-end deductions and the opportunity for rapid return of capital if the research is successful, R & D partnerships may be good vehicles of recourse leveraging.

Movie Syndications

Currently there is only one type of movie syndication available, whereas just a few years ago an investor could choose from many. The movie industry used to be the source of more nonregistered tax shelters offered by more nonlicensed persons, and thus the cause of more dollars lost than any other form of investment. Prior to the Tax Reform Act of 1976, an investor could put money into a production service company that would ultimately "produce" a film. How much the investor received on his money depended on the performance of the movie at the box office. Investors were lured to these investments by promises of 300–400 percent write-offs. However, the IRS investigated the production service company form of syndication and has not allowed the previous tax incentives to stand. Therefore the approach is now in disfavor.

In the "negative pickup syndication," the limited partnership purchases a completed film, the purchase price consisting in part of a cash down payment and in part of a nonrecourse note due in seven to ten years, and payable out of the specified percentage of the receipts from the movie. The syndicate enters into an arrangement for distribution of the movie with an established distributor who arranges for exploitation of the movie through bookings at domestic and foreign theaters. The distributor is paid a fee between 40 percent and 50 percent of the net receipts of the movie, and the distribution costs are deducted. Any proceeds remaining are paid to the partnership and are also used to repay the nonrecourse note.

The objective of these types of movie deals is to generate a large excess write-off the same year the movie was purchased through depreciation and perhaps from investment tax credit applied to the entire leveraged purchase price. The investor should certainly examine the syndicator's track record on past deals and should try to determine if the receipts will be sufficient to meet the nonrecourse note payments. Once the note is retired, the receipts will be profit to the investor. When the receipts are only equal to or less than the note payments, the investor comes out on the losing end of the deal.

Success in a movie limited partnership will depend on public taste, which is both unpredictable and vulnerable to change without warning or reason. The rule of thumb in the industry says that only one or two films in ten earn any profit at all. Hence, diversification is of paramount importance; and most of the public partnerships are set up to invest in five or more films. The tax write-offs can be substantial and the limited partners receive an investment tax credit (a percentage of their share of the production cost) when the film is released; in addition, they are able to take depreciation.

The investor should examine the possibility for profit not only at the box office, but particularly from ancillary markets such as pay-TV or home box office. The audiences for this medium are growing so fast that the partnership may be able to command a higher price for the material. Pre-release sales of ancillary rights can also lower the risk of a box office failure.

The investor must determine where he stands in line to receive a share of the profits, because there may be a lot of people taking their portion before the limited partners—the general partner, the distributor, the stars, screenwriters, and so on.

Important also to the investment program is the inclusion of a *completion guarantee*. Cost overruns are common in film production, and the inclusion of a completion guarantee insures that regardless of weather, strikes, or creative problems, the film will be completed. If the cost is more than a certain percentage of the original budget (for example, 10 percent), the excess will be funded by the guarantee company.

The investor should not invest in any limited partnership with less than a PG rating, as the potential market for worldwide sales would be severely limited.

Today, a successfully packaged film may recoup its production cost entirely from other sources such as network TV, home box office, other pay TV, cable TV, videodiscs and cassettes. A successful producer today can probably expect to receive at least 50 percent of his production budget from ancillary sales.

Tax benefits and an early return of capital may make a movie limited partnership attractive. However, the level of risk is substantially higher because it is difficult to predict the future tastes and interests of the movie-going public. Thus, movie syndications can be one of the most speculative forms of investing. Certainly the questions to be asked of equipment-leasing programs should also be asked of the general partner in a movie partnership.

Some Words of Caution

There are countless other forms of tax-shelter investments, almost too numerous to mention. The Economic Recovery Tax Act of 1981 has taken away many of the so-called benefits previously enjoyed by these programs. However, this does not mean that you should not give them consideration as a tax-shelter investment. Simply apply the questions and suggestions previously discussed to whatever program you are investigating, and, most important, *get professional advice*. This advice may cost you a few dollars, but it could save you thousands in the long run, not to mention avoidance of an IRS audit. Some of the tax shelters not mentioned in detail are:

Cattle breeding	Cattle feeding
Agriculture	Coal
Art and antiques	Miniwarehouse
Sports franchises	Horses

And on and on and on!

The Internal Revenue Service is extremely concerned about tax shelters it considers to be abusive. It recently developed a task force whose primary objective is to seek out and eliminate investments of this type. Over the past few years the IRS has identified approximately 25,000 (involving 19,000 tax returns) and $5.1 billion in adjustments.[1] These "adjustments" generally mean that the investor has to come up with the taxes owed on all money previously written off with these abusive tax shelters.

Watch out for the opinion letter, which has played a major role in the abusive tax-shelter's promotion scheme. The client may feel protected from negligence or civil fraud penalties simply because an attorney has provided an opinion concerning deductibility of a shelter. The IRS may nonetheless prove the claimed loss deductions to be without economic substance, and may impose the 5 percent negligence penalty.

The IRS has identified four types of opinions that cause investors problems.

1. Opinions that knowingly or recklessly misstate the law or facts and are intentionally false or incompetent.

2. Opinions that claim to rely on the factual representations of the promoter even when the evidence is questionable in the light of other facts and circumstances of the transaction.

3. Opinions that never actually come to a conclusion on the tax aspects raised by the particular offering to which they are attached.

4. Opinions that state there is a "reasonable basis" for the taxpayer's claiming of the tax benefits on the basis of which the shelter is promoted, but that indicate, explicitly or implicitly, that, if challenged, the taxpayer would probably lose.

The IRS believes that the creation of abusive shelters will be reduced if related opinions are restricted, since they seem to play a critical role in the promotion of the program to the investors. As a result, in September 1980, the Treasury proposed a new set of standards for attorneys and others who provide opinions. CPAs and attorneys who accept as true the data presented to them by promoters and allow their names to be associated with those data without adequate investigation would be in violation of existing and proposed Circular 230 Rules. Opinions should be based on reasonable expectations of a successful defense against an IRS challenge.

As a final note of caution, remember that if you value the money you are investing, you owe it to yourself to thoroughly examine the product, the company, and the tax benefits. It is not necessarily a case of getting what you pay for. You may have to get less in order to keep your money and not have a visit from the IRS. Greed is the downfall of all tax-shelter investors.

[1] "Tax Shelter: Practice before the Internal Revenue Service," *Federal Register* 45, September 4, 1980, 58594.

Part 7

Editor's Notes:
For
More Sophisticated
Investing

*A*n interesting phenomenon I observed some years ago as I was editing Financial Planner *magazine is that many people who are sophisticated in some areas of life think of themselves as sophisticated investors, even though they aren't, and shouldn't try to be. This part of the book will be particularly helpful to them because it underlines the importance of objective and knowledgeable advice in these areas.*

The discussion starts off with the glamorous investments—gold, silver, platinum, gemstones—as Don McAlvany summarizes the different ways of investing in them and

draws your attention to the risks involved. Chapter 26 by Tom Aaron continues in this line of investments with a consideration of rare coins, stamps, and art, an area in which you may need the advice of an experienced financial planner. Chapter 27 by Dave Barker has a different focus from almost all the others in the book, for it is concerned with risk capital and its domain—commodity futures. Rich White then tackles stock options in Chapter 28, where he relates some important facts and misconceptions as he describes the uses of options in investment and financial planning.

Chapter 25

Gold,
Gemstones,
and Other
Hard Assets

Donald S. McAlvany has been in the securities business for fifteen years and has specialized in the world monetary system. He is owner and president of International Collectors Associates, and editor and publisher of *McAlvany Intelligence Advisor*, a monthly financial newsletter dealing with gold, inflation, the world monetary system, and global geopictures. He has lectured throughout the United States on gold inflation and consults frequently with members of government. He takes large groups of Americans to South Africa annually on political/investment-oriented tours.

Donald S. McAlvany

Whether you are already an investor or a young person just starting to do your financial planning, you witnessed an interesting event in the field of investments not long ago. During the 1970s you saw tangible assets such as gold, silver, rare coins, gemstones, and other collectibles come into their own as viable investment vehicles. Because of high inflation in that period, traditional paper investments such as common stocks, corporate, municipal and government bonds ran a poor second in price appreciation to hard assets. In the 1970s—while the stock market declined over 10 percent, the corporate and municipal bond markets dropped over 30 percent, and the U.S. dollar dropped more than 50 percent in purchasing power—gold, silver, and rare coins appreciated by more than 1000 percent, gemstones by over 700 percent, and most other collectible (hard asset) investments rose in value by at least several hundred percent. Even with a sharp price correction in most tangible investments from 1980 to 1982, their growth record of the past ten years far surpasses most conventional stock and bond investments and has only been rivaled by the impressive rise in oil, gas, and real estate prices.

Now that we have entered an era of deficit spending, high inflation, and soaring interest rates accompanied by violently fluctuating investment markets, accumulating and retaining wealth has become much more difficult for investors. Investors and their advisers, operating in a roller coaster economic environment, have had to discard many of the old investment rules of the 1950s, 1960s, and early 1970s. Liquidity, asset diversification, and inflation hedging have all become important new investment considerations. The ground rules in the battle for investment survival seem to be changing. Regardless of your personal situation, you should update yourself on these new ground rules.

A European-type psychology that considers gold, silver, rare coins, gemstones, and other collectibles not just as *optional*, but as *essential* investment diversifications for unstable, inflationary times, is beginning to take hold in the United States. This old world mind-set, which places tangible assets on an equal footing with more traditional paper investments, is now taking root in large pension funds, banks, stock brokerage firms, as well as in the dynamic financial planning industry, and can be expected to become commonplace during the 1980s.

In the investment environment of the 1980s—which will be a period of potential monetary, economic, and geopolitical uncertainty—investors will be challenged to utilize new creative approaches to portfolio management and diversification. A portion of most investment portfolios will undoubtedly consist of conventional investments such as stocks, bonds, real estate, oil and gas, Treasury bills, money market funds, and so on. But another portion will undoubtedly comprise nonconventional hard assets such as gold and silver coins (or bullion), numismatic (rare) coins, diamonds, or colored gemstones.

Precious Metals (Gold, Silver, and Platinum)

Over the past decade, investments in gold, silver, and platinum by sophisticated U.S. investors and financial institutions, as well as the man in the street, have become both respectable and commonplace—a radical change from the 1960s and early 1970s. This trend should continue among American investors in the 1980s. As growing federal deficits foreshadow continuing inflation, as monetary problems, particularly among the Third World (less-developed countries) continue to spread, and as geopolitical unrest in the Middle East, Africa, Central America, and Eastern Europe proliferates, the prognosis for further substantial price appreciation in precious metals in the 1980s appears very good. Another positive factor for gold prices is the continuing decline of world gold production. Total supplies of gold to the market fell from 1,775 tons per year in 1970 to about 1,350 tons in 1980 (a decline of 25 percent) because of a steady decline in production by the world's number one and two producers, South Africa and Russia. An additional 35 percent decline in world production is likely in the 1980s—a very bullish factor for metals prices.

Precious Metals Price History

Long-term bull markets usually unfold in three distinct phases, the final phase (or leg) being the most spectacular and speculative, and involving the largest public participation. The gold market began its spectacular, decade-long rise in 1971 at $35 per ounce, rising over the next 3½ years until it hit $197.50 in January 1975. For the next twenty months, gold descended to $102.50, with a selling climax in late August 1976—this was *a 50 percent decline*. That market bottom was characterized by negative fundamentals and by extreme pessimism on the part of most investors and advisers. With very little investor interest and virtually no positive fundamentals, gold rose from $102.50 to reach $850 in January 1980. This 3½-year rise terminated with a buying climax accompanied by incredibly bullish sentiment among investors and advisers and extremely bullish fundamentals. From that lofty position, gold plummeted to around $300 by the summer of 1982.

The gold market has now experienced two legs in its long-term bull market, with the third commencing in late 1982. *Leg 1*, as we just noted, saw the fivefold rise from $35 per ounce (September 1971) to $197.50 (January 1975), followed by a sharp twenty-month bear market correction. *Leg 2* saw an 8½-fold rise from $102.50 (August 1976) to $850 (January 1980), followed by a sharp bear market correction. *Leg 3* began with a bear market bottom of $296 on June 21, 1982, and should run from mid-1982 through mid-1985 to mid-1986. *Leg 1* saw little public participation. *Leg 2* saw about

five times greater public participation. *Leg 3* should see massive U.S. participation, including large financial institutions, banks, pension and retirement funds, and up to 10–15 percent of the American public. Most central bankers in Western Europe (who hold over half of their total reserve assets in gold bullion) believe that global monetary, economic, and geopolitical problems in the 1980s will carry gold upward during this third leg to several thousand dollars per ounce.

Silver and platinum have followed similar price movements over the past decade, usually lagging gold in the early stage of a bull move and usually leading gold in the latter stages. Both are somewhat more volatile on the upside and the downside than gold. Silver moved from around $2.00 in the early 1970s to $52 by the spring of 1980, and subsequently back to around $5.00. Platinum moved from around $30 in the early 1970s to almost $1,130 in January 1980, and subsequently back under $300. All three metals tend to move up and down relative to one another, although gold has far more widespread usages (discussed below) than silver and platinum, which are primarily industrial metals. All three metals should move up in tanden in *Leg 3* of the precious metals bull market, with the greatest strength sometimes in gold, sometimes silver, and sometimes platinum. Silver should rise to $100–$125 per ounce in Leg 3, topping out between mid-1985 and mid-1986.

Factors Affecting the Gold Market

Although gold (and to a lesser extent silver and platinum) does have a certain mystique about it, there is no real mystery as to why it was such a spectacular investment in the 1970s, or why it should be an excellent investment in the 1980s. There are practical, fundamental reasons why the gold price does what it does (just as there are for the U.S. stock and bond markets), with the added dimension that gold is a global metal with a global market, and therefore must be analyzed with respect to global economic, monetary, and geopolitical factors, rather than just domestic (U.S.) factors.

Five major factors should be analyzed if one is to understand the world gold market:

1. Demand of oil producing and exporting countries (OPEC)
2. Institutional demand
3. Monetary demand
4. Political demand
5. Inflation hedge demand

OPEC Demand

Since 1973 the OPEC oil producers have experienced a transfer of wealth from the free world amounting to $400 billion. Iraq, Libya, Algeria, Indonesia, the United Arab Emirates, Kuwait, and Saudi Arabia are all believed to have been heavy buyers of gold in recent years. If OPEC placed only 10 percent of its 1980–1982 surplus of $200 billion into gold, this would represent $20 billion in new purchases. Private Arab investors and smaller jewelry and coin buyers could buy additional billions in gold, particularly if Middle East political turmoil increases, as expected.

It has been estimated that the thirteen OPEC nations have a combined investment portfolio totaling $270 billion. If only 5 percent is held in gold ($13.5 billion) and that portfolio is increased to 10 percent gold holdings, that's another $13.5 billion in gold-buying demand. It should be noted that OPEC is forced to nibble slowly on the market so it does not run up the price. The OPEC members have low-profile buying agents making purchases regularly at Dresdner and other West German, Swiss, and London banks. Persian Gulf central banks have only about 3 percent of their reserve assets in gold and are believed to want to increase those gold holdings to 10 percent.

Institutional Demand

In recent years, gold buying by large pension funds and financial institutions in the United States has risen, led by the Alaska state legislature's approval of a 10 percent diversification of the state's $700 million pension funds (that is, $70 million were placed in gold bullion). If all state, local, and corporate pension funds in the United States had total assets of $3 trillion (a conservative estimate), and diversified ⅓ percent per year into gold bullion or gold shares, new buying demand of $10 billion per year would develop.

Large institutional portfolio managers are becoming aware of the relative performance of gold versus stocks and bonds in recent years. Robert S. Salomon, partner in Salomon Brothers, has stated, "Gold in all forms has produced investment yields far outpacing paper stocks and bonds." Salomon showed that on a compounded annual rate of return on investment capital, gold yielded 104 percent in the year ending June 1, 1980, and for the previous five-year period, it yielded an annual return of 28 percent. By comparison, he said, the same twelve-month stocks yielded 12.0 percent, and over a five-year period yielded an average of 6.4 percent per year, and over a ten-year period yielded 6.8 percent. Geoffrey Nichols, chief economist at Argus Research, admitted in the New York Times that institutions had sharply increased their holdings of gold mining stocks. Trade publications of the pension fund industry admit that the "prudent man rule" governing pension funds and other institutions now must permit investment in precious metals and precious metal stocks.

The 1979 Labor Department ruling liberalizing the Employee Retirement Income Security Act (ERISA) regulations, which govern what is "prudent" in a retirement fund investment portfolio, have greatly enhanced the interest in precious metals on the part of large portfolio managers and bank trust officers. Many of these money managers realize that traditional stock and bond investments are simply not protecting their portfolios against the ravages of inflation, which seems likely to continue and accelerate in the 1980s.

Monetary Demand

For centuries, gold (and to a lesser degree silver) has been considered to be money, and until recent years, the paper currency in circulation was thought to be only a warehouse receipt for the gold deposit in the banking system. Even the U.S. Constitution defines "money" as "specie" (gold and silver), and not as the paper currency in circulation. The concept of gold or silver as money or as a backing for the paper currency in circulation—though condemned as archaic by most contemporary politicians and economists—had the singular advantage of limiting the amount of money (currency and credit) that governments could create. In recent years, the supply of money has grown worldwide at a rate of between 8–16 percent per year, whereas the gold supply, which is quite limited, is actually declining.

Over 50 percent of the monetary reserves of the world's central banks are held in gold bullion, and total world government holdings of gold are approximately 1.0 billion ounces (worth about $350 billion). The market value of official gold holdings is now greater than all paper currency reserves in the world combined, and these central banks are accumulating more gold on an ongoing basis. (Central banks quietly accumulated over 230 tons of gold—over 15 percent of world supplies in 1981.) The central banks of the Arab countries and Japan have become particularly active in acquiring gold bullion positions in recent

years, seeking to emulate the central banks in Western Europe.

The simple fact is that because gold has been the only appreciating world monetary asset over the past decade (all currencies are depreciating via inflation), its "unofficial" importance in the world monetary system is growing rapidly. Although the United States, because of pressure from the political and banking systems, will probably not go back on an official gold standard, unofficial gold usage will continue to rise in the 1980s.

Political Demand

Political demand for gold arises whenever there is gross political turmoil in the world, as the smart money of the region moves out of the currency of that region and into a low-profile, bearer-type instrument, such as gold. Political flight capital from the Middle East, resulting from the Iranian hostage crisis and the Soviet invasion of Afghanistan in late 1979 and early 1980, was largely responsible for the surge in gold from $400 to $875 (a factor overlooked by most gold advisers who recommended selling out of gold in the fall of 1979, when it was between $300 and $400). It should be remembered that gold, in addition to being an industrial commodity, a monetary reserve asset, and an inflation hedge, is first and foremost a chaos hedge—a survival vehicle of "first resort." (Diamonds, colored gemstones, silver, and platinum are also recipients of political flight capital.)

The Soviet Union, in the early 1980s, moved into the period that former head of U.S. Air Force Intelligence General George Keegan and former head of the U.S. Defense Intelligence Agency, General Daniel Graham, call the Soviet "window of opportunity"—a three-to-five-year period in which the Soviets will enjoy massive military superiority (conventional and nuclear) over the West. It is believed that the Soviets will be tempted to flex their muscles and initiate substantial military-political expansion during this period, either directly or through surrogates such as the Cubans, East Germans, the Palestine Liberation Organization, or various Soviet-backed "liberation" fronts, particularly in the Middle East, Africa, Central America, and Southeast Asia.

Flight capital can already be seen exiting several of these regions. The Middle East will continue to be the largest source of flight capital into gold. In late 1982 the Soviets had troops massed on the western Afghanistan border for a potential thrust into Iran or western Pakistan (Baluchistan), and high intelligence sources in Washington and London quietly predicted that the Saudi royal family could be overthrown and replaced by a radical regime. In this sort of politically charged environment, similar in some ways to Western Europe in the late 1930s, the potential for surges of flight capital into gold, diamonds, and other precious metals becomes real.

Inflation Hedge Demand

The mechanism of inflation in the United States is far more simple than the politicians would like the public to believe. Inflation is not a rise in wages or prices—it is an expansion of the monetary base (of currency and credit) by the federal government. When you see the word *inflation*, substitute the word *dilution*—which better explains what is happening. Governments, led by our own, are causing inflation and blaming everyone else. From 1955 to 1982, U.S. federal government spending rose from $68 billion to over $700 billion, a tenfold increase. This rise in government spending was much greater than our growth in GNP, productivity, population, or any other parameter for growth. During that twenty-seven-year period, federal welfare and transfer-payment spending rose from $10 billion (15 percent of the budget)

to $350 (50 percent of the budget), an increase of 3500 percent! To finance this explosion in federal spending, the government has floated deficits approaching $325 billion between 1975 and 1980 (with $500 billion in deficits projected for the Reagan years—1981 through 1984).

So, in order to finance burgeoning government programs, we see the budget, the deficits, and the consequent money-supply growth and price inflation cycling higher and higher. And, paradoxically, when deflationary or recessionary symptoms do show up in the economy, the politicians print money still faster to cover up the cracks. A vicious long-term inflation syndrome is the result of this spend-print government policy. At 10 percent inflation, you will lose 50 percent of the purchasing power of your dollars in 7.3 years. At 15 percent inflation, it will take just 5 years, and at 20 percent inflation, half of your purchasing power will disappear in 3.3 years. As people around the world see rising inflation rates, they begin to look for a "stable store of value."

For six thousand years, people have turned to gold as a liquid, stable store of value in unstable times. Two illustrations of this store of value function might be helpful: (1) in the past ten years of above-average inflation, your dollar has dropped over 50 percent in purchasing power, the Dow-Jones Industrial Average has dropped 10 percent, and gold has gone up approximately 1000 percent; and (2) in 1933, you could have bought a first-line man's suit for a $20 gold coin or a $20 bill (they were of equal value in that year), whereas today, if you want to buy a similar first-line suit, you can still use the $20 gold coin to buy the suit, but have to pay over $400 in paper currency. Did the gold coin really go up in value or did it function as a stable store of value? Today, it will buy the same number of loaves of bread, goods or services, or suits of clothes as in 1933. Today, the same $20 bill will not buy the same suit, or the pants, but maybe just the tie or shirt. The obvious conclusion is that historically paper money (via currency or credit) has not been a good store of value because the quantity is infinite and is under the control of the whims of politicians, whereas the supply of gold is finite and is actually decreasing. Hence, gold is sought as a stable store of value in inflationary times.

During the 1972–1974 surge in world inflation (which reached almost 14 percent), as people saw the erosion of their paper assets, inflation hedge demand turned up sharply and a fivefold rise in gold-related investments took place. During the 1976–1980 inflation surge (which reached almost 19 percent) inflation hedge demand helped gold to rise 8½-fold. American buying usually lags the buying in Europe, the Far East, and Latin America, because the people in those regions have experienced monetary turmoil for centuries and have learned how to adjust quickly. It is relatively new to Americans (since about 1968).

The Silver and Platinum Markets

Silver and platinum are primarily industrial commodities (though silver does have a growing hedging function) as opposed to gold, which has industrial demand, monetary demand, inflation-hedging demand, and investment demand, and which functions as a primary international exchange reserve in times of war. Because gold has far wider applications than silver or platinum, it actually rose during the Great Depression, whereas the latter two metals declined.

Nevertheless, in inflationary periods, all precious metals tend to move up together. Many analysts believe that silver will have a greater percentage move in the third leg of the long-term metals bull market, and by the next major peak, platinum will have outpaced the gold price rise by 25 to 50 percent. A case can therefore be made for inclusion of silver (called "the poor man's gold") and platinum in a precious metals portfolio.

Gold, Silver, and Platinum Investment Vehicles

Four Basic Ways to Invest in Gold

Let's first consider the basic ways you can invest in gold:

1. Gold bullion
2. Gold coins
3. Gold futures
4. Gold stocks

Gold Bullion. Gold in the form of bars or wafers is illiquid and generally will have to be assayed prior to resale. It is most appropriate when a person is buying a large quantity, plans to leave it on deposit (that is, in a Swiss bank), and eventually wants to sell it without ever taking physical possession. Gold comes in bars weighing 1, 5, and 10 ounces, or 1 kilo (32.15 ounces) from such well-known refiners as Englehard, Johnson Matthey, and Credit Suisse.

Gold Coins. Low-premium "bullion" coins that trade within a few percent of the bullion content value, are very popular and represent a billion-dollar plus annual market in the United States. These coins, such as the 1-ounce Krugerrand, the 1-ounce Maple Leaf, the 0.98-ounce Austrian 100 Corona, and the 1.20-ounce Mexican 50 Peso, are very liquid, require no assay upon resale, and are concentrated forms of wealth in a convenient and anonymous bearer form. The Krugerrand and Maple Leaf can be purchased (retail) for 5–7 percent above-the-spot gold bullion price, the Austrian 100 Corona at a 2–3 percent premium, and the Mexican 50 Peso at a 5–7 percent premium. Smaller Krugerrands (⅒, ¼, ½ ounce) and smaller Mexian coins (¼, ½, and 1 ounce) are also available, but at somewhat higher premiums.

Gold Commodity Futures. This is a highly speculative approach to gold investing that affords the potential for substantial gains or losses. Because of the inherently volatile and unpredictable nature of the gold market, with global monetary, economic, and political crosscurrents causing sharp up and down (short-term) price movements, gold futures are believed by many commodities experts to be one of the most difficult commodities to trade successfully. Although they are not for longer term, conservative gold investors, gold futures do offer high profit potential for investors willing to take high speculative risk.

Gold Stocks. Shares in gold mining companies are a popular vehicle for gold investors. The largest and best-known gold mines are located in South Africa and often pay excellent dividend income, in some cases over 15 percent. Wide diversification in gold stocks is important, since a gold mine, usually a nondiversified single property, is subject to the physical risks of fire, flood, earthquake, or rockbursts, and can be permanently closed down by such an occurrence. There are also political risks in South Africa and government interference problems in Canada. An individual portfolio of gold shares can be selected or a gold stock mutual fund can be chosen. (There are four gold share mutual funds in the United States.)

Gold bullion coins are the most popular gold investment vehicle in the United States, with the 1 ounce Krugerrand accounting for over 75 percent of total gold coins purchased. Gold jewelry, while popular, should not really be considered an investment vehicle because the retail premium over the actual bullion content usually runs 100–150 percent.

Three Basic Ways to Invest in Silver

Junk Silver Coins. This category consists of bags, half bags, and quarter bags of pre-1965 circulated dimes, quarters, or halves. These coins, which are 90 percent silver, went out of circulation in 1965 when President Lyndon B. Johnson removed the silver from U.S. coinage. They come in $1,000 face value bags, each containing approximately 715 ounces of silver. Bags of circulated silver dollars are also available.

Silver Bars. Silver bars weighing 1, 10, 100, and 1,000 ounces are produced by internationally recognized refineries (for example, Johnson Matthey, Englehard, Credit Suisse). The 100-ounce bars are the most popular. Only "good delivery" bars fabricated by international refiners should be acquired or an assay will be required upon resale.

Uncirculated Silver Dollars. These dollars, minted in the late 1800s and early 1900s, and stored in Federal Reserve vaults until released in the 1950s and 1960s, have appreciated in twenty-nine of the past thirty-two years at an average rate of over 20 percent per year. Actually a quasi-numismatic coin, these silver dollars get a double play from the silver market and from their own rarity.

Silver futures are also available, but are even more speculative than gold futures. Silver stocks are available, too, but usually in more speculative mining shares, which pay almost no dividends.

Three Ways to Invest in Platinum

Platinum Bars. Bars weighing 1 and 10 ounces and 1 kilo (32.15 ounces) are produced by Johnson Matthey, Englehard, or Credit Suisse.

Platinum Futures. As with gold and silver futures, these investments are highly speculative.

Platinum Shares. The best three pure

plays via platinum mining stocks are Impala Platinum, Rustenberg, and Leydenberg (all located in South Africa).

Possible Portfolio Mixes

Some portfolio mixes of these precious metals might be:

1. 50/50, gold/silver (for example, Krugerrands/bags of "junk" silver coins)

2. 40/40/20, gold/silver/platinum (for example, Krugerrands/100-ounce silver bars/1-ounce platinum bars).

3. 33/33/33, gold/silver/uncirculated silver dollars (for example, Krugerrands/100-ounce silver bars/bags or rolls of Morgan or Peace uncirculated silver dollars).

There are a number of reputable precious metals dealers across the country who can assist the investor. One well known national company which can provide precious metals consultation, quotes, and supply gold, silver, and platinum to the investor is International Collectors Associates—Writers Tower #1010, 1660 S. Albion St. Denver, Colorado 80222 (800-525-9556).

Diamonds and Colored Gemstones

For thousands of years man has desired precious gemstones for their aesthetic appeal, for their worth as a store of wealth in times of economic and political instability, and as a symbol of status. The discovery of jewels among the remains of most ancient civilizations is abundant evidence of their enduring intrinsic value. This value is based upon such properties as rarity, beauty, and durability, as well as the fashion of the times. During inflationary periods throughout history, commodities that have intrinsic value have been greatly prized. Gold, silver, and other precious metals have such value because they have

universal acceptance as a *medium of exchange*. Antiques, rare coins, works of art, and other objects have *collector value*, which implies acceptance as valued objects by a more limited group of people. Gemstones have attributes that place them in *both* categories.

Precious stones have a number of unique characteristics that have made them attractive investments.

A Proven Record of Appreciation. Over the past decade diamonds have outperformed most other forms of investment. Colored stones, in only a few short years, have challenged even this performance. (It should be noted that diamonds and colored stones have had a 50–60 percent correction in 1981–1982, the first major price retrenchment in over a decade. Late 1982 appeared to be the bottom area with both diamonds and colored gemstones poised for a new move upward in 1983–1985.

Inflation Hedge. More inflation lies ahead. Deficit spending and excessive printing of paper money are established policies of our government, and are not changing with the different administrations. The price appreciation on diamonds has outstripped inflation drastically, better than almost any other asset. Despite the 1981–1982 pullback, diamonds within the last twenty years have increased four times more than the Consumer Price Index.

Portability. Gemstones are the most compact form of wealth in existence; $20 million worth of diamonds could easily fit within your pocket. In times of political and economic chaos, people have been able to hide and transport large sums of wealth with gemstones owing to their compactness and ability to be concealed easily.

Confidentiality. Unlike many other assets, no governments control or regulate gemstones or their markets. No special licenses or permits are needed to buy, sell, or trade them as a dealer or investor. The transaction between buyer and seller is a totally private and confidential matter. *They are the world's most private investment!*

International Liquidity.   There is a strong worldwide competition for top-quality gems—a world market with recognized values that can be exchanged for currency in any country in the world.

Rarity.   Gemstones have an environment of increasing demand and decreasing supply. Less than 3 percent of all diamonds that are rough mined yield investment-grade stones. This scarcity makes for incredible appreciation potential.

Now that we have examined the positive aspects of gemstone investment, let's consider some *negative* factors to give you a balanced perspective:

1. *No income.* Diamonds and colored stones will not generate cash flow.

2. *Cannot be used as collateral.* At this time in the United States, diamonds and colored stones are difficult to use as collateral for bank loans.

3. *Should be held long time.* Diamonds and colored stones will *not* yield a profit on a short-term basis. (Expect to hold a minimum of three to five years for best results.) The investor may have to wait for favorable market conditions to net the best price for his stone or stones (for example, 1981–1982 was definitely a buyer's market and a poor time to have to liquidate gemstones).

4. *Illiquid.* Diamonds and colored gemstones are definitely not as liquid as gold, silver, stocks, bonds, or even rare coins, but are probably more comparable to real estate with respect to liquidity. The liquidity, however, is enhanced if small markups have been paid when purchased. A maximum 15–20 percent total markup and commission above the true wholesale price for diamonds (for example, the floor prices on the Diamond Club in New York) should be paid! Remember, liquidity can

be defined as a small spread between the bid and offering price.

Precious stone purchases may not be suitable for everyone. If you have an investment portfolio of less than $30,000, you probably should not be investing in gemstones.

Diamonds

During the 1970s, investment-grade diamonds appreciated in excess of 1000 percent. Diamond prices made a sharp surge in early 1980 but by March of that year, the diamond market peaked and began a bear market price decline that would ultimately take the market down 50–60 percent. A number of factors helped precipitate this substantial correction: (1) soaring interest rates (to over 20 percent), (2) certificates of deposit and money market funds, which soaked up massive quantities of investor capital, (3) a temporary decline in inflation figures, (4) consumer optimism over Reaganomics, (5) strength of the dollar, which discouraged foreign investment in domestic diamond exchanges, and (6) bad press on unethical diamond investment firms.

The long-term price outlook is favorable, with a bottom forming in 1982 and a new uptrend developing in 1983–1985.

Colored Stones

The colored stones market is in a revolutionary period. With the incredible increases in diamonds in the past decade, interest has grown in the related area of colored stones, which are thirty to fifty times as rare as diamonds. The year 1982 marked the time to begin looking for investment opportunities in rubies, sapphires, emeralds, and other gems. Many of these stones have seen as much as 1000 percent appreciation or better in the past ten years.

An important factor to remember when considering colored stones as an investment is their origin. Many types of stones come from countries where inflation is as high as 100 percent (for example, Brazil), so they will continue to have inflation-hedge appreciation regardless of our domestic situation. It should be remembered that colored gemstones (as well as diamonds, gold, silver, and so on) have a *global* market and are influenced by global monetary, economic, and geopolitical factors.

Risk Factors in Gemstones

If you invest in gemstones, you should be aware that the greatest risk involved in this type of investment stems from illiquidity. You should also be fully aware that precious stones will generally not yield a profit on a short-term basis.

Another problem is finding highly recognized *independent* laboratories to certify stones. To buy a stone with a certificate issued by the selling company is always taboo. There is too much vested interest to have the objectivity for accurate qualification and quantification of the gem. Use only the following:

Diamonds: Gemological Institute of America (GIA), or European Gemological Laboratory (EGL)

Colored Stones: American Gemological Laboratory (AGL), or United States Gemological Services (USGS) (for some types of semiprecious stones)

Another risk is that of buying a stone that has been marked up excessively. You should demand *full* price disclosure on all gemstone transactions with *maximum* markups of 15–20 percent above the true wholesale price.

Rare (Numismatic) Coins

Rare U.S. coins, dating back to 1793 and minted primarily from gold or silver, are in very low supply owing to the small number originally produced and subsequent coin melting. The supply is even smaller in terms of the ever expanding collector-investor population of several million people. This universe of collectors and investors will probably double in the next ten years and the remaining float of rare coins will slowly disappear.

Numismatic coins should not be considered a substitute for gold and silver bullion coins, but rather a diversification within a precious metals portfolio. During the decade of the 1970s rare U.S. coins appreciated nearly 2000 percent.

Rare U.S. coins are a highly concentrated, readily transported and stored form of wealth; a million dollars in high-grade rare coins could easily fit into a cigarette pack. These coins are subject to no government regulation or exchange controls restricting the international movement of currencies and bullion coins. They would be excluded from any future government confiscation of gold or silver. Numismatic coins offer the investor a low-profile, anonymous-bearer type of investment at a time when many investors are seeking greater privacy. Rare coins function as an excellent counterbalance to smooth out the price fluctuations in a precious metals portfolio.

Rare U.S. coins have appreciated for nearly four decades at rates of 10–25 percent in most years because the supply is strictly limited (no more will ever be produced), while demand is rapidly escalating via collectors and a whole new generation of inflation-conscious investors. Collectors numbering over one million Americans are long-term (often lifetime) holders, who are motivated by the age, beauty, and uniqueness of these coins. Over 75 percent of the limited supply of rare U.S. coins is held by long-term collectors, a factor that lends an underlying price stability not found in most investment vehicles. Investors consist of people, including pension funds and money managers, who are trying to escape the ravages of U.S. inflation in a tangible asset that has consistently outperformed inflation rates. These investors are vying for the small remaining "float" of rare coins not held by long-time collectors. The "thinness" of this float means that small increases in demand will cause large price increases. The supply-demand disparity is further accentuated by the fact that many of these coins have been melted down or lost over the years.

Liquidity is the ability to move out of an asset quickly at or near the purchase price and with a very narrow spread between the bid and offering price. Numismatic coins are not as liquid as bullion coins. However, now that there are over 3,500 U.S. coin dealers and a huge number of investors and collectors, the liquidity of this market has improved sharply in recent years. Liquidity of any asset is increased if a proper purchase price is paid. Rare coin investors should pay a markup (or commission) above true wholesale of no more than 15 percent. Many unscrupulous coin dealers mark up their rare coins 40 percent or more, thus adding substantially to the illiquidity of the coin upon resale. *Caveat emptor*—let the buyer beware!

Accurate definition of the unique physical characteristics of each coin is essential in determining a proper market valuation. Original fabrication differences, tiny scratches, and bag marks can all cause a substantial difference in grade and therefore in the valuation of the coin. Coin grading needs to be done by an expert with years of experience, high integrity, and honesty. Overgrading of numismatic coins is a prevalent abuse in rare coins at the same grade at which they were originally sold.

It should be repeated that rare coins are not a substitute for highly liquid gold and silver bullion coins bought near the free-market bullion price. Rare coins are an excellent diversification within a precious metals portfolio, which can help to iron out cyclical fluctuations in the precious metals markets and provide a highly portable, low-profile, concentrated form of wealth that is a proven inflation hedge. A 10–20 percent diversification of a total precious metals portfolio in rare coins appears to be optimum.

Conclusion

Precious metals (gold, silver, platinum), rare coins (U.S. gold and silver), and gemstones (diamonds and colored stones) all came into their own as viable portfolio diversifications in the inflationary and economically turbulent 1970s. All experienced far-above-average price appreciation and all experienced sharp cyclical price corrections in 1981 and 1982, concurrent with a cyclical downturn in inflation. With the next cyclical upswing in inflation (probably 1983–1985) these hard assets should again experience above-average price appreciation.

All that glitters is not gold (or the other tangibles), but—as in Europe—the tangibles certainly do have a place in most investment portfolios. The precious metals, because of their extreme liquidity, should occupy 10–20 percent of a total portfolio, and rare coins and gemstones, with their lesser liquidity, should be in the 5–7 percent range each. There is nothing mystical about the price appreciation in these assets; global monetary, economic, and geopolitical events (especially inflation) affect their prices favorably. The prognosis is for continuing global monetary and economic problems in the 1980s.

If we can leave you with only one thought for this chapter, it would be this: everyone should have at least a partial diversification in hard assets, both for portfolio insurance and profit potential.

Chapter 26

Collectibles:
Coins,
Stamps,
Art

Thomas E. Aaron has been involved in the field of conceptual financial planning for several years. He is one of the founders and a principal of Multi-Financial Planning Corporation. He is a registered representative of Independent Financial Planners Corporation, and a member of the Tidewater Virginia Chapter of the International Association for Financial Planning, and of the Institute of Certified Financial Planners. Aaron is also a Certified Financial Planner.

Thomas E. Aaron, CFP

The 1970s witnessed the rapid growth and maturing of the financial planning industry. It is not coincidental that interest in collectible items of value intensified during that decade as well. The virtually uncontrolled inflation we experienced in the 1970s and the failure of some conventional investment media to keep pace with it, sent the investing public and the professional planners and advisers scurrying to find ways to cope. In the effort to help clients achieve their financial goals, financial advisers have relearned that there are many roads to the same goal and have refined and improved methods many have used in the past to accumulate wealth. The wealthy for hundreds of years have conserved or added to their riches by assembling portfolios of rare coins or stamps or paintings. Including selected collectibles in reasonable proportion to the remainder of a portfolio is a sound and proven way to increase the safety we all seek on our road to financial independence.

Even though interest in rare coins and stamps has grown tremendously, you may not have considered such media before. You may have collected either or both in the past, but you probably did not consider your collection to be a major investment. Most collectors consider their activity a source of pleasure or recreation, its main benefit being the fulfillment derived from acquiring things of beauty. This chapter is not written from the collector's point of view, however; it expresses the view of the investor. In simple terms, we discuss why you should consider buying things, holding them for a while, and then selling them—we hope at a tidy profit—just as you would a stock or piece of real estate. You will find here a number of statistics, procedures, and suggestions for investing in various collectibles. All performance figures are from sources that are believed to be reliable. There is no assurance, nevertheless, that any of the investments discussed will do as well in the future. In the end, you must be the judge.

Rare Coins

Anyone who is looking for long-term appreciation in value, favorable capital gains tax treatment going out, diversification and balance in their portfolio, and confidentiality and a lack of government interference with their assets should consider at least a modest investment in rare coins. In addition to the pleasure and joy of owning something rare and beautiful, here is what you can get with such an investment.

Potential High Growth. Historically, rare coins have appreciated at a phenomenally high rate. Since about 1950, according to David Hall's *Inside View*, all coins graded MS-65 and above appreciated at an average annual compounded rate of 26.8 percent. This record is truly remarkable and probably is unsurpassed. You may, if you pursue the matter further, run across different appreciation rates. The reason is that the sample underlying these other rates was probably different. Some indices include only silver coins, others only gold. Different grades of coins may have been used also.

Relatively Good Liquidity. There is a worldwide demand for all of these items, and thousands of recognized coin dealers and collectors are willing to buy from you. The best way to liquidate is discussed later in the chapter.

Diversification. There can be no question that the successful investor must be as well diversified as possible within his or her portfolio. A modest percentage of one's investable assets in rare coins, perhaps 5–10 percent, will go a long way toward providing the safety and balance you need to succeed.

Favorable Tax Treatment. One of your major considerations in any investment program is how your profits will be taxed. Every legal effort should be made to reduce or eliminate taxes completely, if possible. Profits from the sale of rare coins, if they have been held for one year, qualify for the favorable long-term capital gains treatment. In addition, they qualify for a deferral of taxes when exchanged for like property of greater value.

Ease of Storage. There is little or no maintenance required for a portfolio of coins. However, they should be kept in a protective case of some type and normally should be secured in a safe-deposit box or vault.

Confidentiality. No titles or certificates are required, and no one knows what you have unless you choose to tell them. Coins are portable, and a million dollars' worth of them could be carried in your hand or pocket.

Contrary to what you may believe, you do not have to be an expert to invest successfully in rare coins. You should, however, do enough research to learn the terms, to develop a feeling for the opportunities available, and then should seek out a well-known, reputable dealer. The ideal dealer would be one who works with investors as well as collectors, and who is actually involved in conducting major auctions. A dealer who works with investors will be better able to recommend what you should buy and why, and can even select your portfolio for you. Many financial planners have taken the time to locate, check out, and establish working arrangements with dealers who offer such services and so would be helpful persons to turn to initially.

Before you enter the arena, you should know what determines whether or not a coin is rare and what factors move the market. Two factors determine the investment grade of a rare coin: its date and its condition. Many people believe the date of a coin is the most significant factor in determining its value. In some cases this is true, but that Indian Head penny dated 1862 given to you by your grandfather, which you have stored in a box in your dresser,

probably isn't worth much. It will surely be worth more than a penny, but probably not a great deal more. While the date is a factor, it is not the most important one. Barring extreme rarity, the most significant factor is the condition of the coin. That 1862 Indian Head could vary in price from 25 cents to $200, depending upon its condition. The one you have is probably the one that is worth about 25 cents—if you can find a buyer.

Most experts would agree that an investment-grade rare coin is an uncirculated coin minted in 1934 or earlier. (There are exceptions, of course, both as to date and to circulation; many of our earlier coins do not exist in uncirculated condition.) Why 1934? Two events, the Pittman Act of 1918 and the Gold Reserve Act of 1934, had an enormous impact on the supply of U.S. coins. The Pittman Act called in silver coins to be melted down into bullion. Over 300 million silver coins were melted down as a result of that event. The Gold Reserve Act called in all gold coinage to be melted down. By the end of 1935, over 72,000 ounces of gold coins were being melted down each month. The American Numismatic Association (ANA) has estimated that as a result of those two events only about 2 percent of all gold and silver coins minted prior to 1934 remain. Of that 2 percent, the ANA estimates that only about 0.5 percent are of investment grade, that is to say MS-60 and above.

It would be useful at this point to learn about the terms used to grade coins. Some dealers may use the General Grading Table, but the ANA system is accepted and understood everywhere. The list below outlines the ANA system.

Essential Elements of the ANA System

Proof. A specially made coin distinguished by sharpness of detail and usually with a brilliant mirror-like surface. Proof refers to the method of manufacture and is not a condition, but normally the term implies perfect mint state, unless otherwise noted.

Mint State. The terms mint state (MS) and uncirculated (Unc.) are used interchangeably to describe coins showing no trace of wear. Such coins may vary to some degree because of blemishes, toning, or slight imperfections, as described in the following three subdivisions.

Perfect Uncirculated (MS-70). Perfect new condition, showing no trace of wear. The finest quality possible, with no evidence of scratches, handling, or contact with other coins. Very few regular issue coins are ever found in this condition.

Choice Uncirculated (MS-65). An above-average uncirculated coin, which may be brilliant or lightly toned and has very few contact marks on the surface or rim.

Uncirculated (MS-60). Has no trace of wear but shows a moderate number of contact marks. The surface may be spotted or may lack some luster.

Choice About Uncirculated (AU-55). Barest evidence of light wear on only the highest points of the design. Most of the mint luster remains.

About Uncirculated (AU-50). Has traces of light wear on many of the high points. At least half of the mint luster is still present.

Choice Extremely Fine (EF-45). Light overall wear shows on highest points. All design details are very sharp. Some of the mint luster is evident.

Extremely Fine (EF-40). Design is lightly worn throughout, but all features are sharp and well defined. Traces of mint luster shown.

Choice Very Fine (VF-30). Light even wear on the surface and highest parts of the design. All lettering and major features are sharp.

Very Fine (VF-20). Shows moderate wear on high points of design. All major details are clear.

Fine (F-12). Moderate to considerable even wear. Entire design is bold with overall pleasing appearance.

Very Good (VF-8). Well worn with main feature clear and bold although rather flat.

Good (G-4). Heavily worn with design visible but faint in areas. Many details are flat.

About Good (AG-3). Very heavily worn with portions of lettering, date, and legends worn smoothly. The date must be barely readable.

There is little need to go too deeply into the grading scale, for you will or should be involved only in a narrow end of it. Investment-grade coins, excepting extreme rarity, are MS-60 and above.

Other than a counterfeit coin against which any reputable dealer guarantees, your greatest risk in investing in rare coins is that they have been overgraded. There can be a difference of two points or more between a commercial coin dealer's grade and an American Numismatic Association Certification Service (ANACS) grade. The commercial dealer may interpret the standards more liberally when grading his coin. ANACS uses the more conservative interpretation. The value of having a coin with an ANACS grade is well illustrated by the fact that a coin with an ANACS certificate can command a premium 30 percent or more over an uncertified coin of the exact description. It is important to know that ANACS is the only universally accepted grading authority. A coin with an ANACS certificate will be graded on both sides. The description MS-65/63 means that the obverse is MS-65 and the reverse MS-63. Dealers with strong guarantees sometimes describe coins similarly.

A two-point differential grade can have meaningful consequences for you and your pocketbook. For example, a 1921S silver dollar graded MS-63 has a value of about $90. The same coin graded M-65 has a value exceeding $1,000. If you bought the coin as an MS-65 and its real grade is MS-63, you can readily see the problem you will have when you try to sell the coin. It might take forty years or more to make up the difference, and, in fact, you might never do so. Unscrupulous dealers may deliberately play this game with you, so beware. Know your dealer!

Most reputable dealers guarantee the accuracy of the grade of coins they sell. Check over the guarantee. It should guarantee that the coins are of a grade equal to or better than an ANACS grade. At least one major dealer guarantees that if his coins turn out to be graded too high, he will refund the full purchase price of the coin plus 15 percent per year for every year the coin was owned. This guarantee happens to be a lifetime guarantee also.

You should also know that there are no bargains in the rare coin business. It would make no sense at all for a dealer, or anyone for that matter, to sell you a coin at a price below the market value. There are too many people, including other dealers, who are willing to pay the price for a properly graded coin. Hence the dealer or other person who offers the MS-65 1921S silver dollar to you for $500 is either out of his mind or thinks he sees one who is!

The case for rare coins is a classic example of supply and demand. The supply factor has been established—what about the demand? There are two forces at work—the growing number of investors and the growing number of collectors. The collectors have made this business work in the past, and they will continue to do so in the future. However, the investor population may soon have a considerable impact on the market. The ANA estimates there were about 500,000 collectors in 1954. By 1975 the number had grown to 12 million. It is estimated there will be 25 million col-

lectors by 1990. At this time collectors account for about 85 percent of the market. The base of rare coins is diminishing. Some are lost in floods, fires, or the like, and others, for various reasons, are withheld from the market. With a growing number of collectors and investors working against a diminishing supply, which way do you think the market will move? David Hall has also reported that all rare coins graded MS-65 and above appreciated at an astounding rate of 47.6 percent for the ten-year period 1970–1979, and at 40.8 percent for 1975–1979. We can only conclude that if you do not participate, you may be missing the boat.

If you have become convinced that you should include rare coins in your portfolio or are leaning toward them, you may be wondering what you should buy, how long you should hold, and how to sell when ready. As suggested earlier, if you have no experience in this field, you should seek out a reliable dealer who works with investors, tell him what your objectives are, and how much you have to invest. If you tell him you are looking for high appreciation over a reasonable holding period, he probably will recommend you buy a portfolio diversified between metals and denominations—that is to say, a portfolio of copper, nickel, silver, and gold coins of various denominations and perhaps paper currency. The number of coins you will be able to buy will depend primarily on the amount you may have to invest. If you buy a diversified portfolio, which you probably should do, you will be up against a minimum investment of about $2,500. For that amount you can probably purchase four or five coins diversified between copper, nickel, and silver. For $5,000, you can probably purchase a portfolio of six to eight coins that might include a gold coin. Following is a sample portfolio of a $10,000 investment furnished by a major coin dealer. Note the diversification of the nine-coin portfolio and note especially the appreciation rates. Those are the average annual compounded rates of appreciation for the period 1977–1982. There are no records available from which to compute appreciation rates for those specimens marked with an asterisk. The rates given were based upon figures reported in *A Guide Book of United States Coins* for coins of a lower grade. It should be noted that higher condition coins, as a rule, have shown higher rates of appreciation than those of the lower grade. The prices of the coins have been omitted, but in 1982 the most valuable coin in the portfolio was the 1879 Liberty Seated Quarter at about $2,600, and the least valuable was the 1913-D Buffalo Nickel (Type One) at about $550. All specimens with a value over $1,000 are marked with a double asterisk.

1884 Indian Head Cent. Grade: Proof 65/65. *Appreciation rate 6.9 percent.

1913-D Buffalo Nickel (Type One). Grade: MS-65/65. Appreciation rate 54.3 percent.

1924 Mercury Dime (Full Split Bands). Grade: MS-65/65. Appreciation rate 54.3 percent.

1929-S Mercury Dime (Full Split Bands). Grade: MS-65/65. Appreciation rate 54.7 percent.

**1879 Liberty Seated Quarter. Grade: Proof 65/63. *Appreciation rate 43.8 percent.

**1884 Nickel Three Cent Piece. Grade: Proof 63/65. *Appreciation rate 41.5 percent.

**1888-S Morgan Dollar. Grade: MS-65/65. Appreciation rate 42.8 percent.

**1903 Liberty $2.50 Gold Piece. Grade: MS 63/63. *Appreciation rate 30.5 percent.

1885-S Liberty $5.00 Gold Piece. Grade: MS-63/63. *Appreciation rate 16.3 percent.

Some major dealers offer a monthly investment program wherein the buyer invests a regular amount each month from as low as $100 per month. Such a program is not recommended unless you invest at least $500 per month. Why? Because it is very difficult to purchase a rare uncirculated coin in grade MS-60 and above for less than $500. It would be virtually impossible to diversify in metal and denomination. A monthly program may be good for the collector but not necessarily so for the investor. You will be much better off in the long run to simply save your money until you have $2,500 and can get four or five coins of higher value, rather than to buy twenty-five coins with a value of $100 each. Remember, the collector is looking for the best-grade coins he can buy for the money he has to spend; for the serious collector, this means the more expensive coin.

If you simply give your dealer the latitude to select your coins for you, he may ask for guidance when it comes to choosing between higher or lower unit price, lower or higher mintage, and lower or higher grade. If that is the case, choose the higher unit price, the lower mintage, and, most important, the higher grade. You may buy fewer coins, but you can be assured you will have a higher grade investment portfolio.

If you select the coins yourself, you will have to decide whether or not you are going to specialize or invest at random. Specializing means investing, for example, only in silver coins, or gold coins, silver dollars, or commemoratives. Whatever you decide, you will have to do a considerable amount of research to judge which coins meet the appreciation criteria you need to achieve your financial goal. This is a lot of work, but it has the advantage not only of making you more knowledgeable, but also of providing you with many entertaining and informative hours spent in research. You might even get hooked and decide to become a collector.

Once your portfolio has been established, how long should you hold it before you sell? The answer to that question is, the longer the better. This is one point in favor of using coins as an investment medium in corporate pension plans. Current regulations prohibit using rare coins or any tangible asset in a self-directed Keogh Plan or Individual Retirement Account, but that could be changed in the future. If you buy rare coins outside a tax-qualified plan, you should plan on holding them for a period of three to five years. The appreciation of rare coins runs in reasonably predictable cycles. Since 1955 there has been an adjustment period in rare coin values about every $5\frac{1}{2}$ years. During an adjustment period, rare coin prices may stagnate and in some instances values may drop somewhat, but ultimately prices will rise again. The situation is quite similar to the price of gasoline in the past. Do you remember when the price of a gallon of gasoline reached fifty cents? When that happened there was considerable consumer resistance. People began selling off their big cars and the high-mileage imported car began to dominate sales. No one then could really believe gas would reach $1 per gallon, even though the experts said it was coming. Eventually we all became accustomed to and accepted prices over $1 per gallon. It was a supply-and-demand phenomenon with gasoline just as it is with rare coins. When the collector finally realizes that he is not going to be able to buy the buffalo nickel he covets for less than $1,000, he will pay it.

The periodic adjustment in prices brings up another reason to buy a diversified portfolio. All types of coins do not necessarily adjust at the same time. Gold coin prices may be flat whereas copper or silver coins are in a strong upward trend. If you ever need money and the only way to get it is to sell off part of your portfolio, you will be thankful to learn that you will not take a loss or have less profit because of a flat market.

When the time comes to liquidate all or part of your portfolio, the two most viable ways to do so are to sell them to a dealer (preferably the one you bought them from), or to offer them at auction. Of the two methods, the auction route is by far the better way to go, for then you can be assured that you will get the best retail price possible for your portfolio. Selling them to the dealer directly will get you only a wholesale price. Offering them at auction could make a significant difference to you, especially if the auction were held in a period of strong rising prices.

Selling coins at auction is not really difficult, especially if you work with a dealer involved with auctions. Most major dealers are. Basically, all you have to do is approach your dealer with what you have to sell and ask him what he thinks the portfolio will bring at auction. The major dealer is constantly in touch with the market, and he will know within reasonable limits what price your portfolio or your specific coin will bring. If you agree to the price quoted, you simply consign the items to the dealer through a consignment contract and send them to him. The standard fee for this is 10 percent of the sales price. Some dealers may reduce that fee if the coins were purchased from them originally. It may take one to three months to liquidate in this way because the description of your coins and perhaps even photographs have to be entered in the auction catalogue. The catalogue recipients also need time to study the catalogue before the auction to determine what they want to buy. If you need funds, a major dealer will usually advance up to 50 percent of the probable sale price and send the remainder after the coins have been sold.

If you are an investor as opposed to a collector, your trip to the auction would be tax deductible under current regulations, as would be the cost of subscriptions to coin periodicals or other reference material. An important factor used by the IRS to determine whether or not you are an investor is the location of your coins. If you keep them at home rather than in a safe-deposit box, you may have a hard time proving you are not a collector.

Rare Stamps

It is said that, considering its size and weight, one of the most valuable objects in the world is a one cent provisional postage stamp printed in British Guiana in 1856. In 1980 this small piece of paper was sold for $850,000. At that time this was reportedly the highest price ever paid for a postage stamp.

Investing in rare stamps can be just as exciting, interesting, and financially and aesthetically rewarding as investing in rare coins. The reasons given earlier for considering investing in rare coins apply to stamps as well. Over the past ten years price appreciation of stamps has paralleled that of coins. The holding period is about the same—a minimum of three to five years. With over 100 suitable auctions every year, stamps are as easy to liquidate as coins, and your best price will normally be realized through an auction. Profits from the sale of stamps have the same favorable capital gains tax treatment as coins and they are eligible for tax-deferred exchange. Stamps need perhaps a bit more care than coins since they can be damaged by high humidity, but in proper storage in a protective case they should remain well preserved. If you use this medium to add diversification to your investment portfolio, you should have about the same percentage ratio as for coins, or about 5–10 percent. Go to the lower figure if you include both coins and stamps.

There are probably more collectors of stamps than there are of coins. The U.S. Postal Service suggests stamp collecting is the most popular hobby in the world and estimates the current number of collectors in the United States to be about 20 million. Collectors account for about 86 percent of the stamp market. Investors account for the remainder.

The philatelist normally does not consider his collection an investment. It is his hobby, not a money-making venture, and collectors are often scornful and perhaps even resentful of the growing numbers of investors who are driving up the prices of the objects of their affection. Indeed, most stamp collections have little value other than the prices paid and the pleasure derived from assembling the collection. Chances are that your father's collection in the attic is not really worth much; on the other hand, there may be something of great value contained in it. Philately is filled with stories of those who yearned for something like a plate block of four 65-cent Zeppelins as a boy in the late 1920s or early 1930s and who, after saving for months, bought them for maybe $3 or $4. Now he might find an eager buyer willing to pay $8,000 for them. These are the fortunate exceptions, however. Along the way something happened that fueled the fire of passion in the collector and hence drove up the prices.

As with coins, the value of a stamp is a function of its rarity, the demand for it by collectors (or investors), and its condition. It is more difficult to define a rare stamp exactly. For investment purposes you could categorize stamps as:

U.S. classics—those printed between 1847 and 1899

Middles—those printed between 1900 and 1924

Moderns—those printed between 1925 and the present

Early airmails—those printed between 1918 and 1935

In general, then, we could say that a rare stamp falls in one or more of the categories above and was printed earlier than perhaps 1935–1940. There are exceptions on either side of this bracket. It is safe to say, though, that most stamps printed after 1940 have little or no value as an investment. For the most part, the collector gathers them for the aesthetic values he derives from his hobby. Then, too, many stamps printed prior to 1935 may be rare indeed, but are not suitable for investing because there is little or no demand for them from collectors. As an investor, you could consider the country in which the stamp was printed (other than the United States) to be another category for determining value. The stamp should have been printed for use as postage rather than for collecting. This should help you to eliminate many specimens printed by smaller countries as a source of revenue and should help you to lean toward countries with a large literate population, a sound economic base, and a well-used postal system.

Although it can be important, the number of stamps printed does not necessarily establish rarity. If you become disposed toward stamp collecting, ultimately you will want to purchase a current *Scott's Standard Postage Stamp Catalogue*. This publication is *the* reference book for collectors. Browsing through the catalogue you may note there were 200 million particular stamps printed in a particular year and that the price range is usually high or low. You may wonder why. Normal reasoning would suggest that a stamp printed in such large numbers could not possibly be rare. What you don't know, though, is how many were shipped to the post office, how many were not sold and subsequently returned and destroyed, how many were used, and how many were not. Finally, the critical factor is collector demand, which in the end determines whether or not the price is high or low and whether the item should be considered an investment-grade stamp.

You enter the alligator pit unprotected if you enter the world of stamp investing without knowledge. Finding a reputable, established dealer who is in touch with the market, and, as with rare coins, one who is accustomed to working with investors as well as collectors, must be your first order of business. You could also find a financial planner who has worked with dealers and has an established relationship with them.

With the possible exception of the Philatelic Foundation, which seems to be headed in the direction of establishing some standards, there is no universally accepted central grading authority for stamps, as there is for coins. The grading system for stamps would seem to be less precise but also less complex than that for coins. However, as you become familiar with it, you should become more comfortable and confident. The U.S Postal Service publishes an inexpensive but thorough encyclopedia of U.S. stamps, entitled *Stamps and Stories*. Included in it are color photographs illustrating some of the features that determine the grade of stamps. The publication advises that "most dealers designate stamp conditions by such terms as 'Superb,' 'Fine' and 'Good.' There are many gradations in range from 'Exceptionally Fine,' 'Very Fine,' and 'Very Good.' " Many prominent dealers consider Extremely Fine (EF) to be synonymous with Superb and break the grades down to Extremely Fine, Very Fine, Fine, and Very Good. Most people seem to agree that stamps held for investment should generally be Very Fine or above, but because of extreme rarity or demand, a stamp graded Fine might be of investment grade.

Stamps graded Superb or Extremely Fine are those of the highest quality. The centering and the color should be perfect and the original gum intact. A Very Fine grade is a well-centered stamp in choice condition. If the stamp is imperforate, there should be very clear margins. A Fine stamp is without flaws; it should have reasonably good centering; perforations do not intrude on the design; and if imperforate, the margins may be close or touching, but do not cut the design.

Other factors also help determine the grade of a stamp. Whether or not it has been used; the degree of cancellation markings; whether or not it is faded, dirty, or stained; whether or not it has been hinged, or has thin spots, tears, or creases—all have a bearing. Because of the more subjective nature of grading, you should buy from a dealer who will give you a strongly written guarantee and who has the ability to back it up.

Investing in rare stamps requires about the same minimum investment as coins, or about $2,500. I know of no major dealer who has a regular monthly investment program for small investments. It is recommended that you allow the dealer to make your selection for you.

Below is a portfolio valued at about $10,000 that was selected by a dealer. All appreciation rates are for the period 1977–1982 and are derived from data published by *Scott's Catalogue of United States Stamps*. Specimens with a value in excess of $1,000 are marked with an asterisk. In 1982 the most expensive specimen was the 1923 Eight Cent Grant, Scott Catalog Number 560, at about $2,000. The least expensive was the 1893 Three Cent Columbian, Scott Catalog Number 232 at about $225. All but three of the portfolio have the original glue and have never been hinged.

*1847 Five Cent Franklin. Very Fine. Appreciation rate 37.2 percent. Scott Catalog Number: 1a.

*1857 Twenty-four Cent Washington. Extremely Fine. Appreciation rate 25.4 percent. Scott Catalog Number: 37.

*1870 Seven Cent Stanton with Grill. Extremely Fine. Appreciation rate 24.9 percent. Scott Catalog Number: 138.

1893 Three Cent Columbian. Extremely Fine. Appreciation rate 30.5 percent. Scott Catalog Number: 232.

1893 Eight Cent Columbian. Extremely Fine. Appreciation rate 30.5 percent. Scott Catalog Number: 236.

1901 Four Cent Pan American. Extremely Fine. Appreciation rate 27.5 percent. Scott Catalog Number: 296.

1904 Ten Cent Louisiana Purchase. Extremely Fine. Appreciation rate 24.6 percent. Scott Catalog Number: 327.

1913 Ten Cent Orange Panama Pacific. Perforated 12. Very Fine. Appreciation rate 25.4 percent. Scott Catalog Number: 400A.

1914 Two Cent Washington. Imperforate Horizontal Coil Pair. Very Fine. Appreciation rate 26.2 percent. Scott Catalog Number: 459.

1923 Eight Cent Grant. Extremely Fine. Appreciation rate 28.9 percent. Scott Catalog Number: 560.

1922 Two Dollar Capitol. Very Fine. Appreciation rate 36.6 percent. Scott Catalog Number: 572.

1918 Sixteen Cent Air Post. Extremely Fine. Appreciation rate 30.6 percent. Scott Catalog Number: C2.

1923 Twenty-four Cent Air Post. Very Fine. Appreciation rate 32.7 percent. Scott Catalog Number: C6.

1933 Fifty Cent Graf Zeppelin. Very Fine. Appreciation rate 28.1 percent. Scott Catalog Number: C18.

Art

Many other intangibles could merit your attention and study for investment purposes. Oriental rugs and antiques may come to mind, and profits may even be made in baseball cards and comic books. Who knows what trivia of the past will suddenly become the hottest investment collectible around. Quality art, of course, is not and never was in the category of trivia. Over the years many of the world's wealthy have added greatly to their wealth by assembling portfolios of the old masters and even the works of contemporary artists. However, one does not have to be wealthy to participate in this profitable and personally satisfying medium. You can spend almost any amount you have when you invest in quality art, but minimums are much the same as they are for coins and stamps, or about $3,000.

The appreciation performance of investment art is similar to that of coins and stamps. A recent Salomon Brothers Annual Survey reported a price appreciation of 22.9 percent for paintings for the year ending June 1, 1981. Since the Salomon survey began in 1968, painting prices have never gone down.

In addition to a steady appreciation potential, paintings offer many of the advantages available from investments in coins and stamps. As in the other two fields, it is virtually mandatory that you depend on the advice of a dealer unless you are knowledgeable.

In the United States the center for art transactions is New York. Hence your adviser should be one who is thoroughly familiar with the New York marketplace. The chance of finding a financial planner who has a working knowledge of investment art or who has established a relationship with a dealer is much less than it is in the area of coins and stamps. Your adviser should understand what you are trying to accomplish and should have some investment experience himself. Some people in art circles do not agree with the concept of buying art only as an investment and resent those who do. Consequently you may find it more difficult to establish a relationship with a suitable adviser.

It is much more difficult to define investment art than it is investment-grade coins or stamps. Paintings are not catalogued by condition or by rarity. There is no such thing as a rare Mona Lisa. Original works of art exist in only one copy. You certainly cannot define investment art by the painter, for every work by an artist is not a masterpiece or even of investment value. Walter and Lucille Rubin, well-known ex-

perts who have advised other investors and collectors for over two decades, suggest you follow these criteria when buying investment quality art:

1. Unless the artist has a track record of sale prices or enjoys major recognitions, avoid contemporary art. No one can predict which artists will make it.

2. Be sure the work is authentic. Buy only through a reputable professional. Unless there is irrefutable evidence of authenticity, buy only signed pieces.

3. Buy works only of established artists who can be found in standard art reference material. Try to buy those who sell with enough frequency to have established a ready market and price level.

4. Buy only pieces that are in good condition. Do not buy pieces that have had or need extensive restoration.

5. Buy only top-quality art. Beware of pieces that do not fall within these guidelines. Otherwise you will have trouble at resale time.

The Rubins point out that most of the pieces you will view at the typical gallery, art shop, or show were painted primarily for decoration. Prices may be high even for decorative paintings, but a high price does not necessarily qualify a piece as an investment. The price to you will be only a function of the profit margin the seller wishes to make—and his stock was probably purchased or painted with a view to its appearance in a particular setting. Although this art may be pleasing to you aesthetically, it will not be pleasing as an investment when you try to sell it.

Where do you purchase investment art? You can buy it at a major gallery, where the price may be marked up over wholesale more than 200 percent; you can purchase it at a major auction, where you will be bidding against professionals who know what they are doing; or you can purchase it through a firm that is specifically oriented toward art investors. You should probably rely on the last type of dealer. There are some financial planners who have sought out a reliable source for investment art and have established working relations. Your financial planner would probably be the best source to turn to at first.

Investment art is not a short-term investment. Rapid appreciation is possible, but you should plan on holding your investment for three to five years, just as you would coins and stamps. When the time comes to sell, you should not be faced with a significant time problem. If you "bought right" to begin with, your piece can be sold at any time between a few days or perhaps four months, depending upon how it is sold. Auctions normally take the longest time, but often provide your greatest financial reward. Here, again, if you have been working with a dealer or firm that is oriented toward the investor, these people will have a finger on the pulse of the marketplace and will be able to give you the best advice about liquidating.

Although investing in quality art can be aesthetically satisfying and financially rewarding, this field is more difficult to participate in than other media, since it is more difficult to find someone who will work with you and advise you on the merits of a piece or a portfolio. Enter the field with caution if you cannot locate a good adviser.

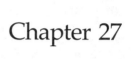

Chapter 27

Trading in the Commodity Futures Market

David Barker, B.A., M.A., has been a commodity trader for more than twelve years. He is a founder and partner of Commodity Systems Development Associates, which, under his direction, has developed a unique capability in the research, development, and testing of computerized technical trading systems with special emphasis on portfolio selection, money management techniques, and risk analysis. He has developed a number of proprietary trading programs for other advisory firms. As an outgrowth of his research work, Barker publishes the highly regarded *Commodity Systems Reports,* an internationally distributed publication specializing in the analysis and testing of many types of technical commodity-trading models.

David Barker, B.A., M.A.

The focus of this chapter is the development and implementation of *profitable trading strategies* in commodity markets. Regardless of one's particular interest in these markets, trading successfully is of utmost importance. However, before proceeding with a discussion of trading systems, we should define a few terms that are essential to an understanding of this subject.

Terminology

1. *Commodity contract* refers to the minimum quantity or basic trading unit for any commodity. Forty thousand pounds of live cattle or five thousand bushels of wheat would be examples of standard contracts in these commodities, and represent the smallest unit normally traded by the majority of commodity traders.

2. *Margin* is the equivalent of a performance bond deposited with your brokerage firm guaranteeing that you will meet the financial obligation associated with trading commodities. In most cases, margin requirements range from 5–15 percent of the actual cash value of the contract.

3. *Leverage* is the inherent result of margined investments. Typically a margin requirement of *10 percent* controls *100 percent* of the profit or loss on a commodity contract. A 10-to-1 leverage is produced in this example.

4. *Buying long* means buying, in the usual investment sense, in anticipation of increasing prices. It also carries with it the contractual obligation to *take delivery* or receive a specified quantity and grade (quality) of a given commodity on a specified date (delivery date).

5. *Selling short* is the reverse of the standard buy-sell sequence; a commodity contract may be sold first in anticipation of lower prices and bought later. As long as the sale price is higher than the buy price, a profit results irrespective of whether the buy or the sell occurred first. Selling short also carries with it the contractual obligation to *deliver* a specified quantity and grade

of a given commodity on a specified date. Unlike selling short in the stock market, commodity contracts need not be borrowed to initiate a short sale transaction.

6. *Offsetting transaction* refers to the contractual obligation to take delivery (buyer) or to deliver (seller) commodities, and it can be met in one of two ways:

Deliver or receive the actual physical commodities. Less than 5 percent of most commodity transactions result in delivery and receipt.

Sell commodity contracts that were purchased earlier or buy (buy back) commodity contracts that were sold (sold short) earlier. These offsetting transactions must occur prior to the commodity contract delivery date and effectively take the trader "out of the market."

7. *Daily trading limits,* which are set by U.S. commodity exchanges, refer to limits on the maximum price change permitted in one trading session for most contract months. The daily trading limit in the live cattle market is currently 1½¢, meaning that prices are not allowed to move up or down more than a cent and a half from the previous day's settlement price during any one trading day.

8. *Trend* denotes sustained directional price movement either up or down.

9. *Congestion* is the opposite of a trend: that is, price behavior is characterized by seemingly random up and down movements.

10. *Entry price* is the price at which either a new long or short position is established.

11. *Protective stops* refer to the price at which unfavorable price movement will cause a trade to be terminated (offset). Since protective stop prices normally move in the same direction as favorable prices, they are sometimes referred to as "trading stops." A trade that is "stopped out" may be either a winning or losing transaction.

12. *Offset and reverse (OAR)* means switching positions from long to short or

vice versa on the same day, usually at the same price.

13. *Reversing system* is a commodity trading system that is *always in the market* either long or short, switching positions as signals are generated.

14. *Equity drawdown* is a drop in total account equity that starts from the previous all-time equity high and lasts until a new equity high is achieved. A drawdown is often expressed as a percentage of total account value.

15. *Closed equity* refers to profit or loss on a completed trade.

16. *Open position equity* refers to unrealized (paper) profit on a trade that is not yet complete.

17. *Total account equity* is the sum of closed and open position equity.

Ingredients of a Successful Trading Plan

Trading commodities profitably is one of the most challenging tasks that anyone can undertake. The profile of the average commodity trader reflects that he is better educated, better capitalized, better paid, and more experienced in business matters than the average person. In short, he is not average. Even so, every study has shown that the majority of commodity traders lose money. The competition is tough. The stakes are high. The potential rewards are extraordinary. The best trading plans will include the following elements, each of which is discussed in some detail.

1. A *trading system* or strategy

2. *Proper capitalization* of the trading account

3. *Diversification* in trading among several different commodities

4. A well-defined *money management* strategy

5. *Psychological fitness*

It is widely recognized that there are two basic types of trading strategies—fundamental and technical. Fundamental trading is discussed first.

The Fundamental Approach

Analyzing supply-demand factors for a particular commodity, the fundamentalist will determine whether prices are higher than, in line with, or below some projected supply-demand *balance price* or fair market value. If current price levels are below the balance price, higher prices could be expected and the fundamental approach would dictate buying the commodity. Conversely, prices significantly above the balance price would suggest selling short in order to profit when prices eventually move lower, toward the balance price. Fundamental trading is the trading method most familiar to investors in stocks, bonds, real estate, or collectibles, depending upon a determination that something is at present either under- or overvalued.

U.S. government reports are the most comprehensive source of supply-demand statistics for most commodities. Because of the enormous resources of large commercial firms dealing in cash commodities, one would expect them to have a trading advantage over the individual fundamentalist. However, sound fundamental trading strategies are the basis for profitability by both large companies and experienced, well-disciplined individual speculators.

Advantages of Fundamental Trading Methods

Fundamentalists employ a trading strategy already familiar to successful investors in other investment media—buying low and selling high.

The fundamental methods give the trader the satisfaction of "being right" since all trades are the result of a rational, well thought-out decision-making process. The fundamentalist never buys wheat when he "thinks" wheat can be expected to go down.

Disadvantages of Fundamental Trading Methods

Econometric models are the most sophisticated of fundamental trading systems and are appropriately the topics of Ph.D. dissertations. The models are typically complex, are difficult to test against historical data, and employ large numbers of factors (parameters). As such, their availability and use is beyond the scope of the average trader.

Implementation on a daily basis is often very time-consuming. They may not be the kind of trading systems that can be used by an individual with a full-time job.

With the exception of econometric models, fundamental trading may be highly subjective, with the result that equally competent individuals may draw very different conclusions after analyzing identical supply-demand figures.

The Technical Approach

Technical trading systems are best developed by analyzing historical data. Although some look at price, volume, and open interest, most are based solely on price. Technical trading models employ a broad range of indicators. Some of the more common models are price channels, moving averages, momentum oscillators, cyclic analysis, and charting techniques based on trend lines or pattern recognition.

Advantages of Technical Trading Methods

Technical trading methods are comparatively simple. In fact, some of the simplest systems are among the best. Complexity is not necessarily an asset.

They are easy to test against historical price data, particularly with computers. Such testing allows the technician to answer the question, How well would the system have performed in the past?

Technical trading systems are easy to operate on a daily basis. By employing a programmable calculator or small home computer, trading decisions can be made in a few minutes each day.

Properly structured, they are totally objective, so the user need not anguish over decisions.

Disadvantages of Technical Trading Methods

The technician does not have the satisfaction of analyzing complex data, making a decision, and experiencing the reward of "being right" when the market responds as predicted.

The technician generally has to wait for a trend to develop before establishing a position. Therefore, profits are realized by buying high and selling higher—an unnatural trading philosophy for most people.

Technical systems usually produce more losing trades than profitable ones, overall success being dependent on profits that are on the average at least twice the size of average losses. Many technical systems are right only 35–40 percent of the time.

The Trading System— A Simple Price Channel

The trading system is defined here as the mechanism that generates buy and sell signals. Since technical systems can be totally objective and are simpler than fundamental econometric models, a technical model, the Simple Price Channel, is used to illustrate system development and implementation. Keep in mind that the system does nothing more than produce buy and sell signals.

Description of the System

The Simple Price Channel is a reversing system; that is, it is always in the market either long or short. Long or short positions are established and maintained by comparing today's close with the theoretical high or low of the Reference Day (day 1) of the price channel. An initial long position is established on the close provided that today's close is above the Reference Day Theoretical High (RDTH). This long position is maintained until the market closes below the Reference Day Theoretical Low (RDTL), at which time the long position is exited and a short position is simultaneously established—OFFSET AND REVERSE (OAR). Since price gaps between one day's close and the next day's high or low effectively distort the daily price range, RDTH and RDTL are defined in such a way that unfilled price gaps are included in the price ranges. Therefore the close immediately prior to day 1 of the price channel has to be evaluated along with the actual high and low of day 1 in order to determine the next day's order. All trading is done on the close using STOP CLOSE ONLY (SCO) orders (see definitions and abbreviations to follow). Both lock-limit and limit-up/limit-down days were taken into consideration in the testing of this model, since trading on the close is often not possible under limit-move conditions.

Definitions and Abbreviations—A Simple Price Channel

1. The High (H), Low (L), and Close (C): the highest, lowest, and settlement price recorded during a trading day.

2. Stop Close Only (SCO): the type of order to buy or sell utilized by this system, and a standard order on many commodity exchanges. An order to BUY ONE CONTRACT OF FEBRUARY PORK BELLIES; 65.40 SCO, instructs your broker to purchase February Bellies on the close (last few minutes of trading) if they are trading at 65.40 OR HIGHER. An order to SELL ONE CONTRACT OF FEBRUARY PORK BELLIES; 62.20 SCO, would instruct the floor broker to sell February Bellies on the close if they are trading at OR BELOW 62.20.

3. Price Channel: price action over N consecutive days, *including today*.

4. Nth Close: today's close.

5. Reference Day (RD): first day of the price channel.

6. Reference Day Theoretical High (RDTH): the high of the Reference Day (day 1) or the previous day's close, whichever is higher.

7. Reference Day Theoretical Low (RDTL): the low of the Reference Day (day 1) or the previous day's close, whichever is lower.

8. OAR: Offset and Reverse.

Systems Operations

In our example, the worksheet (Table 1) and graph (Figure 1) use a ten-day price channel. The optimal values taken from the Optimal Value Summary Table will be different from $N = 10$ days. These optimal parameters for each commodity will enable you to accurately operate and maintain this system.

This system is designed to use STOP CLOSE ONLY (SCO) orders.

1. Select N for each commodity from the Optimal Value Summary Table. Enter the open, high, low, close for $(N + 1)$ days. In our example $N + 1 = 11$ days. The extra day is necessary since RDTH and RDTL often use the close of the day prior to the Reference Day. Directions for computing

Table 1. Worksheet for the Simple Price Channel
Commodity: Sugar   Price Channel in Days = 10

DAY	OPEN	HIGH	LOW	CLOSE	RDTH	RDTL	L/S	BUY PRICE	SELL PRICE
1	13.95	13.98	13.80	13.89					
2	13.80	13.88	13.63	13.71					
3	13.80	14.09	13.80	13.90					
4	13.90	14.00	13.68	13.75					
5	13.60	13.77	13.51	13.73					
6	13.95	14.29	13.90	14.26					
7	14.05	14.25	13.92	14.05					
8	13.95	14.03	13.80	13.82					
9	13.95	14.08	13.83	14.00					
10	14.15	14.42	13.95	13.98					
11	14.10	14.18	13.97	14.14	13.89	13.63	L	14.14	
12	14.35	15.14	14.30	15.14	14.09	13.71	L		
13	15.05	15.30	14.82	14.91	14.00	13.68	L		
14	14.60	14.84	14.52	14.56	13.77	13.51	L		
15	14.55	14.65	14.25	14.33	14.29	13.73	L		
16	14.40	14.44	14.10	14.25	14.26	13.92	L		
17	14.21	14.62	14.15	14.22	14.05	13.80	L		
18	14.40	14.57	14.32	14.41	14.08	13.82	L		
19	14.90	14.90	14.45	14.50	14.42	13.95	L		
20	14.70	15.07	14.64	14.92	14.18	13.97	L		
21	14.85	14.89	14.56	14.76	15.14	14.14	L		
22	14.40	14.43	14.05	14.08	15.30	14.82	S		14.08
23	13.60	13.83	13.50	13.53	14.91	14.52	S		
24	13.47	13.61	13.40	13.60	14.65	14.25	S		
25	13.55	13.63	13.45	13.57	14.44	14.10	S		
26	13.00	13.18	13.00	13.09	14.62	14.15	S		
27	13.15	13.34	13.15	13.32	14.57	14.22	S		
28	13.30	13.34	13.16	13.26	14.90	14.41	S		
29	13.35	13.40	13.25	13.27	15.07	14.50	S		
30	13.35	13.35	13.17	13.23	14.92	14.56	S		
31	13.03	13.20	13.03	13.18	14.76	14.05	S		
32	13.15	13.35	13.15	13.28	14.08	13.50	S		
33	13.30	13.33	13.07	13.13	13.61	13.40	S		
34	12.85	12.92	12.75	12.76	13.63	13.45	S		
35	12.50	12.65	12.48	12.63	13.57	13.00	S		
36	12.53	12.62	12.45	12.56	13.34	13.09	S		
37	12.80	12.89	12.64	12.66	13.34	13.16	S		
38	12.60	12.60	12.47	12.58	13.40	13.25	S		
39	12.60	12.83	12.50	12.74	13.35	13.17	S		
40	13.00	13.04	12.64	12.66	13.23	13.03	S		
41	12.81	12.90	12.67	12.89	13.35	13.15	S		
42	12.95	13.52	12.90	13.27	13.33	13.07	S		
43	13.18	13.71	13.12	13.49	13.13	12.75	L	13.49	

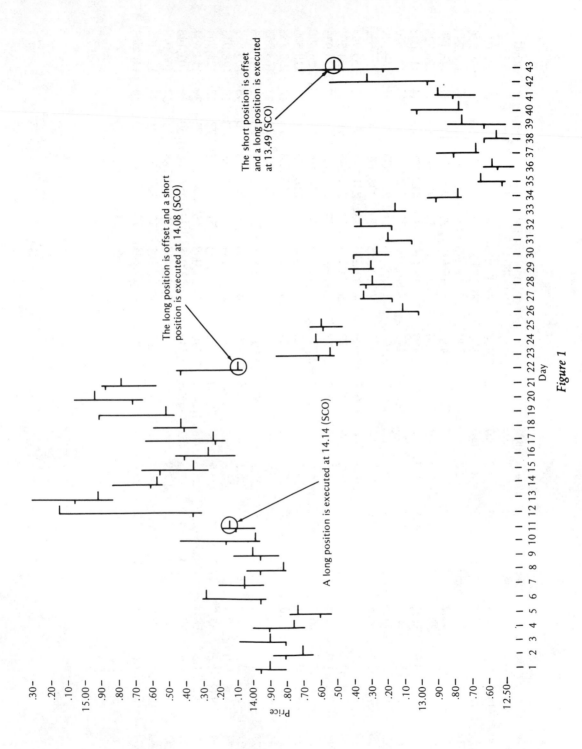

Figure 1

Table 2. Optimization Study for Coffee
Commission = $ 150

N	1975 $K	1976 $K	1977 $K	1978 $K	1979 $K	1980 $K	NBR TRADS	AVWIN $	AVLOS $	MAX# CON LS	MAX$ CON LS	WINS TOT#	WON TOT$	EFF$ %	EFF# %	PROFIT $
10	14.3	29.8	−14.4	24.8	28.3	−2.7	110	5,112	2,424	8	37,076	46	235,166	60	42	80,025
11	−12.3	34.8	−15.1	29.6	10.3	−8.6	110	5,900	2,576	8	37,691	38	224,186	55	35	38,726
12	−9.2	44.6	31.2	33.2	6.2	−2.8	94	6,649	2,347	7	19,478	36	239,363	64	38	103,249
13	−5.8	48.9	44.2	33.5	13.9	8.4	77	7,036	2,455	6	15,619	35	246,274	70	45	143,175
14	−5.1	55.7	30.6	32.1	11.3	2.3	69	7,434	2,730	6	15,619	31	230,460	69	45	126,720
15	−8.5	48.9	36.1	26.6	8.3	2.5	77	6,405	2,413	7	15,619	34	217,781	68	44	114,008
16	−7.4	45.8	60.5	14.1	3.4	7.5	73	6,754	2,475	7	10,556	33	222,881	69	45	123,870
17	−9.5	52.7	71.2	23.6	6.1	25.4	61	7,567	2,168	5	12,446	31	234,593	78	51	169,549
18	−7.5	50.5	86.5	14.8	−3.0	30.2	64	7,954	1,972	7	12,525	30	238,609	78	47	171,551
19	−4.2	49.1	69.1	15.9	−4.7	30.8	64	6,619	2,609	4	11,273	35	231,649	75	55	155,985
20	−7.9	50.7	36.7	20.3	−4.0	28.8	66	7,372	2,683	5	31,114	30	221,149	70	45	124,564
21	−7.5	41.0	74.2	15.9	−11.1	31.5	58	8,289	2,577	5	11,831	27	223,800	74	47	143,925
22	−5.6	36.5	73.1	18.4	−22.6	26.5	58	8,242	2,747	6	14,246	26	214,286	71	45	126,390
23	−6.3	30.8	90.1	16.7	−14.4	23.7	54	9,004	2,520	7	13,440	24	216,105	74	44	140,505
24	−5.2	27.8	84.0	12.8	9.0	25.4	48	10,801	2,224	6	12,150	20	216,023	78	42	153,758
25	−5.4	33.8	86.5	19.0	2.2	27.9	44	11,775	2,390	6	18,870	19	223,721	79	43	163,965
26	−6.6	33.8	82.3	15.6	−6.9	29.7	52	9,854	2,298	8	22,845	22	216,784	76	42	147,855
27	−7.1	30.3	82.0	12.9	9.7	26.1	44	10,605	2,426	4	12,506	20	212,100	78	45	153,885
28	−6.6	29.8	78.9	−8.4	4.6	28.8	50	10,061	2,476	4	12,139	20	201,218	73	40	126,945
29	−8.6	34.8	62.2	7.7	7.1	23.7	50	9,590	2,568	7	14,708	21	201,383	73	42	126,904
30	−8.2	34.8	58.5	4.0	−0.7	26.3	46	10,429	2,610	7	21,008	18	187,718	72	39	114,634
31	−10.0	34.9	59.5	2.3	−4.8	21.3	52	9,235	2,549	8	23,918	20	184,706	69	38	103,148
32	−9.3	34.8	64.1	1.3	−7.7	22.9	52	9,515	2,264	8	28,140	19	180,788	71	37	106,073
33	−10.6	34.8	59.5	4.3	−0.9	25.1	50	11,055	2,295	6	22,103	17	187,928	71	34	112,196
34	−7.6	34.8	63.3	−2.0	−1.2	25.3	44	11,210	2,386	6	21,604	16	179,359	73	36	112,564

35	−7.2	34.8	58.7	−13.5	−5.6	23.8	51	11,938	2,447	8	24,274	15	179,070	67	29	90,964
36	−10.2	31.2	56.0	−14.4	1.9	24.0	55	12,381	2,429	8	25,129	15	185,719	66	27	88,545
37	−10.7	31.3	40.1	−24.8	15.7	22.3	53	10,290	2,452	6	14,790	16	164,644	64	30	73,931
38	−6.6	31.0	56.8	−27.0	22.9	23.2	46	10,167	2,955	6	15,356	18	183,004	69	39	100,271
39	14.1	30.8	50.7	−24.8	21.0	18.4	44	11,763	2,787	6	16,669	16	188,201	71	36	110,156
40	13.1	34.6	48.5	−18.2	25.6	12.8	44	12,244	2,316	5	14,719	15	183,664	73	34	116,490
41	12.4	32.8	41.2	−28.5	28.2	13.5	42	11,550	2,727	7	20,456	15	173,246	70	36	99,626
42	11.4	36.4	41.2	−25.1	25.1	18.3	34	11,343	3,304	3	15,821	15	170,141	73	44	107,366
43	11.4	30.7	41.2	−21.3	34.3	25.4	34	11,502	2,674	5	12,728	15	172,526	77	44	121,729
44	12.3	42.1	45.8	−14.1	30.2	25.4	32	10,985	2,130	3	6,491	16	175,755	84	50	141,668
45	10.5	32.7	45.5	−23.7	30.9	24.9	36	10,546	2,400	3	12,499	16	168,743	78	44	120,739
46	11.3	33.4	38.0	−25.2	33.7	18.7	38	11,262	2,559	6	12,548	15	168,934	74	39	110,070
47	10.4	35.4	42.5	−31.1	36.7	22.1	32	14,321	2,793	10	29,663	12	171,848	75	38	115,984
48	9.3	37.3	30.7	−28.4	39.6	22.1	30	14,828	3,741	5	27,083	12	177,934	73	40	110,603
49	8.3	40.8	30.7	−23.8	37.9	16.9	28	15,852	3,738	6	28,013	11	174,375	73	39	110,835
50	9.8	35.6	25.5	−21.2	35.6	15.4	28	15,420	4,052	7	29,501	11	169,620	71	39	100,733
51	7.7	35.6	18.2	−31.3	33.7	20.6	32	14,835	3,745	9	38,171	11	163,189	67	34	84,540
52	8.5	33.9	29.5	−29.3	38.4	19.3	30	12,929	3,990	8	33,596	13	168,083	71	43	100,256
53	7.7	36.1	47.5	−28.3	34.5	18.0	30	12,344	3,580	6	32,288	14	172,815	75	47	115,541
54	10.4	49.6	50.2	−33.7	32.3	16.8	30	16,409	2,887	8	34,928	11	180,503	77	37	125,644
55	7.3	52.0	48.2	−37.2	38.8	15.2	36	14,101	2,559	7	31,485	13	183,315	76	36	124,448
56	13.3	52.0	48.0	−38.8	39.9	23.6	32	14,673	2,774	5	33,229	13	190,755	78	41	138,041
57	12.4	52.0	44.2	−49.4	31.4	25.1	30	18,560	3,494	7	44,666	10	185,599	73	33	115,718
58	11.7	52.0	44.1	−48.1	33.3	22.9	28	18,200	3,676	7	43,384	10	181,999	73	36	115,834
59	11.5	52.0	42.1	−47.7	36.5	12.8	28	19,564	3,627	7	42,997	9	176,078	72	32	107,156
60	11.3	55.7	42.7	−43.2	34.7	13.0	30	20,174	3,208	8	31,039	9	181,564	70	30	114,184

RDTH and RDTL are found in the "Definitions and Abbreviations" section.

2. On day 11, orders are placed simultaneously to: (1) Buy one contract sugar 13.90 (SCO) (this is 1 point above RDTH); (2) sell one contract sugar 13.62 (SCO) (this is one point below the RDTL). Since the close on day 11 (14.14) is above the RDTH, the order to buy 1 contract is executed and a Long position taken.

3. Each day an order is placed to sell two contracts of sugar 1 point below the RDTL, thus allowing you to offset your Long position and go Short if price action is downward.This order may at times be "out of range" and unnecessary, or price action may not allow a fill providing the close remains higher than the RDTL.

4. On day 22 the close (14.08) drops below the RDTL (14.82). In this situation the Long is offset and a Short position is taken (OAR).

5. Each day an order is placed to buy two contracts of sugar 1 point above the RDTH.

6. On day 43 the close (13.49) is above the RDTH (13.13). In this situation the Short position is offset and a Long position is taken.

Trading Rules

1. Buy Long (BL) when today's close is greater than the RDTH. Use a STOP CLOSE ONLY order.

2. Sell Short (SS) when today's close is less than the RDTL. Use a STOP CLOSE ONLY order.

3. The system is always in the market either Long or Short. After the initial position, the system OFFSETS AND REVERSES (OAR).

4. If, because of limit-move conditions, trading on the close is not possible, trade on the next day's open "at the market."

System Development

The application of computer technology is integral to the development and testing of technical trading systems. A system as easy to operate as the Simple Price Channel can be maintained on a daily basis by anyone who can count (no calculation is required to produce buy and sell signals), but the optimization capability of the computer is critical in system research.

Computer Optimization

Computer optimization answers two important questions about a technical system when applied to historical data:

1. Would the model have produced profitable results in the past?

2. What is the optimal (best) parameter value?

The answers are derived by having the computer test broad sets of parameter values covering several years of data. Since the Simple Price Channel has only one parameter (N, the number of days in the price channel), it is easy for the computer to simply test all values of N between 10 and 100 days. Running through one value of N over six years of historical data for any commodity requires only a few seconds on a large computer system, and is virtually error free. The entire optimization task for the Simple Price Channel over six years of historical data (1975 through 1980) and twenty-five different commodities requires no more than a few hours of computer time.

Examination of the optimization study for coffee (Table 2) reveals that an eighteen-day price channel produced the greatest profit ($171,511) for the 1975–1980 time period.

The Optimal Value Summary table (Table 3) shows the results of testing this system for all twenty-five commodities over the same six-year period. Note the sharp difference from one commodity to the

Table 3. Optimal Value Summary of Simple Price Channel

COMM	N	1975 $K	1976 $K	1977 $K	1978 $K	1979 $K	1980 $K	NBR TRADS	AVWIN $	AVLOS $	MAX# CON LS	MAX$ CON LS	WINS TOT #	WON TOT$	EFF$ %	EFF# %	PROFIT $	LOSS CONFID
Coffee	18	−7.5	50.5	86.5	14.8	−3.0	30.2	64	7,954	1,972	7	12,525	30	238,609	78	47	171,551	12,154
Cocoa	47	5.7	27.7	12.8	5.7	−4.3	6.6	29	5,868	2,416	4	7,965	15	88,020	72	52	54,192	9,097
Sugar	28	30.7	−5.4	−1.8	0.3	2.2	19.2	57	5,890	713	17	11,328	13	76,574	71	23	45,202	13,023
Corn	73	3.4	0.8	1.8	1.1	−1.3	3.3	36	991	272	6	1,575	15	14,863	72	42	9,150	3,084
Wheat	47	11.9	1.2	1.5	−2.7	2.1	4.1	51	1,538	541	5	2,538	22	33,838	68	43	18,150	4,025
Soybeans	50	16.0	3.5	25.3	−4.8	−1.8	17.4	37	4,132	1,266	6	7,413	19	78,500	78	51	55,713	7,458
Soybean meal	33	−1.3	−0.8	10.3	0.8	−1.4	10.4	57	2,018	537	9	5,760	19	38,340	65	33	17,950	6,677
Soybean oil	52	8.8	−3.0	6.8	0.4	−3.5	6.0	47	1,657	420	8	3,414	17	28,174	69	36	15,560	4,623
Live cattle	65	4.1	2.9	−0.7	−0.4	4.2	4.4	31	1,967	770	5	5,820	14	27,540	68	45	14,444	5,823
Pork bellies	53	9.2	8.8	−4.1	12.1	−7.7	10.3	35	3,155	1,152	4	5,672	16	50,479	70	46	28,585	9,179
Live hogs	55	4.0	3.0	2.6	3.5	−0.4	3.4	28	1,491	641	2	1,791	16	23,854	76	57	16,161	2,692
Cotton	46	3.6	9.8	4.2	−5.7	2.9	7.5	38	3,488	924	6	6,305	13	45,350	66	34	22,245	6,521
Lumber	71	−2.6	0.5	−4.1	8.0	5.3	4.2	40	2,160	621	5	3,360	13	28,080	63	33	11,300	5,287
Copper	31	−0.7	4.4	2.2	−8.4	3.3	4.8	55	2,321	659	16	9,375	14	32,500	55	25	5,488	7,101
Gold (IMM)	19	−1.4	−0.5	2.6	2.0	20.4	44.8	77	3,607	589	7	6,690	27	97,380	77	35	67,950	10,620
Platinum	19	1.1	−1.5	−1.3	4.5	13.2	29.3	71	2,266	487	8	5,395	29	65,720	76	41	45,280	8,816
Silver (Chicago)	18	−8.0	−3.4	0.1	−0.5	58.3	240.2	90	11,389	1,564	8	23,125	33	375,825	81	37	286,665	30,415
Ginnie Mae	27	0.0	4.6	−6.8	6.7	6.3	22.4	47	2,677	630	7	3,830	19	50,860	74	40	33,220	5,951
Treasury bills	13	0.0	6.9	−2.0	−4.6	4.1	29.7	74	2,257	454	8	3,825	25	56,425	72	34	34,175	5,360
Treasury bonds	28	0.0	0.0	0.0	0.9	0.8	38.2	24	4,358	1,037	8	7,100	12	52,300	81	50	39,860	6,724
British pound	26	2.9	7.2	6.2	6.7	1.9	3.7	38	2,245	452	4	2,088	17	38,163	80	45	28,663	2,682
Canadian dollar	19	0.0	0.0	3.0	7.0	4.1	0.5	44	1,254	367	6	2,060	19	23,820	72	43	14,650	2,069
Deutsch mark	13	4.1	0.6	4.2	1.4	3.0	11.3	88	1,192	412	6	3,175	38	45,300	69	43	24,700	5,270
Japanese yen	70	0.0	0.0	0.0	15.3	15.9	5.7	7	7,607	556	1	888	5	38,038	97	71	36,925	4,006
Swiss franc	32	0.3	−4.5	14.1	9.6	−2.0	12.7	42	3,054	715	6	6,325	16	48,862	72	38	30,275	8,185

next in the optimal trading values ranging from only thirteen days for Treasury bills and the Deutsch mark, to seventy-three days for corn.

In addition to total profits, other valuable information has been generated by this computer optimization process. Each column in Table 3 provides data in addition to the system's total performance that may be useful in selecting (1) the optimal trading parameter, and (2) the optimal portfolio. Column headings are described as follows:

TTL #TRDS: Total number of trades executed during the six-year period.

AVWIN $: The average dollars won on each winning trade.

AVLOS $: The average dollars lost on each losing trade.

MAX # CON LST and MAX $ CON LST: Maximum number of consecutive losing trades and maximum dollars consecutively lost. These figures take a look at the downside risk.

TTL # WINS: Total number of winning trades.

TTL $ WON: Total dollars won (not to be confused with profits; this does not include losses, just winnings).

EFF$ %: This is a measure of how efficient the system is at creating profits. In our example, .81 means that $81 are won for every $19 lost, or approximately four times as much money is made as lost.

EFF# %: The percentage of profitable trades. This is a measure of reliability, that is, how often you'll be right. It should be noted, however, that with many excellent trading systems, this value is often less than 50 percent, meaning that you're wrong more times than you're right. What is more important is that *even if you lose more times than you win, you will still come out ahead* by keeping your losses small and letting your profits run, that is, minimize losses and maximize profits. That's what optimization is all about.

PROFIT K $: The total net profit for all six years. That's the bottom line.

LOS CNF K$: Another risk measurement. The loss confidence factor is the amount of money, in addition to margin, you would need to "weather" 95 percent of all equity dips. A high figure would indicate the need for more reserves, a small figure, fewer reserves.

Trading a technical system without the benefit of computer optimization is an expensive handicap. In the development of a system it is the single most powerful tool that one can employ.

Capitalization

Commodity trading, because it is a highly margined investment, should be considered only by those who have risk capital. Furthermore, it is necessary to have enough capital to trade like a professional. Undercapitalization makes diversification, portfolio structure, and money management difficult or impossible, and drastically reduces one's chances of profitable trading. For the person with less than $15,000 of risk capital, one might consider one or more of the better public commodity funds being offered through major brokerage firms. Performance results vary greatly, so check several. Some public and private commodity funds have excellent, well-established track records.

Capitalization Guidelines

1. Use only risk capital.

2. Commit no more than one-third of your capital to trading (margin) at any one time.

3. Place a cut-off point on your account at 50 percent. If equity falls below this point, it is time to stop trading, regroup and reexamine your trading strategy.

4. Earn interest on reserves. A Treasury

bill can be used to meet initial margin requirements on many commodities, so you can get T-bill interest on part of the same money you are using to trade cattle. Many brokerage firms now also offer money market funds with check-writing privileges—an excellent way to earn interest on trading reserves.

Using a well-tested trading system, and applying diversification and money management principles, a margin to reserve ratio should give a trader a reasonable expectation of average annual returns of 40–60 percent on total equity. A more conservative investor might commit less than one-third of available capital to trading, anticipating a smaller return with less risk. More aggressive margin allotments will increase the potential return, and the chances of a 50 percent or greater equity drawdown.

Diversification

The importance of diversification cannot be overemphasized. Although trading several commodities is obviously more time-consuming than specializing in one, the benefits of trading a broad portfolio of *unrelated* commodities are as important as the trading system itself. The primary objective of diversification is to limit the size of equity drawdowns by mixing commodities in such a way that, at any one time, losses in one commodity will be offset by gains in another. This is illustrated by the fact that a fully diversified portfolio containing all twenty-five commodities studied with the Simple Price Channel has a loss confidence of $29,795 and total profits of $1,128,053, while a single commodity—silver—had a loss confidence of $30,415 and total profits of only $286,665. In other words, the study suggests that larger reserves would have been required to trade silver alone while earning about one-fourth as much as the fully diversified portfolio of twenty-five commodities.

Portfolio Selection

To be effective, diversification requires not only that different commodities be traded simultaneously, but that the commodities selected be as price independent as possible. The most sophisticated portfolio selection processes involve price correlation studies. However, categorizing commodities into related groups will provide the basis for selecting effective portfolios.

1. Precious metals: gold, silver, platinum

2. Grains and soybeans: corn, wheat, soybeans, bean oil, bean meal

3. Financial instruments: T-bills, T-bonds, Ginnie Mae

4. Foreign currencies: Canadian dollar, Swiss franc, Japanese yen, British pound, Deutsch mark

5. Meats: live cattle, feeder cattle, hogs, pork bellies

6. Stock indexes: Dow-Jones, Standard & Poor's, New York Index

7. Miscellaneous Group:

Sugar	Heating oil
Orange juice	Lumber
Coffee	Copper
Cocoa	Cotton

Individual commodities within any one of the first six groups tend to move in the same direction and at the same rate most of the time. All three stock indices, for example, have highly correlated price movement, and including all three in a trading portfolio would do little for diversification.

Listed in the seventh group are commodities whose price movement does not correlate particularly well with any other individual commodity or commodity group. Lumber, cotton, and copper will, at times, "track with" financial instruments, but will behave independently as often as not.

Selection Guidelines

1. Construct your trading portfolio by selecting one commodity from each of the first six groups and one or more commodities from group seven.

2. If your trading capital is limited, select commodities with the smallest margin requirements in each group. This will allow you to have more groups included in your portfolio.

3. Select a portfolio such that the total portfolio margin requirement is no more than one-third of your available trading capital.

4. If trading capital does not allow the selection of two commodities from each of the first six groups, fill your portfolio out with "group seven" commodities.

Portfolio Balance

After selecting the trading portfolio, an effort should be made to assure that the impact on overall account performance for each commodity is approximately the same. This can be achieved by a consideration of margin as follows:

After determining the amount of risk capital available for commodity trading, an application of the four portfolio selection guidelines might produce a five-commodity portfolio as follows:

	A	B	C	D
GROUP	COM- MODITY	MARGIN	3,500/B	C- ROUNDED
1	Gold	3,500	1.0	1
2	Corn	1,250	2.8	3
3	T-bills	3,000	1.2	1
5	Live cattle	1,500	2.3	2
7	Sugar	2,000	1.8	2

Margins in Column B can be obtained from any brokerage firm. Column C is produced by dividing the largest individual margin (3,500 for gold) by each of the other individual margins. Column D, which is

produced by rounding off the corresponding number in Column C, produces your *balanced* portfolio. When a signal to buy or sell gold is generated, trade one contract. When a corn signal occurs, trade three contracts, and so on for each commodity in the portfolio.

Since margin requirements reflect volatility and, consequently, the size of average profits and losses, it is a good standard with which to develop portfolio balance. As market volatility changes, commodity exchanges adjust margin requirements. It is therefore recommended that portfolios be balanced regularly—quarterly at least.

Money Management

If diversification is as important as the trading system, money management is more important than either. It is also the element of successful trading about which most traders know the least.

No blackjack trading system that I am aware of works because the player wins more hands than the house over the long run. At worst, the house always has about a 1 percent edge on each hand played. Blackjack professionals make money through money management. This is accomplished by card counting, and increasing or decreasing the size of the bet as the probability of winning on an individual hand increases or decreases.

Money management as applied to commodity trading looks at account equity instead of face cards, increasing the number of contracts traded after large equity drawdowns have occurred, and decreasing the number of contracts after equity run-ups. Unfortunately, everything about the application of money management principles is contrary to human emotion; the trader is asked to trade more aggressively when things have been going terribly for some time, and to back off when markets are "hot." Since good markets follow bad, equity always goes up after going down. The principle behind money management attempts to increase the slope of equity increases and decrease the slope of equity drawdowns. Let's consider a simple example of a money management technique that will accelerate the rate of equity increases. The balanced five-commodity portfolio from the section "Portfolio Balance" will be used for illustration. The dollar figures that follow are hypothetical.

1. Balanced portfolio:

COMMODITY	NO. OF CONTRACTS
Gold	1
Corn	3
T-bills	1
Cattle	2
Sugar	2

2. Initial account equity = $50,000
   (3 times total margin)
3. Average equity drawdown = $ 7,500
4. Highest equity = $80,000
5. Current equity = $65,000
6. Current drawdown = $15,000

Since your current drawdown ($15,000) is twice the average ($7,500), it is highly probable that your equity is close to a bottom. At this time a signal is given to buy cattle. Normally your balanced portfolio would indicate going long two contracts. You buy three instead. You have "increased your bet" because your knowledge of the equity characteristics of your system indicates that the probability of profitable trades and an equity upswing is high. Your account could afford the additional contract since it had $15,000 in profits to provide the required margin. If the cattle trade is a winner and marks the beginning of an equity increase, the rate of the increase will be greater with three profitable contracts of cattle than with two.

The science of money management is considerably more complex than the example given here. Standard deviation studies would be an aid in refining the principles. The effort is worthwhile. An average trading system with money management *easily* outperforms the best system without it.

Psychological Fitness

Commodity trading is not for everyone. Equity drawdowns of 30, 40, and occasionally 50 percent or more are a *normal* part of the process of trading profitably over the long run, even with good trading systems. Dominating the trading decisions of thousands of traders, most of whom have a short trading life expectancy, are the emotions of greed and fear. Greed motivates traders to buy heavily at the top of a price run-up. Fear causes the same trader to drop silver from his portfolio after six consecutive losses, only to watch on the sidelines as the next silver trade produces the greatest single trade profit in the history of commodity markets. Greed and fear are the things that make the implementation of money management principles impossible for most traders.

The term "fade the public" used by professional traders working on the floor of the different commodity exchanges means: "Determine what the public is doing, and do the opposite." The assumption is that "the public" is usually wrong. "The public" is undisciplined, emotional, and usually wrong. Systems work—people don't.

Many traders who have reliable information and reliable trading systems still lose money. The reason: lack of discipline! Systems work only if they are followed *absolutely*! If you have available risk capital, are willing to spend considerable time developing or locating a good trading strategy, and above all else, are well disciplined, a systematic trading approach to the commodity futures market may be for you. After all, making money in commodities is easy—30 percent of the time. It is how the other 70 percent is handled that separates the winners from the losers.

Rich White is a former editor of *Financial Planner* magazine who currently works in the publishing and financial fields. His knowledge of options did not originate in his professional work, but rather through his own personal investing and "dabbling." He believes that options have been ignored as a financial planning tool because both listed options and financial planning are relatively new, and that it takes people who are "out exploring" in the market to learn about these new applications.

Chapter 28

Stock Options: Overlooked Financial Planning Tool

Richard T. White

Of all financial planning tools, options are the most misunderstood and overlooked. The typical financial planning guide relegates options to a paragraph under "speculative investments." Its commentary usually runs something like this: "If, after you have finished your financial planning, you have some money left over that you want to blow foolishly, consider options."

Here are some of the most common misconceptions about options, repeated in book after book, and even by some financial advisers who should know better:

1. Options are only for speculators.

2. Most options expire as a worthless investment.

3. People make money in options only in *rapidly* rising markets.

4. Options are not for people whose chief investment goal is income.

5. Option trading generates high transaction costs or brokerage fees.

6. Options are not for people in high tax brackets.

In every case, the popular wisdom is incorrect. In fact:

1. Options are a valuable financial planning tool that can be useful for most investors who own stock.

2. Most options do not expire as worthless investments, particularly when investors have realistic goals for the options within the context of a financial plan.

3. One great benefit of options is the ability to "hedge" in down markets, as well as make a profit in up markets. In other words, you can profit from options when you need to most—when your stocks are bombing out.

4. Options can be a great generator of additional investment income. Later in the chapter, we show you a risk-free way to generate "double dividends" using options.

5. Option investing can control the same positions as stocks at a fraction of the costs and brokerage fees. In other words, you can obtain "credit" toward your stock purchase in the options market even if you can't obtain credit by more conventional means. As we show later in this chapter, the amount of "leverage" you can control in options is virtually limitless.

6. Options can be a valuable tax-planning tool.

Why the confusion over options? First, they are relatively new. "Listed" options (those listed on exchanges and traded at auction, like listed stocks) have been traded for only a little more than a decade. Not until the late 1970s were there enough listed options and trading volume to make options accessible for the average investor. Secondly, options have been given a "fast buck" image by promoters offering schemes to "double your money in fourteen days." You *can* double your money in fourteen days in options, very easily, but you can also lose it *all*. The volatile nature of options has frightened many people away from learning about their financial planning uses. Finally, understanding options (and learning to use them) demands a new psychological orientation to the stock market, which many investors can't seem to take.

Throughout our adult lives, we have been urged to commit our capital to helping American industry grow by investing in common stocks. When we buy stocks, we invest in sound companies with strong management and earnings growth prospects. Then, we sit back and wait (and wait and wait) for the company and its stock to perform.

In this investment school, the emphasis has been on being a *loyal* investor. Your money is tied up in a company for years, and if the stock never rises in value, you still receive dividends and the satisfaction of helping the economy.

Now the investment climate is changing. For starters, we appear to be in an era of permanently high interest rates. Even if rates do not stay at 12–15 percent, they seem destined to stay well above the rate of inflation, and so you must ask yourself before you buy common stocks: "Would I be better off buying bonds? Or keeping the money in a bank or money market fund?" For the next decade, the business motto of the land appears to be, "Cash is king." Do you really want to commit most of your savings to common stocks in such an environment? Maybe we need to decide just what is meant by the term "liquidity."

Liquidity means that you can quickly and easily get to what is yours. It's that simple. If most of your money is invested in common stocks, because you want to grow with America, you may think you have liquidity through the various stock exchanges. In fact, your liquidity is always limited by the willingness of another investor to buy the stocks you may wish to sell, at a price you are willing to accept.

Secondly, the volatility of the market has changed drastically, as has our society. A favorite game used to be chess. Now, we live in the land of video games, which demand lightning-fast reflexes. The same acceleration of activity is at work in the stock market. A "move" that took six months to develop in the market a decade ago now takes a week or two. The bull-bear cycles that once took four or five years have now been compacted into a year or less. As a result, some market gurus now claim that for the smart investor, "There is no such thing as a long-term capital gain." The ability to "time the market" has become as valuable as the ability to select good companies and stocks.

Finally, the economy and markets are so unpredictable that some people who might do well in the stock market simply refuse to play. Many of them remember the Great Depression and fear the kind of giant slide that wipes out investors just when they are most vulnerable to the loss of jobs or income.

Options are uniquely suited to this new investment era. They allow you to take positions in the stock market and still keep your money in a money market fund, earning high interest rates. They allow you to move swiftly and decisively to time the market, without upsetting stock positions that you have held for years. Options allow you to hedge against big drops in the market and general uncertainty. They allow you to limit your risk in market positions to an exact amount.

Given the investment conditions of these times, it is almost inconceivable that an active, intelligent stock market investor would not use options, at least occasionally. It is almost like finding an engineer who still relies on a slide rule, rather than an electronic calculator or computer. Yet, millions of stock buyers have yet to buy or sell their first option, and the major brokerage firms (Merrill Lynch, Dean Witter, and the like) continue to sell options as speculative vehicles.

The rest of this chapter focuses on uses of options specifically in investment and financial planning, rather than speculation. We emphasize the goal and strategy involved, rather than the mechanics, because we assume that a broker skilled in options trading will implement the strategies.

Options Terminology

Here are some basic terms and concepts pertaining to options:

Call Option.   A "call" is the most popular kind of option. About three calls are created for every put (see below). A call is a contract granting the option buyer the right to *buy* 100 shares of stock at the strike price up until the expiration date. The buyer of a call pays a premium to the seller.

Put Options.   A "put" is not the opposite of a call. If you buy one put and one call on the same stock, you do not have nothing. You have a straddle (see below). A put is a contract granting the option buyer the right to *sell* 100 shares of stock at the strike price up until the expiration date. As with calls, the buyer of a put pays a premium to the seller. Puts are usually designated in options listing with a "p" to distinguish them from calls.

Strike Price. The strike price is the price at which the option may be exercised and also the dividing line between an option "in the money" and "out of the money" (see below). The strike price is part of the nomenclature of each option. A June Digital 30 option has a strike price of 30 and an expiration date in June. Please note that contrary to popular belief and some published reports, an option need not be selling at a price above (below in the case of puts) the strike price to make a profit. An option also can make a profit on its time value (see below).

Expiration Date. For the investor's purposes, options expire on the third Friday of the month designated in the option's nomenclature. A June Digital 30 option expires on the third Friday in June. You can trade or sell options at any time up through the expiration date.

Open Interest. This is a very important concept that many options veterans don't understand. Options are not like stock; the supply of them is not fixed. If I am a writer (seller) and you are a buyer, and if we both want to transact the same option at the same price, which is determined through auction bidding, we create new "open interest." For every open interest, there is one new option created. As options approach expiration date, open interest decreases. Writers close their positions by buying, and buyers close by selling. (Incidentally, all the matching of buyers and sellers is done by a company called the Options Clearing Corporation.)

"In the Money" ("Out of the Money"). A call option is in the money when it sells above its strike price. A put is in the money when it sells below its strike price. An in-the-money option has intrinsic value above its time value (see below). The lingo of options says that an option several points

in the money is "deep" in the money. An option is out of the money when it sells below its strike price (call) or above (put).

Time Value (Time Premium). Almost every option buyer pays a price for the time left in the option. The longer the time, usually the more this "time value" costs. The cost of time alone is often referred to as "time premium." For an out-of-the-money option, the total cost (premium) of the option may be considered a time premium.

Straddle. An option straddle is the simultaneous buying of a put and call of the same issue. The effect of a straddle is to make money for the investor when the stock moves rapidly in either direction; however, it may lose money if the stock does not move much.

How Options Work

Over the past decade, hundreds of writers have attempted to explain to the investing public the uses of "puts" and "calls." Today, a Gallup poll would probably find that, except for a few thousand experienced option traders, the investing public is as ignorant of puts and calls as ever. The irony is that options are not intrinsically foreign or complicated. Many people have acquired options to buy or sell real estate without feeling that they were venturing into high finance. When you put down a few dollars to put a piece of merchandise in "layaway," you are engaging in an option transaction, of a sort.

An option is simply an arrangement that allows a *little bit of money*, placed as a down-payment, to secure rights to buy the same goods (usually in the future) at the *full purchase price*. Let's look at this loose definition of options in the context of a real estate sale. Home-buyer *A* knows that he will be moving within a year and will need a new house. He makes an option agreement with homeowner B. By making a downpayment of $5,000, A has the legal right to buy B's house in one year for $60,000. He does not own the house until he pays the full $60,000. All he owns is the intangible "right to buy." He also has the right *not* to exercise the option.

Suppose that by the time the option is about to expire the market value of the home has climbed to $80,000. If buyer A could buy the home at $60,000 and then resell it for $80,000, the option itself has a value of the difference, $20,000. The $5,000 A has paid for the option has effectively *quadrupled* in value. Instead of exercising the option and buying the house, he might sell the option for $20,000 to someone else who would exercise it. Or, he might sell it back to B. In fact, real estate options rarely work quite like this, but listed stock options do.

Let's look at another kind of option. Homeowner B is worried that real estate values in his neighborhood might fall. In the option transaction above, B is not protected against falling values, because if the value of the home fell from $60,000 to $40,000, A almost surely would probably not want to exercise the option to buy. A key characteristic of an option is that the option buyer *can't be forced to exercise*. Otherwise, he has a binding contract, not an option.

B could protect against falling real estate values by himself buying an *option to sell*. This option might say that within the next year, B could sell the house to A for $60,000. If values fall, A would have to buy the house at a price *above* market values.

The first case, in which the home-buyer buys the option is the equivalent of a *"call"* option. The option buyer has a right to call the home away from the seller. The second case is the equivalent of a *"put"* option. The person who buys the option has a right to put the house (or the stock) to the person who sold the option.

In both cases, the option served a similar purpose. For very little money, it allowed the option buyer to control property that would cost a great deal more to buy outright. In finance, this is called leverage. Think of a small child who can balance on a teeter-totter a grown adult, because he has leverage (that is, most of the teeter-totter) on his side. Options give you this kind of leverage with your money.

In terms of ability to buy stock, options give you the same leverage or borrowing clout you might get from a bank, if you were a long-time worthy customer. Options are the "poor man's" ticket to stock market financing. With a stock option, bought at no financing cost or margin requirement, it is not unusual to control as much as twenty times the position that the same money would buy in stock outright. In fact, as we will show, using options, the whole subject of "how much can you borrow" in market investing loses meaning. You can borrow as much as you want. You can control as much as you want. Later, we will show you a way to control substantial stock positions and *get paid* for doing it at the same time, by means of a technique known as "nonstock."

The ability to leverage investments according to your tolerance is the first characteristic of options investing. The second characteristic of options is limited risk of loss. In a stock option, the buyer can never lose more than the amount of "premium" he pays for the option. Please note that this is not the case for the person who sells the option. If the home in the example above had fallen in value to $20,000, a person who sold a put option (thereby agreeing to buy it) for $60,000 would have lost $40,000.

The amount you pay for an option, the $5,000 in the real estate example, is called a "premium."

All options have an "expiration date." The expiration date is the last day on which the option may be exercised. Some options (including listed stock options) may be exercised at *any time* up through the expiration date. Others may be exercised only *on* the expiration date, or for a period prior to it.

Most options also have a "time value," which is a component of the amount you pay for the premium. An option for five years is usually a better bet than an option for five months, because more can happen to prices or market conditions in five years. As options age, they tend to lose their "time value." Listed stock options range in age from one day to nine months.

Before proceeding, we should emphasize one feature of options as a financial planning tool: many of the techniques addressed on the following pages are not applicable (indeed, may not be comprehensible) to the reader who is not already a stock market investor. You do not have to be a market *trader* to use options as a financial planning tool. It is enough to have built up a position in the stock of your own company, if your company's stock has listed options. It is not difficult to explain the mechanics of options to market investors, but it can be trying to translate option dynamics to an investor without market background. If the market is *not* your bag, you have read enough of this chapter. Move on.

One more note: Henceforth in this chapter, it will require a good bit of concentration to understand the opportunities being described in options. Many veteran stock market traders have not yet understood these plain truths and tools. In general, we describe ways to create the equivalent of corporate stock (effortlessly and efficiently) out of thin air, by using options. Be assured that the stock you will create (synthetic stock and "nonstock") is every bit as real, legally and financially, as stock that you buy on the New York Stock Exchange.

The Listed Options Market Today

If you've never before heard about many of the financial planning strategies described in this chapter, don't feel embarrassed. Options are a new ball game. It was not until 1977 that trading in listed put options was allowed, for example. Until recently, only a handful of stocks had listed puts *and* calls traded.

Today, options are the fastest growing sector of the securities industry—in trading volume and in the expanding choices investors have, through new listings. Options are now listed on about 300 stocks on four exchanges—the Chicago Board of Options Exchange (CBOE), the American Exchange, Pacific Exchange, and Philadelphia Exchange. A million options a week, on the average, now trade hands on the largest of the exchanges, the CBOE. The total "open interest" on all exchanges is about 7,000,000 options, or the equivalent of 700 million shares of stock.

Options are growing so fast that one of their strengths is being threatened—that is, their daily price listings in the financial pages of many newspapers, including the *Wall Street Journal*. Options listings take up much more newsprint than stock listings, because a given stock may have a number of option issues traded at a given time (ten to fifteen are not uncommon). If options were traded on every stock listed on the New York Stock Exchange, it would take just about the entire *Wall Street Journal* to list them all!

The expanding volume of options trading adds liquidity to the market. You can watch option prices each day in the newspaper, just like stocks, and usually sell them at close to the quoted price, without difficulty.

Financial Planning Techniques with Options

Options have three main uses in financial planning, all related to stock market investing: (1) as a means of achieving leverage in the market (the equivalent of borrowing money to buy stock); (2) as a means of timing the market, or temporarily negating a stock position; and (3) as a means of hedging or playing the downside of the market. In every case, other techniques are available that will achieve the same end. For example, market leverage can be achieved by buying stock "on margin" using borrowed money. You can temporarily negate a stock position simply by selling stock and buying it back again. Hedging can be achieved by a technique known as "short selling."

In many cases, however, options have economic and psychological advantages. In a margin account, you must pay interest (usually above the prime rate) on money borrowed, and the maximum initial margin allowed under current securities laws is 50 percent. In other words, if you buy $1,000 worth of stock on margin, you must put up at least $500 in cash. Furthermore, you are liable for a dreaded "margin call" if the stock falls in price. As most experienced investors know, margin calls often come at the worst of times, forcing investors to sell right at the bottom of market cycles. On the other hand, the investor using options as a financial planning tool may select whatever degree of leverage fits the plan, never pay margin interest, and never worry about a margin call.

Similarly, many investors feel a psychological attachment to their stocks that prevents them from selling at the appropriate time. For instance, an investor may have temporarily lost his job and need protection from loss of capital; however, he can't part with the stock his grandfather bequeathed him. Also, in selling he may suffer adverse tax consequences, or high brokerage costs. Options may accomplish the same temporary retreat from the market without the trauma, tax consequences, or transaction cost.

The Simulated Stock Position

At today's high interest rates, an investor faces a dilemma: Should he strive for capital gains in the stock market or earn high interest rates by keeping capital in money funds? A simulated stock position, using options, accomplishes both simultaneously.

For example, suppose you wanted to own a strong computer stock (let's say Hewlett Packard) but you have your savings in a money market fund earning 15 percent and are reluctant to give up the interest. If you buy 100 shares of Hewlett at $40 per share, you must take $4,000 out of the money market and transfer it into this stock (which pays a minimal dividend). The Hewlett stock must rise in price $600 per year for you just to break even.

An alternative is to simulate the position by buying Hewlett call options. Let's say that one Hewlett call, giving you the right to purchase 100 shares, costs a $400 premium. Each dollar of the option controls the same position as $10 of stock. After buying the options, you still have $3,600 left in your money fund, earning interest. Depending on how you buy the Hewlett option and how it performs, there may be some "transaction cost" in the option position, but the commission on the option usually will be less than that on an equivalent stock position.

If the Hewlett stock falls rapidly in price, the stock owner could lose a large part of his investment before he can react. But the option buyer's loss is limited to his premium, $400 in this case. The leverage potential is all on the "upside"! On the "downside," you have an automatic discipline that limits the amount you can lose.

Why don't more investors do this? The answer is simple. Most investors, even experienced investors, don't understand the financial planning uses of options. They would not simulate a stock position with $400 worth of options, leaving $3,600 in a money fund. Rather, they might commit $2,000 or even $4,000 to options, thus exposing themselves to more risk than they would ever take in stocks. Successful options investing and financial planning have one common denominator: discipline.

Techniques for Simulating Stock with Options

Once you understand the theory of controlling stock positions with options, for a fraction of the stock cost, you would be wise to let a reliable options broker handle the details. The problem is, what is good for the broker is not necessarily good for the investor.

The key to successful stock simulation is efficiency, and this is achieved in two ways: minimal transaction cost (including brokerage fees), and high leverage. High brokerage fees and "big-time premiums" are transaction costs that reduce the advantages of simulated positions. (Income taxes may be another, but we will avoid discussing that for the moment. See "Financial Planning Problems with Options" later in this chapter.) In general, the higher your leverage in options, the greater your transaction costs. Below are two simulation techniques that provide efficiency in both leverage and transaction costs.

1. **Deep-in-the-money options.** If you purchase a call option with a strike price of $35 and the stock itself is selling at $30, you are buying an option that is already $5 "in the money." It has an intrinsic value of about $5 per share, and unless you are buying options on a very high priced stock, that is often about what you will pay for it. Even if you have six to nine months to go on an option that is "deep" in the money, you usually will not pay that much extra for the time premium. Deep-in-the-money options are very efficient. The deeper they are in-the-money, however, the less leverage you enjoy.

In some cases, if you buy an option that is really deep in the money and if you trade smart, you may be able to buy the option at a discount, rather than a premium. For instance, you might buy an option that is 10 points in the money for 9⅞. Of course, you also lose some of the "limited risk"

feature of options by buying a deep option.

2. **Synthetic stock.** You may need a broker's help and a little credit with your broker to make this one work, but it's a good technique to know about. When you simultaneously buy a *call* option on a stock and sell a *put* on the same stock, at the same strike price, you have effectively created new shares of stock out of thin air. This is known among savvy brokers as synthetic stock, and it is about the most highly leveraged way to buy stock. In some cases, you can buy synthetic stock for almost nothing, because the premium you pay in buying the call is almost offset by the premium you earn in selling the put. In order to sell a put, you usually must demonstrate to your broker that you have the means to buy the stock if it is "put" to you. Usually, you can satisfy this requirement by depositing Treasury bills or having a brokerage house money market fund with sufficient cash reserves. Or, you can use stock as collateral. Synthetic stock behaves exactly as real stock does, with a few exceptions noted below.

Using options as a leveraged way to simulate stock purchases may have its drawbacks for certain investors: options do not pay dividends. If options are traded very actively, they may generate more commissions than stocks traded infrequently. (The life of an options position is only nine months, at most. Beyond that, you must renew the position.) Finally, all options transactions generate short-term gains and losses, and they must be figured in tax planning. Again, you are urged to find a knowledgeable options technician to implement the strategies.

Market Timing and Negative Stock Position

Of all the tools in financial planning, my favorite is "synthetic *non*stock." It is my favorite because almost nobody knows about it or uses it, and also because it sounds a little bit like a creation of Lewis Carroll. But it *works*.

Synthetic nonstock is the opposite of synthetic stock (described above), but it is easier to buy and more often useful to the stockholder. You create synthetic nonstock by buying a put and selling a call on the same stock at the same price. It works best when you already own stock on which options are listed, when the stock pays high dividends, and when you wish to negate market fluctuations in the stock, without sacrificing dividends.

Synthetic nonstock is perhaps the only kind of stock you can buy in which you *get paid* for buying it. You earn money because America is still a land of optimistic investors at heart, and option buyers consistently pay more for a shot at the upside (calls) than the downside (puts). In other words, you will earn more selling someone a little bit of upside (a call) than you will pay for the same bit of downside (a put).

Here is an example of how synthetic nonstock works. Let's says you own 200 shares of AT&T stock, priced at $60 per share. You keep it primarily for the fat 10 percent dividend, and frankly it wouldn't kill you to sell it. Above all, you are getting on toward retirement and you don't rest well thinking what might happen to the stock if the market falls or if the government does something drastic to the phone company. What is the financial planning recommendation? Ah, ha! Synthetic nonstock.

You buy two puts (200 shares equivalent) on AT&T at a strike price of 60 and simultaneously sell two calls at 60. Both options expire in three months. The two calls sells for, let's say $4 each, or bring you a revenue of $800. The two puts you buy cost $3 each, or a total of $600. You have netted $200 on your 200 shares of AT&T, and if you do this four times each year, you will have netted the equivalent of $4 per share *in addition to your regular*

dividend. One way of looking at synthetic nonstock is to consider it a dividend booster. Of course, you have to figure the cost of options commissions against the dividend boost, but even so you can usually come out ahead.

For price appreciation purposes, the nonstock effectively cancels out the stock you own. If the stock falls in price, profit on your put will offset the lost value of the stock. If the price rises, the stock may be called away from you (but then again it may not be). At worst, this is the equivalent of selling the stock at the striking price. A smart nonstock buyer often writes calls at a price higher than the current market price, so that he can gain extra capital gains before the stock reaches the strike price.

Here is an interesting nonstock position with very little risk and a good chance for profit: instead of buying and selling the AT&T options with a strike price of 60, you sell a call at 65 and buy a put at 55. Let's say you still earn the $1 a share net premium on the combined transactions.

Now, for each $1 AT&T rises to 65, you gain on the stock itself. For each dollar AT&T falls, you offset most of your stock loss with a gain on the put option. You can't lose much at all! If the stock falls to, say, $62, you can cancel your nonstock (that is, close both ends of the option position) at a nice option profit, and hope the stock rebounds. If the stock rises, you have your profit on the nonstock transaction ($1 per share) plus your profit on the stock appreciation. It may sound wild, but it gives you a chance to earn up to $6 per share with very little risk (if AT&T goes to 65), and all the while you are making dividends on the stock. You can search the entire stock market and never find a better investment technique for minimizing risk and still giving you a chance for gains.

But that's not all nonstock can do. Perhaps its greatest uses are in tax planning and in market timing. Just remember, nonstock is a way of temporarily negating a stock position with minimal transaction costs or actual impact on a portfolio.

Occasionally, sophisticated stockbrokers go to great pains to effect a position known as the "short sale against the box." The idea of this tax-planning technique is to dispose of a winning position without actually realizing a taxable gain. If your stock rises sharply in November, and you want to get out with a profit but don't wish to report gains until next year, you are an ideal candidate for "the box." The stockbroker sells short the same stock that you own, earning a commission. Later, usually in the next tax year, the broker sells both positions simultaneously, generating two more commissions. Stockbrokers who are wise to the short sales against the box love the technique, because it makes them look erudite and finances their winter vacations.

Synthetic nonstock accomplishes the same purpose and can usually be done at lower brokerage costs. Furthermore, it eliminates the capital expense of a short sale and the liability to pay dividends. Remember, you usually don't pay money to buy synthetic nonstock; you earn cash. In most cases, the advantages of synthetic nonstock far outweigh a short sale against the box on an option stock.

A more common tax-planning situation has to do with the investor who has held a stock many years and built up in it a sizable capital gain. Suddenly, he wants to sell the stock before the next "market bottom," right at the worst tax time to realize capital gains. Considering the impact of capital gains on the relatively new "alternative minimum tax," the unplanned sale of stock can be a devastating tax event. The recourse is simply to buy nonstock in the same stock (if it is an option stock) until it is more advantageous to sell the stock. Perhaps at a later date the investor will reconsider the sale. In that case, the

nonstock can easily be liquidated. All the while it was in force it was probably earning the extra dividend booster.

Here's one last excellent application of nonstock. Suppose you are the executor of an estate and must liquidate a large stock position. You are in no hurry to liquidate. You know the prices at which you would like to sell. You know you do not want to expose the stock to large drops in price. Nonstock makes a lot of sense in this case. It can be fashioned so as to prevent loss, maximize income, and allow the stock to be sold when it rises to a natural "sell point."

Occasionally, financial planners ask, "How can you advocate the *opposite* of stock? That's unpatriotic." The answer is that a short sale may be considered unpatriotic. A purchase of nonstock (or a put option) is not in the least unpatriotic. Enough short sales may drive down the price of stock (in spite of rules to prevent that) and thus undermine the capital system. But it is far-fetched to think that buying puts (which adds the "downside" protection in nonstock) might translate into decreased demand for America's corporate stock. Put options and nonstock allow investors to hedge against unexpected or severe market drops. When more investors become aware of their use, these option vehicles may help to forestall market panics. Thus, nonstock is quite patriotic, as well as potentially profitable.

Option Writing

A number of investment books and articles have suggested that all options techniques are risky and dangerous, except for "covered call writing." Don't believe a word of it! When you buy a simple option, put or call, you risk a little bit of money for a chance to leverage it into a lot, but you can never lose more than the little bit. That does have its risks, but compare them to the big risks in covered call writing.

In a "covered write," you own the stock and write an option against it. For instance, you own IBM at 60 and write an option to sell it for 65. This earns you extra income through the premium that an option buyer pays, less commissions. This premium may work out to be as much as 20 percent per year for a smart writer. However, your ceiling is relatively fixed in covered writing. You can't earn more than the premium and a few points of appreciation in the stock. If the stock zooms up in price, it will be called away from you. You have given up most of your upside in return for fixed income.

But you haven't given up a bit of your downside. The stock can still go as low as zero. That's not exactly a riskless position. As a rule, covered call writers are slaughtered in big bear markets, and they can't usually make up for it in big bull markets, because their upside is limited.

Stockbrokers who use covered writing like the technique, because they can make a great deal of money from it. They make a commission when the stock is bought, when the call is written, when the call is bought back "or covered," and when the stock is called away from the owner. Often, the owner does not really wish to part with the stock, and so he buys back the option and goes through another whole cycle of commissions.

A favorite saying of brokers writing covered calls is that if the stock declines, the covered writer is at least a point or two better off than the person who simply owns the stock, because he has generated premium income. In reality, however, the owner of a falling stock may find that he keeps writing options at lower and lower prices, until the stock is eventually called away at a price well below his initial cost, and perhaps near the bottom of the market cycle.

With that said, we will mention some situations in which call writing does have financial planning applications. Covered writing can have applications in pension plans, Keoghs, and IRAs. It is the only kind of option transaction allowed in those plans, and since stock ownership is usually long-term in pension plan, you may be able to ride out market declines. Here is an innovative approach: write covered calls inside the plan; then, buy put options on the same stocks outside the plan. The puts will help you limit capital losses inside the plan, and will have the effect of allowing premature withdrawals (before age 59½) *without* the 10 percent penalty normally imposed on such withdrawals. Here's how it works: if the stock declines in value (inside the plan), the puts will gain in value (outside the plan). By cashing out the puts, you will have effectively transferred money out of the plan. (This seems to be legal under present law.)

One way to gain access to cash temporarily is to write a deep-in-the-money option against a stock you own. For example, with IBM at 60, you write an option against 100 shares with a strike price of 50. Your premium income is $10 per share, or $1,000. Then, you may either let the stock be called away from you, or you may buy back the option. If IBM declines to 55, you will buy back the option ("close the transaction," by buying 100 calls) at $5 per share. You will have a $500 gain on the option transaction, but the value of your IBM shares will have declined a corresponding amount. In the interim, you will have "loaned" yourself $1,000 from your IBM stock.

We mentioned earlier that nonstock may be an effective tool in liquidating stock or a stock portfolio. The same goes for covered writes. Suppose you know that you will sell a stock if it goes as high as 50. It is now selling for 45. You may place a "limit order" to sell the stock at 50, or you may sell a call at 50. The advantage of selling the call is the extra income it generates.

Options Straddles

Up until about 1981, commodity straddles were a popular year-end tax-planning tool. Then, along came the Economic Recovery Act of 1981, and commodity straddles were as dead as a pork belly. The new tax law left straddles wide open in options, however, as far as the best tax minds have judged.

Here is how a year-end option tax straddle works. In December, you buy (let's say) ten puts and ten calls on IBM at 60. For simplicity, we'll assume the stock is selling at 60 and each of the puts and calls costs $1 per share, or $1,000 each for the ten puts and calls (10 × 100 shares each = 1,000). If in late December the stock is selling at 65, you sell the puts and generate a tax loss, which may be a good part of your premium of $1,000. That is deductible as a tax loss in that tax year. In early January, you sell the calls at a profit, which is reportable in the following tax year. You have, in effect, deferred income into the next tax year. Theoretically, you could keep expanding this deferral each year, and that is exactly what some commodity traders did. When the time came to pay up all the deferred taxes last December, because of the new tax law, they had no choice: they bought options straddles.

You can probably expect the IRS to crack down on listed options straddles soon. Then the only tax game in town will probably be *unlisted* option straddles.

Financial Planning Problems with Options

Be especially careful about these problems:

1. Option profits and option writing premiums produce short-term capital gains, which are taxed at a higher rate than long-term capital gains.

2. You can't use options to get around "wash sale" provisions. A wash sale occurs when an investor sells a security (usually to lock in a tax loss) and then buys the same security back immediately. The law says you must wait thirty days to buy back the same security or an option position substantially similar.

3. In using options as a substitute for a "short sale against the box," you can't stretch a short-term capital gain into a long-term gain. You can't do it with the short sale, either.

4. When you write covered calls, the stock may be called away from you unexpectedly, even if it is out of the money. This frequently happens just before a stock hits an ex-dividend date, and can generate negative tax consequences.

Speculative Options Tips

Once you become familiar with options in financial planning applications, it is a short step to speculating in options for profit. Here are some quick tips to maximize gain and avoid loss:

The best speculative options trader is an active trader. Don't be afraid to take gains and limit losses.

Don't expose too much money to one stock or one side of the market (puts or calls). If an option gets deep in the money, and you still think it is a good bet, "roll it over" to the next strike price. For example, you buy an out-of-the-money call option with a strike price of 45. The option goes to 49, and is four points in the money. Instead of exposing this four points to quick loss, take profits and buy an out-of-the-money 50.

Don't let options near the strike price or in-the-money linger into the last three weeks before expiration date. If the price suddenly goes against you, you don't have much time to recoup.

It is a good practice to buy options, particularly thinly traded or low-priced options, using "limit orders." One technique that often works is the "all or none" limit order, which is allowed by most options exchanges. You say, I want to buy 5 IBM May 60's at ½, "all or none." That prevents what commonly occurs if you do not say "all or none"—namely, you end up buying one or two options at that price, and paying a hefty minimum commission rate.

On the other hand, you should make it a practice to always sell options "at-the-market." If you have ever had a sell limit order placed, and then had the market rampage against you, you know why. Remember, options move faster than stocks. ("At-the-market" means that your order will be transacted at the prevailing price when it reaches the floor of the exchange. A limit order means it will not be transacted unless you get the price you want.)

Part 8

Editor's Notes:
Financial Planning and Retirement

"*Ideally, about half." That's how I usually answer the question, How much of one's financial planning should be directed toward retirement? Ideally, of course, one starts financial planning while one is young enough to make buying a home easier, financing a college education less painful, or taking care of possible catastrophes less traumatic. That long-range planning should also include some attention to retirement needs, which is the subject of this part of the book.*

Dave King starts things off in Chapter 29 by focusing on the self-employed and how they can build up retirement assets through a Keogh plan. Next on the list is the Individual Retirement Account (IRA), the pros and cons of which Herm Kramer discusses in Chapter 30. In Chapter 31 Morris Sahr and Leo Loevner offer a thoughtful discussion of pension and profit-sharing plans; whether you are an employee or employer, you'll find this chapter contains a wealth of material. Finally, in Chapter 32 Stuart Wolk presents an astute analysis of the plight of senior citizens, which will undoubtedly add to your breadth of understanding.*

Chapter 29

A Keogh's Role in Your Financial Plan

David M. King is a highly regarded investment adviser who was the first Certified Financial Planner in Kansas. He is vice-president and registered principal of Investment Management & Research, Incorporated; president of King Financial Services Corporation; president of David M. King and Associates, Limited, Registered Investment Advisors; president of Home Security Services of America; director of Transitions, Incorporated; and a partner of Berdeak Associates. He has written numerous articles, including articles on inflation and taxation, and he copyrighted the inflation tax calculator. He has spoken to groups of financial planners throughout the country and has also given estate planning seminars. King is on the Board of Trustees of the College for Financial Planning and currently is the vice-president of public relations. He served as president of the Institute of Certified Financial Planners from 1978 to 1979 and as chairman of the board in 1980. He is a member of the International Association for Financial Planning and the National Association of Life Underwriters.

David M. King, CFP

If you are a business or professional person who has chosen not to incorporate, you may be overlooking one of the most exciting methods of accumulating substantial wealth for retirement available today. Since Congress passed HR-10 (the Self Employed Individual Retirement Act of 1962), less than 10 percent of the eligible individuals who qualify have established retirement plans. The favorable tax treatment allows the deduction of all contributions, and the tax-free compounding of earnings until retirement allows the dollars normally paid in taxes to build retirement income.

Self-employed individuals fail to establish plans because either they don't understand the value of such plans or do not fully realize the tremendous leverage that the tax benefits give. In this chapter we hope to clear up the mysteries and the myths about Keogh plans for you.

Who Can Establish a Plan?

Any self-employed individual who operates a full-time or part-time unincorporated business and whose earned income comes from personal service can establish such a plan. *Income from dividends, interest, or capital investments that do not require personal service do not qualify* in determining the income on which to base a retirement plan contribution.

You must establish the plan before the end of the fiscal or calendar year.

Contributions are limited to 15 percent of earned income, the maximum being of $15,000. If annual compensation is in excess of $100,000, the rate of employer contributions cannot be less than 7½ percent. One can possibly increase this amount by using a *Defined Benefit Keogh Plan*. This is done by using actuarial assumptions and relatively low earnings estimates. Because of the complications and actuarial costs, few Defined Benefit Keogh plans are used.

Employees

You must cover all employees who meet these requirements:

1. Waiting time, not longer than three years.

2. All full-time employees (1,000 hours a year or more).

3. A spouse can be included in the plan if she is a full-time employee.

4. A plan must be 100 percent vested in the employee at all times.

Voluntary Contributions

Voluntary contributions may be made only if one participating member of the plan is not an owner-employee. Voluntary contributions are limited to 10 percent of earned income, the maximum being $2,500 a year.

Plan Distributions

You may start taking distributions at age 59½ and *must* start taking distributions by the time you are 70½. If you are disabled (as defined by Social Security), you may make withdrawals without penalty.

If you die, your beneficiary may start drawing on your plan. All post-1974 contributions to a plan are taxed as *ordinary income* in the year of distribution.

Distribution may take the form of an annuity for one life *or* a joint and survivor annuity. You may also arrange to make withdrawals over a period of time, not to exceed the normal life expectancy of the participant and spouse.

Rollovers

If an employee leaves the business and all the proceeds of his account in the employer's Keogh plan are paid out to him, he may roll this over to an IRA plan and postpone paying the tax until retirement.

Other Plans

Either the owner or the employee who is a participant in a Keogh plan can also make contributions to an IRA plan. This provision was added in the Economic Recovery Tax Act of 1981.

Permissible Investments

Investments must be made in one of the following ways:

Trust Account. In making contributions to a bank or trust company trustee, either the owner-employee or some other person may direct the investments. Some of the investments that might be used under this method are:

1. Common stock
2. Government or corporate bonds
3. Mutual funds
4. Certain limited partnerships
   Real estate
   Oil income

Prior to 1982, certain so-called hard assets, diamonds, gold, silver, or art objects, could have been contributed; however, ERTA-81 prohibited this for self-directed plans.

Annuity Trust. A trust that uses an annuity, endowment, or life insurance can be established to fund the plan. The trustee does not need to be a bank or a trust company trustee.

Custodial Account. Custodial accounts are generally used with mutual funds, bank certificates of deposit, or annuity, endowment, or life insurance contracts.

Government Bonds. You can use a special series of government bonds that are *nontransferable* and *nonredeemable* until the

holder reaches age 59½, becomes disabled, or dies, whichever occurs first.

The methods you choose to fund your Keogh plan depend a great deal on your personal investment desires and the current economic climate. Should you make a decision now and later want to change investments, under current law, you may do this with all accounts except the retirement bonds.

If you choose the retirement bond route, you are *stuck* until age 59½. Needless to say, these are not as popular as the government would like.

REMEMBER, YOUR KEOGH PLAN IS TAX DEDUCTIBLE AND ALL EARNINGS ACCUMULATE TAX-FREE UNTIL RETIREMENT.

Tables 1 and 2 illustrate what happens

Table 1.
A Retirement Fund Without a Keogh Plan
(Tax Bracket, 39%)

AGE	CONTRIB.	10.00% INTEREST	TAXES	VALUE
45	3660	366	143	3883
46	3660	754	294	8003
47	3660	1166	455	12375
48	3660	1603	625	17013
49	3660	2067	806	21934
50	3660	2559	998	27155
51	3660	3082	1202	32695
52	3660	3636	1418	38573
53	3660	4223	1647	44809
54	3660	4847	1890	51425
55	3660	5509	2148	58446
56	3660	6211	2422	65894
57	3660	6955	2713	73797
58	3660	7746	3021	82182
59	3660	8584	3348	91078
60	3660	9474	3695	100517
61	3660	10418	4063	110532
62	3660	11419	4453	121158
63	3660	12482	4868	132432
64	3660	13609	5308	144393
65	3660	14805	5774	157084
Totals	76,860	131,515	51,291	157,084

when a self-employed individual accumulates funds for retirement with or without a Keogh plan.

Let's assume that John Jones is self-employed, has no employees, and has a taxable income of $40,000 a year, and wants to put away $6,000 a year for retirement. John is forty years old, and we assume an earning rate of 10 percent on each account.

Without a plan, John finds that the $6,000 he wants to lay away will only be $3,660 a year after he pays taxes at a rate of 39 percent. He also finds that his earnings are fully taxed at 39 percent under current tax rates. A retirement fund based on these facts is shown in Table 1.

If we assume a single life annuity rate of $9.00, we can conclude that at age sixty-five with ten years certainty, Jones could expect a retirement income of $1,413 per month.

With a plan, however, his entire $6,000 would work for him and his earnings would accumulate tax-free. Table 2 shows the results of using a plan.

If we use the same annuity rate as in Table 1, the retirement revenue would be $3,788, a gain of 2,375 a month. Without doubt, you can enhance your retirement dollars substantially should you qualify to establish a Keogh plan.

The benefits of using Keogh plans in your retirement efforts should now be apparent. The next questions to deal with concern the factors that may affect your implementation of a Keogh plan.

Question 1: If I have a year of little or no profits, should I be concerned about making a contribution for my employees?
Answer: Many Keogh plans have specific provisions that allow a minimum profit threshold. If the profits of the business do not reach a certain level, no contribution can be made for either the employer or employee. If this is a concern for you, make certain your plan has this provision before you adopt it.

Table 2.
A Retirement Fund with a Keogh Plan
(Tax Bracket, 39%)

AGE	CONTRIB.	10.00% INTEREST	TAXES	VALUE
45	6000	600	0	6600
46	6000	1260	0	13860
47	6000	1986	0	21846
48	6000	2785	0	30631
49	6000	3663	0	40294
50	6000	4629	0	50923
51	6000	5692	0	62615
52	6000	6862	0	75477
53	6000	8148	0	89625
54	6000	9562	0	105187
55	6000	11119	0	122306
56	6000	12831	0	141136
57	6000	14714	0	161850
58	6000	16785	0	184635
59	6000	19063	0	209698
60	6000	21570	0	237268
61	6000	24327	0	267595
62	6000	27360	0	300955
63	6000	30695	0	337650
64	6000	34365	0	378015
65	6000	38401	0	422416
Totals	126,000	296,416	0	422,416

Question 2: If I have a number of employees and want to adopt a Keogh plan, how could I reduce my employee costs?
Answer: Depending on your situation, you may consider a plan that could be integrated with Social Security. This type of plan would allow for no plan contributions for any salary under the Social Security limitations. These plans are complex and difficult to administer; however, if this is a problem relating to the adoption of your Keogh plan, it should be investigated.

Question 3: What are the penalties if I have to terminate my plan prematurely?
Answer: Benefit payments cannot begin until age 59½ unless one is permanently disabled. Any premature distribution is subject to a 10 percent penalty tax and the

owner-employee cannot make contributions to the account in the succeeding five years.

Question 4: I adopted a Keogh Plan and am not happy with my investment decisions. Can I change it?
Answer: Yes, you may adopt a new plan and have the assets of the old plan transferred to it. If you are doing this *make certain* you or your adviser follow the proper steps, so as to avoid constructive receipt of the funds. If you have any questions, check with your legal or tax adviser *before* you do it.

Question 5: Where can I find different Keogh plans to compare?
Answer: Your bank or savings and loan can furnish copies of their plans and you should ask to see their custodial plans and trusteed plans. You should also ask for their charges and penalties. Your securities broker should be able to furnish you with prototype plans of various mutual funds that provide for investment in their fund group, or various trusted plans that provide for investment in stocks, bonds, mutual funds, and limited partnerships. Your insurance agent should be able to provide you with copies of his company's plans and discuss their flexibility and cost.

If you are investigating your choices, the above suggestions should provide you with ample selection. Most people want plans that will provide a wide range of invest-ment choices, so that their plan investments can be adapted to changing economic and personal conditions.

Question 6: How should I invest my Keogh plan dollars?
Answer: You should consider the guidelines that a trustee for a pension or profit-sharing plan follows. He is obliged to look for diversification, income, and safety and to act as a prudent man would with his own wealth. This again points to the importance of flexibility in your Keogh plan investment choices. Only if your plan has the ability to hold several investments can you develop an investment portfolio over the years that can meet this criterion of flexibility.

In summary, the Keogh plan offers the unincorporated business or professional man the opportunity to build substantial retirement assets with *before-tax dollars*. Before adopting any Keogh plan, you should discuss the pros and cons with your financial planner and your legal and tax advisers to make certain the plan will fit your needs on a long-term basis. You should then make investment choices that you think will enable you to meet your financial goals in the years to come.

Only by using a qualified retirement plan can you put the magic of compounding Uncle Sam's tax dollars to work for you, and pay him back when your earnings may be less in retirement.

Chapter 30

IRA—Plus
and Minus

Herman A. Kramer, CLU, CFP

Herman A. Kramer, B.Sc. (Business Management), is nationally known as a pioneer in the financial planning profession. At present he is regional director of agencies for Philadelphia Life Insurance Company, but his business experience over a span of more than twenty years ranges from life insurance and mutual sales to being president of several mutual funds and a securities broker/dealership. He is past president of both the San Francisco and Delaware Valley Chapters of the International Association for Financial Planning. He also served on the national boards of the International Association for Financial Planning and the Institute of Certified Financial Planners. He has also taught the Certified Financial Planner courses at Villanova University. He was one of the first forty-two people in the United States to become a Certified Financial Planner and he is also a Chartered Life Underwriter.

You are the master of at least a part of your retirement fate. An Individual Retirement Account (IRA) can become the bedrock on which other retirement assets can be piled. No matter what the government provides through Social Security, or what your employer provides in pension, profit-sharing, thrift, or stock-ownership plans, *you* control your IRA retirement.

There are pluses and minuses to an IRA but, started early, added to faithfully, and managed wisely, your IRA can be your best source of financial security.

You can set aside up to the first $2,000 you earn each year, or $2,250 if you have a nonearning spouse. Working spouses can set up their own full IRA. The amount put into your IRA each year becomes a total deduction from income, whether you itemize deductions or not. You don't pay federal and, in many states, local income taxes on the amount you contribute. In effect, government has gone into partnership with you in your personal retirement plan. How much the government contributes depends on your top tax bracket. Here's how much you get to put away for your retirement that you would otherwise have to pay in taxes:

YOUR TOP TAX BRACKET (%)	TAX SAVINGS ON A $2,000 CONTRIBUTION	AMOUNT YOU MUST ADD
20	$ 400	$1,600
30	600	1,400
40	800	1,200
50	1,000	1,000

In addition to this tax break, all the earnings inside your IRA accumulate without being taxed.

Your contributions can be invested in a wide variety of things. Virtually the only restriction is that you can't buy collectibles such as coins, stamps, metals, art, rugs, antiques, gems, or alcoholic beverages. Life insurance is also prohibited. A practical restriction will be whether the amount available in your IRA is enough to purchase the particular investment you are interested in and whether you can get a qualified trustee or custodian to hold the asset. For example, you wouldn't be able to buy a $300,000 apartment house with your first $2,000 contribution.

Which investment, or investments, you choose for your IRA dollars should depend on where your IRA fits in with your overall financial planning. Generally, the more time your IRA has to work, the more aggressive you can be with your investment. However, you might want your IRA to be your conservative money so that you can invest your other assets more aggressively.

You can have several IRA accounts, or "pots," as long as each has an appropriate trust or custodian arrangement and you don't exceed the annual contribution limit for all of them combined. You can even change your mind and move them to other investments. How you manage the IRA can affect your overall results. Some accounts, such as those of mutual fund families and self-directed brokerages, allow changes within the account, whereas others do not. For those that don't, you need only close them and open the ones you want. The only restriction is that each pot of money can be moved only once each year. You will have to consider administrative and penalty charges peculiar to each account in your decision-making process.

Typical investments used in IRAs are:

Annuities

Certificates of deposit

Mutual funds

Common stock

Bonds

Government retirement bonds

Real estate limited partnerships

The overall investment result is vitally important. Table 1 shows how well you can do with your $2,000 annual contributions. Your results will depend on the years you have and the compound rate of return you are able to achieve. The amount can be

Table 1. Results of Contributing $2,000 a Year to an IRA

YEARS	CUMULATIVE CONTRIBUTION	Compound Earning Rate			
		7%	10%	12%	15%
1	$ 2,000	$ 2,140	$ 2,200	$ 2,240	$ 2,300
2	4,000	4,430	4,620	4,748	4,946
3	6,000	6,880	7,282	7,558	7,986
4	8,000	9,502	10,210	10,706	11,484
5	10,000	12,306	13,432	14,230	15,508
10	20,000	29,568	35,062	39,310	46,698
15	30,000	53,776	69,900	83,506	109,434
20	40,000	87,730	126,004	161,398	235,620
25	50,000	135,352	216,364	298,668	489,424
30	60,000	202,146	361,886	540,586	999,914
35	70,000	295,826	596,254	966,026	2,026,692
40	80,000	427,220	973,704	1,718,284	4,091,908
45	90,000	611,502	1,581,590	3,042,436	8,245,792

staggering. For example, if you put away $2,000 annually for thirty years and earned an average 10 percent, your $60,000 would grow to $361,886. However, if you earned 15 percent a year, it would grow to $999,914. Historically, these are achievable investment returns. In some economic cycles even greater results have been realized without greater risks.

Meaningful results are possible even if you have only a short time to participate before retirement. In just five years your $10,000 in contributions could grow to $14,230 at a 12 percent compounded return. And, remember, if you don't contribute to an IRA, the government will take a large tax bite out of the $10,000, and you will be left with much less to spend or save.

If you receive a distribution from your employer's qualified pension or profit-sharing plan because it is discontinued or you no longer work for him, you can escape current tax by rolling the amount into an IRA within sixty days. Before doing so, you should examine the alternative of paying the tax due and investing the difference. Special, favorable tax treatment of such distributions might make such a move

smart. Check it out with a tax or financial planning expert.

In an IRA you decide when you want to take all of your accumulated value or start receiving a regular retirement income. It can be during any year when you will be from 59½ to a maximum of 70½ years old. Since everything you receive is taxed as ordinary income, your timing decision should depend on an appraisal of:

1. Your financial needs and desires
2. Taxation laws at the time
3. Your other income
4. Your estate planning needs

A full distribution of the entire account value is advisable only if a relatively small amount has accumulated, or you have an overriding need for a large amount of capital. You would probably want to receive a regular monthly amount to replace the salary you give up when you stop working. At this time, no matter where you invested your contributions during your working years, you should revert to conservative investments, such as quality mutual funds, insurance annuities, bank accounts, or

Table 2.
U.S. Internal Revenue Life Expectancy Table

AGE MALE	FEMALE	REMAINING LIFE EXPECTANCY (YEARS)
59	64	18.9
60	65	18.2
61	66	17.5
62	67	16.9
63	68	16.2
64	69	15.6
65	70	15.0
66	71	14.4
67	72	13.8
68	73	13.2
69	74	12.6
70	75	12.1
71	76	11.6
72	77	11.0
73	78	10.5
74	79	10.1
75	80	9.6

old male with an IRA worth $150,000 at the beginning of the year, you must take $10,000 during the first year of retirement. Since you are expected to live fifteen years, you have to take ¹⁄₁₅ of the $150,000 value in the first year. Then, when you are sixty-six, your life expectancy changes. Now you have to take ¹⁄₁₄.₄ of the remaining value—and so on, as long as you and your money last. If you don't take enough, you'll pay a 50 percent penalty to the government on the amount of the underpayment.

You might want to turn over all, or a portion of your values to an insurance company in exchange for a guaranteed monthly income for life. The same amount would be paid to you monthly, no matter how long you lived. One insurance company currently pays the annuity amounts shown in Table 3 for each $100,000 given them. As an example, let's take the same sixty-five-year-old man having an IRA worth $150,000. He could take his $150,000 and turn it over to the insurance company and receive 1½ times the monthly $1,219 shown in Table 3. This comes to $1,828.50, or $21,942 a year for life. The older you are when you start the arrangement, the more you receive. Of course, if you are in bad health, it is a bad deal.

If you become disabled before you reach age 59½, you are also permitted to take your values just as though you had retired. For this reason, the values in your IRA should be taken into consideration when

government bonds. The peace of mind that a conservative approach brings at this stage of your life is well worth the possible loss of the larger returns a more aggressive one could bring.

You must make annual withdrawals which, if continued at the same rate, would exhaust your account over a period not to exceed your, or your and your spouse's, life expectancy. Table 2 shows what the government believes your life expectancy is. For example, if you are a sixty-five-year-

Table 3. Life Insurance Company Annuity Payments per $100,000 Purchase

STARTING AGE	MALE MONTHLY	YEARLY	FEMALE MONTHLY	YEARLY
60	$1,108	$13,296	$1,019	$12,228
65	1,219	14,628	1,106	13,272
70	1,368	16,416	1,236	14,832

NOTE: Immediate annuity payments quoted by Philadelphia Life Insurance Company, August 1982.

determining how much disability income protection you need.

If you are unfortunate enough to die before you use your IRA values, your heirs will still benefit from them. The choices of how they can receive their shares are many. They can even use them to supplement their own IRAs for their retirement. Distribution of your IRA should be considered in your estate plan.

IRAs are not necessarily for everyone. There are some minuses to consider. Why, for example, should you make a tax-deductible contribution of money on which no tax is due? If you have little or no tax to pay in a year because of other tax planning or circumstances, you would be foolish to contribute to an IRA. Of course, if you are carrying a tax loss back to prior years or forward to future ones, it might make sense. Your tax adviser should help you make that decision.

Young people, just getting started in life, probably are in low tax brackets and are concerned with other important things. Who can forget the struggle to own your own car, furniture, and home? Even the cost of socializing as a young adult can have lifetime implications more important than starting a personal retirement program. But, the young people who do start such a program will be the envy of their peers in the future. They will have the most important element of long-term investment accumulation results working for them—*time*. Remember, the more time your money has to work, the better results you will achieve, if earning rates remain the same.

You must pay the government a 10 percent penalty if you take money from your IRA before the year you turn 59½ or are disabled. In addition, all that you take in a year is added to other income for tax purposes. The penalty you pay cannot be subtracted as a deduction. This might not be as serious as it sounds. After all, your money is not out of reach in your IRA. It is available in an emergency, even though it will be reduced by the penalty and other income tax. However, you might pay less tax then than you would have when you put the contribution into your IRA. For example, if you saved 40 percent tax when you added to your IRA and you pay only the 10 percent penalty when you take some of it out, you are 30 percent ahead. That's not even counting the tax-sheltered accumulation of earnings you have enjoyed in the meantime. Aren't most financial emergencies associated with loss of other income or a tax-deductible catastrophe? If so, there would be little or no additional income tax due that year.

Your IRA might even be used for planned sabbaticals or for other ventures needing cash during a time when your other income is reduced. The planning potential is limited only by your creativity.

IRAs may not be for everyone, but they should be seriously considered in everyone's overall financial plan. After years of having the free services of my wife in my business, I have started paying her a salary. Because of our relationship, neither of us has to pay Social Security taxes on that amount. She can now enjoy her own personal retirement plan and we can take a full, family $4,000 annual IRA deduction. I'm sure there are many more families like us out there. Why not do the same for your nonearning spouse?

Chapter 31

Pension/Profit-Sharing Plans, and ERISA

Morris G. Sahr, Ph.D., is an experienced specialist in personal financial counseling and analysis, individual retirement plans, and group employee benefits. He is president of Cardinal Financial Planning. He has taught at both American University and George Washington University and has been active in a wide variety of community affairs in Virginia. He was a delegate to the White House Conference on Aging and currently serves as state adviser to the U.S. Congressional Advisory Board. Sahr was one of the original founders of the Washington D.C. Chapter of the International Association for Financial Planning and was its first president. He has served continuously as a member of the IAFP's board of directors and has been a contributor to its journal, *Financial Planner*. He is a member of the Institute of Certified Financial Planners.

Morris G. Sahr, Ph.D., CFP
Leo C. Loevner, CPA

Leo C. Loevner has an extensive background in personal and business tax and financial planning for professionals and small businesses. He is currently vice-president of Cardinal Financial Planning. Previously, he was an assistant controller with the Marriott Corporation and with Communications Satellite Corporation. He has also co-authored a book on financial planning. A Certified Public Accountant, Loevner is a member of the District of Columbia Institute of Certified Public Accountants and the American Institute of Certified Public Accountants.

When we think of retirement, we all have different expectations, depending on our age bracket and our defined or undefined goals. Most young adults, for example, pay little attention to the matter of their income forty years from now, whereas middle-aged people think of nothing else. Regardless of age, we can all influence retirement income for ourselves and for our spouse or beneficiaries.

By considering rates of interest, growth factors, mortality schedules, settlement options, and human qualities such as self-discipline and financial temperament, we can determine the future value of our retirement income. Unfortunately, few of us take the time to think constructively about the future or to make enlightened decisions, either early or late in life. If individuals only knew how important it is to consider retirement in their total financial planning, they might place more emphasis on it before beginning employment, rather than after the fact.

Today total benefits received can be as high as 30 percent or more of an employee's base salary. Many employers provide group hospitalization, major medical services, disability income, life insurance, and deferred compensation pensions or profit-sharing plans. Yet, most employees are not fully aware of the actual dollar outlays for these benefits. Furthermore, few recognize that because of tax considerations, if they were to go into the marketplace and attempt to purchase benefits identical to those provided by the employer, they might have to pay 50 percent of their pretax salary. For these and various other reasons, it is incumbent on employees to examine any employment contract with care and to understand fully the terms and conditions of its pension or profit-sharing plan.

The first step in this direction is to learn what questions to ask about a contract that might last the rest of your life! There is nothing more thought provoking than entering into a plan that, in effect, says that no matter if you live, if you die, or if you quit, the contract has a potential value of thousands of dollars. Read it. And if you do not understand it, take it to an independent and knowledgeable third party who can explain to you in lay terms what you are signing and what your employer is agreeing to do. Too many individuals are reluctant to seek the advice of qualified experts such as certified financial planners. Instead, they complain, "No one at the office really knows about this plan—at least no one seems to be able to explain it to me," and they remain ignorant of the benefits they will be entitled to upon retirement.

The tragedy of this experience is twofold. In the first place, the employees never gain the understanding they should have and only compound the problem by going from one job to another without ever knowing what to expect at retirement. One would think, with thousands of dollars at stake—their own dollars—that they would ask some questions. In the second place, too many employees rely on those who have no financial planning expertise or who are unqualified to answer complex questions.

In the past, most people in the United States believed that a guaranteed payment each week to a retired employee was only for workers who were old and needed support because they could no longer earn a living. When pension plans were first introduced, before the turn of the century, they were essentially for disabled individuals. Now, pensions are based upon an employee's age and number of years of service, without consideration of effectiveness or job performance. Now it is common not only to expect a pension, but in some cases to enjoy two or more retirement income streams. However, the multiple retirement benefits that individuals in our society have come to expect are causing monumental problems. The best example is the Social Security system.

Social Security and Its Problems

Much has been said about the solvency of the Social Security fund, or lack of it, but what many workers do not realize is that by the end of this century there will be far more older Americans and not enough younger Americans to pay for Social Security. Also, what is not fully understood is that when an employer has an integrated retirement plan, he is (in simple terms) using a formula based upon two elements, namely, employer and employee dollars. The employee dollars come from FICA contributions during the employee's lifetime. Matching funds along with some additional dollars come from the employer. The employer, like the employee, has accountability only for those additional dollars not directly related to Social Security, since the employer invests those funds. There is no accountability for almost 15 percent of payroll (both employee and employer contributions to Social Security).

Benefits are paid from contributions made by the person standing in the next line. This money is not invested for the future. If you were to conduct your personal financial affairs in this manner, and were to make promises to pay in the future an income based upon a high level of contribution and then give it away immediately to someone else standing next to you, the law might very well step in and put an end to such insanity. In this case, the law supports the situation, and despite the number of well-educated people who assume responsibilities for the maintenance of this program, no one can find an answer to its problems. Thus, a cloud hangs over the Social Security pension system because employees are exposed to a formula that is based upon financial assumptions that cannot be substantiated.

Private pension plans, which cover almost one-half of all employees in the United States in one form or another, have their problems, too. They have over $200 billion in unfunded liabilities. What this means is that even the current private system is not scheduled to have enough dollars to provide for the benefits that employees are expecting at retirement—usually age sixty-five. So, where does this leave you if you are in a pension or profit-sharing plan? To understand the pension system, we should examine the different types of plans and see how they work. The first step, however, is to understand the role that the Employee Retirement Income Security Act of 1974 (ERISA), banks, and Social Security play in the pension system.

ERISA

The Employee Retirement Income Security Act passed by Congress in 1974 provides our current legislation on pension funding. According to this act, a *qualified* pension or profit-sharing plan is an employer-

established program that sets aside dollars from current earnings and sometimes permits employee contributions also. Since a qualified plan is one that has met the test by IRS for acceptable tax status, both the employer and employee may enjoy a number of tax advantages. Employer dollars, for the most part, are deductible. In addition, there is no tax on the earnings nor on any growth while the funds remain in the plan. We call this the *total return*. (See Figure 1 for a comparison of total returns on a qualified plan and on taxable investments outside the plan.) In fact, no tax is paid until the employee starts to receive money from the plan, either in a lump sum or in the form of monthly income. At that point, the tax burden will generally be reduced if the individual has little earned income. Of

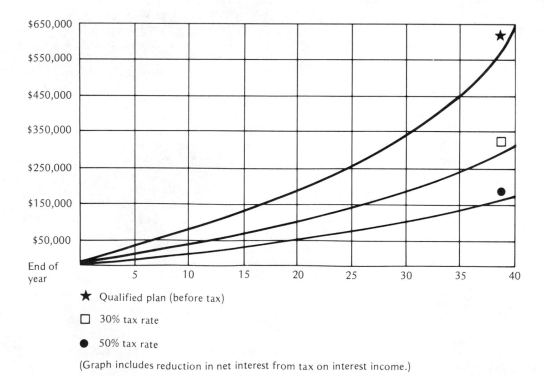

★ Qualified plan (before tax)

☐ 30% tax rate

● 50% tax rate

(Graph includes reduction in net interest from tax on interest income.)

Figure 1. A comparison of $5,000 a year invested in a qualified plan (pension or profit-sharing) with the same amount invested outside of the plan and fully taxable for the same period. The rate of interest is 5 percent. If we use 12 percent—closer to today's rates—then a person in a qualified plan can become a millionaire.

course, even if there is a tax, the employee has had the use of tax dollars that would normally have gone to Uncle Sam. Some individuals compare this situation to having an interest-free loan of about 25 to 50 percent of the tax dollars that they normally would not have seen during their lifetime. If the employee dies prior to receiving this income, his or her family will in most cases receive these dollars free of any estate tax.

Under ERISA, a qualified plan calls for *segregated* contributions. This means that the employer cannot commingle these funds with the general accounts of the business. The money that goes into the pension or profit-sharing plan is deposited directly into a bank or into an insurance or investment company. A trust can be set up to receive these dollars, but a *trustee* must be appointed to invest the money and administer the plan.

ERISA had two broad objectives. First, it attempts to eliminate broken promises to employees; that is, it tries to prevent expected retirement benefits from disappearing because of insufficient funds. Although this does not occur frequently, when it does, the results can be financially devastating for the employee. We now have severe penalties for violators of the law. The second objective of ERISA is to assure people of some form of retirement protection. Those who do not have a pension or profit-sharing plan can now have an Individual Retirement Account (IRA). They can even have an IRA in addition to a pension and profit-sharing plan.

ERISA also enlarged the total responsibilities of the person who creates the plan and assumes the responsibility for making it a reality. We call these *fiduciaries*. Every three years, according to the 1974 act, fiduciaries must submit an accounting, called an *actuarial valuation*, that details what has been done with all the money. Further, fiduciaries have to state in writing what they promise you orally.

Another guarantee that came out of ERISA was the establishment of the *Pension Benefit Guarantee Corporation*, commonly known as *PBGC*. The PBGC provides for insurance protection against the failure of a plan to perform. ERISA also made some significant changes with respect to the admission of employees into a pension plan. Generally speaking, one year is now the maximum waiting period. In addition, *vesting* procedures have been amended (*vesting* refers to the amount of time it takes before the money belongs to you.) Generally, the vesting period is now between five and ten years. This does not necessarily mean that you can get your hands on the money in a lump sum at retirement, but it does mean that after that period of time, if you left a company, you might have something.

Another area of change concerned *portability*, which involves *roll-over* procedures. If a plan states in writing that upon termination you can take the money with you, then you are permitted to transfer the money into another plan or into your own account, which is called an IRA. Generally, it is preferable to take the money, according to the terms of termination, and put it into your own account. One should fully understand, however, that an IRA established on a roll-over from a pension or pension-sharing plan is somewhat different from an IRA established through a month-to-month contribution. That is, an IRA is not really an account; it is a provision of the Internal Revenue Code. If employees decide to take their contributions in the form of a roll-over, they have to put them with one of a number of different institutions—a bank, a savings and loan, an investment company, or an insurance company. It is also possible to move the roll-over from a pension and profit-sharing plan several times during one's lifetime, but this should not be attempted without professional advice.

A qualified financial planner would know best how to maximize the growth of these dollars for the number of years that they would be exposed to earnings before being taken back out to spend. A young person, for example, might want to take this distribution from the pension and profit-sharing plan and put it into real estate, oil and gas, or common stocks, with an effort to maximize the growth. At a later date, these dollars could be put into an annuity, if this proved to be the best option. An older person, on the other hand, might not want to assume any risk and would prefer to put these dollars into guaranteed instruments so that there would not be any loss in the time period prior to receiving this income for retirement purposes.

ERISA also required that full disclosure be made to both employees and the government. Under the act's provisions, employees must be given a detailed annual report on their pension and profit-sharing account, and information must also be available upon request. The reporting requirements to the government were increased considerably, especially with the Department of Labor's requirement that reports be submitted on the money and that an accounting take place every three years to ensure that all promises to employees are being kept.

Pension and Profit-Sharing Plans

Most of the large pension and profit-sharing plans today are with banks, whereas insurance companies, even though their assets are double that of most banks, normally work with medium and small firms. We have to go back in time to understand this situation. Before 1959, banks paid no tax on pension and profit-sharing plans. However, when the Life Insurance Company Tax Act of 1959 was passed, the same tax advantages were accorded to insurance companies. Another factor is that previously banks had more flexibility, and so their investment opportunities yielded higher total returns. But this also changed

when insurance companies expanded their portfolios and were able to obtain the same or higher yields.

Regardless of where the money was invested by the trustee—in commercial or corporate bonds, government bonds, mortgages, or the stock market—it was pooled and averaged with dollars put in years before, mainly at fixed, low-interest rates. Insurance companies could only average the interest, or what we call *portfolio interest*. This was not true at the bank, where dollars could earn a higher rate of interest, and each subsequent plan could relate to the increasing yields. Eventually, insurance companies were able to segregate and separately invest the dollars, given greater flexibility through the plan trustees. Since 1974 insurance companies and banks have both been able to use the "new money" investment opportunities to derive higher yields.

One complication for the *integrated* pension and profit-sharing system is that Social Security increments are now based upon a cost-of-living adjustment, called *COLA*. Meanwhile, although most of the integrated pension and profit-sharing plans reflect assumptions for projected higher income at retirement, the current administration has been proposing the reduction of these benefits. Another problem for *integrated* profit or pension-sharing plans—sometimes referred to as *excess* plans—is that Social Security is being used in a formula to arrive at income at retirement. This income is based upon, once again, employee and employer dollars, including the employer's matching contributions in the Social Security system. The excess plan really deals only with pay *above* the integration level. This means that the excess plan often discriminates in favor of the stockholder and high-income management. Furthermore, there are no governmental prohibitions against this practice.

A *step rate plan* is a variation of the excess plan. Money going to the retirement fund applies to pay below the Social Security integration level, and the excess contributions apply above the integration level.

An *offset plan* is another form of the integrated plan. In this plan, the employer provides specific benefits that are reduced, or offset by the employee's Social Security benefits. The net effect of this approach is to reduce the benefits under the employer's plan, generally corresponding with the increases in Social Security.

Pension or profit-sharing plans may be fully insured, partly insured, or noninsured—depending on the way in which the money is actually put to work. A fully insured plan goes to an insurance company, and the insurance company takes the risk—the mortality, interest (guaranteed), and expenses. A partly insured plan implies just what it says—only part of the money is insured, with the insurance company and employer sharing in varying degrees the remaining risk. A noninsured plan normally calls for the trustee to perform all of the functions without any questions and without an insurance company.

Do you know which type of plan you have? Do you think you ought to know? If you are depending upon a retirement from a pension or profit-sharing plan, maybe you ought to ask!

Type of Plans

Now, let us look at the specific types of pension and profit-sharing plans and see if you can tell which type of plan you have in effect today. The first might be called a *defined contribution* plan (or a *DC* plan). Under a defined contribution, the promise is simply that employer and/or employee dollars are contributory and will be put into the plan to buy the income at a later date; just what it will buy is not predetermined. What goes in? Money goes in on an agreed basis, and it grows (you hope). How much goes in? Generally, no more than 25 percent of your pay. What does it earn? What-

ever the investment will yield. Actually, the individual amounts are not normally in one big pool; that is, there is an accounting for each individual. Generally, these plans favor younger employees. When you have a plan that is integrated with Social Security, the employer, in reality, reflects 7 percent more on the amount going in, according to the total dollar outlay. In other words, an employer can contribute nothing on pay up to the taxable pay Social Security level. Under ERISA, defined contribution plans have received greater emphasis because simplicity is the key element. Accounting methods are less complex, there is no need for PBGC reports, and finally, there are really no reliabilities in a program of this type.

There are different forms of defined contribution plans. First, there is a *money purchase plan*. As this name implies, money goes in and accumulates, and whatever dollars it will buy at retirement will be the benefit. Because these benefits relate to the amount of money that goes into the fund, younger employees, who will have more time to benefit from the compounding effect of these dollars, stand to have a greater income from this plan.

Another form of the DC plan is a profit-sharing plan, whereby a firm shares its profits with its employees. Employees must exercise caution with this program, however, because there is no fixed commitment when the firm has no profits. One of the distinguishing characteristics of the profit-sharing plan is that employees who quit with no vesting generally are not used to reduce the employer's cost. What happens is that the funds are reallocated to everybody else in the plan to increase their benefits. Some employers believe profit-sharing plans help increase profits by motivating employees to work harder. Other employers initiate these plans in anticipation that some employees will quit, thereby increasing the benefits through tax deferrals on the dollars that they might have received. This will depend, in essence, upon the extent of the employer's greed.

Another form of the profit-sharing plan is the *thrift plan*, whereby the employees are encouraged to put in a percentage of their pay with the employer. Such a retirement plan, in its total effect, shows more employee dollars going in over that of employer dollars.

The *target plan* is similar to a money purchase plan in that the dollars represent a set percentage of the employee's pay and a fixed commitment on the employer's part. But the target plan differs in that the annual amount for each employee is based upon age as well as salary; as a result, an older employee receives roughly the same percentage in retirement benefits as other employees. In effect, the target plan is a combination of both a defined benefit plan (more about that in a moment) and a defined contribution plan. The problem is that the benefit is not an exact amount. You make your best guess, but you don't have to correct it as you go down the road. A target plan is adopted when the employer wants the best that can come from a defined contribution plan, but wishes to provide a better benefit for older employees.

In a *defined benefit program* future benefits are predetermined exactly. The employer decides what he is going to pay when the employee retires, and then determines what he must put in to meet that objective. The rules governing the defined benefit approach are being changed, but generally the amount going in can be considerably greater than it is in a defined contribution plan. The earnings on a defined benefit plan are used to reduce the amount that goes in. The accounting on these plans is concerned with the amount that must be put in on a continuing basis. Also, these plans are generally pooled, which means that there are no individual accounts unless, that is, they are fully insured. Defined benefit plans tend to work in the favor of

older employees, since they can accumulate about the same benefits as younger employees.

Defined benefit plans can be subdivided into several types, the first being a *flat benefit* plan, or *stated benefit* plan. This plan stipulates, for example, that 50 percent of the employee's salary will be the retirement benefit, and all employees will have this percentage, regardless of their length of service. The second type, a *unit benefit* plan, provides a small percentage of pay times the years of credited service. In recent years, the government has allowed, as the result of the Tax Reform Act of 1978, a *SEPP*, or *simplified*, employee pension plan. This is nothing more than a modified form of the individual retirement account and allows for greater contributions over and above the normal $2,000 associated with the IRA. The SEPP provides for a maximum contribution of $7,500 per year per employee. This program has its good and bad points. For example, from the standpoint of reporting, it has fewer problems than a true pension or profit-sharing plan. On the other hand, employers have more difficulty determining whether to reallocate in favor of younger or older employees. At present, there are relatively few SEPP programs in effect, but if you are involved in one, make sure you know its advantages.

Another important point is that life insurance may or may not be included in a pension or profit-sharing program. If it is, newer forms of life insurance are a vast improvement over the typical ordinary life plan; they provide for increases without evidence of insurability, and the premiums are normally deductible by the corporation.

Where the Pension Dollars Go

Now that you have some knowledge of pension and profit-sharing plans and understand the guidelines that were established by ERISA, you should be aware that in most of these programs the employer has the sole responsibility for deciding where this money is to be put to work in the marketplace. As mentioned earlier, most pension dollars go to banks or insurance companies. We all know what a bank is, or what it is supposed to be—a repository for funds that provides fixed rates of interest. Banks will also use stocks and other equity-based forms to provide growth for pension and profit-sharing plans. Insurance companies have traditionally used life insurance contracts and fixed annuities to fund pension and profit-sharing plans. But in recent years they have come to use variable annuities, which have a greater amount of dollars exposed to common stocks and mutual funds, which, in turn, are investment companies that can provide a greater opportunity for gowth. An employer can also take advantage of opportunities in real estate in limited areas for some of these programs. Generally, the employee has little control over where these funds are invested, but he or she does have the right under the law to know what's happened to the money.

Through various forms of legislation and public policy, the government has recently provided an atmosphere for encouraging retirement needs to be met by public rather than private sources. The government has attempted to reduce the amount of red tape associated with private pension and profit-sharing plans. This reduction in paperwork came as the result of ERISA and the heavy requirements imposed by that act upon the employer. However, in the last few years new pension and profit-sharing plans have been fewer in number, and more of those in existence have been terminated. The net effect has been a reduction in the benefits that employers are offering to their employees. The law, in effect, raised the cost of such pension and profit-sharing plans while reducing the benefits. Nearly 30 percent of all plans were terminated in the 1970s.

The major thrust of pension and profit-sharing plans was to provide incentives to employees to work harder, do better, and share in the collective fruits of their efforts. But increased legislation has undermined the values of these programs and severely weakened the entire system. The system will be weakened further by the proposed reductions in the Social Security system owing to underfunding and the inability of Americans to rely upon a system currently funded by 13.4 percent of all salary dollars. If Social Security benefits continue to rise, then the incentives of pension and profit-sharing plans will diminish. This, in turn, will reduce employer incentives to provide these plans in the first place. If the government continues to take more dollars from paychecks to fund a program that is sinking, this action will also reduce the employees' demands for money to go into pension and profit-sharing plans. In effect, both ERISA and Social Security are helping to reduce the size of pension and profit-sharing plans.

A demise of the private pension system seems imminent. The final outcome of the retirement situation will probably be determined by the employees themselves. They must learn how to ask intelligent questions and they must learn the current values to be anticipated from all forms of retirement programs, both public and private. And this assessment must be made on an annual basis with the help of a qualified adviser. In performing this duty, the individual will have a much clearer understanding of his or her rights and obligations—that is, rights and obligations under the law, rights and obligations to one's employer, and most important, rights, obligations, and commitments to oneself and one's loved ones in making personal adjustments to account for the errors over which he has no control. Nothing can replace individual initiative in assessing the financial values attached to lifetime goals and objectives.

Chapter 32

Life and Money After Sixty-Five

Stuart R. Wolk, Ph.D., J.D.

Stuart R. Wolk, Ph.D., J.D., is one of the most widely published lawyers in academia, with over thirty journal articles to his credit. He is the senior partner of his own law firm, and he has taught at several major universities, including the U.S. Military Academy (West Point). A judge advocate and former judge in the United States Air Force, he is an active senior reserve adviser on regulatory matters. As associate general counsel for many U.S. corporations, he is also board chairman and officer of several companies.

We are a strange society. Since the early 1970s, we have attempted to define and explain the needs of an ever aging work force and population. Gerontology centers have sprung up all over the United States as part of government policy, university programs, and hospital and health care facilities. Daily we are bombarded by advertisements from religious groups indicating that the old must not be denied love and familial surroundings. Television and movies often depict the elderly as semicrippled, doddering, and lacking total command of their faculties. The financial communities and the United States government have not only fallen into the trap of perpetuating this stereotyping, but they have aided and abetted the misconceptions it has engendered.

Legislation passed by the federal government over recent years has tended to create further problems for the elderly, both psychologically and financially. The Age Discrimination in Employment Statute, for example, ceases protection of workers when they reach age seventy, although some states have increased the upper age limits. The obvious conclusion is that after age seventy, we cease to be worthy of protection; that is, we are told to retire. Individual Retirement Accounts (IRAs) and Keogh plans must be ultimately paid out by 70½ years, and indeed their payout window is extremely narrow (59½ to 70½), especially in the light of the enormous sums that might be accumulated at 12–16 percent or more over periods of up to forty years. However, life does not cease merely because legislation determines that it should be so! What purpose is there to all of our financial advice for those increasingly larger groups of older Americans who, by desire or design, continue to seek gainful and meaningful existence? Obviously, your financial plan, if you are looking forward to the year 2000, must take into account changing life-styles and needs. For most of us, our life will not cease at age sixty-five, but beyond, nor will our various monetary requirements cease after traditional retirement.

What is needed is a rethinking of our views of senior citizen requirements. Financial planning for you, if you are thirty or forty years old, may not encompass spiraling inflation, increased medical complexities, or boredom. The former two are highly speculative and even the best econometric modeling does not indicate the unknown factors. However, boredom and its alleviation are both a financial and psychological problem to be confronted as early as possible by the individual planning his or her financial future and by the financial planning professional involved.

The Need to be Productive

Retirement is not so much a goal as it is a state of being. It is the ability to feel secure about being able not to work, or to work as the mood and inclination motivate. How we program the need to remain active into planning can be illustrated by a farsighted organization started in New York City, Senior Achievers Enterprises, Ltd.® The premise on which it was founded is that productive work is not only possible for senior citizens, but indeed should be performed by them. Fair compensation for effort expended is clearly desired, but a sense of purpose is manifestly as important.

Psychologists have long contended that we ascribe to our senior citizens financial concerns separate from a sense of purpose and importance. Undoubtedly, the need for financial security is a critical factor and requires careful planning and consideration, but it is by no means the entire picture, nor should it be.

Senior Achievers Enterprises, Ltd.® sought to integrate psychological needs by means of financial return, and at the same time hoped to provide a source of useful and productive work. There is no objection to senior citizen centers, but they tend to be both demeaning and nonproductive. Painting, pottery making, dancing, card playing, while good for therapeutic purposes, are terribly wasteful of the accumulated wealth of training, experience, and, yes, even potential residing in most senior Americans. We often view retirement as an end. Total retirement should occur only at death. Since few know when the end will actually take place, financially productive activity must be continued.

Through the acquisition of small neighborhood businesses, Senior Achievers Enterprises, Ltd.® was able to provide adequate work adjustments to meet both the desires and the needs of senior citizens. Virtually all of the employees had some form of income, either in the form of Social Security or a pension. Discussions held with many of them, especially those in their seventies, indicated that it wasn't enough to assuage the fear of being without. The ability to purchase food, clothing, provide for shelter, and, most important, meet medical expenditures far exceeded the realities in most cases.

The more that senior citizens became involved in the day-to-day or every-other-day aspects of corporate activity—running the gamut from executive decision making to outdoor and inside sales—coupled with their renewed sense of purpose and identity, the more their fears of being without diminished. The fortunate seniors who had been better able to provide for their retirement years soon found their surplus funds an embarrassment and were caught between two pulls: (1) the inherent belief in immortality carrying with it the uncertainty of how long they would need their reserves; and (2) a renewed interest in somehow sheltering their money and, at the same time, maintaining optimum liquidity.

What was indeed unique was that as years advanced, more and more similarities than dissimilarities developed concerning financial needs and desires. The wealthier seniors—tired of cruises and winters in Miami as well as of boasting of how successful they had been in life—found themselves, for the most part, concerned with their health and less with their accumulations. The poor, on the other hand, never having acclimated themselves to higher consumptive needs or propensities, also became more concerned with their health and with remaining active than with accumulations as such.

Economic Differences

Economic difficulties are apparent in the three general categories of middle class: lower middle, middle middle, and upper middle. Difficulties are most apparent among middle-class Americans over sixty-five. Their needs are disastrously overlooked. The extremely wealthy, having access to financial planners, can well provide cushioning for senior years far in excess of any capability either to spend or to expend. In the event of catastrophic illness, practically speaking, insurance planning and similar types of financial structuring more than adequately handle most emergencies. On the other end of the spectrum, Medicare, Medicaid, and religious organizations, while certainly not adequate in humanistic terms, tend to provide relief for the poor.

It is in the middle-class groups—where most seek upward economic mobility during work life, coupled with the proportionately ever increasing expenditures—that retirement brings several realizations. Foremost among them is that, in general, members of this group have lived their lives being misled and misdirected, only to find not only social, but economic frustrations in their later years. Persons who have had a sense of financial responsibility for a lifetime of work may suddenly realize that uncertain economic variables have stripped their pensions of real economic worth and, in the absence of other sources of income, they may, in terms of the real world, be more destitute than the poor. The degree of financial adjustment necessary becomes far more dramatic with the middle class after retirement, than with either the poor or the upper class.

While IRA and similar programs may provide financial security forty years down the line for those just entering the work force, for vast numbers of Americans already in their late thirties and forties IRA wealth is more of an illusion. It might well be that the next twenty to thirty years will see a large middle class passing into their golden years only to find that the gold is "fool's gold," and that they have prepared neither financially nor psychologically for the years ahead.

People are living longer in a technologically advancing environment, where the costs of the new society may be just beyond the reach of the majority. Unless steps are taken by the financial planners to help us both recognize and deal with life and money after sixty-five, we may place greater financial burdens on government, through government support and welfare programs, that society as a whole can ill afford. One has only to read the newspapers to question the viability of Social Security. The gnawing issue we all must face is whether the Social Security system can be counted on any longer to provide what it *never* was intended to do—maintain us in our later years through a quasi-pension system. Many of the potential solutions to what otherwise might mark the catastrophic end of middle-class America are painfully simple and well within our capabilities.

Any financial planning for the vast majority of Americans over the age of sixty-five should recognize that the work ethic has been so completely inculcated into our life patterns that just as important as the need for money is the need for self-worth and self-esteem. Financial plans should therefore categorize us by job skills and training, analyzing the potential for continual employment or opportunity for employment. The law has come a long way in this regard, both at the state and federal level, by protecting senior citizens from age discrimination in employment. Further emphasis must be placed on showing that, contrary to the television image, a vast majority of senior Americans are fully capable of performing work and services of some type well into their seventies, eighties, and even nineties. The need to work and be productive goes beyond senior citizens centers, which have become society's way of providing a collection point for elderly people. These centers seek to avoid the embarrassment of having to deal with the senior citizen. Financial planners must encourage employment and must structure financial programs with the continuation of employment in mind. In order to accomplish this, we must know our goals and desires.

Financial Fallacies

One of the fallacies and failings of Keogh and IRA plans is that they assume income will be diminished at ages 59½ through 70. Although this may hold true in some cases, the years between 59½ and 70 should be optimum years for earned income. The sudden influx of taxable funds during this period of time is the worst possible financial situation for most middle-class Americans. The sudden influx of taxable dollars may diminish a considerable portion of the expected benefits of the programs. This is not to say we should disregard the programs; rather, we should recognize that no single plan provides a panacea for all our needs.

This is certainly true for professional middle Americans—doctors, dentists, accountants, lawyers, architects—many of whom continue to earn maximum income well into their seventies. Obviously, consideration must be given to alternative sources of annuity and investment-type programs aimed at meeting the needs of the professional segment of middle America into their senior years.

One of the more common misconceptions perpetuated by planners, economists, and analysts is that all professionals traditionally earn large dollars and therefore must be grouped into one social category. Although many of them do earn large dollars, many others do not, and their only financial advantage lies in the tax benefits of self-employment or partnership operations, rather than in actual gross dollars earned.

In dealing with the nonprofessional seniors, financial planners have overlooked a golden opportunity. Financial planners should be prodding corporations into making increased use of the skills and talents of the senior American. It is obvious to most Americans that financial planning for the year 2000 can no longer be viewed abstractly. We need intelligent, well-trained, sensitive assistance from individuals who understand the senior need, and who can properly exploit both dormant and known talents. What planners must be encouraged to engender (to the extent that corporations are reluctant to make use of senior skills) is the creation of mini-conglomerates along the lines of Senior Achievers Enterprises, Ltd.® This idea would not be as difficult to carry out as we might think at first glance. A careful review of available seniors clearly illustrates the diversity of their skills, which could undoubtedly be organized into small businesses of various types.

Perhaps, the time has come as well to create senior work cooperatives. We live in an era when barter has returned as a means of exchange of goods and services. Why not create a system of barter among senior companies and sales to the general public? This certainly is a self-help alternative to sitting and doing nothing! Humans must remain active if life is to have any purpose or significance.

Even though legislation mandating the continual employment of seniors beyond sixty-five will probably expand rather than contract in the near future, a large segment of the population will still be underemployed and underutilized. If financial planning is to have significance for the average nonprofessional in the golden years, it must do more than advise people on annuities, stock plans, IRAs, and the like. It must be totally integrated as a package for the seniors and designed like the system described above.

Conclusion

The nature and scope of financial planning today encompass the interdisciplinary areas of psychology, psychiatry, and economics. Any projection into the future in purely economic terms is, at best, educated crystal ball gazing. Marketplace variables such as oil embargoes, runaway inflation, devaluations, and monetary definition changes can undo even the most astute of planners, whether professional or amateur.

Events of the past twenty-five years should have clearly shown those in the financial planning fields that far more uncertainty than certainty exists in the marketplace, and that some of the burdens there can still be shouldered by the senior. This requires a far broader comprehension of real life problems than pure economics. Life and money after sixty-five years of age bring a need for more detailed analysis of the peculiar needs of seniors, or soon-to-be-seniors. They should not be treated as a statistical oddity much like the anciety Eskimo placed on an ice flow and pushed out to sea. What a waste!

The financial potential for both the sensitive and involved financial planner and the senior citizen is unlimited as long as ongoing awareness on the part of financial planners precipitates an ongoing relationship through the senior years. To quote the motto of Senior Achievers Enterprises, Ltd.®, "There is no sadness in growing old. There is only sadness in wasted years."

Part 9

Editor's Notes:
You Can't Take It With You

*T*wo interesting questions are at the heart of the discussion in the next four chapters: One, why do so few people take into account the effect inflation will have on their accumulated capital? Two, why do so many high-income people who accumulate large amounts of capital wait so long before deciding what to do with it? These mistakes are common among the young and middle-aged as well as older people. The upcoming chapters can help you avoid making them. In Chapter 33, Al Jeanfreau presents a fascinating, down-to-earth view of economics that proves that the subject has a much wider application than some of us tend to think. Then, in Chapter 34,

Dick Wollack talks about an avenue you may wish to explore—real estate for retirement income, which he points out, is for people of average means just as much as the wealthy. A useful tool for people in all income groups is the subject of Chapter 35, in which Wes Wyatt expertly explains the value of investment and financial planning seminars. Chapter 36 then turns to one of the most neglected areas of financial planning—estate planning. Graydon Calder sets forth some of the basic facts you should know about wills and trusts and urges you not to put off this unpleasant but essential aspect of financial planning.

Chapter 33

Economics and Attitudes for Successful Investing

Al Jeanfreau is an economist who is well-known in both academic and business circles. He is founder and manager of Al Jeanfreau Associates, Incorporated, and is also a lecturer in economics and personal finance at Portland State University. He is an adjunct faculty member for the College for Financial Planning. Jeanfreau has written articles for professional journals and has appeared on the television series "The Money Makers." He also appeared as an adviser in a recent article in *Money* and was featured in the *Financial Planner*. A Certified Financial Planner, he holds memberships in the American Economic Association, the American Institute for Economic Research, the World Future Society, and the Institute of Certified Financial Planners, and is on the national board of directors of the International Association for Financial Planning.

Al Jeanfreau, CFP

My life on earth could be such fun
if I were the only one
to see things as they seem to be
and guide my life accordingly.

But, dear Lord, why did you send
the economist to be my friend
to help me view this world around
for now I don't know up from down.

His world is numbers, charts and graphs
mine's filled with people, birds and grass.
He tries to make his quantified
mine's best when it's unmodified.

You'll understand if I tell him, Lord
that I'll not submit to being his ward.
Since for mass confusion he has no rival
I'd prefer your help with my survival.

A Perspective on Economics

After glancing at that heading, should you read on? After all, economics is said to be a dull subject and who but a full-time student of economics can really understand inflation (much less what causes it), our banking system, the gyrations of interest rates and the stock and bond markets, the balance of payments, the relative values of various currencies, unemployment, and all the other myriad topics that fall within the realm of economics? So why bother with such a heavy subject, which some would insist requires a Ph.D. even to get an inkling of what is going on in the world of economics? Well, let's examine the subject and the prevailing elitist attitude about it.

Why Bother?

If we likened your financial planning effort to sailing a pleasure ship, the condition and position of the ship itself would be the state of your individual financial affairs. The passengers would be your family (or the employees of the company that you might own) and the crew would be analogous to your advisers and business

contacts. If your ultimate port of call was your long-range financial goal, then your responsibility as a captain obviously could not be confined to the hull and decks of your ship. A major and constant consideration would have to be the sea on which your ship is sailing. That sea, with its swells, winds, shoals, and occasional storms, is the economic environment, and you as captain simply cannot choose to ignore that environment. To ignore it is an economic decision, likely to be a disastrous one.

Economists Don't Own Economics

Well, if that analogy holds, then one of your problems might be not knowing how to identify a good navigator to assist in the journey. An ever more popular approach is to engage a qualified financial planner. Let's assume there's also an individual who keeps sending radio bulletins on the weather that you might encounter on your economic sea. But the eventual weather seldom matches the prognostications. This "meteorologist" is analogous to the economist. Author Robert Lekachman has pointed out,

> [Economists] speak in tongues as difficult to comprehend as the dialect of nuclear physicists, molecular biologists, structural linguists, or respectable literary critics. Moreover, most economists are individuals of good will, eager to extirpate poverty, redeem the cities, demolish pollution, feed the hungry, heal the sick, and house the unsheltered. All the same, economists do make the oddest statements and promulgate undue quantities of faulty prophecy and policy prescription.[1]

Where do you find a good economist in whom you might put your trust? Well, I could list a fair number who seem to make a lot of sense and whose arguments are at least consistent, but that would be too simple. Instead, let's consider a suggestion

[1]Robert Lekachman, *Economists at Bay: Why the Expert Will Never Solve Your Problems* (New York: McGraw-Hill, 1976).

that is a bit more radical: with some effort you can become your own best economist—at least, one who is competent enough to select good advisers. That is one of the basic premises of this chapter. The other is that a few adjustments in attitude can make you an even better economist and investment decision maker.

Just What Is Economics?

If we're going to talk about economics relative to your financial planning and investment decisions, perhaps we should try to define economics, because this is where most professional economists get into trouble. It's too easy for them to wind up in left field when they haven't taken the time to locate home plate. There are many definitions, some of them several hundred words long. But a particularly useful definition is one put forth by the Nobel Prize winning economist F. A. Hayek, who stated, "The study of economics is the study of human beings functioning within the society they create." That hardly looks like the definition of a science—it doesn't talk about mathematical models, whisper in the ears of politicians, make projections about the gross national product, or hint at endless statistics. It makes economics look surprisingly like a social science.

In fact, economics was considered a social science from the time Adam Smith wrote *Inquiry into the Nature and Causes of the Wealth of Nations* in 1776 right up to the 1930s, but that idea was overturned when an English economist named John Maynard Keynes suggested during the Great Depression that economics really could be another branch of engineering and that governments could mechanically manipulate the economy to correct its ills. Keynes even provided the mathematical formulas for the politicians to use. Since the appearance of one of Keynes's major works, *The General Theory of Employment, Interest and Money* (1936), the study of economics has

not been the same on our university campuses. A Ph.D. in economics today almost implies a degree in higher mathematics.

Along with Hayek, another prominent economist of the so-called Austrian school was Ludwig Von Mises, who defined economics as the study of human action. His most famous work, *Human Action*, is devoid of a single mathematical formula. If economics is the study of human beings interacting with one another, then the economist, who is supposedly a student of human action, betrays his profession when he tries to manipulate or in any way influence human action, because at that point the economist becomes a political being.

What does that have to do with your making decisions about your finances? Simply this: when economists become involved with the political world, they become biased and lose touch with reality. They see the world as it "ought to be" and in the shape into which they hope to mold it and, as a consequence, they lose touch with reality and no longer see things as they are. Such a state of affairs does not simply mean that most economists are sharing useless information with us but that their advice can be downright dangerous if followed. A critic of Lekachman's book, writing for the *New York Times* "Book Review," has argued:

> The conventional economists of today, who labor under the delusion that they are pure scientists, manage to accomplish little more than misleading politicians and public. This is likely to continue—with possibly horrendous consequences—unless the tradition of social analysis, within which the giants of the profession once worked, is revived.

The whole purpose of putting modern economists in their place is twofold. One is to suggest what economics is not: it is not higher mathematics; it is not owned by economists or politicians; it is not a subject that is beyond your grasp. The second purpose is to prepare the way for a few basic principles of economics that might help give this subject some perspective and that might serve as useful tools in helping you make sound decisions about your money and your financial future in general.

More Perspective and a Bias

Let's assume that your financial goals are not based on some insatiable greed compelling you to try to double your assets every year. Let's also say—at the other end of the spectrum—that it would be undesirable to watch your assets be eroded by taxes and inflation. Instead, let's pick some more "reasonable" middle ground that allows you to define successful investing as simply maintaining the buying power of your assets in the face of taxes and inflation. Now that might seem to be too conservative a position for you to take but, on second thought, you might find it to be the only reasonable investment objective to have because someone in a 40 percent tax bracket, facing 10 percent inflation, would have to have a 25 percent per annum compounded rate of return on investments to gain 5 percent in the buying power of those assets. Have you been attaining 25 percent recently?

Owning vs. Lending

Depending on your age, you might remember when banks boldly displayed the interest rate paid on passbook accounts by painting the 2½ or 3 percent rate in gold leaf in a bank window (that's when money was more stable and the sign could remain painted for some time). It didn't matter so much if the interest rate was low because taxes and inflation were both low at the time. Even though banks and savings and loans are now able to pay 14 percent and higher on certificates of deposit, taxes and inflation still ensure that you come out the

loser. The loss today, however, is considerably larger.

Well, then, how does one get ahead? You could pray for a large inheritance or hope for a winning ticket in the Irish Sweepstakes. Or, you could nurture your hard-earned dollars into a handsome nest egg. How? Well, if savings accounts won't do it for us, and burying our money in the backyard at no interest is even worse, then we must become investors. We must be "owners" of assets that can improve our financial state faster than taxes and inflation erode it.

A Bias

Before we launch into principles of economics and their application, it is important to emphasize the need for professional management when it comes to investing. Regardless of how large or small a portfolio, the individual who has to devote a large amount of time to his business or profession seldom has an investment track record that he's proud of. You have to decide, at some point, what you are going to be doing full time: managing your money, or devoting sufficient time to your job, business, or profession? That doesn't mean an individual cannot become his or her own full-time manager of assets, but it verges on the ridiculous to think that an individual can manage a diversified portfolio of assets alone while devoting full time to earning a living.

Some form of professional management is needed for the bulk of an individual's invested assets. The professional management might come in the form of limited partnerships, investment trusts, investment companies, or investment advisers. Once you have an appreciation for what the professional managers can do for you, *then* the process of investing becomes one of picking the particular types of investments that seem to make sense and doing the shopping for the better professional managers who handle those particular types of investments. You could even go one step further and find a qualified financial planner with whom you feel comfortable and work with that individual from the word "go" on your investment decisions. Now let's talk about a few economics principles and, later on, how to apply them profitably.

Some Useful Economics Principles

Although we can't hope to do more than scratch the surface of the subject of economics, we can profit from examining certain basic principles of economics, for they can be used to evaluate what is presented to us in the media about our economy. This, in turn, can help us to make sound decisions about our money. So, let's jump feet first into a few principles of economics, which in their straightforwardness would at first appear to be obvious to anyone. But, as you digest them and make them your own, you will come to realize that many economists have forgotten them as they delve in their world of mathematical models. It will also become evident that most of our politicians have either never learned these principles or cannot afford to remember them for political reasons.

Man's Material Welfare

A helpful starting point in the field of economics is to look at a relationship described in a small book entitled *How We Live*. The relationship is expressed by means of a few mathematical symbols. It is not to be considered a rigid mathematical formula, but a simple way of expressing a basic principle:

$$MMW = NR + HE \times T$$

This relationship simply means that man's material welfare (*MMW*) is derived from natural resources (*NR*) plus his muscular and mental human energy (*HE*) multiplied by the efficiency of his tools (*T*).

We might say that anything of material value, from food and clothing to a *Voyager* space probe, is the result of combining some naturally occurring building materials with the efforts of people by means of various tools. It becomes apparent that the thing of value might itself be a tool for assisting in creating something else of value.

The relationship also applies to non-material things of value, such as the verbal advice of an accountant. Since, in this case, the "building materials" from nature (the natural resources—*NR*) and the tools (*T*) would not be present, the relationship could be reduced to *MW* (man's welfare) = *HE* (human energy). The usefulness of this and a few other simple principles can be immeasurable in helping us stay out of financial trouble and direct our money into the right places.

Supply and Demand

The next principle is that of *supply and demand*. If you have taken a basic course in economics you have probably come across this principle before. It is nonetheless a useful one to review. When something (an object or a service) is in demand (wanted) by an individual or group of individuals, there is a tendency for another individual or group of individuals to supply (provide) the object or service. This, of course, would be done for some remuneration. It stands to reason that the greater the demand for the object or service, the more possibility there is on the part of those who provide the object or service to earn a profit for doing so. The greatest profit potential lies where the demand is extremely great and the supply rather limited. Conversely, if there is a large supply of the object or service and very little demand, people will not be willing to pay much for what is abundantly available.

This simple principle is applicable not only to the world of economics but also to other aspects of our lives. For instance, a child who is supplied with a great deal of demonstrated love in the home is less apt to make obnoxious demands for attention. Later we'll see how it applies to your financial well-being.

Where Does Government Fit In?

The last principle of note is one that most of the voting citizens in our country have allowed our representatives in government to ignore: generally speaking, government is not a source of goods or services; government usually interferes with the source of goods or services.

Everything produced is produced by the people, and everything that government gives to the people, it must first take from the people. Another way of stating this principle is to say that "there is no such thing as a free lunch." We have all heard that saying. It means that the highways, defense, Social Security payments, welfare payments, low-cost housing subsidies, and all the myriad things that government "gives" us must be paid for by the tax money that it extracts from individuals and businesses.

When the federal government "gives" us more than it taxes us for (in other words, runs a deficit), it does so either by creating the money out of thin air (through the Federal Reserve System) or by borrowing it through the sale of U.S. Treasury bills, notes, and bonds. When the money supply is increased by the Federal Reserve System faster than goods and services become available for purchase, we witness the effects of "inflation"—increases in the price of goods and services (including the price of labor). When the Treasury borrows to fund the deficit, it adds to the existing debt (which is now over $1 trillion) and, in turn,

must pay interest on this debt (which itself runs over $100 billion per year). This madness forces the businesses that depend heavily on debt to compete with the government for borrowed money at higher and higher interest rates.

As a "regulator," the government interferes with the availability of goods and services when it pays farmers to leave land unplanted, remove "surplus" agricultural products from the market, enforce environmental standards, and levy quotas on imported goods, to name a few incidences. There are purported good reasons for the many government regulations, but here we want to consider the effects of the regulations, not their efficacy.

These principles are presented here not because they are utterly inspiring, or because they serve to show up huge governmental debts and financial irresponsibility in general. Rather, the point is to become acquainted with some clear principles of economics that can be immensely useful in evaluating investment risks and opportunities. How can these principles help you?

Applying the Principles for Profit

To make sound investment decisions, you have to find out what is in great demand, relative to the supply, and then supply it. In pursuing this idea, let's tie together the first two principles mentioned earlier into a compatible relationship and proceed with some examples. We said that the greater the difference between the supply and the demand of a given item or service, the greater the opportunity for profit (that is, with a skimpy supply and a strong demand, people are willing to pay more for the item or service). Tying this principle to the first one, the item or service demanded could be *NR* (natural resources in the form of oil, natural gas, timber, metals, water, bauxite, and so on), *HE* (human energy in the form of physical labor or the creative energy of a teacher, architect, manager, and so on), or *T* (tools, such as office equipment and supplies, surgical implements, heavy construction equipment, buildings, books, or any of the thousands upon thousands of items and services that people might use to multiply their muscle power or mental power). So we want to look for "shortages" in any of the items that fall on the right-hand side of the *MMW* relationship. Following are some examples from recent history and a peek at the probable future. These examples are not to be construed as recommendations. The investment vehicles described merely indicate how the principles of economics can be applied in practice.

Energy

In 1970, when crude oil was selling for about $3.00 a barrel, some people began to take seriously the hue and cry of certain analysts who were trying to turn U.S. attention to the "energy crisis" that we were facing. The premise was that there is a limited supply of crude oil and an almost insatiable demand for the products made from oil. Certain enterprising individuals put together limited partnerships to take advantage of this crisis. The partnerships were designed to purchase existing producing oil and natural gas wells to sell the oil and gas for an acceptable net return to the investor, and to give the investor an inflation hedge through the possible increases in oil and gas prices.

This is probably a good place to introduce the effects of that third principle of economics mentioned earlier—the involvement of the federal government. In 1970, crude oil and natural gas prices were regulated by federal mandate. There was some magical dollar figure above which crude oil and natural gas could not be sold, the figure

being about $3.00 in 1970. A major reason for the crisis in the first place was the reality that it was not profitable to drill holes in the ground and search for crude oil (and natural gas) at the prices mandated by the federal government. When Congress finally awoke to that fact, crude oil prices and gas prices were allowed to rise in steps in order to encourage oil and gas exploration. Thus the deregulation in prices was a governmental attempt to solve the problem that it had created. Currently, crude oil prices are deregulated and gas prices are scheduled for deregulation in a few more years. Playing the investment game would have considerably less spice if it were not for the interference of government regulations, which affect every aspect of our economy and, therefore, our investment world.

Many happy investors in this country would say that the tremendous increases in the price of energy have been good news for them, or at least the bad news has been offset by the fact that they own the commodity that cost so much. (Investments in that type of partnership, just as in many other types of vehicles, generally take a $2,500–5,000 minimum initial investment— so we're not talking about something strictly for the wealthy.) Crude oil prices rose to an average of $12.64 in 1979 and by 1982 domestic crude oil was selling for $25.00–$32.00 a barrel (depending on the grade of crude). Remember that we're talking about history. Certain grades of crude oil reached the $34.00 level and have come back several dollars because of the recent "glut." When gas prices are deregulated, it is predicted that the average price of natural gas will at least double.

Although returns on energy investments look quite impressive, remember that if an individual is in a 50 percent tax bracket, half of the current cash flow is gobbled up by taxes. Remember, too, the buying power of each dollar has diminished since 1972 because of inflation.

Also, the so-called "windfall profits" tax is taxing the profits from oil and natural gas; it is not really a tax on profits at all, but a tax on the gross income from the sale of oil. We need not apologize for being cynical about federal regulations and taxing policy, because so little of it makes sense, and so many governmental regulations run counter to one another (for example, an individual can take as a tax deduction the "intangible" costs of drilling an oil well—which is most of the cost—and at the same time have a price ceiling imposed on crude oil as we have experienced until recently; one rule favors oil exploration, and the other discourages it). In any case, those who foresaw the probability of increasing oil and natural gas prices have profited handsomely.

Real Estate

Whenever you hear phrases like "It doesn't matter what you paid for the real estate, inflation will correct any mistakes," be skeptical. This is a form of the "greater fool" theory, which, in effect, says another fool will come along and buy it from you at a higher price. Interestingly, that theory actually worked during most of the 1970s, but when increasing debt in our country encouraged high interest rates, real estate went "flat," in that you could no longer buy just any piece of real estate and expect to sell it in a few years for a profit. Potential buyers were no longer willing or able to pay the high rates for mortgage money. Let's illustrate the opportunities still remaining in real estate by talking about the crisis.

A young married couple desiring to own a house today will have to pay somewhere in the neighborhood of $60,000–$80,000 for a basic house. If they are willing to swallow that challenge they must then find a local bank that has money to lend. If they're successful in doing that, they must then be willing to pay the high interest that would

be demanded by the bank. In all probability they would also have to accept a variable rate loan (pegged to the prevailing interest rates), which could work against them just as easily as it could for them in future years. If they're not discouraged by this point in the game, they must then qualify for the loan. Well, not many young couples can make it through that set of challenges, so what choice do they have? Either move back with mom and dad, or rent.

But what about owning rentals? That could be a good idea, it if wasn't for the challenge of owning and managing local real estate. However, there is another alternative—limited partnerships. Many well-managed limited partnerships in real estate—at least those with a national scope—have purchased properties in the southeastern part of the United States, since business has recently gravitated to that warmer climate, where both energy and labor costs are lower. This influx of business has created a population increase and a demand for housing. That, combined with the fact that rental rates are still quite low across the country (in relation to the cost of the real estate), has made for an excellent investment opportunity since about the mid-1970s. There can be little doubt that rental rates will appreciate strongly and reward the property owner. The profit to be made from the sale of real estate in the near future will depend much more heavily on a particular property's net cash flow than on the "greater fool" theory, as in the past.

Lending

Although high interest rates tend to dampen interest in real estate, there is still a demand for money, and the banks and thrift institutions are short of it. Where then, is the opportunity?

Certain investment trusts have been formed for the purpose of pooling investor capital to lend to builders of new properties and to owners of existing properties. The lending is typically done at rates somewhat lower than would be available from the traditional sources of capital—the banks and savings and loans—but, in order to get the money, the property owner must be willing to give up a percentage of the appreciation of that property from the time the loan is made to perhaps the end of a twelve-year period. In other loans, the property owner gives up a share of the increases in rent or lease income on the property from the date of the loan. In either case, there is a built-in inflation hedge through the appreciation clause or rent-lease clause. At worst, the lender (your trust) is "stuck" with an acceptable return from the interest on the loan and, if there is no inflation, say for the next ten years, the more conservative alternatives for your money—certificates of deposit and money market funds—would probably be paying below what you are receiving from your trust shares. The trust share values might even appreciate as competing interest rates go down.

On the other hand, if inflation persists, the return to your trust shares would go up (because of the appreciation of rent-lease participation) and the trust share value would likely maintain itself and not go down in price, as would other income instruments such as bonds. The current income from this type of trust investment is usually fully taxable, but it makes an excellent vehicle for a qualified retirement plan such as an IRA, Keogh, or corporate pension or profit-sharing plan where taxability is of no concern.

Personal Computers

By the mid-1990s most of us will have computers in our homes probably assisting us in ways that we could not imagine today. Your personal computer will no doubt be able to communicate with your bank and allow you to do your banking via a keyboard. It might allow you to type letters to friends and relatives and transmit those letters instantly to their printer unit or computer screen. Your personal computer might be tied in to your local library, from which you will be able to obtain information directly.

We are now witnessing an increasing demand for the personal computer, and that demand seems to be taking on the proportions of an explosion. However, we also have a large number of companies that are willing to supply that demand. So there does not appear to be current "shortage" in the supply of personal computers. Whether or not there is a great investment opportunity here becomes questionable, for it is difficult to guess the winner among the many competitors who are willing to supply the demanded item. So we have increasing demand for a product, but no shortage of supply.

Cable TV

With the rise of competing technologies, there seems little doubt that the coaxial cable, which is the transmission line for signals sent by cable television stations, will one day lace the majority of the towns in our country. One competing technology that will probably gain some prominence will be the transmission of microwave signals from a central station in a town to the various households, or from a satellite to individual receivers. The advantage of the cable, however, is that it has an "interactive" capability—you can send a signal from your house as well as receive one. So, consumers may eventually want to go beyond simply receiving television shows in their homes via cable to having their personal computers tied to the cable in order to send signals.

A number of partnerships have been formed to buy existing cable stations in smaller towns where the political environment is less "cutthroat" than in most larger

towns. The management of these partnerships attempts to increase the number of
subscriptions in that town and bring in
new services at higher charges. This can
increase the profit of the stations to the
point where they become quite attractive
to a potential buyer upon resale some five
to seven years later.

Stocks

Since the early 1970s it has been difficult
to do anything in the stock market other
than "market timing" or "dollar-cost
averaging" (explained elsewhere in this
book). A healthy, well-managed corporation that creates profits consistently or has
every prospect of creating healthy profits
in the future will reward the holder of its
common stock in the long run. But when
the movement of common stocks is associated with emotional and irrational decisions, the short-term value of an investment is considerably harder to predict.
Rumors of war in the Middle East, the
energy crisis, the real estate crisis, domestic
political events—all of these things create
gyrations in stock prices that are worrying.
For an expanded and, perhaps, more positive view on common stock investing see
the chapter on that topic.

Conclusion

One underlying intent of this chapter
was to sweep away some of the complexity
and confusion about economics and to
show that certain economic principles can
be put to use in making investment decisions. But, the subject of economics is not
really the starting point. Investment decisions rightly begin with the introspective
process of learning about yourself.

Who Am I?

This question is asked not to suggest
that you need to thoroughly analyze yourself from a philosophical or psychological

viewpoint. Rather the question relates to
your financial objectives: Do you want immediate cash flow? Liquidity? A high degree of safety? Long-term growth? Your
answer to these and other similar questions
should strongly influence the particular
types of investment vehicles that you
select. The answers to these questions will
be influenced by certain facts about your
particular financial situation. The answer
to the questions on cash flow and growth,
for example, might depend on when retirement will take place. The answer to the
liquidity and safety questions might depend on the total amount of assets with
which you are working.

Better yet, seek out a competent Certified Financial Planner who can help you
come up with the proper questions and
answers. Naturally, that person's investment philsophy should be at least as well
formulated as your own.

A Step Ahead

Financial success does not have to depend upon things like luck, an inheritance,
or genius. The vast majority of financially
successful people would claim no large
measure of any of these benefits. Rather,
financial success depends upon setting
clearly defined goals and taking one rational step at a time toward the attainment
of those goals. And success as an investor
comes in gathering a kit bag of economics
and financial principles and applying them
in an uncompromising manner. This, more
than anything else, is most likely to keep
you in the winner's circle. Most investors
haven't defined their objectives, nor do
they methodically search out principles by
which they might make rational investment
decisions. To the extent that you set your
objectives and search out investment principles, you will be ahead of the crowd. And
to be highly successful it is not necessary
to be leagues ahead of everyone else. You
simply need to be one step ahead of the
crowd.

Richard G. Wollack, B.A., M.B.A, is a
nationally recognized lecturer and adviser
in the field of real estate. He is president of
Consolidated Capital Institutional Advisers, Incorporated. He was co-founder and
president of First Capital Companies, and
subsequently conducted his own national
real estate investment consulting business.
He has been a featured speaker at conventions of the National Association of Corporate Real Estate Executives, the International Association for Financial Planning,
the Realtors National Marketing Institute,
and the American Association of Individual
Investors. Wollack is a frequent contributor
to national real estate and business periodicals, writes a monthly column for the *National Tax Shelter Digest*, and is a member
of the editorial advisory board of the *Real
Estate Securities Journal*. He is co-author of
Tax-Advantaged Investments, a self-study
program for tax-shelter investment analysis. In addition, he is vice-president of the
California Syndication Forum, and a member of the Western Pension Conference
and of the national board of the International Association for Financial Planning.

Chapter 34

Income Real Estate for Your Retirement Plan

Richard G. Wollack

Suddenly, with the passage of the Economic Recovery Tax Act of 1981 (ERTA), everybody has to start thinking like a professional pension fund manager. Before ERTA, only independent professionals and a small minority of workers not covered by corporate pension plans had any cause to think about managing their own retirement investments. The vast majority of people simply had no control over how their retirement or pension fund dollars were invested.

Now, all that has changed. Since January 1, 1982, everyone with earned income, whether covered by some other retirement plan or not, has become eligible to establish their own, independently managed Individual Retirement Account, or IRA. Whether a part-time worker earning less than $1,000 a year, or one of the highest paid corporate executives in the land, every wage earner should be making decisions about how their retirement dollars are invested.

The rules and alternatives of Individual Retirement Accounts are discussed in detail in Chapter 30, and you should familiarize yourself with that chapter. What is important here is to understand in general how investing in a retirement plan—whether a small individual plan like an IRA or a multi-billion dollar pension fund—differs from personal investing. The rules, objectives, and methods of personal investing, on one hand, and retirement investing on the other, are significantly different. Before discussing how real estate investments can fit into a retirement plan, we need to understand the special characteristics that affect investment decisions for retirement dollars.

Shelter from taxation is the most obvious difference between personal and retirement investing: retirement dollars are pre-tax dollars. Your contributions to an IRA or Keogh plan, or your employer's contributions to your pension plan, are not part of your taxable income for the year contributed. Those dollars, plus the accruing income they earn, remain untaxed until

years later, when you start drawing your retirement benefits. At that time, you are taxed at ordinary tax rates only for the dollars you draw out within a given year. The result of this tax-sheltering aspect of retirement plans is that your retirement investments compound year after year at a much higher rate than your personal investments. Every dollar of retirement investment income can be fully reinvested, without the 20–50 percent IRS "haircut" to which your personal investment income is subjected.

This untaxed compounding of investment income is of more than passing interest. It means that even though your IRA is limited to contributions of only $2,000 per year, its capacity for growth over a number of years is far greater than most people suspect. Table 1 compares the growth rates of tax-sheltered IRA investments to the growth rates of personal investments that are fully taxable.

Considerations for IRA Investing

The untaxed compound growth rate is the prime reason that everybody who is eligible should start contributing to an IRA, if at all possible. Over the years you can build up a significant nest egg much more quickly than you may have thought possible. But beyond the high rate of growth this tax deferral allows, it has further significance in determining what kinds of investments are best suited for retirement plans. Many investments that are popular and appropriate on the personal side because of the tax deductions they generate are inappropriate for retirement plans. Any investment that has tax-shelter benefits as a significant portion of what you are paying for when you purchase it is highly questionable for a retirement plan.

A second important consideration is that retirement plan dollars are not replenishable. If you lose money in a personal investment—if your stocks drop in value, or your

Table 1. IRA Savings vs. Taxable Savings

YEARS LEFT UNTIL AGE 65	WITH IRA ALL TAX BRACKETS	WITHOUT IRA		
		50% TAX BRACKET	40% TAX BRACKET	30% TAX BRACKET
40	$1,718,285	164,048	270,427	436,973
39	1,532,183	153,762	251,064	401,712
38	1,366,020	144,058	233,001	369,183
37	1,217,661	134,905	216,152	339,174
36	1,085,197	126,268	200,434	211,492
35	966,926	118,121	185,772	285,954
30	540,585	83,802	125,976	185,055
20	161,397	38,993	53,903	72,603
10	39,309	14,868	18,748	23,259

NOTE: The table compares the rate at which an annual amount of $2,000 grows when invested within an IRA on a tax-deferred basis with the rate at which the same amount grows when principal and earnings are subject to current taxation. This assumes a 12 percent rate of return.

drilling partnership hits dry holes, or your bonds are battered by high interest rates— you have a number of alternatives to replenish the lost dollars. First, you can deduct your investment losses against current income. Losses within a retirement plan, however, are just that: losses. They cannot be deducted against your income. On the personal investment side, you can work more to earn more money, or you can go on a less expensive vacation, or reduce other expenses. You have considerable flexibility to replace lost personal investment dollars. The opposite is true of retirement investment dollars. You cannot say to the IRS, "Look, I lost $500 in my IRA when the price of my stock dropped, so this year I'm going to contribute $2,500 instead of $2,000." You simply cannot make up for the loss. Thus, you can afford a higher degree of risk exposure in personal investing, whereas in retirement investing, preservation of principal is of paramount importance. Your retirement dollars *must be safe* dollars.

A third important consideration in retirement investing is preservation of purchasing power. For the foreseeable future, at least, it is safe to assume that inflation will continue to advance in this country. In this kind of inflationary environment, if your retirement dollars are earning only 10–12 percent, the purchasing power of your retirement nest egg may be diminishing or showing no real (that is, inflation-adjusted) growth. For this reason, you should be cautious about overweighting fixed-income investments in your retirement portfolio. In order to hedge against inflationary erosion of purchasing power, some of your retirement dollars should be positioned in inflation-sensitive investments that retain a share of value impervious to the inroads of inflation.

A fourth distinguishing characteristic of retirement investing is the liquidity factor. In your personal investments, quick access to your assets can be important. A good part of your personal portfolio should be liquid, so that in the event of a family emergency, sudden business needs, the purchase of a car or house, or other contingencies, you will have the necessary financial flexibilty. Many investors therefore shy away from relatively illiquid investments in their personal portfolio. The liquidity factor is not nearly as important in retirement investing for the simple reason that your retirement dollars are not your contingency dollars. Certainly some of your retirement portfolio can be in a liquid investment vehicle such as a money market fund, which makes an excellent first-stage storage pool for your retirement contributions. You receive a fairly good rate of return, and it is easy to transfer funds from a money market fund to a longer term investment when an appropriate one comes along. But retirement investing is fundamentally long-term investing. You are in it for the long haul. The most important consideration is how many dollars accumulate over a period of twenty to thirty years. Thus an investment that does not mature for five or ten years might be inappropriate for your personal investing, but ideal for your retirement plan.

In summary, your parameters and objectives in a small individual retirement plan are substantially the same as those of the pension fund giants. You want to acquire funds to retire as comfortably as possible; so do the beneficiaries of General Motors' corporate retirement plan. You thus want to achieve the highest rate of growth in your plan that is consistent with safe and prudent investing; so do the professional managers of large pension funds. The amounts of money involved are vastly different, but surprisingly enough, you have virtually the same range of investment alternatives available to you with your personal IRA or Keogh as the professions in charge of major pension funds. For this reason, it is instructive to consider what professional pension fund managers have done in the past, and the direction in which they are now taking their investments.

Pension Fund Investment Strategy

Fifteen or twenty years ago, pension fund managers invested almost exclusively in stocks and bonds. In theory, the two made an ideal combination. Bonds provided fixed income that assured predictable cash flow, while stocks provided equity growth and were a hedge against inflation. During periods of higher interest rates, portfolios could be weighted toward bonds to take advantage of higher cash flows. During periods of rapid economic expansion, they could be weighted toward stocks to take advantage of corporate equity growth. Such was the theory, and it was backed up by the solid performance of the stock and bond markets in the 1950s and 1960s.

The situation changed during the 1970s. In real terms (that is, in terms of purchasing power), the overall value of stock market equity declined by some 50 percent since the high-flying 1960s. Bonds fared even worse. As interest rates climbed higher and higher, the market value of bonds dropped and dropped. If you bought a thirty-year bond yielding 6 percent in the late 1960s, its current market value would at best be fifty cents on the dollar compared to what you paid for it. The value of your bond would have declined by some 75–80 percent.

The gigantic losses of "paper assets" like stocks and bonds during the 1970s have been matched by tremendous growth in the value of "tangible assets" during the same period of time. As the economy foundered, inflation climbed, and interest rates skyrocketed, the store of real value in assets such as real estate increased. While many pension funds and retirement plans have had their assets severely decimated by the loss of value in both stocks and bonds, others have been more fortunate. Some farsighted pension fund managers began positioning themselves in real estate years ago, and the strong growth in real estate over the last decade offset their stock and bond losses.

The decision for a pension fund to go into real estate is not necessarily an easy one. A number of factors about real estate investing are problematic for tax-sheltered pension funds. Just recently, the percentage of the largest pension funds—those with more than $500 million in assets—that had diversified into real estate reached the 35 percent level. Today, the percentage of large funds that have begun diversifying into real estate has climbed to 70 percent. There are two reasons for the tremendous growth in real estate investing in pension funds: one is that real estate, despite its problems for pension funds, has vastly outperformed other investment vehicles; the other is that the financial community has responded to the need for putting real estate in retirement plans by creating new forms of investment that largely avoid the problems of more traditional real estate vehicles.

What problems do traditional methods of investing in real estate create for retirement plans? One has simply been psychological. Traditionally, real estate has not been part of the pension fund program. With fiduciary responsibility for the future welfare of thousands of workers, pension fund managers have followed to an extreme the "prudent man" concept of investing. Legally, their investment decisions must be consistent with what a "prudent man" would do in the same situation. Thus, innovation comes slowly to pension fund management. When a fund manager makes the same decisions that have traditionally been made, and that the vast majority of other fund managers are currently making, it is hard to find fault with this cautious approach. But reality—in the form of horrendous losses in traditional investments—has shown fund managers that traditional investment vehicles are no longer the most prudent ones. At the same time, the innovators among the fund managers have been racking up gains in real estate. Thus, like a jumbo oil tanker that takes miles to slow its speed and shift direction, the major pension funds have gradually altered their view of prudent man investing. Once under way, this change picked up a great deal of speed, and participation in real estate jumped from 35 percent to 70 percent. Today, the pension fund

manager who has *not* diversified into real estate is subject to question, and those who have diversified are well within the consensus of prudent investing.

Another problem with putting real estate into retirement plans concerns their tax-sheltered aspect. Real estate is an extremely attractive investment on the personal side because it can offer tremendous tax advantages to the purchaser. While real estate is being held and its market value is actually climbing, the owner can nonetheless deduct depreciation in value from the income it produces, thus sheltering the income from taxation. What this means is that when you go out to purchase real estate, you pay not only for the value of the land and improvements, but for the value of the depreciation as well. This puts tax-sheltered entities at a disadvantage in purchasing real estate, because their income from real estate will not be affected by depreciation deductions. Thus the same parcel is of higher value to a taxable entity than it is to a tax-exempt entity, where depreciation is wasted.

The leverage involved in traditional real estate investments is also problematic for retirement funds. By paying only 20–40 percent cash and financing the rest of the purchase price, the taxable entity has important advantages, particularly in an inflationary environment. Since virtually all of the payments on a twenty- or thirty-year mortgage during its first few years are for interest rather than principal, the financing cost of leveraged real estate is in large part deductible against other income. More important, you have a larger asset to depreciate. At the same time, since one has only put up a percentage of cash against the value of the property, while the property is growing in value as a whole, a modest appreciation in the market value of the property can translate into a substantial gain in the investor's equity in the property. Because of the deductibility of interest expenses coupled with the enhanced depreciation deductions, and the principal of leveraged appreciation, almost all real estate investing outside of retirement plans has been done on a leveraged basis.

But leverage is not ideal for a retirement plan. Interest and depreciation expenses are not deductible, since a tax-exempt entity is not subject to ordinary income tax in the first place. Secondly, leverage is inherently risky, and goes against the principle of maintaining as much safety as possible in retirement investments. Moreover, if a leveraged property no longer produces income because of uninsured losses or vacancies during periods of economic duress, the investor has the large liability of paying off outstanding loans compounded by the ongoing outflow of financing costs to service these loans.

Finally, retirement plans are subject to a special kind of taxation applied to unrelated business taxable income (UBTI), under circumstances that can often occur with leveraged real estate investments. UBTI is a special tax created by the IRS to apply to a situation of unfair competition that arose when the founder of a particular company left an operating factory to a university endowment fund. Instead of selling the factory and investing the proceeds, the fund started managing the factory, and did rather well. In fact, the fund did so well that the factory's competitors began to complain that the competition was unfair: the tax-exempt fund was able to retain all of its earnings, and could profit on lower margins than its taxable competitors. Thus, regulations regarding unrelated business taxable income were created for all tax-exempt entities, and now most forms of leveraged real estate investments can create UBTI for retirement plans.

How to Avoid Problems of Real Estate in Retirement Plans

With all these drawbacks, it is easy to understand why some pension fund managers were reluctant to plunge into real estate. However, as the alternatives to real estate appeared bleaker and bleaker, ways were found to circumvent some of these difficulties. The simplest and most direct was to buy real estate for 100 percent cash. This reduces the problem of wasted depreciation, since depreciation becomes much less in proportion to the actual dollars invested. Further, it eliminates the exposure to UBTI, which applies only to leveraged real estate investments. In addition, real estate purchased with all cash has little risk exposure, as long as the investment is well selected and well managed. Furthermore, if a property has its income flow seriously reduced owing to adverse economic conditions, the owners are not exposed to the liabilities of large unpaid mortgages and cash outflow for loan maintenance.

A ploy that became popular with doctors, lawyers, and other professionals who administered their own pension plans, was to borrow from their retirement plan and use the proceeds to buy leveraged real estate as a personal investment. This meant that they could still take advantage of depreciation and deductible interest expenses against their personal income, and also take advantage of the augmented equity growth characteristic of leveraged real estate. At the same time, by paying a healthy rate of interst back into their plan, they could assure the steady growth of their retirement dollars. The only real disadvantage to this tactic is that it creates risk exposure for retirement dollars since you borrow your safe dollars from your pension plan to go into transactions that are leveraged and therefore more risky. You do not keep your safe money safe, but expose it to possible loss should economic conditions take an adverse turn. Should the leveraged investment not perform, the banks holding the mortgages will have to be paid off before your retirement plan.

Another form of real estate investing has become common under the pressures of high interest rates and lack of economical financing. You may have heard of this form of creative financing as it applies to the single-family residence market. Most people who go out to buy a home for their family in today's market are stymied by the extremely high interest rates of conventional mortgages. Millions of Americans who under more favorable economic conditions might have expected to purchase a home simply cannot afford the financing costs of today's market. The savings and loans, and the banks, are also frustrated by this situation, for if they cannot make loans, they cannot make a profit at their business. A way around this difficulty came with the development of what is known as a participating mortgage, whereby the bank, or savings and loan, gives the home purchaser a mortgage at several percentage points below prevailing rates, in effect covering the difference itself. In some cases, the bank may also pay part of the downpayment. This enables people who would otherwise be priced out of the market to buy a home. The bank does not do this out of altruism, however. In exchange for covering part of the finance costs of the mortgage, the bank participates in the equity growth of the property. It becomes a partner of the homeowner. In later years when the home is resold, the bank not only receives payout on the unpaid balance of the mortgage, it also takes a good portion of the capital gains resulting from appreciation in the market value of the home.

Major insurance companies and pension plans have been the most aggressive users of this concept of participating debt in the financing of large-scale income real estate investments. They will lend a developer-owner cash for real estate at a favorate rate of interest, below current market rates. Without these favorable rates, the developer-owner would simply be unable to proceed. In exchange for the favorable rate, the developer agrees to pay the lender "additional interest" equal to a certain percentage of the profits when the property is resold. The lender knows it will be receiving at least the stated rate of interest—which might range from 8–12 percent—for the term of the loan. The lender also knows that it will be receiving a substantial amount of additional interest down the line when the property is sold, but the exact amount of dollars is not predetermined. The amount will be known only when the ultimate resale price of the property is established and the lender collects its percentage of the capital gains resulting from the transaction.

More recently, some real estate firms have responded to the glaring needs of smaller pension plans, Keoghs, and IRAs. These smaller retirement plans do not have the capital to enter favorable participating debt situations themselves. Yet their need for diversification into real estate is just as strong as that of the giant pension funds. The result has been the creation of limited partnerships formed to invest capital by loaning money in the form of participating mortgages. Since this kind of partnership has been developed specifically to meet the needs of smaller tax-exempt entities, it is probably more appropriate for your IRA or Keogh than any other form of real estate investing. For that reason, this form of real estate investment deserves your attention.

By investing in such a partnership, you are putting your retirement dollars, in a position similar to the bank's, with many of the advantages the bank normally has in such transactions. To give you an idea of how this kind of investment works, let's look at a more or less typical partnership. Our limited partnership is established specifically for IRAs, Keoghs, and other retirement plans. Through your retirement plan, you may invest in it as a limited partner. Approximately 10 percent of invested dollars go to meet selling costs, commissions, and administrative fees, leaving the retirement partnership about ninety cents on the dollar to be invested. It then lends money to a general partnership that will use the funds borrowed to acquire properties it desires to purchase. The general partnership in turn gives a note to the retirement partnership for each property purchased. This note is secured by a deed of trust on the property. That is, the collateral for performance on the note is the property acquired by the general partnership. In most cases this is a first deed of trust because substantially all of the properties are purchased by the fee owner as if on an all-cash basis, with the retirement partnership as the sole lender.

The property owner is obligated to pay interest to the partnership at the initial rate of 10 percent on the money loaned. At least half of that 10 percent must be paid on a current basis, and any portion deferred also incurs an interest rate of 10 percent.

The notes issued to the partnership by the owner now all have a nine-year due date. The principal must be repaid in full before nine years have elapsed. This puts a horizon on the investment. The fee owner is motivated to add value and resell the properties well before the end of ten years in order to meet the obligations of the notes. As further protection, the owners put up $1,000,000 in cash and another $9,000,000 in personal notes to insure performance on the notes to the limited partnership.

When the properties are sold, all proceeds must go first to pay any outstanding interest or principal on the notes to the limited partnership. After all the debt obligations on the property have been settled, additional interest equal to 75 percent of the appreciation of the property upon resale is also paid to the limited partnership. Only after all the interest and principal on all the notes outstanding from the owners to the limited partnership have been paid in full can the owners begin to realize on their investment. In other words, the owners' share of appreciation on any properties sold earlier than others must be used to retire debt on the unsold properties, and cannot be retained by the owners.

What all this means is that every provision has been made to safeguard the limited partners' investment. They are looking for a basic return of 9 percent on the money they invest originally in the partnership (since only ninety cents on the dollar goes into the secured notes). They have assurance that their outstanding loans are to be repaid before the owners can realize a profit on their investment in the properties. And they have assurance that they will receive 75 percent of the equity growth of the properties in the partnership, paid out to the partnership as additional interest. What characteristics of this structure make it appropriate for retirement plans? Because the partnership is in the position of first lender, rather than owner, the issue of wasted depreciation does not arise. By lending the money to the owners instead of directly purchasing and managing the properties itself, the partnership is in the role of a long-term passive investor, and thus, in accordance with IRS regulations, is not subject to unrelated business taxable income. Being in the "banker's position" of lender also provides a great deal of safety for the capital of the partnership. Should the owners fail to perform on the notes, the partnership has first recourse to title of the properties, which are substantially unencumbered by any other mortgages.

Minimizing the Downside Risk

The fact that the partnership is a lender and its loans are secured by real estate, rather than some other form of business venture, means that downside risk, or risk of loss of principal, is minimized. We'll have more to say about the future of income real estate investing below, but it suffices to note here that the market value of income property is determined by a multiple of its gross revenues, and that the rental rates on established well-managed income properties virtually never go down. While we have seen the market values of single-family residences come down by 10 to 15 percent over the last eighteen months, the market value of large-scale income properties has steadily risen by 10–12 percent during the same period.

Because of the additional interest of 75 percent of the equity growth of the properties, the partnership is positioned to do well in an inflationary environment. Not only is the partnership's principal protected, but the purchasing power of the limited partners' investments will be maintained, and indeed, will probably grow over the years.

The fact that the fee owner uses money loaned from the partnership to purchase properties as if on an all-cash basis also means that favorable purchase terms can be secured. The fee owner does not have to find outside financing, or ask the sellers to carry back loans. Thus, a lower purchase price can often be negotiated. "All-cash" purchases also mean stability and security in the investment. Studies have shown that a pool of unleveraged real estate has the most predictable, consistent price levels over the years, with much less volatility than pooled stock or bond portfolios. We do not want the risk of values shooting up one year, then dropping drastically the next, as economic conditions change. We do want to know that we are maintaining a constant store of value with our investment, so that the purchasing power we put into our investment will still be there when we retire.

We estimate that although the owners are required to pay a minimum of half of the 10 percent initial interest due on the notes to the partnership, the actual current payments on initial interest at the beginning of the partnership will be in the neighborhood of 7 percent, and will gradually rise thereafter. This means that in terms of immediate, current cash flow back to the investor's retirement plan, this kind of participating mortgage partnership will have a higher yield than most traditional leveraged real estate partnerships, where much of the initial cash flows goes to pay for outside financing.

Two other features of the partnership are designed with retirement plans in mind. An annual liquidation option gives the individual retirement plan the opportunity to liquidate its partnership share once each year in accordance with a valuation formula derived from the current net asset value of the partnership as a whole. This feature is particularly important for the smaller IRAs and Keoghs, where changes in the circumstances of the individual covered by the retirement plan can necessitate the early withdrawal of funds from the plan. A second feature is the quarterly appraisal of the total worth of each partnership unit based on the net asset value of the partnership plus the current value of the 75 percent additional interest. This enables the individual investor to see the total value of his interest on a per unit basis, and facilitates the annual report to the IRS of total accrued value that is required of larger retirement plans.

Finally, the size of the pooled fund of the partnership, in excess of $100 million, means that the already low-risk exposure will be further reduced through diversification of the collateral for the participating note. The number of properties purchased in different geographical areas creates an overall stability of performance.

In sum, this kind of partnership offers predictable cash flow, relatively high current yield, low risk, predictable value, freedom from tax complications, safety of principal, and participation in equity growth through the additional interest feature. Designed specifically to allow retirement plans to obtain, in part, some of the benefits associated with real estate without the drawbacks of traditional leveraged ownership pooled funds, its features should serve as a standard of comparison with any form of real estate or real estate related investment you might be considering for your retirement plan.

Is Real Estate O.K. Now?

Is it advisable to consider real estate at all at this particular time? If you have recently attempted to sell a home on the single-family residential market, you may have noticed that there are few buyers around. The prices of single residences have fallen by 10 to 15 percent or more in some parts of the country. People who bought single residences at the peak of the market a few years ago will take a loss if they have to sell at this time. Does this indicate that real estate is a poor investment?

It is important to realize that prices in the single-family residence market and those in the income property markets are not related to each other. The only similarity that single-family residences have to income property is that both are made of bricks and mortar. What we read about single-family housing prices in the morning headlines simply does not apply to income properties.

Supply and demand is what determines prices in the single-family market. Since single-family residences do not produce income, and cannot be operated as a business, their prices are set solely by the number of buyers competing for the houses available on the market. At this time, after the huge run-up in prices during the late 1970s, followed by escalating mortgage rates that have made financing much more expensive than we are used to, there are simply few buyers for homes. Most of us have been priced out of the market. Thus, sellers are having to come down in their asking prices to reach a level buyers can afford.

The pricing of income properties is different. While prices of single-family homes have been dropping, prices of income properties have been consistently rising. Why

is this so, when both markets are subject to the same economic conditions?

For an analogy, we can look back at the gasoline crisis of the mid-1970s. You might think, "What a disaster for the automobile industry." But that generalization is only half true, for the same conditions that were a disaster for the American large auto industry created a bonanza for the Japanese small car industry. Toyota, Datsun, and Honda dealers simply could not import fast enough to keep up with the demand. They were asking hefty premiums over list price, and still had sixty- to ninety-day waiting lists of eager would-be buyers.

Prices of income properties are determined primarily by the amount of income produced. How many landlords do you know who have lowered their rents recently? The same high interest rates that prevent single-family residences from selling have also slowed the construction of income properties. Vacancy rates for apartments and for offices in most parts of the country are extremely low. Rents have been rising steadily. As rents rise, so do the values of income properties.

In the meantime, the Construction Materials Price Index has been rising at even a higher rate than the Consumer Price Index. What this means is that when interest rates come down again, and construction of new income properties picks up, existing properties built when construction costs were relatively much lower will have a cost advantage over new properties. It is likely that new properties will have to charge even higher rents to recover the costs of construction.

The Real Question to Ask

The question you should be asking is not whether income real estate in general is a good investment. Income real estate in general is a good investment. Income real estate has consistently maintained its store of value under all kinds of economic conditions, and there is no reason to think it will not continue to do so. The question you should be asking is, "Is income real estate a good investment for me, personally?" Every investor's goals and needs are different. What is appropriate for one person is inappropriate for another. Also, you should remember that the goals and needs of your tax-exempt retirement fund are distinct from your taxable personal investments.

How, then, do you decide if real estate, or any other form of investment, for that matter, is appropriate for your retirement plan? The investment decisions you make today are going to affect the rest of your life. They should not be made because of your "gut feeling," or because you are under the sway of a salesman's pitch. They should be made on the basis of solid, rational planning for the future, which takes into consideration your personal situation as well as the full range of economic scenarios the future might hold. It is well worth an hour or two of consultation with a qualified professional financial planner, trained to help people identify their financial goals and priorities and to guide them into appropriate investments.

Your retirement investments form a part of your overall financial program. In making decisions about what to put into your IRA or Keogh plan, you want to keep in mind not only the basic ground rules of retirement investing—safety of principal, preservation of purchasing power, appropriate liquidity, and avoidance of tax-deductible investments—but how your retirement investments mesh with your personal investing as well. If you own nothing but real estate on the personal side, then perhaps in interest of diversification you should be making other kinds of investments in your IRA. If, on the other hand, you own mostly stocks and bonds on the personal side, you should give serious consideration to real estate for your retirement plan.

If you have enough funds in your retirement plan to diversify into several investments, income real estate should definitely be among them. You should not make the error of ignoring a relatively safe, inflation-sensitive investment like real estate when inflation is in all likelihood going to be a part of the economic scene for the foreseeable future.

On the other hand, there is nothing sacrosanct about real estate in retirement plans. Diversification is always an important consideration. There is no reason why you should not vary your investment direction from year to year. If you put real estate in your IRA one year, you might buy into a mutual fund the next, and buy bonds another year. These decisions should be based not only on your personal financial plan, but also on the changing economic conditions that affect the desirability of different investments from time to time.

Twelve points should be kept in mind if you and your financial planner come to the conclusion that real estate should be included in your retirement plan:

1. Do not invest retirement dollars for highest possible yield, but consider safety, because lost retirement plan dollars cannot be replenished.

2. Try to find an investment vehicle that minimizes wasted depreciation.

3. Avoid unrelated business taxable income.

4. Is there proven professional management of the partnership? What is its record and reputation?

5. Will the properties be appraised annually (for pension plan annual reports to the IRS)?

6. Is there an identifiable stream of income?

7. Is the investment specifically tailored for retirement plans, or can individuals invest also (programs that try to be all things to all people usually end up being not much to everyone)?

8. Is there at least a minimum liquidity

feature (particularly important for small plans)?

9. Shop around; ask your financial planner to describe at least two or three alternative partnerships.

10. If there is a participating debt structure, do you know who the owners for the properties will be?

11. If there is a participating debt struc-

ture, are the partnership's loans to the owners first mortgages?

12. Is the investment regulated by the SEC?

Here is a final reminder: your retirement plan is a tremendously powerful investment vehicle, provided you do not lose money in it. Safety of principal should always be a primary consideration.

Chapter 35

What You Can Learn From Seminars

Wesley K. Wyatt is one of the nation's top life insurance salesmen, selling multi-millions of life insurance every year. He is president of the Financial Planning Corporation. Wyatt is the author of three books, *How I Became Mr. Insurance in My Community*, *Wes Wyatt's Seminar Selling System*, and *Seminar Selling*. He is also an active speaker and has appeared at professional gatherings throughout the United States, Australia, and New Zealand. He is a registered representative and is also licensed in variable annuities and real estate. He has won many top honors available to insurance professionals.

Wesley K. Wyatt, MDRT

Attending seminars is one of the best ways to gain knowledge on any subject that you are interested in. Seminars are given on just about every subject you can think of. Some seminars charge an attendance fee and some seminars are free. There are short seminars and there are long seminars. There are seminars that you have to travel a long distance to attend and there are seminars in your local area. There are information seminars and there are product seminars. There are seminars put on by just about anyone and everyone, individuals, companies, the government, and organizations of all kinds—so, take your pick. What do you want to learn and how do you want to profit?

Seminars are usually given by people with expertise in the area that the seminar is about. So, when you go to a seminar, have in mind what it is you want to learn from them, picking out those points during the seminar presentation that will apply to you and your use. That is how you can learn and how you can profit by attending seminars.

When you attend a seminar pertaining to a particular interest, you will find others there with the same interest, or like groups getting together to share and discuss ideas. Every occupation and interest group has seminars for these reasons. Salesmen use seminars to tell their story because it is easier to talk to twenty people at one time than it is to talk to one person twenty different times. Attending seminars is a time-saving device for both the people presenting them and for the people attending. You can usually learn the distilled information presented at a seminar much quicker and usually at less cost than you would by trying to seek out or research the information on your own. In this way, everyone's most precious commodity—time—is conserved. Your main objective in attending a seminar is to get information that is pertinent to the subject you are interested in. You want the seminar to help you identify your problem, show what happens if your problem is not solved—in other words, the alternatives—present solutions, and so on. In short, you attend the seminar to find solutions that you can act upon or to help you attain a certain goal.

By attending seminars, you will learn that a great deal of psychology is used by the speaker to motivate people to act or to react. The speaker knows that most people in the audience are really seeking a way to accomplish their goals, whether it be to acquire knowledge or products that will help them build on their plans and dreams. Most people attending seminars are searching for ways to better themselves financially or for the sheer pleasure of knowing more about a particular subject.

When attending a seminar, or thinking about attending one, you will want to find out as much as possible about the background and experience of the people putting it on as well as what will be offered when you do get there. Usually, advance information will be available to give you an idea of what to expect. If it isn't, call or write the people putting on the seminar and tell them what you are looking for and ask whether or not this is the seminar for you to attend. You might also ask for names of others who have attended in the past so you can contact them for their reaction. Don't be afraid to check everything out first, if at all possible. The more preparation you do if you are looking for something specific, the more you will get out of the seminar.

Who attends seminars? Just about everyone who wants to know more about what he or she is doing. Professionals spend a lot of time going to seminars to update their knowledge. If it works for them, it can work for just about anyone. Most people are so busy physically and mentally in their work that they do not have the time to keep up with all the latest advances in their profession. However, don't think you should only attend seminars pertaining to your profession. Seminars can be concerned with special interests or hobbies. You also attend seminars to learn and earn. Let's talk about a few of the things you can expect to learn by attending financial planning seminars. Everyone is concerned about money in these times of high interest and high inflation, especially about how to keep it! How can you tell if you are going to learn anything once you get to the seminar? Here are some things to look for in general.

Is the seminar well organized? How are you greeted when you arrive? Do you have to register or sign a guest book? Are you given any handout material as you arrive or during the seminar? Is the speaker knowledgeable and experienced or new and using a canned sales talk or slides and reading from a prepared script? What kind of presentation equipment and visual illustrations does the speaker have? Can he or she answer questions easily and correctly? Does the performance live up to the billing? Is the seating correct so that you can get the best out of the seminar? Is the lighting proper for the presentation? All of these things are important to you as an attendee. If care is not given to these details, chances are that you will not learn very much from the seminar.

In some seminars, visual aids are an important part of the presentation. If the speaker does not leave the viewgraph or slide on long enough for you to get the message, and the crowd is small enough to permit, you can usually ask the speaker to go back to it or ask to have it on long enough to write it down. Most seminars allow questions, which you should ask at the time you think of them, if at all possible.

When you go to a financial planning seminar, you are entitled to information about the economy and how it works. If all the seminar presenter does is go directly into a slide presentation and reading of a prepared script, you might as well walk out of the seminar if you are looking for someone knowledgeable who can help you work out your financial plans. If, for example, you are attending a seminar on real estate, your financial planning instructor

should have his or her license in real estate and should be abreast of what is happening in this area. He or she should be ready to share with you information about innovations such as the shared equity mortgage that recent tax laws have opened up. He or she should share with you thoughts and ideas on the real estate market and how you as an individual can participate in that market.

You may want to follow up on every facet of investing that you are interested in and attend separate seminars for each. In this way, you'll get more detailed information about each area, rather than bits and pieces crammed into one seminar. Whatever subject a seminar happens to be focusing on, try to glean from it some simple basics or fundamental financial planning concepts. It is helpful if you have a goal established beforehand, so that at the seminar you can look for specific ideas on how to achieve your financial goal.

Many self-help pointers can be picked up from financial planning seminars. For example, tax deferment is treated in many seminars, as is the role of creative financial planning, or methods of balanced financial planning. Some seminars will teach you how to avoid emotional buying decisions and how to recognize high-pressure tactics. This is an important lesson, because you have to take emotion and sentiment out of financial decisions before you can be objective about money.

Look for seminars that try to teach basic concepts about handling money. We all know that before we can climb the ladder of success we must first have the ladder. It is this ladder that you should be trying to acquire in your quest for financial independence by attending seminars. A financial planner's job is not only to tell you what he or she can do for you but, more important, what he or she can keep you from doing to yourself. This brings up another point—the people giving the seminar should have the ability, knowledge, *and* experience (or credentials) to follow through to help you with your planning. Do they have the time and will they take the time to help you, or are they just selling a product?

Finding the right seminar for you depends largely on the area of financial planning you are interested in. Here is a list of possible topics to look for:

How to design a discriminatory medical reimbursement plan for the principals.

How to use pension plans to reduce your federal estate tax liability.

How to design a discriminatory pension plan for stockholders-employees.

How to reward owners with a deferred compensation plan.

How to pass on your business to the oncoming generation.

How to reduce the cost of funding your buy-sell agreement.

How to use the personal holding company technique to freeze the future growth of the business.

How to administer new and existing pension plans at a minimum cost.

Be sure you find the seminar that will fit the problem you are trying to solve. Call around to find the specialist in your area in the field you are interested in. Ask him or her for an evaluation of the proposed seminar.

When you boil down a financial planning seminar, you usually find it covers four basic steps: wealth accumulation, conservation, protection through investments, and growth through business planning. Before you can apply the specific information the seminar gives about those steps, you must give some thought to certain aspects of your financial situation. As we said earlier, it is helpful if you come to a seminar with some idea of your objectives (that is, growth or income), as well as the risks you are willing to take, how your investments would be taxed, how they could be diversified, and the affordability of what you want to do. You should also give some thought to estate planning, the use of wills and trusts. With this thinking as a basis, you will be able to search out the seminars that can be of greatest help to you.

Remember that seminars are a good way to educate yourself. They can be an exciting part of your life by opening new avenues to building and retaining wealth and happiness.

Chapter 36

Straight Talk About Wills and Trusts

Graydon K. Calder is one of the country's leading financial planners. He is the president of Financial Planning Consultants (a Registered Investment Adviser), and a registered principal with a NASD broker/dealer. He is also the author of numerous articles and business courses dealing with every phase of the financial planning process. He has been a contributing editor and consultant to many periodicals such as *Money, Medical Economics,* and *Financial Planner.* Calder served on the national board of directors of the International Association for Financial Planning for five years and is a founder and past president of the San Diego Chapter of the association. Among the first forty-two persons in the United States to receive the Certified Financial Planner professional designation, he currently serves as national president of the Institute of Certified Financial Planners and is a member of the adjunct faculty of the College for Financial Planning. He was selected CFP of the Year in 1975 and again in 1982.

Graydon Calder, CLU, CFP

"Being of sound mind, I spent it all." That sums up what most people would like to do about their last will and testament. However, if you're one of those who would like to take a little more realistic approach to this area of financial planning, read on.

This chapter outlines some of the basic things you should know about wills and trusts in order to develop—with the help of your attorney—an estate distribution plan that fits your needs and desires.

First, here are a few caveats:

1. A number of complex legal concepts are oversimplified here for the sake of clarity. This is not a textbook for attorneys so legal jargon and technical detail are avoided wherever possible.

2. The rules governing this area vary greatly among the states.

3. Basket weaving, woodworking, and flower arranging are excellent do-it-yourself projects—estate planning is not. Therefore, it is strongly recommended that you work with a competent financial planner and a qualified attorney in your area.

Types of Wills

From the standpoint of how a will is created, there are essentially three types.

Holographic Will

A holographic will is one that has been written entirely in your own handwriting and that has been dated and signed. Not all states recognize holographic wills. Many wills of this type have been declared invalid by the courts for technical errors that may seem silly to you, but that nevertheless invalidate the will.

One of the most common errors made is having the will notarized. Remember, a holographic will must have nothing else on the paper other than your own handwriting. There's the classic case of the man who suffered a heart attack while staying in a motel room. Dragging himself to the dresser, he was able to open the top drawer, remove a piece of the complimentary stationery,

and write out his will before expiring. Everything was in proper order for a holographic will. It was dated, signed, and in the handwriting of the testator. Just one problem—the stationery was imprinted with the motel's letterhead, so the will was not admitted to probate.

Some states have an additional requirement that a holographic will must be found among the testator's valuable papers. What valuable papers consist of and where the testator kept his valuable papers are questions of fact. In one state that recognizes holographic wills, a will was found in the decedent's safe-deposit box in the bank, but there was nothing else in the box, so it was declared invalid by the probate court. Another court in the same state held that a holographic will found in the decedent's coat pocket hanging in his bedroom closet was found among his valuable papers and, therefore, valid, because that was where he kept his valuable papers.

An attorney once told of visiting a museum having a display of unusual wills. He thought the most bizarre was one written on the fender of a farm tractor. It seems the farmer was doing some work in his field with the tractor and became pinned under one of the tractor's wheels. When he realized that he was not going to be rescued, he managed to take out his pocket knife and scratch his will out on the fender of the tractor. The will was declared valid by the probate court and is displayed on a shelf in this museum.

Formal or Attested Will

Some people have the mistaken notion that a formal will is one that has been typewritten, but that's not true—a formal or attested will is essentially a "witnessed will." It may be typewritten or written by hand, but the element that distinguishes it from a holographic will is that it is witnessed. The law varies widely among the states, but following are a few major points to be kept in mind.

1. The testator must sign in the presence of

the witnesses or, if he has signed beforehand, he must acknowledge his signature in their presence. In most states only two witnesses are required, but a few states require three.

2. The witnesses must be informed that the document they are being asked to witness is the testator's last will and testament, but it's not necessary for them to read the will or even be familiar with its contents.

3. There's an important thing to keep in mind when the testator owns property in a different state than the one in which he's creating the will. In order to pass title to real property, the will must have the number of witnesses required by the state in which the real property is located.

4. Most states require that the testator and the witnesses all sign in each other's presence.

5. Apparently Pennsylvania is the only state that does not require witnesses at the time the will is executed. After the testator's death, two witnesses may swear to the signature of the testator.

Noncupative Wills

This is the most rarely used type of will and a very small amount of property passes under noncupative wills. A noncupative will is essentially an oral will communicated to witnesses at a time of probable death such as a battlefield situation. The oral will then needs to be reduced to writing by the witnesses and presented to the proper court within a specified number of days after the death of the testator. Some states only allow personal property to pass by a noncupative will.

Estate Distribution Problems

Most of us tend to procrastinate the preparation of a will or a trust. It's hard to say why this is so. Perhaps it's because it's associated with dying, which certainly isn't pleasant to contemplate. It's much more

fun to develop other phases of our financial plan such as funding for a future trip around the world or planning investments for a comfortable retirement but, since none of us get out of this life alive, estate distribution demands our attention.

There are basically two primary ways in which an estate shrinks at death, and a good estate-planning strategy aims at eliminating or reducing the impact of each.

Probate and Administration

Here we're talking about the expense, delay, and publicity associated with settlement of an estate through the probate courts.

Expenses consist primarily of attorney's fees, court costs, and, possibly, executor's fees. In most states the attorney's and executor's fees are set by statute, but many states have adopted the Uniform Probate Code and there are has been a trend in recent years toward charges for actual time and services rendered.

The exasperating *delays* incident to the probate process have been more irritating to many heirs than the expenses involved. Months and, sometimes, years go by before the typical probate estate is settled.

Probate records are a matter of *public record* and are available to anyone who would like to see what the decedent left and to whom he left it.

Death Taxes

The taxes to which an estate might be exposed at the death of the estate owner fall into two general areas: (1) the federal estate tax, and (2) the state inheritance tax. There is a basic difference in philosophy between these two taxes. The federal estate tax is a tax imposed by the federal government upon your right to leave property to others when you die. An inheritance tax, on the other hand, is a tax imposed upon the heirs' right to inherit property from the decedent. A few states have an estate tax, but most have an inheritance tax, and a few have no death taxes at all.

"Just a matter of semantics," you might say. "What difference does it make who the tax is imposed upon? The money to pay the tax comes from the estate in either case." True, but it's important for you to understand that the taxes are calculated in a completely different way. With an estate tax, all includible items are added up and, after certain deductions are made, the tax is calculated from a government table which, with its progressive rates, looks much like an income tax table—the larger the estate, the higher the tax bracket. After the tax has been calculated, you then subtract any unused unified gift and estate tax credit and come up with the amount of tax due.

An inheritance tax, on the other hand, is generally calculated individually for each heir. In most states the amount of inheritance that is exempt from tax and the tax rate on the balance is predicated upon the relationship of the heir to the decedent. Generally speaking, the closer the relationship, the larger the exemption and the lower the tax rate. Conversely, the more distant the relationship, the smaller the exemption and the higher the tax rate. For example, in one state an adult child may inherit the first $20,000 free of inheritance tax and the tax rate on the next $5,000 is 3 percent; then 4 percent on the next $25,000, 6 percent on the next $50,000, and so on. But a cousin would only receive the first $3,000 free of tax and the rate on the next $22,000 would be 10 percent and so on. Both of these areas have to be given consideration in developing an estate distribution plan.

Estate Distribution Strategies

Obviously, dozens of different strategies might be employed in planning for the ultimate distribution of your estate. It's beyond the scope of this chapter to deal with all of them, but we can briefly outline the four most commonly used.

Do Nothing

It may not make sense to refer to doing nothing as an estate distribution strategy, but, according to the American Bar Association, it's the approach that more than 80 percent of Americans have elected to take, if not by choice, then by default. When a person dies without leaving a valid will, he or she is said to have died intestate. Each state has a series of statutes generally referred to as the laws of intestate succession and these laws determine the distribution of your estate. If you insist on doing nothing about an alternative plan, at least become familiar with your state's current laws concerning intestate distribution in order to make sure they don't call for distribution in a manner totally inconsistent with your desires. Most people who make the effort to examine the order of intestate distribution in their state will no doubt be strongly motivated to adopt one of the other estate distribution strategies outlined below.

Create Simple Wills

The vast majority of couples who have created valid wills have had their attorney draft what is commonly referred to as a simple will. Typically, in this approach each person leaves everything to their spouse and, in the event the spouse does not survive them, they leave everything to their children. In addition to the obvious advantage of specifying the desired distribution of your estate, creating a will has many advantages over doing nothing, including the following:

1. You may nominate an executor or executrix and direct that they serve without bond. When you die without leaving a valid will, the probate court appoints an

administrator or administratrix, who must post a bond. The cost of a bond, even on a small estate, will usually far exceed the cost of having had a will drafted.

2. You may nominate a guardian for your minor children. If you die intestate the court will appoint a guardian who may or may not be the person or persons you would have preferred.

In the typcial family situation, the chances are that neither will would be used if something happened to one spouse since they probably hold title to all of their assets as joint tenants or tenants by the entirety. This method of holding title to property has a characteristic called "right of survivorship," which takes precedence over any dispositive provisions in a will.

The wills would be used, however, if something happened to both parents. Remember, one of the important reasons for making a will is to nominate a guardian for minor children. An important point to bring to the attention of all readers with minor children is that this person will become, not only guardian of their persons, but guardian of their assets as well. A court-supervised guardianship has to be established for your minor children and such guardianships have the following inherent drawbacks:

1. They are inconvenient, cumbersome, and expensive. Frequent petitioning of the court for needed actions and annual accounting to the court lead to legal fees and court costs as well as frustration and aggravation. I have watched a guardian petition the court for permission to spend guardianship funds on braces for a teenager's teeth. The judge told her to bring back three estimates from orthodontists in the area. She said she felt like a person getting three repair estimates for an automobile insurance company.

2. Each child's share of the estate is distributed in full at the age of majority, whether they're capable of managing it or not. I have seen substantial sums of money dissipated in a few months by young adults unaccustomed to managing property of any significant size.

3. If your wills called for your children to share equally, then, when distribution is finally made, it must be an equal distribution, regardless of how the relative needs of the children have changed over the years.

4. The way in which the assets of the guardianship may be invested is left up to the investment philosophy of the particular judge involved. I have presented guardianship investment plans to judges on several occasions and have been amazed at some of the responses. One that stands out involved the investment of $50,000 for a youngster who was twelve years old at the time. I worked out what I thought was a conservative and diversified investment plan with a balance between safety of principal, reasonable yield, and enough growth to hedge against inflation. The judge would not even let the guardian and me present the plan. He simply said, "My policy is Government Series E Savings Bonds." When I tried to voice my concerns about inflation and increasing college costs, he quickly interrupted and said, "You don't hear very well, do you?—Series E Bonds—and that's it."

Those of you who have minor children should discuss with your attorney the advisability of using the next estate distribution strategy, simple wills with contingency trust provisions.

Simple Wills With Contingency Trust Provisions

This is the approach that most attorneys take to avoid the guardianship problems mentioned above. A will of this type reads the same as the simple wills already discussed in that everything is typically left to the surviving spouse on the first death. The difference is that at the death of the surviving spouse, which is the "contingency" referred to, all of your assets are left to someone as "trustee" for the benefit of your minor children. This could be an individual (even the same person named as guardian of their persons), or it could be an institution such as a bank or a trust company.

The trustee draws his or her authority from the trust document itself, rather than from the court, so all the expense and inconvenience of court supervision are eliminated. The trustee can be given wide latitude in terms of making distributions according to need and there can even be delayed distribution provisions. For example, each child might be given one-third of his or her share at age twenty-one, another third at age twenty-five, and the remaining third at age thirty—three chances to "blow it," so to speak. You may also give the trustee whatever degree of investment discretion you desire.

The significantly greater flexibility available in this approach makes it worth the relatively small additional expense in initial legal fees for those with minor children. Once again, however, your specific situation should be discussed with a qualified attorney who is familiar with the laws in your area.

Wills With Marital Deduction Trusts

The fourth commonly used estate distribution strategy is most suitable for married couples whose estates are large enough to incur substantial estate or inheritance taxes. The basic concept in this approach is to minimize the total death taxes payable at each spouse's death.

The Economic Recovery Tax Act of 1981 (hereinafter referred to as ERTA) has considerably reduced the number of estates that will be subject to federal estate taxes and has made it possible to totally eliminate federal estate taxes on the death of the first spouse through an unlimited marital de-

duction. However, the larger exemptions (through the unified gift and estate tax credit illustrated in the table below) are being phased in gradually through 1987, so your taxable estate will probably grow as the credit increases.

YEAR	AMOUNT OF CREDIT	EXEMPTION EQUIVALENT
1982	$ 62,800	$225,000
1983	79,300	275,000
1984	96,300	325,000
1985	121,800	400,000
1986	155,800	500,000
1987 and later	192,800	600,000

Let's use an example to illustrate how this marital deduction trust concept works. For the sake of simplicity, we'll jump ahead to 1987 when the maximum credit of $192,800 (equivalent to an exemption of $600,000) is fully phased in and we'll assume that Mr. and Mrs. Brown have a total taxable estate of $1,200,000 and their wills *do not* contain marital deduction trust provisions. We'll also ignore any possible state death taxes. Mr. Brown dies in 1987.

Of course there will be no federal estate tax due upon Mr. Brown's death because of the unlimited marital deduction brought into play by ERTA. However, when Mrs. Brown dies, if we assume the taxable estate is still $1,200,000, her estate will have to pay federal estate taxes on $600,000 ($1,200,000 minus the $600,000 that is exempt). The tax would be roughly $192,800.

Obviously, this is an oversimplified example, but it illustrates the concept. What has happened in this situation is that Mr. Brown has overused the marital deduction. It would have been better for his estate to have incurred a tax of $192,800 because that is the amount of the credit against tax that would have been available to his estate. Let's see how that could have been accomplished by incorporating marital deduction provisions in his will.

Using that approach, the trustee Mr. Brown named in his will would be directed to split his estate into two trusts, usually called "Trust A" and "Trust B." Sometimes they are referred to as the "survivor's trust" and the "residuary trust." The wording of the will would be such that sufficient property would be placed in Trust B (the decedent's trust or residuary trust) to incur a federal estate tax of $192,800. That's just enough to be offset by the credit.

Mrs. Brown will receive all the income from both trusts and will normally be given complete control of Trust A, including the right to revoke it in whole or in part. However, her rights in Trust B need to be more limited. As already mentioned, she may receive all the income from Trust B. She may also be given the right to withdraw the greater of 5 percent of the principal, or $5,000 each year and, in addition, the trustee may be given the discretion to pay out of the principal of Trust B any additional amounts that are necessary for Mrs. Brown to maintain the standard of living to which she was accustomed prior to Mr. Brown's death. She could even be given what is called a "special or limited power of appointment" over Trust B, which would allow her some flexibility in changing the ultimate beneficiaries.

The important point is that, upon Mrs. Brown's death, only the amount in Trust A would be subject to federal estate tax. In our oversimplified example, that amount would be $600,000, on which the tax would be $192,800. Her estate would have a credit of $192,800 against that, hence no tax due. This technique, then, has allowed almost $200,000 more to go to the Browns' heirs rather than to the government.

You can see that by 1987 it will be possible for a man and wife, with proper planning, to pass a taxable estate of $1,200,000 to their heirs without federal estate taxes. As estates become larger than this amount,

a judgment will have to be made about whether to totally avoid federal estate taxes at the first death (by using the maximum marital deduction) with a higher tax at the second spouse's death, or to split the tax burden up over both deaths. This can be a very complex matter and you should seek the assistance of your CFP, CPA, and attorney in arriving at a decision.

Warning

If you already have trust provisions of this type in your wills and the wills were created prior to September 10, 1981, it's very important for you to consult your attorney about the necessity of changing the trust provisions to qualify for the new unlimited marital deduction because the unlimited marital deduction under the new law will not apply to wills or trusts executed prior to thirty days after the date of the law's enactment unless the will makes specific reference to an unlimited marital deduction, or unless state law provides that maximum marital deduction clauses transfer the unlimited marital deduction amount.

Utilizing the marital deduction trust strategy in your wills can eliminate or substantially reduce federal estate taxes. But for this technique to work, it's imperative that you no longer hold title to your assets as joint tenants. Remember, property held in joint tenancy has a characteristic called "right of survivorship" and passes outside of a person's will. If you have marital deduction provisions in your will to minimize death taxes, these provisions will only be effective if you let property pass through your will.

By now you have probably realized that with this technique you have solved one problem and created another. When you held your property as joint tenants, you avoided the expense, delay, and publicity of the probate process, but may not have minimized the impact of death taxes. Incorporating marital deduction provisions in your wills minimizes death taxes but, since this is a testamentary trust (contained in a will), you're back into the probate mess. "Hey," you're saying, "There's gotta be a better way." You're right.

The next estate distribution strategy is a way to "have your cake and eat it too."

Taking the Mystery Out of the Living Trust

Almost everyone nowadays has heard of the living trust as a modern financial planning tool. However, most people have only a vague understanding of what a living trust is, and few are aware of the substantial benefits it can provide.

Very little meaningful information in the area has been made available to the general public. The preponderance of literature on the subject falls into one of two categories:

1. Promotional material distributed by banks and other institutions who would like to act as trustees for a fee.

2. Highly technical articles written by attorneys and accountants, usually dealing with the use of a living trust in a certain specialized situation.

Literature that falls into the latter category is obviously of very little value to the average individual. Much of the material referred to in the first category is well done, but almost always concentrates on the benefits one will receive by using the sponsoring institution as trustee and usually only encourages the placing of a portion of one's assets, such as a securities portfolio, in the trust.

What Is a Living Trust?

Let's explore for a moment the use of a living trust as a holding vehicle for virtually all of one's assets, essentially a "will substitute." There is really nothing mysterious

about a trust. All trusts involve a three-way relationship—the creator of the trust, or *grantor*, places property, such as stocks, bonds, real estate, bank accounts, mutual funds, and so forth, into the legal ownership of a *trustee* who holds and manages the property for the benefit of someone called a *beneficiary*. Sometimes the grantor is referred to as the trustor or settlor. The trustee manages and distributes the property according to instructions that the grantor has spelled out in a legal document know as a declaration of trust or a trust agreement. Each of the three parties referred to above could be different individuals. For instance, Mr. Jones (grantor) might transfer legal title on some property to Mr. Brown (trustee) to be invested and managed for the benefit of Mr. Jones's son (beneficiary). However, Mr. Jones may also place property in trust for the benefit of himself and his wife and he may act as trustee, by wearing three hats, if you will.

There are various ways of classifying trusts. Trusts may be classified as *revocable* (may be amended or cancelled), or *irrevocable* (cannot be amended or cancelled). Trusts may also be classified as *inter-vivos* (created during life, hence "living trust"), or *testamentary* (created under one's last will and testament after death). The type of trust we are discussing in this section is a *revocable living trust*, one that is created right now while the grantor(s) is alive and one that may be amended or revoked at any time before the death of a grantor.

Let's use an example. Assume that Mr. and Mrs. Jones as grantors transfer title to virtually all of their property—securities, bank accounts, real estate, life insurance, and so on—to Mr. Jones as trustee of the Jones Family Trust. Mr. and Mrs. Jones will still need wills, but they will be brief "pour-over" wills meant to pick up the odds and ends of their estate that may not be in the trust and pour them over into the trust at their death. They would also nominate in their wills a guardian for any minor children (guardian of their persons, not their property). But all the dispositive provisions relative to their property are contained in the trust document, not in their wills.

A successor trustee is named to serve in the event Mr. Jones dies or becomes unable to serve. The successor trustee could be Mrs. Jones or another individual, or it could be a bank or trust company.

No Income Tax Savings

How much does such a trust save the Jones family in income taxes? Not a dime. Living trusts are not devices for saving income taxes. Although the trust will have its own tax identification number, it is not required to file an income tax return. The "conduit" principle is used for income tax purposes, which means that all items of income retain their character and are simply passed through to the beneficiaries who, in this example, are also the grantors. All of these items of income, deductions, and credits should then be reported on Mr. and Mrs. Jones's Form 1040.[1]

If the Jones family has a large enough estate to make death taxes a problem, then their attorney may incorporate marital deduction trust provisions to minimize the impact of federal estate taxes and state inheritance taxes. These savings may be substantial. However, as we outlined in the previous section, these same provisions could be included in their wills. What benefits, then, would Mr. and Mrs. Jones be looking for in establishing a living trust?

[1]The Internal Revenue Service used to require trusts of this type to file an "informational" fiduciary tax return (Form 1041), but this is no longer necessary for trusts created after January 1, 1981. If you already have a trust of this type created before January 1, 1981, you may elect the new procedure by filing a final Form 1041 for the current tax year. The final Form 1041 should be clearly marked with a notation on the front of the form, "Final return pursuant to Reg. 1.671-4 as adopted by Treasury Decision 7796."

What Are the Benefits?

First, assets held in a living trust completely bypass the probate process with its court costs, attorney's fees, exasperating delays, and publicity. The late Bing Crosby's will listed cash gifts of $400,000 to fourteen relatives and friends, but the bulk of his estate was governed by a living trust. Each of the bequests made in his will is a matter of public record, but the terms of his living trust are secret. Only those assets not contained in his trust were subject to the expenses and delays of the probate process.

Secondly, Mr. and Mrs. Jones will have the peace of mind that comes from knowing that all of their financial affairs will be managed for them by a successor trustee in the event they become unwilling or unable to manage their own affairs. They may wish to do extended traveling during their retirement years, or some physical incapacity may render them incapable of managing their own financial affairs. In the absence of a living trust, such an occurrence would necessitate the establishment of a court-supervised conservatorship. Such conservatorships are expensive, cumbersome, and inconvenient. They have all of the same disadvantages of a court-supervised guardianship for minors that we discussed earlier.

The living trust concept should be especially appealing to single individuals such as widows and widowers since they do not have a spouse with whom they can jointly register property or who can take care of their affairs in the event of incapacity.

Do you need an attorney to establish a living trust? You definitely do. Each state has different statutes concerning such trusts and drafting such an instrument is a technical job best left to a professional. It's not surprising that many attorneys are somewhat less than enthusiastic about living trusts, especially those who derive a great deal of their income from probate work. However, many attorneys are knowledgeable about living trusts. If you have difficulty finding one in your area, contact a Certified Financial Planner in your area and he or she will be able to give you several names.

To illustrate the concept of the living trust as a holding vehicle for virtually all of a family's assets, we can compare the family trust to a large truck. You and, if you are married, your spouse (grantors) have loaded all of your assets into this truck. You are the driver of the truck (trustee) and sitting next to you in the cab is a relief driver (successor trustee). You have a road map to follow (the trust document). If you become ill or are unable to drive, your relief driver just puts you up in that bed at the rear of the cab, picks up the road map, and slides into the driver's seat.

If you die, your relief driver just reaches over and pushes you out the door, picks up the road map, and keeps "right on truckin." The truck doesn't even slow down for the probate courts.

Visualize a couple of people with wheelbarrows running along beside the truck to pick up any odds and ends of your estate that aren't in the truck. They represent your "pour-over wills." You need these wills for several reasons, including the following:

1. To nominate a guardian for any minor children.

2. To make disposition of your books, furnishings, and other personal effects that are really not practical to put in a trust.

3. To pour over into your trust any items that you may have forgotten to register in the name of the trust.

4. To pour over into your trust any assets of your estate that you didn't even know about. For example, let's say you met death by being run over by a bus. Your estate would probably bring a wrongful death suit against the bus company and would most likely collect a substantial sum

in settlement that would not be in your trust.

It's extremely important that you load the truck. It is amazing to see how many people have created trusts of this type a long time ago without ever changing title to any of their assets. Sometimes their attorney helped them change title to their real property at the time the trust was created, but they never got around to changing the registration on other things like stocks, bank accounts, mutual funds, or limited partnerships. Sometimes, everything was transferred at the time the trust was created, but then the grantor-trustees have been careless about registering subsequently acquired items in the name of the trust. Remember, the living trust will only be effective in avoiding probate to the extent you have transferred property to it.

Some people think that the establishment of a living trust will complicate their lives. This is not really true. Certainly the trustee of such a trust needs to keep accurate records, but that's something you should be doing now anyway. The major drawbacks to a living trust are the initial cost (usually two to four times the cost of ordinary wills), and the minor inconvenience of reregistering each of your assets in the name of the trust. All in all, however, the advantages of the living trust, when it's appropriate, far outweigh its disadvantages.

Certainly, the use of a revocable living trust as the basic framework for a financial plan is not for everyone, but it is a modern financial planning concept that everyone should discuss with an attorney in some detail. Its many benefits are too important to ignore.

Conclusion

Planning a strategy for the disposition of your property after you die is certainly not one of the most pleasant aspects of financial planning. It is, nevertheless, one of the critical elements in a financial plan and probably one of the ones most likely to be put off. Taking the "head in the sand" approach won't make the problems go away. You should work closely with your financial planner and attorney to develop a plan that fits your needs. You'll enjoy much more peace of mind after you have this part of your financial plan in order.

Part 10

Editor's Notes:
Peace of Mind:
The Big Plus

*T*he really big dividend that comes from doing the financial planning so necessary in today's society is the good feeling and peace of mind that it brings you. The psychological effect on most people is tremendous. They find themselves able to enjoy life more, even though they might be forgoing certain extravagant pleasures in favor of putting more aside for the future. Many of them can concentrate more effectively on their work and family.

In line with this theme of peace of mind is the confidence about insurance claims that Dave Goodwin imparts through the details he presents in Chapter 37. Peace of mind also comes from the people we know we can turn to for advice, and Bob Hightower in Chapter 38 discusses the various types of advisers available to assist you—accountants, attorneys, trust officers, stockbrokers, and, of course, financial planners. In Chapter 39 Richard Arnold conveys some of the background information that will help you understand the forces of change in our modern economy and perhaps help you feel less uninformed about the modern financial industry. Chapter 40 follows up with a series of interviews with Louis Kelso, developer of capital theory economics.

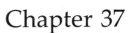 Chapter 37

Dave Goodwin is one of the nation's leading consumerists in all forms of insurance. After being in the insurance business for ten years, he sold his agency, and for the last twenty-two years has served as consultant to both buyers and sellers of insurance. He has taught at the University of Miami, served on the Consumer Advocate's Advisory Board, served on the Florida legislature's Ad Hoc Committee on Automobile Insurance, testified by invitation before state legislative bodies, and addressed the Consumer Participation Subcommittee on the National Association of Insurance Commissioners. He is author of *Stop Wasting Your Dollars*, and of the syndicated newspaper column, "Insurance for Consumers." He was insurance editor of *Boardroom Reports* and his work has appeared in numerous consumer publications. He has appeared on radio and television shows nationwide as an insurance expert and is a frequent podium speaker. Goodwin has been a member of the Board of Regents, College of Financial Planning, an auto section committeeman of the American Risk and Insurance Association, and chairman of the insurance committee of the Miami Beach Taxpayers' Association.

Insurance Claims—Don't Forfeit Your Rights

Dave Goodwin

In general this book deals with "happy" subjects: how to accumulate, multiply, protect, preserve, transfer, enjoy, and extend money and assets. Many would consider the subject of insurance claims glum. But it need not be glum. After all, the purpose of buying any form of insurance is to enjoy the benefit of its protection if or when it's needed. Collecting an insurance claim can and should be (if the cause of the claim can be set aside emotionally) a routine and satisfying experience. Too often, however, it's the reverse, often because the claimant goes about it ineffectively.

This chapter offers a primer on insurance claims. It should be kept with your policies, for you may be making a claim soon. Remember, there are many types of claims. Here are some of the common occurrences involving insurance:

Hospitalization and medical care

Income lost owing to sickness or accident

A workers' compensation claim

Damage to, or theft of, your auto

An accident involving your auto or someone else's

Travel accidents on land, sea, or air

Home, school, or sport accidents

Loss or damage of home or personal property

Liability claims against you involving home, auto, boat, business, and so on

Liability claims you may make against others for injury or property damage

Dental care

Expenses for legal advice

Any of these claims, not to mention the death benefit of a life insurance policy, can be a complex matter. You should know, however, that you can take certain steps to minimize chances of trouble, anguish, and hardship in the handling of insurance claims.

Most claims are settled promptly and fairly, but too often people get less than they should. Sometimes it's the insurer's fault, sometimes the claimant's. Don't assume that because you've had satisfactory claims experiences before, they'll all be easy. Times and insurance philosophies change. Many companies have tightened their claims practices from "liberal" or "fair" to "tight and fight."

Small claims are sometimes settled fast and liberally as a means of buying goodwill and sales referrals by companies that may do just the opposite on large claims. The president of a large medical-expense insurer once boasted: "We automatically deny any claim over $2,000." Some people sue, but many others would rather settle than fight, and they simply forfeit some or all of their benefits.

To get decent claim service, the first step, then is to consider how and where you get your insurance. Other chapters in this book touch on those subjects. The second step is to develop the right perspective. You must realize that all policies are legal contracts. Every policy contains conditions, restrictions, and exclusions. The burden of proof is on you to establish that (1) the policy covers what you're claiming, and (2) the ammount you're claiming is proper. Many people wrongly concentrate on the second—the dollar settlement—and ignore the first—establishing that coverage applies.

When You Have a Claim

On first-party claims (by you, your family members, or other insureds) for reimbursement of property damage or medical bills, your own policy will be involved. Have your agent confirm coverage when his or her office takes the initial claim information. Ask whether there might be coverage complications or questions; if there are, see if they can be clarified before the claim hits the adjuster's office.

It pays to be careful and skeptical. Even agents who want to help their clients can make honest mistakes; for example, some agents (or their office employees) have inadvertently told people that policies don't cover certain situations when in fact they do. If you're told that a policy doesn't cover a situation, feel free to ask for the page and paragraph relating to the loss. If you have doubts, have it checked by another agent, a public adjuster, or an attorney familiar with that type of policy.

If the policy language denies coverage, it often pays to check with experts, particularly when large amounts are involved. One auto policy, for example, said that medical expense benefits would be payable only if the named insured (in this case, the head of the family) was driving at the time of an accident. When a son housed in college had an accident while driving one of the family cars 400 miles from home, the claim was denied. His father took the policy to the insurance commissioner's office, and the company not only paid this claim but was barred for using such restrictive clauses. The policy, it was learned, had not even been approved for public consumption, although many people had bought it.

Keep all advertising, brochures, company or agent proposals, and correspondence relating to your policies. A recent court case was decided in favor of an insured, despite clear and overwhelming policy language against him, because he convinced the court that a sales brochure's language implied coverage that really wasn't there.

In the case of borderline claims, or even some that may seem far from coverage, it pays to delve deeply and pursue all possibilities. In one such situation, an accident-only policy (specifically excluding claims due to sickness) paid its benefits for a man who had a heart attack! The insured had an accident and was lying prone. Paramedics picked him up to put him in an ambulance. While he was being carried, he thrashed around and had a coronary resulting in large medical bills and death. Even though the accident was a separate occurrence, the court connected the two and the man's family collected.

If it's a borderline claim, the odds are in your favor that you'll win. Most courts take the attitude that unclear or ambiguous policy language affecting a claim should be resolved in favor of the policyholder, since in most cases the insurer sold the contract it had created without offering the buyer a chance to negotiate the wording.

Now, having established what coverage you have, pause and consider—perhaps discuss with your insurance adviser— whether or not you should make the claim. There are some claims you should ignore and some you must not ignore. In either case, you should weigh the factors before proceeding.

If there's a possibility that you'll be sued by others, you must report the occurrence promptly. If you don't, your insurer has the right to refuse to defend you or to pay in your behalf if you lose. Similarly, if medical payments to others are involved, you should report the incident, even though you may feel sure that you won't be sued. Most policies place time limits within which you must make claims if possible. If you pass the limit on a claim you want to make, file it with an explanation that you didn't realize you had coverage (or whatever the reason may be). In some cases, claims have been paid years after filing deadlines expired.

To Make (or Not to Make) a Claim

First-party losses not involving the chance of a lawsuit should be weighed as to whether or not they should be claimed. Here are the factors when you have a choice in making a claim:

1. *Will it invite cancellation of your policy?* Your agent should be your guide. Insurers expect claims, of course, and usually take them in stride. But some claims situations invite trouble and cancellation. For example, those involving gross or repeated

carelessness on your part, or conditions inviting further losses (bad electrical wiring) or questionable circumstances (why do you repeatedly lend your car to friends who have accidents?) or false statements (like the "disabled" claimant working full time in his office).

Noncancellable and guaranteed renewable policies, group insurance, and certain other policies cannot be cancelled for individual claim action (short of fraud), and in such cases you don't need to worry about the cancellation factor.

2 *Even if it does invite possible cancellation, should the claim be made anyway?* Generally, if enough money is involved, the answer is yes. Check the availability and price of a replacing policy if your current coverage should be lost. You should also calculate the net effect of your loss on your income tax (assuming you itemize your deductions) if you absorb it. Get Publication 547, *Tax Information on Disasters, Casualty Losses, and Thefts,* free from the IRS. The rules and figures change from time to time, so don't rely on memory in making your decision; get the current facts. If your net, after-tax loss figure is down to a marginal amount, consider the value of your time in making the claim. You may decide it's not worth doing.

Reporting the Claim

There are three important ingredients in an insurance claim: promptness, clarity, and correctness.

To help yourself in each of these areas, make notes about what you've done and when, starting with the occurrence itself. Be sure to gather facts, the names and addresses of witnesses, estimates of damage, and other pertinent data. If a crime was involved—burglary, theft, robbery, larceny, assault, and so on—notify the police. Some policies require police notification and reports even if you're abroad.

Some adjusters settle even if "polizia" is the only word they can recognize on a form.

Report only what you know or what you've seen. If you offer guesses, identify them as such. Don't invent little fibs that make you look better; they can boomerang and cost you all or part of your benefits. In most cases, stretching the truth isn't even necessary. Claimants would get just as much—maybe even more—with the plain facts. (Of course, you're entitled to get the highest possible legitimate estimates for repair or replacement.)

If your claim involves your home or personal property, you should have a written, photographic, or cassette inventory to establish what you had. Good documentation is helpful to an adjuster and valuable to you.

Your next immediate duty—yes, it's dictated in your policies—is to try to prevent further loss or damage. If your windows are smashed, get your insurer's approval for immediate boarding up at its expense. If your property is wide open to looters, ask about protecting it. Do not dispose of your damaged property; even if it's worthless rubble, your adjuster has the right to inspect it. Keep it until you're sure it's all right to remove it.

Working With an Adjuster

The word *adjuster* doesn't have to mean adversary. An adjuster is simply doing a necessary job, hoping to keep claims payments fair. You wouldn't want (nor could you afford) to buy insurance from a company that settled everyone else's claims without an adjuster, so your claim needs to be adjusted, too.

In some cases, the adjuster approves payment of even more than you ask for. This happens, for example, when your estimate for auto damage (or home, or other property) omits something you're entitled to. It may be pure oversight on the part of your estimator and you may have already agreed to settlement when the adjuster boosts the claim.

More often, however, he or she will be concerned about inflated estimates, exaggerations, even outright lies. It's often considered "fair" to get anything that can be gotten from insurance companies by whatever means. Your adjuster may have acquired a thick skin and he may tend to handle your claim matter-of-factly or even coolly. After all, he's human and he often deals with people who are under stress.

Be prepared when you meet with the adjuster. Have your facts in hand. If you're not sure of current values of, say, furniture you bought years ago, do your pricing and homework before your meeting. If you force him or her to make unnecessary repeat calls, you won't be helping your claim. If there's the slightest doubt about anything, review it with your agent before seeing the adjuster. Don't give the adjuster wrong or incomplete statements or hazy facts, thinking you can change them later.

Don't bluff and bluster. He's probably heard it all before. Name-dropping, "casual" mention of your lawyer, big-shot talk—none of it overwhelms him. If you want to use the leverage you have—volume of business with his company, for example—it's best done through your agent, not the adjuster. The agent can speak to the adjuster's superiors, if necessary.

While being careful, assume you'll get a fair settlement until proven otherwise. Later, if it looks as if things aren't going your way, keep the claim open and consider the other avenues we discuss below. Don't waste time. You won't wear them down because time is the insurance company's ally. As weeks and months pass, the company and the adjuster will still be functioning normally; you are the one who will be tied up while settlement dollars earn interest for the insurer.

On the other hand, you need not take any abuse from adjusters. If he or she continually breaks appointments, or is chronically late, call your agent or the claims manager. Your time is valuable, too. If he's gruff or threatening, accurately report his remarks and attitude. If you can prove he's wrong in estimates or statements of value, refute him firmly but politely.

Adjusters make mistakes, of course, not necessarily out of intent or even company directives. Sometimes it is out of ignorance, sometimes out of innocent misjudgment; whatever the cause, a fair company won't begrudge your right to pursue a fair or maximum settlement.

In working with damaged autos, many adjusters use the "Blue Book" or a similar price guide to establish value. Too often, people take such values as a ceiling. Not so! Your auto's value may be much higher than any guide's, and if you have bills or proof, then your settlement should be much higher

Of all the claims in the world of insurance, the one considered easiest to handle (except for the insured) is the last—the death claim. Generally all that's required is a death certificate and some simple policy information. In today's hectic world, however, even such simple claims can have complications, and there are some steps we can take both as insureds and as future beneficiaries.

Millions of dollars are unpaid to beneficiaries because they don't know which life policies existed or which companies carried them. Anguished widows and children—certain that insurance existed—try vainly to locate policies or carriers. The best remedy, of course, is for each insured to have lists of all his policies in the hands of his beneficiaries, lawyer, accountant, business associate, friend, or relative. Lacking that, survivors can look for clues:

In checking account records for premium payments.

In any life application for a list of all other policies then in force.

In bank deposit records for possible dividend checks.

With the accountant or lawyer or business associates, past and present.

With all insurance agents (including property-casualty), stockbrokers, and financial planners the deceased may have known.

With the deceased's doctor(s) for inquiries they may have had about insurance.

Through the Medical Information Bureau (M.I.B.), which serves as a clearinghouse for many insurers (P.O. Box 105, Essex Station, Boston, Mass. 02112), phone (617) 426-3660).

But even if all policies are known, there can be problems. Recently the newspapers told of a man whose body was found in such a state that positive identification was impossible. He had three life policies in three different companies. Two companies paid after they were able to conclude that it was probably their insured's body; the third held out. A company may pay after a seven-year "mysterious disappearance" presumption of death, or it may pay sooner under pressure from an effective agent. Or it may go to court.

What can we learn from tough claim situations? The real lesson is that claims are settled best when there are no puzzles to solve, no presumptions to be made or shattered. There will always be some sticklers, but most can be avoided by simple precautions. If you're flying a commercial line using a ticket in someone else's name, be sure your family knows. Try to avoid situations that could result in a "mysterious disappearance" claim with burdens of proof on your beneficiaries. A simple step is to mail yourself (or your family) a postcard in your handwriting. "Bob Jones decided to stay longer, so I'm using his ticket to Chicago," it might read. If Bob Jones's name appears on the casualty list of that flight, your family's claim shouldn't be extraordinarily delayed or denied.

Handling Problems

Whether claims are big or small, whether they involve property, health, or death, the adjuster simply wants to close them out and go on with the rest, for there are always more coming. Some are so routine that you may not even see an adjuster; he'll handle it by phone and mail. Others may simply be settled by your own agent, for some carriers grant draft-issuing authority for first-party claims up to, say, $500.

While most companies and adjusters want to be fair, there are some who are not and you should be prepared for them. Some learn to use unfair or illegal tricks. One such approach, for example, was to offer a total-loss claimant a short settlement for no valid reason. If the claimaint's policy called for a $50,000 settlement, the adjuster might offer a $40,000 claim draft. If refused, he could "find" another in his briefcase for, say, $44,000. If that was still refused, he could produce another for $48,000—his final offer. Knowing that it's a valid claim for $50,000, he also knows that few attorneys or public adjusters would take the case for a chance at a maximum improvement of only $2,000 to be shared with the claimant. He also knows that most claimants need the money promptly and will forfeit some benefit to get it.

What recourse do you have in such a situation? Plenty! First, inform your agent. Most agents don't know there's a problem with a claim unless you tell them. A good agent won't tolerate such client abuse and will take care of it. Or complain directly to the insurance company president.

Another weapon against unfair adjusters is a complaint to your state insurance commissioner. If you document an adjuster's questionable tactics, he may be in danger of losing his adjuster's license or being otherwise penalized by the state. Often, a call from the commissioner's office will resolve the problem.

If the problem remains, consider a public

adjuster. In situations demanding more time or expertise than you have in wrestling with a tough adjuster, a public adjuster may well be worth the fee (usually 10 percent of the settlement, scaled down for larger claims, but always negotiable). In some parts of the country, public adjusters are used routinely by many, even when no problem exists, but generally it isn't necessary to call them in immediately, especially if you have an effective agent working on your behalf. Some companies consider the immediate introduction of a public adjuster as a sign of hostility.

You should consider an attorney if a great deal is at stake, if your claim seems headed for court, if both sides have gone as far as possible and there's still a wide breach, or if all else has failed. When possible, retain an attorney who is well versed in your type of claim situation.

Settling Claims

You can settle your claim piecemeal if it makes sense. If an extended medical claim runs for more than a month, you can submit bills as you go along and get benefits monthly. You don't need to wait until the incident is concluded before getting paid; just be sure that your claim drafts don't indicate "full or final payment" until appropriate. Similarly, some auto adjusters have delayed paying the collision coverage until, as they put it, "we can finalize the medical payments, too." You don't need to accept that kind of delay; go over his head. You can agree to close out parts of a claim while keeping other parts open.

When you are paid, it will probably be with a draft instead of a check. The two look very much alike but the difference is that the issuer—the insurance company—has the right to change its mind when the draft arrives at its bank. This may happen when higher officers review your claim and decide it was incorrectly settled. Don't delay in depositing claim drafts!

Even after your claim is closed, however, you may not be through. Some policies are reduced by the amount paid on a claim, and original coverage is not automatically regained in such cases. For example, if you carried a $10,000 jewelry floater and recovered $6,000 on a claim, after settlement only $4,000 of coverage would remain unless you add—for an additional premium—coverage for the replacing jewelry. This would be true even if your insurer replaced your lost item in lieu of a cash settlement. After settlement of any claim, review your policy with your insurance adviser and confirm that it covers you properly.

The best defense against unfair settlements of claims is care—care in avoiding accidents or losses, care in how and where you buy your insurance, care in gathering and presenting facts. Mixed with a dose of diplomatic firmness and leverage, your claims problems should be minimal or nil.

Chapter 38

How to Find Experts and Advice

Robert Hightower, CFP

W. Robert Hightower is one of the foremost financial planners in the nation, specializing in tax and investment strategies. He is chief executive officer of W. Robert Hightower Associates and is a registered principal with the National Association of Securities Dealers. He is also president and chairman of HI Securities, Incorporated, and a well-known lecturer and author. Hightower is a licensed real estate broker, a licensed insurance broker, and a past member of the Board of Regents of the College for Financial Planning. He was one of the first in the country to receive the designation of Certified Financial Planner, and served two consecutive terms as president of the Institute of Certified Financial Planners.

The giving and accepting of financial advice is a many faceted and interesting exercise in decision making. The purpose of this chapter is to identify people and professions that frequently come into play in investment decision making. Just as it is almost impossible to make an overall effective investment decision without full disclosure of the facts and the various alternatives, it is equally difficult to make an effective investment decision without full knowledge and recognition of our own limitations, *and* the basic characteristics of those people to whom we frequently turn for advice!

In identifying the players in the investment decision scenario, this chapter also presents some of the questions you might ask various advisers.

You—The Investor

You alone will ultimately be the beneficiary of your investment decision—whether it be good or bad. Therefore, it is extremely important for you to clarify in your mind your relationship with those to whom you will turn for advice. You must evaluate their true capabilities and their relative position to you.

Humans have the faculty of reasoning but too many people still let others do the basic thinking, and it works to their disadvantage. More important, people have the faculty of intuition. Often when you are listening to or considering an investment proposal, you will experience a knowing feeling that something is not right—listen closely to that feeling or "voice"! Many spouses have the ability to objectively evaluate a situation or to ask a question that the other may have forgotten, or is embarrassed to ask. This chapter is addressed to you and your financial mate; you can probably work together more effectively in the evaluation and decision-making process.

One of the first laws of investment decision making is that *there are no stupid questions*! You are entitled to know every conceivable aspect of the investment that you are considering for purchase. Even though the person presenting the investment to you may be highly skilled and knowledgeable, he deserves no more of an apology for your lack of knowledge—and your desire for knowledge—than the doctor who recommends radical surgery. A spouse can be especially perceptive at this point and frequently has a knack for asking clarifying questions when someone appears muddled, uses double-talk, or is just too technical.

As with any other endeavor that you undertake in life, the better prepared you are for the investment interview, the better decision you will make. You would do well to write down the following questions and go over them in your mind prior to any investment interview!

1. I am considering an investment, what is my motive for investing? In other words, am I going to invest because I have been greedy and expect unreasonable profits from an investment? Do I have some extra money in the bank and feel guilty, or frivolous, or unnatural, with this new state of affairs?

2. From what perspective is the salesman talking to me? In other words, does he make a living by having people like me buy the product he is selling? How objective can this individual be? How wide is his investment experience and his product mix? How long has he been in the business—and how much does he know if it has been a very short period of time?

3. Am I being hurried by the salesman to make a decision about this investment? (It is often difficult to make an investment decision without some sense of urgency.) Frequently, sense of urgency is manufactured in order to impel investors to take positive, affirmative action quickly. If you are being rushed and do not feel comfortable, you probably should not make that particular investment! Remember, you are not looking at the last and best deal ever

to be offered to you. There might even be a better one coming up that you can take advantage of, if you still have your cash to invest and have not eliminated your flexibility by making a rash decision!

4. Has this individual gotten my name or called me as a result of some affiliation that lends credibility to that individual but not necessarily to the product that he is selling? Frequently high-credibility organizations are promoted into sponsoring a product that has doubtful, and sometimes negative, effects for you, the investor. When such schemes are put together and their sales talk created, the presentations are generally so beautiful that it is virtually impossible not to invest your money into the schemes. Of course, a large number of worthwhile investments are sponsored by worthwhile organizations. But, be sure you are thinking clearly when you let someone get through your door just because of your emotional affiliations!

5. Am I about to buy an investment that has positive tax effects for me and are these tax effects being used to mask an otherwise poor investment? In other words, is someone selling the smoke instead of the fire—in magic it's called misdirection; in investments it's called economic suicide. With the newly expanded individual retirement account (IRA) and the expanded Keogh for self-employed individuals, every American has an obligation to become better acquainted with investment alternatives. If you are going to buy a tax deduction, be sure that your money is invested in the most productive manner. The difference in the results could be hundreds of thousands of dollars.

6. How do I really feel about the individual presenting this investment, about the investment itself, about my willingness and ability to take the risks involved in any investment? If you generally do not feel comfortable about any aspect of a proposed investment, the second rule of investing

comes into play: *If you don't feel good about it, don't do it!* A little more explanation, study, or time might remove your uneasiness. Remember to consider whether or not you will feel worse if you miss the benefits of the proposed investment; and, decide in favor of your highest comfort level.

7. "Have you invested in this particular investment yourself?" Be sure to look directly in the saleman's face when you ask this question. If he looks you directly in the eye and comes up with a yes, or a good reason for a no, it is one thing; but, if he hems and haws and tries to make excuses, try to find out why he is not doing what he thinks is such a good idea for you to do. But remember that people who make their living selling investments cannot invest in everything that they recommend. There is simply not enough money to invest in everything that the individual handles. However, you might get a great deal of information from his response to this question.

8. Why am I being offered this great opportunity to enrich myself a thousand-fold? Why am I so blessed? By what stroke of luck am I being offered this opportunity? In other words, if you are being offered inside information from some source other than a close relative, be very skeptical of the truth of that offer. If a deal is good, the insiders themselves will surely have taken advantage of it before you hear about it.

Also, beware of relatives with inside information about the latest outstanding opportunity. They tend to be emotional and want company in their new investments or new careers.

The third rule of investing is *there ain't no free lunches!*

The important point to remember is not to default on your judgment and intuition—they work for you from the inside out. Your other advisers all put together do not have your "gut feeling."

As for the technical aspects of investment decisions, try to evaluate closely the players who can promote you into, *or block you from*, excellent opportunity. They can also keep you from making bad investment decisions. In the final analysis, the ball is *always* in your court! Now, let's look at some of the people you can turn to for investment advice.

Accountant

There are many types of accountants, from certified public accountants to general public accountants. The fundamental error people make in turning to an accountant for investment advice is they assume that because he adds and subtracts numbers—and makes them balance—he understands their source, their use, and their final disposition. This is sometimes the case, but, on the whole it is not. It is virtually impossible for an accountant who depends upon you for fees, for food and housing, and other necessities of life to look you in the eye and say "I don't know" when asked the question about the merits of an investment. In the first place an accountant's personality is not inclined to admit that he doesn't know and in the second place it is not politically smart for this adviser to reveal any level of ignorance about the subject. You should not assume investments to be his expertise. If you think about it, an accountant's job is to account; this means adding up, subtracting, and balancing columns of figures. He may know something about tax law, investment philosophy, or some aspect of investing. That is, a tax accountant may be able to inform you about tax law, but he may not be able to accurately inform you about the basic investment theories you happen to be considering.

Questions to your accountant might include:

1. What do you invest in personally? This will give you insight into his investment preferences?

2. If I'm paying more than I want to in taxes, what advice has this man given me in the past to solve this problem?

3. You might want to ask this gentleman what he would do to reduce your tax burden prior to asking about the specific investment at hand. If he has not made specific recommendations in the past, what is it that makes you believe that he has any special information or ability to assist in the evaluation of the suggested investment?

4. Does this accountant ever make recommendations for investment products? If so, what might they be?

Attorney

The first thing to remember about the attorney as an adviser is that he is a trained adversarial person. That is, the attorney is the person who will look for the weak spots! This is an advantage in some cases and a disadvantage in others. The principal benefits are the valid observations an attorney can make about the legal aspects of an investment. One of the greatest problems experienced with attorneys, on the other hand, is that clients find it difficult to assign relative risk to the legal hazards described. Do not expect an attorney to make investment decisions, but to tell you of any perceived risks, as well as their relative importance to the success or failure of the proposed venture. In many cases, the advice of an attorney is not sought when making average investment decisions.

Questions that might be asked of your attorney as you enter into the relationship, or begin to probe about his opinion of a proposed investment would include:

1. In general, how do you feel about the type of investment (for example, oil and gas, cattle or tax shelters) I am considering?

The answer may be quite illuminating as it may indicate some very strong prejudices that this individual possesses.

2. Tell your attorney that you are evaluating an investment opportunity and feel inclined to go along with the investment. Ask him what he might perceive as danger signals. Ask him to show you how to do this investment as opposed to why not to do the investment. This shows that you are making the decision and asking him to participate in it in a positive manner.

3. Ask what kind of investments he personally makes? Try to determine if there are valid economic reasons for his answer.

4. Ask whether he knows the people involved in the sale of this investment or in the overall structure of the investment, that is, the general partners, managers, or other functionaries of the investment. If they have information that is negative, it is certainly worth hearing.

Trust Officer

Basically, trust officers are generally well versed in the working of trusts and wills. These trusts relate to individuals who want to create a living trust or a trust that will be funded at death through the proceeds of your estate. Generally, they will not be able to advise you on the investment. They are bank employees who are bank trained. In most cases, you may not be able to invest in the bank's trust fund, even if you wanted to.

Questions that might be posed to the trust officer would concern his or her perception of the bank and its position in the community. You should certainly ask about creating a trust or will. The information will normally be accurate. You could casually inquire into their own investment activity. It should not be hard to conclude that this is not fertile ground in which to grow your investment decisions.

Stockbroker

Few stockbrokers are asked their opinions about investment proposals, mainly because an obvious conflict of interest exists between a stockbroker who spends his time touting the purchase and sale of common stocks and someone seeking a recommendation. You can be sure that if his advice is sought, you will receive an opinion. Evaluate that opinion as it relates to the source; this is true of all advisers, of course.

Financial Planner

Financial planners can be good, bad, and all shades in between. As in the other professions mentioned, you must be careful and aware! The financial planner is someone who should sit down with you and help you define your objectives, your resources, your liabilities, your prejudices, and your perceptions about economics and investments. Out of this information he should design a financial plan that is suited to you and that will utilize the various investment alternatives available to you (including insurance) in a judicious and objective manner. A financial planner can be anyone who makes a loan, sells insurance, or gives miscellaneous advice. Many people call themselves financial planners but are not really qualified professionals in the field of financial planning. Look behind every designation, including this one.

The most important characteristic that the financial planner brings to your planning activity is that of being an initiator. He or she stimulates you to thought and action. Not only do competent financial planners initiate thoughts and action with clients, they assist in the evaluation process, the formulation of goals, and the ultimate implementation of a plan of action that will move the client in the direction of the achievement of his or her goals. This process is not simple because there are many disciplines to master and all of the disciplines and technical knowledge must be woven through the fabric of human nature and sensitivity to the persons involved.

The level of competence and the objectivity of the planner must be closely scrutinized by you in order to determine if this person is right for you. Financial planners should be willing to discuss with you their professional qualifications, their experience, and their philosophy as it relates to investments and life in general. In this profession more than in any other, you need to understand the individual's personal philosophy and experience because you do not want to buy someone else's prejudices or preferred products!

The financial planner must have a general knowledge of many products, their investment merit, their availability, their tax implications, and their suitability for you. In addition, he must be able to evaluate accounting procedures as they relate to your cash flow and income tax, and your net worth. In addition to knowing the products specifically, he must know stocks, mutual funds, life insurance, disability insurance, casualty insurance, tax shelters, tax-preferred investments such as Keogh, IRA, retirement planning, and the benefits and drawbacks as they relate to incorporation, partnership, and sole practice of a business.

Because of the intensity of the planning discipline and the time the planner must devote to it, you should define your ethical, moral, and financial relationship with the planner. Some financial planners work solely on a fee basis and will work with you in whatever area you desire according to a fee established between you and the planner. Some planners will help you define your goals and aspirations and perhaps will indicate some product, and their compensation will be in the form of commissions derived from that product. Others combine the two forms of compensation and work both on the basis of a fee and a commission. The method of operation must be defined so that there are no surprises or disappointments with respect to your expectation of the planner's objectivity, ability to provide products and to solve problems, or knowledge of various investment alternatives that might fit your needs. Because of the importance of defining a relationship with your financial planner, let's see what you can expect from each type of planner we have defined here.

Fee Only. The fee-only financial planning practitioners tend to work with the high-income investor because their fees must start at a high level in order to pay for the time, experience, and expertise required to discover the problems, evaluate the resources, and apply the solutions to the individual. Because of the time required, a small investor usually cannot afford the services of a fee-only financial planner. This form of planning has become more popular in the past few years as the definition of financial planning and its population of users have become more defined. Because inflation and income tax have affected all of us, we are more aware of the need to employ creative help in our planning. As a result, the marketplace has created a place for highly professional, fee-only planners.

The problem with many fee-only practitioners lies in the area of implementation. The greatest recommendations in the world can be made, but if an individual does not know how to efficiently and effectively enter the marketplace to buy the products or services that are recommended, the plan is incomplete! And, the money spent to evaluate the situation is most often wasted. This is by far the most controversial area of discussion between the fee-only and commission disciplines. It only seems logical that someone who does not make money out of any particular area of investment or insurance will not be as sharp in that area and the changing product within that area as someone who makes a living with those products. This requires close attention if you are considering a fee-only relationship with someone. You would be well-advised to ask about their ability to evaluate and guide you to people who will, in fact, assist you in the purchase of the appropriate products or service. Also, you need to evaluate the cost and ability of the fee-only practitioner to monitor the purchases made so that he can advise you as to their continued effectiveness in your planning to achieve your goals.

One thing to clearly define with your "fee-only" planner is whether or not he has *any* commissionable interest in *any* product he recommends. A number of people have thought that their planners were fee-only, only to discover that was not the case at all.

Commission Only.   The individuals who do not charge for the work that is involved in creating and presenting a financial plan for you have some characteristics that you need to identify and factor into your considerations.

First, you need to know that almost all financial planners *originally* came from a product background, and they were product oriented and commission oriented. This is only natural because, until the industry took form and developed there was no reason for you to pay anyone a fee. The financial planning industry has its roots in the insurance industry and mutual fund industry with a lot of help from the other professions. But, without the initiative and the financial rewards from this group, this industry would not exist today.

The commissioned planner knows that if he does a good job and has the proper license arrangements (life, disability, investments, real estate, investment adviser, and others), that many of the solutions to financial problems rest with financial products that normally carry a stated, and many times a regulated, commissions structure. They are willing to risk that you will need their product to solve a portion of your planning requirements, and, therefore, they will be compensated. This is nothing new. Life insurance people for years gained entry into the homes of America by talking about wills and trusts knowing that life insurance sales normally would follow because of the needs of family protection or estate preservation. The mutual fund salesman of years ago gained entry into your home and talked to you about retirement planning, education for your children, and asset accumulation, knowing that his mutual funds would assist in the accomplishment of these objectives.

The problems associated with commission planners may be difficult for you to discern. One of the main ones is that commission-only planners tend to have a lower self-image than fee-only individuals. As well, they may not have the same basic training and education. For example, someone who comes from the life insurance industry may not be fully acquainted with other areas of investment.

Fee and Commission.   This method of compensation is probably the method that most financial planners utilize in their planning activity with you. The reason for this is that it takes an enormous amount of time and energy for the finanical planner to talk with you and understand your current financial situation, your hopes and desires, your prejudices as they relate to many areas of planning activity, and your sense of urgency and seriousness about defining and achieving your financial goals. Many financial planners have gone to a fee because they themselves are at risk until you finally take action on a plan that can be months in evolving, and that might in the end be unsuccessful for various reasons. Most of these planners will engage in the planning activity with you at a cost that you negotiate and that is based on the time they spend gathering information, organizing, and presenting it to you. Frequently, the fee ceases at the point of recommendation, and should you want to stop at that point you would be free to, having paid for the time commitment taken to that point. Then, if you care to proceed, and if the financial planner is licensed properly, those areas that you care to implement through his office will carry normal commissions associated with the product that you purchase. If you care to purchase products from others, it should be understood that this is an alternative that you reserve for yourself. Some areas of activity may have no commissions, such as helping you obtain a properly drafted will or trust through the attorney of your choice, assisting you in incorporating a business, or designing a retirement plan that has a deferred payoff for the planner.

The financial planning discipline is so personal and so important that it is essential to be sure that you like and respect the person with whom you will be working. If you do not, the relationship will not be successful. Similarly, if he does not like and respect you, it will not be successful. Questions to ask:

1. When you talk about developing a financial plan consistent with my goals and desires, what background and experience will form the basis for your recommendations?

2. Ask the financial planner how he or she is compensated and how they operate their financial planning practice. You need to be sure that your contract is firmly understood by yourself and your planner, or you should not proceed.

3. How does the planner work with your other advisers? He should say that he works with people's accountants and attorneys, but on a professional level. Also, if the planner shows hostility to any of your financial planning team, it is a red flag and one that you need to investigate carefully to see that he does not get confused about the objective of the financial plan and the method of implemention of that plan. Many planners may be intimidated by your other advisers.

4. Ask his opinion about whole life insurance. Probably no other area is so controversial in financial planning than the issue of applying insurance in a financial plan.

5. Since planners get into your personal affairs rather deeply, you should ask how they are doing financially. The answer, if it is not honest, will be apparent on the face of most financial planners, except the most skilled actor. The fact that the financial planner is not as wealthy, or does not make as much money as you does not mean that he cannot effectively work with you for the accomplishment of your financial goals. The profession and art of financial planning takes years to master (if it can be mastered) and it is not financially rewarding in the first years. You will see more in the eyes and body language of your planner than in the verbal answer, in most cases.

His sensitivity to your position, and your feelings will also tell you a good deal. The doggedness with which he pursues your information, his feelings about your position, and your desires for the future will give you insight into his sensitivity to you as an individual and as a potential client.

Finally, if after talking with your proposed financial planner, you do not feel comfortable, do not proceed. Do not proceed unless you can clarify that quiet voice in the back of your mind; otherwise there will probably be disappointments. And, do not forget that in the financial planning process you have an enormous amount of responsibility to provide accurate information and to respond candidly, and much of this response will be based on your gut feeling and your interaction with this person who wants to assist you in this rather complex activity.

Conclusion

Seek the advice of people who have obvious credentials and are capable of meeting your need. Do business only with those people to whom you respond and who respond to you. Closely evaluate the people and the procedure involved.

But, do not duck your responsibility for your own financial activity. No one can think for you, no one can know what is in your heart of hearts. The success of the financial planning activity will, to a large degree, depend on your assuming the responsibility and control for this most important activity!

Chapter 39

Richard W. Arnold, B.S., is assistant to the president and chief financial officer for the Charles Schwab Corporation and its wholly owned subsidiary, Charles Schwab & Company, Incorporated. He is a member of the board of directors of Hamilton Taft & Company. Previously he was vice-president of investment planning for Financial Analysis, Incorporated, and he was special products manager and product specialist at Raychem Corporation. Arnold has written numerous articles, which include a study of problems in small business debt financing and an overview of electronic systems for security trading and execution. He is a registered financial and operations principal of the National Association of Security Dealers and an allied member of the New York Stock Exchange. He is a founding member and treasurer of the Investment Education Council, San Francisco.

It Will Never Be the Same

Richard W. Arnold, B.S.

If you are to perform well in your task of charting a course toward financial security, you must understand some of the forces of change that are underway in our economy. But equally as important is the need to understand the revolution that is occurring in the financial services industry.

As a saver and investor, you are faced with an almost overwhelming array of alternative financial products and services, and an equally confusing diversity of individuals and institutions with whom you may choose to transact business. In fact, recent surveys have indicated that the average investor is a client of approximately twenty different vendors of financial services. You need only to scan the list of chapter titles and authors in this book to appreciate the complexity of the industry.

Yet the type of institutions you deal with and the way in which you interact with them are undergoing massive change at the moment. Lines of distinction between banks, insurance companies, stockbrokers, and investment managers are becoming rapidly blurred as both the regulatory structure and the expanding technology are allowing change through both product diversification and merger. It may even be said that we are close to the point of having only one financial services industry.

The purpose of this chapter is to provide you with some of the background that will help you to understand these changes, and to point you toward some of the changes you will need to make in the ways you deal with vendors of financial products. To begin with, we must look backwards, and study the roots of our present system of regulatory structures.

Regulation of the Financial Industry

At the present time the three major segments of the industry—banking, brokerage, and insurance—are each regulated in entirely different ways. The banks are controlled principally through federal regulation under the auspices of the Federal Reserve Board and the Controller of the Currency. Securities brokerage is a self-regulated industry, in which the federal government—through the Securities and Exchange Commission—has only oversight powers, while the various stock exchanges and the National Association of Securities Dealers perform the principal regulatory functions. Meanwhile, the insurance industry is almost totally controlled by the various state governments with very little federal involvement.

Banking

Banking legislation and regulation stem in great part from the failures of the nation's banking system during the 1920s and 1930s. At the heart of most banking law is a belief that without severe restrictions on the powers of banks there would be excessive concentration of economic influence in the hands of a very few people, and that eventually there could be massive disruption in the economy if this power was left uncontrolled. Thus the key components of bank regulation are *strategic* limitations—controls over *what* the banks may do. In this regard, the Glass-Steagall Act, the McFadden Act, and Regulation Q stand out as the most important restrictions on the nation's bankers.

Glass-Steagall prohibits commercial banks from engaging in investment banking. Prior to the enactment of this statute in 1933, banks that performed conventional commercial lending functions and that managed their clients' money through trust departments were also permitted to both underwrite the issuance of securities and to trade in those securities in the secondary markets. In the aftermath of the stock market crash, it was felt that the New York bankers, particularly J.P. Morgan, wielded too much economic power, and that the risks associated with underwriting were too severe to allow banks to continue in this business. There was also a concern that banks would use their trust departments to buy up any securities the bank was underwriting if it was unable to sell them to outside investors. Glass-Steagall eliminated this potential conflict of interest.

The McFadden Act was designed to restrict the geographical franchise of the banks. It effectively prevented the migration of banks across state lines and permitted individual states to further limit banks to single communities, and even to single branches. While some states, like California, permitted their banks to branch out extensively across the state, others, like both Texas and Illinois, chose to become so-called unit banking states and prohibited any branching.

Regulation Q is one of many credit controls extended by the Federal Reserve Board, and places a limit on the rates of interest that can be paid by banks to their depositors. The principal elements of this regulation are that no bank may pay any interest on demand deposits (checking accounts) and that the rates that may be paid on savings accounts are restricted severely. The intent here was to prevent illiquidity in the banking institutions and to preserve low-cost sources of funds to assist the banks in remaining profitable.

Most of these controls worked well prior to the periods of higher interest rates ushered in during the late 1960s. Then businesses started to bypass the banks by lending their excess funds directly to other businesses and by borrowing even for short periods of time through the securities markets. As a result, a battle developed between the nation's large banks (with Walter Wriston of City Bank in New York as their spokesman) and the Federal Reserve. The banks wanted Regulation Q lifted so they could purchase money at competitive interest rates to fund their corporate customers' borrowing needs. But William McChesney Martin, then head of the Federal Reserve, was concerned that both the farming and real estate industries would

suffer severely if bank costs of funds rose too drastically.

The result was a partial lifting of Regulation Q. Banks were permitted to pay competitive rates for deposits above $100,000 (CDs), and were also allowed to go overseas in their search for funds without restriction as to the rates they could pay in these foreign markets. So began an era of dramatic change for the nation's banks.

In the next fifteen years, large money center banks moved rapidly toward having "purchased" money as the primary source of their funds. The higher cost of these borrowings caused their margins of profit to shrink significantly, so that the return on each asset dollar dropped from about 1.25 percent to less than 0.5 percent. In order to preserve an adequate return on capital, these banks were forced to greatly increase their leverage—the ratio of total assets to actual equity. While in 1965, most big banks had ten cents of equity for each dollar of assets, by 1982 this number had decreased to about three and a half cents.

Meanwhile, the availability of competitive interest rates on large deposits allowed the creation of pools of funds from several small depositors, and the money market fund industry was born.

The growth of the money market funds was fueled by the strenuous support of the securities brokerage industry. Unlike banks, brokers suffer from relatively little strategic restriction, and through the money funds they found an avenue to step into the world of consumer banking.

Brokerage Industry

This freedom from excessive restriction stems in major part from the self-regulated nature of the brokerage industry. As early as 1792, the nation's brokers had banded together in associations that formed the basis of the large stock exchanges and that imposed rules of conduct and ethics on their members. Following the stock market crash of 1929, as new securities law was written, the existence and the strength of these associations were recognized, and in the Maloney Amendment to the Securities Exchange Act of 1934, power was granted to the exchanges to continue in the role of primary regulators of the industry. The act of 1934 also created the National Association of Securities Dealers (the NASD) to oversee the operations of firms that did not belong to any of the established exchanges. The Securites and Exchange Commission (SEC), created by the Securities Act of 1933 and given powers to supervise the registration and issuance of new securities, was given only oversight powers over the self-regulatory organizations in connection with the secondary markets.

Most of the rules of the NASD and the exchanges deal with *how* business is conducted, rather than *what* business is engaged in. Financial and operational controls are severe, and the principal consideration in the regulation is the financial stability of the member firms. In fact, one vital component of the rules up until 1975 was total control over the prices at which brokerage services could be sold.

For many years, the brokerage industry relied on this fixed pricing structure to preserve a reasonable degree of profitability in its organizations. Many brokers will admit that when times were good the partners in the firms were handsomely rewarded, and when times were bad the firms would join together and raise prices. Times change, however, and with the advent of the consumerist movement came the successful challenge by the Justice Department to the fixed price system. In May of 1975, after almost 200 years of price fixing, brokerage rates were made fully competitive.

During this same period, other major changes overcame the brokerage industry. Partnerships had given way to corporate structure and for the first time the management of the brokerage firms had outside shareholders to consider when making strategic decisions. The diversity of products handled by the industry started to increase as management looked for avenues to avoid the extreme cycles of earnings from the basic stock and bond businesses. Finally, with higher interest rates, the brokers began to realize that profits could be significantly increased by focusing attention on the banking aspects of their business, those transactions that allowed them to use customer money left in their hands to lend to other customers at the new high rates.

As with banking, one of the results of this change was an increase in the amount of leverage at work in the securities industry. By 1982 many major firms were operating with equity-to-asset ratios similar to those employed by the major banks.

Insurance Industry

The insurance industry too has undergone rapid change in the last few years of high interest rates. The basic life insurance product was, for many years, principally a savings vehicle that provided an inexpensive source of funds to the underwriting companies. As whole life policies became an uneconomic choice for most consumers, and as the new mutual fund alternatives provided insurance customers with the choice of combining low-cost term life insurance with a regular savings and investment vehicle in the fund of their choice, the industry started to look for avenues to participate in both portions of the transaction.

Many of the insurance agents had long been licensed to sell the policies of more than one company. So it was only natural that these individuals would proceed to license themselves to handle securities products and become mutual fund salesmen. In a very short time, the attractiveness of selling other investment products became obvious, and many insurance agents became financial planners, selling everything from tax shelters to diamonds, from

annuities to stocks and bonds. The underwriting companies saw these changes as crucial to their future, and began to explore ways to broaden their participation in the activities of their agents.

Effects of Regulatory Breakdown

The combined effect of all these changes was the tremendous integration of financial services. The regulatory structures began to break down as banks started to cross state lines with loan production offices to serve corporate clients, as brokers began to pay interest on customer balances and to "sweep" excess balances into money market funds. Perhaps the most important single event of the 1970s was the introduction of the Merrill Lynch cash management account. By joining forces with the progessive Bank One of Ohio, Merrill Lynch was able to offer a single account that performed like a checking account but was actually a stock brokerage account. Here, for the first time, was interstate banking. Here, for the first time, was access to competitive market rates of interest on a "transaction" account.

As with any period of regulatory collapse, small specialty firms that had developed great expertise in one type of transaction began to carve out a significant market share. Discount brokerage firms are probably the best example. By eliminating the cost of providing research and advice to their customers, and by developing some of the most sophisticated transaction-processing technology, these firms were able to execute customer orders for less than half the cost of the large investment banking giants.

By 1982, even the banks had learned to skirt the regulatory restrictions, and three major California banks took bold steps in new directions. Bank of America announced its intention to acquire Charles Schwab & Co., Inc., the nation's largest discount broker, and argued in its application to the Federal Reserve Board that the lack of underwriting and trading functions prevented Schwab from being subject to the Glass-Steagall prohibitions. Security Pacific Bank entered into an agreement to provide similar brokerage services to its customers through Fidelity Brokerage Services—a firm that is operated by one of the country's largest mutual fund managers. What is perhaps most significant, Crocker Bank managed to create a virtual copy of the Merrill Lynch product. Customers could deposit cash and securities, could write checks, use a debit card, place securities orders and borrow money, all through one account, and all the while receive money market rates on any balances in the account. This was accomplished through an arrangement with another specialty brokerage firm, Bradford Securities Processing, and with a money market mutual fund operated by Bradford.

While all this was happening, effectively unregulated firms were expanding their financial services activities. The nation's savings and thrift institutions were in serious trouble, with short-term deposits used to fund long-term loans at fixed interest rates; and several had been acquired by firms from outside the industry. National Steel, Baldwin Piano, Sears Roebuck, and Parker Pen had all entered into the financial services field, and specialty financial companies like American Express were expanding their role through diversification and acquisition.

Technology, too, was having its effect. At the beginning of 1982 there were ten major tests of computerized home banking systems; at the same time, the foundations of large networks of electronic services were already being laid.

What does this all lead to in the future, and what do you, as a saver and investor need to do to prepare for this future?

Future of the Financial Industries

First, you must understand that the ability of the government to regulate stability in the financial markets is all but eliminated. A bank is no longer a bank, and in the future you will have to concern yourself with the safety and potential longevity of the institution you choose. Already it can be said that most people who are leaving balances in savings and loan institutions are doing so either out of ignorance, or a philosophical commitment to the future of residential real estate.

Financial institutions can fail, and many will in the years to come. At present we have federal insurance for most of our savings deposits. You should recognize, however, that many of the new savings vehicles will lack this feature, and some failures will leave devastating effects on local communities. Many institutions will disappear not by failure, but by merger. There are over 14,000 banks in this country, and if the regulations that created this large number disappear, as they almost certainly will, we may see competitive forces reduce the count to less than 2,000.

What, then, will be the nature of the surviving financial institution? A large, highly diversified, and highly technologically based organization will emerge as the vendor of the 1990s. There will, of course, still be small, specialized firms in many segments of the industry, but the financial services supermarket will be dominant.

You will have to learn to use computerized systems in all your financial transactions, and the functions you perform will be broken into four broad categories. Let me first describe the nature of the electronic network that will exist, and then discuss the four types of transactions that will occur.

At the extremities of the network will be home computer terminals. These will not be hooked to your television set, but will be stand-alone appliances in your den or office. Data storage capacity will enable you to make a record of many of your transactions, as well as to keep certain personal files for reference purposes. For most of your electronic connection with the outside world, you will connect over a telephone line to a company that we will call a *gateway*. This gateway service may well be operated by your primary financial services vendor; it will allow you to connect with many other sources of information. The gateway company will offer you certain computer software and services, which will enable you to manipulate the data you have stored and to analyze certain choices you may be facing. Through the gateway, you will connect to a variety of companies that are in the business of data base management. These vendors of information services will provide you with news about the world, with weather predictions, with sports stories, and with complete access to files of information about yourself and transactions you have performed through the network. In addition, they will, upon electronic request, reconnect you with other data base managers who may have more information on a particular subject.

Asset managers will be at the opposite end of the network from you. Here will reside your investment advisers, your banker, your portfolio manager. In many cases a single company may be the gateway, data base manager, and asset manager, but to perform the full range of services, this diversified entity will also allow you to use the network to access other institutions.

As we mentioned before, your transactions will fall into four basic categories. At the lowest end of the spectrum will be simple, purely electronic functions, or "commodity" services. From your home— or from the pocket-sized terminal you will

take everywhere with you—you will instruct your gateway system to deduct $87.34 from your transaction account and to credit Pacific Telephone Account number 555-4680. These commodity services require no human involvement other than your finger on the keyboard, because the size and complexity of the transaction is small enough to be handled in the most cost-efficient manner possible, and simple edits and electronic verification procedures will provide adequate security control.

Level two will involve "monitored" transactions. At this point you will be dealing with enough money, or enough complexity for the service vendor to have an employee observe your transactions to ensure that they meet certain control standards, and that you are satisfied with the results. An example of this level might be the purchase of $20,000 worth of securities. The electronic systems will enable you to originate the trade from your terminal, and to have the order instantaneously transmitted and executed without human involvement (that technology already exists and operates). The human monitor will be there to ensure that you are able to afford the trade, and that no other transaction is due to hit your account that would prevent timely settlement. He will also serve as an extra control against the risk of an error that might result in a $200,000 trade instead of $20,000.

At level three, you will perform "interactive" transactions. In this case, you will need to avail yourself of human consent and support during the electronic process, and an adequate expert will be available to answer your questions and to guide you through the function. In this case you might be searching for a particular type of municipal bond, or you might be arranging financing for your house. The system will ensure that all the data relative to prior transactions are available to the expert with whom you are electronically communicat-

ing, and his answers to your questions will be instantaneously available to you.

Level four transactions will be almost purely "advisory" in nature, and will include such tasks as tax planning, estate planning, or investment consulting. In these cases you will be in direct contact with your chosen expert, either face to face or over the telephone. Both you and your adviser will still have access to the capabilities of the data system, and when complex projections of cash flow analyses are needed, the push of a few buttons will do the trick. As decisions are made, the system will be informed of your choices, and the appropriate documents will be prepared and printed out on a screen for you to attach your digital signature.

How will you learn to cope? Through games, computerized learning systems, and sample transactions. Your children will, of course, have learned most of this in our schools, and will teach you more than they ever have before.

At the end of each year, you will sit at your terminal and type the words "Run 1040." Your home terminal will connect to the gateway, obtain the latest tax preparation software, establish the necessary connections to the data base managers where your files are stored, and will compile your return in a few seconds. Once or twice during the process, the computer will alert you to the fact that more than one reporting alternative exists, and will enable you to review the choices and make your selection. If the choices are too complex, you will be able to connect to a level four adviser, who will call up your data on his own terminal, review the alternatives with you, and give you his input. At the end of your conversation with him, he will punch a few buttons and your account will be charged with the cost of his services. Naturally, in those few rare instances where you have handled cash, you will have stored records in your home data files, and the tax software will ensure that these transactions are also considered in the preparation of your return. Perhaps you will sign your return digitally, and it will be simultaneously transmitted to the IRS system.

This prospect should not frighten, but excite. While so many of the goods and services we consume are becoming ever more expensive, here is one category where the quality should improve greatly while the reduction in paperwork and human involvement will serve to reduce the overall cost. You, as the investor, will have more access to information and be more assured of having considered all important factors before making your investments. And for the first time in your life, you will have a quite accurate idea of where you spent all your hard-earned money.

Chapter 40

Louis O. Kelso, B.S. (Finance), LL.B.,
originated the species of financing
techniques of which the Employee Stock
Ownership Plan (ESOP) is the best known.
A corporate and financial lawyer who
headed his own law firm for many years,
Mr. Kelso is now Chairman of the Board
of Kelso & Co., Inc., a San Francisco investment banking firm specializing in ESOP
financing and other financial designs incorporating the principles of two-factor
economics. His general economic theory
has been set forth in three books and in
many articles, essays, and monographs. In
essence, his theory holds that no economy
can realize the potential of technology to
eliminate poverty and unnecessary toil
until a growing proportion of individuals
and families, and eventually all individuals
and families, become private owners of the
things that are replacing human labor in
the production process. He thus urges governments to enlarge their economic policies
of full labor-worker employment into
policies of economic autonomy based on
employment of every consumer either as a
labor worker, a capital worker (capital
owner), or as both.

Kelso Plans— A Second Income From Ownership

Loren Dunton

This chapter is based on a series of exclusive interviews I have had with Louis Kelso, developer of capital theory economics. He also devised the Employee Stock Ownership Plan (ESOP) and other Kelso techniques for stock financing of every type of business in our free enterprise system. Over 5,000 ESOPs have already generated stock ownership and dividend incomes for hundreds of thousands of workers and managers. Kelso's goal is to bring about economic self-sufficiency by increasing and broadening the ownership of capital. As his ideas are accepted, millions of people will find it easier to reach the goal that this book is about—a better financial future.

More people are now asking why Kelso's ideas for making "stock owners" out of millions of people are not being used even more widely. Kelso Plans would make more people "capital owners," and enable them also to earn dividends from the stock they own instead of only from the work they do.

Those of us interested in financial planning have a vital interest in anything that can make owners out of today's consumers and that will supplement their wages and salaries with income from stock dividends. You will no doubt be intrigued by the following conversation.

DUNTON: As I analyze it, the rich people (including the big stockholders) who now own most of the corporate wealth, think that your theories will hurt them. Is that true? Do the rich have something to fear?

KELSO: No. A capitalist economy starts with the protection of private property, and our Constitution guarantees it. ESOPs do not make rich people poor, but rather make poor people owners of stock, especially in the companies they work for. The most important step that could be taken in this economy towards the protection of rich people and their capital is also to make owners out of the majority who do not own capital today

and as a result are economically underpowered.

DUNTON: How come almost all wealthy people own stock, but so many others do not own stock or any other form of capital?

KELSO: One reason is that wealthy people can borrow money to buy stock or acquire other capital, but the average person can't.

DUNTON: The opportunity to borrow on capital's future earnings to buy stock in the company one works for has been called the real genius of what used to be called "Kelso Plans" but are now called ESOPs or Employee Stock Ownership Plans. Is it genius?

KELSO: No. It's merely common sense!

DUNTON: Well, genius or not, spreading out ownership is certainly not what the Socialists advocate.

KELSO: No. They suggest we do away with private property because only a few people have it and most do not.

DUNTON: So you're saying we shouldn't eliminate the ownership of private property but spread it out to more people using Employee Stock Ownership Plans?

KELSO: Yes. With ESOPs and other financing plans, using the principle behind the ESOP.

DUNTON: We've been using Keynesian economic theory instead of Kelso's for a long time. What has happened to ownership in this country?

KELSO: Despite the presumably good intentions of Roosevelt, Truman, Eisenhower, Kennedy, Johnson, and Carter, the distribution of productive capital today is about the same as it was under Herbert Hoover.

DUNTON: I can remember back then and the big worry for some was how automation would cut out jobs.

KELSO: Senator Russell Long in the *Congressional Record* was quoted as saying:

Some years ago a top Ford official was showing the late Walter Reuther through the very automated plant in Cleveland,

Ohio, and he said to him jokingly, "Walter, you'll have a hard time collecting union dues from these machines," and Walter said, "You are going to have more trouble trying to sell automobiles to them." Both of them let it stop right there. There was a very logical answer to that, the logical answer was that the owners of the machines could buy automobiles and if you increase the number of owners you increase the number of consumers.

DUNTON: Yes, and when he introduced a bill dealing with employee stock ownership, didn't some of his other thoughts in the *Congressional Record* articulate what you have been saying for a long time?

KELSO: Yes. He talked about ownership and access to credit. He said:

A principal objection to private property is that not enough people own some of it. That has been a primary criticism of American capitalism throughout history.

Unfortunately, in many parts of the world capitalism is portrayed simply as an economic system in which a nation's productive wealth is concentrated in the hands of a privileged few. . . .

For the most part, people cannot afford capital ownership. Most working Americans owe rather than own; they accumulate debts rather than wealth. . . .

Expanded ownership or ESOP-type financing is of a different kind. It is producer credit—credit for the acquisition of productive assets rather than for consumer articles.

DUNTON: I like what President [Ronald] Reagan said some years ago:

Capitalism hasn't used the best tool of all in its struggle against socialism—and that's capitalism itself. . . . Could there be a better answer to the stupidity of Karl Marx than millions of workers individually sharing in the ownership of the means of production.

KELSO: Yes, and we could do that if we could change the national economic policy so as to encourage both legitimate employment and the legitimate acquisition of capital ownership.

DUNTON: What else would we have to do?

KELSO: We would also have to modify our banking and financing techniques so as to eliminate the exclusive right of the rich to have access to credit to buy capital and to pay for it out of what it produces.

DUNTON: What do you mean by "exclusive access to credit to buy capital"?

KELSO: For reasons that are mostly historical—certainly not logical—the financing institutions—the banks, insurance companies, savings and loan associations, and venture capitalists—insist upon the existing ownership of capital as a first step to getting access to credit for use in acquiring more capital.

DUNTON: But doesn't that lead to a minority of families using more and more credit to acquire more and more capital and thus to acquire progressively more productive power than they can use?

KELSO: Precisely. The moment a capital owner produces all the income that he and his dependents care to use for consumption, this abuse reaches the height of absurdity. Thereafter, all of his additional income is devoted to acquiring ever more *unnecessary* productive power. After all, the purpose of production is consumption; and in a free market, private property economy, it is consumption by the producer.

DUNTON: Isn't that self-defeating?

KELSO: Yes. Where a majority of consumers are economically underpowered because they don't own capital, our economy becomes depressed. The people with unsatisfied needs and wants lack purchasing power and those with excess purchasing power have no unsatisfied needs and wants.

DUNTON: So they do very little of the additional purchasing that would stimulate the economy.

KELSO: This is exactly what happens. It

happened to the United States in a major way during the 1930s and has been happening every since. Following the lead of the New Deal, governments began redistributing income by welfare, and through loans from those who produce more income than they wish to consume to those who produce less than they need or none.

DUNTON: What do other economists say about this aberration in our economy?

KELSO: I and my co-authors have been pointing this out for nearly twenty-five years, but the economists and other vested interests pretend not to hear.

DUNTON: How long can this go on?

KELSO: Not much longer. High taxes, inflation, and the evil of parasitism were the main issues that elected the Reagan administration in 1980. By "parasitism," of course, I refer to the millions of people who must live on the earnings of others because they themselves are deprived of adequate earning power in an economy where capital produces most of the goods and services.

DUNTON: But I do not see the Reagan administration or even Congress doing anything about it. Shouldn't they be trying to make the underproductive more productive by making capital credit available to them so they can become self-supporting, thus speeding up economic growth?

KELSO: Yes, but the politicians and economists still do not understand that the underproductiveness of consumers who do not have capital working for them is the central defect in the economy. Therefore, they cannot put forth any solution to our problems. We are controlling inflation with unemployment, bankruptcies, slowdown of business, and all the traditional means by which the "dismal science" has always fought inflation. Prosperity is nonexistent, except for the rich, the gamblers in the Wall Street casinos, and the people playing mad

merger and acquisition games in the corporate world.

DUNTON: How long can this go on?

KELSO: Not much longer. America's patience is running out. The governmental power to redistribute income by taxing some and giving to others and by the wealthy lending their excess wealth at high interest rates is raising fierce opposition. "Transfer payments" are the largest reason for taxes at the state level. They are responsible for over half the federal budget. Redistribution is now beginning to violate Machiavelli's law: *A man will forgive you for killing his father before he will forgive you for taking his patrimony.* Total debt in the U.S. economy has passed the $5 trillion mark. Economic growth is stalemated. International trade is crumbling. Poverty is grinding down the unemployed and underemployed who do not own capital. President Reagan has tried to reduce transfer payments in order to curtail deficits, but it is perfectly obvious we cannot reduce redistribution to the underproductive until they can support themselves.

DUNTON: Are other countries suffering from the same malady?

KELSO: Yes, every single one. And the problem is even more disastrous in the developing economies. President Figuardo of Brazil in the first speech in September of 1982 in the current session of the United Nations emphasized this.

DUNTON: What is the significance of the massive use of debt in the U.S. economy and in international banking?

KELSO: In a market economy, debt is a form of redistribution, just as welfare and other transfer payments are, except that debt must be repaid, and with interest. Both are virulent and ongoing. Each constitutes a malady that can only be curtailed by our switching our emphasis in the world of finance and financial planning to making the underproductive more productive and to cease making the excessively productive ever more productive.

DUNTON: I don't know much about market economics but even those of us unsophisticated in that science can see how owning stock, especially in the companies we work for, can make for a better financial future.

Postscript

The prestigious *Forbes* magazine in 1981 ran a feature article about Louis Kelso and his ideas. They titled it: "An Idea Whose Time Has Come?" and in a subtitle asked the question: "What does Senator Long understand that most of our learned economists and vociferous politicians refuse to see?" Their answer: "THAT LOUIS KELSO HAS SOMETHING IMPORTANT TO SAY."

If you agree, write your congressman, and ask any company president you know to at least investigate (with an open mind) how an ESOP might make owners out of his workers.

We are amazed that it took fourteen years for the medical profession to accept Pasteur's germ theory. Let us not provide head-shaking amazement for our children that it took us even longer to accept a new, more logical theory of economics.

Things to Know
and
Places to Go

The National Center for Financial Education is a non-profit corporation for public education, dedicated to helping consumers do a better job of saving, investing, insuring and planning for their financial future.

Merely reading the goals of the NCFE will provide a very clear picture of the NCFE concept and its potential. The goals are:

1. To educate and motivate people to save, invest, insure, and plan more intelligently for their own financial future.

2. To encourage the voluntary allocation of a larger percentage of individual disposable dollars away from spending and into savings and investments.

3. To increase cooperation among all segments of the financial services industry in order to compete more successfully for discretionary income.

4. To encourage government and industry to motivate and reward people who prepare for their own financial future.

All of the goals listed above are aimed at increasing the number of people under our free enterprise system able to retire without depending on government subsidy or Social Security.

The NCFE is an organization for the public, perhaps closer than anything else to the American Association of Retired People. However, most NCFE members will be in their twenties to sixties, interested in preparing ahead of time for a better financial future that, hopefully, will include a long and secure retirement.

It is now obvious those people who, during the 1950s, 1960s, and 1970s, did their financial planning and didn't depend on Social Security to take care of them in the 1980s and 1990s were the smart ones. They are the secure ones—having options, making choices, and enjoying their retirement.

Unfortunately, the financially secure comprise only a small segment of our society, a fact that leads to criticism of our free enterprise system. The media has helped

Appendix A

About the National Center for Financial Education, Inc.

2107 Van Ness Avenue, Suite 301
San Francisco, California 94109
415/474-8496   474-0232

Robert Wick
Director of Communications

millions of people become aware that they cannot, and should not, count on Social Security to provide a comfortable retirement for them no matter how much they have paid into it.

Our surveys show that a great many corporate executives are also conscientiously concerned about their employees' retirement. And the number is growing. It is these enlightened companies—employing tens, hundreds, or thousands of people—who will assist the NCFE in our efforts. We call them Corporate Sponsors and are offering special membership savings and benefits to their employees.

It is also our hope to encourage retired executives from various segments of the

financial services industry to give advice and even to help set up local centers or groups that can get together to share ideas on spending, saving, insuring, investing, and planning. If you or someone you know could benefit, please write for information.

NCFE members will receive a monthly newsletter designed to inform, educate, and motivate. They will also receive names to call for a free hour of consultation, a magazine on financial planning, and other aids, all aimed at helping them "spend smarter now to live better tomorrow."

Here are the firms *within* the financial services industry who have already become Corporate Sponsors and are helping to educate and motivate people.

NAME	EXECUTIVE
Franklin Resources	Charles Johnson, President
Wells Fargo Bank	Richard Rosenberg, Vice-Chairman
Kelso & Co., Inc.	Louis O. Kelso, Chairman of the Board
McNeil Real Estate Partnerships	Robert A. McNeil, Chairman of the Board
Pacific Standard Life Insurance	Clifford Gamble, President and CEO
Lansing Financial Group	Lucile Lansing, President
ITT Life Insurance Corporation	John Helgerson, Vice-President
Hansch Financial Group	Gus Hansch, Chairman
Annuity Services Group	Tom Kelly, President
Multi-Financial Planning Centers	George Diachok, President
Petro Lewis Securities Corporation	Michael Starita, President
R. M. Leary & Co., Inc.	Robert M. Leary, President
Consolidated Capital Companies	Richard G. Wollack, President
E.F Hutton & Company, Inc.	John M. Watts, Vice-President
Insurance Marketing Services, Inc.	George Nordhaus, President
Johnson & Higgins of California	James W. McElvany, Vice-President
The Charles Schwab Corporation	Richard W. Arnold, Chief Financial Off.
Capital Preservation Fund	James M. Benham, Chairman of the Board
Commodities Systems Development Assoc.	Jack King, General Partner
Red Carpet Realty	Robert Dyson, President
John Alden Life Insurance Co.	Stan Dabrowski, Vice-President
Equitec Financial Group	Kenneth Nitzberg, President
California Resources, Inc.	Peter L. Edelmuth, President
Trust Company of America	Hugh S. McCaffery, President
Resource Management, Inc.	Judith Zabalaoui, Chief Exec. Officer
King Financial Services	David M. King, President
Investment Training Institute	Charles D. Lowenstein, President
Walker, Cogswell & Co.	Lewis Walker, President
Cardinal Financial Planning	Morris Sahr, President

The Institute of Certified Financial Planners (ICFP) is a professional association in which regular membership is reserved for practicing financial planners who have earned the CFP designation from The College for Financial Planning, who currently and continuously render financial planning services to the public, and who meet the Institute's continuing education requirements.

All members (including Associates or Provisionals) must subscribe and adhere to the Code of Ethics and the Standards of Practice of the Institute of Certified Financial Planners.

The Certified Financial Planner is a member of a distinguished profession dedicated to serving the financial needs of individuals, families, and businesses.

"Certified Financial Planner" is far more than a title; it is a precise definition of a person's competence, experience, and intelligence in the complex profession of financial planning. Not every person who is described as a financial planner is a CFP; to earn this title the financial planner has demonstrated competence in analyzing and developing personal and business financial plans through the successful completion of a series of rigorous financial planning courses and examinations offered by The College of Financial Planning.

The CFP's area of expertise is in analyzing needs and prudently arranging overall financial plans rather than in promoting individual financial products.

One CFP may be more knowledgeable in a particular field than another and, therefore, may recognize the need to consult with qualified individuals in other specialties and in those areas traditionally and legally set aside for others.

The Institute of Certified Financial Planners

9725 East Hampden Avenue, Suite 33
Denver, Colorado 80231
303/751-7600
Executive Director, Dianna Rampy

Graydon K. Calder,
CLU, CFP

Appendix C

The International Association for Financial Planning, Inc.

5775 Peachtree Dunwoody Rd.
Suite 120C
Atlanta, Georgia 30342

Forrest Wallace Cato

What Is the International Association for Financial Planning?

The International Association for Financial Planning, Inc. (IAFP) is the professional association of those who work with clients in the area of personal and corporate financial planning.

Founded in 1969 under 501 (c) (6) of the Code as a nonprofit association, the IAFP now has chapters in more than 83 cities, with more than 12,000 members located primarily in the United States. Membership also comes from about a dozen other countries.

The philosophy, mission, and Code of Professional Ethics of the IAFP demand continuing education, a unified approach to the solution of the client's financial problems, a dialogue among the professions, and the preservation and enforcement of high ethical standards.

The financial planner believes in: the objective gathering of all relevant financial and emotional data from the client; the preparation of written case solutions and ideas after analysis by members of other professions as required; delivery of the plan, ready for implementation; and finally, periodic review and service.

Membership requirements in the IAFP include a demonstrated professional interest in the financial services industry and a written commitment to abide by the Code of Professional Ethics and Bylaws of the IAFP. In financial planning, we embrace all who sincerely desire to do a better job for their clients. We have members who are compensated by commission only, some by fee only, and many who are compensated by a combination of the two. We come from many different disciplines and represent a true cross section of the financial services industry. Members include registered investment advisers, stockbrokers, insurance agents and brokers, bank trust officers, real estate brokers, accountants, attorneys, and service and product suppliers.

What Does the IAFP Do to Help Insure High Standards of Professional Conduct and Ethics?

The IAFP has a Code of Professional Ethics, established in 1969 and revised in 1982. The basic objective of the Code is to specify and set forth the means to enforce the minimum ethical conduct expected of all members, as professionals, and to facilitate voluntary compliance with standards considerably higher than the required minimums.

The Code of Professional Ethics has three sections: Canons, Rules, and Guidelines. The *Canons* are general goals that express the general concepts and principles of the IAFP. The *Rules* are derived from the Canons and are specific standards of a mandatory and enforceable nature. The Rules prescribe the absolute minimum level of conduct required of every member. The *Guidelines* are designed to assist in interpreting the Canons and Rules, understanding their rationale, and applying them to frequently encountered situations.

To help insure the standards established in the Code, the IAFP's Ethics Committee works with the Ethics Officers in each of the IAFP's 83 chapters to educate chapter members and then alert the National Ethics Committee to members who may be in violation of the Code.

The Ethics procedure allows for potential violators to be indentified by IAFP members, as well as by members of the general public. Violators of the Code of Professional Ethics or the Bylaws may receive one of four decisions from the Ethics Committee. These decisions are: (1) No action; (2) reprimand with specific recommendations as to what would be required to correct actions found to violate the Code; (3) suspension from all association activities and receipt of mailings for a given period of time; (4) removal from membership.

The phrase "financial planner" has become a generic term that is creating confusion in the minds of the consumer and may mean something different to each profes-sional. The IAFP is developing the registry of Financial Planning Practitioners as a means to identify individuals who are involved in the practice of total financial planning and who meet the practice, education, and experience qualifications established by the IAFP. Application to the Registry involves a written application, references, and a personal interview conducted by a local interview committee. Individuals admitted to the Registry agree to take a written examination if and when required for participation in the program. An appeals procedure is available for applicants denied admission to the Registry.

Sixty hours of continuing education are required for each biannual reregistration period. No more than 75 percent of an individual's hours can be in any one field (this emphasizes the broad-based knowledge level required of practitioners). For each four-year reregistration period, no more than 50 percent of the hours may be in any one field. The final determination of an indvidual's admission to the Registry is made by the National Registry Committee, a panel of seven people appointed by the President of the IAFP who serve for one to three years. Implementation date of the Registry is June 30, 1983.

What Is the *Financial Planner* Magazine?

The *Financial Planner* magazine is the official publication of the International Association for Financial Planning. The publication is written by professionals and for professionals, it is not for general consumers.

Loren Dunton produced the first issue of the magazine in January of 1972. The total number of pages was 48, there were 36 pages of editorial comment, 12 pages of ads, and the print run totaled 5,000, most of which was not paid circulation.

The October 1982 issue had 212 pages. That edition had 91 editorial pages and 121 ad pages, with a paid circulation of 13,500, plus an additional bonus distribution of 3,5000, for a total of 17,000. And the magazine continues to grow.

Appendix D

The College for Financial Planning

9725 E. Hampden Avenue
Denver, CO
303/755-7101
William L. Anthes, Ph.D., President

Harry J. Lister, CFP
Chairman (1982–83)

The College for Financial Planning is in the forefront of the challenging and dynamic profession of financial planning. Because of the rapid pace at which change is taking place, importance and scope of both the profession and the College are growing every day.

The College for Financial Planning is an independent, nonprofit educational institution that trains and tests candidates in accordance with rigorous standards established over a decade of continuous growth.

The College for Financial Planning is the only educational institution that confers the Certified Financial Planner (CFP) upon candidates who demonstrate a high level of skill and competence in the analysis of client financial conditions and the development of client-oriented personal financial plans, who pass the College's series of rigorous examinations, and who meet other educational and work experience requirements of the College.

Since its incorporation in 1972, over 4100 candidates have completed the CFP Program and are authorized by the College to use the CFP designation. In addition, over 1200 candidates are enrolled and actively pursuing the CFP Program. The program is approved by the American Council on Education and is presently being offered on the campuses of more than 32 colleges and universities coast to coast.

Objectives of the College are to:

Provide training to persons who are or will be offering financial counseling; investment and risk management advice; counseling relating to retirement, tax, or estate planning; or general personal financial planning and implementation

Provide learning opportunities to such persons through programs of study, courses, textbooks, study guides, special reading materials, continuing education courses, seminars, and classroom instruction by members of an adjunct faculty and affiliated colleges and universities

Advance the knowledge, professionalism,

public recognition, and responsibility of those involved in the field of financial planning and counseling

Advance through its programs and the influence of its activities the financial well-being of the general public

The College for Financial Planning works on three levels:

Through its administration of the CFP Professional Education Program

Through sponsorship of seminars and other continuing educational endeavors

Through support of trade and professional organizations and publications involved in furthering financial planning knowledge and skills

Appendix E

The Chartered Financial Consultant Program

Gordon K. Rose, CLU

Vice-President Student and
  Faculty Services
The American College at Bryn Mawr,
  Pennsylvania

The financial problems of today's families and businesses sometimes seem unsolvable, and past solutions are often not reliable guides to present and future financial planning decisions. What is needed? A professional who can diagnose present and long-range financial planning objectives with skill, confidence, and commitment—someone who will tap other sources of expertise when needed, whose continuous counsel and service can be relied upon in an increasingly complicated financial environment.

This individual will be a uniquely qualified financial professional who will develop and coordinate the implementation of a unified plan to achieve financial growth and security. The individual will have expanded his or her knowledge to help sort out the confusing array of financial opportunities, products, and services.

The profession will be made up of tens of thousands of men and women who are now successful life underwriters, estate planning attorneys, CPAs, trust officers, CPCUs, and investment specialists, who wish to broaden knowledge and skills to enlarge their markets.

The American College at Bryn Mawr provides quality education for these new professionals through its Chartered Financial Consultant program. The program has as its focal point the financial counseling process—an organized approach for formulating, implementing, and monitoring plans to provide clients with comprehensive, coordinated strategies for achieving their financial objectives.

Those who achieve the Chartered Financial Consultant certification from The American College will have successfully completed an extensive ten-course program. That program provides the Chartered Financial Consultant with a comprehensive understanding of the financial services environment and the financial planning process.

The curriculum includes client counseling, economics, income taxation, insurance, investments, financial analysis, tax shelters, real estate, gift and estate tax planning, and planning for business owners and professionals.

Special emphasis is placed on comprehensive fact-finding, counseling techniques, the development of effective working relationships with other financial services professionals, and issues of professionalism and ethics. The program culminates in a comprehensive financial planning case course that provides a practical means of integrating previously covered tools, techniques, and products into the financial planning process.

In addition to completing the rigorous educational requirements, candidates for the Chartered Financial Consultant certification must meet strict experience and ethical requirements, and must pledge to keep their knowledge relevant through lifelong continuing education.

Appendix F

The Masters Program in Financial Sciences

Robert T. LeClair, Ph.D.

Dean, Graduate School of
Financial Sciences
The American College

The need for sound financial planning has never been greater than it is today. In our increasingly complex and unsteady economy, American consumers can no longer afford to go it alone when it comes to deciding how to spend or save their money most effectively. The qualified financial planner offers clients a form of economic insurance: the confidence that, with proper foresight, the ravages of inflation can be decisively resisted.

Graduates of The American College's Master's program are eminently qualified men and women whose commitment to their clients is backed by experience plus knowledge. They are professionals who refuse to accept anything but the best in the standards they set for themselves or in the service they provide to their clients.

Dedicated to professionalism, The American College is famed as a pioneer in the field of nontraditional education. Founded in 1927, the College is a private, nonprofit institution of higher learning for persons concerned with all areas of financial planning, including life insurance estate planning, accounting, banking, and investment.

Through its nontraditional, "open university" approach to education, the college provides the students—many of whom are already established in business with the opportunity to study at centers in all fifty states, the District of Columbia and twenty-five foreign countries. Students may pursue their course work through participation in organized classes in their local communities, informal study groups, or indepedent study.

The American College is best known for its Chartered Life Underwriter (CLU) professional designation program. Through its Graduate School of Financial Sciences the College offers an advanced program leading to the Master of Science in Financial Services degree. Other programs offered to meet the continually expanding needs of insurance and financial planning professionals include the new Chartered Financial Consultant designation program and a

Masters degree program in management. The College also sponsors a variety of workshops, seminars, and intensive learning courses.

The American College is accredited by the Commission on Higher Education of the Middle States Association of Colleges and Schools. Accreditation applies to the College as an institution and to the educational programs of all of its schools. This accreditation is recognized by the other regional accrediting bodies, which together cover institutions chartered in the United States and its possessions.

The Graduate School of Financial Sciences is a truly unusual program. It differs from the conventional MBA degree in that the primary focus is *not* on management of the business enterprise. Instead, greater emphasis is placed on analyzing, planning, implementing, and coordinating complex financial programs for individuals, families, and corporate administrators. Rigorous course work features the integration of substantive content, analytical tools and techniques, and case studies. These courses provide a high level of specialized knowledge and the ability to relate and apply that knowledge to a wide range of client situations.

The Master's degree requires thirty-six credit units of study. Thirty of those credits must be earned in graduate courses, each of which requires the successful completion of a national examination. The remaining six credits must be earned in two weeks of resident study on the College campus leading to successful completion of two seminar courses (three credits each).

Financial Planning Educational Institutions

Forrest Wallace Cato, M.B.A.

The following is a list of institutions (and their offerings) that teach financial planning. It is impossible to perform due diligence functions on educational institutions or their separate offerings. Inclusion of an institution or offering in this listing does not constitute an endorsement. Such listings are provided as an informational service. Other education organizations are beginning to create courses in financial planning.

INSTITUTION	OFFERING
The College for Financial Planning 9725 Hampden Avenue, Suite 200 Denver, CO 80231 303/755-7101	*Certificate:* Certified Financial Planner (CFP)
The American College 270 Bryn Mawr Avenue Bryn Mawr, PA 19010 215/896-4500	*Certificates:* Chartered Life Underwriter (CLU) Chartered Financial Consultant (ChFC) *Degree:* M.S. in Financial Services
Adelphi University Garden City, NY 11530	*Certificates:* Certificate in Financial Planning *Degree:* B.S. in Management and Communication (4 major courses in Financial Planning)

INSTITUTION	OFFERING

Boston University/Metropolitan College
755 Commonwealth Avenue
Boston, MA 02215
617/353-4496

Certificates:
Certificate in Investment Planning

Brigham Young University
395 JKB
Provo, UT 84601
801/378-1211

Degree:
B.S. in Business Management with concentration in finance, emphasis in Financial and Estate Planning
B.S. in Family Science with concentration in Family Financial Planning and Counseling

California State University Long Beach
School of Business
Department of Finance
Long Beach, CA 90840
213/498-4569

Proposed course and college major in Personal Financial Planning (Write for status or details)

Drake University
Cole Hall, Room 204
Des Moines, IA 50311
515/271-3921

Degree:
B.S. and B.A in Finance with concentration in Personal Financial Planning

Georgia State University
College of Business
Department of Insurance
University Plaza
Atlanta, GA 30303
404/658-3840

Degrees:
M.B.A. with major in Insurance and concentration in Financial Planning
Ph.D. with major in insurance and concen- in Financial Planning

Golden Gate University
536 Mission Street
San Francisco, CA 94105
415/442-7272

Certificates:
Certified Financial Planner (CFP) (In cooperation with the College for Financial Planning)

Golden Gate University
818 West 7th Street
Suite 1001
Los Angeles, CA 90017
213/623-6000

Certificates and Degrees:
Same as Golden Gate University, San Francisco

Kirkwood Community College
6301 Kirkwood Blvd., S.W.
P.O. Box 2068
Cedar Rapids, LA 52406
319/398-5411

Certificate:
Money Management Adviser

INSTITUTION	OFFERING
San Diego State University 3092 Lloyd Street San Diego, CA 92119 714/265-5200	*Degrees:* B.B.A. with major in Finance and a concentration in Financial Services M.S. in Business Administration with a concentration in Financial Services
University of California Berkeley Extension 2223 Fulton Street Berkeley, CA 94720 415/642-4111	*Certificate:* Professional designation in Personal Financial Planning
University of California Davis Extension Davis, CA 95616 916/752-0880	*Certificate:* Professional designation in Personal Financial Planning
UCLA Extension Department of Management & Business Post Office Box 24901 Los Angeles, CA 90024 213/825-7031	*Certificate:* Professional designation in Personal Financial Planning
University of Sarasota 2080 Ringling Boulevard Sarasota, FL 33577 813/955-4228	*Degrees:* B.B.A. with Financial Planning major M.B.A. with Financial Planning major NOTE: Experimental learning credits are available for students with work experience in Financial Planning.

In addition to taking the Certified Financial Planner Professional Education Program under the home study mode directly from the College for Financial Planning, candidates may wish to take the Program through one of thirty-three major colleges and universities offering it under a licensing arrangement with the College for Financial Planning. These institutions are:

Bentley College
Center for Cont. Ed.
Waltham, MA 02554

Brookhaven College
Farmers Branch, TX 75234

Broward Community College
Pompano Beach, FL 33063

California Lutheran College
Thousand Oaks, CA 91360

Charles Stewart Mott Community College
Flint, MI 48503

Cleveland State University
Cleveland, OH 44115

College of Mount Saint Vincent
Riverdale, NY 10471

Eastern Washington University
Cheney, WA 99004

Franklin University
Division of Cont. Ed.
Columbus, OH 43215

Fox Valley Tech. Institute
Appleton, WI 54913-2277

George Washington University
Washington, DC 20052

George Washington University–Virginia
Tidewater Center
Hampton, VA 23666

Golden Gate University—L.A.
Los Angeles, CA 90017

Golden Gate University—S.F.
San Francisco, CA 94105

Wm. Rainey Harper College
Palatine, IL 60067

Indiana University
IU/PUI Div. of Cont. Studies
Indianapolis, IN 46202

Jersey City State College
Jersey City, NJ 07305

Metropolitan State College
Denver, CO 80204

Monmouth College
West Long Branch, NJ 07764

Roosevelt University
Chicago, IL 60605

St. John Fisher College
Rochester, NY 14618

St. Vincent College
Latrobe, PA 15650

San Diego State University
San Diego, CA 92182

Scott Community College
Bettendorf, IA 52722

University of Detroit
Detroit, MI 48226

University of Houston
Central Campus
Houston, TX 77002

University of Houston
Downtown College
Houston, TX 77002

University of Miami
Miami, FL

University of Missouri—K.C.
Kansas City, MO 64110

University of So. California
Los Angeles, CA 90007

University of So. California—Valley
Camarillo, CA 93010

University of Tampa/Metro College
Tampa, FL 33606

University of Virginia
Roanoke Regional Center
Roanoke, VA 24018

Appendix H

A Glossary of Financial Planning Terms

ACCIDENT AND HEALTH INSURANCE Coverage paying for medical expenses, disability income, and/or death by accident or loss of eyes or limbs by accident.

ACCIDENT DEATH BENEFIT Insurance for payment of a benefit in case of death by accidental means.

ACCRUED INTEREST Interest accrued on a bond since the last interest payment was made. The buyer of the bond pays the market price plus accrued interest.

ACCUMULATION PLAN A plan for the systematic accumulation of mutal fund shares through periodic investments and reinvestments of income dividends and capital gains distributions.

ACQUISITION COST Immediate costs to an insurer of putting business on the books; commissions, clerical work, inspection fees, medical fees, etc.

ACTUARY An insurance statistician who calculates risk, premiums and related figures.

ADJUSTER A person who investigates and arranges settlement of claims. "Staff," "company" or "independent" adjusters represent insurers; "public" adjusters represent the policyholder for a fee.

ADMINISTRATOR A person appointed by the probate court to administer the estate of a person deceased.

AFFIDAVIT A statement or declaration reduced to writing sworn to or affirmed before some officer who has authority to administer an oath or affirmation.

AGENT One who acts for another called a principal. One who represents another from whom he has derived authority.

AGGRESSIVE GROWTH FUND A mutual fund with an investment objective of substantial capital gains and little income. One aggressive growth fund describes itself as a "speculative mutual fund seeking capital appreciation."

AGL American Gemological Laboratory.

AMERICAN BANKERS ASSOCIATION (ABA) Founded in 1875, it is the voice of organized banking. Its purpose is to keep its members abreast of the rapidly changing needs for banking services, to develop and maintain educated and competent personnel for banks, to spread knowledge and understanding of economic problems, and to elevate the standards of bank management and service.

AMERICAN DEPOSITORY RECEIPT (ADR) A negotiable security evidencing ownership of blocks of a foreign security held on deposit in a foreign branch of an American bank. Often used as the method of trading gold-mining stocks.

AMERICAN INSTITUTE OF BANKING (AIB) A section of The American Bankers Association, founded in 1900 for the purpose of providing an educational program for bank employees. Since the turn of the century hundreds of thousands of bankers have taken courses through the Institute. In addition, about 140,000 persons have earned one or more of the certificates awarded by the Institute. No other industry has matched the efforts of the American Bankers Association in the educational development of career employees.

AMORTIZATION The liquidation of a financial obligation on an installment basis; also, recovery over a period of cost or value.

ANA American Numismatic Association.

ANACS American Nuismatic Association Certification Service.

ANNUAL RENEWABLE TERM (ART) A form of pure protection life insurance that guarantees renewable coverage each year without evidence of insurability (physical examination).

ANNUAL REPORT The formal financial statement issued yearly by a corporation. The annual report shows assets, liabilities, earnings, standing of the company at the close of the business year, performance of the company profit-wise during the year, and other information of interest to shareowners.

ANNUITY A retirement vehicle that provides for the payment of a specific sum of money at uniform intervals of time. Usually purchased from an insurance company, it provides the annuitant with a guaranteed income either immediately or at retirement. Annuities usually pay until death (or for a specific period of time) and provide protection against the possibility of outliving your financial resources.

ANNUITY TRUST One of the vehicles for receiving income from a charitable gift. Provides the donor with an annual income that represents a fixed percentage of at least 5 percent of the initial value of the gift.

APPRECIATE To grow or increase in value.

APPRECIATION PARTICIPATION MORTGAGE (APM) A mortgage through which the lender partici-pates in the appreciation of the property by exchanging a reduction in the mortgage interest rate for a percentage of equity in the property. The mortgagee shares in the appreciation at the time of loan payoff or sale.

ARBITRAGE Dealing in differences. Example: buying on one exchange while simultaneously selling short on another at a higher price.

ASKED PRICE The price asked for a security offered for sale. Quoted, bid, and asked prices are wholesale prices for interdealer trading, and do not represent prices to the public.

ASSESSMENT Additional amounts of capital which a *participant* in a *tax-sheltered program* may be required to furnish beyond his original *subscription*. A given program, depending on the terms, may be either "assessable" or "nonassessable."

ASSET On a balance sheet, that which is owned or receivable.

ASSUMPTION OF MORTGAGE The taking of title to property by a grantee, wherein he assumes liability for payment of an existing note secured by a mortgage or deed of trust against the property; becoming a co-guarantor for the payment of a mortgage or deed of trust note.

ASSURED The insured party, or policyholder.

AUCTION MARKET Dealings on a securities exchange where a two-way auction is continuously in effect.

AUTHORIZED STOCK The total number of shares of stock authorized for issue by a company's shareholders.

AUTOMATIC REINVESTMENT An optional feature of most mutual funds providing for the reinvestment of all income distributions through the automatic purchase of additional shares.

AVERAGES Various ways of measuring the trend of stocks listed on exchanges. Formulas, some very elaborate, have been devised to compensate for stock splits and stock dividends and thus give continuity to the average. In the case of the Dow-Jones Industrial Average, the prices of the 30 stocks are totaled and then divided by a figure that is intended to compensate for past stock splits and stock dividends and that is changed from time to time.

BALANCE SHEET A condensed financial statement showing the nature and amount of a company's assets, liabilities, and capital on a given date. The balance sheet shows in dollar amounts what the company owned, what it owed, and its stockholders' ownership in the company.

BALANCED FUND   A mutual fund that is required to keep a specified percentage of its total assets invested in senior securities.

BALLOON PAYMENT   When the final installment payment on a note is greater than the preceding installment payments and it pays the note in full, such final installment is termed a balloon payment.

BEAR   Someone who believes the market will decline.

BEAR MARKET   A declining market.

BENEFICIARY   (1) One entitled to the benefit of a trust; (2) One who receives profit from an estate, the title of which is vested in a trustee; (3) The lender on the security of a note and deed of trust.

BID AND ASKED   Often referred to as a quotation or quote. The bid is the highest price anyone has declared that he wants to pay for a security at a given time, the asked is the lowest price anyone will take at the same time.

BIG BOARD   A popular term for the New York Stock Exchange, Inc.

BLIND POOL PROGRAM   A *tax-sheltered program* which, at the time sale of *subscriptions* begins, does not have the proceeds of the offering allocated to specific purposes, projects or properties.

BLOCK   A large holding or transaction of stock, popularly considered to be 10,000 shares or more.

BLUE CHIP   A company known nationally for the quality and wide acceptance of its products or services, and for its ability to make money and pay dividends.

BLUE SKY LAWS   A popular name for laws enacted by various states to protect the public against securities frauds. The term is believed to have originated when a judge ruled that a particular stock had about the same value as a patch of blue sky.

BOND   Basically an IOU or promissory note of a corporation, usually issued in multiples of $1000. A bond is evidence of a debt on which the issuing company usually promises to pay the bondholders a specified amount of in-

terest for a specified length of time, and to repay the loan on the expiration date. In every case, a bond represents debt—its holder is a creditor of the corporation and not a part owner, as is the shareholder.

BOND FUND   A mutual fund invested completely in bonds.

BOOK VALUE   An accounting term for the value of a stock determined from a company's records by adding all assets and then deducting all debts and other liabilities, plus the liquidation price of any preferred issues. The sum arrived at is divided by the number of common shares outstanding, and the result is book value per common share. Book value of the assets of a company or a security may have little or no significant relationship to market value.

BROKER   An agent who handles the public's orders to buy and sell securities, commodities, or other property. A commission is charged for this service.

BULL   One who believes the stock market will rise.

BULL MARKET   An advancing stock market.

BUSINESS CYCLE   The long-term boom-recession cycle that has been characteristic of business conditions not only nationally, but on a worldwide basis.

CALL   An option to buy a specified number of shares of a certain security at a definite price within a specified period of time.

CALLABLE   A bond issue, all or part of which may be redeemed by the issuing corporation under definite conditions before maturity. The term also applies to preferred shares, which may be redeemed by the issuing corporation.

CANCELLATION   Termination of a policy. When the company cancels, earned premium is calculated on a pro-rata basis; when the insured cancels, earned premium places a penalty on him via short rate cancellation tables.

CAPITAL   Generally, the money or property used in a business. The term is also used to apply to cash in reserve, savings, or other property of value. In financial reports, it is the total of all assets less the total of all liabilities.

CAPITAL GAIN OR CAPITAL LOSS   Profit or loss from the sale of a capital asset. A capital gain, under current federal income tax laws, may be either short-term (six months or less) or long-term (more than six months).

CAPITAL THEORY ECONOMICS   The theory that economic self-sufficiency is possible in a market economy by increasing and broadening the ownership of capital. One means of doing this is the Employee Stock Ownership Plan.

CASH SURRENDER VALUE   The amount which the policy owner is entitled to receive if he discontinues the coverage.

CASH VALUE INSURANCE   Insurance policies with built-in "savings account" features, e.g., whole and ordinary life.

CATTLE BREEDING   A form of tax-*sheltered investment* involving purchasing, scientific breeding, raising and selling cattle. The tax shelter in cattle breeding is derived principally from: (1) *deductions* for feed, pasturage, labor, rent, *management fees,* and other costs to raise and care for the animals, (2) *depreciation* and (3) *capital gains* treatment on the sale of animals held more than 24 months. Cattle breeding investments are available through both *public programs* and *private programs.*

CATTLE FEEDING   A form of *tax-sheltered investment* involving purchase of feeder calves for feeding under scientifically controlled conditions designed to maximize weight-gain and minimize time, expense and exposure to disease; after the proper amount of weight gain, sale of the animals to meat processors. The tax shelter in cattle feeding is derived principally from *deduction* of prepaid feed costs and *management fees* in the year the animals are purchased. Because the animals are generally sold the second year, the investor deducts the expenses the first year, then recovers that amount plus any profit the following year. Proper timing of purchases and sales makes possible the *deferral* of any year's income over a number of years. Cattle feeding investments are available through both *public programs* and *private programs.*

CBOE   Chicago Board of Options Exchange.

CERTIFICATE OF DEPOSIT (CD)   A formal receipt for funds left with a bank, as a special deposit. Such deposits may bear interest, in which case they are payable at a definite date in the future or after a specified minimum notice of withdrawal; or they may be noninterest bearing, in which case they may be payable on demand or at a future date. These deposits are payable only upon surrender of the formal receipt properly endorsed, and they are carried on the general ledger of the bank under heading Certificate of Deposit rather than on the individual ledgers under the name of the person to whom the certificate was originally issued.

CERTIFIED FINANCIAL PLANNER (CFP)   A designation granted by the College for Financial Planning to individuals who successfully complete a rigorous five-course curriculum.

CHARITABLE REMAINDER TRUST   A trust that donates the principal to a charity at termination of the trust period. *See also* annuity trust.

CHARTERED LIFE UNDERWRITER (CLU)   A designation granted by the American College of Life Underwriters to individuals who pass ten difficult examinations in insurance, economics, estate planning, etc.

COLA   Cost of Living Adjustment.

COLLATERAL   Specific property which a borrower pledges as security for the repayment of a loan, and agrees that the lender shall have the right to sell the collateral for the purpose of liquidating the debt if the borrower fails to repay the loan at maturity or otherwise defaults under the terms of the loan agreement.

COLLEGE FOR FINANCIAL PLANNING   An organization that offers professional training curricula leading the CFP designation (Certified Financial Planner). The courses required include risk management, investments, tax planning, retirement, and estate planning, among others.

COMMERCIAL BANK   A banking corporation which accepts demand deposits subject to check and makes short-term loans to business enterprises, regardless of the scope of its other services.

COMMERCIAL LOAN   A short-term loan made by a bank to a business enterprise for use in the production, manufacture, or distribution of goods or in the financing of related services.

COMMISSION   The broker's fee for purchasing or selling securities or property for a client.

COMMODITIES   Staple products that are basic to many industries and are usually traded in bulk form. Examples include corn, copper, pork, and lumber. Frequently when investors "buy commodities" they are really signing a contract to buy or sell a quantity of the product at some future date, called a commodity future contract.

COMMON STOCKS Certificates representing an undivided interest in the assets of a corporation with no set rate of return. Ownership of common stock provides for corporate voting rights and a share in the future profit (or loss) of the corporation.

COMPOUND INTEREST Interest computed on principal plus interest accrued during a previous period or periods. Interest may be computed monthly, quarterly, or semi-annually for compounding purposes.

COMPTROLLER OF THE CURRENCY An appointed official in the U.S. Treasury Department who is responsible for the chartering, supervision, and liquidation of national banks.

CONVERTIBLE TERM INSURANCE An option offered with some term insurance policies that allows the insured to convert the term policy to a whole life policy at some future date.

CORPORATE INCOME STATEMENT A company's statement of profit and loss (showing revenue, costs, taxes, and profit). One of the three major reports included in corporate financial statements.

CORPORATION A group or body of persons established and treated by law as an individual or unit with rights and liabilities or both, distinct and apart from those of the persons composing it.

CPCU Chartered Property Casualty Underwriter.

CPI Consumer Price Index.

CREATIVE FINANCING Unique and innovative ways of financing a major investment purchase by reducing cash outlay and increasing leverage. Usually in the realm of real estate, it would include arrangements like second mortgages, wraparound mortgages, and appreciation participation mortgages.

CURRENCY Technically, any form of money that serves as a circulating medium including both paper money and metallic money (coins). In banking terminology, however, the term generally refers to paper money only.

CUSTODIAN Any person or organization holding the assets of another. Also used to refer to an adult who agrees to take responsibility for a minor who purchases securities, or to

a bank that serves as a depository for the assets of a mutual fund.

DEBENTURE A promissory note backed by the general credit of a company and usually not secured by a mortgage or lien on any specific property.

DECREASING TERM A type of pure protection life insurance (term) in which the premiums remain the same and face value of coverage decreases over the life of the policy.

DEDUCTION Any reduction of taxable income that ultimately reduces the amount of tax due. The expenses incurred in any business operation are allowable as deductions; however, certain forms of *tax-sheltered investments* offer extraordinarily high deductions, particularly: (1) the *intangible drilling costs* associated with *oil and gas*, (2) *depreciation* and interest costs associated with *real estate, equipment leasing* and *cattle breeding*, particularly when *leverage* is employed, and (3) the feed and maintenance costs associated with *cattle feeding*.

DEED Written instrument which, when properly executed and delivered, conveys title.

DEED OF TRUST Written instrument by which title to land is transferred to a trustee as security for a debt or other obligation.

DEFERRAL A form of tax shelter that results from an investment timed so that *deductions* take place during the investor's high income years, and *capital gains* or other income takes place after retirement or in some other period of reduced income.

DEFERRED ANNUITY An annuity in which income payments begin at some future date, such as a specified age or a stated number of years.

DEFINED BENEFIT PENSION A special form of retirement plan that allows an employer to select the amount of retirement benefit that will be received.

DELIVERY Formal transfer of a deed to the new owner, without the right to recall it. Essential to a valid transfer.

DEPLETION A tax *deduction* granted *oil and gas* and other natural resources in order to encourage exploration for new deposits and development of new supplies by permitting partially tax-free recovery of the costs of exploration and development. Comparable to *depreciation* except that depletion is available.

DEPRECIATION Normally, charges against earnings to write off the cost, less salvage value, of an asset over its estimated useful life. A bookkeeping entry, it does not represent any cash outlay, nor are any funds earmarked for the purpose.

DETERIORATION A form of depreciation evidenced by wear and tear, decay, dry rot, structural defects, etc.

DIRECTOR A person elected by shareholders to establish company policies. The directors elect the president, vice president, and all other operating officers. Directors decide, among other matters, if and when dividends will be paid.

DISCOUNT The amount by which a preferred stock or bond may sell below its par value.

DISCRETIONARY ACCOUNT An account in which the customer gives the broker or someone else discretion, either complete or within specific limits, as to the purchase and sale of securities or commodities, including selection, timing, amount, and price to be paid or received.

DIVERSIFICATION Spreading investments among different companies in different fields. Another type of diversification is also offered by the securities of many individual companies because of the wide range of their activities.

DIVERSIFIED INVESTMENT COMPANY An investment company which, under the Investment Company Act of 1940, must invest 75 percent of its total assets so that not more than 5 percent of total assets are invested in the securities of any one issuer. Also, the company may not own more than 10 percent of the voting securities of any one issuer.

DIVIDEND The payment designated by the board of directors to be distributed pro rata among the shares outstanding. On preferred shares, it is generally a fixed amount. On common shares, the dividend varies with the fortunes of the company and the amount of cash on hand, and it may be omitted if business is poor or the directors determine to withhold earnings to invest in plant and equipment. Sometimes a company will pay a dividend out of past earnings even if it is not currently operating at a profit.

DIVIDEND REINVESTMENT PLAN A mutual fund share account in which dividends are automatically reinvested in additional shares. With this type of account, capital gains distributions are also automatically reinvested. Dividends (but not capital gains) may be invested at offering price (i.e., with a sales charge), but are more commonly reinvested at asset value.

DOLLAR-COST AVERAGING A system of buying securities at regular intervals with a fixed dollar amount. Under this system the investor buys by the dollars' worth rather than by the number of shares. If each investment is of the same number of dollars, payments buy more when the price is low and fewer when it rises. Temporary downswings in price thus benefit the investor if he continues to make periodic purchases in both good times and bad, and the price at which the shares are sold is more than their average cost.

DOUBLE INDEMNITY In accident policies, provision for doubling principal sum benefits when the accident is due to certain perils. In life policies, provision for doubling the face amount if death is caused by an accident.

DOUBLE TAXATION The federal government taxes corporate profits once as corporate income; any part of the remaining profits distributed as dividends to stockholders may be taxed again as income to the recipient stockholder.

DOW-JONES INDUSTRIAL AVERAGE Widely quoted stock averages computed regularly. They include an industrial stock average, a rail average, a utility average, and a combination of the three.

DOW THEORY A theory of market analysis based upon the performance of the Dow-Jones industrial and transportation stock price averages. The theory says that the market is in a basic upward trend if one of these averages advances above a previous important high, accompanied or followed by a similar advance in the other. A dip in both averages below previous important lows is regarded as confirmation of a basic downward trend. The theory does not attempt to predict how long either trend will continue, although it is widely misinterpreted as a method of forecasting future action.

DUAL FUND A closed-end investment company with two classes of shares: income and capital-outstanding. Also designated as a *leveraged fund*.

EARNEST MONEY A sum of money given to bind an agreement or an offer. Receipted for in a "deposit receipt" form.

EMPLOYEE RETIREMENT INCOME SECURITY ACT (ERISA) The 1974 pension reform law act.

ENDORSEMENT A written addition to a policy. Also known as a *rider*. Provisions of an endorsement supersede conflicting clauses of the policy to which it is added.

ENDOWMENT Insurance which pays the face amount to the insured if living on the maturity date, or to a beneficiary if insured dies before that date.

EQUIPMENT LEASING A form of *tax-sheltered investment* involving purchase of *capital assets,* such as airplanes, railroad cars, computers, ships and machinery, leasing those assets to actual users and, ultimately, selling the assets at the end of one or more leasing periods. The tax shelter in equipment leasing is derived principally from *depreciation* resulting from the high use of *leverage*. One type of leasing, railroad rolling stock, provides significant *deferral* possibilities because of favorable depreciation during the first five years. Equipment leasing investments are generally available only as *private programs*.

EQUITY The ownership interest of common and preferred stockholders in a company. Also refers to excess of value of securities over the debit balance in a margin account. Also, the value of a property which remains after all liens and other charges against the property are paid. A property owner's equity generally consists of his or her monetary interest in the property in excess of the mortgage indebtedness. In the case of a long-term mortgage, the owner's equity builds up quite gradually during the first several years because the bulk of each monthly payment is applied, not to the principal amount of the loan, but to the interest.

ESCROW The deposit of instruments and funds with instructions to a third neutral party to carry out the provisions of an agreement or contract; when everything is deposited to enable carrying out the instructions, it is called a complete or perfect escrow.

ESOP Employee Stock Ownership Plan. A plan to spread out ownership of private property. Also known as the *Kelso Plan*.

ESTATE All of a person's property, especially that left by a deceased person.

ESTATE PLANNING A system of planning that ensures your estate will be passed to your chosen heirs with limited red tape and the most favorable tax treatment.

ESTATE TAX A tax assessed on the transfer of wealth in an estate.

EXECUTOR A person named in a will by a decedent to carry out the provisions of the will.

EX-DIVIDEND A synonym for "without dividend." The buyer of a stock selling ex-dividend does not receive the recently declared dividend. Every dividend is payable on a fixed date to all shareholders recorded on the books of the company as of a previous date of record. For example, a dividend may be declared as payable to holders of record on the books of the company on a given Friday. Since five business days are allowed for delivery of stock in a "regular way" transaction on the stock exchange, the exchange would declare the stock "ex-dividend" as of the opening of the market on the preceding Monday. That means anyone who bought it on or after Monday would not be entitled to that dividend. When stocks go ex-dividend, the stock tables include the symbol "x" following the name.

EX-RIGHTS Without the rights. Corporations raising additional money may do so by offering their stockholders the right to subscribe to new or additional stock, usually at a discount from the prevailing market price. The buyer of a stock selling ex-rights is not entitled to the rights.

EXTENDED COVERAGE Addition to a fire policy against loss or damage caused by windstorm, hail, smoke, explosion, riot, riot attending a strike, civil commotion, vehicle and aircraft.

EXTENDED TERM INSURANCE A nonforfeiture option which provides the face amount of insurance for a limited time without further payment of premiums.

EXTRA The short form of "extra dividend." A dividend in the form of stock or cash in addition to the regular or usual dividend the company has been paying.

FACE AMOUNT The amount stated as payable at death of the insured.

FACE VALUE The value of a bond that appears on the face of the bond, unless the value is otherwise specified by the issuing company. Face value is ordinarily the amount the issuing company promises to pay at maturity. Face value is not an indication of market value. It is sometimes referred to as par value.

FAMILY INCOME POLICY A combination of whole life and decreasing term insurance. Beneficiary receives income payments to the end of a specified period if insured dies prior to that date, and the face amount in addition.

"FAMILY OF FUNDS" A system of mutual funds, managed by the same company, that provides the option of switching investments from one type of fund to another, either for free or for a small administrative fee.

FAMILY POLICY Coverage on all or several members of a family in one policy, generally whole life on the husband and smaller amounts of term on the wife and children.

FAMILY TRUST A type of trust that provides income to a spouse and, upon the spouse's death, is automatically disbursed to children.

FEDERAL DEPOSIT INSURANCE COPORATION (FDIC) A corporation established by federal authority to provide insurance on demand and time deposits in participating banks up to a maximum of $20,000 for each depositor.

FEDERAL HOUSING ADMINISTRATION (FHA) Federal government agency which insures loans on residential property.

FEDERAL RESERVE BANKS Federal banking corporations that deal principally with their member banks and with the government. They deal with the general public only to a limited extent.

FEE SIMPLE In modern estates, the term "fee" and "fee simple" are substantially synonymous. The term "fee" is of old English derivation.

FEE SIMPLE ABSOLUTE An estate in real property, by which the owner has the greatest power over the title that it is possible to have, being an absolute estate. In modern use, it expressly establishes the title of real property in the owner, without limitations or end. He may dispose of it by sale, or trade or will, as he chooses.

FICA Federal Insurance Contribution Act.

FIDUCIARY A person in a position of trust and confidence, as between principal and broker; broker as fiduciary owes certain loyalty which cannot be breached under rules of agency.

FINANCIAL STATEMENT A summary of figure facts showing some aspect of the financial condition of a business such as a balance sheet or an income statement.

FINANCING REAL ESTATE Arranging for a loan, giving property as security. Most property is bought partially with borrowed money, so this is an important phase of the real estate business.

FIXED INTEREST An interest rate that does not vary and is guaranteed (can be good or bad!) for the duration of the investment term.

FLOOR The huge trading area of a stock exchange where stocks and bonds are bought and sold.

FLOOR BROKER A member of the stock exchange who executes order on the floor of the exchange to buy or sell any listed securities.

FNMA Fannie Mae.

FRANCHISE A right or privilege conferred by law.

FSLIC Federal Savings and Loan Insurance Corporation.

FULLY MANAGED FUND A mutual fund whose investment policy gives its management complete flexibility as to the types of investments made and the proportions of each. Management is restricted only to the extent that federal or blue sky laws require.

GEMOLOGY The science or study of natural and artificial gemstones.

GENERAL PARTNER The individual (or individuals) who has unlimited liability in a partnership. Usually distinguished from a limited partner in tax-shelter investments, the general partner secures the proper income-producing properties and has the responsibility of managing them on a profitable basis. General partners usually share about 15 percent of the costs and profits.

GIA Gemological Institute of America.

GIFT TAX A tax levied on the transfer of property as a gift. Paid by the giver or donor.

GNMA Ginnie Mae.

GOLD BUILLION Bars of gold that can be purchased on world markets with little markup. Problems include minimum purchases, delivery, storage, and lack of liquidity.

GOVERNMENT BONDS Obligations of the U.S.

government, regarded as the highest grade issues in existence.

GRADUATED PAYMENT MORTGAGES A creative financing technique in which the earlier mortgage payments are lower than they would be with ordinary mortgage financing. Payments gradually increase at a predetermined rate. Successful for first-time, young home buyers, who usually sell the home before the payments become unbearable.

GROSS INCOME Total income from property before any expenses are deducted.

GROSS OPERATING INCOME The total cash available to meet all expenses and debt payment. The words *effective* or *anticipated* could also be used in the term.

GROSS RETURN The gross spendable income plus the principal payments added together creates the gross return before depreciation.

GROSS SPENDABLE This is the cash remaining after deducting the mortgage constants (interest and principal). This is sometimes referred to as the "cash flow."

GROWTH FUND A mutual fund with an investment objective of capital growth and capital gains. Usually, a common stock fund seeking long-term capital growth and future income rather than current income.

GROWTH INVESTMENTS The center portion of the investment pyramid, between the foundation and speculative investments. Middle-of-the-road risk investments. Usually include mutual funds, managed equities, and stocks, among others.

GROWTH STOCK One of the two types of common stock that seeks selling price increases rather than income in the form of dividends for shareholders. *See* income stock.

GUARANTEED RENEWABLE An insurance policy renewable at the option of the insured to a stated age, usually 60 or 65. Premium may be changed only by class.

GUARANTY A written promise by one person (the guarantor) to be liable for the debt of another person (the principal debtor) in the event that the principal debtor fails to perform his obligation and provided the guarantor is notified of that fact by the creditor. A guaranty must be in writing to be enforceable at law.

GUARDIAN An individual appointed by a court to manage the affairs or person (or both) of a minor or a mentally incompetent individual, or corporation appointed by a court to manage the affairs of a minor or a mentally incompetent person.

HARD ASSETS Investments that are tangible as opposed to paper or intangibles. Include metals, gems, art, stamps, collectibles, etc.

HOLDING COMPANY A corporation that owns the securities of another, in most cases with voting control.

HOMEOWNERS POLICY A package policy covering fire, extended coverage, theft, liability and other benefits. Also available to tenants and condominium dwellers.

ICFP Institute of Certified Financial Planners.

INCOME FUND A mutual fund with an investment objective of current income rather than capital growth. Many bond funds are considered income funds.

INCOME STOCK One of the two types of common stock that seeks current income rather than selling price increases or capital growth. *See* growth stock.

INDENTURE A written agreement under which bonds and debentures are issued, setting forth maturity date, interest rate, and other terms.

INDIVIDUAL RETIREMENT ACCOUNT (IRA) A tax-deferred retirement plan; its availability was extended to all workers by the Economic Recovery Tax Act of 1981.

INFLATION A condition of increasing prices, usually caused by an undue expansion in paper money and credit.

INSTITUTION An organization holding substantial investing assets, often for others. Includes banks, insurance companies, investment companies, and pension funds.

INTANGIBLE DRILLING COSTS Expenditures incurred in the drilling and completion of oil and gas wells that are granted a *deduction* from current income for tax purposes. "Intangibles" are the items which have no salvage value (commonly nonmaterial costs such as labor, chemicals, drill-site preparation, etc.) and frequently account for 70% to 90% of the cost of drilling and completing a given well.

INTEREST Payments made by a borrower to a lender for the use of his money. A corporation pays interest on its bonds to its bondholders.

INTERNATIONAL ASSOCIATION FOR FINANCIAL PLANNING (IAFP) The professional association of the financial planner, which also provides training in areas of estate planning, federal taxation and tax sheltering, investment and planning techniques, among others.

INVESTMENT The use of money for the purpose of making more money: to gain income or increase capital or both.

INVESTMENT BANKER Also known as an *underwriter*. The middleman between the corporation issuing new securities and the public. The usual practice is for one or more investment bankers to buy outright from a corporation a new issue of stocks or bonds. The group forms a syndicate to sell the securities to individuals and institutions. Investment bankers also distribute very large blocks of stocks or bonds (perhaps held by an estate).

INVESTMENT COMPANY A company or trust that uses its capital to invest in other companies. There are two principal types: the closed-end and the open-end, or mutual fund. Shares in closed-end investment companies are readily transferable in the open market and are bought and sold like other shares. Capitalization of these companies remains the same unless action is taken to change, which seldom occurs. Open-end funds sell their own new shares to investors, stand ready to buy back their own shares, and are not listed. Open-end funds are so named because their capitalization is not fixed; they issue more shares as people want them.

INVESTMENT COMPANY ACT OF 1940 An act passed by the Congress for the specific purpose of empowering the SEC to regulate investment companies.

INVESTMENT COUNSEL One whose principal business consists of acting as investment adviser, and a substantial part of whose business consists of rendering investment supervisory services.

INVESTMENT PYRAMID A James Barry formula for identifying the mix of investments in individual portfolios. The average percentages include 10–20 percent each in the low risk/foundation investments and the high risk/speculative investments. The remaining 60–80 percent should be in moderate risk/growth investments.

INVESTOR An individual whose principal concerns in the purchase of a security are regular dividend income, safety of the original invest-

ment, and, if possible, capital appreciation.

ISSUE Any of a company's securities, or the act of distributing such securities. Upon the death of a joint tenant, his interest passes, not to his heirs, but to his co-owner.

JOINT AND TWO-THIRDS SURVIVOR ANNUITY An annuity under which joint annuitants receive payments during a joint lifetime. After the demise of one of the annuitants, the other receives two-thirds of the annuity payments in effect during the joint lifetime.

JOINT LIFE INSURANCE A policy insuring two or more lives.

JOINT VENTURE A form of business organization, in this context a *tax-sheltered program*, in which the *sponsor* and the *participants* share jointly in the ownership, management authority and liability. (Contrast with *limited partnership*.)

KEOGH ACCOUNT A tax-deferred retirement plan available to self-employed individuals.

KRUGERRAND A one-ounce gold coin issued by the South African government.

LAND CONTRACT A form of creative finance used in real estate wherein the seller retains legal title to the property until the buyer makes an agreed-upon number of payments to the seller. Usually the buyer has all the benefits of tax deductions and the seller pays the existing mortgage. The technique is usually used when there is a legally enforceable "due on sale" clause in the mortgage.

LEASE A contract between owner and tenant, setting forth conditions upon which tenant may occupy and use the property, and the term of the occupancy.

LEASE OPTION A creative real estate financing technique wherein the buyer, for a consideration, leases a home with the option to buy later when interest rates may be lower. In most cases the monthly payments and the consideration are applied to the purchase price.

LEGAL LIABILITY INSURANCE Coverage for the legal liability incurred by a policyholder, e.g., damage caused by fire to another party due to insured's negligence.

LEGAL LIST A list of investments selected by various states in which certain institutions and fiduciaries, such as insurance companies and banks, may invest. Legal lists are often restricted to high-quality securities and, if possible, capital appreciation.

LETTER OF CREDIT   An instrument issued by a bank to an individual or corporation by means of which the bank substitutes its own credit for that of the individual or corporation.

LETTER OF INTENT PRIVILEGE   In front-end load mutual fund purchases, a discount is allowed for large investors who intend to purchase amounts that qualify for the discount. When the large amounts are not purchased immediately, the fund requests a letter of intent to do so and allows the discounted load to be charged.

LEVEL TERM   A form of pure protection insurance (term) in which the face value and the premiums remain level for the life of the policy.

LEVERAGE   The effect on the per-share earnings of the common stock of a company when large sums must be paid for bond interest or preferred stock dividends or both before the common stock is entitled to share in earnings. Leverage may be advantageous for the common stock when earnings are good, but may work against the common stock when earnings decline. Leverage also refers to mortgage funds used in financing of real estate and oil limited partnerships.

LIABILITIES   All the claims against a corporation. Liabilities include accounts and wages and salaries payable, dividends declared payable, accrued taxes payable, fixed or long-term liabilities such as mortgage bonds, debentures, and bank loans.

LIEN   A claim against property that has been pledged or mortgaged to secure the performance of an obligation. A bond may be secured by a lien against specified property of a company.

LIFE ANNUITY   An annuity that carries no death benefit. Usually, when the annuitant dies, all benefits end, even if there is a surviving spouse.

LIMITED ORDER   An order to buy or sell a stated amount of a security at a specified price, or at a better price.

LIMITED PARTNER   In this context, a participant in a *tax-sheltered program* which has been organized as a *limited partnership*. (See *limited partnership* for details.)

LIMITED PARTNERSHIP   A form of business organization in which some partners exchange their right to participate in management for a limitation on their liability for partnership losses. Commonly, *limited partners* have liability only to the extent of their investment in the business. To establish limited liability, there must be at least one *general partner* who is fully liable for all claims against the business. Limited partnerships are a popular organizational form for *tax-sheltered programs* because of the ease with which tax benefits flow through the partnership to the individual partners. (Contrast with *joint venture*.)

LIMITED PAYMENT LIFE   A type of whole life (cash value) insurance that insures you for life but requires premiums to be paid for a limited number of years. Sometimes named for the periods (20-year paid-up or paid-up at 65), the premiums are higher than if paid for the entire term of the policy.

LIQUIDATING VALUE   When referring to the shares of an open-end investment company, the value at redemption. Usually the net asset value.

LIQUIDATION   The process of converting securities or other property into cash. The dissolution of a company, with cash remaining after sale of its assets and payment of all indebtedness being distributed to the shareholders.

LIQUIDITY   The ability of the market in a particular security to absorb a reasonable amount of buying or selling at reasonable price changes. Liquidity is one of the most important characteristics of a good market.

LISTED STOCK   The stock of a company which is traded on a securities exchange, and for which a listing application and a registration statement, giving detailed information about the company and its operations, have been filed with the Securities & Exchange Commission, unless otherwise exempted, and the exchange itself.

LIVING TRUST   A trust into which you transfer your assets for the eventual benefit of your heirs, made while you are still living. Usually, you can co-manage, with a trustee, all of your property and receive all the income. This type of trust is fully taxed in your estate.

LOCKED IN   An investor is said to be locked in when he has a profit on a security he owns, but does not sell because his profit would immediately become subject to the capital gains tax.

LONG   Signifies ownership of securities. "I am

long 100 U.S. Steel" means the speaker owns 100 shares.

MAGNETIC INK CHARACTER RECOGNITION (MICR) Magnetic Ink Character Recognition is the standards program developed by the American Bankers Association to permit the automatic handling of documents such as bank checks, by electrically reading pre-coded, standardized characters printed on the documents in special magnetic ink.

MANAGEMENT The board of directors, elected by the stockholders, and the officers of the corporation, appointed by the board of directors.

MANAGEMENT FEE The fee paid to the investment manager of a mutual fund. It is usually about one-half of one percent of average net assets annually. Not to be confused with the sales charge, which is the one-time commission paid at the time of purchase as a part of the offering price.

MANIPULATION An illegal operation. Buying or selling a security for the purpose of creating false or misleading appearance of active trading or for the purpose of raising or depressing the price to induce purchase or sale by others.

MARGIN The amount representing the customer's investment or equity in such an investment account. Investment leverage. For example, for each dollar you invest, the broker lends you a specified sum with which you may increase the investment value. The value of the investment is collateral for the loan and the margin agreement allows the broker to liquidate all or part of the investment if the ratio between the amount you invested and the amount you borrowed is not maintained.

MARGIN CALL A demand upon a customer to put up money or securities with the broker. The call is made when a purchase is made or when a customer's equity in a margin account declines below a minimum standard set by the exchange or by the firm.

MARKET ORDER An order to buy or sell a stated amount of a security at the most advantageous price obtainable.

MARKET PRICE In the case of a security, market price is usually considered the last reported price at which the stock or bond sold.

MARKET VALUE (1) The price at which a willing seller would sell and a willing buyer would buy, neither being under abnormal pressure; (2) As defined by the courts, the highest price estimated in terms of money which a property will bring if exposed for sale in the open market allowing a reasonable time to find a purchaser with knowledge of property's use and capabilities for use.

MATURITY The date on which a loan or a bond or a debenture comes due and is to be paid off.

MEMBER FIRM A securities brokerage firm organized as a partnership or corporation and owning at least one seat on the exchange.

MINERAL, OIL, AND GAS LICENSE Special license to deal in such lands.

MONEY PURCHASE PENSION PLAN A defined contribution pension plan in which the employer *must* contribute a certain percentage of each employee's salary each year, regardless of the company's profit.

MORTGAGE An instrument by which the borrower (mortgagor) gives the lender (mortgagee) a lien on real estate as security for a loan. The borrower continues to use the property, and when the loan is repaid, the lien is removed or satisfied.

MORTGAGE BOND A bond secured by a mortgage on a property. The value of the property may or may not equal the value of the so-called mortgage bonds issued against it.

MULTIPLE LISTING A listing, usually an exclusive right to sell, taken by a member of an organization composed of real estate brokers, with the provisions that all members will have the opportunity to find an interested client; a cooperative listing.

MUNICIPAL BOND A bond issued by a state or a political subdivision, such as a county, city, town, or village. The term also designates bonds issued by state agencies and authorities. In general, interest paid on municipal bonds is exempt from federal income taxes and from state and local income taxes within the state of issue.

MUTUAL FUND An open-end investment company that continuously offers new shares to the public in addition to redeeming shares on demand as required by law. While in common use, the term mutual fund has no meaning in law.

NASD The National Association of Securities Dealers, Inc. An association of brokers and dealers in the over-the-counter securities business. The Association has the power to expel members who have been declared guilty of unethical practices. NASD is dedicated to, among other objectives, "adopt, administer and enforce rules of fair practice and rules to prevent fraudulent and manipulative acts and practices, and in general to promote just and equitable principles of trade for the protection of investors."

NASDAQ   An acronym for National Association of Securities Dealers Automated Quotations. An automated information network that provides brokers and dealers with price quotations on securities traded over the counter.

NEGOTIABLE   Refers to a security, title to which is transferable by delivery.

NET ASSET VALUE   A term usually used in connection with investment companies, meaning net asset value per share. It is common practice for an investment company to compute its assets daily by totaling the market value of all securites owned. All liabilities are deducted, and the balance is divided by the number of shares outstanding. The resulting figure is the net asset value per share.

NET CHANGE   The change in the price of a security from the closing price on one day to the closing price on the following day on which the stock is traded. The net change is ordinarily the last figure on the stock price list. The mark $+2\frac{1}{8}$ means up $2.125 a share from the last sale on the previous day the stock traded.

NET OPERATING INCOME   The income earning on and from the improved real estate including the land and the buildings and other improvements placed on it. It is the total dollars after expenses which include taxes, insurance, utilities, maintenance and management fees, etc. It is the yield on the fair market value of the real estate.

NET RETURN   The total yield after taxes earned by the real property.

NET SPENDABLE   The total cash available to the investor to spend after taxes.

NEW ISSUE   A stock or bond sold by a corporation for the first time. Proceeds may be issued to retire outstanding securities of the company, for new plant or equipment, or for additional working capital.

NONCANCELLABLE   Policies that may not be cancelled (during a specified term) by the insurer. But the term "non-can" should not be applied to health policies unless they are also guaranteed renewable.

NONCUMULATIVE   A preferred stock on which unpaid dividends do not accrue. Omitted dividends are, as a rule, gone forever.

NONFORFEITURE   Granting of benefits to the policyholder on the lapsing of his cash value policy. Benefits may be cash surrender value, extended term insurance, or reduced paid-up insurance.

NONPARTICIPATING   Policies that do not include an overcharge in their premiums, hence pay no "dividends."

NUMISMATICS   The study of collecting, or investment in coins. Usually referring to rare coin collections.

NYSE COMMON STOCK INDEX   A composite index covering price movements of all common stocks listed on the "Big Board." It is based on the close of the market December 31, 1965, as 50.00 and is weighted according to the number of shares listed for each issue. The index is computed continuously and printed on the ticker tape each half hour. Point changes in the index are converted to dollars and cents to provide a meaningful measure of changes in the average price of listed stocks.

OASI Old Age Survivor's Insurance.

ODD LOT   An amount of stock less than the established 100-share unit or 10-share unit of trading: from 1 to 99 shares for the great majority of issues, 1 to 9 for so-called inactive stocks. Odd-lot prices are geared to the auction market. On an odd-lot market order, the odd-lot dealer's price is based on the first round-lot transaction that occurs on the floor following receipt at the trading post of the odd-lot order. The differential between the odd-lot price and the "effective" round-lot price is $12\frac{1}{2}$ cents a share. For example: You decide to buy 20 shares of ABC common at the market. Your order is transmitted by your commission broker to the representative of an odd-lot dealer at the post where ABC is traded. A few minutes later there is a 100-share transaction in ABC at $10 a share. The odd-lot price at which your order is immediately filled by the odd-lot dealer is $10.125 a share. If you had sold 20 shares of

ABC, you would have received $9.875 a share.

OFFER   The price at which a person is ready to sell. Opposite of bid, the price at which one is ready to buy.

OIL AND GAS   A form of *tax-sheltered investment* involving drilling, completion, and operation of oil and gas wells. The tax shelter in oil and gas is derived principally from: (1) *deductions* for *intangible drilling costs,* (2) partially tax-free income from *depletion,* and (3) *capital gains.* Oil and gas investments are available through both *public programs* and *private programs,* and vary considerably in risk/reward orientation.

OPEN ACCOUNT   When referring to a mutual fund, a type of account in which the investor may add or withdraw shares at any time. In such an account, dividends may be paid in cash or reinvested at the account holder's option.

OPEN-END INVESTMENT COMPANY   By definition under the 1940 Act, an investment company that has outstanding redeemable shares. Also generally applied to those investment companies which continuously offer new shares to the public and stand ready at any time to redeem their outstanding shares.

OPEN-END MORTGAGE   A mortgage that secures additional advances which a lender may advance to the mortgagor.

OPTION   A right to buy or sell specific securities or properties at a specified price within a specified time.

ORDINARY LIFE INSURANCE   Also known as *straight life* or *whole life.* Premiums are computed to be paid for life.

OVERBOUGHT   An option as to price levels. May refer to a security that has had a sharp rise or to them arket as a whole after a period of vigorous buying which, it may be argued, has left prices "too high."

OVERSOLD   An opinion, the reverse of overbought. A single security or a market that, it is believed, has declined to an unreasonable level.

OVER-THE-COUNTER   A market for securities made up of securities dealers who may or may not be members of a securities exchange. Over-the-counter is mainly a market made over the telephone. Thousands of companies have insufficient shares outstanding, stockholders, or earnings to warrant application for listing on an exchange. Securities of these companies are traded in the over-the-counter market between dealers who act either as principals or as brokers for customers.

PAPER PROFIT   An unrealized profit on a security still held. Paper profits become realized profits only when the security is sold.

PARTNERSHIP   A decision of the Court has defined a partnership in the following terms: "A partnership as between partners themselves may be defined to be a contract of two or more persons to unite their property, labor or skill, or some of them, in prosecution of some joint or lawful business, and to share the profits in certain proportions."

PAR   In the case of a common share, par means a dollar amount assigned to the share by the company's charter. Par value may also be used to compute the dollar amount of the common shares on the balance sheet. Par value has little significance so far as market value of common stock is concerned.

PBGC   Pension Benefit Guarantee Corporation.

PENNY STOCKS   Low-priced issues, often highly speculative, selling at less than $1 a share. Frequently used as a term of disparagement, although a few penny stocks have developed into investment-caliber issues.

PERMANENT LIFE INSURANCE   Generally any life policies except term; policies which accrue cash value, e.g., ordinary life or endowments.

PERSONAL PROPERTY   Any property that is not real property.

POINT   In the case of shares of stock, a point means $1. If ABC shares rise three points, each share has risen $3. In the case of bonds, a *point* means $10, since a bond is quoted as a percentage of $1000. A bond that rises three points gains 3 percent of $1000, or $30 in value. An advance from 87 to 90 would mean an advance in dollar value from $870 to $900 for each $1000 bond. In the case of market averages, the word point means merely that and no more. If, for example, the Dow-Jones Industrial Average rises from 870.25 to 871.25, it has risen a point. A point in this average, however, is not equivalent to $1.

POOLED INCOME FUND   A type of annuity that pools the assets of a number of people, each sharing the income proportionally.

PORTFOLIO   Holdings of securities by an individual or institution. A portfolio may contain bonds, preferred stocks, and common stocks of various types of enterprises.

PREFERRED LIFE INSURANCE   Cash value life insurance.

PREFERRED STOCK   A class of stock with a claim on the company's earnings before payment may be made on the common stock and usually entitled to priority over common stock if the company liquidates. Usually entitled to dividends at a specified rate, when declared by the board of directors and before payment of a dividend on the common stock, depending upon the terms of the issue.

PREMIUM   The amount by which a preferred stock or bond may sell above its par value. In the case of a new issue of bonds or stocks, premium is the amount the market price rises over the original selling price.

PREMIUM WAIVER FEATURE   An optional feature of some insurance policies that waives the continued payment of premiums if you are disabled and unable to pay them.

PRICE-EARNINGS RATIO   The price of a share of stock divided by earnings per share for a 12-month period. For example, a stock selling for $100 a share and earning $5 a share is said to be selling at a price-earnings ratio of 20 to 1.

PRIMARY DISTRIBUTION   Also called *primay offering.* The original sale of a company's securities.

PRINCIPAL   The person for whom a broker executes an order, or a dealer buying or selling for his own account. The term "principal" may also refer to a person's capital or to the face amount of a bond.

PRIVATE PROGRAM   A *tax-sheltered program* which is offered and sold subject to the private offering exemption available under the Securities Act of 1933 and/or some registration exemption granted by the securities regulation authorities of one or more states, i.e., a program which is not registered with the Securities and Exchange Commission. (Contrast with *public program.*)

PROBATE   The judicial process used to establish the validity of a will and carry out its terms. Also used to refer to the judicial proceedings needed to settle an estate.

PROFIT-SHARING PLAN   A retirement plan (or simply a plan for the sharing of profits) through which employees share in the profit of the corporation for which they work. Contributions are only required when there is a profit. (Compare to *money purchase pension.*)

PROFIT TAKING   Selling stock that has appreciated in value since purchase to realize the profit that has been made possible. The term is often used to explain a downturn in the market following a period of rising prices.

PRO FORMA   Latin, meaning "according to form." In financial planning, usually used to refer to an analysis done by a professional regarding the prediction of tax or other financial obligations.

PROPERTY AND CASUALTY INSURANCE   Insurance coverage to provide for the replacement of or compensation for property lost, stolen, damaged, or destroyed.

PROSPECTUS   The document that offers a new issue of securities to the public. It is required under the Securities Act of 1933.

PROXY   Written authorization given by a shareholder to somone else to represent him and vote his shares at a shareholders' meeting

PROXY STATEMENT   Information required by the SEC to be given to stockholders as a prerequisite to solicitation of proxies for a security subject to the requirements of Securities Exchange Act.

PRUDENT MAN RULE   An investment standard. In some states, the law requires that a fiduciary, such as a trustee, may invest the fund's money only in a list of securities designated by the state—the so-called legal list. In other states, the trustee may invest in a security if it is one that a prudent man of discretion and intelligence, who is seeking a reasonable income and preservation of capital, would buy.

PUBLIC PROGRAM   A *tax sheltered program* which is registered with the Securities and Exchange Commission and distributed in a public offering by broker/dealers and/or employees of the sponsor. Public programs are commonly, but no always, organized as *limited partnerships.* (Contrast with *private program.*)

PUT   An option to sell a specified number of shares at a definite price within a specified period of time. The opposite of a call.

QUALIFIED ANNUITY   An annuity that meets IRS requirements for inclusion in group pension plans, Keogh retirement plans, and IRAs.

QUOTATION Often shortened to *quote*. The highest bid to buy and the lowest offer to sell a security in a given market at a given time. If you ask your broker for a quote on a stock, he may come back with something like "45¼ to 45½". This means that $45.25 is the highest price any buyer wanted to pay at the time the quote was given on the floor of the exchange, and that $45.50 was the lowest price any seller would take at the same time.

RALLY A brisk rise following a decline in the general price level of the market, or in an individual stock.

REAL ESTATE A form of *tax-sheltered investment* involving a variety of purchase-construction-operation-sale options, each having distinct investment characteristics: raw land, residential and low-income housing, and other income-producing properties such as office buildings, shopping centers, and industrial and commercial properties. Real estate is the most widely used form of tax shelter; benefits are derived principally from: (1) *deductions* for *depreciation* and interest, (2) *leverage,* and (3) *capital gains.* Real estate investments are available through both *public programs* and *private programs,* offering solutions to a wide range of investment and tax problems.

REAL ESTATE INVESTMENT TRUST (REIT) An equity trust that can hold income properties of all types and offers shares that are publicly traded. Note: this is a modification of a limited partnership that *does not* require net worth or income minimums for the investor.

REALTOR A real estate broker holding active membership in a real estate board affiliated with the National Association of Real Estate Boards.

RECORD DATE The date on which you must be registered as a shareholder on the stock book of a company to receive a declared dividend or, among other things, to vote on company affairs.

RED BOOK The "bible" of coin collection, nicknamed the red book, is actually called *A Guide Book of United States Coins*. It sets down standards for estimating coin condition by comparing with others of the same type and year. The standards were developed by the American Numismatics Association.

REDEMPTION PRICE The price at which a bond may be redeemed before maturity, at the option of the issuing company. Redemption value also applies to the price an open-end investment company must pay to call in certain types of preferred stock. It is usually the net asset value per share—it fluctuates with the value of the company's investment portfolio.

RED HERRING A preliminary prospectus used to obtain indications of interest from prospective buyers of a new issue.

REGISTERED BOND A bond that is registered on the books of the issuing company in the name of the owner. It can be transferred only when endorsed by the registered owner.

REGISTERED REPRESENTATIVE A full-time employee who has met the requirements of an exchange as to background and knowledge of the securities business. Also known as an *account exchange* or *customer's broker.*

REGISTAR Usually a trust company or bank charged with the responsibility of preventing the issuance of more stock than authorized by a company.

REGISTRATION Before a public offering may be made of new securities by a company, or of outstanding securities by controlling stockholders, through the mails or in interstate commerce, the securities must be registered under the Securities Act of 1933. Registration statement is filed with the SEC by the issuer. It must disclose pertinent information relating to the company's operations, securities, management, and purpose of the public offering. On security offerings involving less than $300,000, less information is required.

Before a security must be admitted to dealings on a national securities exchange, it must be registered under the Securities Exchange Act of 1934. The application for registration must be filed with the exchange and the SEC by the company issuing the securities. It must disclose pertinent information relating to the company's operations, securities, and management.

REGULATION Q The regulation extended by the Federal Reserve Board placing a limit on the rates of interest that can be paid by banks to their depositors.

REGULATION T The federal regulation governing the amount of credit that may be advanced by brokers and dealers to customers for the purchase of securities.

REGULATION U   The federal regulation governing the amount of credit that may be advanced by a bank to its customers for the purchase of listed stocks.

RENEWABLE TERM INSURANCE   Term policy renewable at the end of the term at the insured's option and without evidence of insurability, at higher premium.

RETURN   Another term for yield.

RIGHTS   When a company wants to raise more funds by issuing additional securities, it may give its stockholders the opportunity, ahead of others, to buy the new securities in proportion to the number of shares each owns. The piece of paper evidencing this privilege is called a right. Because the additional stock is usually offered to stockholders below the current market price, rights ordinarily have a market value of their own and are actively traded. In most cases they must be exercised within a relatively short period. Failure to exercise or sell rights may result in actual loss to the holder.

ROLLOVER   A method of avoiding the substantial tax bite of a lump sum retirement plan payment, allowing you to roll it over into an IRA or similar vehicle to continue its deferred tax status.

ROUND LOT   A unit of trading or a multiple thereof. On most exchanges the unit of trading is 100 shares in the case of stocks and $1000 par value in the case of bonds. In some inactive stocks, the unit of trading is 10 shares.

RULE OF 72   A simple financial formula for calculating the amount of time it takes an investment to double at any rate of return. Divide the rate of return into 72.

SEAT   A traditional figure of speech for a membership on an exchange. Price and admission requirements vary.

SEC   Securities and Exchange Commission, established by Congress to help protect investors. The SEC administers the Securities Act of 1933, the Securities Exchange Act of 1934, the Trust Indenture Act, the Investment Company Act, the Investment Advisers Act, and the Public Utility Holding Company Act.

SECONDARY DISTRIBUTION   Also known as a *secondary offering*. The redistribution of a block of stock some time after it has been sold by the issuing company. The sale is handled off the exchange by a securities firm or group of firms, and the shares are usually offered at a fixed price that is related to the current market price of the stock. Usually the block is a large one, such as might be involved in the settlement of an estate. The security may be listed or unlisted.

SECOND MORTGAGE   A creative real estate financing technique in which the buyer maintains the original mortgage and "takes back" a second mortgage on the difference between the down payment and the existing first mortgage. Seller financing.

SELLING SHORT   Selling stock not owned. A risky technique of borrowing stock from the broker in anticipation of a drop in stock value that will bring rewards. Instead of looking for market winners, the short seller looks for and bets on losers.

SIMPLIFIED EMPLOYEE PENSION (SEP)   A hybrid IRA pension plan to which your employer can contribute up to 15 percent of your salary or $7,500 (Keogh limits). The plan eliminates substantial paperwork for the employer, hence its name.

SINGLE-PREMIUM DEFERRED ANNUITY (SPDA)   An annuity that is funded with a lump sum payment (single premium) and purchased before the anticipated rate of retirement (deferred).

SINKING FUND   Money regularly set aside by a company to redeem its bonds, debentures, or preferred stock from time to time as specified in the indenture or charter.

SPECIAL OFFERING   Occasionally a large block of stock becomes available for sale that, due to its size and the market in that particular issue, calls for special handling. A notice isprinted on the ticker tape announcing that the stock will be offered for sale on the floor of the exchange at a fixed price. Member firms may buy this stock for customers directly from the seller's broker during trading hours. The price is usually based on the last transaction in the regular auction market. If there are more buyers than stock, allotments are made. Only the seller pays a commission on a special offering.

SPECIALIST   A member of an exchange who has two functions. The first is to maintain an orderly market, insofar as reasonably practicable, in the stocks in which he is registered as a specialist. The exchange expects the specialist to buy or sell for his own account, to a reasonable degree, when there is a temporary disparity between supply and demand. The specialist also acts as a broker's broker. When a commission broker on the exchange floor receives a limit order, say, to buy at $50 a stock then selling at $60, he cannot wait at the post where the stock is traded to see if the price reaches the specified level. So he leaves the order with the specialist, who will try to execute it in the market if and when the stock declines to the specified price. The specialist must put his customers' interests above his own at all times.

SPECULATOR One who is willing to assume a relatively large risk in the hope of gain. His principal concern is to increase his capital rather than his dividend income. The speculator may buy and sell the same day or speculate in an enterprise he does not expect to be profitable for years.

SPLIT The division of the oustanding shares of a corporation into a larger number of shares. A 3-for-1 split by a company with 1 million shares outstanding results in 3 million shares outstanding. Each holder of 100 shares before the 3-to-1 split would have 300 shares, although his proportionate equity in the company would remain the same; 100 parts of 1 million are the equivalent of 300 parts of 3 million.

SPONSOR An entity (or combination of entities) that acts as *general partner*, manager, operator or management company of a *tax-sheltered program,* and provides investment and/or operational expertise.

SPREAD The difference between the bid price and the offering price. Also, the combination of a put and a call "points away" from the market.

STATE BANK A corporation organized under the general banking law of a state and authorized to do a commercial banking business; that is, to receive deposits subject to check and to make loans. It usually performs a variety of other functions as well. In a broader sense, a state bank is any bank chartered by the state.

STATEMENT OF POLICY The SECs statement of its own position as to those things considered "materially misleading" in the offer of shares of open-end investment companies.

STOCK Ownership shares of a corporation.

STOCK CERTIFICATE A certificate that provides physical evidence of stock ownership.

STOCK DIVIDEND A dividend paid in securities rather than cash. The dividend may be additional shares of the issuing company or shares of another company (usually a subsidiary) held by the issuing company.

STOCK EXCHANGE An organization registered under the Securities Exchange Act of 1934 with physical facilities for the buying and selling of securities in a two-way auction.

STOCK POWER An assignment and power of substitution separate from a stock certificate authorizing transfer of the stock on the books of the corporation.

STOCKHOLDER OF RECORD A stockholder whose name is registered on the books of the issuing corporation.

STOP ORDER An order to buy at a price above or to sell below the current market. Stop buy orders are generally used to limit loss or protect unrealized profits on a short sale. Stop sell orders are generally used to protect unrealized profits or limit loss on a holding.

STRAIGHT LIFE ANNUITY An annuity that carries a guarantee of payments to the annuitant for life. All payments stop at death, whether or not the annuitant is survived.

STREET NAME Securities held in the name of a broker instead of his customer's name are said to be carried in a street name. This occurs when the securities have been bought on margin or when the customer wishes the security to be held by the broker.

SUITABILITY RULE The rule of fair practice that requires a member to have reasonable grounds for believing that a recommendation to a customer is suitable on the basis of his financial objectives and abilities.

SYNDICATION In real estate, when two or more individuals pool funds to purchase and manage one or more income-producing properties. A limited partnership is a form of syndication.

TAXABLE INCOME What the government taxes the property on. This amount could be a profit or a loss depending on the leverage used and the depreciation used.

TAX DEDUCTIBLE Expenses that are able to reduce the amount of taxable income. Examples include medical expenses, charitable deductions, and interest paid.

TAX DEFFERAL   A method of tax avoidance that defers the payment of taxes on income until a future time. Rationale: future tax brackets will be lower and the payment of the tax will be made with inflated dollars.

TAX INCENTIVE   Corporate or venture vehicles that include major tax deferring or sheltering characteristics.

TAX-SHELTERED INVESTMENT   An investment that has an expectation of economic profit, made even more attractive because of the timing of the profit or the way it is taxed, generally having some or all of the following characteristics: (a) *capital gains* opportunities; (b) high *deductions*; (c) *deferral* of income; (d) *depletion*; (e) accelerated *depreciation*; (f) *leverage*. The flow-through of tax benefits are a material factor regardless of whether the entity is organized as a *private program* or a *public program*. Common forms of tax-sheltered investments include: *cattle breeding, cattle feeding, equipment leasing, oil and gas, and real estate*.

TAX-SHELTERED PROGRAM   A *tax-sheltered investment* in which flow-through of tax benefits are a material factor regardless of the structure of the legal entity, the vehicle for distribution, or the industry or industries represented. Commonly, a tax-sheltered program is created to mutually benefit a *sponsor* and a group of *participants*. It may be structured as a *limited partnership* or a *joint venture*. Also, it may be organized as a public program or a private program.

TENANTS IN COMMON   A form of registration of property, frequently used with securities. An undivided estate in property where, upon the death of the owner, the undivided estate becomes the property of his heirs or divisees and not of his surviving co-owner.

TENANTS BY THE ENTIRETY   A form of registration of property, usually real estate.

TERM INSURANCE   As opposed to cash value insurance, death protection that is pure and does not include "savings" programs as a part of the policy. Usually issued for a certain period of time, hence "term."

TIME SHARING   A creative financing technique in the field of real estate that allows the use of property on a time-shared basis while building equity for all of the owners. Two types: right-to-use (membership right) and interval ownership (purchase of a particular week or weeks each year).

TIPS   Supposedly "inside" information on corporation affairs.

TRADER   One who buys and sells for his own account for short-term profit.

TRANSFER   This term may refer to two different operations. For one, the delivery of a stock certificate from the seller's brokers to the buyer's broker and legal change of ownership, normally accomplished within a few days. For another, to record the change of ownership on the books of the corporation by the transfer agent. When the purchaser's name is recorded on the books of the company, dividends, notices of meetings, proxies, financial reports, and all pertinent literature sent by the issuer to its securities holders are mailed directly to the new owner.

TRANSFER AGENT   One who keeps a record of the name of each registered shareowner, his or her address, and the number of shares owned, and sees that certificates presented to his office for transfer are properly cancelled and that new certificates are issued in the name of the transferee.

TREASURY BILLS (T-BILLS)   U.S. government paper investments with no stated interest rate. Short-term investment, reaching maturity in 90 days and sold at a discount with competitive bidding.

TREASURY BOND   U.S. government bonds issued in $1000 units with maturity of five years or longer. They are traded on the market like other bonds.

TREASURY NOTE   U.S. government paper, not legally restricted as to interest rates, with maturities from one to five years.

TREASURY STOCK   Stock issued by a company but later reacquired. It may be held in the company's treasury indefinitely, reissued to the public, or retired. Treasury stock receives no dividends and has no vote while held by the company.

TRUST   A legal arrangement within which a person contracts for the management and control of certain assets for self or other benefit.

TRUSTEE   One who holds the legal title to property for the benefit of another.

UMBRELLA LIABILIY   Insurance coverage in excess of underlying liability policies; also provides coverage for many situations excluded by underlying policies, and may also include excess major medical expense coverage.

UNDERWRITER The person who decides for an insurer whether or not a risk will be acceptable, and under what conditions.

UNDERWRITER'S FEE In the sale of mutual funds shares, the difference between the total sales charge and the underwriter's reallowance to the dealer.

UNIT REFUND LIFE ANNUITY A type of annuity that pays on a periodic basis during your lifetime and provides your beneficiary with a lump sum payment based on the dollar amount of your remaining annuity units.

UNLISTED A security not listed on a stock exchange.

VARIABLE ANNUITY An annuity that has the (possible) benefits of high yield by allowing the annuitant to vary the annuity's investment portfolio as the market demands or suggests. One of the best investments available for retirement, although not without some risk.

VARIABLE RATE MORTGAGE A creative financing technique in real estate that allows the interest charged on the mortgage to fluctuate with the rise and fall of market interest rates.

VARIANCE A departure from the general rule.

VENDEE A purchaser; buyer.

VENDOR A seller; one who disposes of a thing in consideration of money.

VERIFICATION Sworn statement before a duly qualified officer to correctness of contents of an instrument.

VEST To bestow upon—such as title of property.

VESTED BENEFITS Those benefits of a retirement, pension or profit-sharing plan that belong to the employee outright. Vesting normally takes place gradually until, after a specified period, the employee is totally vested and is entitled to 100 percent of the retirement account.

VESTED INTEREST An interest that is fixed or determined.

VETERANS'S ADMINISTRATION (VA) A federal government agency, which among other services to veterans, insures or guarantees repayment of home loans borrowed by veterans.

VOTING RIGHT The stockholder's right to vote his stock in the affairs of his company. Most common shares have one vote each. Preferred stock usually has the right to vote when preferred dividends are in default for a specified period. The right to vote may be delegated by the stockholder to another person.

WARRANT A certificate giving the holder the right to purchase securities at a stipulated price within a specified time limit or perpetually. Sometimes a warrant is offered with securities as an inducement to buy.

WHEN ISSUED A short form of "when, as, and if issued." The term indicates a conditional transaction in a security authorized for issuance but not yet actually issued. All "when issued" transactions are on an "if" basis, to be settled if and when the actual security is issued and the exchange or National Association of Securities Dealers rules that the transactions are to be settled.

WHOLE LIFE INSURANCE *See* ordinary life insurance.

WILL A document wherein an individual provides for the distribution of property or wealth after death. State law determines distribution if no will is provided. The three types of wills are: (1) holographic, which is *written entirely* by *hand* and is dated and signed; (2) formal, which is a *witnessed* will; and (3) noncupative which is an *oral* will communicated and witnessed at a time of probable death.

WITHDRAWAL FUND A mutual fund plan that permits monthly or quarterly withdrawal of specified dollar amounts, usually involving the invasion of principal. Alternately, a plan may permit varying withdrawals based on the liquidation of a fixed number of shares monthly or quarterly.

WORKING CAPITAL 1. That portion of a capital of a business enterprise which is not invested in fixed assets but which is kept liquid to provide for day-to-day working needs. 2. In an accounting sense, the excess of current assets over current liabilities.

WORKING CONTROL Theoretically, ownership of 51 percent of a company't voting stock is necessary to exercise control. In practice—and this is particularly true in the case of a large corporation—effective control sometimes can be exerted through ownership, individually or by a group acting in concert, of less than 50 percent.

WORKMEN'S COMPENSATION   Benefits paid a worker for medical care and income replacement for work-connected accident, disease, or death.

WRAPAROUND MORTGAGE   A creative real estate financing technique that is akin to the second mortgage but includes both the original and the second mortgage in a single package, "wrapping" a new mortgage around the other two.

YIELD   Also know as *return*. The dividends or interest paid by a company expressed as a percentage of the current price. A stock with a current market value of $20 a share that has paid $1 in dividends in the preceding 12 months is said to return 5 percent ($1.00/$20.00). The current return on a bond is figured the same way.

Your NCFE Financial Data Form

One of the first steps to improving your financial position, regardless of what it is and regardless of your income level, your age, or your expertise, is to see on paper just what you are spending and where you are now financially.

Kemp Fain
John Austin
Charlotte Beier
Lawrence A. Krause

Financial Inventory Checklist	Balance Sheet

Financial Inventory Checklist

1. Tax returns
   A. Personal and/or business
   B. Partnerships, trusts, etc.

2. Legal documents
   A. Wills
   B. Trust agreements
   C. Business agreements
   D. Domestic separation (decrees, dissolution, child support, etc.)

3. Employment benefits
   A. Descriptive booklets
   B. Account records, annual reports, etc.

4. Income and expense
   A. Salary and bonus totals
   B. Living expenses

5. Insurance policies
   A. Life insurance
   B. Disability insurance
   C. Medical insurance
   D. Home and auto insurance
   E. Other insurance

6. Savings and investments
   A. Savings account and/or certificate of deposit records
   B. Securities (stocks, bonds, etc.) account records
   C. Real estate investment records
   D. Other

7. Other property
   A. Home
   B. Personal property
   C. Checking accounts
   D. Other (antiques, art, etc.)
   E. Precious metals, gems, etc.

8. List of debts
   A. Mortgages
   B. Notes
   C. Installment department store accounts, loan accounts, credit cards, etc.

9. Children's assets

10. Other

Balance Sheet

ASSETS (What I/we own)

Fixed Dollar Assets
Checking accounts $_____
Savings accounts   _____
Bonds   _____
Life insurance cash values _____
Life insurance—term or other _____
Profit-sharing account   _____
Keogh plan   _____
Individual Retirement Acct. _____
Receivables   _____

Equity Dollar Assets
Stocks $_____
Mutual funds   _____
Real estate   _____
Business value   _____
Professional practice values _____
Profit-sharing account   _____
Pension account   _____
Keogh plan   _____
Individual Retirement Acct. _____

Non-Income-Producing Assets
Home and lot $_____
Personal Property   _____
Collectibles   _____

TOTAL ASSETS $_____

LIABILITIES (What I/we owe)
Charge accounts $_____
Notes   _____
Mortgage on home   _____

TOTAL LIABILITIES $_____

MY/OUR NET WORTH $_____

LIVING EXPENSES

Monthly, quarterly or annually. To help us realize where we are actually spending our money, or maybe where we should spend it, we have included some categories not usually found in budget forms.

	Budget	Spent	Goal		Budget	Spent	Goal
Housing:				**Transportation:**			
Mortgage/rent	$	$	$	Car payments	$	$	$
Utilities				Gas, oil & tires			
Telephone				Public transp.			
Maintenance & repair				Maintenance & repair			
Yard maintenance				Licenses & insurance			
Domestic help							
Homeowner prop. ins.							
Property taxes				**Pets:**			
New household purchases				Food	$	$	$
Other (pool, etc.)				Vet. & medicine			
Savings:							
IRAs	$	$	$	**Recreation:**			
Mutual funds				Entertainment	$	$	$
Cash value ins.				Vacations			
				Club dues			
				Other (horses, boats, etc.)			
Food:							
Meals at home	$	$	$				
Meals out				**Medical:**			
Coffee breaks & snacks				Doctors	$	$	$
				Dentists			
				Medicines			
Clothing:				Hospitals			
Essential	$	$	$	Insurance			
Non-essential							
Laundry/ dry cleaning				**TOTALS:**	$	$	$

	Budget	Spent	Goal
Alimony and/or Child Support:			
_____	$_____	$_____	$_____
Personal:			
Grooming	$_____	$_____	$_____
Education	_____	_____	_____
Lessons	_____	_____	_____
Subscriptions	_____	_____	_____
Allowances	_____	_____	_____
_____	_____	_____	_____
Investment Expenses:			
Property upkeep	$_____	$_____	$_____
_____	_____	_____	_____
Gifts & Contributions:			
_____	$_____	$_____	$_____

	Budget	Spent	Goal
Other			
(Unreimbursed bus. exp., etc.)	$_____	$_____	$_____
Cigarettes/etc.	_____	_____	_____
Liquor, beer, soft drinks	_____	_____	_____
TOTAL THIS PAGE	$_____	$_____	$_____
TOTALS PREVIOUS PAGE	$_____	$_____	$_____
GRAND TOTALS:	$_____	$_____	$_____

To get where you want to be
         . . . know where you are
             L.D.

Cash Flow Statement

My (or our) Income:

Salary and/or other earned income	$_____
Bonuses	_____
Business or practice income	_____
Interest	_____
Dividends	_____
Rents	_____
Partnership income	_____
_____	_____
TOTAL INCOME:	$_____
LESS EXPENSES:	_____
NET INCOME:	_____

Adequate Emergency Reserve

Reserve needed (6 months living expenses)	$_____
Less: cash and equivalents	$_____
Reserve deficit (surplus)	$_____
Monthly investment earning ___ % to eliminate deficit	$_____

Assets (What I/We Own)

Checking accounts:

_____ $_____

Savings accounts:

_____ $_____

Business practice (interest):

_____ $_____

Stocks:

_____ $_____

Bonds:

_____ $_____

Life insurance
(term and other):

_____ $_____

Mutual funds:

_____ $_____

Limited partnerships:

_____ $_____

Investment real estate:

_____ $_____

Tangible assets:
(gold, silver, gems)

_____ $_____

Home & other
personal property:

_____ $_____

Life insurance
(Cash Value):

_____ $_____

Employee benefits &
retirement plans:

_____ $_____

Employee stock option plans:

_____ $_____

Income:

_____ $_____

Medical insurance:

_____ $_____

Disability insurance:

_____ $_____

_____ $_____

Retirement/Financial Independence

Monthly retirement income needed at age _____ $_____
Less: Expected retirement plan benefits   − _____
Less: Expected social security benefits   − _____
Less: Expected earnings from capital at work   − _____
Monthly income still needed $_____
Monthly investment earning____ % to provide income needed $_____

Life Insurance: Adequacy Test

Cash needed:
    For education $ _____
    For any mortgages   _____
    For final expenses   _____
    As an emergency fund   _____
    For estate costs   _____

Assets needed to meet income requirement:
    Current income need of $ _____ per month
    less estimated Social Security income of
    $ _____ per month (factor from below)

Total capital needed (assets): $ _____

Less:
    Capital at work $ _____
    + Face amount of insurance $ _____
    − Cash value of insurance $ _____ $ _____

Life insurance needed (surplus): $ _____

Present amount $ _____ vs.   Needed amount $ _____
Present outlay $ _____ vs.   Needed outlay $ _____

*Factors for Various Capital Earning Rates

CAPITAL EARNING RATE AVAILABLE	FACTOR*
6%	200
8%	150
10%	120
12%	100

*Explanation: To understand the use of factors, the number is determined by the following equation:

$$\frac{(\text{Monthly Income needed} \times 12\,\text{months})}{\text{interest rate available}} = \text{Capital NEEDED FOR Investment}$$

Education to Provide for

CHILD	AMOUNT NEEDED	MIDPOINT OF NEED	MONTHLY INVESTMENT EARNING % TO PROVIDE NEED
	$		$
	$		$

Disability Insurance Needed

Monthly disability income needed (at least 60% of present income)	$
Less: Social Security benefits	−
Less: Employee benefits	−
Less: Personal disability income policies	−
Less: Earnings from capital	−
Monthly disability income still needed	$
Present amount $ vs. Needed amount	$
Present outlay $ vs. Needed outlay	$

My—Our Financial Goals

GOAL	WHAT I NEED ($)	WHAT I HAVE ($)	ACTION REQUIRED	WHEN

My/Our Financial Situation at a Glance

YEAR	PERSONAL INCOME	TAXES PAID	NET WORTH	CAPITAL AT WORK
	$			

Contributing Authors

Thomas E. Aaron, CFP
Multi Financial Planning Corp.
47 West Queens Way
Hampton, VA   23669
(804) 627-3120

Dr. William Anthes, President
The College for Financial Planning
9725 E. Hampden Avenue, #200
Denver, CO   80231
(303) 755-7101

Richard W. Arnold
Chief Financial Officer
Charles Schwab & Co., Inc.
One Second Street
San Francisco, CA   94105
(415) 546-1000

Charles M. Atwell, CLU, CFP, ChFC
Director of Financial
    Planning & Analysis
Waddell & Reed, Inc.
P. O. Box 1343
Kansas City, MO   64141
(816) 283-4000

Richard P. Austin, CLU
The Travelers Life, Health &
    Financial Services Department
One Tower Square
Hartford, CT   06115
(203) 928-7846

David Barker
Commodities Systems Development Assoc.
20863 Stevens Creek Blvd., #B2-A
Cupertino, CA   95014
(408) 255-5533

James A. Barry, CFP
Chief Executive Officer
Asset Management Corporation
499 W. Palmetto Park Road
Boca Raton, FL   33432
(305) 368-9120

Lesley Bissett, CFP
Integrated Resources Equity
658 Petaluma Avenue
Long Beach, CA   90815
(213) 420-7738

Graydon K. Calder, CLU, CFP
Financial Planning Consultants
860 Mission Center Court, #103
San Diego, CA   92108
(714) 291-7974

Forrest Wallace Cato
Managing Editor
The *Financial Planner*
5775 Peachtree Dunwoody Road
Atlanta, GA   30342
(404) 257-0110

Kemp P. Fain, Jr., CFP
President
Asset Planning Corporation
238 Peters Road, #103
Knoxville, TN   37923
(615) 690-1231

Philip N. Gainsborough, CFP
Gainsborough Financial Consultants, Inc.
911 Wilshire Blvd.
Los Angeles, CA   90017
(213) 627-9070

Dave Goodwin
Dave Goodwin & Associates
P.O. Drawer 54-6661
Surfside, FL   33154
(305) 531-0071

August C. Hansch, CLU, CFP
Hansch Financial Group
5900 Wilshire Blvd.
Los Angeles, CA   90036
(213) 937-8400

Christopher J. Hegarty
The Stone Financial Group
1036 Sir Francis Drave Blvd.
Kentfield, CA   94904
(415) 459-0363

W. Robert Hightower, CFP
W. Robert Hightower & Associates
P. O. Drawer 30819
Raleigh, NC   27622
(919) 833-1765

Al Jeanfreau, CFP
Al Jeanfreau Associates, Inc.
200 S. W. Market, Suite 821
Portland, OR   97201
(503) 224-5766

Lewis G. Kearns, CFP
6404 Quail Hollow Place
Bradenton, FL   33507
(813) 758-8407

David M. King, CFP
David M. King & Associates
First National Bank Building
Hays, KS   67601
(913) 625-7393

Karen J. Knizley, CFP
Tax & Financial Planning
700 Larkspur Landing Circle, #109
Larkspur, CA   94939
(415) 461-7400

Herman Kramer, CLU, CFP
Regional Director of Agencies
Philadelphia Life Insurance Co.
1414 Lincoln Avenue, #102
San Rafael, CA   94901
(415) 456-2350

Lawrence A. Krause, CFP
Lawrence A. Krause & Associates, Inc.
500 Washington Street, #710
San Francisco, CA   94111
(415) 362-1200

Lucile Lansing
Lansing Financial Group
655 University Avenue, #101
Sacramento, CA   95825
(916) 929-2927

Robert T. LeClair, Ph.D., Dean
Graduate School of Financial Sciences
The American College
Bryn Mawr, PA   19010
(215) 896-4530

Harry J. Lister, CFP, President
JL Financial Services, Inc.
1101 Vermont Avenue, NW
Washington, DC   20005
(202) 842-5675

Leo C. Loevner, CPA
Deposit Management Services
10855 Lee Highway, #200
Fairfax, VA   22030
(703) 385-8040

Thomas McAllister, CFP
McAllister Financial Planning Corp.
2606 Bluffwood-West Drive
Indianapolis, IN   46208
(317) 283-6263

Donald S. McAlvany, President
International Collectors Association
1660 S. Albion Street, #1010
Denver, CO   80222
(303) 758-8536 or (800) 525-9556

Eric H. Medrow, CFP
Hartel & Medrow
P. O. Box 169
Wayne, PA   19087
(215) 688-2600

James Miller, Editor
The Digest
c/o Consolidated Capital Institutional
   Advisors, Inc.
1900 Powell Street, #1000
Emeryville, CA   94608
(800) 772-1870

Lee Pennington, CFP
916 Main Street, #706
Lubbock, TX   79401
(806) 765-7471

Kenneth R. Rouse, CFP, President
Financial Management Consultants
P. O. Box 7265
Colorado Springs, CO   80933
(303) 593-1100

Morris G. Sahr, Ph.D., CFP
Deposit Management Services
10855 Lee Highway, #200
Fairfax, VA   22030
(703) 385-8040

Eileen M. Sharkey, CFP
2755 South Locust, #114
P. O. Box 11153
Denver, CO   80211
(303) 759-4262

Jay A. Smith, CLU
Life Insurance Rx Corporation
P. O. Box 358
Sausalito, CA   94965
(415) 332-2266

Craig Stone
The Stone Financial Group
1036 Sir Francis Drake Blvd.
Kentfield, CA   94904
(415) 459-0363

Beverly Tanner, CFP
Intravest Centaur
700 Larkspur Landing Circle, #109
Larkspur, CA   94939
(415) 461-4800

Venita VanCaspel, CFP
VanCaspel & Company
1540 Post Oak Tower
Houston, TX   77036
(713) 621-9377

Lewis J. Walker, CFP
Walker, Cogswell & Co., Inc.
4340 Georgetown Square, #608
Atlanta, GA   30338
(404) 452-7222

Richard T. White
Magtime, Inc.
310 Madison Avenue, #1211
New York, NY   10017
(212) 794-8787

Stuart R. Wolk, Esquire
Wolk, Maziarz & Kevins
Counsellors at Law
One Craig Court
Montville, NJ   07045
(201) 227-2249

Richard G. Wollack, President
Consolidated Capital Institutional
    Advisors, Inc.
1900 Powell Street
Emeryville, CA   94608
(800) 772-1870

Wesley K. Wyatt, President
Financial Planning Corporation of America, Inc.
Wyatt Building
Stillwater, OK   74074
(405) 372-3177

Index